## Get the eBooks FREE!

(PDF, ePub, Kindle, and liveBook all included)

We believe that once you buy a book from us, you should be able to read it in any format we have available. To get electronic versions of this book at no additional cost to you, purchase and then register this book at the Manning website.

Go to https://www.manning.com/freebook and follow the instructions to complete your pBook registration.

That's it!
Thanks from Manning!

*OCA Java SE 8 Programmer I Certification Guide*

# OCA Java SE 8
# Programmer I
# Certification Guide

MALA GUPTA

MANNING
SHELTER ISLAND

For online information and ordering of this and other Manning books, please visit
www.manning.com. The publisher offers discounts on this book when ordered in quantity.
For more information, please contact

Special Sales Department
Manning Publications Co.
20 Baldwin Road
PO Box 761
Shelter Island, NY 11964
Email: orders@manning.com

©2017 by Manning Publications Co. All rights reserved.

No part of this publication may be reproduced, stored in a retrieval system, or transmitted, in
any form or by means electronic, mechanical, photocopying, or otherwise, without prior written
permission of the publisher.

Many of the designations used by manufacturers and sellers to distinguish their products are
claimed as trademarks. Where those designations appear in the book, and Manning
Publications was aware of a trademark claim, the designations have been printed in initial caps
or all caps.

⊛ Recognizing the importance of preserving what has been written, it is Manning's policy to have
the books we publish printed on acid-free paper, and we exert our best efforts to that end.
Recognizing also our responsibility to conserve the resources of our planet, Manning books
are printed on paper that is at least 15 percent recycled and processed without the use of
elemental chlorine.

Manning Publications Co.
20 Baldwin Road
PO Box 761
Shelter Island, NY 11964

| | |
|---|---|
| Development editor: | Cynthia Kane |
| Technical development editor: | Francesco Bianchi |
| Copy editor: | Linda Recktenwald |
| Proofreader: | Katie Tennant |
| Technical proofreader: | Jean-François Morin |
| Typesetter: | Dennis Dalinnik |
| Cover designer: | Marija Tudor |

ISBN: 9781617293252
Printed in the United States of America
6 7 8 9 10 – SP – 24 23 22 21 20 19

*To Dheeraj, my pillar of strength*

# brief contents

# contents

# preface

Java programmer certifications are designed to tell would-be employers whether you really know your stuff, and cracking the OCA Java SE 8 Programmer Certification is not an easy task. Thorough preparation is crucial if you want to pass the exam the first time with a score that you can be proud of. You need to know Java inside-out, and you need to understand the certification process so that you're ready for the challenging questions you'll face in the exam.

This book is a comprehensive guide to the 1Z0-808 exam. You'll explore a wide range of important Java topics as you systematically learn how to pass the certification exam. Each chapter starts with a list of the exam objectives covered in that chapter. Throughout the book you'll find sample questions and exercises designed to reinforce key concepts and prepare you for what you'll see in the real exam, along with numerous tips, notes, and visual aids.

Unlike many other exam guides, this book provides multiple ways to digest important techniques and concepts, including comic conversations, analogies, pictorial representations, flowcharts, UML diagrams, and, naturally, lots of well-commented code. The book also gives insight into common mistakes people make when taking the exam, and guides you in avoiding traps and pitfalls. It provides

- Complete coverage of exam topics, all mapped to chapter and section numbers
- Hands-on coding exercises, including particularly challenging ones that throw in a twist

- Instruction on what's happening behind the scenes using the actual code from the Java API source
- Mastery of both the concepts and the exam

This book is written for developers with a working knowledge of Java. My hope is that the book will deepen your knowledge and prepare you well for the exam and that you will pass it with flying colors!

# acknowledgments

First and foremost, I thank Dheeraj—my pillar of strength, my best friend, and my husband. His constant guidance, encouragement, and love kept me going. He helped me to get started with this book and got me over the goal line.

My sincere gratitude goes to Marjan Bace, publisher at Manning, for giving me the opportunity to author this book. The Manning team has been wonderful—Michael Stephens ensured that it was worth it for Manning to have a book on this subject. Cynthia Kane, my development editor, is like sunshine. Not only did she help me with the organization of individual chapters and the overall book, but she pulled me through whenever the task of writing a book became overwhelming. It's always a pleasure to work with her. Copyeditor Linda Recktenwald not only applied her magic to sentence and language constructions but also supplemented her editing with valuable suggestions on technical content.

Technical development editor Francesco Bianchi suggested multiple additions and modifications, improving the content of this book. Technical proofreader Jean-François Morin was outstanding in his review. He not only pointed out existing errors but also suggested multiple improvements to the organization of the contents. Proofreader Katie Tennant was extremely capable and talented. She reviewed the final manuscript with great precision.

The technical reviewers on this book did an awesome job of reviewing the contents and sharing their valuable feedback and comments: Andrea Barisone, Andrea Consentino, Anutosh Ghosh, David Blau, Marty Henderson, Mirsad Vojnikovic, Nicola Pedot, Sanjiv Kumar, Simona Russo, Travis Nelson, and Ursin Stauss. I would also like to thank Nicole Butterfield and Donna Clements, review editors, for managing the whole review process and meticulously funneling the feedback to make this book better.

Dennis Dalinnik did an outstanding job of converting the black-and-white hand-drawn illustrations into glorious images. It was amazing to scrutinize the page proofs. I also thank Dennis for adjusting the images in the final page proofs, which was a lot of work. Janet Vail and Mary Piergies were awesome in their expertise at turning all text, code, and images into publishable form. I am also grateful to Candace Gillhoolley for her efforts in promoting the book.

I thank the MEAP readers for buying the book while it was being developed and for their suggestions, corrections, and encouragement.

I would also like to thank my former colleagues Harry Mantheakis, Paul Rosenthal, and Selvan Rajan, whose names I use in coding examples throughout the book. I have always looked up to them.

I thank my daughters, Shreya and Pavni, who often advised me on the images that I created for the book. I thank my family for their unconditional support. The book would have been not been possible without their love and encouragement.

# *about this book*

This book is written for developers with a working knowledge of Java who want to earn the OCA Java SE 8 Programmer Certification. It uses powerful tools and features to make reaching your goal of certification a quick, smooth, and enjoyable experience. This section explains the features used in the book and tells you how to use the book to get the most out of it as you prepare for the certification exam. More information on the exam and on how the book is organized is available in the Introduction.

## *Start your preparation with the chapter-based exam objective map*

I strongly recommend a structured approach to preparing for this exam. To help you with this task, I developed a chapter-based exam objective map, as shown in figure 1. The full version is in the Introduction (table I.3).

| | Exam objectives | Covered in chapter/ section |
|---|---|---|
| **1** | **Java basics** | **Chapters 1 and 3** |
| 1.1 | Define the scope of variables | Section 3.1 |
| 1.2 | Define the structure of a Java class | Section 1.1 |
| 1.3 | Create executable Java applications with a `main` method; run a Java program from | Section 1.2 |

Figure 1  The Introduction to this book provides a list of all exam objectives and the corresponding chapter and section numbers where they are covered. See the full table in the Introduction (table I.3).

The map in the Introduction shows the complete exam objective list mapped to the relevant chapter and section numbers. You can jump to the relevant section number to work on a particular exam topic.

## Chapter-based objectives

Each chapter starts with a list of the exam objectives covered in that chapter, as shown in figure 2. This list is followed by a quick comparison of the major concepts and topics covered in the chapter with real-world objects and scenarios.

| Exam objectives covered in this chapter | What you need to know |
|---|---|
| [1.2] Define the structure of a Java class. | Structure of a Java class, with its components: package and import statements, class declarations, comments, variables, and methods. Difference between the components of a Java class and that of a Java source code file. |
| [1.3] Create executable Java applications with a `main` method; run a Java program from the command line; including console output. | The right method signature for the `main` method to create an executable Java application. The arguments that are passed to the `main` method. |

**Figure 2   An example of the list of exam objectives and brief explanations at the beginning of each chapter**

## Section-based objectives

Each main section in a chapter starts by identifying the exam objective(s) that it covers. Each listed exam topic starts with the exam objective and its subobjective number.

In figure 3, the number "4.4" refers to section 4.4 in chapter 4 (the complete list of chapters and sections can be found in the table of contents). The number "9.4" preceding the exam objective refers to the objective's numbering in the list of exam objectives on Oracle's website (the complete numbered list of exam objectives is given in table I.3 in the Introduction).

### 4.4    ArrayList

> [9.4]   Declare and use an ArrayList of a given type

In this section, I'll cover how to use `ArrayList`, its commonly used methods, and the advantages it offers over an array.

The OCA Java SE 8 Programmer I exam covers only one class from the Java Collection API: `ArrayList`. The rest of the classes from the Java Collection API are covered in the OCP Java SE 8 Programmer II exam (exam number 1Z0-809). One of the reasons

**Figure 3   An example of the beginning of a section, identifying the exam objective that it covers**

## Exam tips

Each chapter provides multiple *exam tip*s to reemphasize the points that are the most confusing, overlooked, or frequently answered incorrectly by candidates and that therefore require special attention for the exam. Figure 4 shows an example.

> **EXAM TIP** An `ArrayList` preserves the order of insertion of its elements. `Iterator`, `ListIterator`, and the enhanced `for` loop will return the elements in the order in which they were added to the `ArrayList`. An iterator (`Iterator` or `ListIterator`) lets you remove elements as you iterate an `ArrayList`. It's not possible to remove elements from an `ArrayList` while iterating it using a `for` loop.

Figure 4   Example of an exam tip; they occur multiple times in a chapter

## Notes

All chapters also include multiple notes that draw your attention to points that should be noted while you're preparing for the exam. Figure 5 shows an example.

> **NOTE** Although the terms *method parameters* and *method arguments* are not the same, you may have noticed that many programmers use them interchangeably. *Method parameters* are the variables that appear in the definition of a method. *Method arguments* are the actual values that are passed to a method while executing it. In figure 3.15, the variables `phNum` and `msg` are method parameters. If you execute this method as `sendMsg("123456", "Hello")`, then the `String` values `"123456"` and `"Hello"` are method arguments. As you know, you can pass literal values or variables to a method. Thus, method arguments can be literal values or variables.

Figure 5   Example note

## Sidebars

Sidebars contain information that may not be directly relevant to the exam but that is related to it. Figure 6 shows an example.

### static classes and interfaces

Certification aspirants frequently ask questions about `static` classes and interfaces, so I'll quickly cover these in this section to ward off any confusion related to them. But note that `static` classes and interfaces are types of nested classes and interfaces that aren't covered by the OCA Java 8 Programmer I exam.

You can't prefix the definition of a top-level class or an interface with the keyword `static`. A top-level class or interface is one that isn't defined within another class or interface. The following code will fail to compile:

```
static class Person {}
```

Figure 6   Example sidebar

## Images

I use a lot of images in the chapters for an immersive learning experience. I believe that a simple image can help you understand a concept quickly, and a little humor can help you to retain information longer.

Simple images are used to draw your attention to a particular line of code (as shown in figure 7).

```
public String replace(char oldChar, char newChar) {
    if (oldChar != newChar) {
        // code to create a new char array and
        // replace the desired char with the new char

        return new String(0, len, buf);
    }
    return this;
}
```

replace creates and returns a new String object. It doesn't modify the existing array value.

**Figure 7   An example image that draws your attention to a particular line of code**

I use pictorial representation of data in arrays (figure 8) and other data types to aid visualization and understanding.

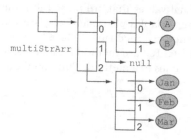

**Figure 8   An example pictorial representation of data in an array**

To reinforce important points and help you retain them longer, a little humor has been added using comic strips (as in figure 9).

**Figure 9   An example of a little humor to help you remember that the `finally` block always executes**

I also use images to group and represent information for quick reference. Figure 10 shows an example of the protected members that can be accessed by derived or unrelated classes in the same or separate packages. I strongly recommend that you try to create a few of your own figures like these.

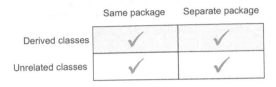

Figure 10   An example of grouping and representing information for quick reference

An image can also add more meaning to a sequence of steps explained in the text. For example, figure 11 seems to bring the Java compiler to life by allowing it to talk with you and convey what it does when it gets to compile a class that doesn't define a constructor. Again, try a few of your own! It'll be fun!

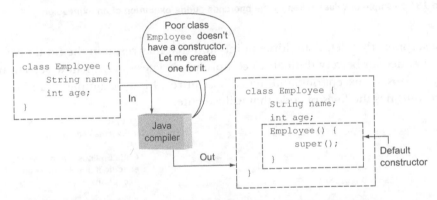

Figure 11   An example pictorial representation of steps executed by the Java compiler when it compiles a class without a constructor

The exam requires that you know multiple methods from classes such as String, StringBuilder, ArrayList, and others. The number of these methods can be overwhelming, but grouping these methods according to their functionality can make this task a lot more manageable. Figure 12 shows an example of an image that groups methods of the String class according to their functionality.

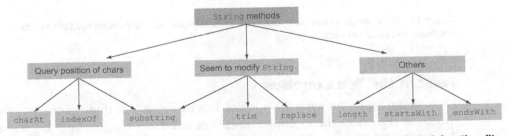

Figure 12   An example image used to group methods of the String class according to their functionality

Expressions that involve multiple operands can be hard to comprehend. Figure 13 is an example of an image that can save you from the mayhem of unary increment and decrement operators used in prefix and postfix notation.

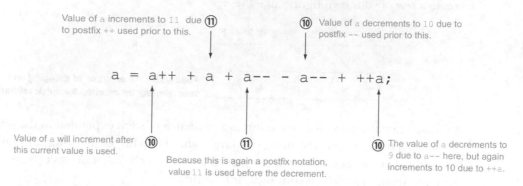

Figure 13   Example of values taken by the operands during execution of an expression

Code snippets that define multiple points and that may result in the nonlinear execution of code can be very difficult to comprehend. These may include selection statements, loops, or exception-handling code. Figure 14 is an example of an image that clearly outlines the lines of code that will execute.

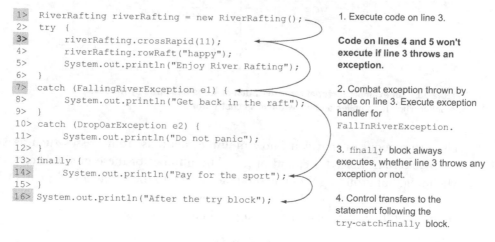

Figure 14   An example of flow of control in a code snippet that may define multiple points of nonlinear execution of code

## Twist in the Tale exercises

Each chapter includes a few Twist in the Tale exercises. For these exercises, I try to use modified code from the examples already covered in a chapter, and the "Twist in the Tale" title refers to modified or tweaked code. These exercises highlight how even small code modifications can change the behavior of your code. They should encourage you to carefully examine all the code in the exam.

My main reason for including these exercises is that on the real exam, you may get to answer more than one question that seems to define exactly the same question and answer options. But on closer inspection, you'll realize that these questions differ slightly and that these differences change the behavior of the code and the correct answer option.

The answers to all the Twist in the Tale exercises are given in the appendix.

## Code indentation

Some of the examples in this book show incorrect indentation of code. This has been done on purpose because on the real exam you can't expect to see perfectly indented code. You should be able to comprehend incorrectly indented code to answer an exam question correctly.

## Review notes

When you're ready to take your exam, don't forget to reread the review notes a day before or on the morning of the exam. These notes contain important points from each chapter as a quick refresher.

## Exam questions

Each chapter concludes with a set of 10 or 11 exam questions. These follow the same pattern as the real exam questions. Attempt these exam questions after completing a chapter.

## Answers to exam questions

The answers to all exam questions provide detailed explanations, including why options are correct or incorrect. Mark your incorrect answers and identify the sections that you need to reread. If possible, draw a few diagrams—you'll be amazed at how much they can help you retain the concepts. Give it a try—it'll be fun!

## Author Online

The purchase of *OCA Java SE 8 Programmer I Certification Guide* includes free access to a private forum run by Manning Publications where you can make comments about the book, ask technical questions, and receive help from the author and other users. You can access and subscribe to the forum at www.manning.com/books/oca-java-se-8-programmer-i-certification-guide. This page provides information on how to get on the forum once you're registered, what kind of help is available, and the rules of conduct in the forum.

Manning's commitment to our readers is to provide a venue where a meaningful dialogue among individual readers and between readers and the author can take place. It's not a commitment to any specific amount of participation on the part of the author, whose contribution to the book's forum remains voluntary (and unpaid). We suggest you try asking the author some challenging questions, lest her interest stray!

The Author Online forum and the archives of previous discussions will be accessible from the publisher's website as long as the book is in print.

> **NOTE** This book uses code styles that you are likely to see on the exam. It often includes practices that aren't recommended on real projects, like poorly indented code or skipping values for brevity, among others, but this is not meant to encourage you to use obscure coding practices.

# about the author

 Mala is passionate about making people employable by bridging the gap between their existing and required skills. In her quest to fulfill this mission, she is authoring books to help IT professionals and students succeed on industry-recognized Oracle Java certifications.

She has master's degrees in computer applications along with multiple other certifications from Oracle. With over 15 years of experience in IT as a developer, architect, trainer, and mentor, she has worked with international training and software services organizations on various Java projects. She is experienced in mentoring teams on technical and software development processes.

She is the founder and lead mentor of a portal (www.ejavaguru.com) that has offered Java courses for Oracle certification since 2006.

Mala is a firm believer in creativity as an essential life skill. To popularize the importance of creativity, innovation, and design in life, she and her daughter started KaagZevar (www.KaagZevar.com)—a platform for nurturing these values.

# about the cover illustration

The figure on the cover of *OCA Java SE 8 Programmer I Certification Guide* is captioned "Morning Habit of a Lady of Quality in Barbary—1700." The illustration is taken from Thomas Jefferys' *A Collection of the Dresses of Different Nations, Ancient and Modern* (four volumes), London, published between 1757 and 1772. The title page states that these are hand-colored copperplate engravings, heightened with gum arabic. Thomas Jefferys (1719–1771) was called "Geographer to King George III." He was an English cartographer who was the leading map supplier of his day. He engraved and printed maps for government and other official bodies and produced a wide range of commercial maps and atlases, especially of North America. His work as a mapmaker sparked an interest in local dress customs of the lands he surveyed and mapped, which are brilliantly displayed in this collection.

Fascination with faraway lands and travel for pleasure were relatively new phenomena in the late 18th century, and collections such as this one were popular, introducing both the tourist as well as the armchair traveler to the inhabitants of other countries. The diversity of the drawings in Jefferys' volumes speaks vividly of the uniqueness and individuality of the world's nations some 200 years ago. Dress codes have changed since then and the diversity by region and country, so rich at the time, has faded away. It's now hard to tell apart the inhabitants of different continents, let alone different towns or regions. Perhaps we have traded cultural diversity for a more varied personal life—certainly for a more varied and fast-paced technological life.

At a time when it is hard to tell one computer book from another, Manning celebrates the inventiveness and initiative of the computer business with book covers based on the rich diversity of regional life of two centuries ago, brought back to life by Jefferys' pictures.

# *Introduction*

---

**This introduction covers**

- Introduction to the Oracle Certified Associate (OCA) Java SE 8 Programmer I Certification (exam number 1Z0-808)
- Importance of the OCA Java SE 8 Programmer certification
- Comparison of the OCA Java SE 8 Programmer I exam to the OCA Java SE 7 Programmer I exam
- Comparison of the OCA Java SE 8 Programmer I exam (1Z0-808) to the OCP Java SE 8 Programmer II exam (1Z0-809)
- Detailed exam objectives, mapped to book chapters
- FAQs on exam preparation and on taking the exam
- Introduction to the testing engine used for the exam

This book is intended specifically for individuals who wish to earn the OCA Java SE 8 Programmer I Certification (exam number 1Z0-808). It assumes that you are familiar with Java and have some experience working with it. If you're completely new to the Java programming language, I suggest that you start your journey with an entry-level book and then come back to this one.

## 1    *Disclaimer*

The information in this chapter is sourced from Oracle.com, public websites, and user forums. Input has been taken from real people who have earned Java certification, including the author. All efforts have been made to maintain the accuracy of the content, but the details of the exam—including the exam objectives, pricing, exam pass score, total number of questions, maximum exam duration, and others—are subject to change per Oracle's policies. The author and publisher of the book shall not be held responsible for any loss or damage accrued due to any information contained in this book or due to any direct or indirect use of this information.

## 2    *Introduction to OCA Java SE 8 Programmer I Certification*

The Oracle Certified Associate (OCA) Java SE 8 Programmer I exam (1Z0-808) covers the fundamentals of Java SE 8 programming, such as the structure of classes and interfaces, variables of different data types, methods, operators, arrays, decision constructs, and loops. The exam includes handling exceptions and a few commonly used classes from the Java API like `String`, `StringBuilder`, and `ArrayList`. This exam doesn't include a lot of Java 8–specific language features. It includes an introduction to functional-style programming with lambda expressions. It partially covers the new Date and Time API.

This exam is one of two steps to earning the title of Oracle Certified Professional (OCP) Java SE 8 Programmer. It certifies that an individual possesses a strong foundation in the Java programming language. Table 1 lists the details of this exam.

Table 1   Details for the OCA Java SE 8 Programmer I exam (1Z0-808)

| | |
|---|---|
| Exam number | 1Z0-808 |
| Java version | Based on Java version 8 |
| Number of questions | 77 |
| Passing score | 65% |
| Time duration | 150 minutes |
| Pricing | US$300 |
| Type of questions | Multiple choice |

## 3    *The importance of OCA Java SE 8 Programmer I Certification*

The OCA Java SE 8 Programmer I exam (1Z0-808) is an entry-level exam in your Java certification roadmap, as shown in figure 1.

This exam is one of two steps to earn the title of OCP Java SE 8 Programmer. The dashed lines and arrows in figure 1 depict the prerequisites for certification. OCP Java Programmer certification (any Java version) is a prerequisite to earn most of the other higher-level certifications in Java.

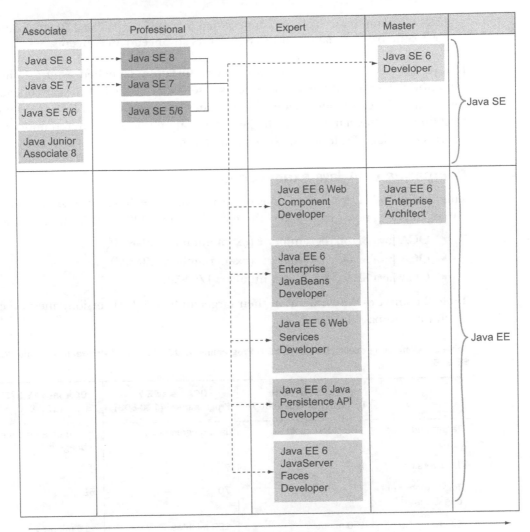

Increasing difficulty level

**Figure 1   OCA Java SE 8 Programmer certification is an entry-level certification in the Java certification roadmap.**

To earn the OCP Java SE 8 Programmer title, you must pass the following two certifications (in any order):

- OCA Java SE 8 Programmer I (1Z0-808)
- OCP Java SE 8 Programmer II (1Z0-809)

 **NOTE**   At the time of writing, Oracle made this exam a prerequisite for passing the 1Z0-809 exam. Earlier, Oracle allowed passing the 1Z0-808 and 1Z0-809 exams in any order. Even when this exam wasn't a prerequisite for passing the

1Z0-809 exam, it was highly recommended to write it first. The 1Z0-808 exam covers the basics of Java, and 1Z0-809 covers advanced Java concepts.

Java Junior Associate (1Z0-811) is a newer certification, launched by Oracle in 2016. It's a novice-level certification for students at secondary schools, two-year colleges, and four-year colleges and universities. All the other Java certifications are career-level certifications. As shown in figure 1, the Java certification tracks are offered under the categories Associate, Professional, Expert, and Master.

## 4    *Comparing OCA Java exam versions*

This section will clear up any confusion surrounding the different versions of the OCA Java exam. As of now, Oracle offers three versions of the OCA certification in Java:

- OCA Java SE 8 Programmer I (exam number: 1Z0-808)
- OCA Java SE 7 Programmer I (exam number: 1Z0-803)
- OCA Java SE 5/SE 6 (exam number: 1Z0-850)

Table 2 compares these exams on their target audience, Java version, question count, duration, and passing score.

Table 2    Comparing exams: OCA Java SE 8 Programmer I, OCA Java SE 7 Programmer I, and OCA Java SE 5/6

|                             | OCA Java SE 8 Programmer I (1Z0-803) | OCA Java SE 7 Programmer I (1Z0-803) | OCA Java SE 5/SE 6 (1Z0-850)      |
|-----------------------------|--------------------------------------|--------------------------------------|-----------------------------------|
| Target audience             | Java programmers                     | Java programmers                     | Java programmers and IT managers  |
| Java version                | 8                                    | 7                                    | 6                                 |
| Total number of questions   | 77                                   | 70                                   | 51                                |
| Exam duration               | 150 minutes                          | 120 minutes                          | 115 minutes                       |
| Passing score               | 65%                                  | 63%                                  | 68%                               |

The OCA Java SE 8 Programmer I Certification adds the following topics to the ones covered by the OCA Java SE 7 Programmer I Certification:

- Features and components of Java
- Wrapper classes
- Ternary constructs
- Some classes from the new Java 8 Date and Time API
- Creating and using lambda expressions
- Predicate interface

Figure 2 shows a detailed comparison of the exam objectives of the OCA Java SE 8 and OCA Java SE 7 Programmer I exams. Here's the legend to understand it:

- *Light gray background*—Main exam objective.
- *Medium gray background*—Covered only in the OCA Java SE 8 exam.
- *Dark gray background*—Although the text or main exam objective of this subobjective differs, it is covered by the other exam.

| OCA Java SE 8 | Objectives common to both exams | OCA Java SE 7 |
|---|---|---|
| | **Java basics** | |
| • Run a Java program from the command line; including console output<br>• Compare and contrast the features and components of Java, such as platform independence, object orientation, encapsulation, and so on | • Define the scope of variables<br>• Define the structure of a Java class<br>• Create executable Java applications with a `main` method<br>• Import other Java packages to make them accessible in your code | |
| | **Working with Java data types** | |
| • Develop code that uses wrapper classes such as `Boolean`, `Double`, and `Integer` | • Declare and initialize variables (including casting of primitive data types)<br>• Differentiate between object reference variables and primitive variables<br>• Know how to read or write to object fields<br>• Explain an object's lifecycle | • Manipulate data using the `StringBuilder` class and its methods<br>• Creating and manipulating Strings |
| | **Using operators and decision constructs** | |
| • Use Java operators, including parentheses to override operator precedence<br>• Ternary constructs | • Test equality between Strings and other objects using `==` and `equals()`<br>• Create `if` and `if/else` and ternary constructs<br>• Use a `switch` statement | • Use Java operators<br>• Use parenthesis to override operator precedence |
| | **Creating and using arrays** | |
| | • Declare, instantiate, initialize and use a one-dimensional array<br>• Declare, instantiate, initialize and use a multi-dimensional array | • Declare and use an `ArrayList` |
| | **Using loop constructs** | |
| | • Create and use `while` loops<br>• Create and use `for` loops, including the enhanced `for` loop<br>• Create and use `do`/`while` loops<br>• Compare loop constructs<br>• Use `break` and `continue` | |
| | **Working with methods and encapsulation** | |
| • Create methods with arguments and return values; including overloaded methods<br>• Create and overload constructors; including impact on default constructors | • Apply the `static` keyword to methods and fields<br>• Apply access modifiers<br>• Apply encapsulation principles to a class<br>• Determine the effect upon object references and primitive values when they are passed into methods that change the values | • Create methods with arguments and return values<br>• Create an overloaded method<br>• Differentiate between default and user defined constructors<br>• Create and overload constructors |

**Figure 2  Comparing exam objectives of the OCA Java SE 8 Programmer I and OCA Java SE 7 Programmer I certifications**

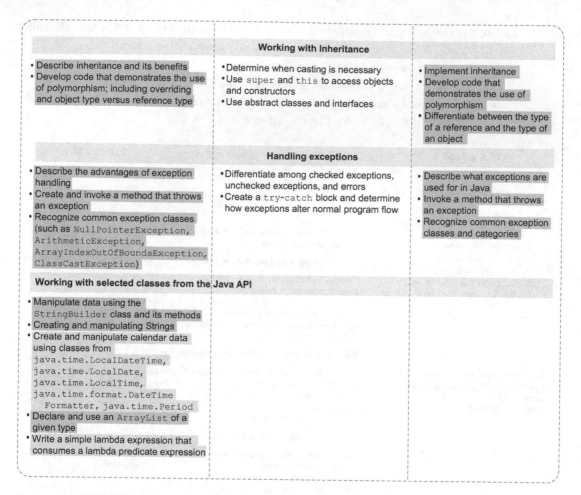

**Working with Inheritance**

| | | |
|---|---|---|
| • Describe inheritance and its benefits<br>• Develop code that demonstrates the use of polymorphism; including overriding and object type versus reference type | • Determine when casting is necessary<br>• Use `super` and `this` to access objects and constructors<br>• Use abstract classes and interfaces | • Implement inheritance<br>• Develop code that demonstrates the use of polymorphism<br>• Differentiate between the type of a reference and the type of an object |

**Handling exceptions**

| | | |
|---|---|---|
| • Describe the advantages of exception handling<br>• Create and invoke a method that throws an exception<br>• Recognize common exception classes (such as `NullPointerException`, `ArithmeticException`, `ArrayIndexOutOfBoundsException`, `ClassCastException`) | • Differentiate among checked exceptions, unchecked exceptions, and errors<br>• Create a `try-catch` block and determine how exceptions alter normal program flow | • Describe what exceptions are used for in Java<br>• Invoke a method that throws an exception<br>• Recognize common exception classes and categories |

**Working with selected classes from the Java API**

| | | |
|---|---|---|
| • Manipulate data using the `StringBuilder` class and its methods<br>• Creating and manipulating Strings<br>• Create and manipulate calendar data using classes from `java.time.LocalDateTime`, `java.time.LocalDate`, `java.time.LocalTime`, `java.time.format.DateTime Formatter`, `java.time.Period`<br>• Declare and use an `ArrayList` of a given type<br>• Write a simple lambda expression that consumes a lambda predicate expression | | |

**Figure 2   Comparing exam objectives of the OCA Java SE 8 Programmer I and OCA Java SE 7 Programmer I certifications** *(continued)*

Figure 3 shows a detailed comparison of the exam objectives of OCA Java SE 5/6 (1Z0-850) and OCA Java SE 7 Programmer I (1Z0-803). It shows objectives that are exclusive to each of these exam versions and those that are common to both. The first column shows the objectives that are included only in OCA Java SE 5/6 (1Z0-850), the middle column shows common exam objectives, and the right column shows exam objectives covered only in OCA Java SE 7 Programmer I (1Z0-803).

| OCA Java SE 5/6 1Z0-850 | Common objectives | OCA Java SE 7 Programmer I 1Z0-803 |
|---|---|---|
| **Algorithm design and implementation**<br>• Algorithm<br>• Pseudocode | **Java basics**<br>• Variable scope<br>• Structure of Java class<br>• `import` and `package` statements<br>• `main` method | |
| | **Working with Java data types** | |
| • Enums | • Primitives, object references<br>• Read/write to object fields<br>• Call methods on objects<br>• `String`s | • `StringBuilder` |
| **Java development fundamentals**<br>• Use of `javac` command<br>• Use of `java` command<br>• Purpose and type of classes in packages<br>  `java.awt`<br>  `javax.swing`<br>  `java.io`<br>  `java.net`<br>  `java.util` | **Operators and decision constructs**<br>• Java operators<br>• `if` and `if-else` constructs<br>• `switch` statement | • Parentheses to override operator precedence<br>• Test equality between `String` and other objects using == and `equals()` |
| | **Creating and using arrays**<br>• One-dimensional arrays<br>• Multidimensional arrays | • `ArrayList` |
| **Java platforms and integration technologies**<br>• Compare and contrast J2SE, J2ME, J2EE<br>• RMI<br>• JDBC, SQL, RDMS<br>• JNDI, messaging, and JMS | **Loop constructs**<br>• `for` and enhanced `for` loops<br>• `while` and `do-while` loops<br>• `break` and `continue` statements | |
| **Client technologies**<br>• HTML, JavaScript<br>• J2ME MIDlets<br>• Applets<br>• Swing | **Methods and encapsulation**<br>• Create methods with arguments and return types<br>• Apply access modifiers<br>• Effect on object references and primitives when they are passed to methods | • Apply `static` keyword to methods and fields<br>• Overloaded constructors and methods<br>• Default and user-defined constructors |
| **Server technologies**<br>• EJB, servlets, JSP, JMS, SMTP, JAX-RBC, WebServices, JavaMail<br>• Servlet and JSP for HTML<br>• EJB session, entity, and message-driven beans<br>• Web tier, business tier, EIS tier | **Inheritance**<br>• Implement inheritance<br>• Polymorphism<br>• Differentiate between type of a reference variable and object<br>• Use abstract classes and interfaces | • Determine when casting is necessary<br>• Use `super` and `this` to access objects and constructors |
| **OOP concepts**<br>• UML diagrams<br>• Association<br>• Composition<br>• Association navigation | | **Handling exceptions**<br>• Exceptions and errors<br>• `try-catch` blocks<br>• Use of exceptions<br>• Methods that throw exceptions<br>• Common exception classes and categories |

**Figure 3  Comparing objectives of exams OCA Java SE 5/6 and OCA Java SE 7 Programmer I**

## 5   Next step: OCP Java SE 8 Programmer II (1Z0-809) exam

After successfully passing the OCA Java SE 8 Programmer I exam, the next step is to take the OCP Java SE 8 Programmer II exam. The OCP Java SE 8 Programmer II certification is designed for individuals who possess advanced skills in the Java programming language. It covers advanced Java features such as threads, concurrency, collections, the Streams API, Java file I/O, inner classes, localization, and others.

## 6   Complete exam objectives, mapped to book chapters, and readiness checklist

Table 3 includes a complete list of exam objectives for the OCA Java SE 8 Programmer I exam, which was taken from Oracle's website. All the objectives are mapped to the book's chapters and the section numbers that cover them.

Table 3   Exam objectives and subobjectives mapped to chapter and section numbers

| | Exam objectives | Covered in chapter/ section |
|---|---|---|
| **1** | **Java basics** | **Chapters 1 and 3** |
| 1.1 | Define the scope of variables | Section 3.1 |
| 1.2 | Define the structure of a Java class | Section 1.1 |
| 1.3 | Create executable Java applications with a `main` method; run a Java program from the command line, including console output | Section 1.2 |
| 1.4 | Import other Java packages to make them accessible in your code | Section 1.3 |
| 1.5 | Compare and contrast the features and components of Java, such as platform independence, object orientation, encapsulation, and so on | Section 1.6 |
| **2** | **Working with Java data types** | **Chapters 2 and 3** |
| 2.1 | Declare and initialize variables (including casting of primitive data types) | Sections 2.1 and 2.3 |
| 2.2 | Differentiate between object reference variables and primitive variables | Sections 2.1 and 2.3 |
| 2.3 | Know how to read and write to object fields | Section 3.6 |
| 2.4 | Explain an object's lifecycle (creation, "dereference by reassignment," and garbage collection) | Section 3.2 |
| 2.5 | Develop code that uses wrapper classes such as `Boolean`, `Double`, and `Integer` | Section 2.5 |
| **3** | **Using Operators and decision constructs** | **Chapters 2, 4, and 5** |
| 3.1 | Use Java operators, including parentheses to override operator precedence | Section 2.4 |
| 3.2 | Test equality between Strings and other objects using `==` and `equals()` | Sections 4.1 and 4.5 |
| 3.3 | Create `if` and `if/else` and ternary constructs | Section 5.1 |
| 3.4 | Use a `switch` statement | Section 5.2 |
| **4** | **Creating and using arrays** | **Chapter 4** |
| 4.1 | Declare, instantiate, initialize, and use a one-dimensional array | Section 4.3 |
| 4.2 | Declare, instantiate, initialize, and use a multidimensional array | Section 4.3 |

**Table 3    Exam objectives and subobjectives mapped to chapter and section numbers**

| | Exam objectives | Covered in chapter/section |
|---|---|---|
| **5** | **Using loop constructs** | **Chapter 5** |
| 5.1 | Create and use `while` loops | Section 5.5 |
| 5.2 | Create and use `for` loops, including the enhanced `for` loop | Sections 5.3 and 5.4 |
| 5.3 | Create and use `do-while` loops | Section 5.5 |
| 5.4 | Compare loop constructs | Section 5.6 |
| 5.5 | Use `break` and `continue` | Section 5.7 |
| **6** | **Working with methods and encapsulation** | **Chapters 1 and 3** |
| 6.1 | Create methods with arguments and return values, including overloaded methods | Sections 3.3 and 3.4 |
| 6.2 | Apply the `static` keyword to methods and fields | Section 1.5 |
| 6.3 | Create and overload constructors, including impact on default constructors | Section 3.5 |
| 6.4 | Apply access modifiers | Section 1.4 |
| 6.5 | Apply encapsulation principles to a class | Section 3.7 |
| 6.6 | Determine the effect on object references and primitive values when they are passed into methods that change the values | Section 3.8 |
| **7** | **Working with inheritance** | **Chapters 1 and 6** |
| 7.1 | Describe inheritance and its benefits | Sections 6.1 and 6.2 |
| 7.2 | Develop code that demonstrates the use of polymorphism, including overriding and object type versus reference type | Sections 6.3 and 6.6 |
| 7.3 | Determine when casting is necessary | Section 6.4 |
| 7.4 | Use `super` and `this` to access objects and constructors | Section 6.5 |
| 7.5 | Use `abstract` classes and interfaces | Sections 1.5, 6.1, 6.2, and 6.6 |
| **8** | **Handling exceptions** | **Chapter 7** |
| 8.1 | Differentiate among checked exceptions, unchecked exceptions, and errors | Section 7.2 |
| 8.2 | Create a `try-catch` block and determine how exceptions alter normal program flow | Section 7.4 |
| 8.3 | Describe the advantages of exception handling | Section 7.1 |
| 8.4 | Create and invoke a method that throws an exception | Sections 7.3 and 7.4 |
| 8.5 | Recognize common exception classes (such as `NullPointerException`, `ArithmeticException`, `ArrayIndexOutOfBoundsException`, `ClassCastException`) | Section 7.5 |
| **9** | **Working with selected classes from the Java API** | **Chapters 4 and 6** |
| 9.1 | Manipulate data using the `StringBuilder` class and its methods | Section 4.2 |
| 9.2 | Creating and manipulating Strings | Section 4.1 |
| 9.3 | Create and manipulate calendar data using classes from `java.time.Local-DateTime`, `java.time.LocalDate`, `java.time.LocalTime`, `java.time.format.DateTimeFormatter`, and `java.time.Period` | Section 4.6 |
| 9.4 | Declare and use an `ArrayList` of a given type | Section 4.4 |
| 9.5 | Write a simple lambda expression that consumes a lambda predicate expression | Section 6.7 |

## 7    FAQs

You might be anxious when you start your exam preparation or even when you think about getting certified. This section can help calm your nerves by answering frequently asked questions on exam preparation and taking the exam.

### 7.1    FAQs on exam preparation

This sections answers frequently asked questions on how to prepare for the exam, including the best approach, study material, preparation duration, types of questions in the exam, and more.

#### WILL THE EXAM DETAILS EVER CHANGE FOR THE OCA JAVA SE 8 PROGRAMMER I EXAM?

Oracle can change the exam details for a certification even after the certification is made live. The changes can be to the exam objectives, pricing, exam duration, exam questions, and other parts. In the past, Oracle has made similar changes to certification exams. Such changes may not be major, but it's always advisable to check Oracle's website for the latest exam information when you start your exam preparation.

#### WHAT IS THE BEST WAY TO PREPARE FOR THIS EXAM?

Generally, candidates use a combination of resources, such as books, online study materials, articles on the exam, free and paid mock exams, and training to prepare for the exam. Different combinations work best for different people, and there's no one perfect formula for preparation. Depending on whether training or self-study works best for you, you can select the method that's most appropriate for you. Combine it with a lot of code practice and mock exams.

#### HOW DO I KNOW WHEN I AM READY FOR THE EXAM?

You can be sure about your exam readiness by *consistently* getting a good score in the mock exams. Generally, a score of 80% and above in approximately three to five mock exams (the more the better) attempted consecutively will assure you of a similar score in the real exam.

#### HOW MANY MOCK TESTS SHOULD I ATTEMPT BEFORE THE REAL EXAM?

Ideally, you should attempt at least five mock exams before you attempt the real exam. The more the better!

#### I HAVE TWO YEARS' EXPERIENCE WORKING WITH JAVA. DO I STILL NEED TO PREPARE FOR THIS CERTIFICATION?

It's important to understand that there's a difference between the practical knowledge of having worked with Java and the knowledge required to pass this certification exam. The authors of the Java certification exams employ multiple tricks to test your knowledge. Hence, you need a structured preparation and approach to succeed in the certification exam.

### What is the ideal time required to prepare for the exam?

The preparation time frame mainly depends on your experience with Java and the amount of time that you can spend to prepare yourself. On average, you will require approximately 150 hours of study over two or three months to prepare for this exam. Again, the number of study hours required depends on individual learning curves and backgrounds.

It's important to be consistent with your exam preparation. You can't study for a month and then restart after, say, a gap of a month or more.

### Does this exam include any unscored questions?

A few of the questions that you write in any Oracle exam may be marked unscored. Oracle's policy states that while taking an exam, you won't be informed as to whether a question will be scored. You may be surprised to learn that as many as 7 questions out of the 77 questions in the OCA Java SE 8 Programmer I exam may be unscored. Even if you answer a few questions incorrectly, you stand a chance of scoring 100%.

Oracle regularly updates its question bank for all its certification exams. These unscored questions may be used for research and to evaluate new questions that can be added to an exam.

### Can I start my exam preparation with the mock exams?

If you are quite comfortable with the Java language features, then yes, you can start your exam preparation with the mock exams. This will also help you to understand the types of questions to expect in the real certification exam. But if you have little or no experience working with Java, or if you're not quite comfortable with the language features of Java, I don't advise you to start with the mock exams. The exam authors often use a lot of tricks to evaluate a candidate in the real certification exam. Starting your exam preparation with mock exams will only leave you confused about the Java concepts.

### Should I really bother getting certified?

Yes, you should, for the simple reason that employers care about the certification of employees. Organizations prefer a certified Java developer over a noncertified Java developer with similar IT skills and experience. The certification can also get you a higher paycheck than uncertified peers with comparable skills.

### Do I need to make any assumptions?

Yes, Oracle has published the following assumptions for candidates on its website (as mentioned previously, Oracle might change the exam details or assumptions, without any prior notice):

- *Missing package and import statements*—If sample code doesn't include package or import statements, and the question doesn't explicitly refer to these missing statements, then assume that all sample code is in the same package, and import statements exist to support them.

- *No file or directory path names for classes*—If a question doesn't state the filenames or directory locations of classes, then assume one of the following, whichever will enable the code to compile and run:
  - All classes are in one file.
  - Each class is contained in a separate file, and all files are in one directory.
- *Unintended line breaks*—Sample code might have unintended line breaks. If you see a line of code that looks like it has wrapped, and this creates a situation where the wrapping is significant (for example, a quoted String literal has wrapped), assume that the wrapping is an extension of the same line, and the line doesn't contain a hard carriage return that would cause a compilation failure.
- *Code fragments*—A code fragment is a small section of source code that's presented without its context. Assume that all necessary supporting code is present and that the supporting environment fully supports the correct compilation and execution of the code shown and its omitted environment.
- *Descriptive comments*—Take descriptive comments, such as "setter and getters go here," at face value. Assume that correct code exists, compiles, and runs successfully to create the described effect.

### WHAT ARE THE TYPES OR FORMATS OF QUESTIONS THAT I CAN EXPECT IN THE EXAM?

The exam uses different formats of multiple choice questions, illustrated in this section by eight example questions with figures.

The examples for all these types of questions show how the following set of topics might be tested using a different question format:

- Correct declaration of the main method
- Passing command-line parameters
- Overloaded methods
- Significance of method parameter names
- Declaration of variables of varargs

**Exam question type 1 (figure 4)**—Includes simple code, but tricky or confusing answer options.

**Figure 4   Exam question type 1**

The answer options in the following example would confuse a reader on whether the command-line values would be concatenated or added as integer values:

```
Given:

class JavaCertQType1 {
    public static void main(String... cmd) {
        main("private", cmd);
    }
    private static void main(String type, String[] args) {
        System.out.println(args[0] + args[1]);
    }
}

What is the output when class JavaCertQType1 is executed using
the following command (choose 1 option):

java JavaCertQType1 1 11 EJava Guru

 ○  1
 ○  1 11
 ○  111
 ○  12
 ○  1 11 EJava Guru
 ○  Compilation error
 ○  Runtime exception
```

**NOTE** In this book, the sample exam questions at the end of each chapter and full mock exam at the end of the book show answer options as lettered (for example, a–d) for ease on discussion. In the exam, however, the answer options aren't numbered or lettered. They're preceded with either a radio button or a check box. Radio buttons are for questions with only one correct answer, and check boxes are for questions with multiple correct answers.

**Exam question type 2 (figure 5)**—Exam questions without code give you a much needed break from reading code. But it isn't always easy to answer them.

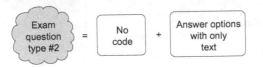

**Figure 5  Exam question type 2**

An example of exam question, type 2:

```
Question2) Assuming that the phrase 'the method main' refers to the method
main that starts an application, select the correct statements (choose 2
options).

 ☐  A class can define multiple methods with the name main, but with
    different signatures.
 ☐  The method main can define its only method parameter of type varargs.
 ☐  Accessibility of the method main can't be restricted to private.
 ☐  A class with overloaded main methods won't compile.
```

**Exam question type 3 (figure 6)**—Reading though and comprehending lots of code can be difficult. The key is to eliminate wrong answers to find the correct answers quickly.

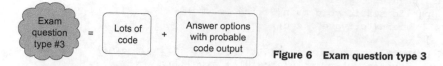

Figure 6   Exam question type 3

An example:

```
Given:

class JavaCertQuesType3 {
    public static void main(String args[]) {
        System.out.println("Spring");
    }
    public static void main(String... args) {
        System.out.println("Summer");
    }
    public static void main(String[] cmd) {
        System.out.println("Autumn");
    }
    public static void main() {
        System.out.println("Winter");
    }
}

What is the output (choose 1 option)?

⊙ Code outputs Spring
⊙ Code outputs Summer
⊙ Code outputs Autumn
⊙ Code outputs Winter
⊙ Compilation error
⊙ Runtime exception
```

**Exam question type 4 (figure 7)**—This type of question is a classic example of "fill in the blank."

Figure 7   Exam question type 4

An example:

```
Given:

class JavaCertQType4 {
    static int c, a = 10, b = 21/2;
    static {
        c = a;
    }
    // INSERT CODE HERE
}

Which options, when inserted individually at //INSERT CODE HERE will
enable class JavaCertQType4 to output value 10 (choose 2)?

☐ public static void main(String... variables) {
      System.out.println(b);
  }

☐ private static void main(String[] commandArgs) {
      System.out.println(b);
  }

☐ public static void main(String args) {
      System.out.println(b);
  }

☐ private static void main() {
      System.out.println(b);
  }
  public static void main(String... method) {
      System.out.println(b);
  }
```

**Exam question type 5 (figure 8)**—This question type will include code, a condition, or both. The answer options will include changes and their results, when applied to the code in the question. Unless otherwise stated, changes in the answer options that you choose are applied individually to the code or the specified situation. Result of a correct answer option won't involve changes suggested in other correct answer options.

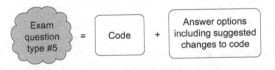

**Figure 8   Exam question type 5**

An example:

```
Given:

1. class JavaCertQType5 {
2.     protected static void main() {
3.         System.out.println("EJavaGuru.com");
4.     }
5.     public static void main(String... method) {
6.         main();
7.         System.out.println("MissionOCAJ8");
8.     }
9. }

Select correct option (choose 2):

☐ Code will compile successfully if code on line 6 is commented.
☐ Code will output the same result if access modifier of main() is
  changed to private at line 2.
☐ Code won't compile if code on line 6 is placed after code on line 7.
☐ The code compiles successfully, but throws a runtime exception.
```

**Exam question type 6 (figure 9)**—Because your mind is programmed to select the correct options, answer this type of question very carefully. My personal tip: cross fingers in one of your hands to remind you that you need to select the *incorrect* statements.

**Figure 9    Exam question type 6**

An example:

```
Given:

1. class JavaCertQType6 {
2.     public static void main(String... method)  {
3.         main();
4.         main(method);
5.     }
6.     protected static void main() {
7.         System.out.println("EJavaGuru");
8.     }
9. }

Select incorrect options (choose 2):

☐ Code will compile successfully only if code on line 3 is commented.
☐ Code will output the same result if access modifier of main() is
  changed to public at line 6.
☐ Code will compile sucessfully and execute without any runtime
  exceptions.
☐ If the order of code on lines 3 and 4 is reversed, the code won't
  output 'EJavaGuru'.
```

**Exam question type 7 (figure 10)**—This question won't include any code in the text of the question; it will state a condition that needs to be implemented using code given in the answer options.

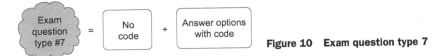

Figure 10    Exam question type 7

An example:

```
Which of the following options can be used to define a main method that
outputs the value of the second and fourth command parameters (choose 2):

☐   public static void main(String... method) {
        for (int i = 1; i < method.size && i < 6; i = i + 2)
            System.out.println(method[i]);
    }

☐   public static void main(String[] main) {
        for (int i = 1; i < main.length && i < 6; i = i + 2)
            System.out.println(main[i]);
    }

☐   public static void main(String... arguments) {
        int ctr = 0;
        while (ctr < arguments.length) {
            if (ctr >= 4) break;
            if (ctr %2 != 0)
                System.out.println(arguments[ctr]);
            ++ctr;
        }
    }

☐   public static void main(String[] arguments) {
        int ctr = 1;
        while (ctr < arguments.length) {
            if (ctr >= 4) break;
            if (ctr %2 == 0)
                System.out.println(arguments[ctr]);
            ++ctr;
        }
    }
```

**Exam question type 8 (figure 11)**—This question includes a pictorial representation of a single or multidimensional array, stating a situation and asking you to select code as input to get the required array formation.

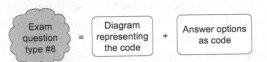

Figure 11    Exam question type 8

An example:

Assuming that the following array and image represents variation of Connect4 game, where a player wins if she places same number in a row or column:

```
char[][] grid = new char[][]{{'7',' ',' ',' '},{'5','7',' ','5'},
{'7','7','5','5'},{'5','7','7','5'}};
```

| 7 |   |   |   |
|---|---|---|---|
| 5 | 7 |   | 5 |
| 7 | 7 | 5 | 5 |
| 5 | 7 | 7 | 5 |

Which of the following assignments would enable a player with number 7 to win (choose 2 options)?

```
☐  grid[0] = new char[]{'7','7',' ',' '};
☐  grid[1] = new char[]{'7','7',' ',' '};
☐  grid[0] = {'7','7',' ',' '};
☐  grid[1] = {'7','7',' ',' '};
☐  grid[0][1] = '7';
☐  grid[1][2] = '7';
☐  grid[0] = new char[4]{'7','7',' ',' '};
☐  grid[1] = new char[4]{'7','7',' ',' '};
```

## 7.2    FAQs on taking the exam

This section contains a list of frequently asked questions related to the exam registration, exam coupon, do's and don'ts while taking the exam, and exam retakes.

### WHERE AND HOW DO I TAKE THIS EXAM?

You can take this exam at an Oracle Testing Center or Pearson VUE Authorized Testing Center. To sit for the exam, you must register for the exam and purchase an exam voucher. The following options are available:

- Register for the exam and pay Pearson VUE directly
- Purchase an exam voucher from Oracle and register at Pearson VUE to take the exam
- Register at an Oracle Testing Center

Look for the nearest testing centers in your area, register yourself, and schedule an exam date and time. Most of the popular computer training institutes also have a testing center on their premises. You can locate a Pearson VUE testing site at www.pearsonvue.com/oracle/, which contains detailed information on locating testing centers and scheduling or rescheduling an exam. At the time of registration, you'll need to provide the following details along with your name, address, and contact numbers:

- Exam title and number (OCA Java SE 8 Programmer I, 1Z0-808)
- Any discount code that should be applied during registration
- Oracle Testing ID/Candidate ID, if you've taken any other Oracle/Sun certification exam
- Your OPN Company ID (if your employer is in the Oracle Partner Network, you can find out the company ID and use any available discounts on the exam fee)

### SHOULD I CARRY MY PHOTO ID PROOF OR ANY OTHER PROOF?

The examination center coordinator will ask you for at least two ID proofs, one of which must include your photograph. If in doubt, please connect with your examination center using email or phone and inquire about the ID requirements.

### HOW LONG IS THE EXAM COUPON VALID?

Each exam coupon is printed with an expiry date. Beware of any discounted coupons that come with an assurance that they can be used past the expiration date.

### CAN I REFER TO NOTES OR BOOKS WHILE TAKING THIS EXAM?

You can't refer to any books or notes while taking this exam. You're not allowed to carry any blank paper for rough work or even your mobile phone inside the testing cubicle.

### WHAT IS THE PURPOSE OF MARKING A QUESTION WHILE TAKING THE EXAM?

By marking a question, you can manage your time efficiently. Don't spend a lot of time on a single question. You can mark a difficult question to defer answering it while taking your exam. The exam gives you an option to review answers to the marked questions at the end of the exam. Also, navigating from one question to another using the Back and Next buttons is usually time consuming. If you're unsure of an answer, mark it and review it at the end.

### CAN I WRITE DOWN THE EXAM QUESTIONS AND TAKE THEM WITH ME?

No. The exam centers no longer provide sheets of paper for the rough work that you may need to do while taking the exam. The testing center will provide you with either erasable or non-erasable boards. If you're provided with a non-erasable board, you may request another one if you need it.

Oracle is quite particular about certification candidates distributing or circulating the memorized questions in any form. If Oracle finds out that this is happening, it may cancel a candidate's certificate, bar that candidate forever from taking any Oracle certification, inform the employer, or take legal action.

### WHAT HAPPENS IF I COMPLETE THE EXAM BEFORE OR AFTER THE TOTAL TIME?

If you complete the exam before the total exam time has elapsed, revise your answers and click the Submit or Finish button. If you have not clicked the Submit button and you use up all the exam time, the exam engine will no longer allow you to modify any of the exam answers and will present the screen with the Submit button.

### WILL I RECEIVE MY SCORE IMMEDIATELY AFTER THE EXAM?

No, you won't. When you click the Submit button, the screen will request you to log in to your Oracle account (CertView) after approximately half an hour to view your score. It also includes the topics you answered incorrectly. The testing center won't give you any hard copies of your certification score. The certificate itself will arrive via mail within six to eight weeks.

### WHAT HAPPENS IF I FAIL? CAN I RETAKE THE EXAM?

It's not the end of the world. Don't worry if you fail. You can retake the exam after 14 days (and the world won't know it's a retake).

But you can't retake a passed exam to improve your score. Also, you can't retake a beta exam.

## 8    *The testing engine used in the exam*

The user interface of the testing engine used for the certification exam is quite simple. (You could even call it primitive, compared to today's web, desktop, and smartphone applications.)

Before you can start the exam, you will be required to accept the terms and conditions of the Oracle Certification Candidate Agreement. Your computer screen will display all these conditions and give you an option to accept the conditions. You can proceed with writing the exam only if you accept these conditions.

Here are the features of the testing engine used by Oracle:

- *Engine UI is divided into three sections*—The UI of the testing engine is divided into the following three segments:
  - *Static upper section*—Displays question number, time remaining, and a check box to mark a question for review
  - *Scrollable middle section*—Displays the question text and the answer options
  - *Static bottom section*—Displays buttons to display the previous question, display the next question, end the exam, and review marked questions
- *Each question is displayed on a separate screen*—The exam engine displays one question on the screen at a time. It doesn't display multiple questions on a single screen, like a scrollable web page. All effort is made to display the complete question and answer options without scrolling, or with little scrolling.
- *Code Exhibit button*—Many questions include code. Such questions, together with their answers, may require significant scrolling to be viewed. Because this can be quite inconvenient, such questions include a Code Exhibit button that displays the code in a separate window.
- *Mark questions to be reviewed*—The question screen displays a check box with the text "Mark for review" at the top-left corner. A question can be marked using this option. The marked questions can be quickly reviewed at the end of the exam.
- *Buttons to display the previous and next questions*—The test includes buttons to display the previous and next questions within the bottom section of the testing engine.

- *Buttons to end the exam and review marked questions*—The engine displays buttons to end the exam and to review the marked questions in the bottom section of the testing engine.
- *Remaining time*—The engine displays the time remaining for the exam at the top right of the screen.
- *Question number*—Each question displays its serial number.
- *Correct number of answer options*—Each question displays the correct number of options that should be selected from multiple options.

On behalf of all at Manning Publications, I wish you good luck and hope that you score very well on your exam.

# *Java basics*

| Exam objectives covered in this chapter | What you need to know |
|---|---|
| [1.2] Define the structure of a Java class. | Structure of a Java class, with its components: package and import statements, class declarations, comments, variables, and methods. Difference between the components of a Java class and that of a Java source code file. |
| [1.3] Create executable Java applications with a `main` method; run a Java program from the command line; including console output. | The right method signature for the `main` method to create an executable Java application. The arguments that are passed to the `main` method. |
| [1.4] Import other Java packages to make them accessible in your code. | Understand packages and import statements. Get the right syntax and semantics to import classes from packages and interfaces in your own classes. |
| [6.4] Apply access modifiers. | Application of access modifiers (`public`, `protected`, default, and `private`) to a class and its members. Determine the accessibility of code with these modifiers. |
| [7.5] Use `abstract` classes and interfaces. | The implication of defining classes, interfaces, and methods as `abstract` entities. |
| [6.2] Apply the `static` keyword to methods and fields. | The implication of defining fields and methods as `static` members. |
| [1.5] Compare and contrast the features and components of Java such as: platform independence, object orientation, encapsulation, etc. | The features and components that are relevant or irrelevant to Java. |

Imagine you're setting up a new IT organization that works with multiple developers. To ensure smooth and efficient working, you'll define a structure for your organization and a set of departments with separate responsibilities. These departments will interact with each other whenever required. Also, depending on confidentiality requirements, your organization's data will be available to employees on an as-needed basis, or you may assign special privileges to only some employees of the organization. This is an example of how organizations might work with a well-defined structure and a set of rules to deliver the best results.

Similarly, Java has a well-defined structure and hierarchy. The organization's structure and components can be compared with Java's class structure and components, and the organization's departments can be compared with Java packages. Restricting access to some data in the organization can be compared to Java's access modifiers. An organization's special privileges can be compared to nonaccess modifiers in Java.

In the OCA Java SE 8 Programmer I exam, you'll be asked questions on the structure of a Java class, packages, importing classes, and applying access and nonaccess modifiers and features and components of Java. Given that information, this chapter will cover the following:

- The structure and components of a Java class
- Understanding executable Java applications
- Understanding Java packages
- Importing Java packages into your code
- Applying access and nonaccess modifiers
- Features and components of Java

## 1.1　*The structures of a Java class and a source code file*

**[1.2]**　Define the structure of a Java class

**NOTE**　When you see a certification objective callout such as the preceding one, it means that in this section we'll cover this objective. The same objective may be covered in more than one section in this chapter or in other chapters.

This section covers the structures and components of both a Java source code file (.java file) and a Java class (defined using the keyword `class`). It also covers the differences between a Java source code file and a Java class.

First things first. Start your exam preparation with a clear understanding of what's required from you in the certification exam. For example, try to answer the following query from a certification aspirant: "I come across the term 'class' with different meanings: class `Person`, the Java source code file (Person.java), and Java bytecode stored in Person.class. Which of these structures is on the exam?" To answer this question, take a look at figure 1.1, which includes the class `Person`, the files Person.java and Person.class, and the relationship between them.

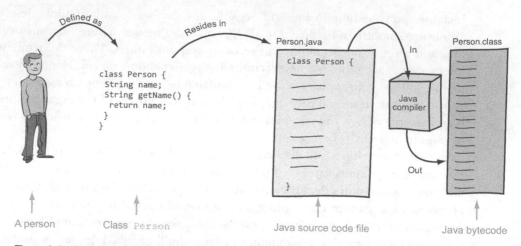

**Figure 1.1   Relationship between the class file `Person` and the files Person.java and Person.class and how one transforms into another**

As you can see in figure 1.1, a person can be defined as a class `Person`. This class should reside in a Java source code file (Person.java). Using this Java source code file, the Java compiler (javac.exe on Windows or javac on Mac OS X/Linux/UNIX) generates bytecode (compiled code for the Java Virtual Machine) and stores it in Person.class. The scope of this exam objective is limited to Java classes (class `Person`) and Java source code files (Person.java).

### 1.1.1  Structure of a Java class

The OCA Java SE 8 Programmer I exam will question you on the structure and components of a Java source file and the classes or interfaces that you can define in it. Figure 1.2 shows the components of a Java class file (interfaces are covered in detail in chapter 6).

In this section, I'll discuss all Java class file components. Let's get started with the `package` statement.

**Java class components**

```
Package statement            ──── 1
Import statements            ──── 2
Comments                     ──── 3a
Class declaration {          ──── 4
        Variables            ──── 5
        Comments             ──── 3b
        Constructors         ──── 6
        Methods              ──── 7
        Nested classes       ┐
        Nested interfaces    ├  Not included in OCA Java SE 8
        Enum                 ┘  Programmer I exam
}
```

**Figure 1.2   Components of a Java class**

**NOTE** The code in this book doesn't include a lot of spaces—it imitates the kind of code that you'll see on the exam. But when you work on real projects, I strongly recommend that you use spaces or comments to make your code readable.

### PACKAGE STATEMENT

All Java classes are part of a package. A Java class can be explicitly defined in a named package; otherwise, it becomes part of a *default* package, which doesn't have a name.

A package statement is used to explicitly define which package a class is in. If a class includes a package statement, it must be the first statement in the class definition:

```
package certification;
class Course {



}
```

The rest of the code for class Course

The package statement should be the first statement in a class.

**NOTE** Packages are covered in detail in section 1.3 of this chapter.

The package statement can't appear within a class declaration or after the class declaration. The following code will fail to compile:

```
class Course {


}
package certification;
```

The rest of the code for class Course

If you place the package statement after the class definition, the code won't compile.

The following code will also fail to compile, because it places the package statement within the class definition:

```
class Course {
package com.cert;
}
```

A package statement can't be placed within the curly braces that mark the start and end of a class definition.

Also, if present, the package statement must appear exactly once in a class. The following code won't compile:

```
package com.cert;
package com.exams;
class Course {
}
```

A class can't define multiple package statements.

### IMPORT STATEMENT

Classes and interfaces in the same package can use each other without prefixing their names with the package name. But to use a class or an interface from another package, you must use its fully qualified name, that is, `packageName.anySubpackageName.ClassName`. For example, the fully qualified name of class `String` is `java.lang.String`.

Because using fully qualified names can be tedious and can make your code difficult to read, you can use the import statement to use the simple name of a class or interface in your code.

Let's look at this using an example class, AnnualExam, which is defined in the package university. Class AnnualExam is associated with the class certification.Exam-Question, as shown using the Unified Modeling Language (UML) *class diagram* in figure 1.3.

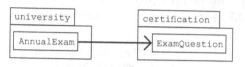

**Figure 1.3   UML representation of the relationship between class AnnualExam and ExamQuestion**

**NOTE**   A UML class diagram represents the static view of an application. It shows entities like packages, classes, interfaces, and their attributes (fields and methods) and also depicts the relationships between them. It shows which classes and interfaces are defined in a package. It depicts the inheritance relationship between classes and interfaces. It can also depict the associations between them—when a class or an interface defines an attribute of another type. All UML representations in this chapter are class diagrams. The exam doesn't cover UML diagrams. But using these quick and simple diagrams simplifies the relationship between Java entities—both on the exam and in your real-world projects.

**NOTE**   Throughout this book, **bold font** will be used to indicate specific parts of code that we're discussing, or changes or modifications in code.

Here's the code for class AnnualExam:

```
package university;
import certification.ExamQuestion;
class AnnualExam {                              Define a variable
    ExamQuestion eq;                            of ExamQuestion
}
```

Note that the import statement follows the package statement but precedes the class declaration. What happens if the class AnnualExam isn't defined in a package? Will there be any change in the code if the classes AnnualExam and ExamQuestion are related, as depicted in figure 1.4?

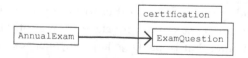

**Figure 1.4   Relationship between the package-less class AnnualExam and ExamQuestion**

In this case, the class `AnnualExam` isn't part of an explicit package, but the class `ExamQuestion` is part of the package `certification`. Here's the code for the class `AnnualExam`:

```
import certification.ExamQuestion;
class AnnualExam {
    ExamQuestion eq;                    ⟵    Define a variable
}                                            of ExamQuestion
```

As you can see in the previous example code, the class `AnnualExam` doesn't define the package statement, but it defines the `import` statement to import the class `certification.ExamQuestion`.

If a package statement is present in a class, the `import` statement must follow the package statement. It's important to maintain the order of the occurrence of the package and `import` statements. Reversing this order will result in your code failing to compile:

```
import certification.ExamQuestion;         The code won't compile because an
package university;                        import statement can't be placed
class AnnualExam {                         before a package statement.
    ExamQuestion eq;
}
```

We'll discuss `import` statements in detail in section 1.3 of this chapter.

**COMMENTS**

You can also add comments to your Java code. Comments can appear at multiple places in a class. A comment can appear before and after a `package` statement, before and after the class definition, as well as before and within and after a method definition. Comments come in two flavors: multiline comments and end-of-line comments.

Multiline comments span multiple lines of code. They start with /* and end with */. Here's an example:

```
class MyClass {
    /*
       comments that span multiple      Multiline comments start
       lines of code                    with /* and end with */.
    */
}
```

Multiline comments can contain special characters. Here's an example:

```
class MyClass {
    /*
       Multi-line comments with
       special characters &%^*{}|\|:;"'    Multiline comment with
       ?/>.<, !@#$%^&*()                   special characters in it
    */
}
```

In the preceding code, the comments don't start with an asterisk on every line. But most of the time when you see a multiline comment in a Java source code file (.java file), you'll notice that it uses an asterisk (*) to start the comment in the next line. Please note that this isn't required—it's done more for aesthetic reasons. Here's an example:

```java
class MyClass {
    /*
     * comments that span multiple
     * lines of code
     */
}
```

**Multiline comments that start with * on a new line—don't they look well organized? The usage of * isn't mandatory; it's done for aesthetic reasons.**

End-of-line comments start with // and, as evident by their name, they're placed at the end of a line of code or on a blank line. The text between // and the end of the line is treated as a comment, which you'd normally use to briefly describe the line of code. Here's an example:

**Brief comment to describe variable fName**

```java
class Person {
    String fName;     // variable to store Person's first name
    String id;        // a 6 letter id generated by the database
}
```

**Brief comment to describe variable id**

Though usage of multiline comments in the following code is uncommon, the exam expects you to know that the code is valid:

```java
String name = /* Harry */ "Paul";
System.out.println(name);
```
**Outputs Paul**

Here's what happens if you include multiline comments within quotes while assigning a string value:

```java
String name = "/* Harry */ Paul";
System.out.println(name);
```
**Outputs /* Harry */ Paul**

When included within double quotes, multiline comments are treated as regular characters and not as comments. So the following code won't compile because the value assigned to variable name is an unclosed string literal value:

```java
String name = "Shre /* ya
                */ Paul";
System.out.println(name);
```
**Won't compile**

In the earlier section on the package statement, you read that a package statement, if present, should be the first line of code in a class. The only exception to this rule is the presence of comments. A comment can precede a `package` statement. The following code defines a `package` statement, with multiline and end-of-line comments:

```
/**
 * @author MGupta          // first name initial + last name    ◁──┐
 * @version 0.1                                                    │
 *                                                              ❶ multiline comment
 * Class to store the details of a monument                        End-of-line
 */                                                                comment within a
package uni;                 // package uni            ◁─❷ End-of-line comment
class Monument {
    int startYear;
    String builtBy;       // individual/ architect     ◁─❸ End-of-line comment
}
// another comment         ◁──┐  End-of-line comment at
                           ❹    the beginning of a line
```

Line ❶ defines an end-of-line code comment within multiline code. This is acceptable. The end-of-line code comment is treated as part of the multiline comment, not as a separate end-of-line comment. Lines ❷ and ❸ define end-of-line code comments. Line ❹ defines an end-of-line code comment at the start of a line, after the class definition.

The multiline comment is placed before the `package` statement, which is acceptable because comments can appear anywhere in your code.

> **Javadoc comments**
> Javadoc comments are special comments that start with `/**` and end with `*/` in a Java source file. These comments are processed by Javadoc, a JDK tool, to generate API documentation for your Java source code files. To see it in action, compare the API documentation of the class `String` and its source code file (String.java).

#### CLASS DECLARATION

The class declaration marks the start of a class. It can be as simple as the keyword `class` followed by the name of a class:

```
                                          Simplest class declaration: keyword
                                          class followed by the class name
class Person {             ◁──
//..        │ A class can define a lot of things here, but we don't
//..        │ need these details to show the class declaration.
}
```

The declaration of a class is composed of the following parts:

- Access modifiers
- Nonaccess modifiers
- Class name

- Name of the base class, if the class is extending another class
- All implemented interfaces, if the class is implementing any interfaces
- Class body (class fields, methods, constructors), included within a pair of curly braces, {}

Don't worry if you don't understand this material at this point. We'll go through these details as we move through the exam preparation.

Let's look at the components of a class declaration using an example:

```
public final class Runner extends Person implements Athlete {}
```

The components of the preceding class declaration can be illustrated as shown in figure 1.5.

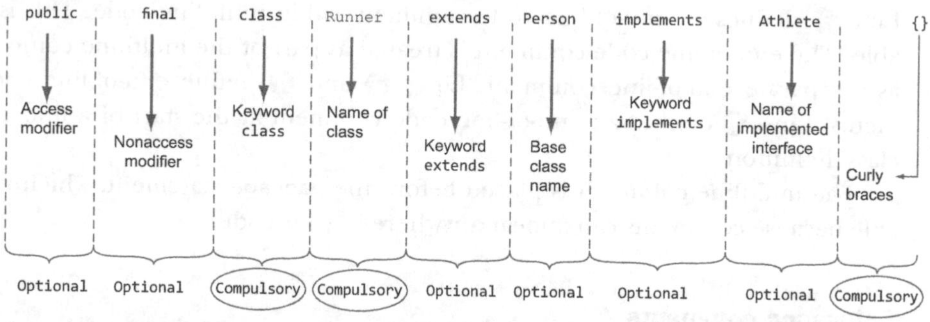

Class declaration components

**Figure 1.5**   **Components of a class declaration**

Table 1.1 summarizes the compulsory and optional components.

**Table 1.1**   **Components of a class declaration**

| Mandatory | Optional |
|---|---|
| Keyword `class` | Access modifier, such as `public` |
| Name of the class | Nonaccess modifier, such as `final` |
| Class body, marked by the opening and closing curly braces, {} | Keyword `extends` together with the name of the base class |
| | Keyword `implements` together with the names of the interfaces being implemented |

We'll discuss the access and nonaccess modifiers in detail in sections 1.4 and 1.5 in this chapter.

## CLASS DEFINITION

A *class* is a design used to specify the attributes and behavior of an object. The attributes of an object are implemented using *variables*, and the behavior is implemented using *methods*. For example, consider a class as being like the design or specification of a mobile phone, and a mobile phone as being an object of that design. The same design can be used to create multiple mobile phones, just as the Java Virtual Machine (JVM) uses a class to create its objects. You can also consider a class as being like a mold that you can use to create meaningful and useful objects. A class is a design from which an object can be created.

Let's define a simple class to represent a mobile phone:

```
class Phone {
    String model;
    String company;
    Phone(String model) {
        this.model = model;
    }
    double weight;
    void makeCall(String number) {
        // code
    }
    void receiveCall() {
        // code
    }
}
```

Points to remember:

- A class name starts with the keyword `class`. Watch out for the case of the keyword `class`. Java is cAsE-sEnSiTivE. `class` (lowercase *c*) isn't the same as `Class` (uppercase *C*). You can't use the word `Class` (uppercase *C*) to define a class.
- The state of a class is defined using attributes or instance variables.
- It isn't compulsory to define all attributes of a class before defining its methods (the variable `weight` is defined after `Phone`'s constructor). But this is far from being optimal for readability.
- The behavior is defined using methods, which may include method parameters.
- A class definition may also include comments and constructors.

 **NOTE** A class is a design from which an object can be created.

## VARIABLES

Revisit the definition of the class `Phone` in the previous example. Because the variables `model`, `company`, and `weight` are used to store the state of an object (also called an *instance*), they're called *instance variables* or *instance attributes*. Each object has its own copy of the instance variables. If you change the value of an instance variable for an object, the value for the same named instance variable won't change for another object. The instance variables are defined within a class but outside all methods in a class.

A single copy of a *class variable* or `static` variable is shared by all the objects of a class. The `static` variables are covered in section 1.5.3 with a detailed discussion of the nonaccess modifier `static`.

### METHODS

Again, revisit the previous example. The methods `makeCall` and `receiveCall` are instance methods, which are generally used to manipulate the instance variables.

A *class method* or *static method* can be used to manipulate the `static` variables, as discussed in detail in section 1.5.3.

### CONSTRUCTORS

Class `Phone` in the previous example defines a single constructor. A class constructor is used to create and initialize the objects of a class. A class can define multiple constructors that accept different sets of method parameters.

## 1.1.2    *Structure and components of a Java source code file*

A Java source code file is used to define Java entities such as a class, interface, enum, and annotation.

> **NOTE**  Java annotations are not on the exam and so won't be discussed in this book.

All your Java code should be defined in Java source code files (text files whose names end with .java). The exam covers the following aspects of the structure of a Java source code file:

- Definition of a class and an interface in a Java source code file
- Definition of single or multiple classes and interfaces within the same Java source code file
- Application of `import` and `package` statements to all the classes in a Java source code file

We've already covered the detailed structure and definition of classes in section 1.1.1. Let's get started with the definition of an interface.

### DEFINITION OF AN INTERFACE IN A JAVA SOURCE CODE FILE

An interface specifies a contract for the classes to implement. You can compare implementing an interface to signing a contract. An interface is a grouping of related methods and constants. Prior to Java 8, interface methods were implicitly abstract. But starting with Java version 8, the methods in an interface can define a default implementation. With Java 8, interfaces can also define `static` methods.

Here's a quick example to help you understand the essence of interfaces. No matter which brand of television each of us has, every television provides the common functionality of changing the channel and adjusting the volume. You can compare the controls of a television set to an interface and the design of a television set to a class that implements the interface controls.

Let's define this interface:

```
interface Controls {
    void changeChannel(int channelNumber);
    void increaseVolume();
    void decreaseVolume();
}
```

The definition of an interface starts with the keyword `interface`. Remember, Java is case-sensitive, so you can't use the word `Interface` (with a capital *I*) to define an interface. This section provides a brief overview of interfaces. You'll work with interfaces in detail in chapter 6.

### DEFINITION OF SINGLE AND MULTIPLE CLASSES IN A SINGLE JAVA SOURCE CODE FILE

You can define either a single class or an interface in a Java source code file or multiple such entities. Let's start with a simple example: a Java source code file called SingleClass.java that defines a single class `SingleClass`:

```
class SingleClass {
    //.. we are not detailing this part
}
```
**Contents of Java source code file SingleClass.java**

Here's an example of a Java source code file, Multiple1.java, that defines multiple interfaces:

```
interface Printable {
    //.. we are not detailing this part
}
interface Movable {
    //.. we are not detailing this part
}
```
**Contents of Java source code file Multiple1.java**

You can also define a combination of classes and interfaces in the same Java source code file. Here's an example:

```
interface Printable {
    //.. we are not detailing this part
}
class MyClass {
    //.. we are not detailing this part
}
interface Movable {
    //.. we are not detailing this part
}
class Car {
    //.. we are not detailing this part
}
```
**Contents of Java source code file Multiple2.java**

No particular order is required to define multiple classes or interfaces in a single Java source code file.

 **EXAM TIP**    The classes and interfaces can be defined in any order of occurrence in a Java source code file.

When you define a `public` class or an interface in a Java source file, the names of the class or interface and Java source file must match. Also, a source code file can't define more than one `public` class or interface. If you try to do so, your code won't compile, which leads to a small hands-on exercise for you that I call *Twist in the Tale*, as mentioned in the preface. The answers to all these exercises are provided in the appendix.

## About the Twist in the Tale exercises

For these exercises, I've tried to use modified code from the examples already covered in the chapter. The *Twist in the Tale* title refers to modified or tweaked code.

These exercises will help you understand how even small code modifications can change the behavior of your code. They should also encourage you to carefully examine all the code in the exam. The reason for these exercises is that in the exam, you may be asked more than one question that seems to require the same answer. But on closer inspection, you'll realize that the questions differ slightly, and this will change the behavior of the code and the correct answer option!

### Twist in the Tale 1.1

Modify the contents of the Java source code file Multiple.java, and define a public interface in it. Execute the code and see how this modification affects your code.

Question: Examine the following content of Java source code file Multiple.java and select the correct options:

```
// Contents of Multiple.java
public interface Printable {
    //.. we are not detailing this part
}
interface Movable {
    //.. we are not detailing this part
}
```

Options:

    **a**  A Java source code file can't define multiple interfaces.

    **b**  A Java source code file can only define multiple classes.

    **c**  A Java source code file can define multiple interfaces and classes.

    **d**  The previous class will fail to compile.

If you need help getting your system set up to write Java, refer to Oracle's "Getting Started" tutorial, http://docs.oracle.com/javase/tutorial/getStarted/.

Twist in the Tale 1.2

Question: Examine the content of the following Java source code file, Multiple2.java, and select the correct option(s):

```
// contents of Multiple2.java
interface Printable {
    //.. we are not detailing this part
}
class MyClass {
    //.. we are not detailing this part
}
interface Movable {
    //.. we are not detailing this part
}
public class Car {
    //.. we are not detailing this part
}
public interface Multiple2 {}
```

Options:

- a  The code fails to compile.
- b  The code compiles successfully.
- c  Removing the definition of class Car will compile the code.
- d  Changing class Car to a nonpublic class will compile the code.
- e  Changing interface Multiple2 to a nonpublic interface will compile the code.

## APPLICATION OF PACKAGE AND IMPORT STATEMENTS IN JAVA SOURCE CODE FILES

In the previous section, I mentioned that you can define multiple classes and interfaces in the same Java source code file. When you use a package or import statement within such Java files, both the package and import statements apply to all the classes and interfaces defined in that source code file.

For example, if you include a package and an import statement in Java source code file Multiple.java (as in the following code), Car, Movable, and Printable will be become part of the same package com.manning.code:

```
// contents of Multiple.java
package com.manning.code;
import com.manning.*;
interface Printable {}
interface Movable {}
class Car {}
```

**Printable, Movable, and Car are part of package com.manning.code.**

**All classes and interfaces defined in package com.manning are accessible to Printable, Movable, and Car.**

**EXAM TIP**   Classes and interfaces defined in the same Java source code file *can't* be defined in separate packages. Classes and interfaces imported using the `import` statement are available to all the classes and interfaces defined in the same Java source code file.

In the next section, you'll create executable Java applications—classes that are used to define an entry point of execution for a Java application.

## 1.2    Executable Java applications

[1.3]   Create executable Java applications with a main method; run a Java program from the command line; including console output.

The OCA Java SE 8 Programmer I exam requires that you understand the meaning of an executable Java application and its requirements, that is, what makes a regular Java class an executable Java class. You also need to know how to execute a Java program from the command line.

### 1.2.1   Executable Java classes versus non-executable Java classes

Doesn't the Java Virtual Machine execute all the Java classes when they are used? If so, what is a non-executable Java class?

An executable Java class, when handed over to the JVM, starts its execution at a particular point in the class—the `main` method. The JVM starts executing the code that's defined in the `main` method. You can't hand over a non-executable Java class (class without a `main` method) to the JVM and ask it to execute it. In this case, the JVM won't know which method to execute because no entry point is marked.

Typically, an application consists of a number of classes and interfaces that are defined in multiple Java source code files. Of all these files, a programmer designates one of the classes as an executable class. The programmer can define the steps that the JVM should execute as soon as it launches the application. For example, a programmer can define an executable Java class that includes code to display the appropriate GUI window to a user and to open a database connection.

In figure 1.6, the classes `Window`, `UserData`, `ServerConnection`, and `UserPreferences` don't define a `main` method. Class `LaunchApplication` defines a `main` method and is an executable class.

**NOTE**   A Java application can define more than one executable class. We choose one (and exactly one) when the time comes to start its execution by the JVM.

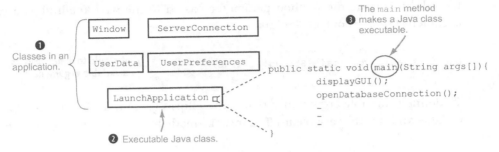

**Figure 1.6   Class `LaunchApplication` is an executable Java class, but the rest of the classes—`Window`, `UserData`, `ServerConnection`, and `UserPreferences`—aren't.**

### 1.2.2   *The main method*

The first requirement in creating an executable Java application is to create a class with a method whose signature (name and method arguments) matches the main method, defined as follows:

```
public class HelloExam {
    public static void main(String args[]) {
        System.out.println("Hello exam");
    }
}
```

This main method should comply with the following rules:

- The method must be marked as a `public` method.
- The method must be marked as a `static` method.
- The name of the method must be main.
- The return type of this method must be `void`.
- The method must accept a method argument of a `String` array or a variable argument (varargs) of type `String`.

Figure 1.7 illustrates the previous code and its related set of rules.

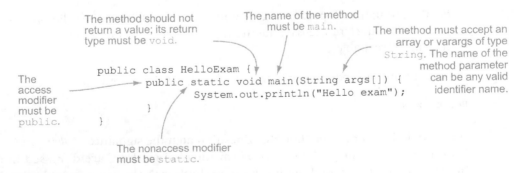

**Figure 1.7   Ingredients of a correct main method**

It's valid to define the method parameter passed to the main method as a variable argument (*varargs*) of type String:

```
public static void main(String... args)
```
⊲─| It's valid to define args as a variable argument.

To define a variable argument variable, the ellipsis (...) must follow the type of the variable and not the variable itself (a mistake made by a lot of new programmers):

```
public static void main(String args...)
```
⊲─| This won't compile. Ellipsis must follow the data type, String.

As mentioned previously, the name of the String array passed to the main method need not be args to qualify it as the correct main method. The following examples are also correct definitions of the main method:

```
public static void main(String[] arguments)
public static void main(String[] HelloWorld)
```
─| The names of the method arguments are arguments and HelloWorld, which is acceptable.

To define an array, the square brackets [] can follow either the variable name or its type. The following is a correct method declaration of the main method:

```
public static void main(String[] args)
public static void main(String minnieMouse[])
```
| The square brackets [] can follow either the variable name or its type.

It's interesting to note that the placement of the keywords public and static can be interchanged, which means that the following are both correct method declarations of the main method:

```
public static void main(String[] args)
static public void main(String[] args)
```
| The placements of the keywords public and static are interchangeable.

**NOTE**  Though both public static and static public are the valid order of keywords to declare the main method, public static is more common and thus more readable.

On execution, the code shown in figure 1.7 outputs the following:

```
Hello exam
```

If a class defines a main method that doesn't match the signature of *the* main method, it's referred to as an *overloaded method* (overloaded methods are discussed in detail in chapter 3). Overloaded methods are methods with the same name but different signatures. For a quick example, class `HelloExam` can define multiple methods with the method name `main`:

```
public class HelloExam {
    public static void main(String args) {
        System.out.println("Hello exam 2");
    }
    public static void main(String args[]) {
        System.out.println("Hello exam");
    }
    public static void main(int number) {
        System.out.println("Hello exam 3");
    }
}
```

JVM will execute this main method.

On execution, JVM will execute *the* main method, resulting in the output `Hello exam`.

## 1.2.3 Run a Java program from the command line

Almost all Java developers work with an Integrated Development Environment (IDE). This exam, however, expects you to understand how to execute a Java application, or an executable Java class, using the command prompt. For this reason, I suggest you work with a simple text editor and command line (even if this might never be the approach you use in the real world).

**NOTE**   If you need help getting your system set up to compile or execute Java applications using the command prompt, refer to Oracle's detailed instructions at http://docs.oracle.com/javase/tutorial/getStarted/cupojava/index.html.

Let's revisit the code shown in figure 1.7:

```
public class HelloExam {
    public static void main(String args[]) {
        System.out.println("Hello exam");
    }
}
```

To execute the preceding code using a command prompt, issue the command `java HelloExam`, as shown in figure 1.8.

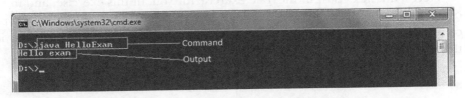

**Figure 1.8   Using the command prompt to execute a Java application**

I mentioned that the main method accepts an array of String as the method parameter. But how and where do you pass the array to the main method? Let's modify the previous code to access and output values from this array:

```
public class HelloExamWithParameters {
    public static void main(String args[]) {
        System.out.println(args[0]);
        System.out.println(args[1]);
    }
}
```

Now let's execute the preceding code using the command prompt, as shown in figure 1.9.

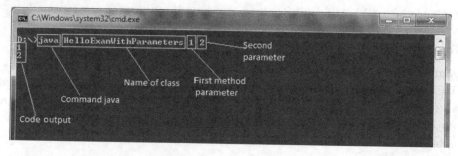

**Figure 1.9  Passing command parameters to a main method**

As you can see from the output shown in figure 1.9, the keyword java and the name of the class aren't passed as command parameters to the main method. The OCA Java SE 8 Programmer I exam will test you on your knowledge of whether the keyword java and the class name are passed on to the main method.

**EXAM TIP**   The method parameters that are passed to the main method are also called command-line parameters or command-line values. As the name implies, these values are passed to a method from the command line.

If you weren't able to follow the code with respect to the arrays and the class String, don't worry; we'll cover the class String and arrays in detail in chapter 4.

Here's the next Twist in the Tale exercise for you. In this exercise, and in the rest of the book, you'll see the names Shreya, Harry, Paul, and Selvan, who are hypothetical programmers also studying for this certification exam. The answer is provided in the appendix, as usual.

**Twist in the Tale 1.3**

One of the programmers, Harry, executed a program that gave the output java one. Now he's trying to figure out which of the following classes outputs these results.

Given that he executed the class using the command java EJava java one one, can you help him figure out the correct option(s)?

```
a  class EJava {
       public static void main(String sun[]) {
           System.out.println(sun[0] + " " + sun[2]);
       }
   }

b  class EJava {
       static public void main(String phone[]) {
           System.out.println(phone[0] + " " + phone[1]);
       }
   }

c  class EJava {
       static public void main(String[] arguments[]) {
           System.out.println(arguments[0] + " " + arguments[1]);
       }
   }

d  class EJava {
       static void public main(String args[]) {
           System.out.println(args[0] + " " + args[1]);
       }
   }
```

---

**Confusion with command-line parameters**

If you've programmed in languages like C, you might get confused by the command-line parameters. Programming languages like C pass the name of a *program* as a command-line argument to the main method. But Java doesn't pass the name of the *class* as an argument to the main method.

## 1.3  *Java packages*

 [1.4]  Import other Java packages to make them accessible in your code

This exam covers importing packages into other classes. But with more than a decade and a half of experience, I've learned that before starting to *import* other packages into your own code, it's important to understand what packages are, the difference between classes that are defined in a package and the classes that aren't defined in a package, and why you need to import packages in your code.

In this section, you'll learn what Java packages are and how to create them. You'll use the import statement, which enables you to use simple names for classes and interfaces defined in separate packages.

### 1.3.1   *The need for packages*

Why do you think we need packages? First, answer this question: do you remember having known more than one Amit, Paul, Anu, or John in your life? Harry knows more than one Paul (six, to be precise), whom he categorizes as managers, friends, and cousins. These are subcategorized by their location and relation, as shown in figure 1.10.

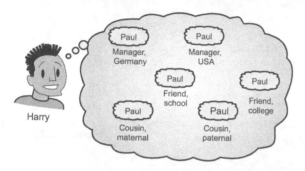

Figure 1.10   Harry knows six Pauls!

Similarly, you can use a package to group together a related set of classes and interfaces (I won't discuss enums here because they aren't covered on this exam). Packages also provide access protection and namespace management. You can create separate packages to define classes for separate projects, such as Android games and online healthcare systems. Further, you can create subpackages within these packages, such as separate subpackages for GUIs, database access, networking, and so on.

> **NOTE**   In real-life projects, you'll rarely work with a package-less class or interface. Almost all organizations that develop software have strict package-naming rules, which are often documented.

All classes and interfaces are defined in a package. If you don't include an explicit `package` statement in a class or an interface, it's part of a *default* package.

### 1.3.2   *Defining classes in a package using the package statement*

You can indicate that a class or an interface is defined in a package by using the `package` statement as the first statement in code. Here's an example:

```
package certification;
class ExamQuestion {                    Variables and
    //..code                            methods
}
```

The class in the preceding code defines an `ExamQuestion` class in the `certification` package. You can define an interface, `MultipleChoice`, in a similar manner:

```
package certification;
interface MultipleChoice {
    void choice1();
```

```
    void choice2();
}
```

Figure 1.11 shows a UML class diagram depicting the relationship of the package certification to the class ExamQuestion and the interface MultipleChoice.

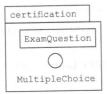

**Figure 1.11   A UML class diagram showing the relationship shared by package** certification, **class** ExamQuestion, **and interface** MultipleChoice

The name of the package in the previous examples is certification. You may use such names for small projects that contain only a few classes and interfaces, but it's common for organizations to use subpackages to define *all* their classes. For example, if the folks at Oracle were to define a class to store exam questions for a Java Associate exam, they might use the package name com.oracle.javacert.associate. Figure 1.12 shows its UML representation, together with the corresponding class definition.

```
package com.oracle.javacert.associate;
class ExamQuestion {
        // variables and methods
}
```

```
com.oracle.javacert.associate

   ExamQuestion
```

**Figure 1.12   A subpackage and its corresponding class definition**

A package is made of multiple sections that go from the more-generic (left) to the more-specific (right). The package name com.oracle.javacert.associate follows a package-naming convention recommended by Oracle and shown in table 1.2.

**Table 1.2   Package-naming conventions used in the package name** com.oracle.javacert.associate

| Package or subpackage name | Its meaning |
| --- | --- |
| com | Commercial. A couple of the commonly used three-letter package abbreviations are<br> ■ gov—for government bodies<br> ■ edu—for educational institutions |
| oracle | Name of the organization |
| javacert | Further categorization of the project at Oracle |
| associate | Further subcategorization of Java certification |

## RULES TO REMEMBER

Here are a few of important rules about packages:

- Per Java naming conventions, package names should all be in lowercase.
- The package and subpackage names are separated using a dot ( . ).
- Package names follow the rules defined for valid identifiers in Java.
- For classes and interfaces defined in a package, the `package` statement is the first statement in a Java source file (a .java file). The exception is that comments can appear before or after a `package` statement.
- There can be a maximum of one `package` statement per Java source code file (.java file).
- All the classes and interfaces defined in a Java source code file are defined in the same package. They can't be defined in separate packages.

**NOTE**   A fully qualified name for a class or interface is formed by prefixing its package name with its name (separated by a dot). The fully qualified name of the class `ExamQuestion` is `certification.ExamQuestion` in figure 1.11 and `com.oracle.javacert.associate.ExamQuestion` in figure 1.12.

## DIRECTORY STRUCTURE AND PACKAGE HIERARCHY

The hierarchy of classes and interfaces defined in packages must match the hierarchy of the directories in which these classes and interfaces are defined in the code. For example, the class `ExamQuestion` in the `certification` package should be defined in a directory with the name "certification." The name of the directory "certification" and its location are governed by the rules shown in figure 1.13.

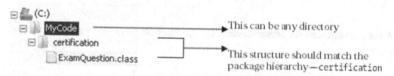

**Figure 1.13   Matching directory structure and package hierarchy**

For the package example shown in figure 1.13, note that there isn't any constraint on the location of the base directory in which the directory structure is defined, as shown in figure 1.14.

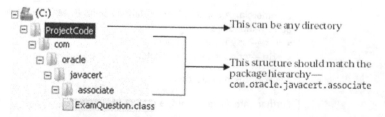

**Figure 1.14   There's no constraint on the location of the base directory to define directories corresponding to package hierarchy.**

##### SETTING THE CLASSPATH FOR PACKAGED CLASSES

To enable the Java Runtime Environment (JRE) to find your classes, add the base directory that contains your packaged Java code to the classpath.

For example, to enable the JRE to locate the `certification.ExamQuestion` class from the previous examples, add the directory C:\MyCode to the classpath. To enable the JRE to locate the class `com.oracle.javacert.associate.ExamQuestion`, add the directory C:\ProjectCode to the classpath.

> **NOTE** You needn't bother setting the classpath if you're working with an IDE. But I strongly encourage you to learn how to work with a simple text editor and how to set a classpath. This can be helpful with your projects at work. The exam expects you to spot code with compilation errors, which isn't easy to do if you didn't learn how to do it without an IDE (IDEs usually include code autocorrection or autocompletion features).

### 1.3.3 *Using simple names with import statements*

The `import` statement enables you to use *simple names* instead of using *fully qualified names* for classes and interfaces defined in separate packages.

Let's work with a real-life example. Imagine your home and your office. Living-Room and Kitchen within your home can refer to each other without mentioning that they exist within the same home. Similarly, in an office, a Cubicle and a Conference-Hall can reference each other without explicitly mentioning that they exist within the same office. But Home and Office can't access each other's rooms or cubicles without stating that they exist in a separate home or office. This situation is represented in figure 1.15.

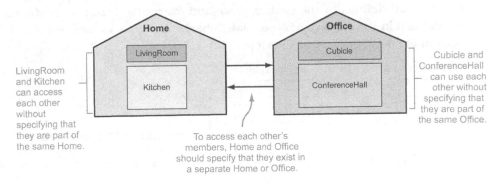

**Figure 1.15   To refer to each other's members, Home and Office should specify that they exist in separate places.**

To refer to the LivingRoom in Cubicle, you *must* specify its complete location, as shown in the left part of the figure 1.16. As you can see in this figure, repeated references to the location of LivingRoom make the description of LivingRoom look tedious and redundant. To avoid this, you can display a notice in Cubicle that all occurrences of LivingRoom refer to LivingRoom in Home and thereafter use its simple name. Home and Office are like Java packages, and this notice is the equivalent of the import statement. Figure 1.16 shows the difference in using fully qualified names and simple names for LivingRoom in Cubicle.

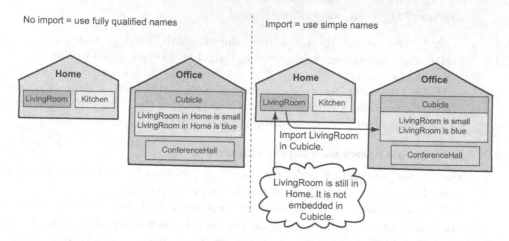

Figure 1.16　LivingRoom can be accessed in Cubicle by using its fully qualified name. It can also be accessed using its simple name if you also use the import statement.

Let's implement the preceding example in code, where classes LivingRoom and Kitchen are defined in the package home and classes Cubicle and ConferenceHall are defined in the package office. Class Cubicle uses (is associated to) class LivingRoom in the package home, as shown in figure 1.17.

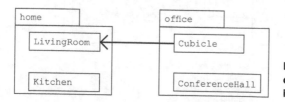

Figure 1.17　A UML representation of classes LivingRoom and Cubicle, defined in separate packages, with their associations

Class Cubicle can refer to class LivingRoom without using an import statement:

```
package office;
class Cubicle {
    home.LivingRoom livingRoom;
}
```

In the absence of an import statement, use the fully qualified name to access class LivingRoom.

Class `Cubicle` can use the simple name for class `LivingRoom` by using the `import` statement:

```
package office;                          import
import home.LivingRoom;          ←┘  statement
class Cubicle {
    LivingRoom livingRoom;       ←┤  No need to use the fully qualified
}                                    name of class LivingRoom
```

 **NOTE** The `import` statement doesn't embed the contents of the imported class in your class, which means that *importing* more classes doesn't increase the size of your own class.

### 1.3.4 *Using packaged classes without using the import statement*

It's possible to use a packaged class or interface without using the `import` statement, by using its fully qualified name:

```
                                 ┤  Missing import
                             ←┤  statement
class AnnualExam {
    certification.ExamQuestion eq;    Define a variable of ExamQuestion
}                                     by using its fully qualified name.
```

But using a fully qualified class name can clutter your code if you create multiple variables of interfaces and classes defined in other packages. *Don't* use this approach in real projects.

 **EXAM TIP** You don't need an explicit `import` statement to use members from the `java.lang` package. Classes and interfaces in this package are automatically imported in *all* other Java classes, interfaces, or enums.

For the exam, it's important to note that you can't use the `import` statement to access multiple classes or interfaces with the same names from different packages. For example, the Java API defines class `Date` in two commonly used packages: `java.util` and `java.sql`. To define variables of these classes in a class, use their fully qualified names with the variable declaration:

```
                                 ┤  import statement
                             ←┤  not required
class AnnualExam {
    java.util.Date date1;        ←────── Variable of type java.util.Date
    java.sql.Date date2;        ←┐
}                                 ┤  Variable of type
                                     java.sql.Date
```

An attempt to use an import statement to import both these classes in the same class will not compile:

```
import java.util.Date;              Code to import classes with the same name
import java.sql.Date;               from different packages won't compile.
class AnnualExam { }
```

An alternate approach (which works well in real projects) is to use the import definition with the class or interface that you use more often and fully reference the one that you use just from time to time:

```
                                  import class you
                                  use often
import java.util.Date;         ←┘
class AnnualExam {
    Date date1;                ←——————— Use simple class name for java.util.Date
    java.sql.Date date2;       ←┐
}
                                  Use fully qualified
                                  name for java.sql.Date
```

### 1.3.5   *Importing a single member versus all members of a package*

You can import either a single member or all members (classes and interfaces) of a package using the import statement. First, revisit the UML notation of the certification package, as shown in figure 1.18.

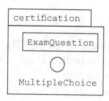

Figure 1.18   A UML representation of the certification package

Examine the following code for the class AnnualExam:

```
                                       Imports only the
import certification.ExamQuestion;  ←┘ class ExamQuestion
class AnnualExam {
    ExamQuestion eq;                   ←— Compiles OK
    MultipleChoice mc;              ←┐
}
                                       Will not compile
```

By using the wildcard character, an asterisk (\*), you can import all the public members, classes, and interfaces of a package. Compare the previous class definition with the following definition of the class AnnualExam:

```
import certification.*;        ←——— Imports all classes and
class AnnualExam {                   interfaces from certification
    ExamQuestion eq;           ←——————— Compiles OK
    MultipleChoice mc;         ←—
}                                    Also compiles OK
```

**NOTE** When overused, using an asterisk to import all members of a package has a drawback. It may be harder to figure out which imported class or interface comes from which package.

When you work with an IDE, it may automatically add import statements for classes and interfaces that you reference in your code.

## 1.3.6 *The import statement doesn't import the whole package tree*

You can't import classes from a subpackage by using an asterisk in the import statement. For example, the UML notation in figure 1.19 depicts the package com.oracle.javacert with the class Schedule and two subpackages, associate and webdeveloper. Package associate contains class ExamQuestion, and package webdeveloper contains class MarkSheet.

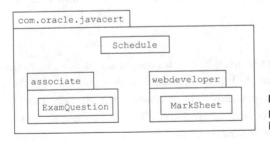

**Figure 1.19  A UML representation of package com.oracle.javacert and its subpackages**

The following import statement will import only the class Schedule. It won't import the classes ExamQuestion and MarkSheet:

```
import com.oracle.javacert.*;      ←——— Imports the class
                                          Schedule only
```

Similarly, the following `import` statement will import all the classes from the packages `associate` and `webdeveloper`:

```
import com.oracle.javacert.associate.*;          Imports class
import com.oracle.javacert.webdeveloper.*;       ExamQuestion only

                                                 Imports class
                                                 MarkSheet only
```

### 1.3.7  *Importing classes from the default package*

What happens if you don't include a package statement in your classes or interfaces? In that case, they become part of a *default, no-name* package. This default package is automatically imported in the Java classes and interfaces defined within the same directory on your system.

For example, the classes `Person` and `Office`, which aren't defined in an explicit package, can use each other if they're defined in the same directory:

```
class Person {                  Not defined in an
    // code                     explicit package
}
class Office {                      Class Person accessible
    Person p;                       in class Office
}
```

A class from a default package can't be used in any named packaged class, regardless of whether they're defined within the same directory or not.

 **EXAM TIP**  Members of a named package can't access classes and interfaces defined in the *default* package.

### 1.3.8  *Static imports*

You can import an individual `static` member of a class or all its `static` members by using the `import static` statement. Although accessible using an instance, the `static` members are better accessed by prefixing their name with the class or interface names. By using `static` import, you can drop the prefix and just use the name of the static variable or method. In the following code, class `ExamQuestion` defines a public `static` variable marks and a `public static` method print:

```
package certification;
public class ExamQuestion {                      public static
    static public int marks;                     variable marks
    public static void print() {
        System.out.println(100);                 public static
    }                                            method print
}
```

The marks variable can be accessed in the class `AnnualExam` using the `import static` statement. The order of the keywords `import` and `static` can't be reversed:

```
package university;
import static certification.ExamQuestion.marks;
class AnnualExam {
    AnnualExam() {
        marks = 20;
    }
}
```

← **Correct statement is import static, not static import**

← **Access variable marks without prefixing it with its class name**

**EXAM TIP** This feature is called *static imports*, but the syntax is `import static`.

To access all `public` and `static` members of class `ExamQuestion` in class `AnnualExam` without importing each of them individually, you can use an asterisk with the `import static` statement:

```
package university;
import static certification.ExamQuestion.*;
class AnnualExam {
    AnnualExam() {
        marks = 20;
        print();
    }
}
```

← **Imports all static members of class ExamQuestion**

**Accesses variable marks and method print without prefixing them with their class names**

Because the variable `marks` and method `print` are defined as `public` members, they're accessible to the class `AnnualExam`. By using the `import static` statement, you don't have to prefix them with their class name.

**NOTE** On real projects, avoid overusing static imports; otherwise, the code might become a bit confusing about which imported component comes from which class.

The accessibility of a class, an interface, and their methods and variables is determined by their access modifiers, which are covered in the next section.

## 1.4 Java access modifiers

 [6.4] Apply access modifiers

In this section, we'll cover all the access modifiers—`public`, `protected`, and `private`—as well as *default access*, which is the result when you don't use an access modifier. We'll also look at how you can use access modifiers to restrict the accessibility of a class and its members in the same and separate packages.

### 1.4.1   *Access modifiers*

Let's start with an example. Examine the definitions of the classes House and Book in the following code and the UML representation shown in figure 1.20.

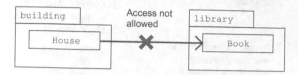

Figure 1.20   **The nonpublic class Book can't be accessed outside the package library.**

```
package building;
class House {}
package library;
class Book {}
```

With the current class definitions, the class House can't access the class Book. Can you make the necessary changes (in terms of the access modifiers) to make the class Book accessible to the class House?

This one shouldn't be difficult. From the discussion of class declarations in section 1.1, you know that a top-level class can be defined only by using the public or default access modifiers. If you declare the class Book using the access modifier public, it'll be accessible outside the package in which it is defined.

> **NOTE**   A top-level class is a class that isn't defined within any other class. A class that is defined within another class is called a *nested* or *inner class*. Nested and inner classes aren't on the OCA Java SE 8 Programmer I exam.

#### WHAT DO THEY CONTROL?

Access modifiers control the accessibility of a class or an interface, including its members (methods and variables), by other classes and interfaces within the same or separate packages. By using the appropriate access modifiers, you can limit access to your class or interface and their members.

#### CAN ACCESS MODIFIERS BE APPLIED TO ALL TYPES OF JAVA ENTITIES?

Access modifiers can be applied to classes, interfaces, and their members (instance and class variables and methods). Local variables and method parameters can't be defined using access modifiers. An attempt to do so will prevent the code from compiling.

#### HOW MANY ACCESS MODIFIERS ARE THERE: THREE OR FOUR?

Programmers are frequently confused about the number of access modifiers in Java because the *default access* isn't defined using an explicit keyword. If a Java class, interface, method, or variable isn't defined using an explicit access modifier, it is said to be defined using the *default access*, also called *package access*.

Java has four access levels:

- public (least restrictive)
- protected

- default
- private (most restrictive)

To understand all of these access levels, we'll use the same set of classes: Book, CourseBook, Librarian, StoryBook, and House. Figure 1.21 depicts these classes using UML notation.

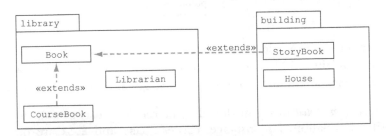

**Figure 1.21 A set of classes and their relationships to help you understand access modifiers**

Classes Book, CourseBook, and Librarian are defined in the package library. The classes StoryBook and House are defined in the package building. Further, classes StoryBook and CourseBook (defined in separate packages) extend class Book. Using these classes, I'll show how the accessibility of a class and its members varies with different access modifiers, from unrelated to derived classes, across packages.

As I cover each of the access modifiers, I'll add a set of instance variables and a method to the class Book with the relevant access modifier. I'll then define code in other classes to access class Book and its members.

### 1.4.2  *Public access modifier*

This is the least restrictive access modifier. Classes and interfaces defined using the public access modifier are accessible across all packages, from derived to unrelated classes.

To understand the public access modifier, let's define the class Book as a public class and add a public instance variable (isbn) and a public method (printBook) to it. Figure 1.22 shows the UML notation.

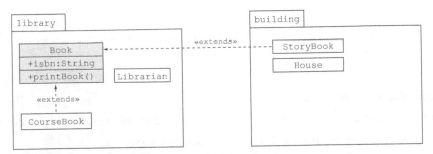

**Figure 1.22  Understanding the public access modifier**

Definition of class `Book`:

```
package library;
public class Book {
    public String isbn;
    public void printBook() {}
}
```

→ **public class Book**

→ **public variable isbn**

→ **public method printBook**

The `public` access modifier is said to be the least restrictive, so let's try to access the `public` class `Book` and its `public` members from class `House`. We'll use class `House` because `House` and `Book` are defined in separate packages and they're *unrelated*.

 **NOTE** The term *unrelated classes* in this chapter refers to classes that don't share inheritance relation. For instance, classes `House` and `Book` are unrelated, if neither `House` derives from `Book` nor `Book` derives from `House`.

Class `House` doesn't enjoy any advantages by being defined in the same package or being a derived class.

Here's the code for class `House`:

```
package building;
import library.Book;
public class House {
    House() {
        Book book = new Book();
        String value = book.isbn;
        book.printBook();
    }
}
```

→ **Class Book is accessible to class House.**

→ **Variable isbn is accessible in House.**

→ **Method printBook is accessible in House.**

In the preceding example, class `Book` and its `public` members—instance variable `isbn` and method `printBook`—are accessible to class `House`. They are also accessible to the other classes: `StoryBook`, `Librarian`, `House`, and `CourseBook`. Figure 1.23 shows the classes that can access a `public` class and its members.

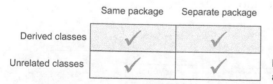

|  | Same package | Separate package |
|---|---|---|
| Derived classes | ✓ | ✓ |
| Unrelated classes | ✓ | ✓ |

**Figure 1.23   Classes that can access a public class and its members**

### 1.4.3  *Protected access modifier*

The members of a class defined using the `protected` access modifier are accessible to

- Classes and interfaces defined in the same package
- All derived classes, even if they're defined in separate packages

Let's add a `protected` instance variable `author` and a method `modifyTemplate` to the class `Book`. Figure 1.24 shows the class representation.

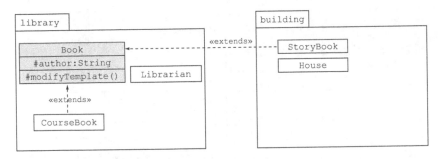

**Figure 1.24** Understanding the `protected` access modifier

Here's the code for the class `Book` (I've deliberately left out its `public` members because they aren't required in this section):

```
package library;
public class Book {
    protected String author;
    protected void modifyTemplate() {}
}
```

Protected
variable author

Protected method
modifyTemplate

Figure 1.25 illustrates how classes from the same and separate packages, derived classes, and unrelated classes access the class `Book` and its `protected` members.

Class `House` fails compilation for trying to access the method `modifyTemplate` and the variable `author`. Following is the compilation error message:

```
House.java:8: modifyTemplate() has protected access in library.Book
        book.modifyTemplate();
            ^
```

 **NOTE** Java code fails compilation because of syntax errors. In such a case, the Java compiler notifies the offending code with its line number and a short description of the error. The preceding code is output from the compilation process. This book uses the command prompt to compile all Java code.

A derived class inherits the protected members of its base class, irrespective of the packages in which they're defined.

Notice that the derived classes `CourseBook` and `StoryBook` inherit class `Book`'s protected member variable `author` and method `modifyTemplate()`. If class `StoryBook`

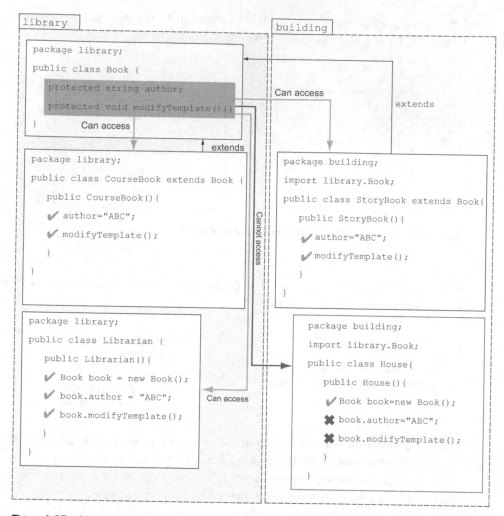

**Figure 1.25** Access of `protected` members of the class `Book` in unrelated and derived classes, from the same and separate packages

tries to instantiate `Book` using a reference variable and then tries to access its protected variable `author` and method `modifyTemplate()`, it won't compile:

```
package building;
import library.Book;
class StoryBook extends Book {
    StoryBook() {
        Book book = new Book();
        String v = book.author;
        book.modifyTemplate();
    }
}
```

**Classes Book and StoryBook defined in separate packages**

**Protected members of class Book are not accessible in derived class StoryBook, if accessed using a new object of class Book.**

**EXAM TIP** A concise but not too simple way of stating the previous rule is this: A derived class can inherit and access `protected` members of its base class, regardless of the package in which it's defined. A derived class in a separate package can't access `protected` members of its base class using reference variables.

Figure 1.26 shows the classes that can access `protected` members of a class or interface.

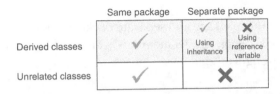

Figure 1.26 Classes that can access protected members

### 1.4.4 *Default access (package access)*

The members of a class defined without using any explicit access modifier are defined with *package accessibility* (also called *default accessibility*). The members with package access are *only* accessible to classes and interfaces defined in the same package. The default access is also referred to as *package-private*. Think of a package as your home, classes as rooms, and things in rooms as variables with default access. These things aren't limited to one room—they can be accessed across all the rooms in your home. But they're still private to your home—you wouldn't want them to be accessed outside your home. Similarly, when you define a package, you might want to make members of classes accessible to all the other classes across the same package.

**NOTE** Although the package-private access is as valid as the other access levels, in real projects it often appears as the result of inexperienced developers forgetting to specify the access mode of Java components.

Let's define an instance variable `issueCount` and a method `issueHistory` with default access in class `Book`. Figure 1.27 shows the class representation with these new members.

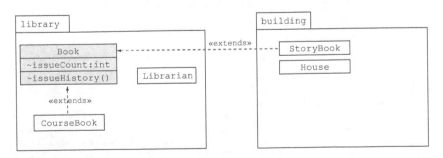

Figure 1.27 Understanding class representation for default access

Here's the code for the class Book (I've deliberately left out its public and protected members because they aren't required in this section):

```
package library;
public class Book {
    int issueCount;
    void issueHistory() {}
}
```

**Public class Book**

**Variable issueCount with default access**

**Method issueHistory with default access**

You can see how classes from the same package and separate packages, derived classes, and unrelated classes access the class Book and its members (the variable issueCount and the method issueHistory) in figure 1.28.

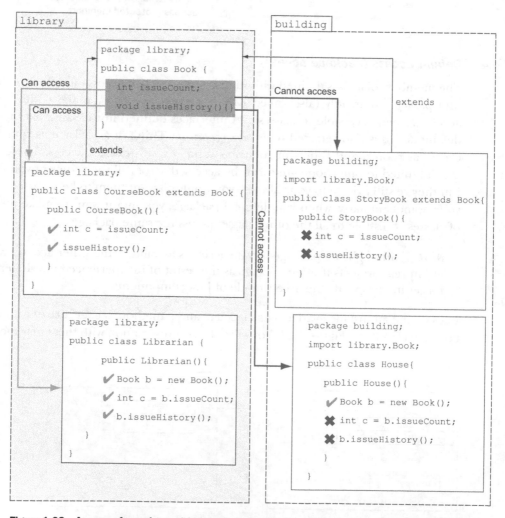

**Figure 1.28  Access of members with default access to the class Book in unrelated and derived classes from the same and separate packages**

Because the classes `CourseBook` and `Librarian` are defined in the same package as the class `Book`, they can access the variables `issueCount` and `issueHistory`. Because the classes `House` and `StoryBook` don't reside in the same package as the class `Book`, they can't access the variables `issueCount` and `issueHistory`. The class `StoryBook` throws the following compilation error message:

```
StoryBook.java:6: issueHistory() is not public in library.Book; cannot be
    accessed from outside package
        book.issueHistory();
          ^
```

Class `House` is unaware of the existence of `issueHistory()`—it fails compilation with the following error message:

```
House.java:9: cannot find symbol
symbol  : method issueHistory()
location: class building.House
        issueHistory();
```

### DEFINING A CLASS BOOK WITH DEFAULT ACCESS

What happens if we define a class with default access? What will happen to the accessibility of its members if the class itself has default (package) accessibility?

Consider this situation: Assume that Superfast Burgers opens a new outlet on a beautiful island and offers free meals to people from all over the world, which obviously includes inhabitants of the island. But the island is inaccessible by all means (air and water). Would awareness of the existence of this particular Superfast Burgers outlet make any sense to people who don't inhabit the island? An illustration of this example is shown in figure 1.29.

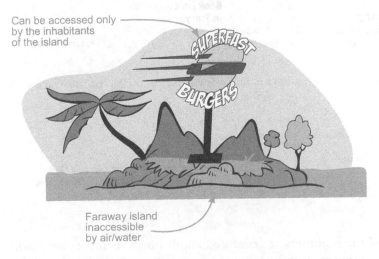

Can be accessed only by the inhabitants of the island

Faraway island inaccessible by air/water

**Figure 1.29  This Superfast Burgers can't be accessed from outside the island because the island is inaccessible by air and water.**

The island is like a package in Java, and Superfast Burgers is like a class defined with default access. In the same way that Superfast Burgers can't be accessed from outside the island in which it exists, a class defined with default (package) access is visible and accessible only from within the package in which it's defined. It can't be accessed from outside the package in which it resides.

Let's redefine the class Book with default (package) access, as follows:

```
package library;
class Book {
    //.. class members
}
```
← **Class Book now has default access.**

The behavior of class Book remains the same for the classes CourseBook and Librarian, which are defined in the same package. But class Book can't be accessed by classes House and StoryBook, which reside in a separate package.

Let's start with the class House. Examine the following code:

```
package building;
import library.Book;
public class House {}
```
← **Class Book isn't accessible in class House.**

Class House generates the following compilation error message:

```
House.java:2: library.Book is not public in library; cannot be accessed from
    outside package
import library.Book;
```

Here's the code of class StoryBook:

```
package building;
import library.Book;
class StoryBook extends Book {}
```
**Book isn't accessible in StoryBook.**

**StoryBook can't extend Book.**

Figure 1.30 shows which classes can access members of a class or interface with default (package) access.

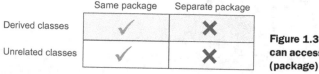

| | Same package | Separate package |
|---|---|---|
| Derived classes | ✓ | ✗ |
| Unrelated classes | ✓ | ✗ |

**Figure 1.30　The classes that can access members with default (package) access**

Because a lot of programmers are confused about which members are made accessible by using the protected and default access modifiers, the exam tip offers a simple and interesting rule to help you remember their differences.

> **EXAM TIP**  Default access can be compared to package-private (accessible only within a package), and `protected` access can be compared to package-private + *kids* ("kids" refer to derived classes). Kids can access `protected` methods only by inheritance and not by reference (accessing members by using the dot operator on an object).

### 1.4.5   private access modifier

The `private` access modifier is the most restrictive access modifier. The members of a class defined using the `private` access modifier are accessible only to themselves. It doesn't matter whether the class or interface in question is from another package or has extended the class—`private` members are *not* accessible outside the class in which they're defined. `private` members are accessible only to the classes and interfaces in which they're defined.

Let's see this in action by adding a `private` method `countPages` to the class `Book`. Figure 1.31 depicts the class representation using UML.

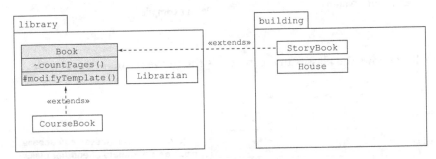

**Figure 1.31   Understanding the `private` access modifier**

Examine the following definition of the class `Book`:

```
package library;
class Book {
    private void countPages() {}
    protected void modifyTemplate() {
        countPages();
    }
}
```

**private method**

**Only Book can access its own private method countPages.**

None of the classes defined in any of the packages (whether derived or not) can access the `private` method `countPages`. But let's try to access it from the class `CourseBook`. I chose `CourseBook` because both of these classes are defined in the same package, and `CourseBook` extends the class `Book`. Here's the code of `CourseBook`:

```
package library;
class CourseBook extends Book {
    CourseBook() {
        countPages();
    }
}
```

◁─┤ **CourseBook extends Book.**

◁─┐ **CourseBook can't access private method countPages.**

Because the class `CourseBook` tries to access private members of the class `Book`, it won't compile. Similarly, if any of the other classes (`StoryBook`, `Librarian`, `House`, or `Course-Book`) tries to access the `private` method `countPages()` of class `Book`, it won't compile.

Here's an interesting situation: do you think a `Book` instance can access its private members using a reference variable? The following code won't compile—even though variable `b1` is of type `Book`, it's trying to access its private method `countPages` outside `Book`:

```
class TestBook {
    public static void main(String args[]) {
        Book b1 = new Book();
        b1.countPages();                ◁─┐ Won't compile
    }
}
```

Figure 1.32 shows the classes that can access the `private` members of a class.

|                    | Same package | Separate package |
|--------------------|:------------:|:----------------:|
| Derived classes    | ✗            | ✗                |
| Unrelated classes  | ✗            | ✗                |

**Figure 1.32  No classes can access `private` members of another class**

 **NOTE**  For your real projects, it *is* possible to access private members of a class outside them, using *Java reflection*. But Java reflection isn't on the exam. So don't consider it when answering questions on the accessibility of private members.

### 1.4.6  Access modifiers and Java entities

Can every access modifier be applied to all the Java entities? The simple answer is *no*. Table 1.3 lists the Java entities and the access modifiers that can be used with them.

**Table 1.3  Java entities and the access modifiers that can be applied to them**

| Entity name | `public` | `protected` | `private` |
|-------------|:--------:|:-----------:|:---------:|
| Top-level class, interface, enum | ✓ | ✗ | ✗ |
| Class variables and methods | ✓ | ✓ | ✓ |
| Instance variables and methods | ✓ | ✓ | ✓ |
| Method parameter and local variables | ✗ | ✗ | ✗ |

What happens if you try to code the combinations for an X in table 1.3? None of these combinations will compile. Here's the code:

```
protected class MyTopLevelClass {}
private class MyTopLevelClass {}
protected interface TopLevelInterface {}
```
**Won't compile—top-level class and interfaces can't be defined with protected and private access.**

```
void myMethod(private int param) {}
void myMethod(int param) {
    public int localVariable = 10;
}
```
**Won't compile—method parameters and local variables can't be defined using any explicit access modifiers.**

Watch out for these combinations on the exam. It's simple to insert these small and invalid combinations in any code snippet and still make you believe that you're being tested on a rather complex topic like threads or concurrency.

> **EXAM TIP** Watch out for invalid combinations of a Java entity and an access modifier. Such code won't compile.

### Twist in the Tale 1.4

The following task was assigned to a group of programmers: "How can you declare a class `Curtain` in a package `building` so that it isn't visible outside the package `building`?"

These are the answers submitted by Paul, Shreya, Harry, and Selvan. Which of these do you think is correct and why? (You can check your Twist in the Tale answers in the appendix.)

| Programmer name | Submitted code |
|---|---|
| Paul | `package building;`<br>`public class Curtain {}` |
| Shreya | `package building;`<br>`protected class Curtain {}` |
| Harry | `package building;`<br>`class Curtain {}` |
| Selvan | `package building;`<br>`private class Curtain {}` |

Your job title may assign special privileges or responsibilities to you. For example, if you work as a Java developer, you may be responsible for updating your programming skills or earning professional certifications in Java. Similarly, you can assign special privileges, responsibilities, and behaviors to your Java entities by using *nonaccess modifiers*, which are covered in the next section.

## 1.5 *Nonaccess modifiers*

> **[7.5]** Use abstract classes and interfaces

> **[6.2]** Apply the static keyword to methods and fields

This section discusses the nonaccess modifiers `abstract`, `final`, and `static`. Access modifiers control the accessibility of your class and its members outside the class and the package. Nonaccess modifiers change the default behavior of a Java class and its members.

For example, if you add the keyword `abstract` to the definition of a class, it can't be instantiated. Such is the magic of the nonaccess modifiers.

You can characterize your classes, interfaces, methods, and variables with the following nonaccess modifiers (though not all are applicable to each Java entity):

- `abstract`
- `static`
- `final`
- `synchronized`
- `native`
- `strictfp`
- `transient`
- `volatile`

The OCA Java SE 8 Programmer I exam covers only three of these nonaccess modifiers: `abstract`, `final`, and `static`, which I'll cover in detail. To ward off any confusion about the rest of the modifiers, I'll describe them briefly here:

- `synchronized`—A synchronized method can't be accessed by multiple threads concurrently. You can't mark classes, interfaces, or variables with this modifier.
- `native`—A native method calls and makes use of libraries and methods implemented in other programming languages such as C or C++. You can't mark classes, interfaces, or variables with this modifier.
- `transient`—A transient variable isn't serialized when the corresponding object is serialized. The `transient` modifier can't be applied to classes, interfaces, or methods.
- `volatile`—A volatile variable's value can be safely modified by different threads. Classes, interfaces, and methods can't use this modifier.
- `strictfp`—Classes, interfaces, and methods defined using this keyword ensure that calculations using floating-point numbers are identical on all platforms. This modifier can't be used with variables.

Now let's look at the three nonaccess modifiers that are on the exam.

### 1.5.1 *abstract modifier*

When added to the definition of a class, interface, or method, the abstract modifier changes its default behavior. Because it is a nonaccess modifier, abstract doesn't change the accessibility of a class, interface, or method.

Let's examine the behavior of each of these with the abstract modifier.

#### ABSTRACT CLASS

When the abstract keyword is prefixed to the definition of a concrete class, it changes it to an abstract class, even if the class doesn't define any abstract methods. The following code is a valid example of an abstract class:

```
abstract class Person {
    private String name;
    public void displayName() { }
}
```

An abstract class can't be instantiated, which means that the following code will fail to compile:

```
class University {
    Person p = new Person();
}
```
**This line of code won't compile.** ←⏋

Here's the compilation error thrown by the previous class:

```
University.java:4: Person is abstract; cannot be instantiated
    Person p = new Person();
                   ^
1 error
```

**EXAM TIP** An abstract class may or may not define an abstract method. But a concrete class can't define an abstract method.

#### ABSTRACT INTERFACE

An interface is an abstract entity by default. The Java compiler automatically adds the keyword abstract to the definition of an interface. Thus, adding the keyword abstract to the definition of an interface is redundant. The following definitions of interfaces are the same:

```
interface Movable {}
abstract interface Movable {}
```
←⏋ **Interface defined without the explicit use of keyword abstract**

←⏋ **Interface defined with the explicit use of keyword abstract**

**ABSTRACT METHOD**

An abstract method doesn't have a body. Usually, an abstract method is implemented by a derived class. Here's an example:

```
abstract class Person {
    private String name;
    public void displayName() { }        This isn't an abstract method.
    public abstract void perform();      It has an empty body: {}.
}
                                         This is an abstract method.
                                         It isn't followed by {}.
```

**EXAM TIP**   A method with an empty body isn't an `abstract` method.

**ABSTRACT VARIABLES**

None of the different types of variables (instance, `static`, local, and method parameters) can be defined as `abstract`.

**EXAM TIP**   Don't be tricked by code that tries to apply the nonaccess modifier `abstract` to a variable. Such code won't compile.

### 1.5.2   *final modifier*

The keyword `final` can be used with the declaration of a class, variable, or method. It can't be used with the declaration of an interface.

**FINAL CLASS**

A class that's marked `final` can't be extended by another class. The class `Professor` won't compile if the class `Person` is marked as `final`, as follows:

```
final class Person {}
class Professor extends Person {}        Won't compile
```

**FINAL INTERFACE**

An interface can't be marked as `final`. An interface is `abstract` by default and marking it with `final` will prevent your interface from compiling:

```
final interface MyInterface{}            Won't compile
```

**FINAL VARIABLE**

A `final` variable can't be reassigned a value. It can be assigned a value only once. See the following code:

```
class Person {
    final long MAX_AGE;
    Person() {                           Compiles successfully: value
        MAX_AGE = 99;                    assigned once to final variable
    }
}
```

Compare the previous example with the following code, which tries to reassign a value to a final variable:

```
class Person {
    final long MAX_AGE = 90;
    Person() {                        Won't compile;
        MAX_AGE = 99;                 reassignment not allowed
    }
}
```

It's easy to confuse reassigning a value to a `final` variable with *calling* a method on a `final` variable, which might change the state of the object that it refers to. If a reference variable is defined as a `final` variable, you can't reassign another object to it, but you can call methods on this variable (that modify its state):

```
class Person {
    final StringBuilder name = new StringBuilder("Sh");   Can call methods on
    Person() {                                            a final variable that
        name.append("reya");                              change its state
        name = new StringBuilder();
    }                                    Won't compile. You can't reassign
}                                        another object to a final variable.
```

**FINAL METHOD**

A `final` method defined in a base class can't be overridden by a derived class. Examine the following code:

```
class Person {
    final void sing() {
        System.out.println("la..la..la..");
    }
}
class Professor extends Person {
    void sing() {                                   Won't compile
        System.out.println("Alpha.. beta.. gamma");
    }
}
```

If a method in a derived class has the same method signature as its base class's method, it's referred to as an *overridden method*. Overridden methods are discussed along with polymorphism in chapter 6.

### 1.5.3 *static modifier*

The nonaccess modifier `static` can be applied to the declarations of variables, methods, classes, and interfaces. We'll examine each of them in following sections.

**STATIC VARIABLES**

static variables belong to a class. They're common to all instances of a class and aren't unique to any instance of a class. static attributes exist independently of any instances of a class and may be accessed even when no instances of the class have been created. You can compare a static variable with a shared variable. A static variable is shared by all the objects of a class.

 **NOTE**   A class and an interface can declare static variables. This section covers declaration and usage of static variables that are defined in a class. Chapter 6 covers interfaces and their static variables in detail.

Think of a static variable as being like a common bank vault that's shared by the employees of an organization. Each of the employees accesses the same bank vault, so any change made by one employee is visible to all the other employees, as illustrated in figure 1.33.

**Figure 1.33   Comparing a shared bank vault with a static variable**

Figure 1.34 defines a class Emp that defines a non-static variable name and a static variable bankVault.

```
class Emp {
    String name;
    static int bankVault;
}
```
> We want this value to be shared by all the objects of class Emp.

**Figure 1.34   Definition of the class Emp with a static variable bankVault and non-static variable name**

It's time to test what we've been discussing up to this point. The following `TestEmp` class creates two objects of the class `Emp` (from figure 1.34) and modifies the value of the variable `bankVault` using these separate objects:

```
class TestEmp {
    public static void main(String[] args) {
    Emp emp1 = new Emp();
        Emp emp2 = new Emp();
        emp1.bankVault = 10;
        emp2.bankVault = 20;
        System.out.println(emp1.bankVault);
        System.out.println(emp2.bankVault);
        System.out.println(Emp.bankVault);
    }
}
```

**Reference variables emp1 and emp2 refer to separate objects of class Emp.**

**Variable bankVault of variable emp1 is assigned a value of 10.**

**Variable bankVault of variable emp2 is assigned a value of 20.**

**This will print 20.**

**This will also print 20.**

**This will print 20 as well.**

In the preceding code example, `emp1.bankVault`, `emp2.bankVault`, and `Emp.bank-Vault` all refer to the *same* `static` attribute: `bankVault`.

**EXAM TIP** Even though you can use an object reference variable to access `static` members, it's not advisable to do so. Because `static` members belong to a class and not to individual objects, using object reference variables to access `static` members may make them appear to belong to an object. The preferred way to access them is by using the class name. The `static` and `final` nonaccess modifiers can be used together to define *constants* (variables whose value can't change).

In the following code, the class `Emp` defines the constants `MIN_AGE` and `MAX_AGE`:

```
class Emp {
    public static final int MIN_AGE = 20;
    static final int MAX_AGE = 70;
}
```

**Constant MIN_AGE**

**Constant MAX_AGE**

Although you can define a constant as a non-`static` member, it's common practice to define constants as `static` members, because doing so allows the constant values to be used across objects and classes.

**STATIC METHODS**

`static` methods aren't associated with objects and can't use any of the instance variables of a class. You can define `static` methods to access or manipulate `static` variables:

```
class Emp {
    String name;
    static int bankVault;
    static int getBankVaultValue() {
        return bankVault;
    }
}
```

**static method getBankVaultValue returns the value of static variable bankVault.**

It's a common practice to use static methods to define *utility methods*, which are methods that usually manipulate the method parameters to compute and return an appropriate value:

```
static double interest(double num1, double num2, double num3) {
    return(num1+num2+num3)/3;
}
```

The following utility (static) method doesn't define input parameters. The method averageOfFirst100Integers computes and returns the average of numbers 1 to 100:

```
static double averageOfFirst100Integers() {       ◁──┐   Method averageOfFirst100Integers
    int sum = 0;                                          doesn't define method parameters.
    for (int i=1; i <= 100; ++i) {
        sum += i;
    }
    return (sum)/100;
}
```

The nonprivate static variables and methods are inherited by derived classes. The static members aren't involved in runtime polymorphism. You can't override the static members in a derived class, but you can redefine them.

Any discussion of static methods and their behavior can be quite confusing if you aren't aware of inheritance and derived classes. But don't worry if you don't understand all of it. I'll cover derived classes and inheritance in chapter 6. For now, note that a static method can be accessed using the name of the object reference variables and the class in a manner similar to static variables.

**WHAT CAN A STATIC METHOD ACCESS?**

Neither static methods nor static variables can access the non-static variables and methods of a class. But the reverse is true: non-static variables and methods can access static variables and methods because the static members of a class exist even if no instances of the class exist. static members are forbidden from accessing instance methods and variables, which can exist only if an instance of the class is created.

Examine the following code:

```
class MyClass {
    static int x = count();              ◁──┤   Compilation
    int count() { return 10; }                   error
}
```

This is the compilation error thrown by the previous class:

```
MyClass.java:3: nonstatic method count() cannot be referenced from a static
    context
    static int x = count();
                   ^
1 error
```

The following code is valid:

```
class MyClass {
    static int x = result();
    static int result() { return 20; }
    int nonStaticResult() { return result(); }
}
```

**static variable referencing a static method**

**Non-static method using static method**

 **EXAM TIP** static methods and variables can't access the instance members of a class.

Table 1.4 summarizes the access capabilities of static and non-static members.

**Table 1.4 Access capabilities of static and non-static members**

| Member type | Can access static attribute or method? | Can access non-static attribute or method? |
|---|---|---|
| static | Yes | No |
| Non-static | Yes | Yes |

### ACCESSING STATIC MEMBERS FROM A NULL REFERENCE

Because static variables and methods belong to a class and not to an instance, you can access them using variables, which are initialized to null. Watch out for such questions in the exam. Such code won't throw a runtime exception (NullPointer-Exception to be precise). In the following example, the reference variable emp is initialized to null:

```
class Emp {
    String name;
    static int bankVault;
    static int getBankVaultValue() {
        return bankVault;
    }
}
class Office {
    public static void main(String[] args) {
        Emp emp = null;
        System.out.println(emp.bankVault);
        System.out.println(emp.getBankVaultValue());
    }
}
```

**Outputs 0**

 **EXAM TIP** You can access static variables and methods using a null reference.

**static classes and interfaces**

Certification aspirants frequently ask questions about `static` classes and interfaces, so I'll quickly cover these in this section to ward off any confusion related to them. But note that `static` classes and interfaces are types of nested classes and interfaces that aren't covered by the OCA Java 8 Programmer I exam.

You can't prefix the definition of a top-level class or an interface with the keyword `static`. A top-level class or interface is one that isn't defined within another class or interface. The following code will fail to compile:

```
static class Person {}
static interface MyInterface {}
```

But you can define a class and an interface as a `static` member of another class. The following code is valid:

```
class Person {
    static class Address {}
    static interface MyInterface {}
}
```
← **Also known as a static nested class**

The next section covers features of Java that led to its popularity two decades ago, and which still hold strong.

## 1.6  *Features and components of Java*

> [1.5]   Compare and contrast the features and components of Java such as: platform independence, object orientation, encapsulation, etc.

The Java programming language was released in 1995. It was developed mainly to work with consumer appliances. But it soon became very popular with web browsers, to deliver dynamic content (using applets), which didn't require it to be recompiled for separate platforms. Let's get started with the distinctive features and components of Java, which still make it a popular programming language.

**NOTE**   The exam will question you on the features and components of Java that are relevant or irrelevant to it.

### 1.6.1  *Valid features and components of Java*

Java offers multiple advantages over other languages and platforms.

#### PLATFORM INDEPENDENCE

This feature is one of main reasons of Java's phenomenal rise since its release. It's also referred to as "write once, run anywhere" (WORA)—a slogan created by Sun Microsystems[TM] to highlight Java's platform independence.

Java code can be executed on multiple systems without recompilation. Java code is compiled into *bytecode,* to be executed by a *virtual machine*—the Java Virtual Machine (JVM). A JVM is installed on platforms with different OSs like Windows, Mac, or Linux. A JVM interprets bytecodes to machine-specific instructions for execution. The implementation details of a JVM are machine-dependent and might differ across platforms, but all of them interpret the same bytecode in a similar manner. Bytecode generated by a Java compiler is supported by all platforms with a JVM.

Other popular programming languages like C and C++ compile their code to a host system. So the code must be recompiled for separate platforms.

### OBJECT ORIENTATION
Java emulates real-life object definition and behavior. In real life, state and behavior are tied to an object. Similarly, all Java code is defined within classes, interfaces, or enums. You need to create their objects to use them.

### ABSTRACTION
Java lets you abstract objects and include only the required properties and behavior in your code. For example, if you're developing an application that tracks the population of a country, you'll record a person's name, address, and contact details. But for a health-tracking system, you might want to include health-related details and behavior as well.

### ENCAPSULATION
With Java classes, you can encapsulate the state and behavior of an object. The state or the fields of a class are protected from unwanted access and manipulation. You can control the level of access and modifications to your objects.

### INHERITANCE
Java enables its classes to inherit other classes and implement interfaces. The interfaces can inherit other interfaces. This saves you from redefining common code.

### POLYMORPHISM
The literal meaning of polymorphism is "many forms." Java enables instances of its classes to exhibit multiple behaviors for the same method calls. You'll learn about this in detail in chapter 6.

### TYPE SAFETY
In Java, you must declare a variable with its data type *before* you can use it. This means that you have compile-time checks that ensure you never assign to a variable a value of the wrong type.

### AUTOMATIC MEMORY MANAGEMENT
Unlike other programming languages like C or C++, Java uses garbage collectors for automatic memory management. They reclaim memory from objects that are no longer in use. This frees developers from explicitly managing the memory themselves. It also prevents memory leaks.

### MULTITHREADING AND CONCURRENCY

Java has supported multithreading and concurrency since it was first released—supported by classes and interfaces defined in its core API.

### SECURITY

Java includes multiple built-in security features (though not all are covered in this exam) to control access to your resources and execution of your programs.

Java is type safe and includes garbage collection. It provides secure class loading, and verification ensures execution of legitimate Java code.

The Java platform defines multiple APIs, including cryptography and public key infrastructure. Java applications that execute under a security manager control access to your resources, like reading or writing to file. Access to a resource can be controlled using a policy file. Java enables you to define digital signatures, certificates, and keystores to secure code and file exchanges. Signed code is distributed for execution.

With features like encapsulation and data hiding, Java secures the state of its objects. Java applets execute in browsers and don't allow code to be downloaded to a system, thus enabling security for browsers and the systems that run them.

### 1.6.2  *Irrelevant features and components of Java*

The exam might also include some terms that are irrelevant.

### SINGLE-THREADED

Java supports multithreading programming with inbuilt classes and interfaces. You can create and use single threads, but the Java language isn't single-threaded. Even when you create single threads of execution, Java executes its own processes like garbage collection in separate threads. Java isn't a single-threaded language.

### RELATED TO JAVASCRIPT

Java isn't related to JavaScript (except for the similarity in their name). JavaScript is a programming language used in web pages to make them interactive.

## 1.7    Summary

This chapter started with a look at the structure of a Java class. Although you should know how to work with Java classes, Java source code files (.java files), and Java bytecode files (.class files), the OCA Java SE 8 Programmer I exam will question you only on the structure and components of the first two—classes and source code—not on Java bytecode.

We discussed the components of a Java class and of Java source code files. A class can define multiple components, namely, `import` and `package` statements, variables, constructors, methods, comments, nested classes, nested interfaces, annotations, and enums. A Java source code file (.java) can define multiple classes and interfaces.

We then covered the differences and similarities between executable and nonexecutable Java classes. An executable Java class defines the entry point (`main` method) for the JVM to start its execution. The `main` method should be defined with the required method signature; otherwise, the class will fail to be categorized as an executable Java class.

Packages are used to group together related classes and interfaces. They also provide access protection and namespace management. The import statement is used to import classes and interfaces from other packages. In the absence of an import statement, classes and interfaces should be referred to by their fully qualified names (complete package name plus class or interface name).

Access modifiers control the access of classes and their members within a package and across packages. Java defines four access modifiers: public, protected, default, and private. When default access is assigned to a class or its member, no access modifier is prefixed to it. The absence of an access modifier is equal to assigning the class or its members with default access. The least restrictive access modifier is public, and private is the most restrictive. protected access sits between public and default access, allowing access to derived classes outside a package.

We covered the abstract and static nonaccess modifiers. A class or a method can be defined as an abstract member. abstract classes can't be instantiated. Methods and variables can be defined as static members. All the objects of a class share the same copy of static variables, which are also known as class-level variables.

Finally, we covered the features and components of Java that make it a popular choice.

## 1.8 Review notes

This section lists the main points covered in this chapter.

The structure of a Java class and source code file:

- The OCA Java SE 8 Programmer I exam covers the structure and components of a Java class and Java source code file (.java file). It doesn't cover the structure and components of Java bytecode files (.class files).
- A class can define multiple components. All the Java components you've heard of can be defined within a Java class: import and package statements, variables, constructors, methods, comments, nested classes, nested interfaces, annotations, and enums.
- This exam doesn't cover the definitions of nested classes, nested interfaces, annotations, and enums.
- If a class defines a package statement, it should be the first statement in the class definition.
- The package statement can't appear within a class declaration or after the class declaration.
- If present, the package statement should appear exactly once in a class.
- The import statement allows usage of simple names, nonqualified names of classes, and interfaces.

- The `import` statement can't be used to import multiple classes or interfaces with the same name.
- A class can include multiple `import` statements.
- If a class includes a `package` statement, all the `import` statements should follow the `package` statement.
- If present, an `import` statement must be placed before any class or interface definition.
- Comments are another component of a class. Comments are used to annotate Java code and can appear at multiple places within a class.
- A comment can appear before or after a `package` statement, before or after the class definition, and before, within, or after a method definition.
- Comments come in two flavors: multiline and end-of-line comments.
- Comments can contain any special characters (including characters from the Unicode charset).
- Multiline comments span multiple lines of code. They start with `/*` and end with `*/`.
- End-of-line comments start with `//` and, as the name suggests, are placed at the end of a line of code or a blank line. The text between `//` and the end of the line is treated as a comment.
- Class declarations and class definitions are components of a Java class.
- A Java class may define zero or more instance variables, methods, and constructors.
- The order of the definition of instance variables, constructors, and methods doesn't matter in a class.
- A class may define an instance variable before or after the definition of a method and still use it.
- A Java source code file (.java file) can define multiple classes and interfaces.
- A `public` class can be defined only in a source code file with the same name.
- `package` and `import` statements apply to all the classes and interfaces defined in the same source code file (.java file).

Executable Java applications:

- An executable Java class is a class that, when handed over to the Java Virtual Machine (JVM), starts its execution at a particular point in the class. This point of execution is the `main` method.
- For a class to be executable, the class should define a `main` method with the signature `public static void main(String args[])` or `public static void main(String... args)`. The positions of `static` and `public` can be interchanged, and the method parameter can use any valid name.
- A class can define multiple methods with the name `main`, provided that the signature of these methods doesn't match the signature of the `main` method

defined in the previous point. These *overloaded* versions aren't considered the main method.

- The main method accepts an array of type String containing the method parameters passed to it by the JVM.
- The keyword java and the name of the class aren't passed on as command parameters to the main method.

Java packages:

- You can use packages to group together a related set of classes and interfaces.
- By default, all classes and interfaces in separate packages and subpackages aren't visible to each other.
- The package and subpackage names are separated using a dot.
- All classes and interfaces in the same package are visible to each other.
- An import statement allows the use of simple names for packaged classes and interfaces defined in other packages.
- You can't use the import statement to access multiple classes or interfaces with the same names from different packages.
- You can import either a single member or all members (classes and interfaces) of a package using the import statement.
- You can't import classes from a subpackage by using the wildcard character, an asterisk (*), in the import statement.
- A class from a default package can't be used in any named packaged class, regardless of whether it's defined within the same directory or not.
- You can import an individual static member of a class or all its static members by using a static import statement.
- An import statement can't be placed before a package statement in a class. Any attempt to do so will cause the compilation of the class to fail.
- The members of default packages are accessible only to classes or interfaces defined in the same directory on your system.

Java access modifiers:

- The access modifiers control the accessibility of your class and its members outside the class and package.
- Java defines four access levels: public, protected, default, and private.
- Java defines three access modifiers: public, protected, and private.
- The public access modifier is the least restrictive access modifier.
- Classes and interfaces defined using the public access modifier are accessible to related and unrelated classes outside the package in which they're defined.
- The members of a class defined using the protected access modifier are accessible to classes and interfaces defined in the same package and to all derived classes, even if they're defined in separate packages.

- The members of a class defined without using an explicit access modifier are defined with package accessibility (also called default accessibility).
- The members with package access are accessible only to classes and interfaces defined in the same package.
- A class defined using default access can't be accessed outside its package.
- The members of a class defined using a `private` access modifier are accessible only to the class in which they're defined. It doesn't matter whether the class or interface in question is from another package or has extended the class. Private members are not accessible outside the class in which they're defined.
- The `private` access modifier is the most restrictive access modifier.

Nonaccess modifiers:

- The nonaccess modifiers change the default properties of a Java class and its members.
- The nonaccess modifiers covered by this exam are `abstract`, `final`, and `static`.
- The `abstract` keyword, when prefixed to the definition of a concrete class, can change it to an `abstract` class, even if it doesn't define any `abstract` methods.
- An abstract class can't be instantiated.
- An interface is implicitly `abstract`. The Java compiler automatically adds the keyword `abstract` to the definition of an interface (which means that adding the keyword `abstract` to the definition of an interface is redundant).
- An abstract method doesn't have a body. When a non-abstract class extends a class with an abstract method, it must implement the method.
- A variable can't be defined as an `abstract` variable.
- The `static` modifier can be applied to inner classes, inner interfaces, variables, and methods. Inner classes and interfaces aren't covered in this exam.
- A method can't be defined as both `abstract` and `static`.
- `static` attributes (fields and methods) are common to all instances of a class and aren't unique to any instance of a class.
- `static` attributes exist independently of any instances of a class and may be accessed even when no instances of the class have been created.
- `static` attributes are also known as *class fields* or *class methods* because they're said to belong to their class, not to any instance of that class.
- A `static` variable or method can be accessed using the name of a reference object variable or the name of a class.
- A `static` method or variable can't access non-`static` variables or methods of a class. But the reverse is true: non-`static` variables and methods can access `static` variables and methods.
- `static` classes and interfaces are a type of nested classes and interfaces, but they aren't covered in this exam.

- You can't prefix the definition of a top-level class or an interface with the keyword static. A top-level class or interface is one that isn't defined within another class or interface.

Features and components of Java:

- *Object orientation*—Java emulates real-life object definition and behavior. It uses classes, interfaces, or enums to define all its code.
- *Abstraction*—Java lets you abstract objects and include only the required properties and behavior in your code.
- *Encapsulation*—The state or the fields of a class are protected from unwanted access and manipulation.
- *Inheritance*—Java enables its classes to inherit other classes and implement interfaces. The interfaces can inherit other interfaces.
- *Polymorphism*—Java enables instances of its classes to exhibit multiple behaviors for the same method calls.
- *Type safety*—In Java, you must declare a variable with its data type before you can use it.
- *Automatic memory management*—Java uses garbage collectors for automatic memory management. They reclaim memory from objects that are no longer in use.
- *Multithreading and concurrency*—Java defines classes and interfaces to enable developers to develop multithreaded code.
- Java isn't a single-threaded language.

## 1.9   Sample exam questions

**Q1-1.** Given:

```
class EJava {
    //..code
}
```

Which of the following options will compile?

a   ```
package java.oca.associate;
class Guru {
    EJava eJava = new EJava();
}
```

b   ```
package java.oca;
import EJava;
class Guru {
    EJava eJava;
}
```

c   ```
package java.oca.*;
import java.default.*;
class Guru {
    EJava eJava;
}
```
```

```
d  package java.oca.associate;
   import default.*;
   class Guru {
       default.EJava eJava;
   }
```

e  None of the above

**Q1-2.** The following numbered list of Java class components is not in any particular order. Select the acceptable order of their occurrence in any Java class (choose all that apply):

1  comments
2  import statement
3  package statement
4  methods
5  class declaration
6  variables

  a  1, 3, 2, 5, 6, 4
  b  3, 1, 2, 5, 4, 6
  c  3, 2, 1, 4, 5, 6
  d  3, 2, 1, 5, 6, 4

**Q1-3.** Which of the following examples defines a correct Java class structure?

```
a  #connect java compiler;
   #connect java virtual machine;
   class EJavaGuru {}
```

```
b  package java compiler;
   import java virtual machine;
   class EJavaGuru {}
```

```
c  import javavirtualmachine.*;
   package javacompiler;
   class EJavaGuru {
       void method1() {}
       int count;
   }
```

```
d  package javacompiler;
   import javavirtualmachine.*;
   class EJavaGuru {
       void method1() {}
       int count;
   }
```

```
e  #package javacompiler;
   $import javavirtualmachine;
   class EJavaGuru {
       void method1() {}
       int count;
   }
```

```
f  package javacompiler;
   import javavirtualmachine;
   Class EJavaGuru {
       void method1() {}
       int count;
   }
```

**Q1-4.** Given the following contents of the Java source code file MyClass.java, select the correct options:

```
// contents of MyClass.java
package com.ejavaguru;
import java.util.Date;
class Student {}
class Course {}
```

    **a** The imported class, java.util.Date, can be accessed only in the class Student.

    **b** The imported class, java.util.Date, can be accessed by both the Student and Course classes.

    **c** Both of the classes Student and Course are defined in the package com.ejavaguru.

    **d** Only the class Student is defined in the package com.ejavaguru. The class Course is defined in the default Java package.

**Q1-5.** Given the following definition of the class EJavaGuru,

```
class EJavaGuru {
    public static void main(String[] args) {
        System.out.println(args[1]+":"+ args[2]+":"+ args[3]);
    }
}
```

what is the output of EJavaGuru, if it is executed using the following command?

```
java EJavaGuru one two three four
```

    **a** one:two:three

    **b** EJavaGuru:one:two

    **c** java:EJavaGuru:one

    **d** two:three:four

**Q1-6.** Which of the following options, when inserted at //INSERT CODE HERE, will print out EJavaGuru?

```
public class EJavaGuru {
    // INSERT CODE HERE
    {
        System.out.println("EJavaGuru");
    }
}
```

```
a  public void main (String[] args)
b  public void main(String    args[])
c  static public void main      (String[] array)
d  public static void main (String args)
e  static public main (String args[])
```

**Q1-7.** What is the meaning of "write once, run anywhere"? Select the correct options:

a Java code can be written by one team member and executed by other team members.

b It is for marketing purposes only.

c It enables Java programs to be compiled once and can be executed by any JVM without recompilation.

d Old Java code doesn't need recompilation when newer versions of JVMs are released.

**Q1-8.** A class Course is defined in a package com.ejavaguru. Given that the physical location of the corresponding class file is /mycode/com/ejavaguru/Course.class and execution takes place within the mycode directory, which of the following lines of code, when inserted at // INSERT CODE HERE, will import the Course class into the class MyCourse?

```
// INSERT CODE HERE
class MyCourse {
    Course c;
}
```

a  import mycode.com.ejavaguru.Course;

b  import com.ejavaguru.Course;

c  import mycode.com.ejavaguru;

d  import com.ejavaguru;

e  import mycode.com.ejavaguru*;

f  import com.ejavaguru*;

**Q1-9.** Examine the following code:

```
class Course {
    String courseName;
}
class EJavaGuru {
    public static void main(String args[]) {
        Course c = new Course();
        c.courseName = "Java";
        System.out.println(c.courseName);
    }
}
```

Which of the following statements will be true if the variable courseName is defined as a private variable?

   **a** The class EJavaGuru will print Java.

   **b** The class EJavaGuru will print null.

   **c** The class EJavaGuru won't compile.

   **d** The class EJavaGuru will throw an exception at runtime.

**Q1-10.** Given the following definition of the class Course,

```
package com.ejavaguru.courses;
class Course {
    public String courseName;
}
```

what's the output of the following code?

```
package com.ejavaguru;
import com.ejavaguru.courses.Course;
class EJavaGuru {
    public static void main(String args[]) {
        Course c = new Course();
        c.courseName = "Java";
        System.out.println(c.courseName);
    }
}
```

   **a** The class EJavaGuru will print Java.

   **b** The class EJavaGuru will print null.

   **c** The class EJavaGuru won't compile.

   **d** The class EJavaGuru will throw an exception at runtime.

**Q1-11.** Given the following code, select the correct options:

```
package com.ejavaguru.courses;
class Course {
    public String courseName;
    public void setCourseName(private String name) {
        courseName = name;
    }
}
```

   **a** You can't define a method argument as a private variable.

   **b** A method argument should be defined with either public or default accessibility.

   **c** For overridden methods, method arguments should be defined with protected accessibility.

   **d** None of the above.

## 1.10  *Answers to sample exam questions*

**Q1-1.** Given:

```
class EJava {
    //..code
}
```

Which of the following options will compile?

    **a**  package java.oca.associate;
```
    class Guru {
        EJava eJava = new EJava();
    }
```

    **b**  package java.oca;
```
    import EJava;
    class Guru {
        EJava eJava;
    }
```

    **c**  package java.oca.*;
```
    import java.default.*;
    class Guru {
        EJava eJava;
    }
```

    **d**  package java.oca.associate;
```
    import default.*;
    class Guru {
        default.EJava eJava;
    }
```

    **e**  **None of the above**

Answer: e

Explanation: A class that isn't defined in a package gets implicitly defined in Java's default package. But such classes can't be accessed by classes or interfaces, which are explicitly defined in a package.

    Option a is incorrect. The EJava class isn't defined in a package, so it can't be accessed by the Guru class, which is defined in the java.oca.associate package.

    Options b, c, and d won't compile. Option b uses invalid syntax in the import statement. Options c and d try to import classes from nonexistent packages—*java.default* and *default.*

**Q1-2.** The following numbered list of Java class components is not in any particular order. Select the correct order of their occurrence in a Java class (choose all that apply):

**1** comments

**2** import statement

**3** package statement

**4** methods

**5** class declaration

**6** variables

  **a** **1, 3, 2, 5, 6, 4**

  **b** **3, 1, 2, 5, 4, 6**

  **c** 3, 2, 1, 4, 5, 6

  **d** **3, 2, 1, 5, 6, 4**

Answer: a, b, d

Explanation: The comments can appear anywhere in a class. They can appear before and after package and import statements. They can appear before or after a class, method, or variable declaration.

The first statement (if present) in a class should be a package statement. It can't be placed after an import statement or a declaration of a class.

The import statement should follow a package statement and be followed by a class declaration.

The class declaration follows the import statements, if present. It's followed by the declaration of the methods and variables.

Answer c is incorrect. None of the variables or methods can be defined before the definition of a class or interface.

**Q1-3.** Which of the following examples defines a correct Java class structure?

```
a   #connect java compiler;
    #connect java virtual machine;
    class EJavaGuru {}
```

```
b   package java compiler;
    import java virtual machine;
    class EJavaGuru {}
```

```
c   import javavirtualmachine.*;
    package javacompiler;
    class EJavaGuru {
        void method1() {}
        int count;
    }
```

```
d   package javacompiler;
    import javavirtualmachine.*;
    class EJavaGuru {
        void method1() {}
        int count;
    }
```

```
e  #package javacompiler;
   $import javavirtualmachine;
   class EJavaGuru {
       void method1() {}
       int count;
   }

f  package javacompiler;
   import javavirtualmachine;
   Class EJavaGuru {
       void method1() {}
       int count;
   }
```

Answer: d

Explanation: Option a is incorrect because #connect isn't a statement in Java. # is used to add comments in UNIX.

Option b is incorrect because a package name (Java compiler) can't contain spaces. Also, java virtual machine isn't a valid package name to be imported in a class. The package name to be imported can't contain spaces.

Option c is incorrect because a package statement (if present) must be placed before an import statement.

Option e is incorrect. #package and $import aren't valid statements or directives in Java.

Option f is incorrect. Java is case-sensitive, so the word class is not the same as the word Class. The correct keyword to define a class is class.

**Q1-4.** Given the following contents of the Java source code file MyClass.java, select the correct options:

```
// contents of MyClass.java
package com.ejavaguru;
import java.util.Date;
class Student {}
class Course {}
```

a   The imported class, java.util.Date, can be accessed only in the class Student.

**b   The imported class, java.util.Date, can be accessed by both the Student and Course classes.**

**c   Both of the classes Student and Course are defined in the package com.ejava-guru.**

d   Only the class Student is defined in the package com.ejavaguru. The class Course is defined in the default Java package.

Answer: b, c

Explanation: You can define multiple classes, interfaces, and enums in a Java source code file.

Option a is incorrect. The `import` statement applies to all the classes, interfaces, and enums defined within the same Java source code file.

Option d is incorrect. If a `package` statement is defined in the source code file, all the classes, interfaces, and enums defined within it will exist in the same Java package.

**Q1-5.** Given the following definition of the class `EJavaGuru`,

```
class EJavaGuru {
    public static void main(String[] args) {
        System.out.println(args[1]+":"+ args[2]+":"+ args[3]);
    }
}
```

what is the output of the previous class, if it is executed using the following command?

```
java EJavaGuru one two three four
```

- **a** `one:two:three`
- **b** `EJavaGuru:one:two`
- **c** `java:EJavaGuru:one`
- **d** `two:three:four`

Answer: d

Explanation: The command-line arguments passed to the `main` method of a class do not contain the word *Java* and the name of the class.

Because the position of an array is zero-based, the method argument is assigned the following values:

args[0] -> one
args[1] -> two
args[2] -> three
args[3] -> four

The class prints `two:three:four`.

**Q1-6.** Which of the following options, when inserted at `//INSERT CODE HERE`, will print out `EJavaGuru`?

```
public class EJavaGuru {
    // INSERT CODE HERE
    {
        System.out.println("EJavaGuru");
    }
}
```

**a** `public void main (String[] args)`
**b** `public void main(String     args[])`
**c** `static public void main     (String[] array)`
**d** `public static void main (String args)`
**e** `static public main (String args[])`

Answer: c

Explanation: Option a is incorrect. This option defines a valid method but not a valid `main` method. The `main` method should be defined as a `static` method, which is missing from the method declaration in option a.

Option b is incorrect. This option is similar to the method defined in option a, with one difference. In this option, the square brackets are placed after the name of the method argument. The `main` method accepts an array as a method argument, and to define an array, the square brackets can be placed after either the data type or the method argument name.

Option c is correct. Extra spaces in a class are ignored by the Java compiler.

Option d is incorrect. The `main` method accepts an array of `String` as a method argument. The method in this option accepts a single `String` object.

Option e is incorrect. It isn't a valid method definition and doesn't specify the return type of the method. This line of code will not compile.

**Q1-7.** What is the meaning of "write once, run anywhere"? Select the correct options:

**a** Java code can be written by one team member and executed by other team members.
**b** It is for marketing purposes only.
**c** **It enables Java programs to be compiled once and can be executed by any JVM without recompilation.**
**d** Old Java code doesn't need recompilation when newer versions of JVMs are released.

Answer: c

Explanation: Platform independence, or "write once, run anywhere," enables Java code to be compiled once and run on any system with a JVM. It isn't for marketing purposes only.

**Q1-8.** A class `Course` is defined in a package `com.ejavaguru`. Given that the physical location of the corresponding class file is `/mycode/com/ejavaguru/Course.class` and execution takes place within the mycode directory, which of the following lines of code, when inserted at // INSERT CODE HERE, will import the Course class into the class MyCourse?

```
// INSERT CODE HERE
class MyCourse {
    Course c;
}
```

  a  import mycode.com.ejavaguru.Course;

  **b  import com.ejavaguru.Course;**

  c  import mycode.com.ejavaguru;

  d  import com.ejavaguru;

  e  import mycode.com.ejavaguru*;

  f  import com.ejavaguru*;

Answer: b

Explanation: Option a is incorrect. The base directory, mycode, in which package com.ejavaguru is defined, must not be included in the import statement.

Options c and e are incorrect. The class's physical location isn't specified in the import statement.

Options d and f are incorrect. ejavaguru is a package. To import a package and its members, the package name should be followed by .*, as follows:

```
import com.ejavaguru.*;
```

**Q1-9.** Examine the following code:

```
class Course {
    String courseName;
}
class EJavaGuru {
    public static void main(String args[]) {
        Course c = new Course();
        c.courseName = "Java";
        System.out.println(c.courseName);
    }
}
```

Which of the following statements will be true if the variable courseName is defined as a private variable?

  a  The class EJavaGuru will print Java.

  b  The class EJavaGuru will print null.

  c  The **class EJavaGuru won't compile.**

  d  The class EJavaGuru will throw an exception at runtime.

Answer: c

Explanation: If the variable `courseName` is defined as a `private` member, it won't be accessible from the class `EJavaGuru`. An attempt to do so will cause it to fail at compile time. Because the code won't compile, it can't execute.

**Q1-10.** Given the following definition of the class `Course`,

```
package com.ejavaguru.courses;
class Course {
    public String courseName;
}
```

what's the output of the following code?

```
package com.ejavaguru;
import com.ejavaguru.courses.Course;
class EJavaGuru {
    public static void main(String args[]) {
        Course c = new Course();
        c.courseName = "Java";
        System.out.println(c.courseName);
    }
}
```

- a  The class `EJavaGuru` will print `Java`.
- b  The class `EJavaGuru` will print `null`.
- **c  The class `EJavaGuru` will not compile.**
- d  The class `EJavaGuru` will throw an exception at runtime.

Answer: c

Explanation: The class will fail to compile because a nonpublic class can't be accessed outside a package in which it's defined. The class `Course` therefore can't be accessed from within the class `EJavaGuru`, even if it's explicitly imported into it. If the class itself isn't accessible, there's no point in accessing a public member of a class.

**Q1-11.** Given the following code, select the correct options:

```
package com.ejavaguru.courses;
class Course {
    public String courseName;
    public void setCourseName(private String name) {
        courseName = name;
    }
}
```

- a  **You can't define a method argument as a `private` variable.**
- b  A method argument should be defined with either `public` or default accessibility.

c For overridden methods, method arguments should be defined with protected accessibility.

d None of the above.

Answer: a

Explanation: You can't add an explicit accessibility keyword to the method parameters. If you do, the code won't compile.

# Working with Java data types

2

| Exam objectives covered in this chapter | What you need to know |
|---|---|
| [2.2] Differentiate between object reference variables and primitive variables. | The primitive data types in Java, including scenarios when a particular primitive data type should or can't be used. Similarities and differences between the primitive data types.<br>Similarities and differences between primitive and object reference variables. |
| [2.1] Declare and initialize variables (including casting of primitive data types). | Declaration and initialization of primitives and object reference variables.<br>Literal values for primitive and object reference variables. |
| [2.5] Develop code that uses wrapper classes such as Boolean, Double, and Integer. | How and when values are boxed and unboxed when used with wrapper classes. |
| [3.1] Use Java operators; including parentheses to override operator precedence. | Use of assignment, arithmetic, relational, and logical operators with primitives and object reference variables.<br>Valid operands for an operator. Output of an arithmetic expression.<br>Determine the equality of two primitives.<br>How to override the default operator precedence by using parentheses. |

Imagine that you've just purchased a new home. You'll likely need to buy different-sized containers to store different types of food items, because one size can't fit all.

Also, you might move around food items in your home—perhaps because of a change in the requirements over time (you wish to eat it or you wish to store it).

Your new kitchen is an analogy for how Java stores its data using different data types, and manipulates the data using operators. The food items are like data types in Java, and the containers used to store the food are like variables in Java. The change in the requirements that triggers a change in the state of food items can be compared to the processing logic. The agents of change (fire, heat, or cooling) that change the state of the food items can be compared to Java operators. You need these agents of change so that you can process the raw food items to create delicacies.

In the OCA Java SE 8 Programmer I exam, you'll be asked questions on the various data types in Java, such as how to create and initialize them and what their similarities and differences are. The exam will also question you on using the Java operators. This chapter covers the following:

- Primitive data types in Java
- Literal values of primitive Java data types
- Object reference variables in Java
- Valid and invalid identifiers
- Usage of Java operators
- Modification of default operator precedence via parentheses

## 2.1 Primitive variables

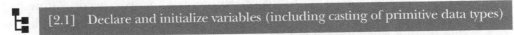

[2.1] Declare and initialize variables (including casting of primitive data types)

[2.2] Differentiate between object reference variables and primitive variables

In this section, you'll learn all the primitive data types in Java, their literal values, and the process of creating and initializing primitive variables. A variable defined as one of the primitive data types is a *primitive variable*.

Primitive data types, as the name suggests, are the simplest data types in a programming language. In the Java language, they're predefined. The names of the primitive types are quite descriptive of the values that they can store. Java defines the following eight primitive data types:

- `char`
- `byte`
- `short`
- `int`
- `long`
- `float`
- `double`
- `boolean`

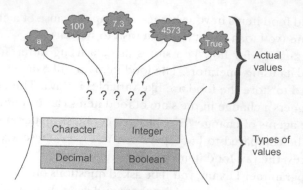

Figure 2.1   **Matching a value with its corresponding type**

Examine figure 2.1 and try to match the given value with the corresponding type. This should be a simple exercise. Table 2.1 provides the answers.

Table 2.1   **Matching a value with its corresponding data type**

| Character values | Integer values | Decimal values | Boolean |
|---|---|---|---|
| a | 100<br>4573 | 7.3 | true |

In the preceding exercise, I categorized the data that you need to store as follows: character, integer, decimal, and Boolean values. This categorization will make your life simpler when confronted with selecting the most appropriate primitive data type to store a value. For example, to store an integer value, you need a primitive data type that's capable of storing integer values; to store decimal numbers, you need a primitive data type that can store decimal numbers. Simple, isn't it?

Let's map the types of data that the primitive data types can store, because it's always easy to group and remember information.

 **NOTE**   The category *Boolean* is not the same as the primitive data type `boolean` or wrapper class `Boolean`. Java primitive data types and class names are displayed using code font.

The primitive data types can be categorized as follows: Boolean, character, and numeric (further categorized as integral and floating-point) types. Take a look at this categorization in figure 2.2.

As shown in figure 2.2, the `char` primitive data type is an unsigned numeric data type. It can only store positive integers. The rest of the numeric data types (`byte`, `short`, `int`, `long`, `float`, and `double`) are signed numeric data types (they can store both negative and positive values). The categorization in figure 2.2 will help you further associate each data type with the value that it can store. Let's start with the Boolean category.

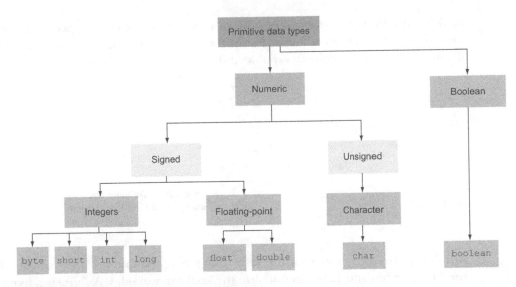

**Figure 2.2   Categorization of primitive data types**

### 2.1.1   *Category: Boolean*

The Boolean category has only one data type: boolean. A boolean variable can store one of two values: true or false. It's used in scenarios where only two states can exist. See table 2.2 for a list of questions and their probable answers.

**Table 2.2   Suitable data that can be stored using a boolean data type**

| Question | Probable answers |
|---|---|
| Did you purchase the exam voucher? | Yes/No |
| Did you log in to your email account? | Yes/No |
| Did you tweet about your passion today? | Yes/No |
| Tax collected in financial year 2001–2002 | Good question! But it can't be answered as yes/no. |

**EXAM TIP**   In this exam, the questions test your ability to select the best suitable data type for a condition that can only have two states: yes/no or true/false. The correct answer here is the boolean type.

Here's some code that defines boolean primitive variables:

```
boolean voucherPurchased = true;
boolean examPrepStarted = false;
```

In some languages, such as JavaScript, you don't need to define the type of a variable before you use it. In JavaScript, the compiler defines the type of the variable according to the value that you assign to it. Java, in contrast, is a strongly typed language. You must declare a variable and define its type before you can assign a value to it. Figure 2.3 illustrates defining a boolean variable and assigning a value to it.

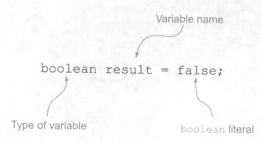

Variable name

```
boolean result = false;
```

Type of variable

boolean literal

**Figure 2.3   Defining and assigning a primitive variable**

Another point to note here is the value that's assigned to a boolean variable. I used the literals true and false to initialize the boolean variables. A *literal* is a fixed value that doesn't need further calculations in order for it to be assigned to any variable. true and false are the only two boolean literals.

**NOTE**   There are only two boolean literal values: true and false.

### 2.1.2   *Category: signed numeric*

The numeric category defines two subcategories: integers and floating point (also called decimals). Let's start with the integers.

#### INTEGERS: BYTE, INT, SHORT, LONG

When you can count a value in whole numbers, the result is an integer. It includes both negative and positive numbers. Table 2.3 lists probable scenarios in which the data can be stored as integers.

**Table 2.3   Data that can be categorized as numeric (nondecimal numbers) data type**

| Situation | Can be stored as integers? |
| --- | --- |
| Number of friends on Facebook | Yes |
| Number of tweets posted today | Yes |
| Number of photographs uploaded for printing | Yes |
| Your body temperature | Not always |

You can use the byte, short, int, and long data types to store integer values. Wait a minute: why do you need so many types to store integers?

Each one of these can store a different range of values. The benefits of the smaller ones are obvious: they need less space in memory and are faster to work with. Table 2.4

lists all these data types, along with their sizes and the ranges of the values that they can store.

**Table 2.4** Ranges of values stored by the signed numeric Java primitive data types

| Data type | Size | Range of values |
|-----------|------|-----------------|
| byte | 8 bits | –128 to 127, inclusive |
| short | 16 bits | –32,768 to 32,767, inclusive |
| int | 32 bits | –2,147,483,648 to 2,147,483,647, inclusive |
| long | 64 bits | –9,223,372,036,854,775,808 to 9,223,372,036,854,775,807, inclusive |

The OCA Java SE 8 Programmer I exam may ask you questions about the range of integers that can be assigned to a byte data type, but it won't include questions on the ranges of integer values that can be stored by short, int, or long data types. Don't worry—you don't have to memorize the ranges for all these data types!

Here's some code that assigns literal values to primitive numeric variables within their acceptable ranges:

```
byte num = 100;
short sum = 1240;
int total - 48764;
long population = 214748368;
```

The default type of a nondecimal number is int. To designate an integer literal value as a long value, add the suffix L or l (L in lowercase), as follows:

```
long fishInSea = 764398609800L;
```

Integer literal values come in four flavors: binary, decimal, octal, and hexadecimal:

- *Binary number system*—A base-2 system, which uses only 2 digits, 0 and 1.
- *Octal number system*—A base-8 system, which uses digits 0 through 7 (a total of 8 digits). Here the decimal number 8 is represented as octal 10, decimal 9 as 11, and so on.
- *Decimal number system*—The base-10 number system that you use every day. It's based on 10 digits, from 0 through 9 (a total of 10 digits).
- *Hexadecimal number system*—A base-16 system, which uses digits 0 through 9 and the letters A through F (a total of 16 digits and letters). Here the number 10 is represented as A or a, 11 as B or b, 12 as C or c, 13 as D or d, 14 as E or e, and 15 as F or f.

Let's take quick look at how you can convert integers in the decimal number system to the other number systems. Figures 2.4, 2.5, and 2.6 show how to convert the decimal number 267 to the octal, hexadecimal, and binary number systems.

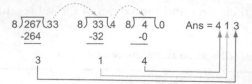

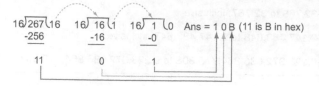

Figure 2.4   **Converting an integer from decimal to octal**

Figure 2.5   **Converting an integer from decimal to hexadecimal**

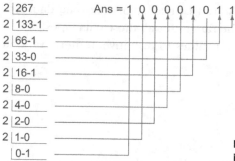

Figure 2.6   **Converting an integer from decimal to binary**

**EXAM TIP**   In the exam, you won't be asked to convert a number from the decimal number system to the octal and hexadecimal number systems and vice versa. But you can expect questions that ask you to select valid literals for integers. The figures 2.4–2.6 will help you understand these number systems better and retain this information longer, which will in turn enable you to answer questions correctly during the exam.

You can assign integer literals in base decimal, binary, octal, and hexadecimal. For octal literals, use the prefix 0; for binary, use the prefix 0B or 0b; and for hexadecimal, use the prefix 0X or 0x. Here's an example of each of these:

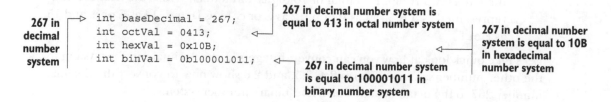

**267 in decimal number system**

```
int baseDecimal = 267;
int octVal = 0413;
int hexVal = 0x10B;
int binVal = 0b100001011;
```

**267 in decimal number system is equal to 413 in octal number system**

**267 in decimal number system is equal to 10B in hexadecimal number system**

**267 in decimal number system is equal to 100001011 in binary number system**

Java 7 introduced the use of underscores as part of the literal values. Grouping individual digits or letters of literal values makes them more readable. The underscores have no effect on the values. The following is valid code:

```
long baseDecimal = 100_267_760;
long octVal = 04_13;
long hexVal = 0x10_BA_75;
long binVal = 0b1_0000_10_11;
```

**More-readable literal values in binary, decimal, octal, and hexadecimal that use underscores to group digits and letters**

### RULES TO REMEMBER

Here's a quick list of rules for usage of underscores in the numeric literal values:

- You can place an underscore right after the prefix 0, which is used to define an octal literal value.
- You can't start or end a literal value with an underscore.
- You can't place an underscore right after the prefixes 0b, 0B, 0x, and 0X, which are used to define binary and hexadecimal literal values.
- You can't place an underscore prior to an L suffix (the L suffix is used to mark a literal value as long).
- You can't use an underscore in positions where a string of digits is expected (see the following example).

Because you're likely to be questioned on valid and invalid uses of underscores in literal values on the exam, let's look at some invalid examples:

```
int intLiteral = _100;
int intLiteral2 = 100_999_;
long longLiteral = 100_L;
```

**Can't start or end a literal value with an underscore**

**Can't place an underscore prior to suffix L**

The following line of code will compile successfully but will fail at runtime:

```
int i = Integer.parseInt("45_98");
```

**Invalid use of underscore where a string of digits is expected**

Because a String value can accept underscores, the compiler will compile the previous code. But the runtime will throw an exception stating that an invalid format of value was passed to the method parseInt.

Here's the first Twist in the Tale exercise of this chapter for you to attempt. It uses multiple combinations of underscores in numeric literal values. See if you can get all of them right (answers in the appendix).

### Twist in the Tale 2.1

Let's use the primitive variables `baseDecimal`, `octVal`, `hexVal`, and `binVal` defined earlier in this section and introduce additional code for printing the values of all these variables. Determine the output of the following code:

```java
class TwistInTaleNumberSystems {
public static void main (String args[]) {
        int baseDecimal = 267;
        int octVal = 0413;
        int hexVal = 0x10B;
        int binVal = 0b100001011;
        System.out.println (baseDecimal + octVal);
        System.out.println (hexVal + binVal);
    }
}
```

Here's another quick exercise—let's define and initialize some `long` primitive variables that use underscores in the literal values assigned to them. Determine which of these does this job correctly:

```java
long var1 = 0_100_267_760;
long var2 = 0_x_4_13;
long var3 = 0b_x10_BA_75;
long var4 = 0b_10000_10_11;
long var5 = 0xa10_AG_75;
long var6 = 0x1_0000_10;
long var7 = 100__12_12;
```

## FLOATING-POINT NUMBERS: FLOAT AND DOUBLE

You need floating-point numbers where you expect decimal numbers. For example, can you define the probability of an event occurring as an integer? Table 2.5 lists probable scenarios in which the corresponding data is stored as a floating-point number.

Table 2.5   Data that's stored as floating-point numbers

| Situation | Is the answer a floating-point number? |
|---|---|
| Orbital mechanics of a spacecraft | Yes (very precise values are required) |
| Probability of your friend request being accepted | Yes; probability is between 0.0 (none) and 1.0 (sure) |
| Speed of Earth revolving around the sun | Yes |
| Magnitude of an earthquake on the Richter scale | Yes |

In Java, you can use the `float` and `double` primitive data types to store decimal numbers. `float` requires less space than `double`, but it can store a smaller range of values than `double`. `float` is less precise than `double`. `float` can't represent accurately some numbers even if they're in range. The same limitation applies to `double`—even if it's a data type that offer more precision. Table 2.6 lists the sizes and ranges of values for `float` and `double`.

**Table 2.6   Range of values for decimal numbers**

| Data type | Size | Range of values |
|-----------|------|-----------------|
| float | 32 bits | +/–1.4E–45 to +/–3.4028235E+38, +/–infinity, +/–0, NaN |
| double | 64 bits | +/–4.9E–324 to +/–1.7976931348623157E+308, +/–infinity, +/–0, NaN |

Here's some code in action:

```
float average = 20.129F;
float orbit = 1765.65f;
double inclination = 120.1762;
```

Did you notice the use of the suffixes F and f while initializing the variables `average` and `orbit` in the preceding code? The default type of a decimal literal is `double`, but by suffixing a decimal literal value with F or f, you tell the compiler that the literal value should be treated like a `float` and not a `double`.

You can also assign a literal decimal value in scientific notation as follows:

```
double inclination2 = 1.201762e2;
```
⟵ **120.1762 is same as 1.201762e2 (the latter is expressed in scientific notation)**

You can also add the suffix D or d to a decimal number value to specify that it's a double value. Because the default type of a decimal number is `double`, the use of the suffix D or d is redundant. Examine the following line of code:

```
double inclination = 120.1762D;
```
⟵ **120.1762D is same as 120.1762**

Starting with Java version 7, you can also use underscores with the floating-point literal values. The rules are generally the same as previously mentioned for numeric literal values; the following rules are specific to floating-point literals:

- You can't place an underscore prior to a D, d, F, or f suffix (these suffixes are used to mark a floating-point literal as `double` or `float`).
- You can't place an underscore adjacent to a decimal point.

Let's look at some examples that demonstrate the invalid use of underscores in floating-point literal values:

```
float floatLiteral = 100._48F;
double doubleLiteral = 100_.87;
```
| **Can't use underscore adjacent to a decimal point**

```
float floatLiteral2 = 100.48_F;
double doubleLiteral2 = 100.87_d;
```
**Can't use underscore
prior to suffix F, f, D, or d**

### 2.1.3   *Category: character (unsigned integer)*

The character category defines only one data type: char. A char is an unsigned integer. It can store a single 16-bit Unicode character; that is, it can store characters from virtually all the existing scripts and languages, including Japanese, Korean, Chinese, Devanagari, French, German, and Spanish. Because your keyboard may not have keys to represent all these characters, you can use a value from \u0000 (or 0) to a maximum value of \uffff (or 65,535) inclusive. The following code shows the assignment of a value to a char variable:

```
char c1 = 'D';
```
◄─┤ **Use single quotes to assign
a char, not double quotes.**

A very common mistake is using double quotes to assign a value to a char. The correct option is single quotes. Figure 2.7 shows a conversation between two (hypothetical) programmers, Paul and Harry.

**Figure 2.7   Never use double quotes to assign a letter as a char value.**

What happens if you try to assign a char using double quotes? The code will fail to compile, with this message:

```
Type mismatch: cannot convert from String to char
```

**EXAM TIP**   Never use double quotes to assign a letter to a char variable. Double quotes are used to assign a value to a variable of type String.

Internally, Java stores char data as an unsigned integer value (positive integer). It's therefore acceptable to assign a positive integer value to a char, as follows:

```
char c1 = 122;
```
◄──── **Assign z to c1**

**NOTE** The exam will test you on multiple (obscure) techniques like assigning an unsigned integer value to a char data type. But I don't recommend using these on real projects. Please write code that's readable and easy to maintain.

The integer value 122 is equivalent to the letter z, but the integer value 122 is not equal to the Unicode value \u0122. The former is a number in base 10 (uses digits 0–9) and the latter is a number in base 16 (uses digits 0–9 and letters a–f—lower- or upper-case). \u is used to mark the value as a Unicode value. You must use quotes to assign Unicode values to char variables. Here's an example:

```
char c2 = '\u0122';
System.out.println("c1 = " + c1);
System.out.println("c2 = " + c2);
```

Figure 2.8 shows the output of the preceding code on a system that supports Unicode characters.

c1 = z
c2 = Ģ

**Figure 2.8  The output of assigning a character using the integer value 122 versus the Unicode value \u0122**

As mentioned earlier, char values are unsigned integer values, so if you try to assign a negative number to one, the code won't compile. Here's an example:

```
char c3 = -122;          ◄——— Fails to compile
```

But you can forcefully assign a negative number to a char type by casting it to char, as follows:

```
char c3 = (char)-122;                    ◄—┐ Compiles successfully
System.out.println("c3 = " + c3);
```

In the previous code, note how the literal value –122 is prefixed by (char). This practice is called *casting.* Casting is the forceful conversion of one data type to another data type.

You can cast only compatible data types. For example, you can cast a char to an int and vice versa. But you can't cast an int to a boolean value or vice versa. When you cast a bigger value to a data type that has a smaller range, you tell the compiler that you know what you're doing, so the compiler proceeds by chopping off any extra bits that may not fit into the smaller variable. Use casting with caution—it may not always give you the correct converted values.

Figure 2.9 shows the output of the preceding code that cast a value to c3 (the value looks weird!).

c3 = ͆

**Figure 2.9  The output of assigning a negative value to a character variable**

The char data type in Java doesn't allocate space to store the sign of an integer. If you try to forcefully assign a negative integer to char, the sign bit is stored as the part of the integer value, which results in the storage of unexpected values.

**EXAM TIP**   The exam will test your understanding of the possible values that can be assigned to a variable of type char, including whether an assignment will result in a compilation error. Don't worry—it won't test you on the value that's actually displayed after assigning arbitrary integer values to a char!

### 2.1.4   *Confusion with the names of the primitive data types*

If you've previously worked in another programming language, there's a good chance that you might get confused with the names of the primitive data types in Java and other languages. For example, C defines a primitive short int data type. But short and int are two separate primitive data types in Java. The OCA Java SE 8 Programmer I exam will test you on your ability to recognize the names of the primitive data types, and the answers to these questions may not be immediately obvious. An example follows:

Question: What is the output of the following code?

```
public class MyChar {
    public static void main(String[] args) {
        int myInt = 7;
        bool result = true;
        if (result == true)
            do
                System.out.println(myInt);
            while (myInt > 10);
    }
}
```

   **a**  It prints 7 once.
   **b**  It prints nothing.
   **c**  Compilation error.
   **d**  Runtime error.

The correct answer is (c). This question tries to trick you with complex code that doesn't use any if constructs or do-while loops! As you can see, it uses an incorrect data type name, bool, to declare and initialize the variable result. Therefore, the code will fail to compile.

**EXAM TIP**   Watch out for questions that use incorrect names for the primitive data types. For example, there isn't any bool primitive data type in Java. The correct data type is boolean. If you've worked with other programming languages, you might get confused trying to remember the exact names of all the primitive data types used in Java. Remember that just two of the primitive data types—int and char—are shortened; the rest of the primitive data types (byte, short, long, float, and double) are not.

## 2.2 Identifiers

Identifiers are names of packages, classes, interfaces, methods, and variables. Though identifying a valid identifier is not explicitly included in the exam objectives, there's a good chance that you'll encounter a question similar to the following that will require you to identify valid and invalid identifiers:

Question: Which of the following lines of code will compile successfully?

  **a** `byte exam_total = 7;`

  **b** `int exam-Total = 1090;`

The correct answer is (a). Option (b) is incorrect because hyphens aren't allowed in the name of a Java identifier. Underscores are allowed.

### 2.2.1 Valid and invalid identifiers

Table 2.7 contains a list of rules that will enable you to correctly define valid (and invalid) identifiers, along with some examples.

Table 2.7 Ingredients of valid and invalid identifiers

| Properties of valid identifiers | Properties of invalid identifiers |
| --- | --- |
| Unlimited length | Same spelling as a Java reserved word or keyword (see table 2.8) |
| Starts with a letter ( a–z, upper- or lowercase), a currency sign, or an underscore | Uses special characters: !, @, #, %, ^, &, *, ( , ), ', :, ;, [, /, \, } |
| Can use a digit (not at the starting position) | Starts with a Java digit (0–9) |
| Can use an underscore (at any position) | |
| Can use a currency sign (at any position): ¤, $, £, ¢, ¥, and others | |

| Examples of valid identifiers | Examples of invalid identifiers |
| --- | --- |
| `customerValueObject` | `7world` (identifier can't start with a digit) |
| `$rate, £Value, _sine` | `%value` (identifier can't use special char %) |
| `happy2Help, nullValue` | `Digital!`, `books@manning` (identifier can't use special char ! or @) |
| `Constant` | `null, true, false, goto` (identifier can't have the same name as a Java keyword or reserved word) |

You can't define a variable with the same name as Java keywords or reserved words. As these names suggest, they're reserved for specific purposes. Table 2.8 lists Java keywords, reserved words, and literals that you can't use as identifier names.

**Table 2.8  Java keywords and reserved words that can't be used as names for Java variables**

| abstract | default | goto | package | this |
|----------|---------|------|---------|------|
| assert | do | if | private | throw |
| boolean | double | implements | protected | throws |
| break | else | import | public | transient |
| byte | enum | instanceof | return | true |
| case | extends | int | short | try |
| catch | false | interface | static | void |
| char | final | long | strictfp | volatile |
| class | finally | native | super | while |
| const | float | new | switch | |
| continue | for | null | synchronized | |

Let's combat some of the common mistakes when determining correct and incorrect variables using the following variable declarations:

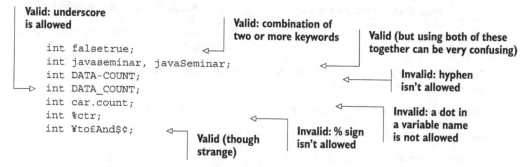

Next, let's look at the object reference variables and how they differ from the primitive variables.

## 2.3    *Object reference variables*

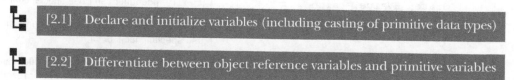

[2.1]   Declare and initialize variables (including casting of primitive data types)

[2.2]   Differentiate between object reference variables and primitive variables

The variables in Java can be categorized into two types: *primitive variables* and *reference variables*. In this section, along with a quick introduction to reference variables, we'll cover the basic differences between reference variables and primitive variables.

Reference variables are also known as *object reference variables* or *object references*. I use these terms interchangeably in this text.

### 2.3.1 *What are object reference variables?*

Objects are instances of classes, including both predefined and user-defined classes. For a reference type in Java, the variable name evaluates to the address of the location in memory where the object referenced by the variable is stored. An object reference is, in fact, a memory address that points to a memory area where an object's data is located.

Let's quickly define a barebones class, `Person`, as follows:

```
class Person {}
```

When an object is instantiated with the `new` operator, a memory address value to that object is returned. That address is usually assigned to the reference variable. Figure 2.10 shows a line of code that creates a reference variable `person` of type `Person` and assigns an object to it.

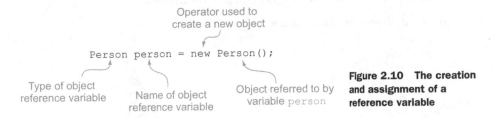

**Figure 2.10   The creation and assignment of a reference variable**

When the statement shown in figure 2.10 executes, three things happen:

- A new `Person` object is created.
- A variable named `person` is created in the stack with an empty (`null`) value.
- The variable `person` is assigned the memory address value where the object is located.

Figure 2.11 contains an illustration of a reference variable and the object it refers to in memory.

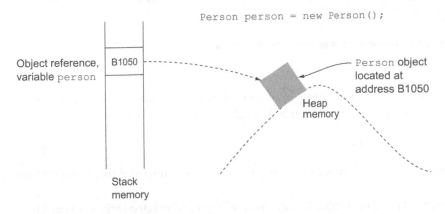

**Figure 2.11   An object reference variable and the referenced object in memory**

You can think of an object reference variable as a *handle* to an object that allows you access to that object's attributes. The following analogy will help you understand object reference variables, the objects that they refer to, and their relationship. Think of objects as analogous to *dogs*, and think of object references as analogous to *leashes*. Although this analogy won't bear too much analysis, the following comparisons are valid:

- A leash not attached to a dog is a reference object variable with a `null` value.
- A dog without a leash is a Java object that's not referred to by any object reference variable.
- Just as an unleashed dog might be picked up by animal control, an object that isn't referred to by a reference variable is liable to be garbage collected (removed from memory by the JVM).
- Several leashes may be tethered to a single dog. Similarly, a Java object may be referenced by multiple object reference variables.

Figure 2.12 illustrates this analogy.

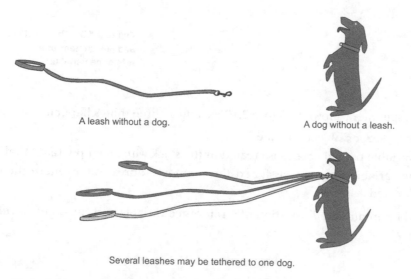

A leash without a dog.                    A dog without a leash.

Several leashes may be tethered to one dog.

**Figure 2.12   Dog leash analogy for understanding objects**

The default value of all types of object reference variables is `null`. You can also assign a `null` value to a reference variable explicitly. Here's an example:

```
Person person = null;
```

In this case, the reference variable `person` can be compared to a leash without a dog.

**NOTE**   The literal value for all types of object reference variables is `null`.

### 2.3.2 Differentiating between object reference variables and primitive variables

Just as men and women are fundamentally different (according to John Gray, author of *Men Are from Mars, Women Are from Venus*), primitive variables and object reference variables differ from each other in multiple ways. The basic difference is that primitive variables store the actual values, whereas reference variables store the addresses of the objects they refer to.

Let's assume that a class `Person` is already defined. If you create an `int` variable `a` and an object reference variable `person`, they will store their values in memory, as shown in figure 2.13.

```
int a = 77;
Person person = new Person();
```

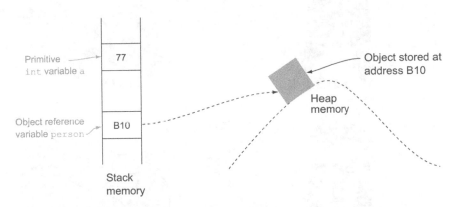

**Figure 2.13** Primitive variables store the actual values, whereas object reference variables store the addresses of the objects they refer to.

Other important differences between primitive variables and object reference variables are shown in figure 2.14 as a conversation between a girl and a boy. The girl represents an object reference variable and the boy represents a primitive variable. (Don't worry if you don't understand all of these analogies. They'll make much more sense after you read related topics in later chapters.)

In the next section, you'll start manipulating these variables using operators.

**Figure 2.14   Differences between object reference variables and primitive variables**

**Figure 2.14   Differences between object reference variables and primitive variables** *(continued)*

## 2.4   *Operators*

[3.1]  Use Java operators; including parentheses to override operator precedence

In this section, you'll use different types of operators—assignment, arithmetic, relational, and logical—to manipulate the values of variables. You'll write code to determine the equality of two primitive data types. You'll also learn how to modify the default precedence of an operator by using parentheses. For the OCA Java SE 8 Programmer I exam, you should be able to work with the operators listed in table 2.9.

**Table 2.9  Operator types and the relevant operators**

| Operator type | Operators | Purpose |
|---|---|---|
| Assignment | =, +=, -=, *=, /= | Assign value to a variable |
| Arithmetic | +, -, *, /, %, ++, -- | Add, subtract, multiply, divide, and modulus primitives |
| Relational | <, <=, >, >=, ==, != | Compare primitives |
| Logical | !, &&, \|\| | Apply NOT, AND, and OR logic to primitives |

**NOTE**  Not all operators can be used with all types of operands. For example, you can determine whether a number is greater than another number, but you can't determine whether true is greater than false or a number is greater than true. Take note of this as you learn the usage of all the operators on this exam.

### 2.4.1  *Assignment operators*

The assignment operators that you need to know for the exam are =, +=, -=, *=, and /=.

The simple assignment operator, =, is the most frequently used operator. It's used to initialize variables with values and to reassign new values to them.

The +=, -=, *=, and /= operators are short forms of addition, subtraction, multiplication, and division with assignment. The += operator can be read as "first add and then assign," and -= can be read as "first subtract and then assign." Similarly, *= can be read as "first multiply and then assign," /= can be read as "first divide and then assign," and %= can be read as "first modulus and then assign." If you apply these operators to two operands, a and b, they can be represented as follows:

```
a -= b is equal to a = a - b
a += b is equal to a = a + b
a *= b is equal to a = a * b
a /= b is equal to a = a / b
a %= b is equal to a = a % b
```

Let's have a look at some valid lines of code:

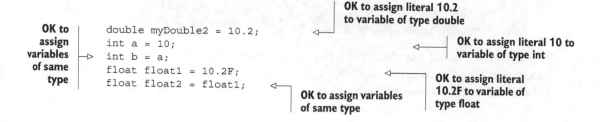

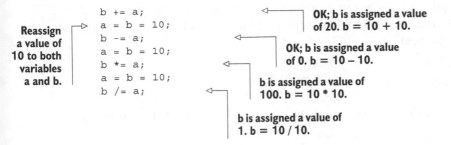

**Reassign a value of 10 to both variables a and b.**

```
b += a;
a = b = 10;
b -= a;
a = b = 10;
b *= a;
a = b = 10;
b /= a;
```

OK; b is assigned a value of 20. b = 10 + 10.

OK; b is assigned a value of 0. b = 10 – 10.

b is assigned a value of 100. b = 10 * 10.

b is assigned a value of 1. b = 10 / 10.

Next let's look at some invalid lines of code:

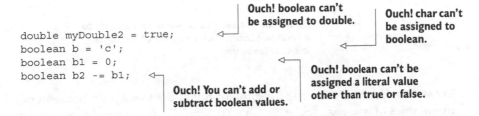

```
double myDouble2 = true;
boolean b = 'c';
boolean b1 = 0;
boolean b2 -= b1;
```

Ouch! boolean can't be assigned to double.

Ouch! char can't be assigned to boolean.

Ouch! boolean can't be assigned a literal value other than true or false.

Ouch! You can't add or subtract boolean values.

Now let's try to squeeze the variables that can store a larger range of values into variables with a shorter range. Try the following assignments:

```
long num = 100976543356L;
int val = num;
```

Compiler won't allow this

It's similar to what's shown in figure 2.15, where someone is forcefully trying to squeeze a bigger value (`long`) into a smaller container (`int`).

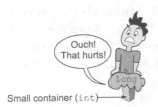

Small container (`int`)

**Figure 2.15  Assigning a bigger value (`long`) to a variable (`int`) that's only capable of storing a smaller value range**

You can still assign a bigger value to a variable that can only store smaller ranges by explicitly casting the bigger value to a smaller value. By doing so, you tell the compiler that you know what you're doing. In that case, the compiler proceeds by chopping off any extra bits that may not fit into the smaller variable. Beware! Though chopping off extra bits will make a bigger value fit in a smaller data type, the remaining bits won't represent the original value and can produce unexpected results.

Compare the previous assignment example (assigning a long to an int) with the following example that assigns a smaller value (int) to a variable (long) that's capable of storing bigger value ranges:

```
int intVal = 1009;
long longVal = intVal;        ⟵┘ Allowed
```

An int can easily fit into a long because there's enough room for it (as shown in figure 2.16).

Big container (long) ⟶ int

**Figure 2.16   Assigning a smaller value (int) to a variable (long) that's capable of storing a larger value range**

**EXAM TIP**   You can't use the assignment operators to assign a boolean value to variables of type char, byte, int, short, long, float, or double, or vice versa.

You can also assign multiple values on the same line using the assignment operator. Examine the following lines of code:

**Define and initialize variables on the same line** ⟶
```
int a = 7, b = 10, c = 8;
a = b = c;
System.out.println(a);        ⟵┐ Prints 8
```
❶ **Assignment starts from right; the value of c is assigned to b and the value of b is assigned to a**

On the line tagged ❶, the assignment starts from right to left. The value of variable c is assigned to the variable b, and the value of variable b (which is already equal to c) is assigned to the variable a. This is proved by the fact that line 3 prints 8, and not 7!

The next Twist in the Tale throws in a few twists with variable assignment and initialization. Let's see if you can identify the incorrect ones (answers in the appendix).

**Twist in the Tale 2.2**

Let's modify the assignment and initialization of the boolean variables used in previous sections. Examine the following code initializations and select the incorrect answers:

```
public class Foo {
    public static void main (String args[]) {
        boolean b1, b2, b3, b4, b5, b6;     // line 1
        b1 = b2 = b3 = true;                // line 2
        b4 = 0;                             // line 3
        b5 = 'false';                       // line 4
        b6 = yes;                           // line 5
    }
}
```

a The code on line 1 will fail to compile.

b Can't initialize multiple variables like the code on line 2.

c The code on line 3 is correct.

d Can't assign `'false'` to a `boolean` variable.

e The code on line 5 is correct.

---

## 2.4.2 Arithmetic operators

Let's take a quick look at each of these operators, together with a simple example, in table 2.10.

**Table 2.10   Use of arithmetic operators with examples**

| Operator | Purpose | Usage | Answer |
|---|---|---|---|
| + | Addition | `12 + 10` | `22` |
| - | Subtraction | `19 - 29` | `-10` |
| * | Multiplication | `101 * 45` | `4545` |
| / | Division (quotient) | `10 / 6`<br>`10.0 / 6.0` | `1`<br>`1.6666666666666667` |
| % | Modulus (remainder in division) | `10 % 6`<br>`10.0 % 6.0` | `4`<br>`4.0` |
| ++ | Unary increment operator; increments value by 1 | `++var` or `var++` | `11` (assuming value of `var` is 10) |
| -- | Unary decrement operator; decrements value by 1 | `--var` or `var--` | `9` (assuming value of `var` is 10) |

**EXAM TIP**   You can use unary increment and decrement operators with variables but not with literal values. If you do, the code won't compile.

When you apply the addition operator to `char` values, their corresponding ASCII values are added and subtracted. Here's a quick example (the ASCII value of character a is 97):

```
char char1 = 'a';
System.out.println(char1);              Outputs a
System.out.print(char1 + char1);        Outputs 194
```

And the following code outputs 0:

```
char char1 = 'a';
System.out.print(char1 - char1);        Outputs 0
```

**EXAM TIP**    You can use all arithmetic operators with the char primitive data type, including unary increment and decrement operators.

### IMPLICIT WIDENING OF DATA TYPES IN AN ARITHMETIC OPERATION

All byte, short, and char values are automatically widened to int when used as operands for arithmetic operations. If a long value is involved somewhere, then everything, including int values, is widened to long. This explains why you can't assign the sum of two byte values to a short type:

```
byte age1 = 10;
byte age2 = 20;
short sum = age1 + age2;        Fails to
                                compile
```

The preceding code fails with the following error message:

```
incompatible types: possible lossy conversion from int to short
short sum = age1 + age2;
                  ^
1 error
```

**EXAM TIP**    For arithmetic operations with data types char, byte, short, or int, all operand values are widened to int. If an arithmetic operation includes the data type long, all operand values are widened to long. If an arithmetic operation includes a data type of float or double, all operand values are widened to double.

But if you modify the preceding example and define variables age1 and age2 as final variables, then the compiler *is assured* that their sum, value 30, can be assigned to a variable of type short, without any loss of precision. In this case, the compiler is good to assign the sum of age1 and age2 to sum. Here's the modified code:

```
final byte age1 = 10;
final byte age2 = 20;           Compiles
short sum = age1 + age2;        successfully
```

### ++ AND -- (UNARY INCREMENT AND DECREMENT OPERATORS)

The operators ++ and -- are unary operators; they work with a single operand. They're used to increment or decrement the value of a variable by 1.

Unary operators can also be used in prefix and postfix notation. In *prefix notation*, the operator appears before its operand:

```
int a = 10;                     Operator ++ in
++a;                            prefix notation
```

In *postfix notation*, the operator appears after its operand:

```
int a = 10;                     Operator ++ in
a++;                            postfix notation
```

When these operators aren't part of an expression, the postfix and prefix notations behave in exactly the same manner:

```
int a = 20;              ⟵── Assign 20 to a
int b = 10;         ⟵┐
++a;                    └ Assign 10 to b
b++;
System.out.println(a);   ⟵┘ Prints 21
System.out.println(b);  ⟵┐
                          └ Prints 11
```

When a unary operator is used in an expression, its placement with respect to its operand decides whether its value will increment or decrement before the evaluation of the expression or after the evaluation of the expression. See the following code, where the operator ++ is used in prefix notation:

```
int a = 20;          ⟵┘ Assign 20 to a
int b = 10;                ⟵── Assign 10 to b        │ Assign 20 − (++10), that
int c = a - ++b;                            ⟵┘        │ is, 20–11, or 9, to c
System.out.println(c);               ⟵┐ Prints 9
System.out.println(b);  ⟵┐            └
                          └ Prints 11
```

In the preceding example, the expression a - ++b uses the increment operator (++) in prefix notation. Therefore, the value of variable b increments to 11 before it's subtracted from 20, assigning the result 9 to the variable c.

When ++ is used in postfix notation with an operand, its value increments after it's been used in the expression:

```
int a = 50;          ⟵┘ Assign 50 to a
int b = 10;                ⟵── Assign 10 to b        │ Assign 50 − (10++), that
int c = a - b++;                            ⟵┘        │ is, 50–10, or 40, to c
System.out.println(c);               ⟵┐ Prints 40
System.out.println(b);  ⟵┐            └
                          └ Prints 11
```

The interesting part here is that the value of b is printed as 11 in both cases because the value of the variable increments (or decrements) as soon as the expression in which it's used is evaluated.

The same logic applies to the unary operator, --. Here's an example:

```
double d = 20.0;     ⟵┘ Assign 20.0 to d
double e = 10.0;           ⟵── Assign 10.0 to e      │ Assign 20.0 * (--10.0), that
double f = d * --e;                         ⟵┘        │ is, 20.0 * 9.0, or 180.0, to f
System.out.println(f);               ⟵┐ Prints 180.0
System.out.println(e);  ⟵┐            └
                          └ Prints 9.0
```

Let's use the unary decrement operator (--) in postfix notation and see what happens:

```
double d = 20.0;        ⟵┘  Assign 20.0 to d
double e = 10.0;             ⟵── Assign 10.0 to e        │ Assign 20.0 * (10.0--), that is,
double f = d * e--;                              ⟵──────┘ 20.0 * 10.0, or 200.0, to f
System.out.println(f);                     ⟵┐  Prints 200.0
System.out.println(e);    ⟵┐             Prints 200.0
                            └ Prints 9.0
```

Let's check out some example code that uses unary increment and decrement operators in both prefix and postfix notation in the same line of code. What do you think the output of the following code will be?

```
int a = 10;
a = a++ + a + a-- - a-- + ++a;
System.out.println(a);
```

The output of this code is 32. The expression on the right-hand side evaluates from left to right, with the following values, which evaluate to 32:

```
a = 10 + 11 + 11 - 10 + 10;
```

The evaluation of an expression starts from left to right. For a prefix unary operator, the value of its operand increments or decrements just before its value is used in an expression. For a postfix unary operator, the value of its operand increments or decrements just after its value is used in an expression. Figure 2.17 illustrates what's happening in the preceding expression.

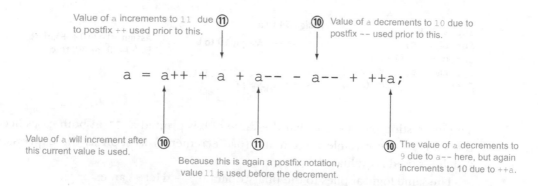

**Figure 2.17**  **Evaluation of an expression that has multiple occurrences of unary operators in postfix and prefix notation**

For the exam, it's important for you to have a good understanding of, and practice in, using postfix and prefix operators. In addition to the expressions shown in the previous examples, you can also find them in use as conditions in `if` statements, `for` loops, and `do-while` and `while` loops.

The next Twist in the Tale exercise will give you practice with unary operators used in prefix and postfix notation (answer in the appendix).

**Twist in the Tale 2.3**

Let's modify the expression used in figure 2.17 by replacing all occurrences of unary operators in prefix notation with postfix notations and vice versa. So `++a` changes to `a++`, and vice versa. Similarly, `--a` changes to `a--`, and vice versa. Your task is to evaluate the modified expression and determine the output of the following code:

```
int a = 10;
a = ++a + a + --a - --a + a++;
System.out.println (a);
```

Try to form the expression by replacing the values of variable a in the expression and explain each of them, the way it was done for you in figure 2.17.

---

### 2.4.3 Relational operators

Relational operators are used to check one condition. You can use these operators to determine whether a primitive value is equal to another value or whether it is less than or greater than the other value.

These relational operators can be divided into two categories:

- Comparing greater (>, >=) and lesser values (<, <=)
- Comparing values for equality (==) and inequality (!=)

The operators <, <=, >, and >= work with all types of numbers, both integers (including `char`) and floating point, that can be added and subtracted. Examine the following code:

```
int i1 = 10;
int i2 = 20;
System.out.println(i1 >= i2);          ←┘ Prints false
long long1 = 10;
long long2 = 20;
System.out.println(long1 <= long2);    ←┘ Prints true
```

The second category of operators is covered in the following section.

**EXAM TIP** You can't compare incomparable values. For example, you can't compare a `boolean` with an `int`, a `char`, or a floating-point number. If you try to do so, your code will not compile.

**COMPARING PRIMITIVES FOR EQUALITY (USING == AND !=)**

The operators == (equal to) and != (not equal to) can be used to compare all types of primitives: char, byte, short, int, long, float, double, and boolean. The operator == returns the boolean value true if the primitive values that you're comparing are equal, and false otherwise. The operator != returns true if the primitive values that you're comparing are *not* equal, and false otherwise. For the same set of values, if == returns true, != will return false. Sounds interesting!

Examine the following code:

```
int a = 10;
int b = 20;
System.out.println(a == b);          Prints false
System.out.println(a != b);            Prints true
boolean b1 = false;
System.out.println(b1 == true);      Prints false
System.out.println(b1 != true);        Prints true
System.out.println(b1 == false);      Prints true
System.out.println(b1 != false);      Prints false
```

Remember that you can't apply these operators to incomparable types. In the following code snippet, the code that compares an int variable to a boolean variable will fail to compile:

```
int a = 10;
boolean b1 = false;                  Causes
System.out.println(a == b1);         compilation error
```

Here's the compilation error:

```
incomparable types: int and boolean
System.out.println(a == b1);
                     ^
```

 **EXAM TIP**  The result of the relational operation is always a boolean value. You can't assign the result of a relational operation to a variable of type char, int, byte, short, long, float, or double.

**COMPARING PRIMITIVES USING THE ASSIGNMENT OPERATOR (=)**

It's a very common mistake to use the assignment operator, =, in place of the equality operator, ==, to compare primitive values. Before reading any further, check out the following code:

```
int a = 10;
int b = 20;
System.out.println(a = b);          ❶ Prints 20 (this is not
boolean b1 = false;                   a boolean value!)
System.out.println(b1 = true);       ❷ Prints true
System.out.println(b1 = false);        Prints false
```

In the previous example, ❶ isn't comparing the variables a and b. It's assigning the value of the variable b to a and then printing out the value of the variable a, which is 20. Similarly, ❷ isn't comparing the variable b1 with the boolean literal true. It's assigning the boolean literal true to variable b1 and printing out the value of the variable b1.

> **NOTE** You can't compare primitive values by using the assignment operator, =.

### 2.4.4 Logical operators

Logical operators are used to evaluate one or more expressions. These expressions should return a boolean value. You can use the logical operators AND, OR, and NOT to check multiple conditions and proceed accordingly. Here are a few real-life examples:

- *Case 1 (for managers)*—Request promotion if customer is extremely happy with the delivered project AND you think you deserve to be in your boss's seat!
- *Case 2 (for students)*—Accept job proposal if handsome pay and perks OR awesome work profile.
- *Case 3 (for entry-level Java programmers)*—If NOT happy with current job, change it.

In each of these example cases, you're making a decision (request promotion, accept job proposal, or change job) only if a set of conditions is satisfied. In case 1, a manager may request a promotion only if *both* the specified conditions are met. In case 2, a student may accept a new job if *either* of the conditions is true. In case 3, an entry-level Java programmer may change their current job if *not* happy with the current job, that is, if the specified condition (being happy with the current job) is false.

As illustrated in these examples, if you wish to proceed with a task when *both* the conditions are true, use the logical AND operator, &&. If you wish to proceed with a task when *either* of the conditions is true, use the logical OR operator, ||. If you wish to reverse the outcome of a boolean value, use the negation operator, !.

Time to look at some code in action:

```
int a = 10;
int b = 20;
System.out.println(a > 20 && b > 10);
System.out.println(a > 20 || b > 10);
System.out.println(! (b > 10));
System.out.println(! (a > 20));
```

❶ **Prints false**
❷ **Prints true**
❸ **Prints false**
❹ **Prints true**

❶ prints false because both of the conditions, a > 20 and b > 10, are not true. The first one (a > 20) is false. ❷ prints true because one of these conditions (b > 10) is true. ❸ prints false because the specified condition, b > 10, is true. ❹ prints true because the specified condition, a > 20, is false.

Table 2.11 will help you understand the result of using these logical operators.

**Table 2.11** Outcome of using `boolean` literal values with the logical operators AND, OR, and NOT

| Operators && (AND) | Operator \|\| (OR) | Operator ! (NOT) |
|---|---|---|
| `true  && true  → true`<br>`true  && false → false`<br>`false && true  → false`<br>`false && false → false`<br>`true && true && false →`<br>`false` | `true  \|\| true  → true`<br>`true  \|\| false → true`<br>`false \|\| true  → true`<br>`false \|\| false → false`<br>`false \|\| false \|\| true →`<br>`true` | `!true  → false`<br>`!false → true` |

Here's a summary of this table:

- *Logical* AND *(&&)*—Evaluates to `true` if *all* operands are `true`; `false` otherwise.
- *Logical* OR *(\|\|)*—Evaluates to `true` if *any or all* the operands are `true`.
- *Logical negation* *(!)*—Negates the `boolean` value. Evaluates to `true` for `false` and vice versa.

The operators `|` and `&` can also be used to manipulate individual bits of a number value, but I won't cover this usage here, because it's not on this exam.

**&& AND \|\| ARE SHORT-CIRCUIT OPERATORS**

Another interesting point to note with respect to the logical operators `&&` and `||` is that they're also called *short-circuit* operators because of the way they evaluate their operands to determine the result. Let's start with the operator `&&`.

The `&&` operator returns `true` only if both the operands are `true`. If the first operand to this operator evaluates to `false`, the result can *never* be `true`. Therefore, `&&` does not evaluate the second operand. Similarly, the `||` operator does not evaluate the second operator if the first operand evaluates to `true`.

```
int marks = 8;
int total = 10;
System.out.println(total < marks && ++marks > 5);     ❶ Prints false
System.out.println(marks);                            ❷ Prints 8
System.out.println(total == 10 || ++marks > 10);      ❸ Prints true
System.out.println(marks);                            ❹ Prints 8
```

In the first print statement ❶, because the first condition, `total < marks`, evaluates to `false`, the next condition, `++marks > 5`, isn't even evaluated. As you can see ❷, the output value of `marks` is still `8` (the value to which it was initialized on line 1)! Similarly, in the next comparison ❸, because `total == 10` evaluates to `true`, the second condition, `++marks > 10`, isn't evaluated. Again, this can be verified when the value of `marks` is printed again ❹, and the output is `8`.

**NOTE**   All the relational and logical operators return a `boolean` value, which can be assigned to a primitive `boolean` variable.

The purpose of the next Twist in the Tale is to encourage you to play with code that uses short-circuit operators. To determine whether a boolean expression passed as an operand to the short-circuit operators evaluates, you can apply a unary increment operator (in postfix notation) to the variable used in the expression. Compare the new variable value with the old value to verify whether the expression was evaluated (answers in the appendix).

**Twist in the Tale 2.4**

As you know, the short-circuit operators && and || may not evaluate both their operands if they can determine the result of the expression by evaluating just the first operand. Examine the following code and circle the expressions that you think will evaluate. Draw a square around the expressions that you think may not execute. (For example, on line 1, both a++ > 10 and ++b < 30 will evaluate.)

```
class TwistInTaleLLogicalOperators {
    public static void main (String args[]) {
        int a = 10;
        int b = 20;
        int c = 40;
        System.out.println(a++ > 10 || ++b < 30);       // line1
        System.out.println(a > 90 && ++b < 30);
        System.out.println(!(c>20) && a==10 );
        System.out.println(a >= 99 || a <= 33 && b == 10);
        System.out.println(a >= 99 && a <= 33 || b == 10);
    }
}
```

**Example use of the short-circuit operator && in real projects**

The logical operator && is often used in code to check whether an object reference variable has been assigned a value before invoking a method on it:

```
String name = "hello";
if (name != null && name.length() > 0)
    System.out.println(name.toUpperCase());
```

### 2.4.5 *Operator precedence*

What happens if you use multiple operators within a single line of code with multiple operands? Which one should be treated like the king and given preference over the others?

Don't worry. Java already has a rule in place for just such a situation. Table 2.12 lists the precedence of operators: the operator on top has the highest precedence, and operators within the same group have the same precedence and are evaluated from left to right.

**Table 2.12   Precedence of operators**

| Operator | Precedence |
|---|---|
| Postfix | Expression++, expression-- |
| Unary | ++expression, --expression, +expression, -expression, ! |
| Multiplication | * (multiply), / (divide), % (remainder) |
| Addition | + (add), - (subtract) |
| Relational | <, >, <=, >= |
| Equality | ==, != |
| Logical AND | && |
| Logical OR | \|\| |
| Assignment | =, +=, -=, *=, /=, %= |

 **NOTE**   Table 2.12 is limited to the operators that are part of the OCA exam. You can access the complete list at https://docs.oracle.com/javase/tutorial/java/nutsandbolts/operators.html.

Let's execute an expression that uses multiple operators (with different precedence) in an expression:

```
int int1 = 10, int2 = 20, int3 = 30;
System.out.println(int1 % int2 * int3 + int1 / int2);
```
❶ **Prints 300**

Because this expression ❶ defines multiple operators with different precedence, it's evaluated as follows:

```
(((int1 % int2) * int3)) + (int1 / int2)
(((10 % 20) * 30)) + (10 / 20)
( (10      * 30)) + (0)
( 300 )
```

What if you don't want to evaluate the expression in this way? The remedy is simple: use parentheses to override the default operator precedence. Here's an example that adds int3 and int1 before multiplying by int2:

```
int int1 = 10, int2 = 20, int3 = 30;
System.out.println(int1 % int2 * (int3 + int1) / int2);
```
**Prints 20!**

 **NOTE**   You can use parentheses to override the default operator precedence. If your expression defines multiple operators and you're unsure how your expression will be evaluated, use parentheses to evaluate in your preferred order. The inner parentheses are evaluated prior to the outer ones, following the same rules of classic algebra.

## 2.5 *Wrapper classes*

> [2.5] Develop code that uses wrapper classes such as Boolean, Double, and Integer.

Java defines a wrapper class for each of its primitive data types. The wrapper classes are used to wrap primitives in an object, so they can be added to a collection object. They enable all types to be treated like object instances. Wrapper classes help you write cleaner code, which is easy to read. For this exam, you should be able to write code that uses these wrapper classes.

### 2.5.1 *Class hierarchy of wrapper classes*

All the wrapper classes are *immutable*—classes that don't allow changes to the state of their instances after initialization. They share multiple usage details and methods. Figure 2.18 shows their hierarchy.

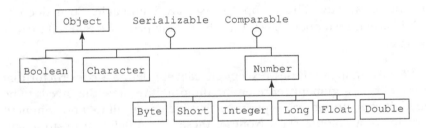

**Figure 2.18** **Hierarchy of wrapper classes**

All the numeric wrapper classes extend the class `java.lang.Number`. Classes `Boolean` and `Character` directly extend the class `Object`. All the wrapper classes implement the interfaces `java.io.Serializable` and `java.lang.Comparable`. All these classes can be serialized to a stream, and their objects define a natural sort order.

### 2.5.2 *Creating objects of the wrapper classes*

You can create objects of all the wrapper classes in multiple ways:

- *Assignment*—By assigning a primitive to a wrapper class variable (autoboxing)
- *Constructor*—By using wrapper class constructors
- *Static methods*—By calling static method of wrapper classes, like, `valueOf()`

For example:

```
Boolean bool1 = true;
Character char1 = 'a';          Autoboxing
Byte byte1 = 10;
Double double1 = 10.98;
```

```
Boolean bool2 = new Boolean(true);
Character char2 = new Character('a');       Constructors that
Byte byte2 = new Byte((byte)10);            accept primitive value
Double double2 = new Double(10.98);


//Character char3 = new Character("a");    ◄──┐  Won't compile
Boolean bool3 = new Boolean("true");              (if uncommented)
Byte byte3 = new Byte("10");               Constructor that
Double double3 = new Double("10.98");      accepts String


Boolean bool4 = Boolean.valueOf(true);
Boolean bool5 = Boolean.valueOf(true);
Boolean bool6 = Boolean.valueOf("TrUE");   Using static
Double double4 = Double.valueOf(10);       method valueOf()
```

You can create objects of the rest of the wrapper classes (`Short`, `Integer`, `Long`, and `Float`) in a similar manner. All the wrapper classes define constructors to create an object using a corresponding primitive value or as a `String`.

Another interesting point to note is that neither of these classes defines a default no-argument constructor. The wrapper classes are immutable. So it doesn't make sense to initialize the wrapper objects with the default primitive values if they can't be modified later.

**EXAM TIP**   All wrapper classes (except `Character`) define a constructor that accepts a `String` argument representing the primitive value that needs to be wrapped. Watch out for exam questions that include a call to a no-argument constructor of a wrapper class. None of these classes define a no-argument constructor.

You can assign a primitive value directly to a reference variable of its wrapper class type—thanks to *autoboxing*. The reverse is *unboxing*, when an object of a primitive wrapper class is converted to its corresponding primitive value. I'll discuss autoboxing and auto-unboxing, in detail, in the next section.

### 2.5.3   *Retrieving primitive values from the wrapper classes*

All wrapper classes define methods of the format *primitive*Value(), where the term *primitive* refers to the exact primitive data type name. Table 2.13 shows a list of the classes and their methods to retrieve corresponding primitive values.

**Table 2.13   Methods to retrieve primitive values from wrapper classes**

| Boolean | Character | Byte, Short, Integer, Long, Float, Double |
|---------|-----------|-------------------------------------------|
| booleanValue() | charValue() | byteValue(), shortValue(), intValue(), longValue(), floatValue(), doubleValue() |

It's interesting to note that all numeric wrapper classes define methods to retrieve the value of the primitive value they store, as a `byte`, `short`, `int`, `long`, `float`, or `double`.

> **EXAM TIP** All six numeric wrapper classes inherit all six `***Value()` methods from their common superclass, `Number`.

### 2.5.4 *Parsing a string value to a primitive type*

To get a primitive data type value corresponding to a string value, you can use the static utility method parse*DataType*, where *DataType* refers to the type of the return value. Each wrapper class (except `Character`) defines a method to parse a `String` to the corresponding primitive value, as listed in table 2.14.

**Table 2.14 List of *parseDataType* methods in wrapper classes**

| Class name | Method |
| --- | --- |
| Boolean | `public static boolean parseBoolean(String s)` |
| Character | `no corresponding parsing method` |
| Byte | `public static byte parseByte(String s)` |
| Short | `public static short parseShort (String s)` |
| Integer | `public static int parseInt(String s)` |
| Long | `public static long parseLong(String s)` |
| Float | `public static float parseFloat(String s)` |
| Double | `public static double parseDouble(String s)` |

All these parsing methods throw `NumberFormatExceptions` for invalid values. Here are some examples:

```
Long.parseLong("12.34");
```
← **Throws NumberFormatException:** **12.34 isn't a valid long**

```
Byte.parseByte("1234");
```
← **Throws NumberFormatException:** **1234 is out of range for byte**

```
Boolean.parseBoolean("true");
```
← **Returns boolean true**

```
Boolean.parseBoolean("TrUe");
```
← **No exceptions; the String argument isn't case-sensitive**

> **EXAM TIP** All parse methods (listed in table 2.14) throw `NumberFormat-Exception` except `Boolean.parseBoolean()`. This method returns `false` whenever the string it parses is not equal to "true" (case-insensitive comparison).

## 2.5.5   *Difference between using the valueOf method and constructors of wrapper classes*

The valueOf() method returns an object of the corresponding wrapper class when it's passed an argument of a primitive type or String. So what is the difference between the valueOf() method and constructors of these classes, which also accept method arguments of a primitive type and String?

Wrapper classes Byte, Short, Integer, and Long cache objects with values in the range of -128 to 127. The Character class caches objects with values 0 to 127. These classes define inner static classes that store objects for the primitive values -128 to 127 or 0 to 127 in an array. If you request an object of any of these classes, from this range, the valueOf() method returns a reference to a predefined object; otherwise, it creates a new object and returns its reference:

```
Long var1 = Long.valueOf(123);
Long var2 = Long.valueOf("123");
System.out.println(var1 == var2);
```
← **Prints true; var1 and var2 refer to the same cached object.**

```
Long var3 = Long.valueOf(223);
Long var4 = Long.valueOf(223);
System.out.println(var3 == var4);
```
← **Prints false; var3 and var4 refer to different objects.**

 **EXAM TIP**   Wrapper classes Float and Double don't cache objects for any range of values.

In the case of the Boolean class, the cached instances are accessible directly because only two exist: static constants Boolean.TRUE and Boolean.FALSE.

## 2.5.6   *Comparing objects of wrapper classes*

You can compare objects of wrapper classes for equality by using the method equals or the comparison operator, that is, ==. Method equals() always compares the primitive value stored by a wrapper instance, and == compares object references. The operator == returns true if the variables being compared to refer to the same instance.

Refer to the preceding section on valueOf(). Wrapper classes like Character, Byte, Short, Integer, and Long cache wrapper objects for values 0 to 127 or -128 to 127. Depending on how you initialize wrapper instances, they might or might not refer to the same instances. The following example initializes Integer variables using constructors, the static method valueOf, and autoboxing (covered in the next section). Let's compare these references using ==:

```
Integer i1 = new Integer(10);
Integer i2 = new Integer(10);
```
**Constructors always create new instances.**

```
Integer i3 = Integer.valueOf(10);
Integer i4 = Integer.valueOf(10);
```
**valueOf returns a cached copy for int value 10.**

```
Integer i5 = 10;
Integer i6 = 10;
```
**Autoboxing returns a cached copy for applicable values.**

```
System.out.println(i1 == i2);
System.out.println(i3 == i4);
System.out.println(i4 == i5);
System.out.println(i5 == i6);
```

Here's the output of the preceding code:

```
false
true
true
true
```

As evident from the output of the preceding code, `Integer` instances created using the method `valueOf` and autoboxing for `int` value `10` refer to the same instance. If you replace `==` with `equals()` in the preceding lines of code, they will output `true`:

```
System.out.println(i1.equals(i2));
System.out.println(i3.equals(i4));      Output
System.out.println(i4.equals(i5));      true
System.out.println(i5.equals(i6));
```

But the same isn't applicable for `Integer` instances created for `int` value `200` and compared using `==` (because they aren't stored in the `Integer` cache):

```
Integer i1 = new Integer(200);
Integer i2 = new Integer(200);

Integer i3 = Integer.valueOf(200);
Integer i4 = Integer.valueOf(200);

Integer i5 = 200;
Integer i6 = 200;

System.out.println(i1 == i2);      Return false—no
System.out.println(i3 == i4);      cached copies for
System.out.println(i4 == i5);      int value 200
System.out.println(i5 == i6);
```

Again, if you replace `==` with `equals()` in the preceding code, the code will output `true` for all comparisons.

 **EXAM TIP**   Cached instances exist for the wrapper `Boolean` class for the values `true` and `false`. The `Character` class caches instances with values from `0` to `127`. Classes `Byte`, `Short`, `Integer`, and `Long` cache instances for values `-127` to `128`. No cached instances exist for the `Float` and `Double` wrapper classes.

The method `equals` compares the values stored by wrapper instances. The comparison operator `==` compares reference variables—checking whether they refer to the same instance.

> **Using hashCode() and equals() to determine equality of wrapper class instances**
>
> Instances of wrapper classes can be used with the Java collection framework, as keys, with classes that support key-value pairs (like `HashMap`). These classes use `hashCode()` and `equals()` to determine the equality of instances. Because the collection framework classes (apart from `ArrayList`) aren't on this exam, I don't cover them in this book.

You can't compare wrapper instances for equality using `equals()` or `==`, if they aren't of the same class. The code won't compile for instances that are compared using `==`. When compared using `equals()`, the output will be `false`:

```
Integer obj1 = 100;
Short obj2 = 100;

System.out.println(obj1.equals(obj2));        Outputs false
System.out.println(obj1 == obj2);             Doesn't compile
```

**EXAM TIP**   Objects of different wrapper classes with same values are not equal. Using `equals()` with such instances will return `false`. If you use `==` with such instances, the code won't compile.

The next section covers autoboxing and unboxing, used by the compiler to convert primitive values to wrapper objects and vice versa.

### 2.5.7 Autoboxing and unboxing

*Autoboxing* is the automatic conversion of a primitive data type to an object of the corresponding wrapper class (you *box* the primitive value). *Unboxing* is the reverse process (you *unbox* the primitive value), as shown in figure 2.19.

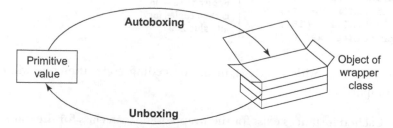

**Figure 2.19**   Autoboxing and unboxing

The wrapper classes use autoboxing and unboxing features quite frequently:

```
Double d1 = new Double(12.67);
System.out.println(d1.compareTo(21.68));      Prints -1, since
                                               12.67 < 21.68
```

Compare the use of the preceding method against the following method defined by the class `Double`:

```
public int compareTo(Double anotherDouble)
```

Wait—did I just mention that the `compareTo()` method defined in the class `Double` accepts an object of the class `Double` and not a `double` primitive data type? Then why does the preceding code compile? The answer is autoboxing. Java converted the primitive `double` to an object of the class `Double` (by using the `valueOf()` method), so it works correctly. The Java compiler converted it to the following at runtime:

```
Double d1 = new Double(12.67D);
System.out.println(d1.compareTo(Double.valueOf(21.68D)));
```

Now examine the following code (an example of unboxing with autoboxing):

```
public class Unboxing {
    public static void main (String args[]) {
        ArrayList<Double> list = new ArrayList<Double>();        List of
        list.add(12.12);                                         Double
        list.add(11.24);                                         Autoboxing—add double
        Double total = 0.0;
        for (Double d : list)
            total += d;                        Unbox to use operator
    }                                          += with total
}
```

In the preceding code, at the end of execution of the `for` loop, `total` will be assigned a `Double` value of `23.36`. The arithmetic operators like `+=` can't be used with objects. So why do you think the code compiles? In this example, the Java compiler converted the preceding code to the following at runtime:

```
public class Unbox {
    public static void main(String args[]) {
        ArrayList list = new ArrayList();
        list.add(new Double(12.12D));
        list.add(new Double(11.24D));
        Double total = Double.valueOf(0.0D);
        for(Iterator iterator = list.iterator(); iterator.hasNext();) {
            Double d = (Double)iterator.next();
            total = total.doubleValue() + d.doubleValue();
        }
    }
}
```

In the previous section, I mentioned that wrapper classes are immutable. So what happens when you *add* a value to the variable `total`, a `Double` object? In this case, the variable `total` refers to a *new* `Double` object.

 **EXAM TIP** Wrapper classes are immutable. Adding a primitive value to a wrapper class variable doesn't modify the value of the object it refers to. The wrapper class variable is assigned a new object.

Here's another interesting question. What happens if you pass `null` as an argument to the following method?

```
public int increment(Integer obj) {
    return ++i;
}
```

Because the Java compiler would call `obj.intValue()` to get `obj`'s `int` value, passing `null` to the `increment()` method will throw a `NullPointerException`.

**EXAM TIP**   Unboxing a wrapper reference variable, which refers to `null`, will throw a `NullPointerException`.

## 2.6   *Summary*

In this chapter, we started with the primitive data types in Java, including examples of where to use each of the kinds and their literal values. We also categorized the primitives into character type, integer type, and floating type. Then we covered the ingredients of valid and invalid Java identifiers. We covered the differences between primitive and reference types.

We discussed the operators used to manipulate primitives (limited to the ones required for the OCA Java SE 8 Programmer I exam). We also covered the conditions in which a particular operator can be used. For example, if you wish to check whether a set of conditions is true, you can use the logical operators. It's also important to understand the operand types that can be used for each of these operators. For example, you can't use `boolean` operands with the operators `>`, `>=`, `=<`, and `<`.

We discussed the wrapper classes, including their class hierarchy, creating their instances, retrieving primitive values stored by wrapper class instance, parsing string values to primitive types, and comparing instances of wrapper classes. At the end of the chapter, we covered autoboxing and unboxing.

## 2.7   *Review notes*

Primitive data types:

- Java defines eight primitive data types: `char`, `byte`, `short`, `int`, `long`, `float`, `double`, and `boolean`.
- Primitive data types are the simplest data types.
- Primitive data types are predefined by the programming language. A user can't define a primitive data type in Java.
- It's helpful to categorize the primitive data types as Boolean, numeric, and character data types.

The `boolean` data type:

- The `boolean` data type is used to store data with only two possible values. These two possible values may be thought of as yes/no, 0/1, true/false, or any other combination. The actual values that a `boolean` can store are `true` and `false`.

- `true` and `false` are literal values.
- A literal is a fixed value that doesn't need further calculations to be assigned to any variable.

Numeric data types:

- Numeric values can be stored as either integers or decimal numbers.
- `byte`, `short`, `int`, and `long` can be used to store integers.
- The `byte`, `short`, `int`, and `long` data types use 8, 16, 32, and 64 bits, respectively, to store their values.
- `float` and `double` can be used to store decimal numbers.
- The `float` and `double` data types use 32 and 64 bits, respectively, to store their values.
- The default type of integers—that is, nondecimal numbers—is `int`.
- To designate an integer literal value as a `long` value, add the suffix `L` or `l` to the literal value.
- Numeric values can be stored in binary, octal, decimal, and hexadecimal number formats. This exam won't ask you to convert a number from one number system to another.
- Literal values in the decimal number system use digits from 0 to 9 (a total of 10 digits).
- Literal values in the octal number system use digits from 0 to 7 (a total of 8 digits).
- Literal values in the hexadecimal number system use digits from 0 to 9 and letters from A to F (a total of 16 digits and letters).
- Literal values in the binary number system use digits 0 and 1 (a total of 2 digits).
- The literal values in the octal number system start with the prefix `0`. For example, `0413` in the octal number system is `267` in the decimal number system.
- The literal values in the hexadecimal number system start with the prefix `0x`. For example, `0x10B` in the hexadecimal number system is `267` in the decimal number system.
- The literal values in the binary number system start with the prefix `0b` or `0B`. For example, the decimal value `267` is `0B100001011` in the binary system.
- Starting with Java 7, you can use underscores within the Java literal values to make them more readable. `0B1_0000_10_11`, `0_413`, and `0x10_B` are valid binary, octal, and hexadecimal literal values.
- The default type of a decimal number is `double`.
- To designate a decimal literal value as a `float` value, add the suffix `F` or `f` to the literal value.
- The suffixes `D` and `d` can be used to mark a literal value as a `double` value. Though it's allowed, doing so is not required because the default value of decimal literals is `double`.

Character primitive data types:

- A char data type can store a single 16-bit Unicode character; that is, it can store characters from virtually all the world's existing scripts and languages.
- You can use values from \u0000 (or 0) to a maximum of \uffff (or 65,535 inclusive) to store a char. Unicode values are defined in the hexadecimal number system.
- Internally, the char data type is stored as an unsigned integer value (only positive integers).
- When you assign a letter to a char, Java stores its integer equivalent value. You may assign a positive integer value to a char instead of a letter, such as 122.
- The literal value 122 is not the same as the Unicode value \u0122. The former is a decimal number and the latter is a hexadecimal number.
- Single quotes, not double quotes, are used to assign a letter to a char variable.

Valid identifiers:

- A valid identifier starts with a letter (a–z, upper- or lowercase), a currency sign, or an underscore. There is no limit to its length.
- A valid identifier can contain digits but not in the starting place.
- A valid identifier can use the underscore and currency sign at any position of the identifier.
- A valid identifier can't have the same spelling as a Java keyword, such as switch.
- A valid identifier can't use any special characters, including !, @, #, %, ^, &, *, (, ), ', :, ;, [, /, \, and }.

Assignment operators:

- Assignment operators can be used to assign or reassign values to all types of variables.
- A variable can't be assigned to an incompatible value. For example, character and numeric values can't be assigned to a boolean variable and vice versa.
- += and -= are short forms of addition/subtraction and assignment.
- += can be read as "first add and then assign" and -= can be read as "first subtract and then assign."

Arithmetic operators:

- Arithmetic operators can't be used with the boolean data type. Attempting to do so will make the code fail to compile.
- ++ and -- are unary increment and decrement operators. These operators work with single operands.
- Unary operators can be used in prefix or postfix notation.
- When the unary operators ++ and -- are used in prefix notation, the value of the variable increments/decrements just before the variable is used in an expression.

- When the unary operators ++ and -- are used in postfix notation, the value of the variable increments/decrements just after the variable is used in an expression.
- By default, unary operators have a higher precedence than multiplication operators and addition operators.

Relational operators:

- Relational operators are used to compare values for equality (==) and inequality (!=). They're also used to determine whether two numeric values are greater than (>, >=) or less than (<, <=) each other.
- You can't compare incomparable values. For example, you can't compare a boolean with an int, a char, or a floating-point number. If you try to do so, your code will not compile.
- The operators equal to (==) and not equal to (!=) can be used to compare all types of primitives: char, byte, short, int, long, float, double, and boolean.
- The operator == returns true if the primitive values being compared are equal.
- The operator != returns true if the primitive values being compared are *not* equal.
- The result of the relational operator is always a boolean value.

Logical operators:

- You can use the logical operators to determine whether a set of conditions is true or false and proceed accordingly.
- Logical AND (&&) evaluates to true if all operands are true and false otherwise.
- Logical OR (||) evaluates to true if any or all the operands are true.
- Logical negation (!) negates the boolean value. It evaluates to true for false and vice versa.
- The result of a logical operation is always a boolean value.
- The logical operators && and || are also called short-circuit operators. If these operators can determine the output of the expression with the evaluation of the first operand, they don't evaluate the second operand.
- The && operator returns true only if both of the operands are true. If the first operand to this operator evaluates to false, the result can never be true. Therefore, && does not evaluate the second operand.
- Similarly, the || operator returns true if any of the operands is true. If the first operand to this operator evaluates to true, the result can never be false. Therefore, || does not evaluate the second operator.

Wrapper classes:

- The wrapper classes are used to wrap primitives in an object, so they can be added to a collection object.
- All the wrapper classes are immutable.

- You can create objects of all the wrapper classes in multiple ways:
  - *Assignment*—By assigning a primitive to a wrapper class variable (autoboxing)
  - *Constructor*—By using wrapper class constructors
  - *Static methods*—By calling the static method of wrapper classes, like `valueOf()`
- All wrapper classes (except `Character`) define a constructor that accepts a `String` argument representing the primitive value that needs to be wrapped.
- None of the wrapper class defines a no-argument constructor.
- You can assign a primitive value directly to a reference variable of its wrapper class type, called autoboxing. The reverse is unboxing, when an object of a primitive wrapper class is converted to its corresponding primitive value.
- All wrapper classes define methods of the format *primitive*Value(), where the term *primitive* refers to the exact primitive data type name.
- To get a primitive data type value corresponding to a string value, you can use the static utility method parse*DataType*, where *DataType* refers to the type of the return value.
- The `valueOf()` method returns an object of the corresponding wrapper class when it's passed an argument of a primitive type or `String`.
- You can compare objects of wrapper classes for equality by using the method equals or the comparison operator, `==`.
- The method `equals` always compares the primitive value stored by a wrapper instance and `==` compares object references. The operator `==` returns `true` if the variables being compared refer to the same instance.
- In the case of the `Boolean` class, the cached instances are accessible directly because only two exist: the static constants `Boolean.TRUE` and `Boolean.FALSE`.
- The `Character` class caches instances with values from `0` to `127`. Classes `Byte`, `Short`, `Integer`, and `Long` cache instances for values `-128` to `127`. No cached instances exist for the `Float` and `Double` wrapper classes.
- Wrapper classes are immutable. Adding a primitive value to a wrapper class variable doesn't modify the value of the object it refers to. The wrapper class variable is assigned a new object.
- Unboxing a wrapper reference variable, which refers to `null`, will throw a `NullPointerException`.

## 2.8  *Sample exam questions*

**Q2-1.** Given:

```
int myChar = 97;
int yourChar = 98;
System.out.print((char)myChar + (char)yourChar);

int age = 20;
System.out.print(" ");
System.out.print((float)age);
```

What is the output?

a 195 20.0

b 195 20

c ab 20.0

d ab 20

e Compilation error

f Runtime exception

**Q2-2.** Which of the options are correct for the following code?

```
public class Prim {                                 // line 1
    public static void main(String[] args) {        // line 2
        char a = 'a';                               // line 3
        char b = -10;                               // line 4
        char c = '1';                               // line 5
        integer d = 1000;                           // line 6
        System.out.println(++a + b++ * c - d);      // line 7
    }                                               // line 8
}                                                   // line 9
```

a Code at line 4 fails to compile.

b Code at line 5 fails to compile.

c Code at line 6 fails to compile.

d Code at line 7 fails to compile.

**Q2-3.** What is the output of the following code?

```
public class Foo {
    public static void main(String[] args) {
        int a = 10;
        long b = 20;
        short c = 30;
        System.out.println(++a + b++ * c);
    }
}
```

a 611

b 641

c 930

d 960

**Q2-4.** Given:

```
Boolean buy = new Boolean(true);
Boolean sell = new Boolean(true);
System.out.print(buy == sell);
```

```
boolean buyPrim = buy.booleanValue();
System.out.print(!buyPrim);

System.out.print(buy && sell);
```

What is the output?

**a** falsefalsefalse

**b** truefalsetrue

**c** falsetruetrue

**d** falsefalsetrue

**e** Compilation error

**f** Runtime exception

**Q2-5.** Which of the following options contain correct code to declare and initialize variables to store whole numbers?

**a** bit a = 0;

**b** integer a2 = 7;

**c** long a3 = 0x10C;

**d** short a4 = 0512;

**e** double a5 = 10;

**f** byte a7 = -0;

**g** long a8 = 123456789;

**Q2-6.** Select the options that, when inserted at // INSERT CODE HERE, will make the following code output a value of 11:

```
public class IncrementNum {
    public static void main(String[] args) {
        int ctr = 50;
        // INSERT CODE HERE
        System.out.println(ctr % 20);
    }
}
```

**a** ctr += 1;

**b** ctr =+ 1;

**c** ++ctr;

**d** ctr = 1;

**Q2-7.** What is the output of the following code?

```
int a = 10;
int b = 20;
int c = (a * (b + 2)) - 10-4 * ((2*2) - 6;
System.out.println(c);
```

a  218

b  232

c  246

d  Compilation error

**Q2-8.** What is true about the following lines of code?

```
boolean b = false;
int i = 90;
System.out.println(i >= b);
```

a  Code prints true

b  Code prints false

c  Code prints 90 >= false

d  Compilation error

**Q2-9.** Examine the following code and select the correct options:

```
public class Prim {                                          // line 1
    public static void main(String[] args) {                 // line 2
        int num1 = 12;                                       // line 3
        float num2 = 17.8f;                                  // line 4
        boolean eJavaResult = true;                          // line 5
        boolean returnVal = num1 >= 12 && num2 < 4.567       // line 6
                      || eJavaResult == true;
        System.out.println(returnVal);                       // line 7
    }                                                        // line 8
}                                                            // line 9
```

a  Code prints false

b  Code prints true

c  Code will print true if code on line 6 is modified to the following:

```
boolean returnVal = (num1 >= 12 && num2 < 4.567) || eJavaResult == true;
```

d  Code will print true if code on line 6 is modified to the following:

```
boolean returnVal = num1 >= 12 && (num2 < 4.567 || eJavaResult == false);
```

**Q2-10.** Given:

```
boolean myBool = false;                              // line 1
int yourInt = 10;                                    // line 2
float hisFloat = 19.54f;                             // line 3
System.out.println(hisFloat = yourInt);              // line 4
System.out.println(yourInt > 10);                    // line 5
System.out.println(myBool = false);                  // line 6
```

What is the result?

a   ```
true
true
false
```

b   ```
10.0
false
false
```

c   ```
false
false
false
```

d   Compilation error

## 2.9   *Answers to sample exam questions*

**Q2-1.** Given:

```
int myChar = 97;
int yourChar = 98;
System.out.print((char)myChar + (char)yourChar);

int age = 20;
System.out.print(" ");
System.out.print((float)age);
```

What is the output?

   a   **195 20.0**

   b   195 20

   c   ab 20.0

   d   ab 20

   e   Compilation error

   f   Runtime exception

Answer: a

Explanation: When a char primitive data type is used as an operand to arithmetic operators, its corresponding ASCII value is used in the arithmetic operation. Though (char)myChar explicitly casts int variable myChar to char type, its value 97 is used in the arithmetic operation. When literal value 20 is explicitly cast to a float type, it outputs its value as a decimal number, that is, 20.0.

**Q2-2.** Which of the options are correct for the following code?

```
public class Prim {                             // line 1
    public static void main(String[] args) {    // line 2
        char a = 'a';                           // line 3
        char b = -10;                           // line 4
        char c = '1';                           // line 5
```
```

```
        integer d = 1000;                         // line 6
        System.out.println(++a + b++ * c - d);    // line 7
    }                                             // line 8
}                                                 // line 9
```

**a** **Code at line 4 fails to compile.**

**b** Code at line 5 fails to compile.

**c** **Code at line 6 fails to compile.**

**d** **Code at line 7 fails to compile.**

Answer: a, c, d

Explanation: Option (a) is correct. The code at line 4 fails to compile because you can't assign a negative value to a primitive char data type without casting.

Option (c) is correct. There is no primitive data type with the name "integer." The valid data types are int and Integer (a wrapper class with *I* in uppercase).

Option (d) is correct. The variable d remains undefined on line 7 because its declaration fails to compile on line 6. So the arithmetic expression (++a + b++ * c - d) that uses variable d fails to compile. There are no issues with using the variable c of the char data type in an arithmetic expression. The char data types are internally stored as unsigned integer values and can be used in arithmetic expressions.

**Q2-3.** What is the output of the following code?

```
public class Foo {
    public static void main(String[] args) {
        int a = 10;
        long b = 20;
        short c = 30;
        System.out.println(++a + b++ * c);
    }
}
```

**a** **611**

**b** 641

**c** 930

**d** 960

Answer: a

Explanation: The prefix increment operator (++) used with the variable a will increment its value before it's used in the expression ++a + b++ * c. The postfix increment operator (++) used with the variable b will increment its value after its initial value is used in the expression ++a + b++ * c.

Therefore, the expression ++a + b++ * c evaluates with the following values:

```
11 + 20 * 30
```

Because the multiplication operator has a higher precedence than the addition operator, the values 20 and 30 are multiplied before the result is added to the value 11.
The example expression evaluates as follows:

```
(++a + b++ * c)
= 11 + 20 * 30
= 11 + 600
= 611
```

**EXAM TIP**   Although questions 2-2 and 2-3 seemed to test you on your understanding of operators, they actually tested you on different topics. Question 2-2
tested you on the name of the primitive data types. Beware! The real exam
has many such questions. A question that may seem to test you on threads
may actually be testing you on the use of a do-while loop!

**Q2-4.** Given:

```
Boolean buy = new Boolean(true);
Boolean sell = new Boolean(true);
System.out.print(buy == sell);

boolean buyPrim = buy.booleanValue();
System.out.print(!buyPrim);

System.out.print(buy && sell);
```

What is the output?

- a  `falsefalsefalse`
- b  `truefalsetrue`
- c  `falsetruetrue`
- d  **`falsefalsetrue`**
- e  Compilation error
- f  Runtime exception

Answer: d

Explanation: The Boolean instances buy and sell are created using constructors.
Constructors don't refer to existing instances in cache; they create new instances.
Because the comparison operator == compares object references and not the primi-
tive value stored by a wrapper instance, buy == sell returns false.

The method booleanValue() can be used to get the primitive boolean value
stored by a Boolean wrapper instance. So buy.booleanValue() returns false. Because
wrapper instances can be used with arithmetic and logical operators, buy && sell compiles, returning true.

**Q2-5.** Which of the following options contain correct code to declare and initialize variables to store whole numbers?

   **a** `bit a = 0;`

   **b** `integer a2 = 7;`

   **c** `long a3 = 0x10C;`

   **d** `short a4 = 0512;`

   **e** `double a5 = 10;`

   **f** `byte a7 = -0;`

   **g** `long a8 = 123456789;`

Answer: c, d, f, g

Explanation: Options (a) and (b) are incorrect. There are no primitive data types in Java with the names `bit` and `integer`. The correct names are `byte` and `int`.

   Option (c) is correct. It assigns a hexadecimal literal value to the variable a3.

   Option (d) is correct. It assigns an octal literal value to the variable a4.

   Option (e) is incorrect. It defines a variable of type `double`, which is used to store decimal numbers, not integers.

   Option (f) is correct. `-0` is a valid literal value.

   Option (g) is correct. `123456789` is a valid integer literal value that can be assigned to a variable of type `long`.

**Q2-6.** Select the options that, when inserted at `// INSERT CODE HERE`, will make the following code output a value of 11:

```
public class IncrementNum {
    public static void main(String[] args) {
        int ctr = 50;
        // INSERT CODE HERE
        System.out.println(ctr % 20);
    }
}
```

   **a** `ctr += 1;`

   **b** `ctr =+ 1;`

   **c** `++ctr;`

   **d** `ctr = 1;`

Answer: a, c

Explanation: To output a value of 11, the value of the variable `ctr` should be 51 because 51%20 is 11. Operator `%` outputs the remainder from a division operation. The current value of the variable `ctr` is 50. It can be incremented by 1 using the correct assignment or increment operator.

   Option (b) is incorrect. Java does not define a `=+` operator. The correct operator is `+=`.

Option (d) is incorrect because it's assigning a value of 1 to the variable `result`, not incrementing it by 1.

**Q2-7.** What is the output of the following code?

```
int a = 10;
int b = 20;
int c = (a * (b + 2)) - 10-4 * ((2*2) - 6;
System.out.println(c);
```

    a  218

    b  232

    c  246

    d  **Compilation error**

Answer: d

Explanation: First of all, whenever you answer any question that uses parentheses to override operator precedence, check whether the number of opening parentheses matches the number of closing parentheses. This code won't compile because the number of opening parentheses doesn't match the number of closing parentheses.

Second, you may not have to answer complex expressions in the real exam. Whenever you see overly complex code, look for other possible issues in the code. Complex code may be used to distract your attention from the real issue.

**Q2-8.** What is true about the following lines of code?

```
boolean b = false;
int i = 90;
System.out.println(i >= b);
```

    a  Code prints `true`

    b  Code prints `false`

    c  Code prints `90 >= false`

    d  **Compilation error**

Answer: d

Explanation: The code will fail to compile; hence, it can't execute. You can't compare incomparable types, such as a `boolean` value with a number.

**Q2-9.** Examine the following code and select the correct options:

```
public class Prim {                              // line 1
    public static void main(String[] args) {     // line 2
        int num1 = 12;                           // line 3
        float num2 = 17.8f;                      // line 4
```

```
        boolean eJavaResult = true;                    // line 5
        boolean returnVal = num1 >= 12 && num2 < 4.567 // line 6
                        || eJavaResult == true;
        System.out.println(returnVal);                 // line 7
                                                       // line 8
    }                                                  // line 9
}
```

**a**  Code prints `false`

**b**  **Code prints `true`**

**c**  **Code will print `true` if code on line 6 is modified to the following:**

```
boolean returnVal = (num1 >= 12 && num2 < 4.567) || eJavaResult == true;
```

**d**  Code will print `true` if code on line 6 is modified to the following:

```
boolean returnVal = num1 >= 12 && (num2 < 4.567 || eJavaResult == false);
```

Answer: b, c

Explanation: Option (a) is incorrect because the code prints `true`.

Option (d) is incorrect because the code prints `false`.

The code in option (c) uses parentheses to indicate which expression should evaluate prior to the rest. Here are the steps of execution:

```
boolean returnVal = (num1 >= 12 && num2 < 4.567) || eJavaResult == true;
returnVal = false || eJavaResult == true;
returnVal = true;
```

The original code in the question doesn't use parentheses to group the expressions. In this case, because the operator `&&` has a higher operator precedence than `||`, the expression `'num1 >= 12 && num2 < 4.567'` will be the first expression to execute. Here are the steps of execution:

```
boolean returnVal = num1 >= 12 && num2 < 4.567 || eJavaResult == true;
returnVal = false || eJavaResult == true;
returnVal = true;
```

**Q2-10.** Given:

```
boolean myBool = false;                         // line 1
int yourInt = 10;                               // line 2
float hisFloat = 19.54f;                        // line 3
System.out.println(hisFloat = yourInt);         // line 4
System.out.println(yourInt > 10);               // line 5
System.out.println(myBool = false);             // line 6
```

What is the result?

**a**  `true`
    `true`
    `false`

    **b**  `10.0`
       `false`
       `false`

    **c**  `false`
       `false`
       `false`

    **d** Compilation error

Answer: b

Explanation: The expression `myBool = false` uses the assignment operator (`=`) and not a comparison operator (`==`). This expression assigns the `boolean` literal `false` to `myBool`; it doesn't compare `false` with `myBool`. Watch out for similar (trick) assignments in the exam, which may *seem* to be comparing values.

# Methods and encapsulation

| Exam objectives covered in this chapter | What you need to know |
|---|---|
| [1.1] Define the scope of variables. | Variables can have multiple scopes: class, instance, method, and local.<br>Accessibility of a variable in a given scope. |
| [2.3] Know how to read or write to object fields. | Object fields can be read from and written to by directly accessing instance variables and calling methods.<br>The correct notation to call methods on an object.<br>Methods may or may not change the value of instance variables.<br>Access modifiers affect access to instance variables and methods that can be called using a reference variable.<br>Nonstatic methods can't be called on uninitialized objects. |
| [2.4] Explain an Object's Lifecycle (creation, "dereference by reassignment" and garbage collection). | Differences between when an object is declared, initialized, accessible, and eligible to be collected by Java's garbage collection.<br>Garbage collection in Java. |
| [6.1] Create methods with arguments and return values; including overloaded methods. | Creation of methods with correct return types and method argument lists.<br>Creation of methods with the same names, but a different set of argument lists. |

| Exam objectives covered in this chapter | What you need to know |
|---|---|
| [6.3] Create and overload constructors; including impact on default constructors. | Like regular methods, constructors can be overloaded. A default constructor isn't the same as a no-argument constructor. Java defines a no-argument constructor when no user-defined constructors are created. User-defined constructors can be overloaded. |
| [6.5] Apply encapsulation principles to a class. | Need for and benefits of encapsulation. Definition of classes that correctly implement the encapsulation principle. |
| [6.6] Determine the effect upon object references and primitive values when they are passed into methods that change the values. | Object references and primitives are treated in a different manner when passed to methods. Unlike reference variables, the values of primitives are never changed in the calling method when they're passed to methods. |

Look around, and you'll find multiple examples of *well-encapsulated objects.* For instance, most of us use the services of a bank, which applies a set of well-defined processes that enable us to secure our money and valuables (a bank vault). The bank may require input from us to execute some of its processes, such as depositing money into our accounts. But the bank may or may not inform us about the results of other processes; for example, it may inform us about an account balance after a transaction, but it likely won't inform us about its recruitment plans for new employees.

In Java, you can compare a bank to a well-encapsulated class and the bank processes to Java methods. In this analogy, your money and valuables are like object fields in Java. You can also compare inputs that a bank process requires to Java's method parameters and compare the bank process result to a Java method's return value. Finally, you can compare the set of steps that a bank executes when it opens a bank account to constructors in Java.

In the exam, you must answer questions about methods and encapsulation. This chapter will help you get the correct answers by covering the following:

- Defining the scope of variables
- Explaining an object's life cycle
- Creating methods with primitive and object arguments and return values
- Creating overloaded methods and constructors
- Reading and writing to object fields
- Calling methods on objects
- Applying encapsulation principles to a class

Let's get started with the scope of variables.

## 3.1    Scope of variables

[1.1]   Define the scope of variables

The scope of a variable specifies its life span and its visibility. In this section, we'll cover the scopes of variables, including the domains in which they're accessible. Here are the available scopes of variables:

- Local variables (also known as method-local variables)
- Method parameters (also known as method arguments)
- Instance variables (also known as attributes, fields, and nonstatic variables)
- Class variables (also known as static variables)

As a rule of a thumb, the scope of a variable ends when the brackets of the block of code it's defined in get closed. This might be hard to understand now, but it will become clearer when you go through the examples. Let's get started by defining local variables.

### 3.1.1    Local variables

*Local variables* are defined within a method. They may or may not be defined within code constructs such as `if-else` constructs, looping constructs, or `switch` statements. Typically, you'd use local variables to store the intermediate results of a calculation. Compared to the other three variable scopes listed previously, they have the shortest scope (life span).

In the following code, a local variable avg is defined within the method getAverage():

```
class Student {
    private double marks1, marks2, marks3;          Instance variables
    private double maxMarks = 100;
    public double getAverage() {                        Local variable avg
        double avg = 0;
        avg = ((marks1 + marks2 + marks3) / (maxMarks*3)) * 100;
        return avg;
    }
    public void setAverage(double val) {          This code won't compile
        avg = val;                                because avg is inaccessible
    }                                             outside the method getAverage.
}
```

As you can see, the variable avg, defined locally in the method getAverage, can't be accessed outside it, in the method setAverage. The scope of this local variable, avg, is depicted in figure 3.1. The unshaded area marks where avg is accessible, and the shaded area is where it won't be available.

**NOTE**   The life span of a variable is determined by its scope. If the scope of a variable is limited to a method, its life span is also limited to that method. You may notice that these terms are used interchangeably.

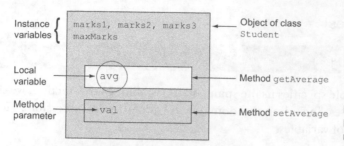

Instance variables { `marks1, marks2, marks3` `maxMarks`  ← Object of class `Student`

Local variable — (avg)  ← Method `getAverage`

Method parameter — `val`  ← Method `setAverage`

**Figure 3.1   You can access the local variable avg only within the method getAverage.**

Let's define another variable, avg, local to the `if` block of an `if` statement (code that executes when the `if` condition evaluates to `true`):

```java
public double getAverage() {
    if (maxMarks > 0) {
        double avg = 0;                                   ← Variable avg is
        avg = (marks1 + marks2 + marks3)/(maxMarks*3) * 100;   local to if block
        return avg;
    }
    else {
        avg = 0;          Variable avg can't be accessed because it's
        return avg;       local to the if block. Variables local to the if
    }                     block can't be accessed in the else block.
}
```

In this case, the scope of the local variable avg is reduced to the `if` block of the `if-else` statement defined within the getAverage method. The scope of this local variable avg is depicted in figure 3.2, where the unshaded area marks where avg is accessible, and the shaded part marks the area where it won't be available.

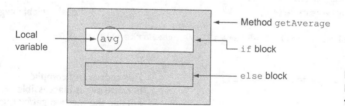

Local variable — (avg)

← Method `getAverage`

└ `if` block

← `else` block

**Figure 3.2   The scope of local variable avg is part of the if statement.**

Similarly, loop variables aren't accessible outside the loop body:

```java
public void localVariableInLoop() {                 Variable ctr is defined
    for (int ctr = 0; ctr < 5; ++ctr) {             within the for loop
        System.out.println(ctr);
    }
    System.out.println(ctr);         Variable ctr isn't accessible outside
}                                    the for loop; this line won't compile.
```

**EXAM TIP**   The local variables topic is a favorite of OCA Java SE 8 Programmer I exam authors. You're likely to be asked a question that seems to be about a rather complex topic, such as inheritance or exception handling, but instead it'll be testing your knowledge on the scope of a local variable.

Can a local variable be accessed in a method, before its declaration? No. A *forward reference* to local variables isn't allowed:

```
public void forwardReference() {
    int a = b;                        Won't
    int b = 20;                       compile
}
```

If you reverse the declaration of the variables in the preceding example, the code will compile:

```
public void noForwardReference() {
    int b = 20;                       No forward reference;
    int a = b;                        code compiles
}
```

The scope of a local variable depends on the location of its declaration within a method. The scope of local variables defined within a loop, if-else, or switch construct or within a code block (marked with {}) is limited to these constructs. Local variables defined outside any of these constructs are accessible across the complete method.

The next section discusses the scope of method parameters.

### 3.1.2   Method parameters

The variables that accept values in a method signature are called *method parameters.* They're accessible only in the method that defines them. In the following example, a method parameter val is defined for the method setTested:

```
class Phone {
    private boolean tested;
    public void setTested(boolean val) {     Method parameter val is accessible
        tested = val;                        only in method setTested
    }
    public boolean isTested() {              Variable val can't be accessed
        val = false;                         in method isTested
        return tested;
    }                                        This line of code
}                                            won't compile.
```

In the preceding code, you can access the method parameter val only within the method setTested. It can't be accessed in any other method.

The scope of the method parameter val is depicted in figure 3.3. The unshaded area marks where the variable is accessible, and the shaded part marks where it won't be available.

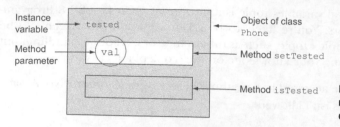

Figure 3.3  **The scope of the method parameter val, which is defined in the method setTested**

The scope of a method parameter may be as long as that of a local variable or longer, but it can never be shorter. The following method, isPrime, defines a method parameter, num, and two local variables, result and ctr:

```
boolean isPrime(int num) {
    if (num <= 1) return false;
    boolean result = true;
    for (int ctr = num-1; ctr > 1; ctr--) {
        if (num%ctr == 0) result = false;
    }
    return result;
}
```

**Method parameter num**

**Local variable result**

**Local variable ctr**

The scope of the method parameter num is as long as the scope of the local variable result. Because the scope of the local variable ctr is limited to the for block, it's shorter than the method parameter num. The comparison of the scope of all of these three variables is shown in figure 3.4, where the scope of each variable (defined in an oval) is shown by the rectangle enclosing it.

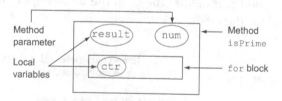

Method parameter

Local variables

Method isPrime

for block

Figure 3.4  **Comparison of the scope of method parameters and local variables**

Let's move on to instance variables, which have a larger scope than method parameters.

### 3.1.3  *Instance variables*

*Instance* is another name for an object. Hence, an *instance variable* is available for the life of an object. An instance variable is declared within a class, outside all the methods. It's accessible to all the instance (or nonstatic) methods defined in a class.

In the following example, the variable `tested` is an instance variable—it's defined within the class `Phone`, outside all the methods. It can be accessed by all the methods of class `Phone`:

```
class Phone {
    private boolean tested;
    public void setTested(boolean val) {
        tested = val;
    }
    public boolean isTested() {
        return tested;
    }
}
```

Instance variable
`tested`

Variable tested is accessible
in method setTested

Variable tested is also
accessible in method isTested

The scope of the instance variable `tested` is depicted in figure 3.5. As you can see, the variable `tested` is accessible across the object of class `Phone`, represented by the unshaded area. It's accessible in the methods `setTested` and `isTested`.

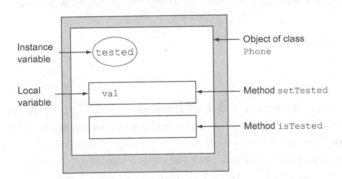

Instance variable

Local variable

Object of class
`Phone`

Method `setTested`

Method `isTested`

**Figure 3.5  The instance variable
`tested` is accessible across the
object of class `Phone`.**

 **EXAM TIP**  The scope of an instance variable is longer than that of a local variable or a method parameter.

Class variables, covered in the next section, have the largest scope of all types of variables.

### 3.1.4  Class variables

A *class variable* is defined by using the keyword `static`. A class variable belongs to a class, not to individual objects of the class. A class variable is shared across all objects—objects don't have a separate copy of the class variables.

You don't even need an object to access a class variable. It can be accessed by using the name of the class in which it's defined:

```
package com.mobile;
class Phone {
    static boolean softKeyboard = true;
}
```

Class variable
softKeyboard

Let's try to access this variable in another class:

```
package com.mobile;
class TestPhone {
    public static void main(String[] args) {
        Phone.softKeyboard = false;              ◄──┘  Accesses the class variable by
        Phone p1 = new Phone();                         using the name of the class. It
        Phone p2 = new Phone();                         can be accessed even before any
        System.out.println(p1.softKeyboard);            of the class's objects exist.
        System.out.println(p2.softKeyboard);     ◄──┘  Prints false. A class
        p1.softKeyboard = true;                         variable can be read by
        System.out.println(p1.softKeyboard);            using objects of the class.
        System.out.println(p2.softKeyboard);     ◄──┘  A change in the
        System.out.println(Phone.softKeyboard);         value of this variable
    }                                                   will be reflected
}                                                       when the variable is
                                                        accessed via objects
                                                        or class name.
```

**Accesses the class variable by using the name of the class. It can be accessed even before any of the class's objects exist.**

**Prints false. A class variable can be read by using objects of the class.**

**Prints false**

**Prints true**

**A change in the value of this variable will be reflected when the variable is accessed via objects or class name.**

As you can see in the preceding code, the class variable softKeyboard is accessible using all the following:

- Phone.softKeyboard
- p1.softKeyboard
- p2.softKeyboard

It doesn't matter whether you use the name of the class (Phone) or reference to an object (p1) to access a class variable. You can change the value of a class variable using either of them because they all refer to a single shared copy. When you access static variable softKeyboard, Java refers to the *type* of reference variables p1 and p2 (which is Phone) and not to the objects referred to by them. So accessing a static variable using a null reference won't throw an exception:

```
Phone p1 = null;                               Won't throw an exception,
System.out.println(p1.softKeyboard);     ◄──┘  even though p1 is set to null
```

The scope of the class variable softKeyboard is depicted in figure 3.6. As you can see, a single copy of this variable is accessible to all the objects of the class Phone. The variable softKeyboard is accessible even without the existence of any Phone instance. The class variable softKeyboard is made accessible by the JVM when it loads the Phone class into memory. The scope of the class variable softKeyboard depends on its access modifier and that of the Phone class. Because the class Phone and the class variable softKeyboard are defined using default access, they're accessible only within the package com.mobile.

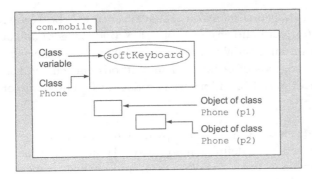

**Figure 3.6   The scope of the class variable `softKeyboard` is limited to the package `com.mobile` because it's defined in the class `Phone`, which is defined with default access. The class variable `softKeyboard` is shared and accessible across all objects of the class `Phone`.**

#### COMPARING THE USE OF VARIABLES IN DIFFERENT SCOPES

Here's a quick comparison of the use of the local variables, method parameters, instance variables, and class variables:

- Local variables are defined within a method and are normally used to store the intermediate results of a calculation.
- Method parameters are used to pass values to a method. These values can be manipulated and may also be assigned to instance variables.
- Instance variables are used to store the state of an object. These are the values that need to be accessed by multiple methods.
- Class variables are used to store values that should be shared by all the objects of a class.

### 3.1.5   *Overlapping variable scopes*

In the previous sections on local variables, method parameters, instance variables, and class variables, did you notice that some of the variables are accessible in multiple places within an object? For example, all four variables will be accessible in a loop within a method.

This overlapping scope is shown in figure 3.7. The variables are defined in ovals and are accessible within all methods and blocks, as illustrated by their enclosing rectangles.

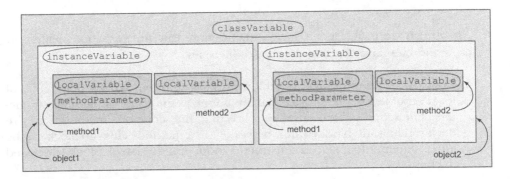

**Figure 3.7   The scopes of variables can overlap.**

As shown in figure 3.7, an individual copy of `classVariable` can be accessed and shared by multiple objects (`object1` and `object2`) of a class. Both `object1` and `object2` have their own copy of the instance variable `instanceVariable`, so `instanceVariable` is accessible across all the methods of `object1`. The methods `method1` and `method2` have their own copies of `localVariable` and `methodParameter` when used with `object1` and `object2`.

> **NOTE**   The scope of `instanceVariable` overlaps with the scope of `local-Variable` and `methodParameter`, defined in `method1`. Hence, all three of these variables (`instanceVariable`, `localVariable`, and `methodParameter`) can access each other in this overlapped area. But `instanceVariable` can't access `localVariable` and `methodParameter` outside `method1`.

### COMPARING THE SCOPE OF VARIABLES

Figure 3.8 compares the life spans of local variables, method parameters, instance variables, and class variables.

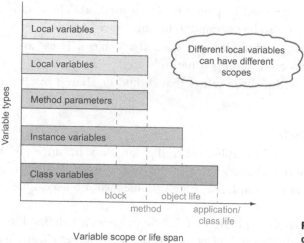

**Figure 3.8   Comparing the scope, or life span, of all four variables**

As you can see in figure 3.8, local variables have the shortest scope or life span, and class variables have the longest scope or life span.

> **EXAM TIP**   Different local variables can have different scopes. The scope of local variables may be shorter than or as long as the scope of method parameters. The scope of local variables is less than the scope of a method if they're declared in a sub-block (within braces `{}`) in a method. This sub-block can be an `if` statement, a `switch` construct, a loop, or a `try-catch` block (discussed in chapter 7).

### VARIABLES WITH THE SAME NAME IN DIFFERENT SCOPES

The fact that the scopes of variables overlap results in interesting combinations of variables within different scopes but with the same names. Some rules are necessary to prevent conflicts. In particular, you can't define a `static` variable and an instance variable with the same name in a class:

```java
class MyPhone {
    static boolean softKeyboard = true;
    boolean softKeyboard = true;
}
```

**Won't compile. Class variable and instance variable can't be defined using the same name in a class.**

Similarly, local variables and method parameters can't be defined with the same name. The following code defines a method parameter and a local variable with the same name, so it won't compile:

```java
void myMethod(int weight) {
    int weight = 10;
}
```

**Won't compile. Method parameter and local variable can't be defined using the same name in a method.**

A class can define local variables with the same name as the instance or class variables, also referred to as *shadowing*. The following code defines a class variable and a local variable, softKeyboard, with the same name, and an instance variable and a local variable, phoneNumber, with the same name, which is acceptable:

```java
class MyPhone {
    static boolean softKeyboard = true;          
    String phoneNumber;
    void myMethod() {
        boolean softKeyboard = true;        
        String phoneNumber;
    }
}
```

**Class variable softKeyboard**

**Instance variable phoneNumber**

**Local variable softKeyboard can coexist with class variable softKeyboard**

**Local variable phoneNumber can coexist with instance variable phoneNumber**

**NOTE** Defining variables with the same name in overlapping scopes can be a dangerous coding practice. It's usually accepted only in very specific situations, like constructors and setters. Please write code that's easy to read, comprehend, and maintain.

What happens when you assign a value to a local variable that has the same name as an instance variable? Does the instance variable reflect this modified value? This question provides the food for thought in this chapter's first Twist in the Tale exercise. It should help you remember what happens when you assign a value to a local variable when an instance variable already exists with the same name in the class (answer in the appendix).

The class `Phone` defines a local variable and an instance variable, `phoneNumber`, with the same name. Examine the definition of the method `setNumber`. Execute the class on your system and select the correct output of the class `TestPhone` from the given options:

```
class Phone {
    String phoneNumber = "123456789";
    void setNumber () {
        String phoneNumber;
        phoneNumber = "987654321";
    }
}
class TestPhone {
    public static void main(String[] args) {
        Phone p1 = new Phone();
        p1.setNumber();
        System.out.println (p1.phoneNumber);
    }
}
```

    **a**  123456789

    **b**  987654321

    **c**  No output

    **d**  The class `Phone` will not compile.

In this section, you worked with variables in different scopes. When variables go out of scope, they're no longer accessible by the remaining code. In the next section, you'll see how an object is created and made accessible and then inaccessible.

## 3.2    *Object's life cycle*

 [2.4]   Explain an Object's Lifecycle (creation, "dereference by reassignment" and garbage collection)

The OCA Java SE 8 Programmer I exam will test your understanding of when an object is created, when it can be accessed, and when it can be dereferenced. The exam also tests your ability to determine the total number of objects that are accessible at a particular line of code. Primitives aren't objects, so they're not relevant in this section.

Unlike some other programming languages, such as C, Java doesn't allow you to allocate or deallocate memory yourself when you create or destroy objects. Java manages the memory for allocating objects and reclaiming the memory occupied by unused objects.

The task of reclaiming unused memory is taken care of by Java's garbage collector, which is a low-priority thread. It runs periodically and frees up space occupied by unused objects.

Java also provides a method called `finalize`, which is accessible to all the classes. The method `finalize` is defined in the class `java.lang.Object`, which is the base class of all Java classes. All Java classes can override the method `finalize`, which executes just before an object is garbage collected. In theory, you can use this method to free up resources being used by an object, although doing so isn't recommended because its execution isn't guaranteed to happen.

An object's life cycle starts when it's created and lasts until it goes out of scope or is no longer referenced by a variable. When an object is accessible, it can be referenced by a variable and other classes can use it by calling its methods and accessing its variables. I'll discuss these stages in detail in the following subsections.

### 3.2.1  An object is born

An object comes into the picture when you use the keyword operator new. You can initialize a reference variable with this object. Note the difference between declaring a variable and initializing it. The following is an example of a class `Person` and a class `ObjectLifeCycle`:

```
class Person {}                 ←——— Class Person
class ObjectLifeCycle {
    Person person;              ←— Declaring a reference
}                                  variable of type Person
```

In the preceding code, no objects of class `Person` are created in the class `ObjectLife-Cycle`; it declares only a variable of type `Person`. An object is created when a reference variable is initialized:

```
class ObjectLifeCycle2 {
    Person person = new Person();   ←— Declaring and initializing
}                                      a variable of type Person
```

The difference in variable declaration and object creation is illustrated in figure 3.9, where you can compare a baby name to a reference variable and a real baby to an object. The left box in figure 3.9 represents variable declaration, because the baby hasn't been born yet. The right box in figure 3.9 represents object creation.

Syntactically, an object comes into being by using the new operator. But the `String` class is an exceptional case here. `String` reference variables can also be initialized by using string literal values:

```
class ObjectLifeCycle3 {
    String obj1 = new String("eJava");   ←— String object
    String obj2 = "Guru";                    referenced by obj1
}                                         ←— Another String object
                                             referenced by obj2
```

Figure 3.9   The difference between declaring a reference variable and initializing a reference variable

**NOTE**   Initializing a reference variable and an instance is not same. Initializing a reference variable might not always result in the creation of a new instance. In chapter 4, we'll cover in detail how String *literal values* are pooled in a *String pool* by JVM. Although using the new operator always creates a new String object, using a String literal value to initialize a String reference variable might not always create a new String object.

What happens when you create a new object without assigning it to any reference variable? Let's create a new object of class Person in class ObjectLifeCycle2 without assigning it to any reference variable (modifications in bold):

```
class ObjectLifeCycle2 {
    Person person = new Person();
    ObjectLifeCycle2() {                        An unreferenced
        new Person();                           object
    }
}
```

In the preceding example, an object of the class Person is created, but it can't be accessed using any reference variable. Creating an object in this manner will execute the relevant constructors of the class.

**EXAM TIP**   Watch out for a count of instances created in a given code—the ones that are eligible for garbage collection and the ones that aren't.

In the next section, you'll learn what happens after an object is created.

### 3.2.2   *Object is accessible*

Once an object is created, it can be accessed using its reference variable. It remains accessible until it goes out of scope or its reference variable is explicitly set to null. Also, if you reassign another object to an initialized reference variable, the previous object becomes inaccessible *from that variable.* You can access and use an object within other classes and methods.

Look at the following definition of the class `Exam`:

```
class Exam {
    String name;
    public void setName(String newName) {
        name = newName;
    }
}
```

The class `ObjectLife1` declares a variable of type `Exam`, creates its object, calls its method, sets it to `null`, and then reinitializes it:

```
class ObjectLife1 {
    public static void main(String args[]) {
        Exam myExam = new Exam();                    ❶ Object        ❷ Access
        myExam.setName("OCA Java Programmer 1");        creation          method
        myExam = null;                                                ❸ Set reference
        myExam = new Exam();                         ❹ Another          variable to null
        myExam.setName("PHP");          ❺ Access       object
    }                                     method      creation
}
```

The preceding example creates two objects of the class `Exam` using the same reference variable `myExam`. Let's walk through what's happening in the example:

- ❶ creates a reference variable `myExam` and initializes it with an object of class `Exam`.
- ❷ calls method `setName` on the object referenced by the variable `myExam`.
- ❸ assigns a value `null` to the reference variable `myExam` such that the object referenced by this variable is no longer accessible through `myExam`.
- ❹ creates a new object of class `Exam` and assigns it to the reference variable `myExam`.
- ❺ calls method `setName` on the second `Exam` object, created in method `main`.

When ❹ creates another object of class `Exam` and assigns it to the variable `myExam`, what happens to the first object created by ❶? Because the first object can no longer be accessed using any variable, it's considered garbage by Java and deemed eligible to be sent to the garbage bin by Java's garbage collector. As mentioned earlier, the garbage collector is a low-priority thread that reclaims the space used by unused or unreferenced objects in Java.

What happens when an object become inaccessible? You'll find out in the next section.

### 3.2.3 *Object is inaccessible*

An object can become inaccessible if it goes out of scope or is dereferenced by reassignment.

### VARIABLE GOES OUT OF SCOPE

An object can become inaccessible if it goes out of scope:

```java
public void myMethod() {
    int result = 88;
    if (result > 78) {
        Exam myExam1 = new Exam();          ❶  Scope of local
        myExam1.setName("Android");             variable myExam1
    }
    else {
        Exam myExam2 = new Exam();          ❷  Start of else block
        myExam2.setName("MySQL");
    }
}                                           ❸  End of else block
```

In the preceding code, the variable myExam1 is a local variable defined within the if block. Its scope starts from the line where it's declared until the end of the if block, marked with a closing brace ❶. After this closing brace, the object referred by the variable myExam1 is no longer accessible. It goes out of scope and is marked as eligible for garbage collection by Java's garbage collector. Similarly, the object referred to by the variable myExam2 becomes inaccessible at the end of the else block, marked with a closing brace ❸.

**EXAM TIP**   When an object goes out of scope, it can no longer be referenced and is marked for garbage collection.

### DEREFERENCING BY REASSIGNMENT

A variable that already refers to an instance can be assigned another instance. In this case, the earlier instance is dereferenced and becomes eligible for garbage collection. Let's work with a modified version of a previous code example:

```java
class Exam {
    String name;
    public Exam(String name) {
        this.name = name;
    }
}
class ObjectLife2 {
    public static void main(String args[]) {        ❶     ❷
        Exam myExam = new Exam("PHP");
        myExam = null;
        myExam = new Exam("SQL");                          ❸
        myExam = new Exam("Java");

        Exam yourExam = new Exam("PMP");             ❹
        yourExam = myExam;                        ❺
    }                                          ❻
}
```

In the preceding code, an Exam instance is created and assigned to the variable myExam ❶. At ❷ myExam is set to null before being assigned another Exam instance ❸.

The code at ❹ reassigns yet another Exam instance to myExam, without explicitly setting it to null. Again, the instance created at ❸ is dereferenced. After the execution of ❹, two MyExam instances are dereferenced by reassignment and are eligible for garbage collection.

At ❺, another variable, yourExam, is initialized using an Exam instance. At ❻, the variable myExam is assigned to the variable yourExam. This dereferences the Exam instance, which was assigned to yourExam earlier.

Figure 3.10 shows how Exam instances are referred to by the variables myExam and yourExam. The Exam instances highlighted using gray boxes represent unreferenced objects.

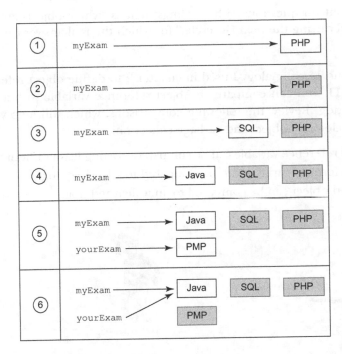

Figure 3.10 Objects can be dereferenced by reassignment of variables.

 **EXAM TIP**   An instance is dereferenced by reassignment when a variable is either explicitly set to null or is assigned another instance or reference variable.

### 3.2.4   *Garbage collection*

In the OCA Java SE 8 Programmer I exam, you're likely to answer questions on garbage collection for code that has multiple variable declarations and initializations. The exam may query you on the total number of objects that are eligible for garbage collection after a particular line of code.

## AUTOMATIC MEMORY MANAGEMENT

The garbage collector is a low-priority thread that marks the objects eligible for garbage collection in the JVM and then clears the memory of these objects. It enables automatic memory management because programmers aren't required to mark these instances themselves.

## WHEN IS AN OBJECT GARBAGE COLLECTED?

You can determine only which objects are *eligible* to be garbage collected. You can *never* determine when a particular object *will* be garbage collected. A user can't control or determine the execution of a garbage collector. It's controlled by the JVM.

**EXAM TIP**   Watch out for questions with wordings such as "which objects are sure to be collected during the next GC cycle," for which the real answer can never be known.

Let's revisit the dog and leash analogy I used in chapter 2 to define object reference variables. In figure 3.11, you can compare an object reference variable with a leash and an object with a dog. Review the following comparisons, which will help you to understand the life cycle of an object and garbage collection:

- An uninitialized reference variable can be compared to a dog leash without a dog.
- An initialized reference variable can be compared to a leashed dog.
- An unreferenced object can be compared to an unleashed dog.

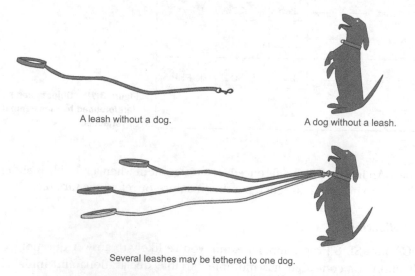

A leash without a dog.

A dog without a leash.

Several leashes may be tethered to one dog.

**Figure 3.11   Comparing object reference variables and objects to dog leashes and leashed and unleashed dogs**

You can compare Java's garbage collector to animal control. The way animal control picks up untethered dogs is like the way Java's garbage collector reclaims the memory used by unreferenced objects.

### USING SYSTEM.GC() OR RUNTIME.GETRUNTIME().GC()

As a programmer, you can't start execution of Java's garbage collector. You can only *request* it to be started by calling `System.gc()` or `Runtime.getRuntime().gc()`. But calling this method doesn't guarantee when the garbage collector would start (the call can even be ignored by the JVM). Watch out for exam questions that query you on the number of instances that have been garbage collected after calling `System.gc()`. It won't *guarantee* any count, at any line of code.

### GARBAGE COLLECTING REFERENCED OBJECTS

The garbage collector can also reclaim memory from a group of referenced objects. This group of variables is referred to as an *island of isolation.*

An instance can be referred to by multiple variables. So when you assign `null` to one of these variables, the instances can still be referenced using other variable(s). But a group of instances with no *external reference* becomes eligible for garbage collection. Let's work with an example:

```
class Exam {
    private String name;
    private Exam other;
    public Exam(String name) {
        this.name = name;
    }
    public void setExam(Exam exam) {
        other = exam;
    }
}
class IslandOfIsolation {
    public static void main(String args[]) {
        Exam php = new Exam("PHP");
        Exam java = new Exam("Java");

        php.setExam(java);
        java.setExam(php);

        php = null;
        java = null;
    }
}
```

**1** Initialize variable php

**2** Initialize variable java

**3** Assign object referred by java to php.exam

**4** Assign object referred by php to java.exam

**5** Assign null to php

**6** Assign null to java

In the preceding example, an `Exam` instance can refer to an object of its own type, using its field `other`. At **1** and **2**, two variables, `php` and `java`, are created and initialized using Exam instances. At **3**, `java` is assigned to `php.other`. At **4**, `php` is assigned to `java.other`. At **5**, when `php` is set to `null`, the instance referred to by it *isn't* eligible for garbage collection because it can still be referenced using `java.other`. At **6**, when `java` is also set to `null`, both the objects referred to by `java` and `php` become eligible for garbage collection. As shown in figure 3.12, even though both these objects can be referred to by each other, they can no longer be referenced in the method main. They form an *island of isolation*. Java's garbage collector can determine such groups of instances.

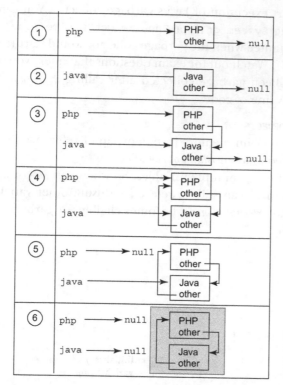

Figure 3.12   **A group of instances with no external references forms an island of isolation, which is eligible for garbage collection.**

Now that you're familiar with an object's life cycle, you can create methods that accept primitive data types and objects as method arguments; these methods return a value, which can be either a primitive data type or an object.

## 3.3   *Create methods with arguments and return values*

[6.1]   Create methods with arguments and return values; including overloaded methods

In this section, you'll work with the definitions of methods, which may or may not accept input parameters and may or may not return any values.

A method is a group of statements identified with a name. Methods are used to define the behavior of an object. A method can perform different operations, as shown in figure 3.13.

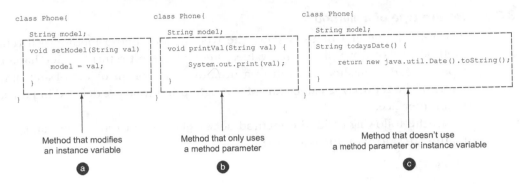

Figure 3.13  **Different types of methods**

a  The method setModel can access and modify the state of a Phone instance.
b  The method printVal uses only the method parameter passed to it.
c  The method todaysDate initializes a java.util.Date instance and returns its String presentation.

In the following subsections, you'll learn about the components of a method:

- Return type
- Method parameters
- return statement
- Access modifiers (covered in chapter 1)
- Nonaccess modifiers (covered in chapter 1)

Figure 3.14 shows the code of a method accepting method parameters and defining a return type and a return statement.

Let's get started with a discussion of the return type of a method.

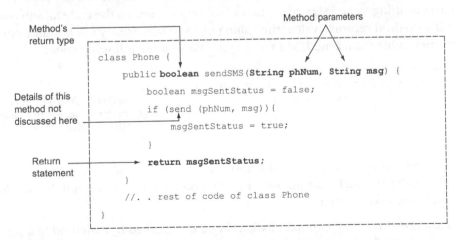

Figure 3.14  **An example of a method that accepts method parameters and defines a return type and a return statement**

### 3.3.1  *Return type of a method*

The return type of a method states the type of value that a method will return. A method may or may not return a value. One that doesn't return a value has a return type of void. A method can return a primitive value or an object of any class. The name of the return type can be any of the eight primitive types defined in Java, a class, or an interface.

In the following code, the method setWeight doesn't return any value, and the method getWeight returns a value:

```
class Phone {
    double weight;
    void setWeight(double val) {          Method with
        weight =val;                      return type void
    }
    double getWeight() {              Method with
        return weight;               return type double
    }
}
```

If a method doesn't return a value, you can't assign the result of that method to a variable. What do you think is the output of the following class TestMethods, which uses the preceding class Phone?

```
class TestMethods {
    public static void main(String args[]) {
        Phone p = new Phone();                    Because the method
        double newWeight = p.setWeight(20.0);     setWeight doesn't
    }                                             return any value, this
}                                                 line won't compile.
```

The preceding code won't compile because the method setWeight doesn't return a value. Its return type is void. Because the method setWeight doesn't return a value, there's nothing to be assigned to the variable newWeight, so the code fails to compile.

If a method returns a value, the calling method may or may not bother to store the returned value from a method in a variable. Look at the following code:

```
class TestMethods2 {
    public static void main(String args[]) {
        Phone p = new Phone();            Method getWeight returns a
        p.getWeight();                    double value, but this value
    }                                     isn't assigned to any variable.
}
```

In the preceding example, the value returned by the method getWeight isn't assigned to any variable, which isn't an issue for the Java compiler. The compiler will happily compile the code for you.

**EXAM TIP**  You can optionally assign the value returned by a method to a variable. If you don't assign the returned value from a method, it's neither a compilation error nor a runtime exception.

The value that you return from a method must be assignable to the variable to which it's being assigned. For instance, the return value of getWeight() in Phone is double. You can assign the return value of getWeight() to a variable of type double but not to a variable of type int (without an explicit cast). Here's the code:

```
class EJavaTestMethods2 {
    public static void main(String args[]) {
        Phone p = new Phone();
        double newWeight = p.getWeight();
        int newWeight2 = p.getWeight();
    }
}
```

❶ Will compile

❷ Won't compile

In the preceding code, ❶ will compile successfully because the return type of the method getWeight is double and the type of the variable newWeight is also double. But ❷ won't compile because the double value returned from method getWeight can't be assigned to variable newWeight2, which is of type int. You can make it happen by an explicit cast:

```
class EJavaTestMethods2 {
    public static void main(String args[]) {
        Phone p = new Phone();
        double newWeight = p.getWeight();
        int newWeight2 = (int)p.getWeight();
    }
}
```

Will compile

Will compile with an explicit cast

But an explicit cast won't work with data types that aren't compatible:

```
class EJavaTestMethods2 {
    public static void main(String args[]) {
        Phone p = new Phone();
        double newWeight = p.getWeight();
        boolean newWeight2 = (boolean)p.getWeight();
    }
}
```

Will compile

Won't compile; double can't be casted to boolean

We've discussed how to transfer a value out from a method. To transfer a value into a method, you can use method arguments.

### 3.3.2 *Method parameters*

*Method parameters* are the variables that appear in the definition of a method and specify the type and number of values that a method can accept. In figure 3.15, the variables phNum and msg are the method parameters.

You can pass multiple values to a method as input. Theoretically, no limit exists on the number of method parameters that can be defined by a method, but practically it's not a good idea to define more than three method parameters. It's cumbersome to

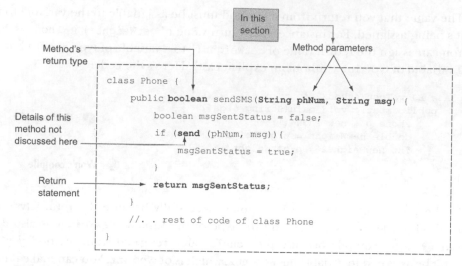

**Figure 3.15    An example of a method that accepts method parameters and defines a return type and a `return` statement**

use a method with too many method parameters because you have to cross-check their types and purposes multiple times to ensure that you're passing the right values at the right positions.

> **NOTE**    Although the terms *method parameters* and *method arguments* are not the same, you may have noticed that many programmers use them interchangeably. *Method parameters* are the variables that appear in the definition of a method. *Method arguments* are the actual values that are passed to a method while executing it. In figure 3.15, the variables phNum and msg are method parameters. If you execute this method as sendMsg("123456", "Hello"), then the String values "123456" and "Hello" are method arguments. As you know, you can pass literal values or variables to a method. Thus, method arguments can be literal values or variables.

A method may accept zero or multiple method arguments. The following example accepts two int values and returns their average as a double value:

```
double calcAverage(int marks1, int marks2) {        ⟵ Multiple method
    double avg = 0;                                    parameters: marks1
    avg = (marks1 + marks2)/2.0;                       and marks2
    return avg;
}
```

The following example shows a method that doesn't accept any method parameters:

```
void printHello() {
    System.out.println("Hello");
}
```

If a method doesn't accept any parameters, the parentheses that follow the name of the method are empty. Because the keyword void is used to specify that a method doesn't return a value, you may think it's correct to use the keyword void to specify that a method doesn't accept any method parameters, but this is incorrect. The following is an invalid definition of a method that accepts no parameters:

```java
void printHello(void) {
    System.out.println("Hello");          Won't compile
}
```

You can define a parameter that can accept variable arguments (varargs) in your methods. Following is an example of the class Employee, which defines a method days-OffWork that accepts variable arguments:

```java
class Employee {
    public int daysOffWork(int... days) {
        int daysOff = 0;
        for (int i = 0; i < days.length; i++)
            daysOff += days[i];
        return daysOff;
    }
}
```

The ellipsis ( . . . ) that follows the data type indicates that the method parameter days may be passed an array or multiple comma-separated values. Reexamine the preceding code example and note the usage of the variable days in the method daysOff-Work—it works like an array. When you define a variable-length argument for a method, Java creates an array behind the scenes to implement it.

You can define only one variable argument in a parameter list, and it must be the last variable in the parameter list. If you don't comply with these two rules, your code won't compile:

```java
class Employee {
    public int daysOffWork(String... months, int... days) {     Won't compile.
        int daysOff = 0;                                         You can't define
        for (int i = 0; i < days.length; i++)                    multiple variables
            daysOff += days[i];                                  that can accept
        return daysOff;                                          variable
    }                                                            arguments.
}
```

If your method defines multiple method parameters, the variable that accepts variable arguments must be the last one in the parameter list:

```java
class Employee {
    public int daysOffWork(int... days, String year) {     Won't compile; if
        int daysOff = 0;                                   multiple parameters
        for (int i = 0; i < days.length; i++)              are defined, the
            daysOff += days[i];                            variable argument
        return daysOff;                                    must be the last in
    }                                                      the list.
}
```

**EXAM TIP**   In the OCA exam, you may be questioned on the valid return types for a method that doesn't accept any method parameters. Note that there are no valid or invalid combinations of the number and type of method parameters that can be passed to a method and the value that it can return. They're independent of each other.

You can pass any type and number of parameters to a method, including primitives, objects of a class, or objects referenced by an interface.

**RULES TO REMEMBER**

Here are some points to note with respect to defining method parameters:

- You can define multiple parameters for a method.
- The method parameter can be a primitive type or object.
- The method's parameters are separated by commas.
- Each method parameter is preceded by the name of its type. Each method parameter must have an explicit type declared with its name. You can't declare the type once and then list the parameters separated by commas, as you can for variables.

### 3.3.3   *Return statement*

A return statement is used to exit from a method, with or without a value. For methods that define a return type, the return statement must be immediately followed by a return value. For methods that don't return a value, the return statement can be used without a return value to exit a method. Figure 3.16 illustrates the use of a return statement.

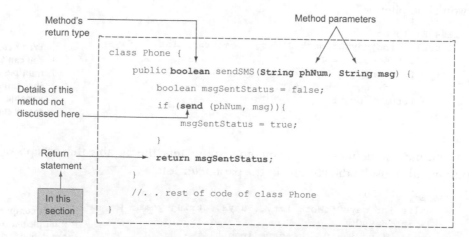

**Figure 3.16   An example of a method that accepts method parameters and defines a return type and a `return` statement**

In this example, we'll revisit the previous example of method `calcAverage`, which returns a value of type `double`, using a `return` statement:

```
double calcAverage(int marks1, int marks2) {
    double avg = 0;
    avg = (marks1 + marks2)/2.0;
    return avg;                          return
}                                        statement
```

The methods that don't return a value (the return type is `void`) aren't required to define a `return` statement:

```
void setWeight(double val) {             return statement not required for
    weight = val;                        methods with return type void
}
```

But you can use the `return` statement in a method even if it doesn't return a value. Usually this statement is used to define an early exit from a method:

```
void setWeight(double val) {                         Method with return
    if (val < -1) return;    This code compiles successfully;   type void can use
    weight = val;            control exits the method if this    return statement
}                           condition is true.
```

Also, the `return` statement must be the last statement to *execute* in a method, if present. The return statement transfers control out of the method, which means that there's no point in defining any code after it. The compiler will fail to compile such code:

```
                            The return statement
                            must be the last statement
void setWeight(double val) {   to execute in a method.
    return;                                   This code can't execute
    weight = val;                             due to the presence of the
}                                             return statement before it.
```

Note that there's a difference in the `return` statement being the last statement in a method and being the last statement to execute in a method. The `return` statement need not be the *last statement* in a method, but it must be the *last statement to execute* in a method:

```
void setWeight(double val) {
    if (val < 0)
        return;
    else
        weight = val;
}
```

In the preceding example, the `return` statement isn't the last statement in this method. But it's the last statement to execute for method parameter values of less than zero.

**RULES TO REMEMBER WHEN DEFINING A RETURN STATEMENT**

Here are some items to note when defining a return statement:

- For a method that returns a value, the return statement must be followed immediately by a value.
- For a method that doesn't return a value (return type is void), the return statement must *not* be followed by a return value.
- If the compiler determines that a return statement isn't the last statement to *execute* in a method, the method will fail to compile.

Do you think we've covered all the rules for defining a method? Not yet! Do you think you can define multiple methods in a class with the same name? You can, but you need to be aware of some additional rules, which are discussed in the next section.

## 3.4　*Create an overloaded method*

> [6.1]　Create methods with arguments and return values; including overloaded methods

*Overloaded methods* are methods with the same name but different method parameter lists. In this section, you'll learn how to create and use overloaded methods.

Imagine that you're delivering a lecture and need to instruct the audience to take notes using paper, a smartphone, or a laptop—whichever is available to them for the day. One way to do this is give the audience a list of instructions as follows:

- Take notes using paper.
- Take notes using a smartphone.
- Take notes using a laptop.

Another method is to instruct them to "take notes" and then provide them with the paper, a smartphone, or a laptop they're supposed to use. Apart from the simplicity of the latter method, it also gives you the flexibility to add other media on which to take notes (such as one's hand, some cloth, or the wall) without needing to remember the list of all the instructions.

This second approach, providing one set of instructions (with the same name) but a different set of input values can be compared to using overloaded methods in Java, as shown in figure 3.17.

Again, overloaded methods are methods that are defined in the same class with the same name, but with different method argument lists. As shown in figure 3.17, overloaded methods make it easier to add methods with similar functionality that work with different sets of input values.

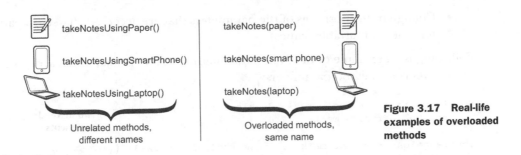

**Figure 3.17  Real-life examples of overloaded methods**

Let's work with an example from the Java API classes that we all use frequently: System .out.println(). The println method accepts multiple types of method parameters:

```
int intVal = 10;
System.out.println(intVal);
```
Prints an int value

```
boolean boolVal = false;
System.out.println(boolVal);
```
Prints a boolean value

```
String name = "eJava";
System.out.println(name);
```
Prints a string value

When you use the method println, you know that whatever you pass to it as a method argument will be printed to the console. Wouldn't it be crazy to use methods like printlnInt, printlnBool, and printlnString for the same functionality? I think so, too. But opinions change across different conditions. At times, you might use specific methods instead of overloading because it reads well and avoids confusion. As you work with more code, you'll be able to judge these situations for yourself.

**RULES TO REMEMBER FOR DEFINING OVERLOADED METHODS**
Here are a few rules for defining overloaded methods:

- Overloaded methods must have method parameters different from one another.
- Overloaded methods may or may not define a different return type.
- Overloaded methods may or may not define different access levels.
- Overloaded methods can't be defined by only changing their return type or access modifiers or both.

Next, I'll describe in detail the preceding rules—valid argument list, return types, and access level to define overloaded methods.

### 3.4.1  Argument list

Overloaded methods accept different lists of arguments. The argument lists can differ in terms of any of the following:

- Change in the number of parameters that are accepted
- Change in the types of parameters that are accepted

- Change in the positions of the parameters that are accepted (based on parameter type, not variable names)

Following is an example of the overloaded method `calcAverage`, which accepts different numbers of method parameters:

```java
double calcAverage(int marks1, double marks2) {          ◁──┐ Two method
    return (marks1 + marks2)/2.0;                               arguments
}
double calcAverage(int marks1, int marks2, int marks3) { ◁──┐ Three method
    return (marks1 + marks2 + marks3)/3.0;                      arguments
}
```

The preceding code is an example of the simplest flavor of overloaded methods. You can also define overloaded methods in which the difference in the argument list is in the types of the parameters that are accepted:

```java
double calcAverage(int marks1, double marks2) {  ◁──┐ Arguments:
    return (marks1 + marks2)/2.0;                        int, double
}
double calcAverage(char marks1, char marks2) {   ◁──┐ Arguments:
    return (marks1 + marks2)/2.0;                        char, char
}
```

But you can't define overloaded methods by just switching an array parameter into a vararg or vice versa (unless the vararg or array item type doesn't remain the same). Behind the scenes, varargs are implemented as arrays. So the following overloaded methods won't compile:

```java
double calcAverage(int[] marks) {   ◁──┐ Arguments:
    //return a double value                array
}
double calcAverage(int... marks) {  ◁──┐ Arguments:
    //return a double value                int... (varags)
}
```

The methods are also correctly overloaded if they change only the positions of the parameters that are passed to them:

```java
double calcAverage(double marks1, int marks2) {  ◁──┐ Arguments:
    return (marks1 + marks2)/2.0;                        double, int
}
double calcAverage(int marks1, double marks2) {  ◁──┐ Arguments:
    return (marks1 + marks2)/2.0;                        int, double
}
```

Although you might argue that the arguments being accepted are one and the same, with only their positions differing, the Java compiler treats them as different argument lists. The compiler can understand which method implementation you want to call by looking at the *sequence* of arguments you specified in your code. Hence, the preceding code is a valid example of overloaded methods.

But an issue arises when you try to execute this method using values that can be passed to both versions of the overloaded methods. In this case, the code will fail to compile:

```
class MyClass {
    double calcAverage(double marks1, int marks2) {      ◁──  ❶ Method parameters:
        return (marks1 + marks2)/2.0;                             double and int
    }
    double calcAverage(int marks1, double marks2) {      ◁──  ❷ Method parameters:
        return (marks1 + marks2)/2.0;                             int and double
    }
    public static void main(String args[]) {             ❸ Compiler can't determine
        MyClass myClass = new MyClass();                     which overloaded method
        myClass.calcAverage(2, 3);                  ◁──      calcAverage should be called
    }
}
```

In the preceding code, ❶ defines the method calcAverage, which accepts two method parameters: a double and an int. ❷ defines the overloaded method calcAverage, which accepts two method parameters: an int and a double. Because an int literal value can be passed to a variable of type double, literal values 2 and 3 can be passed to both of the overloaded methods declared at ❶ and ❷. Because this method call is dubious, ❸ fails to compile.

### 3.4.2 Return type

Methods can't be defined as overloaded methods if they differ only in their return types, because return type is not part of a method signature:

```
double calcAverage(int marks1, int marks2) {      ◁──  Return type of method
    return (marks1 + marks2)/2.0;                         calcAverage is double
}
int calcAverage(int marks1, int marks2) {         ◁──  Return type
    return (marks1 + marks2)/2;                           is int
}
```

Methods in the preceding code can't be termed overloaded methods.

### 3.4.3 Access level

Methods can't be defined as overloaded methods if they differ only in their access levels:

```
public double calcAverage(int marks1, int marks2) {      ◁──  Access—public
    return (marks1 + marks2)/2.0;
}
private double calcAverage(int marks1, int marks2) {     ◁──  Access—private
    return (marks1 + marks2)/2.0;
}
```

If you define overloaded `calcAverage` methods as shown in the preceding code, the code won't compile.

In the next section, you'll create special methods called constructors, which are used to create objects of a class.

## 3.5    *Constructors of a class*

> [6.3]    Create and overload constructors; including impact on default constructors

In this section, you'll create constructors, learn the differences between default and user-defined constructors, and create overloaded constructors.

What happens when you open a new bank account? Depending on the services your bank provides, you may be assigned a new bank account number, provided with a checkbook, and given access to a new online account the bank has created for you. These details are created and returned to you as part of setting up your new bank account.

Compare these steps with what a constructor does in Java, as illustrated in figure 3.18.

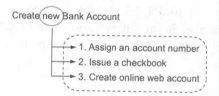

**Figure 3.18   The series of steps that may be executed when you create a new bank account. These steps can be compared with what a constructor does in Java.**

*Constructors* are special methods that create and return an object of the class in which they're defined. Constructors have the same name as the class in which they're defined, and they don't specify a return type—not even `void`.

A constructor can accomplish the following tasks:

- Call the superclass's constructor; this can be an implicit or explicit call.
- Initialize all the instance variables of a class with their default values.

Constructors come in two flavors: user-defined constructors and default constructors, which we'll cover in detail in the next sections.

### 3.5.1    *User-defined constructors*

The author of a class has full control over the definition of the class. An author may or may not define a constructor in a class. If the author defines a constructor in a class, it's known as a *user-defined constructor*. Here the word *user* doesn't refer to another person or class that uses this class but instead refers to the person who created the class. It's called "user-defined" because it's not created by the Java compiler.

Figure 3.19 shows a class `Employee` that defines a constructor.

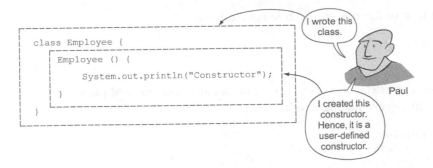

**Figure 3.19   A class, `Employee`, with a constructor defined by the user Paul**

Here's a class, `Office`, that creates an object of class `Employee`:

```
class Office {
    public static void main(String args[]) {
        Employee emp = new Employee();
    }
}
```
❶ **Constructor is called on object creation**

In the preceding example, ❶ creates an object of class `Employee` using the keyword new, which triggers the execution of the `Employee` class constructor. The output of the class `Office` is as follows:

```
Constructor
```

Because a constructor is called as soon as an object is created, you can use it to assign default values to the instance variable of your class, as follows (modified and additional code is highlighted in bold):

```
class Employee {
    String name;                              Instance variable
    int age;
    Employee() {
        age = 20;                             ←——— Initialize age
        System.out.println("Constructor");
    }
}
```

Let's create an object of the class `Employee` in the class `Office` and see if there's any difference:

```
class Office {
    public static void main(String args[]) {
        Employee emp = new Employee();
        System.out.println(emp.age);          ←—— Access and print the
    }                                              value of variable age
}
```

The output of the preceding code is as follows:

```
Constructor
20
```

Because a constructor is a method, you can also pass method parameters to it, as follows (changes are highlighted in bold):

```
class Employee {
    String name;
    int age;
    Employee(int newAge, String newName) {
        name = newName;
        age = newAge;
        System.out.println("Constructor");
    }
}
```

You can use this constructor in the class Office by passing to it the required method arguments, as follows:

```
class Office {
    public static void main(String args[]) {
        Employee emp = new Employee(30, "Pavni Gupta");
    }
}
```

Revisit the use and declaration of the previously mentioned constructors. Note that a constructor is called when you create an object of a class. A constructor does have an implicit return type, which is the class in which it's defined. It creates and returns an object of its class, which is why you can't define a return type for a constructor. Also note that you can define constructors using any of the four access levels.

**EXAM TIP**   You can define a constructor using all four access levels: public, protected, default, and private.

What happens if you define a return type for a constructor? Java will treat it as another method, not a constructor, which also implies that it won't be called implicitly when you create an object of its class:

```
class Employee {
    void Employee() {
        System.out.println("Constructor");
    }
}
class Office {
    public static void main(String args[]) {
        Employee emp = new Employee();
    }
}
```

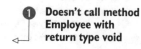

❶ Doesn't call method Employee with return type void

In the preceding example, ❶ won't call the method Employee with the return type void defined in the class Employee. Because the method Employee defines its return type as void, it's no longer treated as a constructor.

If the class Employee defines the return type of the method Employee as void, how can Java use it to create an object? The method (with the return type void) is treated as any other method in the class Employee. This logic applies to all the other data types: if you define the return type of a constructor to be any data type—such as char, int, String, long, double, or any other class—it'll no longer be treated as a constructor.

How do you execute such a method? By calling it explicitly, as in the following code (modified code is in bold):

```
class Employee {
    void Employee() {
        System.out.println("not a Constructor now");
    }
}
class Office {
    public static void main(String args[]) {
        Employee emp = new Employee();
        emp.Employee();                    Prints "not a
    }                                      Constructor now"
}
```

Note that the Employee method in the preceding code is called like any other method defined in the class Employee. It doesn't get called automatically when you create an object of the class Employee. As you can see in the preceding code, it's allowed to define a method that's not a constructor in a class with the same name. Interesting.

But note that the authors of the OCA exam also found this interesting, and you're likely to get a few tricky questions regarding this concept. Don't worry: with the right information under your belt, you're sure to answer them correctly.

**EXAM TIP**  A constructor must not define any return type. Instead, it creates and returns an object of the class in which it's defined. If you define a return type for a constructor, it'll no longer be treated as a constructor. Instead, it'll be treated as a regular method, even though it shares the same name as its class.

### INITIALIZER BLOCKS VERSUS CONSTRUCTORS

An *initializer block* is defined within a class, not as a part of a method. It executes for every object that's created for a class. In the following example, the class Employee defines an initializer block:

```
class Employee {
    {
        System.out.println("Employee:initializer");     Initializer block
    }
}
```

In the following code, the class `TestEmp` creates an object of the class `Employee`:

```
class TestEmp {
    public static void main(String args[]) {          Prints
        Employee e = new Employee();                  Employee:initializer
    }
}
```

If you define both an initializer and a constructor for a class, both of these will execute. The initializer block will execute prior to the constructor:

```
class Employee {
    Employee() {
        System.out.println("Employee:constructor");        Constructor
    }
    {
        System.out.println("Employee:initializer");        Initializer block
    }
}
class TestEmp {
    public static void main(String args[]) {          Creates an object of class
        Employee e = new Employee();                  Employee; calls both the
    }                                                 initializer block and the
}                                                     constructor
```

The output of the class `TestEmp` is as follows:

```
Employee:initializer
Employee:constructor
```

If a class defines multiple initializer blocks, their order of execution depends on their placement in a class. But all of them execute before the class's constructor:

```
class Employee {
    {
        System.out.println("Employee:initializer 1");        Initializer block 1
    }
    Employee() {
        System.out.println("Employee:constructor");          Constructor
    }
    {
        System.out.println("Employee:initializer 2");        Initializer block 2
    }
}
class TestEmp {
    public static void main(String args[]) {
        Employee e = new Employee();
    }
}
```

Here's the output of the preceding code:

```
Employee:initializer 1
Employee:initializer 2
Employee:constructor
```

Does the preceding code example leave you wondering why you need both an initializer block and a constructor, if both of these execute upon the creation of an object? Initializer blocks are used to initialize the variables of anonymous classes. An *anonymous class* is a type of inner class. In the absence of a name, anonymous classes can't define a constructor and rely on an initializer block to initialize their variables upon the creation of an object of their class. Because inner classes aren't on this exam, I won't discuss how to use an initializer block with an anonymous inner class.

A lot of action can happen within an initializer block: It can create local variables. It can access and assign values to instance and static variables. It can call methods and define loops, conditional statements, and `try-catch-finally` blocks. Unlike constructors, an initializer block can't accept method parameters.

 **NOTE** Loops and conditional statements are covered in chapter 5, and `try-catch-finally` blocks are covered in chapter 7.

## 3.5.2 *Default constructor*

In the previous section on user-defined constructors, I discussed how a constructor is used to create an object. What happens if you don't define any constructor in a class?

The following code is an example of the class `Employee` that doesn't define a constructor:

```
class Employee {
    String name;
    int age;
}
```
**No constructor is defined
in class Employee.**

You can create objects of this class in another class (`Office`), as follows:

```
class Office {
    public static void main(String args[]) {
        Employee emp = new Employee();
    }
}
```
**Class Employee doesn't
define a constructor,
but this code compiles
successfully.**

In this case, which method creates the object of the class `Employee`? Figure 3.20 shows what happens when a class (`Employee`) is compiled that doesn't define any constructor. In the absence of a user-defined constructor, Java inserts a *default constructor*. This constructor doesn't accept any method arguments. It calls the constructor of the super (parent) class and assigns default values to all the instance variables.

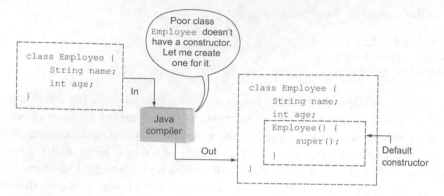

**Figure 3.20  When the Java compiler compiles a class that doesn't define a constructor, the compiler creates one for it.**

**EXAM TIP**    The accessibility of a default constructor matches the accessibility of its class. Java creates a public default constructor for a public class. It creates a default constructor with package access for a class with package-level access.

What happens if you add another constructor to the class `Employee`, as in the following example?

```
class Employee {
    String name;
    int age;
    Employee(int newAge, String newName) {
        name = newName;
        age = newAge;
        System.out.println("User defined Constructor");
    }
}
```
User-defined constructor

In this case, upon recompilation, the Java compiler will notice that you've defined a constructor in the class `Employee`. It won't add a default constructor to it, as shown in figure 3.21.

In the absence of a no-argument constructor, the following code will fail to compile:

```
class Office {
    public static void main(String args[]) {
        Employee emp = new Employee();            ⟵  Won't compile
    }
}
```

**EXAM TIP**    Java defines a default constructor if and only if you don't define a constructor. If a class doesn't define a constructor, the compiler will add a default, no-argument constructor to the class. But if you modify the class later by adding a constructor to it, the Java compiler will remove the default, no-argument constructor that it initially added to the class.

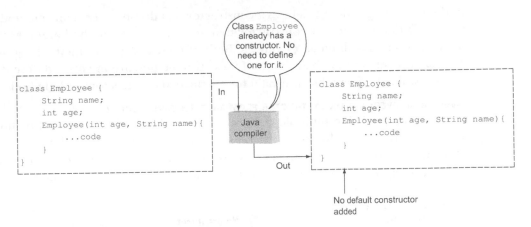

**Figure 3.21  When a class with a constructor is compiled, the Java compiler doesn't add a default constructor to it.**

### 3.5.3  *Overloaded constructors*

In the same way in which you can overload methods in a class, you can also overload the constructors in a class. *Overloaded constructors* follow the same rules as discussed in the previous section for overloaded methods. Here's a quick recap:

- Overloaded constructors must be defined using different argument lists.
- Overloaded constructors can't be defined by just a change in the access levels.

Because constructors don't define a return type, there's no point in defining invalid overloaded constructors with different return types.

The following is an example of an `Employee` class that defines four overloaded constructors:

```
class Employee {
    String name;
    int age;
    Employee() {                           ❶ No-argument
        name = "John";                       constructor
        age = 25;
    }
    Employee(String newName) {             ❷ Constructor with one
        name = newName;                      String argument
        age = 25;
    }
    Employee(int newAge, String newName) { ❸ Constructor with two
        name = newName;                      arguments—int and String
        age = newAge;
    }
    Employee(String newName, int newAge) { ❹ Constructor with two
        name = newName;                      arguments—String and int
        age = newAge;
    }
}
```

In the preceding code, ❶ defines a constructor that doesn't accept any method arguments. ❷ defines another constructor that accepts a single method argument. Note the constructors defined at ❸ and ❹. Both of these accept two method arguments, `String` and `int`. But the placement of these two method arguments is different in ❸ and ❹, which is acceptable and valid for overloaded constructors and methods.

### INVOKING AN OVERLOADED CONSTRUCTOR FROM ANOTHER CONSTRUCTOR

It's common to define multiple constructors in a class and reuse their functionality across constructors. Unlike overloaded methods, which can be invoked using the name of a method, overloaded constructors are invoked by using the keyword `this`—an implicit reference that's accessible to all objects that refer to an object itself:

```
class Employee {
    String name;                        ❶  No-argument
    int age;                                constructor        ❷  Invokes constructor
    Employee() {                                                   that accepts two
        this(null, 0);                                             method arguments
    }
    Employee(String newName, int newAge) {
        name = newName;                 ❸  Constructor that
        age = newAge;                       accepts two method
    }                                       arguments
}
```

The code at ❶ creates a no-argument constructor. At ❷, this constructor calls the overloaded constructor by passing to it values `null` and `0`. ❸ defines an overloaded constructor that accepts two method arguments.

Because a constructor is defined using the name of its class, it's a common mistake to try to invoke a constructor from another constructor using the class's name:

```
class Employee {
    String name;
    int age;
    Employee() {
        Employee(null, 0);              Won't compile—you can't
    }                                   invoke a constructor within a
    Employee(String newName, int newAge) {   class by using the class's name.
        name = newName;
        age = newAge;
    }
}
```

Also, when you invoke an overloaded constructor using the keyword `this`, it must be the first statement in your constructor:

```
class Employee {
    String name;
    int age;
    Employee() {
        System.out.println("No-argument constructor");
```

```
        this(null, 0);
    }
    Employee(String newName, int newAge) {
        name = newName;
        age = newAge;
    }
}
```

Won't compile—the call to
the overloaded constructor
must be the first statement
in a constructor.

You can't call two (or more) constructors within a constructor because the call to a constructor must be the first statement in a constructor:

```
class Employee {
    String name;
    int age;
    Employee() {
    }
    Employee(String newName, int newAge) {
        name = newName;
        age = newAge;
    }
    Employee(String newName, int newAge, boolean create) {
        this();
        this(newName, newAge);
        if (create)
            System.out.println(10);
    }
}
```

Won't compile; can't include
calls to multiple constructors
in a constructor

That's not all: you can't call a constructor from any other method in your class. None of the other methods of the class Employee can invoke its constructor.

### RULES TO REMEMBER

Here's a quick list of rules to remember for the exam for defining and using overloaded constructors:

- Overloaded constructors must be defined using different argument lists.
- Overloaded constructors can't be defined by just a change in the access levels.
- Overloaded constructors may be defined using different access levels.
- A constructor can call another overloaded constructor by using the keyword this.
- A constructor can't invoke a constructor by using its class's name.
- If present, the call to another constructor must be the first statement in a constructor.
- You can't call multiple constructors from a constructor.
- A constructor can't be invoked from a method (except by instantiating a class using the new keyword).

The next Twist in the Tale exercise hides an important concept within its code, which you can get to know only if you execute the modified code (answer in the appendix).

**Twist in the Tale 3.2**

Let's modify the definition of the class `Employee` that I used in the section on over-loaded constructors, as follows:

```
class Employee {
    String name;
    int age;
    Employee() {
        this ();
    }
    Employee (String newName, int newAge) {
        name = newName;
        age = newAge;
    }
}
```

Question: What is the output of this modified code, and why?

Now that you've seen how to create methods and constructors, and their overloaded variants, we'll turn to how all of these can be used to access and modify object fields in the next section.

## 3.6   Accessing object fields

   [2.3]   Know how to read or write to object fields

In this section, you'll learn what object fields are and how to read, initialize, and modify them. You'll also learn the correct notation used to call methods on objects. Access modifiers also determine whether you can call a method on an object.

### 3.6.1   What is an object field?

An *object field* is another name for an instance variable defined in a class. I've often seen certification aspirants who are confused over whether the object fields are the same as instance variables of a class.

Here's an example of the class `Star`:

```
class Star {
    double starAge;
    public void setAge(double newAge) {
        starAge = newAge;
    }
    public double getAge() {
        return starAge;
    }
}
```

❶ Instance variable—
    starAge

❷ Setter method—
    setAge

❸ Getter method—
    getAge

In the preceding example, ❶ defines an instance variable, starAge. ❷ defines a *setter* method, setAge. A *setter* (or *mutator*) method is used to set the value of a variable. ❸ defines a *getter* (or *accessor*) method, getAge. A *getter* method is used to retrieve the value of a variable. In this example, the object field is starAge, not age or newAge. The name of an object field is not determined by the name of its *getter* or *setter* methods.

---

### JavaBeans properties and object fields

The reason for the confusion over the name of the object field is that Java classes can also be used to define visual or nonvisual components called *JavaBeans*, which are used in visual and nonvisual environments like Spring, Hibernate, and others. These classes are supposed to define getter and setter methods to retrieve and set the properties of the visual components. If a visual JavaBean component defines a property such as age, then the name of its getter and setter methods will be getAge and setAge. For a JavaBean, you don't have to worry about the name of the variable that's used to store the value of this property. In a JavaBean, an object field thisIsMyAge can be used to store the value of its *property* age.

Note that the JavaBeans I mentioned aren't Enterprise JavaBeans. Enterprise Java-Beans are used in enterprise applications written in Java, which run on servers.

---

### 3.6.2 Read and write object fields

The OCA Java SE 8 Programmer I exam will test you on how to read values from and write them to fields of an object, which can be accomplished by any of following:

- Using methods to read and write object fields
- Using constructors to write values to object fields
- Directly accessing instance variables to read and write object fields

 **EXAM TIP** Although object fields can be manipulated by direct access, it isn't a recommended practice. It makes an object vulnerable to invalid data. Such a class isn't well encapsulated.

This exam objective (2.3) will also test your understanding of how to assign different values to the same object fields for multiple objects. Let's start with an example:

```
class Employee {
    String name;                    ❶  Object fields
    int age;
    Employee() {
        age = 22;                        ⟵┐  Assign value
    }                                    ❷   to age
    public void setName(String val) {
        name = val;                      ⟵┐  Assign val
    }                                    ❸   to name
    public void printEmp() {
        System.out.println("name = " + name + " age = " + age);
    }
}
```

In the class Employee, ❶ defines two object fields: name and age. It defines a (no-argument) constructor. And ❷ assigns a value of 22 to its field age. This class also defines a method setName, where ❸ assigns the value passed to it to the object field name. The method printEmp is used to print the values of object fields name and age.

The following is the definition of a class, Office, which creates two instances, e1 and e2, of the class Employee and assigns values to its fields. Let's look at the definition of the class Office:

```
class Office {
    public static void main(String args[]) {
        Employee e1 = new Employee();
        Employee e2 = new Employee();
        e1.name = "Selvan";
        e2.setName("Harry");
        e1.printEmp();
        e2.printEmp();
    }
}
```

This is the output of the preceding code:

```
name = Selvan age = 22
name = Harry age = 22
```

Figure 3.22 defines object diagrams (a diagram with the name and type of an object, the name of the object's fields, and their corresponding values), which will help you to better understand the preceding output.

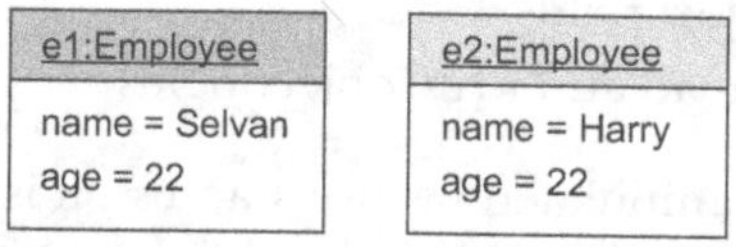

Figure 3.22   Two objects of the class Employee

You can access the object field name of the object of the class Employee either by using its variable name or by using the method setName. The following line of code assigns a value Selvan to the field name of object e1:

```
e1.name = "Selvan";
```

The following line of code uses the method setName to assign a value of Harry to the field name of object e2:

```
e2.setName("Harry");
```

Because the constructor of the class Employee assigns a value of 22 to the variable age, objects e1 and e2 both contain the same value, 22.

What happens if you don't assign any value to an object field and try to print out its value? All the instance variables (object fields) are assigned their default values if you try to access or read their values before writing any values to them:

```
class Employee {                          Object field:
    String name;                          name        Object field:
    int age;                                          age
    public void printEmp() {
        System.out.println("name = " + name + " age = " + age);
    }
}
class Office {
    public static void main(String args[]) {
        Employee e1 = new Employee();
        e1.printEmp();
    }
}
```

The output of the preceding code is as follows (the default value of an object is `null` and `int` is `0`):

```
name = null age = 0
```

What happens if you change the access modifier of the variable `name` to `private`, as shown here (modified code in bold)?

```
class Employee {
    private String name;                  Object field with
    int age;                              private access
    Employee() {
        age = 22;                         Assign value
    }                                     to age
    public void setName(String val) {
        name = val;                       Assign val
    }                                     to name
    public void printEmp() {
        System.out.println("name = " + name + " age = " + age);
    }
}
```

Nonprivate object field

You won't be able to set the value of the object field `name` as follows:

```
e1.name = "Selvan";
```

This line of code won't compile. Instead, it complains that the variable `name` has private access in the class `Employee` and can't be accessed from any other class:

```
Office.java:6:  name has private access in Employee
        e1.name = "Selvan";
```

When you answer questions on reading values from and writing them to an object field, watch out for the following points in the exam:

- Access modifier of the object field
- Access modifiers of methods used to read and write the value of the object field
- Constructors that assign values to object fields

### 3.6.3  Calling methods on objects

You can call methods defined in a class using an object reference variable. In this exam objective, this exam will specifically test you on the following:

- The correct notation used to call a method on an object reference variable
- The right number of method parameters that must be passed to a method
- The return value of a method that's assigned to a variable

Java uses the dot notation (.) to execute a method on a reference variable. Suppose the class Employee is defined as follows:

```
class Employee {                          ◄────── Class Employee
    private String name;
    public void setName(String val) {
        name = val;                       ◄─┐  Method setName
    }
}
```

You can create an object of class Employee and call the method setName on it like this:

```
Employee e1 = new Employee();
e1.setName("Java");
```

The following method invocations aren't valid in Java:

```
e1->setName("Java");
e1->.setName("Java");        Invalid method
e1-setName("Java");          invocations
```

When you call a method, you must pass to it the exact number of method parameters that are defined by it. In the previous definition of the Employee class, the method set-Name defines a method parameter of type String. You can pass a literal value or a variable to a method, as a method parameter. The following code invocations are correct:

```
                             Passing literal value
                             as method parameter
Employee e1 = new Employee();
String anotherVal = "Harry";
e1.setName("Shreya");                   Passing variable as
e1.setName(anotherVal);                 method parameter
```

**EXAM TIP**   A call to a method must be followed by passing values to all its method parameters. For a method that defines one or more method parameters, you can't call the method followed by () to indicate it doesn't need to be passed values.

If the parameter list of the called method defines a variable argument at the rightmost position, you can call the method with a variable number of arguments. Let's add a method `daysOffWork` in the class `Employee` that accepts a variable list of arguments (modifications in bold):

```
class Employee {
    private String name;
    public void setName(String val) {
        name = val;
    }
    public int daysOffWork(int... days) {
        int daysOff = 0;
        for (int i = 0; i < days.length; i++)
            daysOff += days[i];
        return daysOff;
    }
}
```

You can call this method using a variable list of arguments:

```
Class Test {
    public static void main(String args[]) {
        Employee e = new Employee();
        System.out.println(e.daysOffWork(1, 2, 3, 4));    ◄──  Call method
        System.out.println(e.daysOffWork(1, 2, 3));       ◄──  daysOffWork with four
    }                                                          method arguments
}
```

Call method **daysOffWork** with four method arguments

Call method **daysOffWork** with three method arguments

The output of the preceding code is as follows:

```
10
6
```

**EXAM TIP**   Methods that accept varargs parameters can be called with a different count of actual arguments. Also, a method that accepts a vararg can be invoked with an array in place of the vararg.

Let's add the method `getName` to the class `Employee` that returns a `String` value (changes in bold):

```
class Employee {
    private String name;
    public void setName(String val) {
        name = val;
    }
```

```
    public String getName() {
        return name;
    }
}
```

You can assign the `String` value returned from the method `getName` to a `String` variable or pass it on to another method, as follows:

```
Employee e1 = new Employee();
Employee e2 = new Employee();
String name = e1.getName();
e2.setName(e1.getName());
```
**Assign method's return value to a variable**

**Pass method's return value to another method**

In the preceding code, the return type of the method `setName` is `void`; therefore, you can't use it to assign a value to a variable:

```
Employee e1 = new Employee();
String name = e1.setName();
```
**Won't compile**

Also, you can't assign a return value of a method to an incompatible variable, as follows:

```
Employee e1 = new Employee();
int val = e1.getName();
```
**You can't assign the String returned from method getName to an int variable.**

You can read and write object fields either by using methods or by directly accessing the instance variables of a class. But it's not a good idea to enable access to the instance variables outside a class.

In the next section, you'll see the risks of exposing instance variables outside a class and the benefits of a well-encapsulated class.

## 3.7   *Apply encapsulation principles to a class*

 [6.5]   Apply encapsulation principles to a class

As the heading of this section suggests, we'll apply the encapsulation principle to a class. A well-encapsulated object doesn't expose its internal parts to the outside world. It defines a set of methods that enables the users of the class to interact with it.

As an example from the real world, you can compare a bank to a well-encapsulated class. A bank doesn't expose its internal parts—for example, its vaults and bank accounts—to the outside world, just as a well-encapsulated class in Java shouldn't expose the variables that it uses to store the state of an object outside that object. The way a bank defines a set of procedures (such as key access to vaults and verification before money withdrawals) to protect its internal parts is much like the way a well-encapsulated class defines methods to access its variables.

### 3.7.1    *Need for encapsulation*

The private members of a class—its variables and methods—are used to hide information about a class. Why would you need to hide class information? Compare a class with yourself. Do you want everyone else to know about all of your weaknesses? Do you want everyone else to be able to control your mind? The same applies to a class that you define in Java. A class may need a number of variables and methods to store an object's state and define its behavior. But it wouldn't like all the other classes to know about it. Here's a quick list of reasons to encapsulate the state of a Java object:

- To prevent an external object from performing dangerous operations
- To hide implementation details, so that the implementation can change a second time without impacting other objects
- To minimize the chance of *coupling*

Let's work with an example. Here's the definition of the class Phone:

```
class Phone {
    String model;
    String company;
    double weight;
    void makeCall(String number) {
    }
    void receiveCall() {
    }
}
```

**Instance variables that store the state of an object of Phone**

**Methods; details not relevant at this point**

Because the variable weight isn't defined as a private member, any other class (in the same package) can access it and write any value to it, as follows:

```
class Home {
    public static void main() {
        Phone ph = new Phone();
        ph.weight = -12.23;
    }
}
```

**Assign a negative weight to Phone**

### 3.7.2    *Apply encapsulation*

In the previous section, you might have noticed that the object fields of a class that isn't well encapsulated are exposed outside the class. This approach enables the users of the class to assign arbitrary values to the object fields.

Should this be allowed? For example, going back to the example of the Phone class discussed in section 3.7.1, how can the weight of a phone be a negative value?

Let's resolve this issue by defining the variable weight as a private variable in the class Phone, as follows (irrelevant changes have been omitted):

```
class Phone {
    private double weight;
}
```

But now this variable won't be accessible in the class Home. Let's define methods using this variable, which can be accessible outside the class Phone (changes in bold):

```
class Phone {
    private double weight;
    public void setWeight(double val) {
        if (val >= 0 && val <= 1000) {
            weight =val;                        ← Negative and weight
        }                                          over 1,000 not allowed
    }
    public double getWeight() {
        return weight;
    }
}
```

The method setWeight doesn't assign the value passed to it as a method parameter to the instance variable weight if it's a negative value or a value greater than 1,000. This behavior is known as *exposing object functionality using public methods.*

Let's see how this method is used to assign a value to the variable weight in the class Home:

```
class Home {                                         Assign a negative
    public static void main(String[] args) {         weight to Phone object
        Phone ph = new Phone();
        ph.setWeight(-12.23);
Prints 0.0 ──→  System.out.println(ph.getWeight());  Assign weight > 1,000
        ph.setWeight(77712.23);                       to Phone object
Prints 0.0 ──→  System.out.println(ph.getWeight());
        ph.setWeight(12.23);                          Assign weight in
        System.out.println(ph.getWeight());          allowed range
    }
}                                                    Prints 12.23
```

Note that when the class Home tries to set the value of the variable to -12.23 or 77712.23 (out-of-range values), those values aren't assigned to the Phone's private variable weight. It accepts the value 12.23, which is within the defined range.

On the OCA Java SE 8 Programmer I exam, you may also find the term *information hiding. Encapsulation* is the concept of defining variables and the methods together in a class. *Information hiding* originated from the application and purpose of the concept of encapsulation. These terms are also used interchangeably.

 **EXAM TIP** The terms *encapsulation* and *information hiding* are used interchangeably. By exposing object functionality only through methods, you can prevent your private variables from being assigned any values that don't fit your requirements. One of the best ways to create a well-encapsulated class is to define its instance variables as private variables and allow access to these variables using public methods.

The next Twist in the Tale exercise has a little hidden trick about determining a correctly encapsulated class. Let's see if you can find it (answer in the appendix).

**Twist in the Tale 3.3**

Let's modify the definition of the class `Phone` that I previously used to demonstrate the encapsulation principle in this section. Given the following definition of class `Phone`, which of the options, when replacing the code on lines 1–3, makes it a well-encapsulated class?

```
class Phone {
    public String model;
    double weight;                              //LINE1
    public void setWeight(double w) {weight = w;}  //LINE2
    public double getWeight() {return weight;}  //LINE3
}
```

Options:

**a** 
```
public double weight;
private void setWeight(double w) { weight = w; }
private double getWeight() {    return weight; }
```

**b** 
```
public double weight;
void setWeight(double w) { weight = w; }
double getWeight() {    return weight; }
```

**c** 
```
public double weight;
protected void setWeight(double w) { weight = w; }
protected double getWeight() {    return weight; }
```

**d** 
```
public double weight;
public void setWeight(double w) { weight = w; }
public double getWeight() {    return weight; }
```

**e** None of the above

Well-encapsulated classes don't expose their instance variables outside their class. What happens when the methods of these classes modify the state of the method arguments that are passed to them? Is this acceptable behavior? I'll discuss what happens in the next section.

## 3.8 *Passing objects and primitives to methods*

[6.6]  Determine the effect upon object references and primitive values
       when they are passed into methods that change the values

In this section, you'll learn the difference between passing object references and primitives to a method. You'll determine the effect on object references and primitive values when they're passed into methods that change the values.

Object references and primitives behave in a different manner when they're passed to a method because of the differences in how these two data types are internally stored by Java. Let's start with passing primitives to methods.

### 3.8.1 *Passing primitives to methods*

The value of a primitive data type is copied and passed to a method. Hence, the variable whose value was copied doesn't change:

```
class Employee {
    int age;
    void modifyVal(int a) {                     ① Method modifyVal
        a = a + 1;                                 accepts method
        System.out.println(a);                     argument of type int
    }
}
class Office {
    public static void main(String args[]) {
        Employee e = new Employee();
        System.out.println(e.age);              ⟵  Prints 0
        e.modifyVal(e.age);                        ⟵  Calls method
        System.out.println(e.age);      ⟵           modifyVal on an object
    }                                    Prints 0  ② of class Employee
}
```

The output of the preceding code is as follows:

```
0
1
0
```

**NOTE**  In the preceding code, method `modifyVal` *seems* to accept and modify the argument passed to it. This book includes such code because you might see similar code on the exam, which doesn't follow coding or naming conventions. But please follow the coding conventions when you write code on real projects.

The method `modifyVal` ① accepts a method argument a of type `int`. In this method, the variable a is a method parameter and holds a copy of the value that's passed to it. The method increments the value of the method parameter a and prints its value.

When the class `Office` calls the method `modifyVal` ②, it passes a copy of the value of the object field age to it. The method `modifyVal` never accesses the object field age. Hence, after the execution of this method, the value of the method field age prints as 0 again.

What happens if the definition of the class `Employee` is modified as follows (modifications in bold):

```
class Employee {
    int age;
    void modifyVal(int age) {
        age = age + 1;
```

```
        System.out.println(age);
    }
}
```

The class Office will still print the same answer because the method modifyVal
defines a method parameter with the name age (do you remember the topic on variable scopes covered earlier in this chapter?). Note the following important points
related to passing a method parameter to a method:

- It's OK to define a method parameter with the same name as an instance variable (or object field). But this is not a recommended practice.
- Within a method, a method parameter takes precedence over an object field.
  When the method modifyVal refers to the variable age, it refers to the method
  parameter age, not the instance variable age. To access the instance variable
  age within the method modifyVal, the variable name age needs to be prefixed
  with the keyword this (this is a keyword that refers to the object itself).

The keyword this is discussed in detail in chapter 6.

 **EXAM TIP**  When you pass a primitive variable to a method, its value remains
the same after the execution of the method. The value doesn't change,
regardless of whether the method reassigns the primitive to another variable
or modifies it.

## 3.8.2  *Passing object references to methods*

There are two main cases:

- When a method reassigns the object reference passed to it to another variable
- When a method modifies the state of the object reference passed to it

**WHEN METHODS REASSIGN THE OBJECT REFERENCES PASSED TO THEM**

When you pass an object reference to a method, the method can assign it to another
variable. In this case, the state of the object, which was passed on to the method,
remains intact. When a method is passed a reference value, a copy of the reference (that
is, the memory address) is passed to the invoked method. The callee can do whatever it
wants with its copy without ever altering the original reference held by the caller.

The following code example explains this concept. Suppose you have the following definition of the class Person:

```
class Person {
    private String name;
    Person(String newName) {
        name = newName;
    }
    public String getName() {
        return name;
    }
```

```
        public void setName(String val) {
            name = val;
        }
    }
```

What do you think is the output of the following code?

```
class Test {
    public static void swap(Person p1, Person p2) {
        Person temp = p1;
        p1 = p2;
        p2 = temp;
    }
    public static void main(String args[]) {
        Person person1 = new Person("John");
        Person person2 = new Person("Paul");
        System.out.println(person1.getName()
                            + ":" + person2.getName());
        swap(person1, person2);
        System.out.println(person1.getName()
                            + ":" + person2.getName());
    }
}
```

**Method to swap two object references**

**Creates object** ❶

❷ **Prints John:Paul before passing objects referred by variable person1 and person2 to method swap**

**Executes method swap**

❸ **Prints John:Paul after method swap completes execution**

In the preceding code, ❶ creates two object references, person1 and person2, illustrated in step 1 of figure 3.23. The boxed values represent objects of the class Person. ❷ prints John:Paul—the value of person1.name and person2.name.

The code then calls the method swap and passes to it the objects referred to by person1 and person2. When these objects are passed as arguments to the method swap, the method arguments p1 and p2 also refer to these objects. This behavior is illustrated in step 2 in figure 3.23.

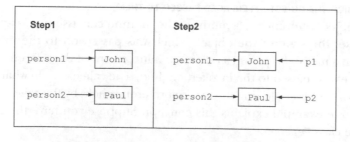

**Figure 3.23   Objects of class Person, referred to by variables person1, person2, p1, and p2**

The method swap defines three lines of code:

- Person temp = p1: makes temp refer to the object referred to by p1
- p1 = p: makes p1 refer to the object referred to by p2
- p2 = temp: makes p2 refer to the object referred to by temp

These three steps are represented in figure 3.24.

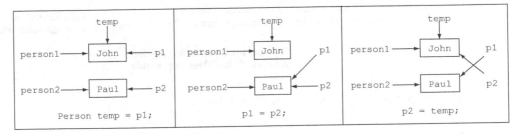

**Figure 3.24   The change in the objects referred to by variables during the execution of the method swap**

As you can see in figure 3.24, the reference variables person1 and person2 are still referring to the objects that they passed to the method swap. Because no change was made to the values of the objects referred to by variables person1 and person2, line ❸ from the previous page prints John:Paul again.

The output of the preceding code is as follows:

```
John:Paul
John:Paul
```

## WHEN METHODS MODIFY THE STATE OF THE OBJECT REFERENCES PASSED TO THEM

Let's see how a method can change the state of an object so that the modified state is accessible in the calling method. Assume the same definition of the class Person, listed again for your convenience:

```
class Person {
    private String name;
    Person(String newName) {
        name = newName;
    }
    public String getName() {
        return name;
    }
    public void setName(String val) {
        name = val;
    }
}
```

What's the output of the following code?

```
class Test {
    public static void resetValueOfMemberVariable(Person p1) {
        p1.setName("Rodrigue");
    }
    public static void main(String args[]) {
        Person person1 = new Person("John");
        System.out.println(person1.getName());
```

**Create an object reference person1**

**Print person1.name before passing it to resetValueOfMemberVariable**

```
        resetValueOfMemberVariable(person1);
        System.out.println(person1.getName());
    }
}
```

**Pass person1 to method resetValueOfMemberVariable**

**Print person1.name after passing it to resetValueOfMemberVariable**

The output of the preceding code is as follows:

```
John
Rodrigue
```

The method `resetValueOfMemberVariable` accepts the object referred to by `person1` and assigns it to the method parameter `p1`. Now both variables, `person1` and `p1`, refer to the same object. `p1.setName("Rodrigue")` modifies the value of the object referred to by the variable `p1`. Because the variable `person1` also refers to the same object, `person1.getName()` returns the new name, `Rodrigue`, in the method `main`. This sequence of actions is represented in figure 3.25.

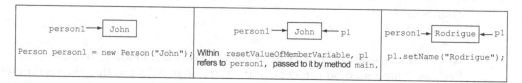

**Figure 3.25   Modification of the state of an object passed to the method `resetValueOfMember-Variable`**

## 3.9   *Summary*

I started this chapter by discussing the scope of these variables: local, method parameter, instance, and class. Often these variables' scopes overlap each other.

I also covered the constructors of a class: the user-defined and default constructors. Java inserts a default constructor in a class that doesn't define any constructor. You can modify the source code of such a class, add a constructor, and recompile the class. Upon recompilation, the Java compiler removes the automatically generated constructor.

I then covered the subobjective of reading from and writing to object fields. The terms *object fields* and *instance variables* have the same meaning and are used interchangeably. You can read from and write to object fields by directly accessing them or by using accessor methods. I also showed you how to apply encapsulation principles to a class and explained why doing so is useful.

Finally, I explained the effect on references and primitives when they're passed into methods that change their values. When you pass a primitive value to a method, its value never changes for the calling method. When you pass an object reference variable to a method, a change in its value may be reflected in the calling method—if the called method modifies an object field of the object passed to it. If the called method assigns a new object reference to the method argument before modifying the value of its fields, these changes aren't visible in the calling method.

## 3.10 Review notes

This section lists the main points covered in this chapter.

Scope of variables:

- Variables can have multiple scopes: class, instance, local, and method parameters.
- Local variables are defined within a method. Loop variables are local to the loop within which they're defined.
- The scope of local variables is less than the scope of a method if they're declared in a sub-block (within braces, {}) in a method. This sub-block can be an `if` statement, a `switch` construct, a loop, or a `try-catch` block (discussed in chapter 7).
- Local variables can't be accessed outside the method in which they're defined.
- In a method, a local variable can't be accessed before its declaration.
- Instance variables are defined and accessible within an object. They're accessible to all the instance methods of a class.
- Class variables are shared by all the objects of a class—they can be accessed even if there are no objects of the class.
- Method parameters are used to accept arguments in a method. Their scope is limited to the method where they're defined.
- A method parameter and a local variable can't be defined using the same name.
- Class and instance variables can't be defined using the same name.
- Local and instance variables can be defined using the same name. In a method, if a local variable exists with the same name as an instance variable, the local variable takes precedence.

Object's life cycle:

- An object's life cycle starts when it's initialized and lasts until it goes out of scope or is no longer referenced by a variable.
- When an object is alive, it can be referenced by a variable, and other classes can use it by calling its methods and accessing its variables.
- Declaring a reference object variable isn't the same as creating an object.
- An object is created using the operator `new`. Strings have special shorthand built into the compiler. Strings can be created by using double quotes, as in `"Hello"`.
- An object is marked as eligible for garbage collection when it can no longer be accessed.
- An object can become inaccessible if it can no longer be referenced by any variable, which happens when a reference variable is explicitly set to `null` or when it goes out of scope.

- The garbage collector can also reclaim memory from a group of referenced objects. This group of variables is referred to as island of isolation.
- You can be sure only about whether objects are marked for garbage collection. You can never be sure about whether an object has been garbage collected.

Creating methods with arguments and return values:

- The return type of a method states the type of value that a method will return.
- You can define multiple method parameters for a method.
- The method parameter can be of a primitive type or an object of a class or interface.
- The method parameters are separated by commas.
- Unlike the declaration of a local variable, or instance and class fields, *each* method parameter must be preceded by its type. This isn't allowed: `void description(String name, age) {}`.
- You can define only one variable argument in a parameter list, and it must be the final variable in the parameter list. If these two rules aren't followed, your code won't compile.
- For a method that returns a value, the `return` statement must be followed immediately by a compatible value.
- For a method that doesn't return a value (return type is `void`), the `return` statement must not be followed by a return value.
- If there's code that can be executed only after a `return` statement, the class will fail to compile.
- A method can optionally accept method arguments.
- A method may optionally return a value.
- A method returns a value by using the keyword `return` followed by the name of a variable, whose value is passed back to the calling method.
- The returned value from a method may or may not be assigned to a variable. If the value is assigned to a variable, the variable type should be compatible with the type of the return value.
- A `return` statement should be the last statement in a method. Statements placed after the `return` statement aren't accessible and fail to compile.
- A method can take zero or more parameters but can return only zero or one value.

Creating an overloaded method:

- Overloaded methods accept different lists of arguments. The argument lists can differ by
  - Changes in the number of parameters that are accepted
  - Changes in the types of parameters that are accepted
  - Changes in the positions of parameters that are accepted
- Methods can't be defined as overloaded methods if they differ only in their return types or access levels.

Constructors of a class:

- Constructors are special methods defined in a class that create and return an object of the class in which they're defined.
- Constructors have the same name as the class, and they don't specify a return type—not even `void`.
- User-defined constructors are defined by the developer.
- If a class defines multiple initializer blocks, their order of execution depends on their placement in a class. But all of them execute before a class's constructor.
- Default constructors are defined by Java, but only if the developer doesn't define any constructor in a class.
- You can define a constructor using the four access levels: `public`, `protected`, default, and `private`.
- Accessibility of a default constructor matches the accessibility of its class. Java creates a public default constructor for a public class. It creates a default constructor with package access for a class with package-level access.
- If you define a return type for a constructor, it'll no longer be treated like a constructor. It'll be treated like a regular method, even though it shares the same name as its class.
- An *initializer block* is defined within a class, not as a part of a method. It executes for every object that's created for a class.
- If you define both an initializer and a constructor for a class, both of these will execute. The initializer block will execute prior to the constructor.
- Unlike constructors, an initializer block can't accept method parameters.
- An initializer block can create local variables. It can access and assign values to instance and static variables. It can call methods and define loops, conditional statements, and `try-catch-finally` blocks.

Overloaded constructors:

- A class can also define overloaded constructors.
- Overloaded constructors must be defined using different argument lists.
- Overloaded constructors can't be defined by just a change in the access levels.
- Overloaded constructors may be defined using different access levels.
- A constructor can call another overloaded constructor by using the keyword `this`.
- A constructor can't invoke a constructor by using its class's name.
- If present, a call to another constructor must be the first statement in a constructor.

Accessing object fields:

- An object field is another name for an instance variable defined in a class.
- An object field can be read either by directly accessing the variable (if its access level permits) or by using a method that returns its value.

- Although object fields can be manipulated by direct access, it isn't a recommended practice. It makes the object vulnerable to invalid data. Such a class isn't well encapsulated.
- An object field can be written either by directly accessing the variable (if its access level permits) or by using constructors and methods that accept a value and assign it to the instance variable.
- You can call methods defined in a class using an object reference variable.
- You can't call two (or more) constructors within a constructor because the call to a constructor must be the first statement in a constructor.
- When calling a method, it must be passed the correct number and type of method arguments.
- A call to a method must be followed by passing values to all its method parameters. For a method that defines one or more method parameters, you can't call the method followed by () to indicate it doesn't need to be passed values.
- Methods that accept varargs can be called with different counts of actual arguments.

Applying encapsulation principles to a class:

- A well-encapsulated object doesn't expose the internal parts of an object outside it. It defines a set of well-defined interfaces (methods), which enables the users of the class to interact with it.
- A class that isn't well encapsulated is at risk of being assigned undesired values for its variables by the callers of the class, which can make the state of an object unstable.
- The terms *encapsulation* and *information hiding* are used interchangeably.
- To define a well-encapsulated class, define its instance variables as private variables. Allow access or manipulation to these variables using methods.

Passing objects and primitives to methods:

- Objects and primitives behave in different manners when they're passed to a method, because of differences in the way these two data types are internally stored by Java.
- When you pass a primitive variable to a method, its value remains the same after the execution of the method. This doesn't change, regardless of whether the method reassigns the primitive to another variable or modifies it.
- When you pass an object to a method, the method can modify the object's state by executing its methods. In this case, the modified state of the object is reflected in the calling method.

## 3.11   *Sample exam questions*

**Q3-1.** Which option defines a well-encapsulated class?

a
```
class Template {
    public String font;
}
```

b
```
class Template2 {
    public String font;
    public void setFont(String font) {
        this.font = font;
    }
    public String getFont() {
        return font;
    }
}
```

c
```
class Template3 {
    private String font;
    public String author;
    public void setFont(String font) {
        this.font = font;
    }
    public String getFont() {
        return font;
    }
    public void setAuthor(String author) {
        this.author = author;
    }
    public String getAuthor() {
        return author;
    }
}
```

d   None of the above


**Q3-2.** Examine the following code and select the correct option(s):

```
public class Person {
    public int height;
    public void setHeight(int newHeight) {
        if (newHeight <= 300)
            height = newHeight;
    }
}
```

a   The height of a Person can never be set to more than 300.

b   The preceding code is an example of a well-encapsulated class.

c   The class would be better encapsulated if the height validation weren't set to 300.

d   Even though the class isn't well encapsulated, it can be inherited by other classes.

**Q3-3.** Which of the following methods correctly accepts three integers as method arguments and returns their sum as a floating-point number?

**a** 
```
public void addNumbers(byte arg1, int arg2, int arg3) {
    double sum = arg1 + arg2 + arg3;
}
```

**b** 
```
public double subtractNumbers(byte arg1, int arg2, int arg3) {
    double sum = arg1 + arg2 + arg3;
    return sum;
}
```

**c** 
```
public double numbers(long arg1, byte arg2, double arg3) {
    return arg1 + arg2 + arg3;
}
```

**d** 
```
public float wakaWakaAfrica(long a1, long a2, short a977) {
    double sum = a1 + a2 + a977;
    return (float)sum;
}
```

**Q3-4.** Which of the following statements are true?

**a** If the return type of a method is `int`, the method can return a value of type `byte`.

**b** A method may or may not return a value.

**c** If the return type of a method is `void`, it can define a `return` statement without a value, as follows:

```
return;
```

**d** A method may or may not accept any method arguments.

**e** A method must accept at least one method argument or define its return type.

**f** A method whose return type is `String` can't return `null`.

**Q3-5.** Given the following definition of class `Person`,

```
class Person {
    public String name;
    public int height;
}
```

what is the output of the following code?

```
class EJavaGuruPassObjects1 {
    public static void main(String args[]) {
        Person p = new Person();
        p.name = "EJava";
        anotherMethod(p);
        System.out.println(p.name);
        someMethod(p);
        System.out.println(p.name);
    }
```

```
    static void someMethod(Person p) {
        p.name = "someMethod";
        System.out.println(p.name);
    }
    static void anotherMethod(Person p) {
        p = new Person();
        p.name = "anotherMethod";
        System.out.println(p.name);
    }
}
```

a  anotherMethod
   anotherMethod
   someMethod
   someMethod

b  anotherMethod
   EJava
   someMethod
   someMethod

c  anotherMethod
   EJava
   someMethod
   EJava

d  Compilation error

## Q3-6. What is the output of the following code?

```
class EJavaGuruPassPrim {
    public static void main(String args[]) {
        int ejg = 10;
        anotherMethod(ejg);
        System.out.println(ejg);
        someMethod(ejg);
        System.out.println(ejg);
    }
    static void someMethod(int val) {
        ++val;
        System.out.println(val);
    }
    static void anotherMethod(int val) {
        val = 20;
        System.out.println(val);
    }
}
```

a  20
   10
   11
   11

b  20
   20
   11
   10

   c  20
      10
      11
      10

   d  Compilation error

**Q3-7.** Given the following signature of method eJava, choose the options that correctly overload this method:

```
public String eJava(int age, String name, double duration)
```

   a  `private String eJava(int val, String firstName, double dur)`

   b  `public void eJava(int val1, String val2, double val3)`

   c  `String eJava(String name, int age, double duration)`

   d  `float eJava(double name, String age, byte duration)`

   e  `ArrayList<String> eJava()`

   f  `char[] eJava(double numbers)`

   g  `String eJava()`

**Q3-8.** Given the following code,

```
class Course {
    void enroll(long duration) {
        System.out.println("long");
    }
    void enroll(int duration) {
        System.out.println("int");
    }
    void enroll(String s) {
        System.out.println("String");
    }
    void enroll(Object o) {
        System.out.println("Object");
    }
}
```

what is the output of the following code?

```
class EJavaGuru {
    public static void main(String args[]) {
        Course course = new Course();
        char c = 10;
        course.enroll(c);
        course.enroll("Object");
    }
}
```

   a  Compilation error

   b  Runtime exception

c `int`
`String`

d `long`
`Object`

**Q3-9.** Examine the following code and select the correct options:

```java
class EJava {
    public EJava() {
        this(7);
        System.out.println("public");
    }
    private EJava(int val) {
        this("Sunday");
        System.out.println("private");
    }
    protected EJava(String val) {
        System.out.println("protected");
    }
}
class TestEJava {
    public static void main(String[] args) {
        EJava eJava = new EJava();
    }
}
```

a The class `EJava` defines three overloaded constructors.

b The class `EJava` defines two overloaded constructors. The private constructor isn't counted as an overloaded constructor.

c Constructors with different access modifiers can't call each other.

d The code prints the following:

```
protected
private
public
```

e The code prints the following:

```
public
private
protected
```

**Q3-10.** Select the incorrect options:

a If a user defines a `private` constructor for a `public` class, Java creates a `public` default constructor for the class.

b A class that gets a default constructor doesn't have overloaded constructors.

c A user can overload the default constructor of a class.

d The following class is eligible for a default constructor:

```java
class EJava {}
```

e The following class is also eligible for a default constructor:

```
class EJava {
        void EJava() {}
}
```

## 3.12 Answers to sample exam questions

Q3-1. Which option defines a well-encapsulated class?

a
```
class Template {
    public String font;
}
```

b
```
class Template2 {
    public String font;
    public void setFont(String font) {
        this.font = font;
    }
    public String getFont() {
        return font;
    }
}
```

c
```
class Template3 {
    private String font;
    public String author;
    public void setFont(String font) {
        this.font = font;
    }
    public String getFont() {
        return font;
    }
    public void setAuthor(String author) {
        this.author = author;
    }
    public String getAuthor() {
        return author;
    }
}
```

d **None of the above**

Answer: d

Explanation: Options (a), (b), and (c) are incorrect because they all define a public instance variable. A well-encapsulated class should be like a capsule, hiding its instance variables from the outside world. The only way you should access and modify instance variables is through the public methods of a class to ensure that the outside world can access only the variables the class allows it to. By defining methods to assign values to its instance variables, a class can control the range of values that can be assigned to them.

**Q3-2.** Examine the following code and select the correct option(s):

```
public class Person {
    public int height;
    public void setHeight(int newHeight) {
        if (newHeight <= 300)
            height = newHeight;
    }
}
```

    **a**  The height of a Person can never be set to more than 300.

    **b**  The preceding code is an example of a well-encapsulated class.

    **c**  The class would be better encapsulated if the height validation weren't set to 300.

    **d**  **Even though the class isn't well encapsulated, it can be inherited by other classes.**

Answer: d

Explanation: This class isn't well encapsulated because its instance variable `height` is defined as a `public` member. Because the instance variable can be directly accessed by other classes, the variable doesn't always use the method `setHeight` to set its height. The class `Person` can't control the values that can be assigned to its public variable `height`.

**Q3-3.** Which of the following methods correctly accepts three integers as method arguments and returns their sum as a floating-point number?

    **a**  
```
public void addNumbers(byte arg1, int arg2, int arg3) {
    double sum = arg1 + arg2 + arg3;
}
```

    **b**  
```
public double subtractNumbers(byte arg1, int arg2, int arg3) {
    double sum = arg1 + arg2 + arg3;
    return sum;
}
```

    **c**  
```
public double numbers(long arg1, byte arg2, double arg3) {
    return arg1 + arg2 + arg3;
}
```

    **d**  
```
public float wakaWakaAfrica(long a1, long a2, short a977) {
    double sum = a1 + a2 + a977;
    return (float)sum;
}
```

Answer: b, d

Explanation: Option (a) is incorrect. The question specifies the method should return a decimal number (type `double` or `float`), but this method doesn't return any value.

    Option (b) is correct. This method accepts three integer values that can be automatically converted to an integer: `byte`, `int`, and `int`. It computes the sum of these integer values and returns it as a decimal number (data type double). Note that the name of the method is subtractNumbers, which doesn't make it an invalid option. Practically, you wouldn't name a method subtractNumbers if it's adding them. But syntactically and technically, this option meets the question's requirements and is a correct option.

Option (c) is incorrect. This method doesn't accept integers as the method arguments. The type of the method argument arg3 is double, which isn't an integer.

Option (d) is correct. Even though the name of the method seems weird, it accepts the correct argument list (all integers) and returns the result in the correct data type (float).

**Q3-4.** Which of the following statements are true?

    a   **If the return type of a method is int, the method can return a value of type byte.**

    b   **A method may or may not return a value.**

    c   **If the return type of a method is void, it can define a return statement without a value, as follows:**

```
return;
```

    d   **A method may or may not accept any method arguments.**

    e   A method should accept at least one method argument or define its return type.

    f   A method whose return type is String can't return null.

Answer: a, b, c, d

Explanation: Option (e) is incorrect. There's no constraint on the number of arguments that can be passed to a method, regardless of whether the method returns a value.

Option (f) is incorrect. You can't return the value null for methods that return primitive data types. You can return null for methods that return objects (String is a class and not a primitive data type).

**Q3-5.** Given the following definition of class Person,

```
class Person {
    public String name;
    public int height;
}
```

what is the output of the following code?

```
class EJavaGuruPassObjects1 {
    public static void main(String args[]) {
        Person p = new Person();
        p.name = "EJava";
```

```
        anotherMethod(p);
        System.out.println(p.name);
        someMethod(p);
        System.out.println(p.name);
    }
    static void someMethod(Person p) {
        p.name = "someMethod";
        System.out.println(p.name);
    }
    static void anotherMethod(Person p) {
        p = new Person();
        p.name = "anotherMethod";
        System.out.println(p.name);
    }
}
```

**a**  anotherMethod
    anotherMethod
    someMethod
    someMethod

**b**  **anotherMethod**
    **EJava**
    **someMethod**
    **someMethod**

**c**  anotherMethod
    EJava
    someMethod
    EJava

**d**  Compilation error

Answer: b

Explanation: The class `EJavaGuruPassObject1` defines two methods, `someMethod` and `anotherMethod`. The method `someMethod` modifies the value of the object parameter passed to it. Hence, the changes are visible within this method and in the calling method (method `main`). But the method `anotherMethod` reassigns the reference variable passed to it. Changes to any of the values of this object are limited to this method. They aren't reflected in the calling method (the `main` method).

**Q3-6.** What is the output of the following code?

```
class EJavaGuruPassPrim {
    public static void main(String args[]) {
        int ejg = 10;
        anotherMethod(ejg);
        System.out.println(ejg);
        someMethod(ejg);
        System.out.println(ejg);
    }
```

```
static void someMethod(int val) {
    ++val;
    System.out.println(val);
}
static void anotherMethod(int val) {
    val = 20;
    System.out.println(val);
}
}
```

a    20
     10
     11
     11

b    20
     20
     11
     10

c    20
     10
     11
     10

d  Compilation error

Answer: c

Explanation: When primitive data types are passed to a method, the values of the variables in the calling method remain the same. This behavior doesn't depend on whether the primitive values are reassigned other values or modified by addition, subtraction, or multiplication—or any other operation.

**Q3-7.** Given the following signature of method eJava, choose the options that correctly overload this method:

```
public String eJava(int age, String name, double duration)
```

a   `private String eJava(int val, String firstName, double dur)`
b   `public void eJava(int val1, String val2, double val3)`
c   `String eJava(String name, int age, double duration)`
d   `float eJava(double name, String age, byte duration)`
e   `ArrayList<String> eJava()`
f   `char[] eJava(double numbers)`
g   `String eJava()`

Answer: c, d, e, f, g

Explanation: Option (a) is incorrect. Overloaded methods can change the access modifiers, but changing the access modifier alone won't make it an overloaded method. This option also changes the names of the method parameters, but that doesn't make any difference to a method signature.

Option (b) is incorrect. Overloaded methods can change the return type of the method, but changing the return type won't make it an overloaded method.

Option (c) is correct. Changing the placement of the types of the method parameters overloads it.

Option (d) is correct. Changing the return type of a method and the placement of the types of the method parameters overloads it.

Option (e) is correct. Changing the return type of a method and making a change in the parameter list overloads it.

Option (f) is correct. Changing the return type of a method and making a change in the parameter list overloads it.

Option (g) is correct. Changing the parameter list also overloads a method.

**Q3-8.** Given the following code,

```
class Course {
    void enroll(long duration) {
        System.out.println("long");
    }
    void enroll(int duration) {
        System.out.println("int");
    }
    void enroll(String s) {
        System.out.println("String");
    }
    void enroll(Object o) {
        System.out.println("Object");
    }
}
```

what is the output of the following code?

```
class EJavaGuru {
    public static void main(String args[]) {
        Course course = new Course();
        char c = 10;
        course.enroll(c);
        course.enroll("Object");
    }
}
```

- a  Compilation error
- b  Runtime exception
- c  `int`
     `String`
- d  `long`
     `Object`

Answer: c

Explanation: No compilation issues exist with the code. You can overload methods by changing the type of the method arguments in the list. Using method arguments with data types having a base-derived class relationship (Object and String classes) is acceptable. Using method arguments with data types for which one can be automatically converted to the other (int and long) is also acceptable.

When the code executes course.enroll(c), char can be passed to two overloaded enroll methods that accept int and long. The char gets expanded to its nearest type—int—so course.enroll(c) calls the overloaded method that accepts int, printing int. The code course.enroll("Object") is passed a String value. Although String is also an Object, this method calls the specific (not general) type of the argument passed to it. So course.enroll("Object") calls the overloaded method that accepts String, printing String.

**Q3-9.** Examine the following code and select the correct options:

```
class EJava {
    public EJava() {
        this(7);
        System.out.println("public");
    }
    private EJava(int val) {
        this("Sunday");
        System.out.println("private");
    }
    protected EJava(String val) {
        System.out.println("protected");
    }
}
class TestEJava {
    public static void main(String[] args) {
        EJava eJava = new EJava();
    }
}
```

a  **The class EJava defines three overloaded constructors.**

b  The class EJava defines two overloaded constructors. The private constructor isn't counted as an overloaded constructor.

c  Constructors with different access modifiers can't call each other.

d  **The code prints the following:**

   **protected**
   **private**
   **public**

e  The code prints the following:

   public
   private
   protected

Answer: a, d

Explanation: You can define overloaded constructors with different access modifiers in the same way that you define overloaded methods with different access modifiers. But a change in only the access modifier can't be used to define overloaded methods or constructors. `private` methods and constructors are also counted as overloaded methods.

The following line of code calls `EJava`'s constructor, which doesn't accept any method argument:

```
EJava eJava = new EJava();
```

The no-argument constructor of this class calls the constructor that accepts an `int` argument, which in turn calls the constructor with the `String` argument. Because the constructor with the `String` constructor doesn't call any other methods, it prints `protected` and returns control to the constructor that accepts an `int` argument. This constructor prints `private` and returns control to the constructor that doesn't accept any method argument. This constructor prints `public` and returns control to the `main` method.

**Q 3-10.** Select the incorrect options:

**a** **If a user defines a private constructor for a public class, Java creates a public default constructor for the class.**

**b** A class that gets a default constructor doesn't have overloaded constructors.

**c** **A user can overload the default constructor of a class.**

**d** The following class is eligible for default constructor:

```
class EJava {}
```

**e** The following class is also eligible for a default constructor:

```
class EJava {
        void EJava() {}
}
```

Answer: a, c

Explanation: Option (a) is incorrect. If a user defines a constructor for a class with any access modifier, it's no longer an eligible candidate to be provided with a default constructor.

Option (b) is correct. A class gets a default constructor only when it doesn't have any constructor. A default or an automatic constructor can't exist with other constructors.

Option (c) is incorrect. A default constructor can't coexist with other constructors. A default constructor is automatically created by the Java compiler if the user doesn't define any constructor in a class. If the user reopens the source code file and adds a constructor to the class, upon recompilation no default constructor will be created for the class.

Option (d) is correct. Because this class doesn't have a constructor, Java will create a default constructor for it.

Option (e) is also correct. This class also doesn't have a constructor, so it's eligible for the creation of a default constructor. The following isn't a constructor because the return type of a constructor isn't void:

```
void EJava() {}
```

It's a regular and valid method, with the same name as its class.

# Selected classes from the Java API and arrays

| Exam objectives covered in this chapter | What you need to know |
|---|---|
| **[9.2]** Creating and manipulating Strings | How to initialize String variables using = (assignment) and new operators. Use of the operators =, +=, !=, and == with String objects. Pooling of string literal values. Literal value for class String. Use of methods from class String. Immutable String values. All the String methods manipulate and return a new String object. |
| **[3.2]** Test equality between Strings and other objects using == and equals(). | How to determine the equality of two String objects.<br>Differences between using operator == and method equals() to determine equality of String objects. |
| **[9.1]** Manipulate data using the StringBuilder class and its methods. | How to create StringBuilder classes and how to use their commonly used methods.<br>Difference between StringBuilder and String classes. Difference between methods with similar names defined in both of these classes. |
| **[4.1]** Declare, instantiate, initialize, and use a one-dimensional array. | How to declare, instantiate, and initialize one-dimensional arrays using single and multiple steps. The do's and don'ts of each of these steps. |
| **[4.2]** Declare, instantiate, initialize, and use a multidimensional array. | How to declare, instantiate, and initialize multidimensional arrays using single and multiple steps, with do's and don'ts for each of these steps. Accessing elements in asymmetric multidimensional arrays. |

| Exam objectives covered in this chapter | What you need to know |
|---|---|
| **[9.4]** Declare and use an `ArrayList` of a given type. | How to declare, create, and use an `ArrayList`. Advantages of using an `ArrayList` over arrays. Use of methods that add, modify, and delete elements of an `ArrayList`. |
| **[9.3]** Create and manipulate calendar data using classes from `java.time.LocalDateTime`, `java.time.LocalDate`, `java.time.LocalTime`, `java.time.format.DateTimeFormatter`, `java.time.Period`. | How to store dates and times using classes `LocalDate`, `LocalTime`, and `LocalDateTime`. Identify the factory methods to instantiate date and time objects. Use instance methods of date and time classes. Use `Period` to add or subtract duration (days, months, or years) to and from date objects. Use `DateTimeFormatter` to format or parse date and time objects. |

In the OCA Java SE 8 Programmer I exam, you'll be asked many questions about how to create, modify, and delete `String` objects, `StringBuilder` objects, arrays, `ArrayList` objects, and date/time objects. To prepare you for such questions, in this chapter I'll provide insight into the variables you'll use to store these objects' values, along with definitions for some of their methods. This information should help you apply all the methods correctly.

In this chapter, we'll cover the following:

- Creating and manipulating `String` and `StringBuilder` objects
- Using common methods from classes `String` and `StringBuilder`
- Creating and using one-dimensional and multidimensional arrays in single and multiple steps
- Accessing elements in asymmetric multidimensional arrays
- Declaring, creating, and using an `ArrayList` and understanding the advantages of an `ArrayList` over arrays
- Using methods that add, modify, and delete elements of an `ArrayList`
- Creating date and time objects using the classes `LocalDate`, `LocalTime`, and `LocalDateTime`
- Manipulating date objects using the class `Period`
- Formatting and parsing date and time objects using `DateTimeFormatter`

Let's get started with the class `String`.

## 4.1 Welcome to the world of the String class

In this section, we'll cover the class String defined in the Java API in the java.lang package. The String class represents character strings. We'll create objects of the class String and work with its commonly used methods, including indexOf(), substring(), replace(), charAt(), and others. You'll also learn how to determine the equality of two String objects.

The String class is perhaps the most-used class in the Java API. You'll find instances of this class being used by every other class in the Java API. How many times do you think you've used the class String? Don't answer that question—it's like trying to count your hair.

Although many developers find the String class to be one of the simplest to work with, this perception can be deceptive. For example, in the String value "Shreya", at which index do you think r is stored—second or third? The correct answer is second because the first letter of a String is stored at index 0 and not index 1. You'll learn many other facts about the String class in this section.

Let's start by creating new objects of this class.

### 4.1.1 Creating String objects

You can create objects of the class String by using the new operator or by using String literal values (values within double quotes). You can assign a String literal value to a String reference variable by using the assignment operator (=). But you may have noticed a *big* difference in how these objects are stored and referred to by Java.

Let's create two String objects with the value "Paul" using the operator new:

```
String str1 = new String("Paul");
String str2 = new String("Paul");
System.out.println(str1 == str2);
```

**Create two String objects by using the operator new**

**Comparing the objects referred to by the variables str1 and str2 prints false.**

Figure 4.1 illustrates the previous code.

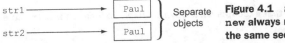

str1 ——————————→ Paul

str2 ——————————→ Paul

Separate objects

**Figure 4.1** String objects created using the operator new always refer to separate objects, even if they store the same sequence of characters.

In the previous code, a comparison of the String reference variables str1 and str2 prints false. The operator == compares the addresses of the objects referred to by the variables str1 and str2. Even though these String objects store the same sequence of characters, they refer to separate objects stored at separate locations.

Let's initialize two String variables with the value "Harry" using the assignment operator (=). Figure 4.2 illustrates the variables str3 and str4 and the objects referred to by these variables.

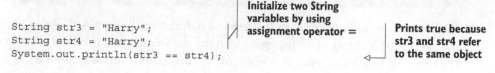

```
String str3 = "Harry";
String str4 = "Harry";
System.out.println(str3 == str4);
```

**Initialize two String variables by using assignment operator =**

**Prints true because str3 and str4 refer to the same object**

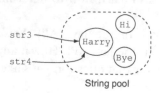

String pool

**Figure 4.2**  String **objects created using the assignment operator (=) may refer to the same object if they store the same sequence of characters.**

In the preceding example, the variables str1 and str2 referred to different String objects, even if they were created using the same sequence of characters. In the case of variables str3 and str4, the objects are created and stored in a *pool* of String objects. Before creating a new object in the pool, Java searches for an object with similar contents. When the following line of code executes, no String object with the value "Harry" is found in the pool of String objects:

```
String str3 = "Harry";
```

As a result, Java creates a String object with the value "Harry" in the pool of String objects referred to by the variable str3. This action is depicted in figure 4.3.

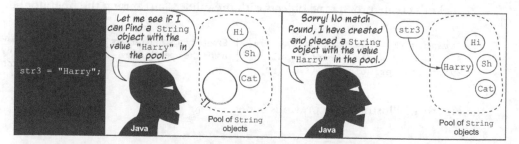

**Figure 4.3**  **The sequence of steps that executes when Java is unable to locate a** String **in a pool of** String **objects**

When the following line of code executes, Java is able to find a String object with the value "Harry" in the pool of String objects:

```
String str4 = "Harry";
```

Java doesn't create a new `String` object in this case, and the variable `str4` refers to the existing `String` object `"Harry"`. As shown in figure 4.4, both variables `str3` and `str4` refer to the same `String` object in the pool of `String` objects.

**Figure 4.4   The sequence of actions that executes when Java locates a *String* in the pool of *String* objects**

You can also create a `String` object by enclosing a value within double quotes (`"`):

```
System.out.println("Morning");
```
◁— **Creates a new String object with value Morning in the String constant pool**

These values are reused from the `String` constant pool if a matching value is found. If a matching value isn't found, the JVM creates a `String` object with the specified value and places it in the `String` constant pool:

```
String morning1 = "Morning";
System.out.println("Morning" == morning1);
```

Compare the preceding example with the following example, which creates a `String` object using the operator `new` and (only) double quotes and then compares their references:

```
String morning2 = new String("Morning");
System.out.println("Morning" == morning2);
```
◁— **This String object is not placed in the String constant pool.**

The preceding code shows that object references of `String` objects that exist in the `String` constant pool and object references of `String` objects that don't exist in the `String` constant pool don't refer to the same `String` object, even if they define the same `String` value.

**NOTE**   The terms *String constant pool* and *String pool* are used interchangeably and refer to the same pool of `String` objects. Because `String` objects are immutable, the pool of `String` objects is also called the *String constant pool*. You may see either of these terms on the exam.

You can also invoke other overloaded constructors of the class String to create its objects by using the operator new:

```
String girl = new String("Shreya");
char[] name = new char[]{'P','a','u','l'};
String boy = new String(name);
```

⟵┐ **String constructor that accepts a String**

⟵ **String constructor that accepts a char array**

You can also create objects of String using the classes StringBuilder and String-Buffer:

```
StringBuilder sd1 = new StringBuilder("String Builder");
String str5 = new String(sd1);
StringBuffer sb2 = new StringBuffer("String Buffer");
String str6 = new String(sb2);
```

⟵┐ **String constructor that accepts object of StringBuilder**

⟵ **String constructor that accepts object of StringBuffer**

Because String is a class, you can assign null to it, as shown in the next example:

```
String empName = null;
```

⟵ **null is a literal value for objects.**

**EXAM TIP**    The default value for String is null.

## COUNTING STRING OBJECTS

To test your understanding of the various ways in which a String object can be created, the exam may question you on the total number of String objects created in a given piece of code. Count the total number of String objects created in the following code, assuming that the String constant pool doesn't define any matching String values:

```
class ContString {
    public static void main(String... args) {
        String summer = new String("Summer");        ⟵➊
        String summer2 = "Summer";                   ⟵➋
        System.out.println("Summer");                ⟵➌
        System.out.println("autumn");                ⟵➍
        System.out.println("autumn" == "summer");    ⟵➎
        String autumn = new String("Summer");        ⟵➏
    }
}
```

I'll walk through the code with you step by step to calculate the total number of String objects created:

- The code at ➊ creates a new String object with the value "Summer". This object is not placed in the String constant pool.
- The code at ➋ creates a new String object with the value "Summer" and places it in the String constant pool.

- The code at ❸ doesn't need to create any new String object. It reuses the String object with the value "Summer" that already existed in the String constant pool.

- The code at ❹ creates a new String object with the value "autumn" and places it in the String constant pool.

- The code at ❺ reuses the String value "autumn" from the String constant pool. It creates a String object with the value "summer" in the String constant pool (note the difference in the case of letters—Java is case-sensitive and "Summer" is not the same as "summer").

- The code at ❻ creates a new String object with the value "Summer".

The previous code creates a total of five String objects.

**EXAM TIP**  If a String object is created using the keyword new, it always results in the creation of a new String object. String objects created this way are never pooled. When a variable is assigned a String literal using the assignment operator, a new String object is created only if a String object with the same value isn't found in the String constant pool.

### 4.1.2  *The class String is immutable*

The concept that the class String is immutable is an important point to remember. Once created, the contents of an object of the class String can never be modified. The immutability of String objects helps the JVM reuse String objects, reducing memory overhead and increasing performance.

As shown previously in figure 4.4, the JVM creates a pool of String objects that can be referenced by multiple variables across the JVM. The JVM can make this optimization only because String is immutable. String objects can be shared across multiple reference variables without any fear of changes in their values. If the reference variables str1 and str2 refer to the same String object value "Java", str1 need not worry for its lifetime that the value "Java" might be changed through the variable str2.

Let's take a quick look at how the immutability of the class String is implemented by the authors of this class:

- The class String stores its values in a private variable of the type char array (char value[]). Arrays are fixed in size and don't grow once initialized.

- This value variable is marked as final in the class String. Note that final is a nonaccess modifier, and a final variable can be initialized only once.

- None of the methods defined in the class String manipulate the individual elements of the array value.

I'll discuss each of these points in detail in the following sections.

**Code from Java API classes**

To give you a better understanding of how the classes `String`, `StringBuilder`, and `ArrayList` work, I'll explain the variables used to store these objects' values, along with definitions for some of their methods. My purpose is not to overwhelm you but to prepare you. The exam won't question you on this subject, but these details will help you retain relevant information for the exam and implement similar requirements in code for practical projects.

The source code of the classes defined in the Java API is shipped with the Java Development Kit (JDK). You can access it by unzipping the src.zip archive from your JDK's installation folder.

The rest of this section discusses how the authors of the Java API have implemented immutability in the class `String`.

### STRING USES A CHAR ARRAY TO STORE ITS VALUE

Here's a partial definition of the class `String` from the Java source code file (String.java) that includes the array used to store the characters of a `String` value (the relevant code is in bold):

```
public final class String
    implements java.io.Serializable, Comparable<String>, CharSequence
{
    private final char value[];
}
```

The rest of the code
of the class String

The value array is used
for character storage.

The arrays are fixed in size—they can't grow once they're initialized.

Let's create a variable name of type `String` and see how it's stored internally:

```
String name = "Selvan";
```

Figure 4.5 shows a UML representation (class diagram on the left and object diagram on the right) of the class `String` and its object name, with only one relevant variable, value, which is an array of the type char and is used to store the sequence of characters assigned to a `String`.

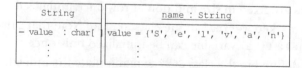

| String | name : String |
|---|---|
| – value : char[ ] | value = {'S', 'e', 'l', 'v', 'a', 'n'} |

**Figure 4.5   UML representations of the class `String` and a `String` object with `String`'s instance attribute value**

As you can see in figure 4.5, the `String` value Selvan is stored in an array of type char. In this chapter, I'll cover arrays in detail, as well as how an array stores its first value at position 0.

**Figure 4.6  Mapping characters stored by a String with the positions at which they're stored**

Figure 4.6 shows how Selvan is stored as a char array.

What do you think you'll get when you request that this String return the character at position 4? If you said a and not v, you got the right answer (as in figure 4.6).

### STRING USES FINAL VARIABLE TO STORE ITS VALUE

The variable value, which is used to store the value of a String object, is marked as final. Review the following code snippet from the class String.java:

```
private final char value[];          value is used for
                                     character storage.
```

The basic characteristic of a final variable is that it can initialize a value only once. By marking the variable value as final, the class String makes sure that it can't be reassigned a value.

### METHODS OF STRING DON'T MODIFY THE CHAR ARRAY

Although we can't reassign a value to a final char array (as mentioned in the previous section), we can reassign its individual characters. Wow—does this mean that the statement "Strings are immutable" isn't completely true?

No, that statement is still true. The char array used by the class String is marked private, which means that it isn't accessible outside the class for modification. The class String itself doesn't modify the value of this variable either.

All the methods defined in the class String, such as substring, concat, toLowerCase, toUpperCase, trim, and so on, which *seem* to modify the contents of the String object on which they're called, create and return a new String object rather than modify the existing value. Figure 4.7 illustrates the partial definition of String's replace method.

```
public String replace(char oldChar, char newChar) {
    if (oldChar != newChar) {
        // code to create a new char array and
        // replace the desired char with the new char

        return new String(0, len, buf);
    }
    return this;                                    replace creates and
}                                                   returns a new String
                                                    object. It doesn't modify
                                                    the existing array value.
```

**Figure 4.7  The partial definition of the method replace from the class String shows that this method creates and returns a new String object rather than modifies the value of the String object on which it's called.**

I reiterate that the previous code from the class String will help you relate the theory to the code and understand how and why a particular concept works. If you understand a particular concept well in terms of how and why it works, you'll be able to retain that information longer.

> **EXAM TIP**   Strings are immutable. Once initialized, a String value can't be modified. All the String methods that return a modified String value return a new String object with the modified value. The original String value always remains the same.

### 4.1.3   *Methods of the class String*

Figure 4.8 categorizes the methods that are on the exam into groups: ones that query the positions of characters, ones that seem to modify String, and others.

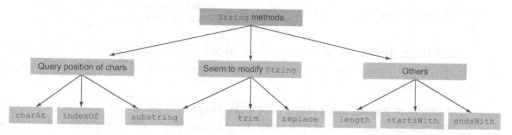

**Figure 4.8   Categorization of the String methods**

Categorizing the methods in this way will help you better understand these methods. For example, the methods charAt(), indexOf(), and substring() query the position of individual characters in a String. The methods substring(), trim(), and replace() seem to be modifying the value of a String.

#### CHARAT()

You can use the method charAt(int index) to retrieve a character at a specified index of a String:

```
String name = new String("Paul");
System.out.println(name.charAt(0));      |  Prints P
System.out.println(name.charAt(2));      <———— Prints u
```

Figure 4.9 illustrates the previous string, Paul.

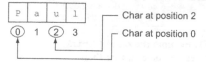

| P | a | u | l |     — Char at position 2

(0)  1  (2)  3     — Char at position 0

**Figure 4.9   The sequence of characters of "Paul" stored by String and the corresponding array index positions**

Because the last character is placed at index 3, the following code will throw an exception at runtime:

```
System.out.println(name.charAt(4));
```

> **NOTE** As a quick introduction, a *runtime exception* is a programming error determined by the Java Runtime Environment (JRE) during the execution of code. These errors occur because of the inappropriate use of another piece of code (exceptions are covered in detail in chapter 7). The previous code tries to access a nonexistent index position, so it causes an exception.

### INDEXOF()

You can search a String for the occurrence of a char or a String. If the specified char or String is found in the target String, this method returns the first matching position; otherwise, it returns -1:

```
String letters = "ABCAB";
System.out.println(letters.indexOf('B'));     ←┘ Prints 1
System.out.println(letters.indexOf("S"));     ←┘ Prints –1
System.out.println(letters.indexOf("CA"));    ←── Prints 2
```

Figure 4.10 illustrates the previous string ABCAB.

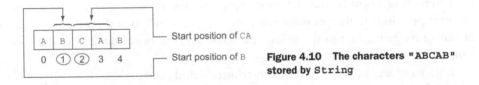

Start position of CA

Start position of B

**Figure 4.10   The characters "ABCAB" stored by String**

By default, the indexOf() method starts its search from the first char of the target String. If you wish, you can also set the starting position, as in the following example:

```
String letters = "ABCAB";
System.out.println(letters.indexOf('B', 2));    ←┘ Prints 4
```

### SUBSTRING()

The substring() method is shipped in two flavors. The first returns a substring of a String from the position you specify to the end of the String, as in the following example:

```
String exam = "Oracle";
String sub = exam.substring(2);       | Prints acle
System.out.println(sub);              ←┘
```

Figure 4.11 illustrates the previous example.

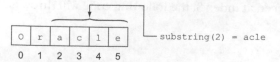

substring(2) = acle

**Figure 4.11   The** `String "Oracle"`

You can also specify the end position with this method:

```
String exam = "Oracle";
String result = exam.substring(2, 4);
System.out.println(result);
```
**Prints ac**

Figure 4.12 illustrates the `String` value "Oracle", including both a start point and an end point for the method `substring`.

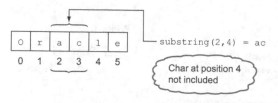

substring(2,4) = ac

Char at position 4
not included

**Figure 4.12   How the method** `substring` **looks for the specified characters from the start until the end position**

An interesting point is that the `substring` method doesn't include the character at the end position. In the previous example, `result` is assigned the value ac (characters at positions 2 and 3), not the value acl (characters at positions 2, 3, and 4). Here's a simple way to remember this rule:

Length of `String` returned by substring() = end - start

**EXAM TIP**   The `substring` method doesn't include the character at the end position in its return value.

### TRIM()

The `trim()` method returns a new `String` by removing all the leading and trailing *white space* in a `String`. White spaces are blanks (new lines, spaces, or tabs).

Let's define and print a `String` with leading and trailing white space. (The colons printed before and after the `String` determine the start and end of the `String`.)

```
String varWithSpaces = " AB CB    ";
System.out.print(":");
System.out.print(varWithSpaces);
System.out.print(":");
```
**String with white space**

**Prints : AB CB    :**

Here's another example that trims the leading and trailing white space:

```
System.out.print(":");
System.out.print(varWithSpaces.trim());
System.out.print(":");
```
**Prints :AB CB:**

Note that this method doesn't remove the space *within* a String.

### REPLACE()

This method will return a new String by replacing all the occurrences of a char with another char. Instead of specifying a char to be replaced by another char, you can also specify a sequence of characters—a String to be replaced by another String:

```
String letters = "ABCAB";
System.out.println(letters.replace('B', 'b'));        ⟵    Prints AbCAb
System.out.println(letters.replace("CA", "12"));        ⟵    Prints AB12B
```

Notice the type of the method parameters passed on this method: either char or String. You can't mix these parameter types, as the following code shows:

```
String letters = "ABCAB";
System.out.println(letters.replace('B', "b"));        Won't compile
System.out.println(letters.replace("B", 'b'));
```

Again, notice that this method doesn't—or can't—change the value of the variable letters. Examine the following line of code and its output:

```
System.out.println(letters);        ⟵    Prints ABCAB because previous replace() method
                                          calls don't affect the char[] array within letters
```

### LENGTH()

You can use the length() method to retrieve the length of a String. Here's an example showing its use:

```
System.out.println("Shreya".length());        ⟵    Prints 6
```

> **EXAM TIP**   The length of a String is one number greater than the position that stores its last character. The length of String "Shreya" is 6, but its last character, a, is stored at position 5 because the positions start at 0, not 1.

### STARTSWITH() AND ENDSWITH()

The method startsWith() determines whether a String starts with a specified prefix, specified as a String. You can also specify whether you wish to search from the start of a String or from a particular position. This method returns true if a match is found and false otherwise:

```
String letters = "ABCAB";
System.out.println(letters.startsWith("AB"));        ⟵    Prints true
System.out.println(letters.startsWith("a"));        ⟵    Prints false
System.out.println(letters.startsWith("A", 3));        ⟵    Prints true
```

The method endsWith() tests whether a String ends with a particular suffix. It returns true for a matching value and false otherwise:

```
System.out.println(letters.endsWith("CAB"));          ◄─────┐  Prints true
System.out.println(letters.endsWith("B"));            ◄────────  Prints true
System.out.println(letters.endsWith("b"));            ◄──────  Prints false
```

### METHOD CHAINING

It's common practice to use multiple String methods in a single line of code, as follows:

```
String result = "Sunday  ".replace(' ', 'Z').trim().concat("M n");
System.out.println(result);                           ◄──────┐  Prints SundayZZM n
```

The methods are evaluated from left to right. The first method to execute in this example is replace, not concat.

Method chaining is one of the favorite topics of the exam authors. You're sure to encounter a question on method chaining in the OCA Java SE 8 Programmer I exam.

**EXAM TIP**   When chained, the methods are evaluated from left to right.

Note that there's a difference between calling a chain of methods on a String object versus doing the same and then reassigning the return value to the same variable:

```
String day = "SunDday";
day.replace('D', 'Z').substring(3);        ◄─── Calls methods replace and substring on day
System.out.println(day);
day = day.replace('D', 'Z').substring(3);  ◄───
System.out.println(day);
```

Prints Zday (for first block) — **String is immutable—no change in the value variable day; prints SunDday**

Calls methods replace and substring on day, and assigns the result back to variable day

Because String objects are immutable, their values won't change if you execute methods on them. You can, of course, reassign a value to a reference variable of type String. Watch out for related questions in the exam.

Although the next Twist in the Tale exercise may seem simple, with only two lines of code, appearances can be deceptive (answers in the appendix).

### Twist in the Tale 4.1

Let's modify some of the code used in the previous section. Execute this code on your system. Which answer correctly shows its output?

```
String letters = "ABCAB";
System.out.println(letters.substring(0, 2).startsWith('A'));
```

   a   true
   b   false

   **c** AB

   **d** ABC

   **e** Compilation error

---

### 4.1.4 *String objects and operators*

Of all the operators that are on this exam, you can use just a handful with the String objects:

- Concatenation: + and +=
- Equality: == and !=

In this section, we'll cover the concatenation operators. We'll cover the equality operators in the next section (4.1.5).

Concatenation operators (+ and +=) have a special meaning for Strings. The Java language has additional functionality defined for these operators for String. You can use the operators + and += to concatenate two String values. Behind the scenes, string concatenation is implemented by using the StringBuilder (covered in the next section) or StringBuffer (similar to StringBuilder) classes.

But remember that a String is immutable. You can't modify the value of any existing object of String. The + operator enables you to create a new object of the class String with a value equal to the concatenated values of multiple Strings. Examine the following code:

```
String aString = "OCJA"+"Cert"+"Exam";      ⟵  aString contains
                                                OCJACertExam
```

Here's another example:

```
int num = 10;
int val = 12;
String aStr = "OCJA";
String anotherStr = num + val + aStr;
System.out.println(anotherStr);      ⟵  Prints 22OCJA
```

Why do you think the value of the variable anotherStr is 22OCJA and not 1012OCJA? The + operator can be used with the primitive values, and the expression num + val + aStr is evaluated from left to right. Here's the sequence of steps executed by Java to evaluate the expression:

- Add operands num and val to get 22.
- Concatenate 22 with OCJA to get 22OCJA.

If you wish to treat the numbers stored in variables num and val as String values, modify the expression as follows:

```
anotherStr = "" + num + val + aStr;      ⟵  Evaluates to
                                             1012OCJA
```

**A practical tip on String concatenation**

During my preparation for my Java Programmer certification, I learned how the output changes in String concatenation when the order of values being concatenated is changed. At work, it helped me to quickly debug a Java application that was logging incorrect values to a log file. It didn't take me long to discover that the offending line of code was `logToFile("Shipped:" + numReceived() + inTransit());`. The methods were returning correct values individually, but the return values of these methods were not being added. They were being *concatenated* as `String` values, resulting in the unexpected output.

One solution is to enclose the `int` addition within parentheses, as in `logToFile("Shipped:"+ (numReceived() + inTransit()));`. This code will log the text `"Shipped"` with the sum of the numeric values returned by the methods `numReceived()` and `inTransit()`.

When you use `+=` to concatenate `String` values, ensure that the variable you're using has been initialized (and doesn't contain `null`). Look at the following code:

```
String lang = "Java";
lang += " is everywhere!";                    ←──|  lang is assigned
String initializedToNull = null;                    "Java is everywhere"
initializedToNull += "Java";
System.out.println(initializedToNull);        ←──|  Prints nullJava
```

## 4.1.5   *Determining equality of Strings*

The correct way to compare two `String` values for equality is to use the `equals` method defined in the `String` class. This method returns a `true` value if the object being compared to it isn't `null`, is a `String` object, and represents the same sequence of characters as the object to which it's being compared.

**EQUALS METHOD**
The following listing shows the method definitions of the `equals` method defined in class `String` in the Java API.

**Listing 4.1   Method definition of the `equals` method from the class `String`**

```
public boolean equals(Object anObject) {
    if (this == anObject) {
        return true;
    }
    if (anObject instanceof String) {
        String anotherString = (String)anObject;
        int n = count;
        if (n == anotherString.count) {
            char v1[] = value;
            char v2[] = anotherString.value;
            int i = offset;
            int j = anotherString.offset;
```

❶ Returns true if the object being compared to is the same object

❷ Executes statements in if construct if anObject is of type String

❸ Continues comparison if the length of String values being compared is equal

```
        while (n-- != 0) {
            if (v1[i++] != v2[j++])
                return false;
        }
            return true;
    }
}
    return false;
}
```

**④** Compares individual String characters;
returns false if there's a mismatch with
any individual String character

**⑤** Returns true if all characters of String anObject
successfully matched with this object

**⑥** Returns false if the object being compared
to is not of type String or the lengths of
the compared Strings don't match

In listing 4.1, the equals method accepts a method parameter of type Object and returns a boolean value. Let's walk through the equals method defined by the class String:

- **❶** compares the object reference variables. If the reference variables are the same, they refer to the same object.
- **❷** compares the type of the method parameter to this object. If the method parameter passed to this method is not of type String, **❻** returns false.
- **❸** checks whether the lengths of the String values being compared are equal.
- **❹** compares the individual characters of the String values. It returns false if a mismatch is found at any position. If no mismatch is found, **❺** returns true.

**COMPARING REFERENCE VARIABLES TO INSTANCE VALUES**
Examine the following code:

```
String var1 = new String("Java");
String var2 = new String("Java");
System.out.println(var1.equals(var2));      Prints true
System.out.println(var1 == var2);           Prints false
```

The operator == compares the reference variables, that is, whether the variables refer to the same object. Hence, var1 == var2 in the previous code prints false. Now examine the following code:

```
String var3 = "code";
String var4 = "code";
System.out.println(var3.equals(var4));      Prints true
System.out.println(var3 == var4);           Prints true
```

Even though comparing var3 and var4 using the operator == prints true, you should *never* use this operator for comparing String values. The variables var3 and var4 refer to the same String object created and shared in the pool of String objects. (We discussed the pool of String objects in section 4.1.1 earlier in this chapter.) The == operator won't always return the value true, even if the two objects store the same String values.

**EXAM TIP**   The operator == compares whether the reference variables refer to the same objects, and the method `equals` compares the `String` values for equality. Always use the `equals` method to compare two `Strings` for equality. Never use the == operator for this purpose.

You can use the operator != to compare the inequality of objects referred to by `String` variables. It's the inverse of the operator ==. Let's compare the usage of the operator != with the operator == and the method `equals()`:

```
String var1 = new String("Java");
String var2 = new String("Java");
System.out.println(var1.equals(var2));        ⟵┐ Prints true
System.out.println(var1 == var2);             ⟵┘ Prints false
System.out.println(var1 != var2);             ⟵── Prints true
```

The following example uses the operators != and == and the method `equals` to compare `String` variables that refer to the same object in the `String` constant pool:

```
String var3 = "code";
String var4 = "code";
System.out.println(var3.equals(var4));        ⟵┐ Prints true
System.out.println(var3 == var4);             ⟵┘ Prints true
System.out.println(var3 != var4);             ⟵── Prints false
```

As you can see, in both of the previous examples the operator != returns the inverse of the value returned by the operator ==.

### EQUALITY OF VALUES RETURNED BY STRING METHODS

Do you think the `String` values returned by methods are stored in the `String` pool? Will they return `true` when their variable references are compared using the == operator? Let's find out:

```
String lang1 = "Java";
String lang2 = "JaScala";

String returnValue1 = lang1.substring(0,1);
String returnValue2 = lang2.substring(0,1);
                                                          ┐ Outputs false
System.out.println(returnValue1 == returnValue2);       ⟵┘
System.out.println(returnValue1.equals(returnValue2));  ⟵── Outputs true
```

In the preceding code, the call to `lang1.substring()` and `lang2.subtring()` will return `"Ja"`. But these string values aren't stored in the `String` pool. This is because these substrings are created using the new operator in `String`'s method `substring` (and other `String` methods). This is confirmed by comparing their reference variables using the == operator, which returns `false`.

**EXAM TIP**  Watch out for the exam questions that test you on using the `==` operator with `String` values returned by methods of the class `String`. Because these values are created using the `new` operator, they aren't placed in the `String` pool.

Because `Strings` are immutable, we also need a mutable sequence of characters that can be manipulated. Let's work with the other type of string on the OCA Java SE 8 Programmer I exam: `StringBuilder`.

## 4.2  *Mutable strings: StringBuilder*

    [9.1]   Manipulate data using the StringBuilder class and its methods

The class `StringBuilder` is defined in the package `java.lang`, and it has a mutable sequence of characters. You should use the class `StringBuilder` when you're dealing with larger strings or modifying the contents of a string often. Doing so will improve the performance of your code. Unlike `StringBuilder`, the `String` class has an immutable sequence of characters. Every time you modify a string that's represented by the `String` class, your code creates new `String` objects instead of modifying the existing one.

 **EXAM TIP**  You can expect questions on the need for the `StringBuilder` class and its comparison with the `String` class.

Let's work with the methods of the class `StringBuilder`. Because `StringBuilder` represents a mutable sequence of characters, the main operations on `StringBuilder` are related to the modification of its value by adding another value at the end or at a particular position, deleting characters, or changing characters at a particular position.

### 4.2.1  *The StringBuilder class is mutable*

In contrast to the class `String`, the class `StringBuilder` uses a non–final char array to store its value. Following is a partial definition of the class `AbstractStringBuilder` (the superclass of the class `StringBuilder`). It includes the declaration of the variables `value` and `count`, which are used to store the value of `StringBuilder` and its length, respectively (the relevant code is in bold):

```
abstract class AbstractStringBuilder implements Appendable, CharSequence {
    /**
     * The value is used for character storage.
     */
    char value[];
    /**
     * The count is the number of characters used.
     */
    int count;
//.. rest of the code
}
```

This information will come in handy when we discuss the methods of class String-Builder in the following sections.

### 4.2.2   *Creating StringBuilder objects*

You can create objects of the class StringBuilder using multiple overloaded constructors, as follows:

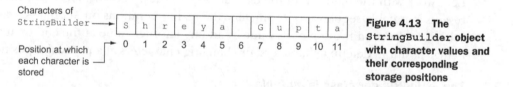

```
class CreateStringBuilderObjects {
    public static void main(String args[]) {
        StringBuilder sb1 = new StringBuilder();
        StringBuilder sb2 = new StringBuilder(sb1);
        StringBuilder sb3 = new StringBuilder(50);
        StringBuilder sb4 = new StringBuilder("Shreya Gupta");
    }
}
```

**①** No-argument constructor

**②** Constructor that accepts a StringBuilder object

**③** Constructor that accepts an int value specifying initial capacity of StringBuilder object

**④** Constructor that accepts a String

**①** constructs a StringBuilder object with no characters in it and an initial capacity of 16 characters. **②** constructs a StringBuilder object that contains the same set of characters as contained by the StringBuilder object passed to it. **③** constructs a String-Builder object with no characters and an initial capacity of 50 characters. **④** constructs a StringBuilder object with an initial value as contained by the String object. Figure 4.13 illustrates StringBuilder object sb4 with the value Shreya Gupta.

Characters of StringBuilder ⟶

| S | h | r | e | y | a | | G | u | p | t | a |
|---|---|---|---|---|---|---|---|---|---|---|---|
| 0 | 1 | 2 | 3 | 4 | 5 | 6 | 7 | 8 | 9 | 10 | 11 |

Position at which each character is stored

**Figure 4.13**   The StringBuilder object with character values and their corresponding storage positions

When you create a StringBuilder object using its default constructor, the following code executes behind the scenes to initialize the array value defined in the class StringBuilder itself:

```
StringBuilder() {
    value = new char[16];
}
```

Creates an array of length 16

When you create a StringBuilder object by passing it a String, the following code executes behind the scenes to initialize the array value:

```
public StringBuilder(String str) {
    value = new char[str.length() + 16];
    append(str);
}
```

Creates an array of length 16+ str.length

The creation of objects for the class StringBuilder is the basis for the next Twist in the Tale exercise. Your task in this exercise is to look up the Java API documentation or the Java source code to answer the question. You can access the Java API documentation in a couple of ways:

- View it online at http://docs.oracle.com/javase/8/docs/api/.
- Download it to your system from http://www.oracle.com/technetwork/java/javase/documentation/jdk8-doc-downloads-2133158.html. Accept the license agreement and click the link for jdk-8u66-docs-all.zip to download it. (These links may change eventually as Oracle updates its website.)

The answer to the following Twist in the Tale exercise is given in the appendix.

---

**Twist in the Tale 4.2**

Take a look at the Java API documentation or the Java source code files and answer the following question:

Which of the following options (there's just one correct answer) correctly creates an object of the class StringBuilder with a default capacity of 16 characters?

- **a** StringBuilder name = StringBuilder.getInstance();
- **b** StringBuilder name = StringBuilder.createInstance();
- **c** StringBuilder name = StringBuilder.buildInstance();
- **d** None of the above

---

### 4.2.3 *Methods of class StringBuilder*

You'll be pleased to learn that many of the methods defined in the class String-Builder work exactly like the versions in the class String—for example, methods such as charAt, indexOf, substring, and length. We won't discuss these again for the class StringBuilder. In this section, we'll discuss the other main methods of the class StringBuilder: append, insert, and delete.

Figure 4.14 shows the categorization of this class's methods.

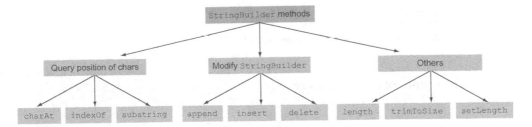

**Figure 4.14  Categorization of StringBuilder methods**

**APPEND()**

The append method adds the specified value at the end of the existing value of a
StringBuilder object. Because you may want to add data from multiple data types to
a StringBuilder object, this method has been overloaded so that it can accept data of
any type.

This method accepts all the primitives, String, char array, and Object, as method
parameters, as shown in the following example:

```
class AppendStringBuilder {
    public static void main(String args[]) {          Appends boolean
        StringBuilder sb1 = new StringBuilder();
        sb1.append(true);                          ◄──       Appends int
        sb1.append(10);                              ◄──
        sb1.append('a');                                ◄──   Appends char
        sb1.append(20.99);                              ◄──
        sb1.append("Hi");                            ◄──     Appends double
        System.out.println(sb1);       ◄──
    }                                   ◄── Appends String
}                                    Prints
                                     true10a20.99Hi
```

You can append a complete char array, StringBuilder, or String or its subset as follows:

```
StringBuilder sb1 = new StringBuilder();         Starting with position 1
char[] name = {'J', 'a', 'v', 'a', '8'};         append 3 characters,
sb1.append(name, 1, 3);              ◄──          position 1 inclusive
System.out.println(sb1);          ◄── Prints ava
```

Because the method append also accepts a method parameter of type Object, you can
pass it any object from the Java API or your own user-defined object:

```
class AppendStringBuilder2 {
    public static void main(String args[]) {        Append String
        StringBuilder sb1 = new StringBuilder();
        sb1.append("Java");                      ◄──        Append object
        sb1.append(new Person("Oracle"));      ◄──          of class Person
        System.out.println(sb1);        ◄──
    }                                     Doesn't print
}                                        JavaOracle
class Person {
    String name;
    Person(String str) { name = str; }
}
```

The output of the previous code is

```
JavaPerson@126b249
```

In this output, the hex value (126b249) that follows the @ sign may differ on your system.

When you append an object's value to a `StringBuilder`, the method `append` calls the static `String.valueOf()` method. The version taking an `Object` parameter returns the four-letter string "null" if the parameter is `null`; otherwise, it calls its `toString` method. If the `toString` method has been overridden by the class, then the method `append` adds the `String` value returned by it to the target `StringBuilder` object. In the absence of the overridden `toString` method, the `toString` method defined in the class `Object` executes. For your information, the default implementation of the method `toString` in the class `Object` returns the name of the class followed by the @ char and unsigned hexadecimal representation of the hash code of the object (the value returned by the object's `hashCode` method).

**EXAM TIP** For classes that haven't overridden the `toString` method, the `append` method results in appending the output from the default implementation of method `toString` defined in the class `Object` (if the parameter isn't `null`).

It's interesting to take a quick look at how the `append` method works for the class `StringBuilder`. Following is a partial code listing of the method `append` that accepts a boolean parameter (as explained in the comments):

```
public AbstractStringBuilder append(boolean b) {
    if (b) {
        int newCount = count + 4;
        if (newCount > value.length)
            expandCapacity(newCount);
        value[count++] = 't';
        value[count++] = 'r';
        value[count++] = 'u';
        value[count++] = 'e';
    } else {
        ...
    }
    return this;
}
```

❶ Adds 4 (length of "true") to count, which holds the number of characters in the StringBuilder

❷ Checks if value array is long enough and expands if required

❸ Adds the text "true", letter by letter

Code to append false

❶ and ❷ determine whether the array `value` can accommodate four additional characters corresponding to the boolean literal value `true`. At ❷, the call to expand-Capacity() increases the capacity of the array `value` (used to store the characters of a `StringBuilder` object) if it isn't big enough. ❸ adds individual characters of the boolean value `true` to the array `value`.

### INSERT()

The `insert` method is as powerful as the `append` method. It also exists in multiple flavors (read: overloaded methods) that accept any data type. The main difference between the `append` and `insert` methods is that the `insert` method enables you to insert the requested data at a particular position, but the append method allows you to add the requested data only at the end of the StringBuilder object:

```
class InsertStringBuilder {
    public static void main(String args[]) {
        StringBuilder sb1 = new StringBuilder("Bon");
        sb1.insert(2, 'r');                          Inserts r at
        System.out.println(sb1);                     position 2
    }
}                                                    Prints Born
```

Figure 4.15 illustrates the previous code.

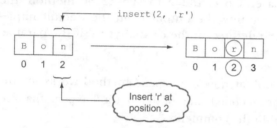

**Figure 4.15   Inserting a char using the method** insert **in** StringBuilder

As with String objects, the first character of StringBuilder is stored at position 0. Hence, the previous code inserts the letter r at position 2, which is occupied by the letter n. You can also insert a complete char array, StringBuffer, or String or its subset, as follows:

```
StringBuilder sb1 = new StringBuilder("123");      Insert at sb1 position 1,
char[] name = {'J', 'a', 'v', 'a'};                values ava from String name
sb1.insert(1, name, 1, 3);
System.out.println(sb1);                            Prints 1ava23
```

Figure 4.16 illustrates the previous code.

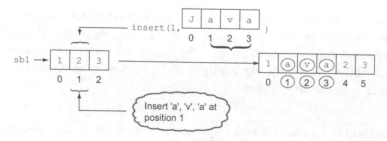

**Figure 4.16   Inserting a substring of** String **in** StringBuilder

**EXAM TIP** Take note of the start and end positions when inserting a value in a `StringBuilder`. Multiple flavors of the insert method defined in `String-Builder` may confuse you because they can be used to insert either single or multiple characters.

### DELETE() AND DELETECHARAT()

The method `delete` removes the characters in a substring of the specified `String-Builder`. The method `deleteCharAt` removes the `char` at the specified position. Here's an example showing the method `delete`:

```
class DeleteStringBuilder {
    public static void main(String args[]) {
        StringBuilder sb1 = new StringBuilder("0123456");
        sb1.delete(2, 4);
        System.out.println(sb1);
    }
}
```

❶ **Removes characters at positions starting from 2 to 4, excluding 4**

**Prints 01456**

❶ removes characters at positions 2 and 3. The `delete` method doesn't remove the letter at position 4. Figure 4.17 illustrates the previous code.

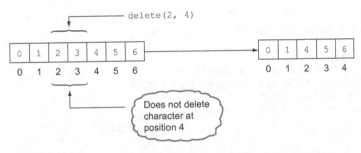

**Figure 4.17 The method `delete(2,4)` doesn't delete the character at position 4.**

The method `deleteCharAt` is simple. It removes a single character, as follows:

```
class DeleteStringBuilder {
    public static void main(String args[]) {
        StringBuilder sb1 = new StringBuilder("0123456");
        sb1.deleteCharAt(2);
        System.out.println(sb1);
    }
}
```

**Deletes character at position 2**

**Prints 013456**

 **EXAM TIP** Combinations of the `deleteCharAt` and insert methods can be quite confusing.

### TRIM()

Unlike the class `String`, the class `StringBuilder` doesn't define the method `trim`. An attempt to use it with this class will prevent your code from compiling. The only reason I'm describing a nonexistent method here is to ward off any confusion.

### REVERSE()

As the name suggests, the reverse method reverses the sequence of characters of a `StringBuilder`:

```
class ReverseStringBuilder {
    public static void main(String args[]) {
        StringBuilder sb1 = new StringBuilder("0123456");
        sb1.reverse();
        System.out.println(sb1);                    ⟵┐  Prints
    }                                                  │  6543210
}
```

 **EXAM TIP**   You can't use the method `reverse` to reverse a substring of `String-Builder`.

### REPLACE()

Unlike the `replace` method defined in the class `String`, the `replace` method in the class `StringBuilder` replaces a sequence of characters, identified by their positions, with another `String`, as in the following example:

```
class ReplaceStringBuilder {
    public static void main(String args[]) {
        StringBuilder sb1 = new StringBuilder("0123456");
        sb1.replace(2, 4, "ABCD");
        System.out.println(sb1);             ⟵┐  Prints
    }                                          │  01ABCD456
}
```

Figure 4.18 shows a comparison of the replace methods defined in the classes `String` and `StringBuilder`.

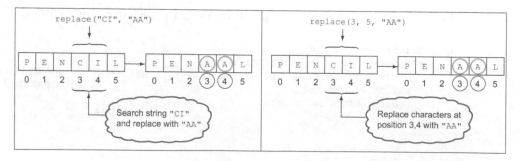

**Figure 4.18  Comparing the `replace` methods in `String` (left) and `StringBuilder` (right). The method `replace` in `String` accepts the characters to be replaced. The method `replace` in `StringBuilder` accepts a position to be replaced.**

**SUBSEQUENCE()**

Apart from using the method `substring`, you can also use the method `subSequence` to retrieve a subsequence of a `StringBuilder` object. This method returns objects of type `CharSequence`:

```
class SubSequenceStringBuilder {
    public static void main(String args[]) {
        StringBuilder sb1 = new StringBuilder("0123456");
        System.out.println(sb1.subSequence(2, 4));
        System.out.println(sb1);
    }
}
```

**Prints 23**

**Prints 0123456**

The method `subsequence` doesn't modify the existing value of a `StringBuilder` object.

### 4.2.4 A quick note on the class StringBuffer

Although the OCA Java SE 8 Programmer I exam objectives don't mention the class `StringBuffer`, you may see it in the list of (incorrect) answers in the OCA exam.

The classes `StringBuffer` and `StringBuilder` offer the same functionality, with one difference: the methods of the class `StringBuffer` are synchronized where necessary, whereas the methods of the class `StringBuilder` aren't. What does this mean? When you work with the class `StringBuffer`, only one thread out of multiple threads can execute your method. This arrangement prevents any inconsistencies in the values of the instance variables that are modified by these (synchronized) methods. But it introduces additional overhead, so working with synchronized methods and the `StringBuffer` class affects the performance of your code.

The class `StringBuilder` offers the same functionality as offered by `StringBuffer`, minus the additional feature of synchronized methods. Often your code won't be accessed by multiple threads, so it won't need the overhead of thread synchronization. If you need to access your code from multiple threads, use `StringBuffer`; otherwise use `StringBuilder`.

## 4.3 Arrays

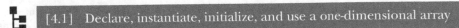

[4.1]  Declare, instantiate, initialize, and use a one-dimensional array

[4.2]  Declare, instantiate, initialize, and use a multidimensional array

In this section, I'll cover declaration, allocation, and initialization of one-dimensional and multidimensional arrays. You'll learn about the differences between arrays of primitive data types and arrays of objects.

### 4.3.1   *What is an array?*

An array is an object that stores a collection of values. The fact that an array itself is an object is often overlooked. I'll reiterate: an array is an object itself; it stores references to the data it stores. Arrays can store two types of data:

- A collection of primitive data types
- A collection of objects

An array of primitives stores a collection of values that constitute the primitive values themselves. (With primitives, there are no objects to reference.) An array of objects stores a collection of values, which are in fact heap-memory addresses or pointers. The addresses point to (reference) the object instances that your array is said to store, which means that object arrays store references (to objects) and primitive arrays store primitive values.

The members of an array are defined in contiguous (continuous) memory locations and hence offer improved access speed. (You should be able to quickly access all the students of a class if they all can be found next to each other.)

The following code creates an array of primitive data and an array of objects:

```
class CreateArray {
    public static void main(String args[]) {                Array of
        int intArray[] = new int[] {4, 8, 107};            primitive data
        String objArray[] = new String[] {"Harry", "Shreya",
                                          "Paul", "Selvan"};    Array of
    }                                                           objects
}
```

I'll discuss the details of creating arrays shortly. The previous example shows one of the ways to create arrays. Figure 4.19 illustrates the arrays `intArray` and `objArray`. Unlike `intArray`, `objArray` stores references to `String` objects.

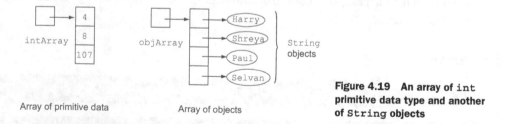

**Figure 4.19   An array of `int` primitive data type and another of `String` objects**

   **NOTE**   Arrays are objects and refer to a collection of primitive data types or other objects.

In Java, you can define one-dimensional and multidimensional arrays. A *one-dimensional array* is an object that refers to a collection of scalar values. A two-dimensional (or more) array is referred to as a *multidimensional array*. A two-dimensional array refs to a collection of objects in which each of the objects is a one-dimensional array. Similarly, a three-dimensional array refers to a collection of two-dimensional arrays, and so on. Figure 4.20 depicts a one-dimensional array and multidimensional arrays (two-dimensional and three-dimensional).

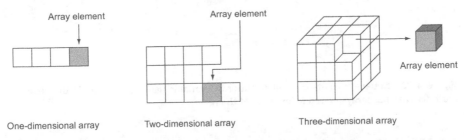

**Figure 4.20   One-dimensional and multidimensional (two- and three-dimensional) arrays**

Note that multidimensional arrays may or may not contain the same number of elements in each row or column, as shown in the two-dimensional array in figure 4.20.

Creating an array involves three steps, as follows:

- Declaring the array
- Allocating the array
- Initializing the array elements

You can create an array by executing the previous steps using separate lines of code or you can combine these steps on the same line of code. Let's start with the first approach: completing each step on a separate line of code.

### 4.3.2   Array declaration

An array declaration includes the array *type* and array *variable*, as shown in figure 4.21. The type of objects that an array can store depends on its type. An array type is followed by one or more empty pairs of square brackets [].

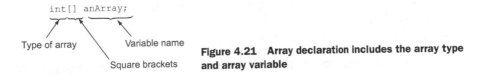

**Figure 4.21   Array declaration includes the array type and array variable**

To declare an array, specify its type, followed by the name of the array variable. Here's an example of declaring arrays of int and String values:

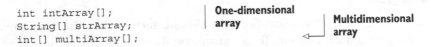

```
int intArray[];
String[] strArray;
int[] multiArray[];
```

The number of bracket pairs indicates the depth of array nesting. Java doesn't impose any theoretical limit on the level of array nesting. The square brackets can follow the array type or its name, as shown in figure 4.22.

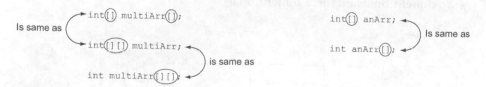

Figure 4.22   **Square brackets can follow either the variable name or its type. In the case of multidimensional arrays, it can follow both of them.**

 **NOTE**   In an array declaration, placing the square brackets next to the type (as in `int []` or `int [] []`) is preferred because it makes the code easier to read by showing the array types in use.

The array declaration only creates a variable that refers to `null`, as shown in figure 4.23.

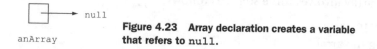

Figure 4.23   **Array declaration creates a variable that refers to `null`.**

Because no elements of an array are created when it's declared, it's invalid to define the size of an array with its declaration. The following code won't compile:

```
int intArray[2];
String[5] strArray;
int[2] multiArray[3];
```

**Array size can't be defined with the array declaration. This code won't compile.**

An array type can be any of the following:

- Primitive data type
- Interface
- Abstract class
- Concrete class

We declared an array of an `int` primitive type and a concrete class `String` previously. I'll discuss some complex examples with abstract classes and interfaces in section 4.3.7.

 **NOTE**   Arrays can be of any data type other than `null`.

### 4.3.3   *Array allocation*

As the name suggests, array allocation will allocate memory for the elements of an array. When you allocate memory for an array, you should specify its dimensions, such as the number of elements the array should store. Note that the size of an array can't expand or reduce once it is allocated. Here are a few examples:

```
int intArray[];                    Array
String[] strArray;                 declaration
int[] multiArr[];
intArray = new int[2];             Note use of keyword new
strArray = new String[4];          to allocate an array
multiArr = new int[2][3];
```

Because an array is an object, it's allocated using the keyword new, followed by the type of value that it stores, and then its size. The code won't compile if you don't specify the size of the array or if you place the array size on the left of the = sign, as follows:

```
                                        Won't compile; array
                                        size missing
intArray = new int[];
intArray[2] = new int;        Won't compile; array
                              size placed incorrectly
```

The size of the array must evaluate to an int value. You can't create an array with its size specified as a floating-point number. The following line of code won't compile:

```
                              Won't compile; can't define size of
intArray = new int[2.4];      an array as a floating-point number
```

Java accepts an expression to specify the size of an array, as long as it evaluates to an int value. The following are valid array allocations:

```
                                   2*5 evaluates to
                                   an integer value.
strArray = new String[2*5];
int x = 10, y = 4;                      This is acceptable; expression x*y
strArray = new String[x*y];             evaluates to an integer value.
strArray  = new String[Math.max(2, 3)];
                                   This is acceptable; Math.max(2,3)
                                   returns an int value.
```

Let's allocate the multidimensional array multiArr, as follows:

```
int[] multiArr[];          Array declaration
multiArr = new int[2][3];                 OK to define size in
                                          both square brackets
```

You can also allocate the multidimensional array multiArr by defining size in only the first square brackets:

```
multiArr = new int[2][];          OK to define the size in only
                                  the first square bracket
```

It's interesting to note the difference between what happens when the multidimensional array `multiArr` is allocated by defining sizes for a single dimension or for both of its dimensions. This difference is shown in figure 4.24.

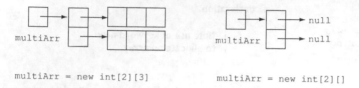

```
multiArr = new int[2][3]        multiArr = new int[2][]
```

**Figure 4.24   The difference in array allocation of a two-dimensional array when it's allocated using values for only one of its dimensions and for both of its dimensions**

You can't allocate a multidimensional array as follows:

```
int[] multiArr[];                    Multidimensional
multiArr = new int[];                array declaration
multiArr = new int[][3];             Nonmatching
                                     square brackets ❶
                          Size in first square
                       ❷ bracket missing
```

❶ won't compile because there's a mismatch in the number of square brackets on both sides of the assignment operator (=). The compiler required `[][]` on the right side of the assignment operator, but it finds only `[]`. ❷ won't compile because you can't allocate a multidimensional array without including a size in the first square bracket and defining a size in the second square bracket.

Once allocated, the array elements store their default values. For arrays that store objects, all the allocated array elements store `null`. For arrays that store primitive values, the default values depend on the exact data types stored by them.

 **EXAM TIP**   Once allocated, all the array elements store their default values. Elements in an array that store objects default to `null`. Elements of an array that store primitive data types store `0` for integer types (`byte`, `short`, `int`, `long`); `0.0` for decimal types (`float` and `double`); `false` for `boolean`; or `\u0000` for `char` data.

### 4.3.4   *Array initialization*

You can initialize an array as follows:

```
                                          Array declaration
int intArray[];
intArray = new int[2];                    Array allocation
for (int i=0; i<intArray.length; i++) {
    intArray[i] = i + 5;                  ❶ Initializes array
}                                            using a for loop
```

```
intArray[0] = 10;          ❷ Reinitializes individual
intArray[1] = 1870;           array elements
```

In the preceding code, ❶ uses a for loop to initialize the array `intArray` with the required values. ❷ initializes the individual array elements without using a `for` loop. Note that all array objects use their public immutable field `length` to access their array size.

Similarly, a `String` array can be declared, allocated, and initialized as follows:

```
                                      Array declaration
String[] strArray;                ←─┘
strArray = new String[4];                   Array allocation
for (int i=0; i<strArray.length; i++) { ←─┘
    strArray[i] = new String("Hello" + i);       Initializes array
}                                                 using a for loop
strArray[1] = "Summer";
strArray[3] = "Winter";      Initializes array without
strArray[0] = "Autumn";      using a for loop
strArray[2] = "Spring";
```

When you initialize a two-dimensional array, you can use nested `for` loops to initialize its array elements. Also notice that to access an element in a two-dimensional array, you should use two array position values, as follows:

```
                                    Array declaration
int[] multiArr[];                ←─┘
multiArr = new int[2][3];                   Array allocation
for (int i=0; i<multiArr.length; i++) {  ←─┘
    for (int j=0; j<multiArr[i].length; j++) {
        multiArr[i][j] = i + j;                  Initializes array
    }                                            using a for loop
}
multiArr[0][0] = 10;
multiArr[1][2] = 1210;       Initializes array without
multiArr[0][1] = 110;        using a for loop
multiArr[0][2] = 1087;
```

What happens when you try to access a nonexistent array index position? The following code creates an array of size 2 but tries to access its array element at index 3:

```
                                      Length of
                                      intArray is 2      3 isn't a valid index
int intArray[] = new int[2];      ←─┘                    position for intArray.
System.out.println(intArray[3]);  ←─┘
```

The previous code will throw a runtime exception, `ArrayIndexOutOfBoundsException`. For an array of size 2, the only valid index positions are 0 and 1. All the rest of the array index positions will throw the exception `ArrayIndexOutOfBoundsException` at runtime.

**NOTE**　Don't worry if you can't immediately absorb all the information related to exceptions here. Exceptions are covered in detail in chapter 7.

The Java compiler doesn't check the range of the index positions at which you try to access an array element. You may be surprised to learn that the following line of code will compile successfully even though it uses a negative array index value:

```java
int intArray[] = new int[2];
System.out.println(intArray[-10]);
```

Length of
intArray is 2

Will compile successfully even
though it tries to access array
element at negative index

Although the previous code compiles successfully, it will throw the exception Array-IndexOutOfBoundsException at runtime. Code to access an array element will fail to compile if you don't pass it a char, byte, short, or int data type (wrapper classes are not on this exam, and I don't include them in this discussion):

```java
int intArray[] = new int[2];
System.out.println(intArray[1.2]);
```

Won't compile; can't specify array
index using floating-point number

**EXAM TIP**　Code to access an array index will throw a runtime exception if you pass it an invalid array index value. Code to access an array index will fail to compile if you don't use a char, byte, short, or int.

Also, you can't remove array positions. For an array of objects, you can set a position to the value null, but it doesn't remove the array position:

```java
String[] strArray = new String[] {"Autumn", "Summer",
                                  "Spring", "Winter"};
strArray[2] = null;
for (String val : strArray)
    System.out.println(val);
```

❶ Define an array
of String objects

❷ Can you remove an
array position like this?

❸ Outputs
four values

❶ creates an array of String and initializes it with four String values. ❷ sets the value at array index 2 to null. ❸ iterates over all the array elements. As shown in the following output, four (not three) values are printed:

```
Autumn
Summer
null
Winter
```

### 4.3.5　*Combining array declaration, allocation, and initialization*

You can combine all the previously mentioned steps of array declaration, allocation, and initialization into one step, as follows:

```java
int intArray[] = {0, 1};
String[] strArray = {"Summer", "Winter"};
int multiArray[][] = { {0, 1}, {3, 4, 5} };
```

Notice that the previous code

- Doesn't use the keyword new to initialize an array
- Doesn't specify the size of the array
- Uses a single pair of braces to define values for a one-dimensional array and multiple pairs of braces to define a multidimensional array

All the previous steps of array declaration, allocation, and initialization can be combined in the following way, as well:

```
int intArray2[] = new int[]{0, 1};
String[] strArray2 = new String[]{"Summer", "Winter"};
int multiArray2[][] = new int[][]{ {0, 1}, {3, 4, 5}};
```

Unlike the first approach, the preceding code uses the keyword new to initialize an array.
    If you try to specify the size of an array with the preceding approach, the code won't compile. Here are a few examples:

```
int intArray2[] = new int[2]{0, 1};
String[] strArray2 = new String[2]{"Summer", "Winter"};
int multiArray2[][] = new int[2][]{ {0, 1}, {3, 4, 5}};
```

 **EXAM TIP**   When you combine an array declaration, allocation, and initialization in a single step, you can't specify the size of the array. The size of the array is calculated by the number of values that are assigned to the array.

Another important point to note is that if you declare and initialize an array using two separate lines of code, you'll use the keyword new to initialize the values. The following lines of code are correct:

```
int intArray[];
intArray = new int[]{0, 1};
```

But you can't miss the keyword new and initialize your array as follows:

```
int intArray[];
intArray = {0, 1};
```

### 4.3.6   *Asymmetrical multidimensional arrays*

At the beginning of this section, I mentioned that a multidimensional array can be asymmetrical. An array can define a different number of columns for each of its rows.
    The following example is an asymmetrical two-dimensional array:

```
String multiStrArr[][] = new String[][]{
                                    {"A", "B"},
                                    null,
                                    {"Jan", "Feb", "Mar"},
                            };
```

Figure 4.25 shows this asymmetrical array.

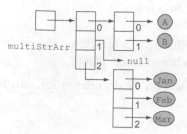

**Figure 4.25   An asymmetrical array**

As you might have noticed, `multiStrArr[1]` refers to a null value. An attempt to access any element of this array, such as `multiStrArr[1][0]`, will throw an exception. This brings us to the next Twist in the Tale exercise (answers are in the appendix).

**Twist in the Tale 4.3**

Modify some of the code used in the previous example as follows:

```
Line1> String multiStrArr[][] = new String[][]{
Line2>                                  {"A", "B"},
Line3>                                  null,
Line4>                                  {"Jan", "Feb", null},
Line5>                                  };
```

Which of the following individual options are true for the previous code?

a   Code on line 4 is the same as {"Jan", "Feb", null, null},.

b   No value is stored at `multiStrArr[2][2]`.

c   No value is stored at `multiStrArr[1][1]`.

d   Array `multiStrArr` is asymmetric.

## 4.3.7   *Arrays of type interface, abstract class, and class Object*

In the section on array declaration, I mentioned that the type of an array can also be an interface or an abstract class. What values do elements of these arrays store? Let's look at some examples.

### INTERFACE TYPE

If the type of an array is an interface, its elements are either null or objects that implement the relevant interface type. For example, for the interface `MyInterface`, the array `interfaceArray` can store references to objects of either the class `MyClass1` or `MyClass2`:

```
interface MyInterface {}
class MyClass1 implements MyInterface {}
```

```
class MyClass2 implements MyInterface {}
class Test {
MyInterface[] interfaceArray = new MyInterface[]
                                {
                                        new MyClass1(),
                                        null,
                                        new MyClass2()
                                };
}
```

## ABSTRACT CLASS TYPE

If the type of an array is an `abstract` class, its elements are either `null` or objects of concrete classes that extend the relevant `abstract` class:

```
abstract class Vehicle{}
class Car extends Vehicle {}
class Bus extends Vehicle {}
class Test {
        Vehicle[] vehicleArray = { new Car(),
                                   new Bus(),        ←┐  null is a valid
                                   null};             │  element.
}
```

Next, I'll discuss a special case in which the type of an array is `Object`.

## OBJECT

Because all classes extend the class `java.lang.Object`, elements of an array whose type is `java.lang.Object` can refer to any object. Here's an example:

```
interface MyInterface {}
class MyClass1 implements MyInterface {}
abstract class Vehicle{}
class Car extends Vehicle {}
class Test {
Object[] objArray = new Object[] {
                    new MyClass1(),                    null is a valid
                    null,                          ←┐  element.
                    new Car(),
                    new java.util.Date(),
                    new String("name"),
                    new Integer [7]                ←┐  Array element of type Object
        };                                       ❶  can refer to another array
    }
```

❶ is valid code. Because an array is an object, the element of the array of `java.lang` `.Object` can refer to another array. Figure 4.26 illustrates the previously created array, `objArray`.

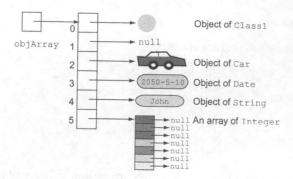

**Figure 4.26    An array of class `Object`**

### 4.3.8    *Members of an array*

Array objects have the following `public` members:

- `length`—The public variable `length` stores the number of elements of the array.
- `clone()`—This method overrides the method `clone` defined in the class `Object` but doesn't throw checked exceptions. The return type of this method is the same as the array's type. For example, for an array of type `Type[]`, this method returns `Type[]`.
- *Inherited methods*—Methods inherited from the class `Object`, except the method `clone`.

As mentioned in the earlier section on the `String` class, a `String` uses the method `length()` to retrieve its length. With an array, you can use the array's variable `length` to determine the number of the array's elements. In the exam, you may be tricked by code that tries to access the *length* of a `String` using the variable `length`. Note the correct combination of class and member used to access its length:

- `String`—Retrieve length using the method `length()`
- *Array*—Determine element count using the variable `length`

I have an interesting way to remember this rule. As opposed to an array, you'll invoke a *lot* of methods on `String` objects. So you use the *method* `length()` to retrieve the length of `String` and the *variable* `length` to retrieve the length of an array.

## 4.4    *ArrayList*

   [9.4]   Declare and use an ArrayList of a given type

In this section, I'll cover how to use `ArrayList`, its commonly used methods, and the advantages it offers over an array.

The OCA Java SE 8 Programmer I exam covers only one class from the Java Collection API: `ArrayList`. The rest of the classes from the Java Collection API are covered in the OCP Java SE 8 Programmer II exam (exam number 1Z0-809). One of the reasons to include this class in the Java Associate exam could be how frequently this class is used by all Java programmers.

ArrayList is one of the most widely used classes from the Collections framework. It offers the best combination of features offered by an *array* and the *List* data structure. The most commonly used operations with a list are *add items to a list, modify items in a list, delete items from a list,* and *iterate over the items.*

One frequently asked question by Java developers is, "Why should I bother with an ArrayList when I can already store objects of the same type in an array?" The answer lies in the ease of use of an ArrayList. This is an important question, and this exam contains explicit questions on the practical reasons for using an ArrayList.

You can compare an ArrayList with a resizable array. As you know, once it's created, you can't increase or decrease the size of an array. On the other hand, an ArrayList automatically increases and decreases in size as elements are added to or removed from it. Also, unlike arrays, you don't need to specify an initial size to create an ArrayList.

Let's compare an ArrayList and an array with real-world objects. Just as a balloon can increase and decrease in size when it's inflated or deflated, an ArrayList can increase or decrease in size as values are added to it or removed from it. One comparison is a cricket ball, because it has a predefined size. Once created, like an array, it can't increase or decrease in size.

Here are a few more important properties of an ArrayList:

- It implements the interface List.
- It allows null values to be added to it.
- It implements all list operations (add, modify, and delete values).
- It allows duplicate values to be added to it.
- It maintains its insertion order.
- You can use either Iterator or ListIterator to iterate over the items of an ArrayList.
- It supports generics, making it type safe. (You have to declare the type of the elements that should be added to an ArrayList with its declaration.)

### 4.4.1  Creating an ArrayList

The following example shows you how to create an ArrayList:

```
import java.util.ArrayList;                               ① Import
public class CreateArrayList {                              java.util.ArrayList
    public static void main(String args[]) {
        ArrayList<String> myArrList = new ArrayList<String>();
    }                                                    Declare an
}                                                   ArrayList object ②
```

Package java.util isn't implicitly imported into your class, which means that ① imports the class ArrayList in the class CreateArrayList defined previously. To create an `ArrayList`, you need to inform Java about the type of the objects that you want to store in this collection of objects. ❷ declares an `ArrayList` called `myArrList`, which can store `String` objects specified by the name of the class `String` between the angle brackets (`<>`). Note that the name `String` appears twice in the code at ❷, once on the left side of the equal sign and once on the right. Do you think the second one seems redundant? Congratulations, Oracle agrees with you. Starting with Java version 7, you can omit the object type on the right side of the equal sign and create an `Array-List` as follows:

```
ArrayList<String> myArrList = new ArrayList<>();
```

<— **Missing object type on right of = works in Java version 7 and above**

Many developers still work with Java SE versions prior to version 7, so you're likely to see some developers still using the older way of creating an `ArrayList`.

Take a look at what happens behind the scenes (in the Java source code) when you execute the previous statement to create an `ArrayList`. Because you didn't pass any arguments to the constructor of class `ArrayList`, its no-argument constructor will execute. Examine the definition of the following no-argument constructor defined in the class `ArrayList.java`:

```
/**
 * Constructs an empty list with an initial capacity of ten.
 */
public ArrayList() {
    this(10);
}
```

Because you can use an `ArrayList` to store any type of `Object`, `ArrayList` defines an instance variable `elementData` of type `Object[]` to store all its individual elements. Following is a partial code listing from class `ArrayList`:

```
/**
 * The array buffer into which the elements of the ArrayList are stored.
 * The capacity of the ArrayList is the length of this array buffer.
 */
private transient Object[] elementData;
```

Figure 4.27 illustrates the variable `elementData` shown within an object of `ArrayList`.

Object of `ArrayList`

**Figure 4.27**   Variable `elementData` shown within an object of `ArrayList`

Here's the definition of the constructor from the class ArrayList (ArrayList.java), which initializes the previously defined instance variable, elementData:

```
/**
 * Constructs an empty list with the specified initial capacity.
 *
 * @param   initialCapacity   the initial capacity of the list
 * @exception IllegalArgumentException if the specified initial capacity
 *              is negative
 */
public ArrayList(int initialCapacity) {
    super();
    if (initialCapacity < 0)
        throw new IllegalArgumentException("Illegal Capacity: "+
                                            initialCapacity);
    this.elementData = new Object[initialCapacity];
}
```

Wait a minute. Did you notice that an ArrayList uses an array to store its individual elements? Does that make you wonder why on earth you would need another class if it uses a type (array, to be precise) that you already know how to work with? The simple answer is that you wouldn't want to reinvent the wheel.

For an example, answer this question: to decode an image, which of the following options would you prefer?

- Creating your own class using characters to decode the image
- Using an existing class that offers the same functionality

Obviously, it makes sense to go with the second option. If you use an existing class that offers the same functionality, you get more benefits with less work. The same logic applies to ArrayList. It offers you all the benefits of using an array with none of the disadvantages. It looks and behaves like an expandable array that's modifiable.

**NOTE**  An ArrayList uses an array to store its elements. It provides you with the functionality of a dynamic array.

I'll cover how to add, modify, delete, and access the elements of an ArrayList in the following sections. Let's start with adding elements to an ArrayList.

### 4.4.2  Adding elements to an ArrayList

Let's begin by adding String objects to an ArrayList, as follows:

```
import java.util.ArrayList;
public class AddToArrayList {
    public static void main(String args[]) {
        ArrayList<String> list = new ArrayList<>();
        list.add("one");                                  ❶ Add element
        list.add("two");                                    at the end
        list.add("four");
        list.add(2, "three");         ←⎤  Add element at
    }                                  ❷  specified position
}
```

You can add a value to an ArrayList either at its end or at a specified position. ❶ adds elements at the end of list. ❷ adds an element to list at position 2. Please note that the first element of an ArrayList is stored at position 0. Hence, at ❷ the String literal value "three" will be inserted at position 2, which was occupied by the literal value "four". When a value is added to a place that's already occupied by another element, the values shift by a place to accommodate the newly added value. In this case, the literal value "four" shifted to position 3 to make way for the literal value "three" (see figure 4.28).

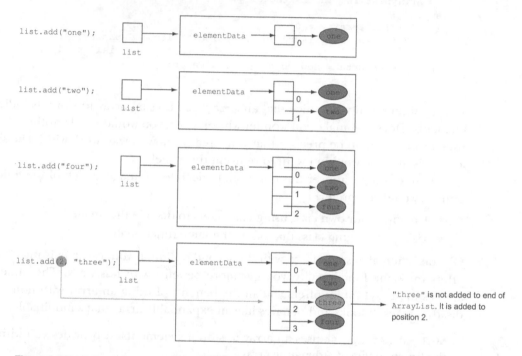

**Figure 4.28   Code that adds elements to the end of an ArrayList and at a specified position**

Let's see what happens behind the scenes in an ArrayList when you add an element to it. Here's the definition of the method add from the class ArrayList:

```
/**
 * Appends the specified element to the end of this list.
 *
 * @param e element to be appended to this list
 * @return <tt>true</tt> (as specified by {@link Collection#add})
 */
public boolean add(E e) {
    ensureCapacity(size + 1);      // Create another array with
                                   // the increased capacity
                                   // and copy existing elements to it.
```

```
        elementData[size++] = e;        // Store the newly added variable
                                        // reference at the
                                        // end of the list.

        return true;
    }
```

When you add an element to the end of the list, the ArrayList first checks whether its instance variable elementData has an empty slot at the end. If there's an empty slot at its end, it stores the element at the first available empty slot. If no empty slots exist, the method ensureCapacity creates another array with a higher capacity and copies the existing values to this newly created array. It then copies the newly added value at the first available empty slot in the array.

When you add an element at a particular position, an ArrayList creates a new array (only if there's not enough room left) and inserts all its elements at positions other than the position you specified. If there are any subsequent elements to the right of the position that you specified, it shifts them by one position. Then it adds the new element at the requested position.

> **PRACTICAL TIP**  Understanding how and why a class works in a particular manner will take you a long way in regard to both the certification exam and your career. This understanding should help you retain the information for a longer time and help you answer questions in the certification exam that are designed to verify your practical knowledge of using this class. Finally, the internal workings of a class will enable you to make informed decisions on using a particular class at your workplace and writing efficient code.

### 4.4.3  *Accessing elements of an ArrayList*

Before we modify or delete the elements of an ArrayList, let's see how to access them. To access the elements of an ArrayList, you can use get(), an enhanced for loop, Iterator, or ListIterator.

The following code accesses and prints all the elements of an ArrayList using the enhanced for loop (code to access elements is in bold):

```
import java.util.ArrayList;
public class AccessArrayList {
    public static void main(String args[]) {
        ArrayList<String> myArrList = new ArrayList<>();
        myArrList.add("One");
        myArrList.add("Two");
        myArrList.add("Four");
        myArrList.add(2, "Three");
        for (String element : myArrList) {              ❶ Code to access
            System.out.println(element);                   ArrayList elements
        }
    }
}
```

The output of the previous code is as follows:

```
One
Two
Three
Four
```

❶ defines the enhanced for loop to access all the elements of the myArrList.

Let's look at how to use a ListIterator to loop through all the values of an ArrayList:

```java
import java.util.ArrayList;
import java.util.ListIterator;
public class AccessArrayListUsingListIterator {
    public static void main(String args[]) {
        ArrayList<String> myArrList = new ArrayList<String>();
        myArrList.add("One");
        myArrList.add("Two");
        myArrList.add("Four");
        myArrList.add(2, "Three");
        ListIterator<String> iterator = myArrList.listIterator();      ❶ Get the
        while (iterator.hasNext()) {                                        iterator
            System.out.println(iterator.next());      ❸ Call next() to get    Use hasNext()
        }                                                the next item        to check
    }                                                    from iterator        whether more
}                                                                      ❷ elements exist
```

❶ gets the iterator associated with ArrayList myArrList. ❷ calls the method has-Next on iterator to check whether more elements of myArrList exist. The method hasNext returns a boolean true value if more of its elements exist and false otherwise. ❸ calls the method next on iterator to get the next item from myArrList.

The previous code prints out the same results as the code that preceded it, the code that used an enhanced for loop to access ArrayList's elements. A ListIterator doesn't contain any reference to the *current* element of an ArrayList. ListIterator provides you with a method (hasNext) to check whether more elements exist for an ArrayList. If true, you can extract its *next* element using the method next().

Note that an ArrayList preserves the insertion order of its elements. ListIterator and the enhanced for loop will return to you the elements in the order in which you added them.

**EXAM TIP**   An ArrayList preserves the order of insertion of its elements. Iterator, ListIterator, and the enhanced for loop will return the elements in the order in which they were added to the ArrayList. An iterator (Iterator or ListIterator) lets you remove elements as you iterate an ArrayList. It's not possible to remove elements from an ArrayList while iterating it using a for loop.

### 4.4.4 *Modifying the elements of an ArrayList*

You can modify an ArrayList by either replacing an existing element in the Array-List or modifying all of its existing values. The following code uses the set method to replace an element in an ArrayList:

```
import java.util.ArrayList;
public class ReplaceElementInArrayList {
    public static void main(String args[]) {
        ArrayList<String> myArrList = new ArrayList<String>();
        myArrList.add("One");
        myArrList.add("Two");
        myArrList.add("Three");                          Replace ArrayList element
        myArrList.set(1, "One and Half");          ◁——  at position 1 ("Two") with
        for (String element:myArrList)                   "One and Half"
            System.out.println(element);
    }
}
```

The output of the previous code is as follows:

```
One
One and Half
Three
```

You can also modify the existing values of an ArrayList by accessing its individual elements. Because Strings are immutable, let's try this with StringBuilder. Here's the code:

```
import java.util.ArrayList;
public class ModifyArrayListWithStringBuilder {
    public static void main(String args[]) {
        ArrayList<StringBuilder> myArrList =
                                    new ArrayList<StringBuilder>();
        myArrList.add(new StringBuilder("One"));
        myArrList.add(new StringBuilder("Two"));
        myArrList.add(new StringBuilder("Three"));
        for (StringBuilder element : myArrList)          ❶ Access ArrayList elements
            element.append(element.length());              and modify them
        for (StringBuilder element : myArrList)
            System.out.println(element);
    }
}
```

The output of this code is as follows:

```
One3
Two3
Three5
```

❶ accesses all the elements of myArrList and modifies the element value by appending its length to it. The modified value is printed by accessing myArrList elements again.

### 4.4.5   *Deleting the elements of an ArrayList*

ArrayList defines two methods to remove its elements, as follows:

- remove(int index)—This method removes the element at the specified position in this list.

- remove(Object o)—This method removes the first occurrence of the specified element from this list, if it's present.

Let's take a look at some code that uses these removal methods:

```
import java.util.ArrayList;
public class DeleteElementsFromArrayList {
    public static void main(String args[]) {
        ArrayList<StringBuilder> myArrList = new ArrayList<>();
        StringBuilder sb1 = new StringBuilder("One");
        StringBuilder sb2 = new StringBuilder("Two");
        StringBuilder sb3 = new StringBuilder("Three");
        StringBuilder sb4 = new StringBuilder("Four");
        myArrList.add(sb1);
        myArrList.add(sb2);
        myArrList.add(sb3);
        myArrList.add(sb4);                         Removes element
        myArrList.remove(1);                 ◁      at position 1
        for (StringBuilder element:myArrList)
            System.out.println(element);            Prints One,
        myArrList.remove(sb3);                      Three, and Four
        myArrList.remove(new StringBuilder("Four"));  ◁  Removes
        System.out.println();                            Three from list
        for (StringBuilder element : myArrList)
            System.out.println(element);            Prints One
    }                                               and Four
}
```

**Doesn't** ❶
**remove**
**Four**

The output of the previous code is as follows:

```
One
Three
Four
One
Four
```

❶ tries to remove the StringBuilder with the value "Four" from myArrList. The removal of the specified element fails because of the manner in which the object references are compared for equality. Objects are compared for equality using their equals() method, which isn't overridden by the class StringBuilder. So two StringBuilder objects are equal if their object references (the variables that store them) point to the same object. You can always override the equals method in your own class to change this default behavior. The following is an example using the class MyPerson:

```
import java.util.ArrayList;
class MyPerson {
```

```
        String name;
        MyPerson(String name) { this.name = name; }
        @Override
        public boolean equals(Object obj) {
            if (obj instanceof MyPerson) {
                MyPerson p = (MyPerson)obj;
                boolean isEqual = p.name.equals(this.name);
                return isEqual;
            }
            else
                return false;
        }
    }
public class DeleteElementsFromArrayList2 {
    public static void main(String args[]) {
        ArrayList<MyPerson> myArrList = new ArrayList<MyPerson>();
        MyPerson p1 = new MyPerson("Shreya");
        MyPerson p2 = new MyPerson("Paul");
        MyPerson p3 = new MyPerson("Harry");
        myArrList.add(p1);
        myArrList.add(p2);
        myArrList.add(p3);
        myArrList.remove(new MyPerson("Paul"));
        for (MyPerson element:myArrList)
            System.out.println(element.name);
    }
}
```

**❶ Method equals** — null and objects of type other than MyPerson can't be equal to this object.

**Cast obj to MyPerson**

Compare name of method parameter to that of this object's name

**❷ Removes Paul**

Prints Shreya and Harry

At ❶, the method equals in the class MyPerson overrides the method equals in the class Object. It returns false if a null value is passed to this method. It returns true if an object of MyPerson is passed to it with a matching value for its instance variable name.

At ❷, the method remove removes the element with the name Paul from myArr-List. As mentioned earlier, the method remove compares the objects for equality before removing it from ArrayList by calling the method equals.

When elements of an ArrayList are removed, the remaining elements are rearranged at their correct positions. This change is required to retrieve all the remaining elements at their correct new positions.

### 4.4.6  *Other methods of ArrayList*

Let's briefly discuss the other important methods defined in ArrayList.

#### ADDING MULTIPLE ELEMENTS TO AN ARRAYLIST

You can add multiple elements to an ArrayList from another ArrayList or any other class that's a subclass of Collection by using the following overloaded versions of method addAll:

- addAll(Collection<? extends E> c)
- addAll(int index, Collection<? extends E> c)

The method addAll(Collection<? extends E> c) appends all the elements in the specified collection to the end of this list in the order in which they're returned by the specified collection's Iterator. If you aren't familiar with generics, and the parameters of this method look scary to you, don't worry—other classes from the Collection API aren't on this exam.

Method addAll(int index, Collection<? extends E> c) inserts all the elements in the specified collection into this list, starting at the specified position.

In the following code example, all elements of ArrayList yourArrList are inserted into ArrayList myArrList, starting at position 1:

```
ArrayList<String> myArrList = new ArrayList<String>();
myArrList.add("One");
myArrList.add("Two");
ArrayList<String> yourArrList = new ArrayList<String>();
yourArrList.add("Three");
yourArrList.add("Four");
myArrList.addAll(1, yourArrList);         ◁─┤  Add elements of
for (String val : myArrList)                    yourArrList to
    System.out.println(val);                     myArrList
```

The output of the previous code is as follows:

```
One
Three
Four
Two
```

The elements of yourArrList aren't removed from it. The objects that are stored in yourArrList can now be referred to from myArrList.

What happens if you modify the *common* object references in these lists, myArrList and yourArrList? We have two cases here: in the first one, you *reassign* the object reference using either of the lists. In this case, the value in the second list will remain unchanged. In the second case, you *modify* the internals of any of the common list elements—in this case, the change will be reflected in both of the lists.

**EXAM TIP**   This is also one of the favorite topics of the exam authors. In the exam, you're likely to encounter a question that adds the same object reference to multiple lists and then tests you on your understanding of the state of the same object and reference variable in all the lists. If you have any questions on this issue, please refer to the section on reference variables (section 2.3).

It's time for our next Twist in the Tale exercise. Let's modify some of the code that we've used in our previous examples and see how it affects the output (answers in the appendix).

What is the output of the following code?

```
ArrayList<String> myArrList = new ArrayList<String>();
String one = "One";
String two = new String("Two");
myArrList.add(one);
myArrList.add(two);
ArrayList<String> yourArrList = myArrList;
one.replace("O", "B");
for (String val : myArrList)
    System.out.print(val + ":");
for (String val : yourArrList)
    System.out.print(val + ":");
```

   **a** One:Two:One:Two:

   **b** Bne:Two:Bne:Two:

   **c** One:Two:Bne:Two:

   **d** Bne:Two:One:Two:

### CLEARING ARRAYLIST ELEMENTS

You can remove all the `ArrayList` elements by calling `clear` on it. Here's an example:

```
ArrayList<String> myArrList = new ArrayList<String>();
myArrList.add("One");
myArrList.add("Two");
myArrList.clear();
for (String val:myArrList)
    System.out.println(val);
```

The previous code won't print out anything because there are no more elements in `myArrList`.

### ACCESSING INDIVIDUAL ARRAYLIST ELEMENTS

In this section, we'll cover the following methods for accessing elements of an `ArrayList`:

- `get(int index)`—This method returns the element at the specified position in this list.
- `size()`—This method returns the number of elements in this list.
- `contains(Object o)`—This method returns `true` if this list contains the specified element.
- `indexOf(Object o)`—This method returns the index of the first occurrence of the specified element in this list, or `-1` if this list doesn't contain the element.
- `lastIndexOf(Object o)`—This method returns the index of the last occurrence of the specified element in this list, or `-1` if this list doesn't contain the element.

You can retrieve an object at a particular position in `ArrayList` and determine its size as follows:

```
ArrayList<String> myArrList = new ArrayList<String>();
myArrList.add("One");
myArrList.add("Two");
String valFromList = myArrList.get(1);          Prints Two—element
System.out.println(valFromList);                at position 1
System.out.println(myArrList.size());           Prints 2
```

Behind the scenes, the method `get` will check whether the requested position exists in the `ArrayList` by comparing it with the array's size. If the requested element isn't within the range, the `get` method throws a `java.lang.IndexOutOfBoundsException` error at runtime.

All the remaining three methods—`contains`, `indexOf`, and `lastIndexOf`—require you to have an unambiguous and strong understanding of how to determine the equality of objects. `ArrayList` stores objects, and these three methods will compare the values that you pass to these methods with all the elements of the `ArrayList`.

By default, objects are considered equal if they are referred to by the same variable (the `String` class is an exception with its pool of `String` objects). If you want to compare objects by their state (values of the instance variable), override the `equals` method in that class. I've already demonstrated the difference in how equality of objects of a class is determined, when the class overrides its `equals` method and when it doesn't, in section 4.4.5 with an overridden `equals` method in the class `MyPerson`.

Let's see the usage of all these methods:

```
public class MiscMethodsArrayList3 {
    public static void main(String args[]) {
        ArrayList<StringBuilder> myArrList =                          Adds sb1 to
                        new ArrayList<StringBuilder>();               the ArrayList
        StringBuilder sb1 = new StringBuilder("Jan");
        StringBuilder sb2 = new StringBuilder("Feb");
        myArrList.add(sb1);                                           Adds sb2
        myArrList.add(sb2);                                           to the
        myArrList.add(sb2);                                           ArrayList
        System.out.println(myArrList.contains(new StringBuilder("Jan")));
        System.out.println(myArrList.contains(sb1));                 Prints
        System.out.println(myArrList.indexOf(new StringBuilder("Feb")));  true
        System.out.println(myArrList.indexOf(sb2));
        System.out.println(myArrList.lastIndexOf(                    Prints 1
                        new StringBuilder("Feb")));
        System.out.println(myArrList.lastIndexOf(sb2));
    }                                                                Prints 2
}
```

Annotations (left margin): **Adds sb2 to the ArrayList again**, **Prints false**, **Prints –1**, **Prints –1**

The output of the previous code is as follows:

```
false
true
-1
1
-1
2
```

Take a look at the output of the same code using a list of `MyPerson` objects that has overridden the `equals` method. First, here's the definition of the class `MyPerson`:

```
class MyPerson {
    String name;
    MyPerson(String name) { this.name = name; }
    @Override
    public boolean equals(Object obj) {
        if (obj instanceof MyPerson) {
            MyPerson p = (MyPerson)obj;
            boolean isEqual = p.name.equals(this.name);
            return isEqual;
        }
        else
            return false;
    }
}
```

**Overridden equals method in class MyPerson; it returns true for same String values for instance variable name**

The definition of the class `MiscMethodsArrayList4` follows:

```
public class MiscMethodsArrayList4 {
    public static void main(String args[]) {
        ArrayList<MyPerson> myArrList = new ArrayList<MyPerson>();
        MyPerson p1 = new MyPerson("Shreya");
        MyPerson p2 = new MyPerson("Paul");
        myArrList.add(p1);
        myArrList.add(p2);
        myArrList.add(p2);
        System.out.println(myArrList.contains(new MyPerson("Shreya")));
        System.out.println(myArrList.contains(p1));
        System.out.println(myArrList.indexOf(new MyPerson("Paul")));
        System.out.println(myArrList.indexOf(p2));
        System.out.println(myArrList.lastIndexOf(new MyPerson("Paul")));
        System.out.println(myArrList.lastIndexOf(p2));
    }
}
```

**Adds p1 to ArrayList**

**Adds p2 to ArrayList**

**Adds p2 to ArrayList again**

**Prints true**

**Prints true**

**Prints 1**

**Prints 1**

**Prints 2**

**Prints 2**

As you can see from the output of the preceding code, equality of the objects of the class `MyPerson` is determined by the rules defined in its `equals` method. Two objects of the class `MyPerson` with the same value for its instance variable name are considered to be equal. `myArrList` stores objects of the class `MyPerson`. To find a target object, `myArrList` will rely on the output given by the `equals` method of the class `MyPerson`; it won't compare the object references of the stored and target objects.

**EXAM TIP**  An `ArrayList` can store duplicate object values.

### CLONING AN ARRAYLIST

The method `clone` defined in the class `ArrayList` returns a *shallow copy* of this `Array-List` instance. "Shallow copy" means that this method creates a new instance of the `ArrayList` object to be cloned. Its element references are copied, but the objects themselves are not.

Here's an example:

```
public class MiscMethodsArrayList5 {
    public static void main(String args[]) {
        ArrayList<StringBuilder> myArrList = new ArrayList<StringBuilder>();
        StringBuilder sb1 = new StringBuilder("Jan");
        StringBuilder sb2 = new StringBuilder("Feb");
        myArrList.add(sb1);
        myArrList.add(sb2);
        myArrList.add(sb2);
        ArrayList<StringBuilder> assignedArrList = myArrList;
        ArrayList<StringBuilder> clonedArrList =
                (ArrayList<StringBuilder>)myArrList.clone();
        System.out.println(myArrList == assignedArrList);
        System.out.println(myArrList == clonedArrList);
        StringBuilder myArrVal = myArrList.get(0);
        StringBuilder assignedArrVal = assignedArrList.get(0);
        StringBuilder clonedArrVal = clonedArrList.get(0);
        System.out.println(myArrVal == assignedArrVal);
        System.out.println(myArrVal == clonedArrVal);
    }
}
```

**①** Assigns object referred to by myArrList to assignedArrList

**②** Clones myArrList and assigns it to clonedArrList

**③** Prints true

**④** Prints false

**⑤** All of these reference variables refer to the same object.

**⑥** Prints true

**⑦** Prints true

Let's go through the previous code:

- **①** assigns the object referred to by `myArrList` to `assignedArrList`. The variables `myArrList` and `assignedArrList` now refer to the same object.
- **②** assigns a *copy* of the object referred to by `myArrList` to `clonedArrList`. The variables `myArrList` and `clonedArrList` refer to different objects. Because the method `clone` returns a value of the type `Object`, it's cast to `ArrayList<String-Builder>` to assign it to `clonedArrList` (don't worry if you can't follow this line—casting is covered in chapter 6).
- **③** prints `true` because `myArrList` and `assignedArrList` refer to the same object.
- **④** prints `false` because `myArrList` and `clonedArrList` refer to separate objects, because the method `clone` creates and returns a new object of `ArrayList` (but with the same list members).
- **⑤** proves that the method `clone` didn't copy the elements of `myArrList`. All the variable references `myArrVal`, `AssignedArrVal`, and `clonedArrVal` refer to the same objects.
- Hence, both **⑥** and **⑦** print `true`.

**CREATING AN ARRAY FROM AN ARRAYLIST**

You can use the method `toArray` to return an array containing all the elements in an `ArrayList` in sequence from the first to the last element. As mentioned earlier in this chapter (refer to figure 4.27 in section 4.4.1), an `ArrayList` uses a private variable, `elementData` (an array), to store its own values. Method `toArray` doesn't return a reference to this array. It creates a new array, copies the elements of the `ArrayList` to it, and then returns it.

Now comes the tricky part. No references to the returned array, which is itself an object, are maintained by the `ArrayList`. But the references to the individual `ArrayList` elements are copied to the returned array and are still referred to by the `ArrayList`.

This implies that if you modify the returned array by, say, swapping the position of its elements or by assigning new objects to its elements, the elements of `ArrayList` won't be affected. But if you modify the state of (mutable) elements of the returned array, then the modified state of elements will be reflected in the `ArrayList`.

## 4.5    *Comparing objects for equality*

[3.2]   Test equality between Strings and other objects using == and equals()

In section 4.1, you saw how the class `String` defined a set of rules to determine whether two `String` values are equal and how these rules were coded in the method `equals`. Similarly, any Java class can define a set of rules to determine whether its two objects should be considered equal. This comparison is accomplished using the method `equals`, which is described in the next section.

### 4.5.1    *The method equals in the class java.lang.Object*

The method `equals` is defined in class `java.lang.Object`. All the Java classes directly or indirectly inherit this class. Listing 4.2 contains the default implementation of the method `equals` from the class `java.lang.Object`.

**Listing 4.2    Implementation of `equals` method from class `java.lang.Object`**

```
public boolean equals(Object obj) {
    return (this == obj);
}
```

As you can see, the default implementation of the `equals` method only compares whether two object variables refer to the same object. Because instance variables are used to store the state of an object, it's common to compare the values of the instance variables to determine whether two objects should be considered equal.

### 4.5.2    *Comparing objects of a user-defined class*

Let's work with an example of the class `BankAccount`, which defines two instance variables: `acctNumber` of type `String`, and `acctType` of type `int`. The `equals` method compares the values of these instance variables to determine the equality of two objects of the class BankAccount.

Here's the relevant code:

```
class BankAccount {
    String acctNumber;
    int acctType;
    public boolean equals(Object anObject) {
        if (anObject instanceof BankAccount) {              ←——  Check whether you're
            BankAccount b = (BankAccount)anObject;                comparing the same
            return (acctNumber.equals(b.acctNumber) &&  ←——      type of objects
                acctType == b.acctType);
        }                                                   ←——  Two bank objects are
        else                                                     considered equal if
            return false;                                        they have the same
    }                                                            values, for instance
}                                                                variables acctNumber
                                                                 and acctType.
```

Let's verify the working of this equals method in the following code:

```
class Test {
    public static void main(String args[]) {
        BankAccount b1 = new BankAccount();
        b1.acctNumber = "0023490";
        b1.acctType = 4;
        BankAccount b2 = new BankAccount();
        b2.acctNumber = "11223344";
        b2.acctType = 3;
        BankAccount b3 = new BankAccount();
        b3.acctNumber = "11223344";
        b3.acctType = 3;                                      ❶  Prints false
        System.out.println(b1.equals(b2));   ←——
        System.out.println(b2.equals(b3));          ←——  ❷  Prints true
        System.out.println(b1.equals(new String("abc")));  ←——
    }                                                     ❸  Prints false
}
```

❶ prints false because the value of the reference variables b1 and b2 don't match. ❷ prints true because the values of the reference variables b2 and b3 match each other. ❸ passes an object of type String to the method equals defined in the class Bank-Account. This method returns false if the method parameter passed to it is not of type BankAccount. Hence, ❸ prints false.

Even though the following implementation is unacceptable for classes used in the real world, it's still correct syntactically:

```
class BankAccount {
    String acctNumber;
    int acctType;
    public boolean equals(Object anObject) {
        return true;
    }
}
```

The previous definition of the `equals` method will return `true` for any object that's compared to an object of the class `BankAccount` because it doesn't compare any values. Let's see what happens when you compare an object of the class `String` with an object of class `BankAccount` and vice versa using `equals()`:

```
class TestBank {
    public static void main(String args[]) {
        BankAccount acct = new BankAccount();
        String str = "Bank";
        System.out.println(acct.equals(str));
        System.out.println(str.equals(acct));
    }
}
```

**1** **Prints true**

**2** **Prints false**

In the preceding code, **1** prints `true`, but **2** prints `false`. The `equals` method in the class `String` returns `true` only if the object that's being compared to is a `String` with the same sequence of characters.

**EXAM TIP**  In the exam, watch out for questions about the correct implementation of the `equals` method (refer to section 4.5.4) to compare two objects versus questions about the `equals` methods that simply compile correctly. If you'd been asked whether `equals()` in the previous example code would compile correctly, the correct answer would be yes.

### 4.5.3 *Incorrect method signature of the equals method*

It's a common mistake to write an `equals` method that accepts an instance of the class itself. In the following code, the class `BankAccount` doesn't override `equals()`; it overloads it:

```
class BankAccount {
    String acctNumber;
    int acctType;
    public boolean equals(BankAccount obj) {          Type of method parameter
        if (obj != null) {                            is BankAccount, not Object
                    return (acctNumber.equals(obj.acctNumber) &&
                acctType == obj.acctType);
        }
        else
            return false;
    }
}
```

Although the previous definition of `equals()` may seem to be flawless, what happens when you try to add and retrieve an object of the class `BankAccount` (as shown in the preceding code) from an `ArrayList`? The method `contains` defined in the class `ArrayList` compares two objects by calling the object's `equals` method. It does not compare object references.

In the following code, see what happens when you add an object of the class Bank-Account to an `ArrayList` and then try to verify whether the list contains a `BankAccount` object with the same instance variable's values for `acctNumber` and `acctType` as the object being searched for:

```
class TestMethodEquals {
    public static void main(String args[]) {
        BankAccount b1 = new BankAccount();
        b1.acctNumber = "0023490"; b1.acctType = 4;
        ArrayList <BankAccount> list = new ArrayList<BankAccount>();
        list.add(b1);
        BankAccount b2 = new BankAccount();
        b2.acctNumber = "0023490"; b2.acctType = 4;
        System.out.println(list.contains(b2));
    }
}
```

**Adds object b1 to list** ❷

❶ **Object b1**

❸ **Creates b2 with same state as b1**

❹ **Prints false**

❶ and ❸ define objects b1 and b2 of the class `BankAccount` with the same state. ❷ adds b1 to the list. ❹ compares the object b2 with the objects added to the list.

An `ArrayList` uses the method `equals` to compare two objects. Because the class `BankAccount` didn't follow the rules for correctly defining (overriding) the method `equals`, `ArrayList` uses the method `equals` from the base class `Object`, which compares object references. Because the code didn't add b2 to `list`, it prints `false`.

What do you think will be the output of the previous code if you change the definition of the method `equals` in the class `BankAccount` so that it accepts a method parameter of type `Object`? Try it for yourself!

**EXAM TIP**　The method `equals` defines a method parameter of type `Object`, and its return type is `boolean`. Don't change the name of the method, its return type, or the type of method parameter when you define (*override*) this method in your class to compare two objects.

### 4.5.4　*Contract of the equals method*

The Java API defines a *contract* for the `equals` method, which should be taken care of when you implement it in any of your classes. I've pulled the following contract explanation directly from the Java API documentation:[1]

*The `equals` method implements an equivalence relation on non-null object references:*

- *It is reflexive: for any non-null reference value x, x.equals(x) should return `true`.*
- *It is symmetric: for any non-null reference values x and y, x.equals(y) should return `true` if and only if y.equals(x) returns `true`.*
- *It is transitive: for any non-null reference values x, y, and z, if x.equals(y) returns `true` and y.equals(z) returns `true`, then x.equals(z) should return `true`.*

---

[1]　The Java API documentation for `equals` can be found on the Oracle site: http://docs.oracle.com/javase/8/docs/api/java/lang/Object.html#equals(java.lang.Object).

- *It is consistent: for any non-null reference values* x *and* y, *multiple invocations of* x.equals(y) *consistently return* true *or consistently return* false, *provided no information used in* equals() *comparisons on the objects is modified.*
- *For any non-null reference value* x, x.equals(null) *should return* false.

As per the contract, the definition of the equals method that we defined for the class BankAccount in an earlier example violates the contract for the equals method. Take a look at the definition again:

```
public boolean equals(Object anObject) {
    return true;
}
```

This code returns true, even for null values passed to this method. According to the contract of the method equals, if a null value is passed to the equals method, the method should return false.

**EXAM TIP**  You may get to answer explicit questions on the contract of the equals method. An equals method that returns true for a null object passed to it will violate the contract. Also, if the equals method modifies the value of any of the instance variables of the method parameter passed to it, or of the object on which it is called, it will violate the equals contract.

---

### The hashCode() method

A lot of programmers are confused about the role of the method hashCode in determining the equality of objects. The method hashCode is *not* called by the equals method to determine the equality of two objects. Because the hashCode method is not on the exam, I'll discuss it quickly here to ward off any confusion about this method.

The method hashCode is used by the collection classes (such as HashMap) that store *key-value* pairs, where a *key* is an object. These collection classes use the hashCode of a *key* to search efficiently for the corresponding *value*. The hashCode of the *key* (an object) is used to specify a *bucket* number, which should store its corresponding *value*. The hashCode values of two *distinct* objects can be the same. When these collection classes find the right bucket, they call the equals method to select the correct *value* object (that shares the same *key* values). The equals method is called even if a *bucket* contains only one object. After all, it might be the same hash but a different equals, and there is no match to get!

According to the Java documentation, when you override the equals method in your class, you should also override the hashCode method. If you don't, objects of your classes won't behave as required if they're used as *keys* by collection classes that store *key-value* pairs. This method is not discussed in detail in this chapter because it isn't on the exam. But don't forget to override it with the method equals in your real-world projects.

## 4.6    Working with calendar data

> [9.3]   Create and manipulate calendar data using classes from
> java.time.LocalDateTime, java.time.LocalDate, java.time.LocalTime,
> java.time.format.DateTimeFormatter, java.time.Period

The new Date and Time API in Java 8 simplifies working with date and time objects. It includes classes and interfaces with simple and informative method names. As you work with the classes LocalDate, LocalTime, LocalDateTime, Period, and DateTime-Formatter in this section, you'll notice that these classes define methods with similar names (which have similar purposes). Table 4.1 lists the method prefix, its type, and its use (from Oracle Java documentation).

Table 4.1   Method prefixes, types, and their uses in the Date and Time API in Java 8

| Prefix | Method type | Use |
|--------|-------------|-----|
| of | static | Creates an instance where the factory is primarily validating the input parameters, not converting them. |
| from | static | Converts the input parameters to an instance of the target class, which may involve losing information from the input. |
| parse | static | Parses the input string to produce an instance of the target class. |
| format | instance | Uses the specified formatter to format the values in the temporal object to produce a string. |
| get | instance | Returns a part of the state of the target object. |
| is | instance | Queries the state of the target object. |
| with | instance | Returns a copy of the target object with one element changed; this is the immutable equivalent to a set method on a JavaBean. |
| plus | instance | Returns a copy of the target object with an amount of time added. |
| minus | instance | Returns a copy of the target object with an amount of time subtracted. |
| to | instance | Converts this object to another type. |
| at | instance | Combines this object with another. |

**NOTE**   The preceding table might not *seem* to add a lot of value at this point. But as you go through the following sections, you'll realize the similarity in the names of the methods that are defined in the date and time classes.

Let's get started with the class LocalDate.

### 4.6.1 *LocalDate*

To store dates like a birthday or anniversary, visiting a place, or starting a job, school, or college, you don't need to store the time. LocalDate will work perfectly in this case.

LocalDate can be used to store dates like 2015-12-27 without time or time zones. LocalDate instances are immutable and hence safe to be used in a multithreaded environment.

#### CREATING LOCALDATE

The LocalDate constructor is marked private, so you must use one of the factory methods to instantiate it. The static method of() accepts year, month, and day of month:

```
LocalDate date1 = LocalDate.of(2015, 12, 27);           ← Accept month
LocalDate date2 = LocalDate.of(2015, Month.DECEMBER, 27);  ← as int value
                                                           ← Accept month as
                                                             enum constant
```

> **NOTE** In the new Date and Time API, introduced with Java 8, January is represented by int value 1 and not 0. The old Calendar-based API hasn't changed in Java 8 and still uses 0-based month numbering.

To get the current date from the system clock, use the static method now():

```
LocalDate date3 = LocalDate.now();
```

You can also parse a string in the format 2016-02-27 to instantiate LocalDate. Here's an example:

```
LocalDate date2 = LocalDate.parse("2025-08-09");
```

> **EXAM TIP** If you pass invalid values to parse() or of(), you'll get Date-TimeParseException. The format of the string passed to parse() must be exactly of the format 9999-99-99. The month and date values passed to parse() must be of two digits; a single digit is considered an invalid value. For days and months with values 1–9, pass 01–09.

#### QUERYING LOCALDATE

You can use instance methods like getXX() to query LocalDate on its year, month, and date values. The date can be queried as day-of-month, day-of-week, and day-of-year. The month value can be retrieved as the enum constant Month or as an int value:

```
LocalDate date = LocalDate.parse("2020-08-30");
System.out.println(date.getDayOfMonth());
System.out.println(date.getDayOfWeek());
System.out.println(date.getDayOfYear());
System.out.println(date.getMonth());
System.out.println(date.getMonthValue());
System.out.println(date.getYear());
```

The output of the preceding code looks like this:

```
30
SUNDAY
243
AUGUST
8
2020
```

You can use the instance methods `isAfter()` or `isBefore()` to determine whether a date is chronologically before or after another date:

```
LocalDate shreyaBday = LocalDate.parse("2002-08-30");
LocalDate paulBday = LocalDate.parse("2002-07-29");

System.out.println(shreyaBday.isAfter(paulBday));       ⟵┐   Outputs true
System.out.println(shreyaBday.isBefore(paulBday));          │
System.out.println(shreyaBday.isBefore(shreyaBday));    │   Outputs false
```

### MANIPULATING LOCALDATE

The `LocalDate` class defines methods with the names `minusXX()`, `plusXX()`, and `withXX()` to manipulate the date values. The API architects have used the names that make their purpose explicit. Because `LocalDate` is an immutable class, all the methods create and return a copy. The `minusXX()` methods return a copy of the date with the specified days, months, or years subtracted from it:

```
LocalDate bday = LocalDate.of(2052,03,10);
System.out.println(bday.minusDays(10));
System.out.println(bday.minusMonths(2));
System.out.println(bday.minusWeeks(30));
System.out.println(bday.minusYears(1));
```

Here's the output of the preceding code:

```
2052-02-29
2052-01-10
2051-08-13
2051-03-10
```

 **EXAM TIP**   `LocalDate` is immutable. All the methods that seem to manipulate its value return a copy of the `LocalDate` instance on which it's called.

The `plusXX()` methods return a copy of the date instance after adding the specified days, months, or years to it:

```
LocalDate launchCompany = LocalDate.of(2016,02,29);
System.out.println(launchCompany.plusDays(1));
System.out.println(launchCompany.plusMonths(1));
System.out.println(launchCompany.plusWeeks(7));
System.out.println(launchCompany.plusYears(1));
```

Here's the output of the preceding code:

```
2016-03-01
2016-03-29
2016-04-18
2017-02-28
```

**EXAM TIP**   All additions, subtractions, or replacements to `LocalDate` consider leap years.

The `withXX()` methods return a copy of the date instance replacing the specified day, month, or year in it:

```
LocalDate firstSex = LocalDate.of(2036,02,28);
System.out.println(firstSex.withDayOfMonth(1));
System.out.println(firstSex.withDayOfYear(1));
System.out.println(firstSex.withMonth(7));
System.out.println(firstSex.withYear(1));
```

The output of the preceding code looks like this:

```
2036-02-01
2036-01-01
2036-07-28
0001-02-28
```

**CONVERTING TO ANOTHER TYPE**

The `LocalDate` class defines methods to convert it to `LocalDateTime` and `long` (representing the epoch date).

The `LocalDate` class defines overloaded `atTime()` instance methods. These methods combine `LocalDate` with time to create and return `LocalDateTime`, which stores both the date and time (the `LocalDateTime` class is covered in the next section):

```
LocalDate interviewDate = LocalDate.of(2016,02,28);
System.out.println(interviewDate.atTime(16, 30));
System.out.println(interviewDate.atTime(16, 30, 20));
System.out.println(interviewDate.atTime(16, 30, 20, 300));
System.out.println(interviewDate.atTime(LocalTime.of(16, 30)));
```

Here's the output of the preceding code:

```
2016-02-28T16:30
2016-02-28T16:30:20
2016-02-28T16:30:20.000000300
2016-02-28T16:30
```

**EXAM TIP**   If you pass any invalid hours, minutes, or seconds value to the method `atTime`, it will throw a `DateTimeException` at runtime.

You can use the method `toEpochDay()` to convert `LocalDate` to the *epoch date*—the count of days from January 1, 1970:

```
LocalDate launchBook = LocalDate.of(2016,2,8);
LocalDate aDate = LocalDate.of(1970,1,8);
System.out.println(launchBook.toEpochDay());
System.out.println(aDate.toEpochDay());
```

Here's the output of the preceding code:

```
16839
7
```

**NOTE**   In standard date and time, the *epoch date* refers to January 1, 1970, 00:00:00 GMT.

### 4.6.2   *LocalTime*

To store times like breakfast, conference talk start time, or in-store sale end time, you can use `LocalTime`. It stores time in the format hours-minutes-seconds (without a time zone) and to nanosecond precision. So you're sure to see methods that accept nanoseconds as method arguments or methods that return this value. Like `LocalDate`, `LocalTime` is also immutable and hence safe to be used in a multithreaded environment.

#### CREATING LOCALTIME

The `LocalTime` constructor is private, so you must use one of the factory methods to instantiate it. The static method `of()` accepts hours, minutes, seconds, and nanoseconds:

```
                                                  Hours and      Hours,
                                                  minutes        minutes, and
                                                                 seconds
LocalTime timeHrsMin =  LocalTime.of(12, 12);        ◄─┘
LocalTime timeHrsMinSec =  LocalTime.of(0, 12, 6);         ◄─┘
LocalTime timeHrsMinSecNano =  LocalTime.of(14, 7, 10, 998654578);   ◄─┐

                                                  Hours, minutes, seconds,
                                                  and nanoseconds
```

The `of()` method uses a 24-hour clock to specify the hour value. What happens if you pass out-of-range values for hours, minutes, or seconds to `of()`? In this case, you'll get a runtime exception, `DateTimeException`. You'll get a compiler error if the range of values passed to a method doesn't comply with the method's argument type. Here's an example:

```
                                                          Runtime
                                                          exception
LocalTime timeHrsMin =  LocalTime.of(120, 12);        ◄─┘
LocalTime timeHrsMin2 =  LocalTime.of(9986545781, 12);     ◄─┐
                                                          Compilation
                                                          error
```

**EXAM TIP**   `LocalTime` doesn't define a method to pass a.m. or p.m. Use values 0–23 to define hours. If you pass out-of-range values to either hours, minutes, or seconds, you'll get a runtime exception.

To get the current time from the system clock, use the static method `now()`:

```
LocalDate date3 =  LocalTime.now();
```

You can parse a string to instantiate `LocalTime` by using its static method `parse()`. You can either pass a string in the format 15:08:23 (hours:minutes:seconds) or parse any text using `DateTimeFormatter` (covered in the next section):

```
LocalTime time = LocalTime.parse("15:08:23");
```

 **EXAM TIP** If you pass invalid string values to `parse()`, the code will compile but will throw a runtime exception. If you don't pass a `DateTimeFormatter`, the format of the string passed to `parse()` must be exactly of the format 99:99:99. The hours and minutes values passed to `parse()` must be two digits; a single digit is considered an invalid value. For hours and minutes with the value 0–9, pass 00–09.

### USING LOCALTIME CONSTANTS

You can use constants from the `LocalTime` class to work with predefined times:

- `LocalTime.MIN`—Minimum supported time, that is, 00:00
- `LocalTime.MAX`—Maximum supported time, that is, 23:59:59.999999999
- `LocalTime.MIDNIGHT`—Time when the day starts, that is, 00:00
- `LocalTime.NOON`—Noontime, that is, 12:00

Does that make you wonder whether the minimum and midnight times are equal? See for yourself; the following code outputs `true`:

```
System.out.println(LocalTime.MIN.equals(LocalTime.MIDNIGHT));    ⟵— Outputs true
```

### QUERYING LOCALTIME

You can use instance methods like `getXX()` to query `LocalTime` on its hour, minutes, seconds, and nanoseconds. All these methods return an `int` value:

```
LocalTime time = LocalTime.of(16, 20, 12, 98547);
System.out.println(time.getHour());
System.out.println(time.getMinute());
System.out.println(time.getSecond());
System.out.println(time.getNano());
```

Here's the output:

```
16
20
12
98547
```

**EXAM TIP**   The correct method names for querying LocalTime are get-Hour(), getMinute(), getSecond(), and getNano(). Watch out for exam questions that use invalid method names like *getHours(), getMinutes(), getSeconds(),* or *getNanoSeconds().*

You can use the instance methods isAfter() and isBefore() to check whether a time is after or before the specified time. The following code outputs true:

```
LocalTime shreyaFinishTime = LocalTime.parse("17:09:04");
LocalTime paulFinishTime = LocalTime.parse("17:09:12");
if(shreyaFinishTime.isBefore(paulFinishTime))
    System.out.println("Shreya wins");
else
    System.out.println("Paul wins");
```

**Outputs
Shreya wins**

### MANIPULATING LOCALTIME

You can use the instance methods minusHours(), minusMinutes(), minusSeconds(), and minusNanos() to create and return a copy of LocalTime instances with the specified period subtracted. The method names are self-explanatory. For example, minus-Hours(int) returns a copy of a LocalTime instance with the specified period in hours subtracted. The following example calculates and outputs the time when Shreya should leave from her office to watch a movie, given that the movie starts at 21:00 hours and it takes 35 minutes to commute to the movie theater:

```
LocalTime movieStartTime = LocalTime.parse("21:00:00");
int commuteMin = 35;
LocalTime shreyaStartTime = movieStartTime.minusMinutes(commuteMin);
System.out.println("Start by " + shreyaStartTime + " from office");
```

Here's the output of the preceding code:

```
Start by 20:25 from office
```

**EXAM TIP**   Unlike the get*XXX*() methods, minus*XXX*() methods use the plural form: getHour() versus minusHours(), getMinute() versus minusMinutes(), getSecond() versus minusSeconds(), and getNano() versus minusNanos().

The plusHours(), plusMinutes(), plusSeconds(), and plusNanos() methods accept long values and add the specified hours, minutes, seconds, or nanoseconds to time, returning its copy as LocalTime. The following example uses the addSeconds() and isAfter() methods to add seconds to a time and compares it with another time:

```
int worldRecord = 10;
LocalTime raceStartTime = LocalTime.of(8, 10, 55);
LocalTime raceEndTime = LocalTime.of(8, 11, 11);
if (raceStartTime.plusSeconds(worldRecord).isAfter(raceEndTime))
    System.out.println("New world record");
else
    System.out.println("Try harder");
```

The output of the preceding code looks like this:

```
Try harder
```

> **EXAM TIP**    LocalTime is immutable. Calling any method on its instance won't modify its value.

The withHour(), withMinute(), withSecond(), and withNano() methods accept an int value and return a copy of LocalTime with the specified value altered. In the following example, a new LocalTime instance with the minute value 00 is created:

```
LocalTime startTime = LocalTime.of(5, 7, 9);
if (startTime.getMinute() < 30)
    startTime = startTime.withMinute(0);
System.out.println(startTime);
```

Here's the output:

```
05:00:09
```

**COMBINING WITH ANOTHER TYPE**

The LocalTime class defines the atDate() method to combine a LocalDate with itself to create LocalDateTime:

```
LocalTime time = LocalTime.of(14, 10, 0);
LocalDate date = LocalDate.of(2016,02,28);
LocalDateTime dateTime = time.atDate(date);
System.out.println(dateTime);
```

Here's the output:

```
2016-02-28T14:10
```

> **EXAM TIP**    The class LocalTime defines the method atDate(), which can be passed a LocalDate instance to create a LocalDateTime instance.

### 4.6.3    *LocalDateTime*

If you want to store both date and time (without the time zone), use the class LocalDateTime. It stores a value like 2050-06-18T14:20:30:908765 (year-month-dayThours :minutes:seconds:nanoseconds).

> **NOTE**    The LocalDateTime class uses the letter *T* to separate date and time values in its printed value.

You can consider this class to offer the functionality of both the LocalDate and LocalTime classes. This class defines similar methods as those defined by the LocalDate and

LocalTime classes. So instead of discussing individual methods of this class, here's an example that covers the important methods of this class:

**Parse String to LocalDateTime**

```
LocalDateTime prizeCeremony = LocalDateTime.parse("2050-06-05T14:00:00");
LocalDateTime dateTimeNow = LocalDateTime.now();

if (prizeCeremony.getMonthValue() == 6)
    System.out.println("Can't invite president");
else
    System.out.println("President invited");

LocalDateTime chiefGuestDeparture =
                      LocalDateTime.parse("2050-06-05T14:30:00");

if (prizeCeremony.plusHours(2).isAfter(chiefGuestDeparture))
    System.out.println("Chief Guest will leave before ceremony completes");

LocalDateTime eventMgrArrival = LocalDateTime.of(2050, 6, 5, 14, 30, 0);
if (eventMgrArrival.isAfter(prizeCeremony.minusHours(3)))
    System.out.println("Manager is supposed to arrive 3 hrs earlier");
```

**Get current date and time**

**Retrieve month as integer value**

**Instantiate LocalDateTime using separate int values**

**Check whether a LocalDateTime instance is before another LocalDateTime instance**

In the next section, you'll discover how you can perform calculations with date and time using the Period class.

### 4.6.4   *Period*

People often talk about periods of years, months, or days. With the Java 8 Date API, you can use the Period class to do so. The Period class represents a date-based amount in years, months, and days, like 2 years, 5 months, and 10 days. To work with a time-based amount in seconds and nanoseconds, you can use the Duration class.

**NOTE**   The Duration class can be used to store amounts of time like 1 hour, 36 minutes, or 29.4 seconds. But this class isn't explicitly covered in this exam (and this book). It's covered in the OCP Java SE 8 Programmer II exam.

You can add or subtract Period instances from the LocalDate and LocalDateTime classes. Period is also an immutable class and hence safe to use in a multithreaded environment. Let's get started by instantiating Period.

**INSTANTIATING PERIOD**

With a private constructor, the Period class defines multiple factory methods to create its instances. The static methods of(), ofYears(), ofMonths(), ofWeeks(), and ofDays() accept int values to create periods of years, months, weeks, or days:

**1 year, 2 months, and 7 days**

```
Period period1 = Period.of(1, 2, 7);
Period period2 = Period.ofYears(2);
```

**2 years**

```
Period period3 = Period.ofMonths(5);
Period period4 = Period.ofWeeks(10);
Period period5 = Period.ofDays(15);
```

←— **5 months**

←— **10 weeks**

**15 days**

**EXAM TIP**   A period of 35 days is not stored as 1 month and 5 days. Its individual elements, that is, days, months, and years, are stored the way it is initialized.

You can also define negative periods by passing negative integer values to all the preceding methods. Here's a quick example:

```
Period period6 = Period.ofDays(-15);
```

←——— **Period of -15 days**

**EXAM TIP**   You can define positive or negative periods of time. For example, you can define `Period` instances representing 15 or -15 days.

You can also parse a string to instantiate `Period` by using its static method `parse`. This method parses string values of the format *PnYnMnD* or *PnW*, where *n* represents a number and the letters (*P, Y, M, D,* and *W*) represent parse, year, month, day, and week. These letters can exist in lower- or uppercase. Each string must start with the letter *p* or *P* and must include at least one of the four sections, that is, year, month, week, or day. For the string format PnW, the count of weeks is multiplied by 7 to get the number of days. You can also define negative periods using `parse()`. If you precede the complete string value passed to `parse()` with a negative sign (-), it's applied to all values. If you place a negative sign just before an individual number, it applies only to that section. Here are some examples to instantiate a period of five years (notice the use of uppercase and lowercase letters and + and – signs):

```
Period p5Yrs1 = Period.parse("P5y");
Period p5Yrs2 = Period.parse("p5y");
Period p5Yrs3 = Period.parse("P5Y");
Period p5Yrs4 = Period.parse("+P5Y");
Period p5Yrs5 = Period.parse("P+5Y");
Period p5Yrs6 = Period.parse("-P-5Y");
System.out.println(p5Yrs1 + ":" + p5Yrs2);
```

**Period of
5 years**

←— **Outputs P5Y:P5Y**

The following examples define periods of separate durations:

```
Period p5Yrs7 = Period.parse("P5y1m2d");
Period p5Yrs8 = Period.parse("p9m");
Period p5Yrs9 = Period.parse("P60d");
Period p5Yrs10 = Period.parse("-P5W");
```

When passed to `System.out.println()`, the variables in the preceding code will result in the following output:

```
P5Y1M2D
P9M
P60D
P-35D
```

**EXAM TIP**  If you pass invalid string values to `parse()`, the code will compile but will throw a runtime exception.

You can also use the static method `between(LocalDate dateInclusive, LocalDate dateExclusive)` to instantiate `Period`:

```
LocalDate carnivalStart = LocalDate.of(2050, 12, 31);
LocalDate carnivalEnd = LocalDate.of(2051, 1, 2);

Period periodBetween = Period.between(carnivalStart, carnivalEnd);
System.out.println(periodBetween);
```
← **Outputs P2D**

**EXAM TIP**  The static method `between` accepts two `LocalDate` instances and returns a `Period` instance representing the number of years, days, and months between the two dates. The first date is included, but the second date is excluded in the returned `Period`. Here's a quick way to remember it: period = end date − start date.

#### MANIPULATING LOCALDATE AND LOCALDATETIME USING PERIOD

In everyday life, it's common to add or subtract periods of days, months, or years from a date. The `Period` class implements the interface `TemporalAmount`, so it can be used with the methods `plus()` and `minus()` defined in the classes `LocalDateTime` and `LocalDate`. The following example adds a period of a day to a `LocalDate` instance:

```
LocalDate date = LocalDate.of(2052, 01, 31);
System.out.println(date.plus(Period.ofDays(1)));
```

Here's the output of the preceding code:

```
2052-02-01
```

What happens when you add a period of a month to January 31 of any year? Do you get the last day of February or the first day of March? The following example adds a period of a month to a `LocalDateTime` instance:

```
LocalDateTime dateTime = LocalDateTime.parse("2052-01-31T14:18:36");
System.out.println(dateTime.plus(Period.ofMonths(1)));
```

The output of the preceding code looks like this:

```
2052-02-29T14:18:36
```

**EXAM TIP**    Because `Period` instances can represent positive or negative periods (like 15 days or -15 days), you can subtract days from a `LocalDate` or `LocalDateTime` by calling the method plus.

Similarly, you can use the method `minus()` with the classes `LocalDate` and `LocalDate-Time` to subtract a period of years, months, weeks, or days:

```
LocalDateTime dateTime = LocalDateTime.parse("2020-01-31T14:18:36");
System.out.println(dateTime.minus(Period.ofYears(2)));

LocalDate date = LocalDate.of(2052, 01, 31);
System.out.println(date.minus(Period.ofWeeks(4)));
```

Here's the output:

```
2018-01-31T14:18:36
2052-01-03
```

### QUERYING PERIOD INSTANCES

You can use the instance methods `getYears()`, `getMonths()`, and `getDays()` to query a `Period` instance on its years, months, and days. All these methods return an `int` value:

```
Period period = Period.of(2,4,40);
System.out.println(period.getYears());
System.out.println(period.getMonths());
System.out.println(period.getDays());
```

The preceding code outputs the following:

```
2
4
40
```

**EXAM TIP**    When you initialize a `Period` instance with days more than 31 or months more than 12, it doesn't recalculate its years, months, or days components.

You can query whether any of three units of a `Period` is negative using the methods `isNegative` and `isZero`. A `Period` instance is zero if all three units are zero. The `isNegative` method returns `true` if at least one of its three components is strictly negative (<0):

```
Period days5 = Period.of(0,0,5);
System.out.println(days5.isZero());          ◁── Outputs false

Period daysMinus5 = Period.of(0,0,-5);
System.out.println(daysMinus5.isNegative()); ◁── Outputs true
```

### MANIPULATING PERIOD

You can use the instance methods `minus(TemporalAmount)`, `minusDays(long)`, `minus-Weeks(long)`, `minusMonths(long)`, `minusYears(long)`, and `multipliedBy(int)` to create and return a copy of `Period` instances with the specified period subtracted or modified. The method names are self-explanatory. For an example, `minusDays(long)` returns a copy of a `Period` instance with the specified days subtracted. You can use the following example to send out reminders to your friends (limited to printing a message) for an event, say a birthday celebration, if it's due in 10 days:

```
LocalDate bday = LocalDate.of(2020, 10, 29);
LocalDate today = LocalDate.now();
Period period10Days = Period.of(0, 0, 10);

if (bday.minus(period10Days).isBefore(today))
    System.out.println("Time to send out reminders to friends");
```

**EXAM TIP**  In the class `Period`, both the get*XXX*() methods and minus*XXX*() methods use the plural form: `getYears()`, `minusHours()`.

What happens when you subtract a `Period` representing one month (P1M) from a `Period` representing 10 days (P10D)? Would you get a `Period` representing 20 days or a `Period` representing -1 month and 10 days? Let's find out using the following code, which also includes quick sample code on the usage of all the minus*XXX* methods:

```
Period period10Days = Period.of(0, 0, 10);
Period period1Month = Period.of(0, 1, 0);

System.out.println(period10Days.minus(period1Month));
System.out.println(period10Days.minusDays(5));
System.out.println(period10Days.minusMonths(5));
System.out.println(period10Days.minusYears(5));
```

Here's the output:

```
P-1M10D
P5D
P-5M10D
P-5Y10D
```

**EXAM TIP**  When you subtract `Period` instances using the minus*XXX*() methods, the individual elements are subtracted. Subtracting P10D from P1M returns P1M-10D and not P20D.

The `Period` class defines `multipliedBy(int)`, which multiplies each element in the period by the integer value:

```
Period year1Month9Day20 = Period.of(1, 9, 20);
System.out.println(year1Month9Day20.multipliedBy(2));
System.out.println(year1Month9Day20.multipliedBy(-2));
```
    **Outputs**
    **P2Y18M40D**

    **Outputs**
    **P-2Y-18M-40D**

**EXAM TIP**  The method `multipliedBy(int)` in the class `Period` is used to modify all elements of a `Period` instance. `Period` doesn't define a "divideBy()" method. Both the get*XXX*() methods and minus*XXX*() methods use the plural form `getYears()`, `minusHours()`.

The plus(TemporalAmount), plusDays(long), plusWeeks(long), plusMonths(long), and plusYears(long) methods add to Period instances and return the modified value as a Period. Like the minus*XXX*() methods, all the plus*XXX*() methods add individual elements:

```
Period period5Month = Period.of(0, 5, 0);
Period period10Month = Period.of(0, 10, 0);
Period period10Days = Period.of(0, 0, 10);

System.out.println(period5Month.plus(period10Month));
System.out.println(period10Days.plusDays(35));
System.out.println(period10Days.plusMonths(5));
System.out.println(period10Days.plusYears(5));
```

The output of the preceding code is as follows:

```
P15M
P45D
P5M10D
P5Y10D
```

 **EXAM TIP**  Adding a Period of 10 months to a Period of 5 months gives 15 months, not 1 year and 3 months.

The withDays(), withMonths(), and withYears() methods accept an int value and return a copy of Period with the specified value altered.

**CONVERTING TO ANOTHER TYPE**

The method toTotalMonths() returns the total number of months in the period by multiplying the number of years by 12 and adding the number of months:

```
System.out.println(Period.of(10,5,40).toTotalMonths());          ⟵——— Outputs 125
```

A Period can be used as an argument to the LocalDate one-parameter plus() and minus() methods. What happens when you want to add 3 months and 10 days to a given date? The number of months per year is constant but the number of days per month isn't. A glimpse at the plus() and minus() methods in the LocalDate source code shows that years are converted to months and months are always handled before days.

In the next section, you'll work with the class DateTimeFormatter.

### 4.6.5  *DateTimeFormatter*

Defined in the package java.time.format, the class DateTimeFormatter can be used to format and parse date and time objects. In this section, you'll use this class to format or parse date and time objects using predefined constants (like ISO_LOCAL_DATE), using patterns (like yyyy-MM-dd) or localized styles like *long* or *short*.

The first step to format or parse a date or time object is to access a DateTime-Formatter and then call format or parse methods on either date or time objects or

DateTimeFormatter. Let's work in detail with these steps, starting with multiple ways to instantiate or access a DateTimeFormatter object.

### INSTANTIATE OR ACCESS DATETIMEFORMATTER

You can instantiate or access a DateTimeFormatter object in multiple ways:

- By calling a static of*XXX* method, passing it a FormatStyle value
- By access public static fields of DateTimeFormatter
- By using the static method ofPattern and passing it a string value

Starting with the first option, you can instantiate a DateTimeFormatter to work with date, time, or date/time objects by calling its of*XXX* static method and passing it a FormatStyle value (FormatStyle.FULL, FormatStyle.LONG, FormatStyle.MEDIUM, or FormatStyle.SHORT):

```
DateTimeFormatter formatter1 =
                DateTimeFormatter.ofLocalizedDate(FormatStyle.MEDIUM);
DateTimeFormatter formatter2 =
                DateTimeFormatter.ofLocalizedTime(FormatStyle.FULL);
DateTimeFormatter formatter3 =
                DateTimeFormatter.ofLocalizedDateTime(FormatStyle.LONG);
DateTimeFormatter formatter4 =
                DateTimeFormatter.ofLocalizedDateTime(FormatStyle.SHORT,
                                                      FormatStyle.SHORT);
```

 **NOTE**   The methods ofLocalizedDate, ofLocalizedTime, and ofLocalized-DateTime format date and time objects according to the locale (language, region, or country) of the system on which your code executes. So the output might vary slightly across systems.

Table 4.2 shows how a date or time object will be formatted by using the different FormatStyle values.

**Table 4.2**   Examples of how FormatStyle affects formatting of a date (say, August 11, 2057) or time (say, 14 hours, 30 minutes, and 15 seconds) object

| FormatStyle | Example |
| --- | --- |
| FormatStyle.FULL | Saturday, August 11, 2057 |
| FormatStyle.LONG | August 11, 2057 |
| FormatStyle.MEDIUM | Aug 11, 2057 |
| FormatStyle.SHORT | 8/11/57 |
| FormatStyle.FULL | |
| FormatStyle.LONG | |
| FormatStyle.MEDIUM | 2:30:15 PM |
| FormatStyle.SHORT | 2:30 PM |

You can access a DateTimeFormatter object by using the public and static fields of this class:

```
DateTimeFormatter formatter5 = DateTimeFormatter.ISO_DATE;
```

Table 4.3 lists a few predefined formatters that are relevant for this exam.

**Table 4.3** Predefined formatters in the class DateTimeFormatter and an example of how they format a date (say, August 11, 2057) or time (say, 14 hours 30 minutes, and 15 seconds) object

| Predefined formatter | Example |
|---|---|
| BASIC_ISO_DATE | 20570811 |
| ISO_DATE/ISO_LOCAL_DATE | 2057-08-11 |
| ISO_TIME/ISO_LOCAL_TIME | 14:30:15.312 |
| ISO_DATE_TIME/ISO_LOCAL_DATE_TIME | 2057-08-11T14:30:15.312 |

You can instantiate a DateTimeFormatter using a pattern (of letters and symbols) by using the static method ofPattern and passing it a string value:

```
DateTimeFormatter formatter6= DateTimeFormatter.ofPattern("yyyy MM dd");
```

You can use the preceding code to format a date, say August 11, 2057, as 2057 08 11. Table 4.4 lists the letters that can be used to define such patterns.

**Table 4.4** Letters used to define patterns for DateTimeFormatter and examples of how they would format a date (say, August 11, 2057) or time (say, 14 hours, 30 minutes, and 15 seconds) object

| Symbol | Meaning | Example |
|---|---|---|
| y, Y | year | 2057; 57 |
| M | month of year | 8; 08; Aug; August |
| D | day of year | 223 |
| d | day of month | 11 |
| E | day of week | Sat |
| e | localized day of week | 7; Sat |
| a | a.m. or p.m. of day | pm |
| h | clock hour of a.m./p.m. | 03 |
| H | hour of day | 14 |
| m | minute of hour | 30 |
| s | second of minute | 15 |
| ` | escape for text | |

**EXAM TIP**   A DateTimeFormatter can define rules to format or parse a date object, time object, or both.

### FORMAT DATE OR TIME OBJECTS USING DATETIMEFORMATTER

To format a date or time object, you can use either the instance format method in date/time objects or the instance format method in the DateTimeFormatter class. Behind the scenes, the format method in date and time objects simply calls the format method in DateTimeFormatter. Table 4.5 lists the available format methods.

**NOTE**   TemporalAccessor is an interface, implemented by the classes Local-Date, LocalTime, and LocalDateTime. You won't get explicit questions on this interface on the exam.

**Table 4.5   format methods in the classes LocalDate, LocalTime, LocalDateTime, and Date-TimeFormatter**

| Defined in | Return type | Method signature and description |
|---|---|---|
| LocalDate | String | format(DateTimeFormatter)<br>Formats this date object using the specified DateTimeFormatter |
| LocalTime | String | format(DateTimeFormatter)<br>Formats this time object using the specified DateTimeFormatter |
| LocalDateTime | String | format(DateTimeFormatter)<br>Formats this date/time object using the specified DateTimeFormatter |
| DateTimeFormatter | String | format(TemporalAccessor)<br>Formats a date/time object using this formatter |

**EXAM TIP**   Watch out for the count and type of arguments passed to the instance method format. When calling format on a LocalDate, LocalTime, or LocalDateTime instance, pass a DateTimeFormatter instance as a method parameter. When calling format on DateTimeFormatter, pass a LocalDate, LocalTime, or LocalDateTime instance as a method argument.

The method format in DateTimeFormatter formats a date or time object to a String using the rules of the formatter. The following example formats a LocalDate object using the style FormatStyle (styles are listed in table 4.2):

```
DateTimeFormatter formatter =
                DateTimeFormatter.ofLocalizedDate(FormatStyle.LONG);
LocalDate date = LocalDate.of(2057,8,11);
System.out.println(formatter.format(date));
```
⟵| **Outputs August 11, 2057**

What happens if you pass a time object (LocalTime) instead of a date object (Local-Date) in the preceding code? Will it compile or execute successfully (changes are shown in bold)?

```
DateTimeFormatter formatter =
                  DateTimeFormatter.ofLocalizedDate(FormatStyle.LONG);
LocalTime time = LocalTime.now();
System.out.println(formatter.format(time));                ⟵ Throws runtime
                                                                exception
```

The preceding code will compile successfully but won't execute. It will throw a runtime exception because the formatter defines rules to format a date object (created using ofLocalizedDate()), but its format() is passed a time object.

 **EXAM TIP** If you pass a date object to the method format on a DateTimeFormatter instance that defines rules to format a time object, it will throw a runtime exception.

Formatting date and time objects using DateTimeFormatter, which are created using string patterns, is interesting (and confusing). Take note of the case of the letters used in the patterns. *M* and *m* or *D* and *d* are not the same. Also, using a pattern letter doesn't specify the count of digits or texts. For an example, using *Y* or *YYYY* to format a date object returns the same results. Following are examples that use different patterns:

```
LocalDate date = LocalDate.of(2057,8,11);
LocalTime time = LocalTime.of(14,30,15);

DateTimeFormatter d1 = DateTimeFormatter.ofPattern("y");
DateTimeFormatter d2 = DateTimeFormatter.ofPattern("YYYY");
DateTimeFormatter d3 = DateTimeFormatter.ofPattern("Y M D");
DateTimeFormatter d4 = DateTimeFormatter.ofPattern("e");

DateTimeFormatter t1 = DateTimeFormatter.ofPattern("H h m s");
DateTimeFormatter t2 = DateTimeFormatter.ofPattern("'Time now:'HH mm a");

System.out.println(d1.format(date));
System.out.println(d2.format(date));
System.out.println(d3.format(date));
System.out.println(d4.format(date));

System.out.println(t1.format(time));
System.out.println(t2.format(time));
```

Here's the output of the preceding code:

```
2057
2057
2057 8 223
7
14 2 30 15
Time now:14 30 PM
```

**EXAM TIP**   If you're confused between *M, m, D,* and *d,* remember that an upper-case letter represents a bigger duration period. So *M* is for month and *m* is for minutes. Similarly, *D* represents day of year; *d* represents day of month.

You can also format date and time objects by calling the `format` method in date or time objects and passing it a `DateTimeFormatter` instance.

**NOTE**   If you access Java's source code, you'll notice that the `format` and `parse` methods in date and time classes simply call the `format` and `parse` methods on a `DateTimeFormatter` instance.

### PARSE DATE OR TIME OBJECTS USING DATETIMEFORMATTER

To parse a date or time object, you can use either the static `parse` method in date/time objects or the instance `parse` method in the `DateTimeFormatter` class. Behind the scenes, the `parse` method in date/time objects simply calls the `parse` method in `DateTimeFormatter`. Table 4.6 lists the available parse methods.

**EXAM TIP**   The parse methods are defined as static methods in the classes `LocalDate`, `LocalTime`, and `LocalDateTime`. The class `DateTimeFormatter` defines the parse method as an instance method.

**Table 4.6   parse methods in the classes** `LocalDate`, `LocalTime`, `LocalDateTime`, **and** `Date-TimeFormatter`

| Defined in | Return type | Method signature and description |
|---|---|---|
| LocalDate | LocalDate | `parse(CharSequence)`<br>Creates a `LocalDate` instance using a text string such as 2057-08-11, parsed using `DateTimeFormatter.ISO_LOCAL_DATE` |
| LocalDate | LocalDate | `parse(CharSequence, DateTimeFormatter)`<br>Creates a `LocalDate` instance, parsing text using the specified formatter |
| LocalTime | LocalTime | `parse(CharSequence)`<br>Creates a `LocalTime` instance using a text string such as 14:40, parsed using `DateTimeFormatter.ISO_LOCAL_TIME` |
| LocalTime | LocalTime | `parse(CharSequence, DateTimeFormatter)`<br>Creates a `LocalTime` instance, parsing text using the specified formatter |
| LocalDateTime | LocalDateTime | `parse(CharSequence)`<br>Creates a `LocalDateTime` instance using a text string such as 2057-08-11T14:40, parsed using `DateTimeFormatter.ISO_LOCAL_DATE_TIME` |

**Table 4.6** parse methods in the classes `LocalDate`, `LocalTime`, `LocalDateTime`, and `Date-TimeFormatter`

| Defined in | Return type | Method signature and description |
|---|---|---|
| `LocalDateTime` | `LocalDateTime` | `parse(CharSequence, DateTimeFormatter)`<br>Creates a `LocalDateTime` instance, parsing text using the specified formatter |
| `DateTimeFormatter` | `TemporalAccessor` | `parse(CharSequence)`<br>Parses text using the rules of `DateTimeFormatter`, returning a temporal object |

**EXAM TIP** When calling parse on `LocalDate`, `LocalTime`, or `LocalDateTime` instances, you might not specify a formatter. In this case `DateTimeFormatter.ISO_LOCAL_DATE`, `DateTimeFormatter.ISO_LOCAL_TIME`, and `DateTimeFormatter.ISO_LOCAL_DATE_TIME` are used to parse text, respectively.

Let's work with the method parse of `LocalDate`, `LocalTime`, or `LocalDateTime` to parse a string value using a `DateTimeFormatter`, producing a date or time object:

```
DateTimeFormatter d1 = DateTimeFormatter.ofPattern("yyyy-MM-dd");
LocalDate date = LocalDate.parse("2057-01-29", d1 );
```

The following line throws a `DateTimeParseException` because this mechanism works *only if* all components are present. For example, the pattern yyyy-MM-dd with "2057-01-29" works fine. The component order doesn't matter; hence, using dd-yyyy-MM to parse "29-2057-01" works too and yields January 29, 2057 as well:

```
DateTimeFormatter d1 = DateTimeFormatter.ofPattern("yyyy");
LocalDate date = LocalDate.parse("2057", d1);
```

Similarly, you can call the parse method to create instances of `LocalTime` and `LocalDateTime`.

## 4.7 Summary

In this chapter, you learned about the `String` class, its properties, and its methods. Because this is one of the most frequently used classes in Java, I'll reiterate that a good understanding of this class in terms of why its methods behave in a particular manner will go a long way toward helping you successfully complete the OCA Java SE 8 Programmer I exam.

You learned how to initialize `String` variables using the operator new and the assignment operator (=) with `String` literals. You also learned the differences between how `String` objects are stored using these two approaches. If you use the assignment operator to initialize your `String` variables, they're stored in a common pool of `String` objects (also known as the `String` constant pool) that can be used by others.

This storage is possible because String objects are immutable—that is, their values can't be changed.

You learned how a char array is used to store the value of a String object. This helps explain why the methods charAt(), indexOf(), and substring() search for the first character of a String at position 0, not position 1. We also reviewed the methods replace(), trim(), and substring(), which seem to modify the value of a String but will never be able to do so because String objects are immutable. You also learned the methods length(), startsWith(), and endsWith().

Because not all operators can be used with Strings, you learned about the ones that can be used with String: +, +=, ==, and !=. You also learned that the equality of Strings can be determined using the method equals. By using the operator ==, you can only determine whether both of the variables are referring to the same object; it doesn't compare the values stored by Strings. As with all the other object types, you can assign null to a String variable.

You worked with the class StringBuilder, which is defined in the package java.lang and is used to store a mutable sequence of characters. The class String-Builder is usually used to store a sequence of characters that needs to be modified often—such as when you're building a query for database applications. Like the String class, StringBuilder also uses a char array to store its characters. Many of the methods defined in the class StringBuilder work exactly as defined by the class String, such as the methods charAt, indexOf, substring, and length. The append method is used to add characters to the end of a StringBuilder object. The insert method is another important StringBuilder method that's used to insert either single or multiple characters at a specified position in a StringBuilder object. The class String-Builder offers the same functionality as offered by the class StringBuffer, minus the additional feature of methods that are synchronized where needed.

An array is an object that stores a collection of values. An array can store a collection of primitive data types or a collection of objects. You can define one-dimensional and multidimensional arrays. A one-dimensional array is an object that refers to a collection of scalar values. A two-dimensional (or more) array is referred to as a multidimensional array. A two-dimensional array refers to a collection of objects, where each of the objects is a one-dimensional array. Similarly, a three-dimensional array refers to a collection of two-dimensional arrays, and so on. Arrays can be declared, allocated, and initialized in a single step or in multiple steps. A two-dimensional array doesn't need to be symmetrical, and each of its rows can define different numbers of members. You can define arrays of primitives, interfaces, abstract classes, and concrete classes. All arrays are objects and can access the variable length and methods inherited from the class java.lang.Object.

ArrayList is a resizable array that offers the best combination of features offered by an array and the List data structure. You can add objects to an ArrayList using the method add. You can access the objects of an ArrayList by using an enhanced for loop or by using the get() method or an iterator. An ArrayList preserves the order of insertion of its elements. `ListIterator`, `Iterator`, and the enhanced `for` loop will return the elements in the order in which they were added to the `ArrayList`. You can modify the elements of an `ArrayList` using the method `set`. You can remove the elements of an `ArrayList` by using the method `remove`, which accepts the element position or an object. You can also add multiple elements to an `ArrayList` by using the method `addAll`. The method `clone` defined in the class `ArrayList` returns a shallow copy of this `ArrayList` instance. *Shallow copy* means that the method creates a new instance of the `ArrayList` to be cloned, but the `ArrayList` elements aren't copied.

You can compare the objects of your class by overriding the `equals` method. The `equals` method is defined in the class `java.lang.Object`, which is the base class of all classes in Java. The default implementation of the method `equals` only compares the object references for equality. Because instance variables are used to store the state of an object, it's common to compare the values of these variables to determine whether two objects should be considered equal in the `equals` method. The Java API documentation defines a contract for the `equals` method. In the exam, for a given definition of the method `equals`, it is important to note the differences between an `equals` method that compiles successfully, one that fails compilation, and one that doesn't follow the contract.

The Date and Time API in Java 8 simplifies how you work with the date and time classes. You worked with `LocalDate`, which is used to store only dates of the format 2016-08-14. `LocalTime` stores time in the format 14:09:65:23 (hours:minutes:seconds :nanoseconds). The class `LocalDateTime` stores both date and time. The class `Period` is used to work with a duration of, say, a period of 4 months or 4 days. The class `DateTimeFormatter` is used to format date and time using a predefined or custom format.

## 4.8   *Review notes*

This section lists the main points covered in this chapter.

The class `String`:

- The class `String` represents an immutable sequence of characters.
- A `String` variable can be initialized by using the operator `new` or by using the assignment operator with `String` literal values.
- `String` objects created using a `String` literal without the `new` operator are placed in a *pool* of `String` objects. Whenever the JRE receives a new request to initialize a `String` variable using the assignment operator, it checks whether a `String` object with the same value already exists in the pool. If one is found, it returns the object reference for the existing `String` object from the pool.
- `String` objects created using the operator `new` are never placed in the pool of `String` objects.
- The comparison operator (`==`) compares `String` references, whereas the `equals` method compares the `String` values.
- None of the methods defined in the class `String` can modify its value.

- The method `charAt(int index)` retrieves a character at a specified index of a `String`.
- The method `indexOf` can be used to search a `String` for the occurrence of a `char` or a `String`, starting from the first position or a specified position.
- The method `substring` can be used to retrieve a portion of a `String` object. The `substring` method doesn't include the character at the end position.
- The `trim` method will return a new `String` by removing all the leading and trailing white spaces from a `String`. This method doesn't remove any white space *within* a `String`.
- You can use the method `length` to retrieve the length of a `String`.
- The method `startsWith` determines whether a `String` starts with a specified `String`.
- The method `endsWith` determines whether a `String` ends with a specified `String`.
- It's a common practice to use multiple `String` methods in a single line of code. When chained, the methods are evaluated from left to right.
- You can use the concatenation operators `+` and `+=` and comparison operators `!=` and `==` with `String` objects.
- The Java language provides special support for concatenating `String` objects by using the operators `+` and `+=`.
- The right technique for comparing two `String` values for equality is to use the method `equals` defined in the `String` class. This method returns a `true` value if the object being compared isn't `null` and is a `String` object that represents the same sequence of characters as the object to which it's being compared.
- The comparison operator `==` determines whether both of the reference variables are referring to the same `String` objects. Hence, it's not the right operator for comparing `String` values.

The class `StringBuilder`:

- The class `StringBuilder` is defined in the package `java.lang` and represents a mutable sequence of characters.
- The `StringBuilder` class is very efficient when a user needs to modify a sequence of characters often. Because it's mutable, the value of a `String-Builder` object can be modified without the need to create a new `String-Builder` object.
- A `StringBuilder` object can be created using its constructors, which can accept either a `String` object, another `StringBuilder` object, an `int` value to specify the capacity of `StringBuilder`, or nothing.
- The methods `charAt`, `indexOf`, `substring`, and `length` defined in the class `StringBuilder` work in the same way as methods with the same names defined in the class `String`.

- The append method adds the specified value at the end of the existing value of a StringBuilder object.
- The insert method enables you to insert characters at a specified position in a StringBuilder object. The main difference between the append and insert methods is that the insert method enables you to insert the requested data at a particular position, whereas the append method allows you to add the requested data only at the end of the StringBuilder object.
- The method delete removes the characters in a substring of the specified StringBuilder. The method deleteCharAt removes the char at the specified position.
- Unlike the class String, the class StringBuilder doesn't define the method trim.
- The method reverse reverses the sequence of characters of a StringBuilder.
- The replace method in the class StringBuilder replaces a sequence of characters, identified by their position, with another String.
- In addition to using the method substring, you can also use the method subSequence to retrieve a subsequence of a StringBuilder object.

Arrays:

- An array is an object that stores a collection of values.
- An array itself is an object.
- An array can store two types of data—a collection of primitive data types and a collection of objects.
- You can define one-dimensional and multidimensional arrays.
- A one-dimensional array is an object that refers to a collection of scalar values.
- A two-dimensional (or more) array is referred to as a multidimensional array.
- A two-dimensional array refers to a collection of objects, in which each of the objects is a one-dimensional array.
- Similarly, a three-dimensional array refers to a collection of two-dimensional arrays, and so on.
- Multidimensional arrays may or may not contain the same number of elements in each row or column.
- The creation of an array involves three steps: declaration of an array, allocation of an array, and initialization of array elements.
- An array declaration is composed of an array type, a variable name, and one or more occurrences of [].
- Square brackets can follow either the variable name or its type. In the case of multidimensional arrays, it can follow both of them.
- An array declaration creates a variable that refers to null.
- Because no elements of an array are created when it's declared, it's invalid to define the size of an array with its declaration.

- Array allocation allocates memory for the elements of an array. When you allocate memory for an array, you must specify its dimensions, such as the number of elements the array should store.

- Because an array is an object, it's allocated using the keyword new, followed by the type of value that it stores, and then its size.

- Once allocated, all the array elements store their default values. Elements of an array that store objects refer to null. Elements of an array that store primitive data types store 0 for integer types (byte, short, int, long), 0.0 for decimal types (float and double), false for boolean, or /u0000 for char data.

- To access an element in a two-dimensional array, use two array position values.

- You can combine all the steps of array declaration, allocation, and initialization into a single step.

- When you combine array declaration, allocation, and initialization in a single step, you can't specify the size of the array. The size of the array is calculated by the number of values that are assigned to the array.

- You can declare and allocate an array but choose not to initialize its elements (for example, int[] a = new int[5];).

- The Java compiler doesn't check the range of the index positions at which you try to access an array element. The code throws an ArrayIndexOutOfBounds-Exception exception if the requested index position doesn't fall in the valid range at runtime.

- A multidimensional array can be asymmetrical; it may or may not define the same number of columns for each of its rows.

- The type of an array can also be an interface or abstract class. Such an array can be used to store objects of classes that inherit from the interface type or the abstract class type.

- The type of an array can also be java.lang.Object. Because all classes extend the java.lang.Object class, elements of this array can refer to any object.

- All the arrays are objects and can access the variable length, which specifies the number or components stored by the array.

- Because all arrays are objects, they inherit and can access all methods from the class Object.

ArrayList:

- ArrayList is one of the most widely used classes from the Collections framework. It offers the best combination of features offered by an array and the List data structure.

- An ArrayList is like a resizable array.

- Unlike arrays, you may not specify an initial size to create an ArrayList.

- ArrayList implements the interface List and allows null values to be added to it.

- ArrayList implements all list operations (add, modify, and delete values).

- `ArrayList` allows duplicate values to be added to it and maintains its insertion order.
- You can use either `Iterator` or `ListIterator` or an enhanced `for` loop to iterate over the items of an `ArrayList`.
- `ArrayList` supports generics, making it type safe.
- Internally, an array of type `java.lang.Object` is used to store the data in an `ArrayList`.
- You can add a value to an `ArrayList` either at its end or at a specified position by using the method `add`.
- An iterator (`Iterator` or `ListIterator`) lets you remove elements as you iterate through an `ArrayList`. It's not possible to remove elements from an `ArrayList` while iterating through it using a `for` loop.
- An `ArrayList` preserves the order of insertion of its elements. `ListIterator` and the enhanced `for` loop will return the elements in the order in which they were added to the `ArrayList`.
- You can use the method `set` to modify an `ArrayList` by either replacing an existing element in `ArrayList` or modifying its existing values.
- `remove(int)` removes the element at the specified position in the list.
- `remove(Object o)` removes the first occurrence of the specified element from the list, if it's present.
- You can add multiple elements to an `ArrayList` from another `ArrayList` or any other class that's a subclass of `Collection` by using the method `addAll`.
- You can remove all the `ArrayList` elements by calling the method `clear` on it.
- `get(int index)` returns the element at the specified position in the list.
- `size()` returns the number of elements in the list.
- `contains(Object o)` returns `true` if the list contains the specified element.
- `indexOf(Object o)` returns the index of the first occurrence of the specified element in the list, or -1 if the list doesn't contain the element.
- `lastIndexOf(Object o)` returns the index of the last occurrence of the specified element in the list, or -1 if the list doesn't contain the element.
- The method `clone` defined in the class `ArrayList` returns a shallow copy of this `ArrayList` instance. *Shallow copy* means that the method creates a new instance of the `ArrayList` to be cloned, but the `ArrayList` elements aren't copied.
- You can use the method `toArray` to return an array containing all the elements in `ArrayList` in sequence from the first to the last element.

Comparing objects for equality:

- Any Java class can define a set of rules to determine whether two objects should be considered equal.
- The method `equals` is defined in the class `java.lang.Object`. All the Java classes directly or indirectly inherit this class.

- The default implementation of the equals method only checks whether two object variables refer to the same object.
- Because instance variables are used to store the state of an object, it's common to compare the values of the instance variables to determine whether two objects should be considered equal.
- When you override the equals method in your class, make sure that you use the correct method signature for the equals method.
- The Java API defines a contract for the equals method, which should be taken care of when you implement the method in any of your classes.
- According to the contract of the method equals, if a null value is passed to it, the method equals should return false.
- If the equals method modifies the value of any of the instance variables of the method parameter passed to it, or of the object on which it is called, it will violate the contract.

LocalDate:

- LocalDate can be used to store dates like 2015-12-27 without time or time zones.
- LocalDate instances are immutable.
- The LocalDate constructor is marked private.
- Use LocalDate's overloaded static method of() to instantiate it:
  - public static LocalDate of(int year, int month, int dayOfMonth)
  - public static LocalDate of(int year, Month month, int dayOfMonth)
- The of() methods will throw a DateTimeException when values passed to it are out of range.
- In date classes released with Java 8, the January month is represented by int value 1 and not 0. The date classes defined with or prior to Java 7 represent January using 0.
- LocalDate's static method now() returns the current date from the system clock as a LocalDate instance.
- Use LocalDate's static method parse() to parse a string in the format 2016-02-27 to instantiate LocalDate.
- If you pass invalid values to parse() or of(), you'll get a DateTimeParse-Exception. The format of the string passed to parse() must be exactly of the format 9999-99-99. The month and date values passed to parse() must be of two digits; a single digit is considered an invalid value. For days and months with a value 1–9, pass 01–09.
- You can use LocalDate's instance methods like get*XX*() to query LocalDate on its year, month, and date values:
  - getDayOfMonth()
  - getDayOfWeek()
  - getDayOfYear()

- – getMonth()
- – getMonthValue()
- – getYear()
- LocalDate's instance minus*XX*() methods return a copy of its value after subtracting the specified days, months, weeks, or years from it:
  - – minusDays()
  - – minusMonths()
  - – minusWeeks()
  - – minusYears()
- LocalDate is immutable. All the methods that seem to manipulate its value return a copy of the LocalDate instance on which it's called.
- The plus*XX*() methods return a copy of LocalDate's value after adding the specified days, months, or year to it:
  - – plusDays()
  - – plusMonths()
  - – plusWeeks()
  - – plusYears()
- The with*XX*() methods return a copy of LocalDate's value replacing the specified day, month, or year in it:
  - – withDayOfMonth()
  - – withDayOfYear()
  - – withMonth()
  - – withYear()
- All additions, subtractions, or replacements to LocalDate consider leap years.
- Despite the verbs used in the previous methods (*add, subtract, replace*), none of them actually modifies an existing LocalDate—all of them return a new instance with the requested changes applied.
- The LocalDate class defines overloaded atTime() instance methods. These methods combine LocalDate with time to create and return LocalDateTime, which stores both the date and time.
- Use the method toEpochDay() to convert LocalDate to the epoch date—the count of days from January 1, 1970.

LocalTime:

- It stores time in the format hours-minutes-seconds (without a time zone).
- It stores time to nanosecond precision.
- LocalTime is immutable.
- You can instantiate LocalTime using LocalTime's static method of() that accepts hours, minutes, seconds, and nanoseconds.
- The of() method uses a 24-hour clock to specify the hour value.

- The of() method will throw a runtime exception, DateTimeException, if you pass an invalid range of values to it.
- LocalTime doesn't define a method to pass a.m. or p.m. Use values 0–23 to define hours. If you pass out-of-range values to either hours, minutes, or seconds, you'll get a runtime exception.
- To get the current time from the system clock, use the static method now().
- You can parse a string to instantiate LocalTime by using its static method parse(). You can either pass a string in the format 15:08:23 (hours:minutes:seconds) or parse any text using DateTimeFormatter.
- If you pass invalid string values to parse(), the code will compile but will throw a runtime exception. If you don't pass a DateTimeFormatter, the format of the string passed to parse() must be exactly of the format 99:99:99. The hours and minutes values passed to parse() must be of two digits; a single digit is considered an invalid value. For hours and minutes with a value 0–9, pass 00–09.
- You can use constants from the LocalTime class to work with predefined times:
  - LocalTime.MIN—Minimum supported time, that is, 00:00
  - LocalTime.MAX—Maximum supported time, that is, 23:59:59.999999999
  - LocalTime.MIDNIGHT—Time when day starts, that is, 00:00
  - LocalTime.NOON—Noontime, that is, 12:00
- You can use instance methods like get*XX*() to query LocalTime on its hour, minutes, seconds, and nanoseconds. All these methods return an int value.
- The correct method names to query LocalTime are getHour(), getMinute(), getSecond(), and getNano(). Watch out for exam questions that use invalid method names like getHours(), getMinutes(), getSeconds(), or getNanoSeconds().
- You can use the instance methods isAfter() and isBefore() to check whether a time is after or before the specified time.
- You can use the instance methods minusHours(), minusMinutes(), minusSeconds(), and minusNanos() to create and return a copy of LocalTime instances with the specified period subtracted.
- Unlike the get*XXX*() methods, the minus*XXX*() methods use the plural form: getHour() versus minusHours(), getMinute() versus minusMinutes(), getSecond() versus minusSeconds(), and getNano() versus minusNanos().
- The plusHours(), plusMinutes(), plusSeconds(), and plusNanos() methods accept long values and add the specified hours, minutes, seconds, or nanoseconds to time, returning its copy as LocalTime.
- LocalTime is immutable. Calling any method on an instance won't modify its value.
- The withHour(), withMinute(), withSecond(), and withNano() methods accept an int value and return a copy of LocalTime with the specified value altered.
- The class LocalTime defines the method atDate(), which can be passed a LocalDate instance to create a LocalDateTime instance.

`LocalDateTime`:

- `LocalDateTime` stores a value like 2050-06-18T14:20:30:908765 (year-month-dayThours:minutes:seconds:nanoseconds).
- The `LocalDateTime` class uses the letter *T* to separate date and time values in its printed value.
- You can consider this class to offer the functionality of both the `LocalDate` and `LocalTime` classes. This class defines similar methods as those defined by the `LocalDate` and `LocalTime` classes.

`Period`:

- The `Period` class represents a date-based amount in years, months, and days, like 2 years, 5 months, and 10 days. To work with time-based amounts in seconds and nanoseconds, you can use the `Duration` class.
- You can add or subtract `Period` instances from `LocalDate` and `LocalDateTime` classes.
- `Period` is an immutable class.
- The `Period` class defines multiple factory methods to create its instances. The static methods of `of()`, `ofYears()`, `ofMonths()`, `ofWeeks()`, and `ofDays()` accept int values to create periods of years, months, weeks, or days.
- A `Period` of 35 days is not stored as 1 month and 5 days. Its individual elements, that is, days, months, and years, are stored the way it is initialized.
- You can define positive or negative periods of time. You can define `Period` instances representing 15 or -15 days.
- You can also parse a string to instantiate `Period` by using its static method parse. This method parses string values of the format PnYnMnD or PnW, where *n* represents a number and the letters (*P, Y, M, D,* and *W*) represent parse, year, month, day, and week. These letters can exist in lower- or uppercase. Each string must start with the letter *p* or *P* and must include at least one of the four sections, that is, year, month, week, or day.
- If you pass invalid string values to `parse()`, the code will compile but will throw a runtime exception.
- You can also use the static method `between(LocalDate dateInclusive, Local-Date dateExclusive)` to instantiate `Period`.
- The static method `between` accepts two `LocalDate` instances and returns a `Period` instance representing number of years, days, and months between the two dates. The first date is included, but the second date is excluded in the returned `Period`.
- The `Period` class implements the interface `TemporalAmount`, so it can be used with the methods `plus()` and `minus()` defined in the classes `LocalDateTime` and `LocalDate`.

- Because `Period` instances can represent positive or negative periods (like 15 days or -15 days), you can subtract days from a `LocalDate` or `LocalDateTime` by calling the method `plus`.

- Similarly, you can use the method `minus()` with classes `LocalDate` and `Local-DateTime` to subtract a period of years, months, weeks, or days.

- You can use the instance methods `getYears()`, `getMonths()`, and `getDays()` to query a `Period` instance on its years, months, and days. All these methods return an `int` value.

- When you initialize a `Period` instance with days more than 31 or months more than 12, it doesn't recalculate its years, months, or days components.

- You can query whether any of three units of a `Period` is negative using the methods `isNegative` and `isZero`. A `Period` instance is negative if all three of its units are zero.

- You can use instance methods `minus(TemporalAmount)`, `minusDays(long)`, `minusMonths(long)`, `minusYears(long)`, and `multipliedBy(int)` to create and return a copy of `Period` instances with the specified period subtracted or modified.

- In the class `Period`, both the get*XXX*() methods and minus*XXX*() methods use the plural form: `getYears()`, `minusHours()`.

- When you subtract a `Period` instance using the minus*XXX*() methods, its individual elements are subtracted. Subtracting P10D from P1M returns P1M-10D and not P20D.

- The method `multipliedBy(int)` in the class `Period` is used to modify all elements of a `Period` instance. `Period` doesn't define *divideBy*.

- Adding a `Period` of 10 months to a `Period` of 5 months gives 15 months, not 1 year and 3 months.

- The method `toTotalMonths()` returns the total number of months in the period by multiplying the number of years by 12 and adding the number of months.

DateTimeFormatter

- Defined in the package `java.time.format`, the class `DateTimeFormatter` can be used to format and parse date and time objects.

- A `DateTimeFormatter` can define rules to format or parse a date object, time object, or both.

- You can instantiate or access a `DateTimeFormatter` object in multiple ways:
  - By calling a static of*XXX* method, passing it a `FormatStyle` value
  - By accessing public static fields of `DateTimeFormatter`
  - By using a static method `ofPattern` and passing it a string value

- To instantiate a `DateTimeFormatter` using of*XXX* methods, pass it a `Format-Style` value (`FormatStyle.FULL`, `FormatStyle.LONG`, `FormatStyle.MEDIUM`, or `FormatStyle.SHORT`).

- You can access a DateTimeFormatter object by using the public and static fields of this class: BASIC_ISO_DATE, ISO_DATE, ISO_TIME, and ISO_DATE_TIME.
- The method format in DateTimeFormatter formats a date or time object to a String using the rules of the formatter.
- To parse a date or time object, you can use either the parse method in date/time objects or the parse method in the DateTimeFormatter class.

## 4.9    Sample exam questions

**Q4-1.** What is the output of the following code?

```
class EJavaGuruArray {
    public static void main(String args[]) {
        int[] arr = new int[5];
        byte b = 4; char c = 'c'; long longVar = 10;
        arr[0] = b;
        arr[1] = c;
        arr[3] = longVar;
        System.out.println(arr[0] + arr[1] + arr[2] + arr[3]);
    }
}
```

a   4c010

b   4c10

c   113

d   103

e   Compilation error

**Q4-2.** What is the output of the following code?

```
class EJavaGuruArray2 {
    public static void main(String args[]) {
        int[] arr1;
        int[] arr2 = new int[3];
        char[] arr3 = {'a', 'b'};
        arr1 = arr2;
        arr1 = arr3;
        System.out.println(arr1[0] + ":" + arr1[1]);
    }
}
```

a   0:0

b   a:b

c   0:b

d   a:0

e   Compilation error

**Q4-3.** Which of the following are valid lines of code to define a multidimensional int array?

a  `int[][] array1 = {{1, 2, 3}, {}, {1, 2,3, 4, 5}};`
b  `int[][] array2 = new array() {{1, 2, 3}, {}, {1, 2,3, 4, 5}};`
c  `int[][] array3 = {1, 2, 3}, {0}, {1, 2,3, 4, 5};`
d  `int[][] array4 = new int[2][];`

**Q4-4.** Which of the following statements are correct?

a  The following code executes without an error or exception:

```
ArrayList<Long> lst = new ArrayList<>();
lst.add(10);
```

b  Because `ArrayList` stores only objects, you can't pass an element of an `Array-List` to a `switch` construct.
c  Calling `clear()` or `remove()` on an `ArrayList` will remove all its elements.
d  If you frequently add elements to an `ArrayList`, specifying a larger capacity will improve the code efficiency.
e  Calling the method `clone()` on an `ArrayList` creates its shallow copy; that is, it doesn't clone the individual list elements.

**Q4-5.** Which of the following statements are correct?

a  An `ArrayList` offers a resizable array, which is easily managed using the methods it provides. You can add and remove elements from an `ArrayList`.
b  Values stored by an `ArrayList` can be modified.
c  You can iterate through elements of an `ArrayList` using a for loop, `Iterator`, or `ListIterator`.
d  An `ArrayList` requires you to specify the total number of elements before you can store any elements in it.
e  An `ArrayList` can store any type of object.

**Q4-6.** What is the output of the following code?

```
import java.util.*;                                              // line 1
class EJavaGuruArrayList {                                       // line 2
    public static void main(String args[]) {                    // line 3
        ArrayList<String> ejg = new ArrayList<>();              // line 4
        ejg.add("One");                                         // line 5
        ejg.add("Two");                                         // line 6
        System.out.println(ejg.contains(new String("One")));   // line 7
        System.out.println(ejg.indexOf("Two"));                // line 8
        ejg.clear();                                            // line 9
        System.out.println(ejg);                               // line 10
```

```
        System.out.println(ejg.get(1));              // line 11
    }                                                 // line 12
}                                                     // line 13
```

a Line 7 prints true.

b Line 7 prints false.

c Line 8 prints -1.

d Line 8 prints 1.

e Line 9 removes all elements of the list ejg.

f Line 9 sets the list ejg to null.

g Line 10 prints null.

h Line 10 prints [].

i Line 10 prints a value similar to ArrayList@16356.

j Line 11 throws an exception.

k Line 11 prints null.

**Q4-7.** What is the output of the following code?

```
class EJavaGuruString {
    public static void main(String args[]) {
        String ejg1 = new String("E Java");
        String ejg2 = new String("E Java");
        String ejg3 = "E Java";
        String ejg4 = "E Java";
        do
            System.out.println(ejg1.equals(ejg2));
        while (ejg3 == ejg4);
    }
}
```

a true printed once

b false printed once

c true printed in an infinite loop

d false printed in an infinite loop

**Q4-8.** What is the output of the following code?

```
class EJavaGuruString2 {
    public static void main(String args[]) {
        String ejg = "game".replace('a', 'Z').trim().concat("Aa");
        ejg.substring(0, 2);
        System.out.println(ejg);
    }
}
```

a gZmeAZ

b gZmeAa

c  gZm

d  gZ

e  game

## Q4-9. What is the output of the following code?

```
class EJavaGuruString2 {
    public static void main(String args[]) {
        String ejg = "game";
        ejg.replace('a', 'Z').trim().concat("Aa");
        ejg.substring(0, 2);
        System.out.println(ejg);
    }
}
```

a  gZmeAZ

b  gZmeAa

c  gZm

d  gZ

e  game

## Q4-10. What is the output of the following code?

```
class EJavaGuruStringBuilder {
    public static void main(String args[]) {
        StringBuilder ejg = new StringBuilder(10 + 2 + "SUN" + 4 + 5);
        ejg.append(ejg.delete(3, 6));
        System.out.println(ejg);
    }
}
```

a  12S512S5

b  12S12S

c  1025102S

d  Runtime exception

## Q4-11. What is the output of the following code?

```
class EJavaGuruStringBuilder2 {
    public static void main(String args[]) {
        StringBuilder sb1 = new StringBuilder("123456");
        sb1.subSequence(2, 4);
        sb1.deleteCharAt(3);
        sb1.reverse();
        System.out.println(sb1);
    }
}
```

   **a** 521

   **b** Runtime exception

   **c** 65321

   **d** 65431

**Q4-12.** What is the output of the following code?

```
String printDate = LocalDate.parse("2057-08-11")
                     .format(DateTimeFormatter.ISO_DATE_TIME);
System.out.println(printDate);
```

   **a** August 11, 2057T00:00

   **b** Saturday Aug 11,2057T00:00

   **c** 08-11-2057T00:00:00

   **d** Compilation error

   **e** Runtime exception

## 4.10 *Answers to sample exam questions*

**Q4-1.** What is the output of the following code?

```
class EJavaGuruArray {
    public static void main(String args[]) {
        int[] arr = new int[5];
        byte b = 4; char c = 'c'; long longVar = 10;
        arr[0] = b;
        arr[1] = c;
        arr[3] = longVar;
        System.out.println(arr[0] + arr[1] + arr[2] + arr[3]);
    }
}
```

   **a** 4c010

   **b** 4c10

   **c** 113

   **d** 103

   **e** **Compilation error**

Answer: e

Explanation: The code in this question won't compile due to

```
arr[3] = longVar;
```

The preceding line of code tries to assign a value of type long to a variable of type int. Because Java doesn't support implicit narrowing conversions (for example, long to int in this case), the assignment fails. Also, this code tries to trick you regarding your understanding of the following:

- Assigning a char value to an int array element (arr[1] = c)
- Adding a byte value to an int array element (arr[0] = b)
- Whether an unassigned int array element is assigned a default value (arr[2])
- Whether arr[0] + arr[1] + arr[2] + arr[3] prints the sum of all these values or a concatenated value

When answering questions in the OCA Java SE 8 Java Programmer I exam, be careful about such tactics. If any of the answers lists a compilation error or a runtime exception as an option, look for obvious lines of code that could result in it. In this example, arr[3] = longVar will result in a compilation error.

**Q4-2.** What is the output of the following code?

```
class EJavaGuruArray2 {
    public static void main(String args[]) {
        int[] arr1;
        int[] arr2 = new int[3];
        char[] arr3 = {'a', 'b'};
        arr1 = arr2;
        arr1 = arr3;
        System.out.println(arr1[0] + ":" + arr1[1]);
    }
}
```

- a  0:0
- b  a:b
- c  0:b
- d  a:0
- e  **Compilation error**

Answer: e

Explanation: Because a char value can be assigned to an int value, you might assume that a char array can be assigned to an int array. But we're talking about arrays of int and char primitives, which aren't the same as a primitive int or char. Arrays themselves are reference variables, which refer to a collection of objects of similar type.

**Q4-3.** Which of the following are valid lines of code to define a multidimensional int array?

- a  `int[][] array1 = {{1, 2, 3}, {}, {1, 2,3, 4, 5}};`
- b  `int[][] array2 = new array() {{1, 2, 3}, {}, {1, 2,3, 4, 5}};`
- c  `int[][] array3 = {1, 2, 3}, {0}, {1, 2,3, 4, 5};`
- d  `int[][] array4 = new int[2][];`

Answer: a, d

Explanation: Option (b) is incorrect. This line of code won't compile because new array() isn't valid code. Unlike objects of other classes, an array isn't initialized using the keyword new followed by the word array. When the keyword new is used to initialize an array, it's followed by the type of the array, not the word array.

Option (c) is incorrect. To initialize a two-dimensional array, all of these values must be enclosed within another pair of curly braces, as shown in the code in option (a).

**Q4-4.** Which of the following statements are correct?

a The following code executes without an error or exception:

```
ArrayList<Long> lst = new ArrayList<>();
lst.add(10);
```

b Because ArrayList stores only objects, you can't pass element of an ArrayList to a switch construct.

c Calling clear() or remove() on an ArrayList will remove all its elements.

d **If you frequently add elements to an ArrayList, specifying a larger capacity will improve the code efficiency.**

e **Calling the method clone() on an ArrayList creates its shallow copy; that is, it doesn't clone the individual list elements.**

Answer: d, e

Explanation: Option (a) is incorrect. The default type of a non-floating numeric literal value is int. You can't add an int to an ArrayList of type Long. You can pass values of type Long or long to its add method.

Option (b) is incorrect. Starting with Java 7, switch also accepts variables of type String. Because a String can be stored in an ArrayList, you can use elements of an ArrayList in a switch construct.

Option (c) is incorrect. Only clear() will remove all elements of an ArrayList.

Option (d) is correct. An ArrayList internally uses an array to store all its elements. Whenever you add an element to an ArrayList, it checks whether the array can accommodate the new value. If it can't, ArrayList creates a larger array, copies all the existing values to the new array, and then adds the new value at the end of the array. If you frequently add elements to an ArrayList, it makes sense to create an ArrayList with a bigger capacity because the previous process isn't repeated for each ArrayList insertion.

Option (e) is correct. Calling clone() on an ArrayList will create a separate reference variable that stores the same number of elements as the ArrayList to be cloned. But each individual ArrayList element will refer to the same object; that is, the individual ArrayList elements aren't cloned.

**Q4-5.** Which of the following statements are correct?

a **An `ArrayList` offers a resizable array, which is easily managed using the methods it provides. You can add and remove elements from an `ArrayList`.**

b **Values stored by an `ArrayList` can be modified.**

c **You can iterate through elements of an `ArrayList` using a for loop, `Iterator`, or `ListIterator`.**

d An `ArrayList` requires you to specify the total elements before you can store any elements in it.

e **An `ArrayList` can store any type of object.**

Answer: a, b, c, e

Explanation: Option (a) is correct. A developer may prefer using an `ArrayList` over an array because it offers all the benefits of an array and a list. For example, you can easily add or remove elements from an `ArrayList`.

Option (b) is correct.

Option (c) is correct. An `ArrayList` can be easily searched, sorted, and have its values compared using the methods provided by the Collection framework classes.

Option (d) is incorrect. An array requires you to specify the total number of elements before you can add any element to it. But you don't need to specify the total number of elements that you may add to an `ArrayList` at any time in your code.

Option (e) is correct.

**Q4-6.** What is the output of the following code?

```
import java.util.*;                                              // line 1
class EJavaGuruArrayList {                                        // line 2
    public static void main(String args[]) {                      // line 3
        ArrayList<String> ejg = new ArrayList<>();                // line 4
        ejg.add("One");                                           // line 5
        ejg.add("Two");                                           // line 6
        System.out.println(ejg.contains(new String("One")));     // line 7
        System.out.println(ejg.indexOf("Two"));                   // line 8
        ejg.clear();                                              // line 9
        System.out.println(ejg);                                  // line 10
        System.out.println(ejg.get(1));                           // line 11
    }                                                             // line 12
}                                                                 // line 13
```

a **Line 7 prints `true`.**

b Line 7 prints `false`.

c Line 8 prints `-1`.

d **Line 8 prints `1`.**

e **Line 9 removes all elements of the list `ejg`.**

f Line 9 sets `ejg` to `null`.

g Line 10 prints `null`.

 h  **Line 10 prints** [].
 i  Line 10 prints a value similar to `ArrayList@16356`.
 j  **Line 11 throws an exception.**
 k  Line 11 prints `null`.

Answer: a, d, e, h, j

Explanation: Line 7: The method `contains` accepts an object and compares it with the values stored in the list. It returns `true` if the method finds a match and `false` otherwise. This method uses the `equals` method defined by the object stored in the list. In the example, the `ArrayList` stores objects of class `String`, which has overridden the `equals` method. The `equals` method of the `String` class compares the values stored by it. This is why line 7 returns the value `true`.

Line 8: `indexOf` returns the index position of an element if a match is found; otherwise, it returns -1. This method also uses the `equals` method behind the scenes to compare the values in an `ArrayList`. Because the `equals` method in the class `String` compares its values and not the reference variables, the `indexOf` method finds a match in position 1.

Line 9: The `clear` method removes all the individual elements of an `ArrayList` such that an attempt to access any of the earlier `ArrayList` elements will throw a runtime exception. It doesn't set the `ArrayList` reference variable to `null`.

Line 10: `ArrayList` has overridden the `toString` method such that it returns a list of all its elements enclosed within square brackets. To print each element, the `toString` method is called to retrieve its `String` representation.

Line 11: The `clear` method removes all the elements of an `ArrayList`. An attempt to access the (nonexistent) `ArrayList` element throws a runtime `IndexOutOfBounds-Exception` exception.

This question tests your understanding of `ArrayList` and determining the equality of `String` objects.

**Q4-7.** What is the output of the following code?

```
class EJavaGuruString {
    public static void main(String args[]) {
        String ejg1 = new String("E Java");
        String ejg2 = new String("E Java");
        String ejg3 = "E Java";
        String ejg4 = "E Java";
        do
            System.out.println(ejg1.equals(ejg2));
        while (ejg3 == ejg4);
    }
}
```

 a  `true` printed once
 b  `false` printed once

    c  **true printed in an infinite loop**

    d  `false` printed in an infinite loop

Answer: c

Explanation: `String` objects that are created without using the `new` operator are placed in a pool of `Strings`. Hence, the `String` object referred to by the variable `ejg3` is placed in a pool of `Strings`. The variable `ejg4` is also defined without using the `new` operator. Before Java creates another `String` object in the `String` pool for the variable `ejg4`, it looks for a `String` object with the same value in the pool. Because this value already exists in the pool, it makes the variable `ejg4` refer to the same `String` object. This, in turn, makes the variables `ejg3` and `ejg4` refer to the same `String` objects. Hence, both of the following comparisons will return `true`:

- `ejg3 == ejg4` (compare the object references)
- `ejg3.equals(ejg4)` (compare the object values)

Even though the variables `ejg1` and `ejg2` refer to different `String` objects, they define the same values. So `ejg1.equals(ejg2)` also returns `true`. Because the loop condition (`ejg3==ejg4`) always returns `true`, the code prints `true` in an infinite loop.

**Q4-8.** What is the output of the following code?

```
class EJavaGuruString2 {
    public static void main(String args[]) {
        String ejg = "game".replace('a', 'Z').trim().concat("Aa");
        ejg.substring(0, 2);
        System.out.println(ejg);
    }
}
```

    a  gZmeAZ

    b  **gZmeAa**

    c  gZm

    d  gZ

    e  game

Answer: b

Explanation: When chained, methods are evaluated from left to right. The first method to execute is `replace`, not `concat`. `Strings` are immutable. Calling the method `substring` on the reference variable `ejg` doesn't change the contents of the variable `ejg`. It returns a `String` object that isn't referred to by any other variable in the code. In fact, none of the methods defined in the `String` class modify the object's own value. They all create and return new `String` objects.

**Q4-9.** What is the output of the following code?

```
class EJavaGuruString2 {
    public static void main(String args[]) {
        String ejg = "game";
        ejg.replace('a', 'Z').trim().concat("Aa");
        ejg.substring(0, 2);
        System.out.println(ejg);
    }
}
```

- a  gZmeAZ
- b  gZmeAa
- c  gZm
- d  gZ
- e  **game**

Answer: e

Explanation: `String` objects are immutable. It doesn't matter how many methods you execute on a `String` object; its value won't change. Variable `ejg` is initialized with the `String` value `"game"`. This value won't change, and the code prints game.

**Q4-10.** What is the output of the following code?

```
class EJavaGuruStringBuilder {
    public static void main(String args[]) {
        StringBuilder ejg = new StringBuilder(10 + 2 + "SUN" + 4 + 5);
        ejg.append(ejg.delete(3, 6));
        System.out.println(ejg);
    }
}
```

- a  **12S512S5**
- b  12S12S
- c  1025102S
- d  Runtime exception

Answer: a

Explanation: This question tests your understanding of operators, `String`, and `StringBuilder`. The following line of code returns `12SUN45`:

```
10 + 2 + "SUN" + 4 + 5
```

The + operator adds two numbers but concatenates the last two numbers. When the + operator encounters a `String` object, it treats all the remaining operands as `String` objects.

Unlike the String objects, StringBuilder objects are mutable. The append and delete methods defined in this class change its value. ejg.delete(3, 6) modifies the existing value of the StringBuilder to 12S5. It then appends the same value to itself when calling ejg.append(), resulting in the value 12S512S5.

**Q4-11.** What is the output of the following code?

```
class EJavaGuruStringBuilder2 {
    public static void main(String args[]) {
        StringBuilder sb1 = new StringBuilder("123456");
        sb1.subSequence(2, 4);
        sb1.deleteCharAt(3);
        sb1.reverse();
        System.out.println(sb1);
    }
}
```

   a   521

   b   Runtime exception

   c   **65321**

   d   65431

Answer: c

Explanation: Like the method substring, the method subSequence doesn't modify the contents of a StringBuilder. Hence, the value of the variable sb1 remains 123456, even after the execution of the following line of code:

```
sb1.subSequence(2, 4);
```

The method deleteCharAt deletes a char value at position 3. Because the positions are zero-based, the digit 4 is deleted from the value 123456, resulting in 12356. The method reverse modifies the value of a StringBuilder by assigning to it the reverse representation of its value. The reverse of 12356 is 65321.

**Q4-12.** What is the output of the following code?

```
String printDate = LocalDate.parse("2057-08-11")
                     .format(DateTimeFormatter.ISO_DATE_TIME);
System.out.println(printDate);
```

   a   August 11, 2057T00:00

   b   Saturday Aug 11,2057T00:00

   c   08-11-2057T00:00:00

   d   Compilation error

   e   **Runtime exception**

Answer: e

Explanation: The example code in this question calls `LocalDate.parse()`, passing it a string value but no `DateTimeFormatter` instance. In this case, the text 2057-08-11 is parsed using `DateTimeFormatter.ISO_LOCAL_DATE`. `LocalDate.parse()` returns a `LocalDate` instance.

The example code then calls the `format` method on a `LocalDate` instance, using `DateTimeFormatter.ISO_DATE_TIME`. The code compiles successfully because the `format` method accepts a `DateTimeFormatter` instance. But `format()` throws an exception at runtime because it tries to format a `LocalDate` instance using a formatter (`ISO_DATE_TIME`) that defines rules for a date/time object. When no matching time values are found in a `LocalDate` object, an exception is thrown.

**EXAM TIP**   The parse method is defined as a static method in classes `Local-Date`, `LocalTime`, and `LocalDateTime`. The class `DateTimeFormatter` defines the method parse as an instance method. But `format()` is defined as an instance method by all. The example code wouldn't have compiled if the order of calling `parse()` and `format()` was reversed:

```
String printDate = LocalDate.format(DateTimeFormatter.ISO_DATE_TIME)
                      .parse("2057-08-11");
```

# Flow control

| Exam objectives covered in this chapter | What you need to know |
|---|---|
| **[3.3]** Create `if` and `if/else` and ternary constructs. | How to use `if`, `if-else`, `if-else-if-else`, and nested `if` constructs. The differences between using these `if` constructs with and without curly braces `{ }`. How to use a ternary construct. How it compares with `if` and `if-else` constructs. |
| **[3.4]** Use a `switch` statement. | How to use a `switch` statement by passing the correct type of arguments to the `switch` statement and `case` and `default` labels. The change in the code flow when `break` and `return` statements are used in the `switch` statement. |
| **[5.1]** Create and use `while` loops. | How to use the `while` loop, including determining when to apply the `while` loop. |
| **[5.2]** Create and use `for` loops including the enhanced `for` loop. | How to use `for` and enhanced `for` loops. The advantages and disadvantages of the `for` loop and enhanced `for` loop. Scenarios when you may not be able to use the enhanced `for` loop. |
| **[5.3]** Create and use `do/while` loops. | Creation and use of `do-while` loops. Every `do-while` loop executes at least once, even if its condition evaluates to `false` for the first iteration. |

| Exam objectives covered in this chapter | What you need to know |
|---|---|
| **[5.4]** Compare loop constructs. | The differences and similarities between `for`, enhanced `for`, `do-while`, and `while` loops. Given a scenario or a code snippet, knowing which is the most appropriate loop. |
| **[5.5]** Use `break` and `continue`. | The use of `break` and `continue` statements. A `break` statement can be used within loops and `switch` statements. A `continue` statement can be used only within loops. The difference in the code flow when a `break` or `continue` statement is used. Identify the right scenarios for using `break` and `continue` statements. |

We all make multiple decisions on a daily basis, and we often have to choose from a number of available options to make each decision. These decisions range from the complex, such as selecting what subjects to study in school or which profession to choose, to the simple, such as what food to eat or what clothes to wear. The option you choose can potentially change the course of your life, in a small or big way. For example, if you choose to study medicine at a university, you may become a research scientist; if you choose fine arts, you may become a painter. But deciding whether to eat pasta or pizza for dinner isn't likely to have a huge impact on your life.

You may also repeat particular sets of actions. These actions can range from eating an ice cream cone every day, to phoning a friend until you connect, to passing exams at school or university in order to achieve a desired degree. These repetitions can also change the course of your life: you might relish having ice cream every day or enjoy the benefits that come from earning a higher degree.

In Java, the selection statements (`if` and `switch`) and looping statements (`for`, enhanced `for`, `while`, and `do-while`) are used to define and choose among different courses of action, as well as to repeat lines of code. You use these types of statements to define the flow of control in code.

In the OCA Java SE 8 Programmer I exam, you'll be asked how to define and control the flow in your code. To prepare you, I'll cover the following topics in this chapter:

- Creating and using `if`, `if-else`, ternary, and `switch` constructs to execute statements selectively
- Creating and using loops: `while`, `do-while`, `for`, and enhanced `for`
- Creating nested constructs for selection and iteration statements
- Comparing the `do-while`, `while`, `for`, and enhanced `for` loop constructs
- Using `break` and `continue` statements

In Java, you can execute your code conditionally by using either the `if` or `switch` construct. Let's start with the `if` construct.

## 5.1    *The if, if-else, and ternary constructs*

   [3.3]   Create if and if/else and ternary constructs

In this section, we'll cover if, if-else, and ternary constructs. We'll examine what happens when these constructs are used with and without curly braces {}. We'll also cover nested if, if-else, and ternary constructs.

### 5.1.1    *The if construct and its flavors*

An if construct enables you to execute a set of statements in your code based on the result of a condition. This condition must always evaluate to a boolean or a Boolean value. You can specify a set of statements to execute when this condition evaluates to true or false. (In many Java books, the terms *constructs* and *statements* are used interchangeably.)

Multiple flavors of the if statement are illustrated in figure 5.1:

- if
- if-else
- if-else-if-else

In figure 5.1, *condition1* and *condition2* refer to a variable or an expression that must evaluate to a boolean or a Boolean value; *statement1*, *statement2*, and *statement3* refer to either a single line of code or a code block.

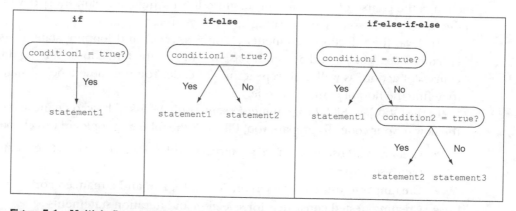

**Figure 5.1    Multiple flavors of the if statement: if, if-else, and if-else-if-else**

**EXAM TIP**    In Java, *then* isn't a keyword, so it must not be used with the if statement.

Let's look at the use of the `if` statement flavors by first defining a set of variables: score, result, name, and `file`, as follows:

```
int score = 100;
String result = "";
String name = "Lion";
java.io.File file = new java.io.File("F");
```

Figure 5.2 shows the use of `if`, `if-else`, and `if-else-if-else` constructs and compares them by showing the code side by side.

| if | if-else | if-else-if-else |
|---|---|---|
| `if (name.equals("Lion"))`  `score = 200;` | `if (name.equals("Lion"))`  `score = 200;` `else`  `score = 300;` | `if (score == 100)`  `result = "A";` `else if (score == 50)`  `result = "B";` `else if (score == 10)`  `result = "C";` `else`  `result = "F";` |

**Figure 5.2   Multiple flavors of `if` statements implemented in code**

Let's quickly go through the code used in figure 5.2's `if`, `if-else`, and `if-else-if-else` statements. In the following example code, if the condition `name.equals("Lion")` evaluates to `true`, a value of 200 is assigned to the variable `score`:

```
if (name.equals("Lion"))
    score = 200;
```
**Example of if construct**

In the following example, if the condition `name.equals("Lion")` evaluates to `true`, a value of 200 is assigned to the variable `score`. If this condition were to evaluate to `false`, a value of 300 would be assigned to the variable `score`:

```
if (name.equals("Lion"))
    score = 200;
else
    score = 300;
```
**Example of if-else construct**

In the following example, if `score` is equal to 100, the variable `result` is assigned a value of A. If `score` is equal to 50, the variable `result` is assigned a value of B. If `score` is equal to 10, the variable `result` is assigned a value of `C`. If `score` doesn't match any of 100, 50, or 10, a value of `F` is assigned to the variable `result`. An `if-else-if-else` construct can use different conditions for all its `if` constructs:

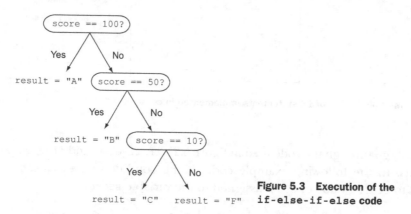

```
if (score == 100)
    result = "A";
else if (score == 50)
    result = "B";
else if (score == 10)
    result = "C";
else
    result = "F";
```

| Condition 1 -> |
| score == 100 |

| Condition 2 -> |
| score == 50 |

| Condition 3 -> |
| score == 10 |

If none of previous conditions evaluates to true, execute else statement

 **NOTE** Chapters in this book use the code style that you're likely to see on the exam. The exam code style often includes practices that aren't recommended on real projects, like poorly indented code or skipping usage of braces for brevity. This book doesn't encourage you to use such obscure coding practices. Please write code that's easy to read, comprehend, and maintain.

**Figure 5.3 Execution of the `if-else-if-else` code**

Figure 5.3 illustrates the preceding code and makes several points clear:

- The last `else` statement is part of the last `if` construct, not any of the `if` constructs before it.
- The `if-else-if-else` is an `if-else` construct in which the `else` part defines another `if` construct. A few other programming languages, such as Python and Shell Script, use `elif`; Perl and Ruby use `elsif`; and VB uses `ElseIf` to define `if-else-if` constructs. If you've programmed with any of these languages, note the difference in Java. The following code is equal to the preceding code:

```
if (score == 100)
    result = "A";
```

```
else
    if (score == 50)
        result = "B";
    else
        if (score == 10)
            result = "C";
        else
            result="F";
```

Again, note that none of the preceding `if` constructs use *then* to define the code to execute if a condition evaluates to `true`. Unlike other programming languages, *then* isn't a keyword in Java and isn't used with the `if` construct.

**EXAM TIP**   The `if-else-if-else` is an `if-else` construct in which the `else` part defines another `if` construct.

The `boolean` expression used as a condition for the `if` construct can also include an assignment operation. The following Twist in the Tale exercise throws in a twist by modifying the value of a variable that the `if` statement is comparing. Let's see if you can answer it correctly (answer in the appendix).

### Twist in the Tale 5.1

Modify the code used in the preceding example as follows. What is the output of this code?

```
String result = "1";
int score = 10;
if ((score = score+10) == 100)
    result = "A";
else if ((score = score+29) == 50)
    result = "B";
else if ((score = score+200) == 10)
    result = "C";
else
    result = "F";
System.out.println(result + ":" + score);
```

   **a**  A:10

   **b**  C:10

   **c**  A:20

   **d**  B:29

   **e**  C:249

   **f**  F:249

### 5.1.2   *Missing else blocks*

What happens if you don't define the `else` statement for an `if` construct? It's acceptable to define one course of action for an `if` construct as follows (omitting the `else` part):

```
boolean testValue = false;
if (testValue == true)
    System.out.println("value is true");
```

But you can't define the `else` part for an `if` construct, skipping the `if` code block. The following code won't compile:

```
boolean testValue = false;
if (testValue == true)
else                                          Won't
    System.out.println("value is false");     compile
```

But an empty code block that follows `if` works well:

```
boolean testValue = false;
if (testValue == true) {}
else
    System.out.println("value is false");
```

Here's another interesting and bizarre piece of code:

```
int score = 100;                          ❶  Missing then
if((score=score+10) > 110);                  or else part
```

❶ is a valid line of code, even if it doesn't define either the *then* or `else` part of the `if` statement. In this case, the `if` condition evaluates and that's it. The `if` construct doesn't define any code that should execute based on the result of this condition.

> **NOTE**   Using `if(testValue==true)` is the same as using `if(testValue)`. Similarly, `if(testValue==false)` is the same as using `if(!testValue)`. This book includes examples of both these approaches. Many programming beginners find the latter approach (without the explicit `==`) confusing.

### 5.1.3   *Implications of the presence and absence of {} in if-else constructs*

You can execute a single statement or a block of statements when an `if` condition evaluates to `true` or `false`. An `if` block is marked by enclosing one or more statements within a pair of curly braces `{}`. An `if` block will execute a single line of code if there are no braces but will execute an unlimited number of lines if they're contained within a block (defined using braces). The braces are optional if there's only one line in the `if` statement.

The following code executes only one statement of assigning the value 200 to the variable `score` if the expression used in the `if` statement evaluates to `true`:

```
String name = "Lion";
int score = 100;
if (name.equals("Lion"))
    score = 200;
```

What happens if you want to execute another line of code if the value of the variable name is equal to Lion? Is the following code correct?

```
String name = "Lion";
int score = 100;
if (name.equals("Lion"))
    score = 200;
    name = "Larry";
```
**Set name to Larry**

**NOTE**  The preceding code is a good example to suggest that you must use braces in code on your real-world project to avoid errors.

The statement `score = 200;` executes if the `if` condition is `true`. Although it looks like the statement `name = "Larry";` is part of the `if` statement, it isn't. It will execute regardless of the result of the `if` condition because of the lack of braces { }.

**EXAM TIP**  In the exam, watch out for code that uses misleading indentation in `if` constructs. In the absence of a defined code block (marked with { }), only the statement following the `if` construct will be considered part of it.

What happens to the same code if you define an `else` part for your `if` construct, as follows?

```
String name = "Lion";
int score = 100;
if (name.equals("Lion"))
    score = 200;
    name = "Larry";
else
    score = 129;
```
**This statement isn't part of the if construct.**

In this case, the code won't compile. The compiler will report that the `else` part is defined without an `if` statement. If this leaves you confused, examine the following code, which is indented in order to emphasize the fact that the `name = "Larry"` line isn't part of the `else` construct:

```
String name = "Lion";
int score = 100;
if (name.equals ("Lion"))
    score = 200;
name = "Larry";
else
    score = 129;
```
**This statement isn't part of the if construct.**

**The else statement seems to be defined without a preceding if construct.**

If you want to execute multiple statements for an if construct, define them within a block of code. You can do so by defining all this code within curly braces {}. Here's an example:

```
String name = "Lion";
int score = 100;
if (name.equals("Lion")) {
    score = 200;
    name = "Larry";
}
else
    score = 129;
```

**Start of code block**

**Statements to execute if (name.equals("Lion")) evaluates to true**

**End of code block**

Similarly, you can define multiple lines of code for the else part. The following example does so incorrectly:

```
String name = "Lion";
if (name.equals("Lion"))
    System.out.println("Lion");
else
    System.out.println("Not a Lion");
    System.out.println("Again, not a Lion");
```

❶ **Not part of the else construct; will execute regardless of value of variable name**

The output of the preceding code is as follows:

```
Lion
Again, not a Lion
```

Although the code at ❶ *looks* like it will execute only if the value of the variable name matches the value Lion, this is not the case. It's indented incorrectly to trick you into believing that it's a part of the else block. The preceding code is the same as the following code (with correct indentation):

```
String name = "Lion";
if (name.equals("Lion"))
    System.out.println("Lion");
else
    System.out.println("Not a Lion");
System.out.println("Again, not a Lion");
```

**Not part of the else construct; will execute regardless of value of variable name**

If you wish to execute the last two statements in the preceding code only if the if condition evaluates to false, you can do so by using {}:

```
String name = "Lion";
if (name.equals("Lion"))
    System.out.println("Lion");
else {
    System.out.println("Not a Lion");
    System.out.println("Again, not a Lion");
    }
```

**Now part of the else construct; will execute only when if condition evaluates to false**

You can define another statement, construct, or loop to execute for an `if` condition, without using { }, as follows:

```
String name = "Lion";
if (name.equals("Lion"))
    for (int i = 0; i < 3; ++i)
        System.out.println(i);
```

An if condition

A for loop is a single construct that will execute if name.equals("Lion") evaluates to true.

This code is part of the for loop defined on the previous line.

`System.out.println(i)` is part of the `for` loop, not an unrelated statement that follows the `for` loop. So this code is correct and gives the following output:

```
0
1
2
```

### 5.1.4 Appropriate versus inappropriate expressions passed as arguments to an if statement

The result of a variable or an expression used in an `if` construct must evaluate to `true` or `false`. Assume the following definitions of variables:

```
int score = 100;
boolean allow = false;
String name = "Lion";
```

Let's look at a few examples of some of the valid variables and expressions that can be passed to an `if` statement:

```
(score == 100)
(name == "Lio")
(score <= 100 || allow)
(allow)
```

Evaluates to true

Evaluates to false

Evaluates to true

Evaluates to false

Using `==` is simply wrong for comparing two `String` objects for equality. As mentioned in chapter 4, the correct way for comparing two `String` objects is to use the `equals` method from the `String` class. But comparing two `String` values using `==` is a valid expression that returns a `boolean` value, and it may be used in the exam.

Now comes the tricky part of passing an assignment operation to an `if` construct. What do you think is the output of the following code?

```
boolean allow = false;
if (allow = true)
    System.out.println("value is true");
else
    System.out.println("value is false");
```

This is assignment, not comparison.

You may think that because the value of the boolean variable allow is set to false, the preceding code output's value is false. Revisit the code and notice that the assignment operation allow = true assigns the value true to the boolean variable allow. Also, its result is also a boolean value, which makes it eligible to be passed on as an argument to the if construct.

Although the preceding code has no syntactical errors, there's a *logical error*—an error in the program logic. The correct code to compare a boolean variable with a boolean literal value is as follows:

```
boolean allow = false;
if (allow == true)
    System.out.println("value is true");
else
    System.out.println("value is false");
```

This is comparison.

**EXAM TIP** Watch out for code in the exam that uses the assignment operator (=) to compare a boolean value in the if condition. It won't compare the boolean value; it'll assign a value to it. The correct operator for comparing a boolean value is the equality operator (==).

### 5.1.5 *Nested if constructs*

A nested if construct is an if construct defined within another if construct. Theoretically, there's no limit on the number of levels of nested if and if-else constructs.

Whenever you come across nested if and if-else constructs, you need to be careful about determining the else part of an if statement. If the preceding statement didn't make a lot of sense, look at the following code and determine its output:

```
int score = 110;
if (score > 200)
    if (score <400)
        if (score > 300)
            System.out.println(1);
        else
            System.out.println(2);
else
    System.out.println(3);
```

❶ if (score>200)

❷ if (score<400)

❸ To which if does this else belong?

Based on the way the code is indented, you may believe that the else at ❸ belongs to the if defined at ❶. But it belongs to the if defined at ❷. Here's the code with the correct indentation:

```
int score = 110;
if (score > 200)
    if (score <400)
        if (score > 300)
            System.out.println(1);
```

```
        else
            System.out.println(2);
else
        System.out.println(3);
```

> This else belongs to the if
> with condition (score<400).

Next, you need to understand how to do the following:

- Define an `else` for an outer `if` other than the one that it'll be assigned to by default.
- Determine to which `if` an `else` belongs in nested `if` constructs.

Both of these tasks are simple. Let's start with the first one.

### DEFINING AN ELSE FOR AN OUTER IF
The key point is to use curly braces, as follows:

```
int score = 110;
if (score > 200) {
    if (score < 400)
        if (score > 300)
            System.out.println(1);
        else
            System.out.println(2);
}
else
    System.out.println(3);
```

**①** Start if construct for score > 200

**②** End if construct for score > 200

**③** else for score > 200

Curly braces at **①** and **②** mark the start and end of the `if` condition (`score > 200`) defined at **①**. Hence, the `else` at **③** that follows **②** belongs to the `if` defined at **①**.

### DETERMINING TO WHICH IF AN ELSE BELONGS
If code uses curly braces to mark the start and end of the territory of an `if` or `else` construct, it can be simple to determine which `else` goes with which `if`, as mentioned in the previous section. When the `if` constructs don't use curly braces, don't be confused by the code indentation, which may or may not be correct.

Try to match the `if`s with their corresponding `else`s in the following poorly indented code:

```
if (score > 200)
if (score < 400)
if (score > 300)
    System.out.println(1);
else
    System.out.println(2);
else
    System.out.println(3);
```

Start working from the inside out, with the innermost `if-else` statement, matching each `else` with its nearest unmatched `if` statement. Figure 5.4 shows how to match the `if-else` pairs for the preceding code, marked with **①**, **②**, and **③**.

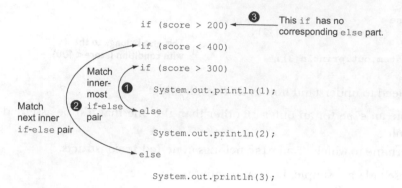

**Figure 5.4   How to match `if-else` pairs for poorly indented code**

Figure 5.5 shows how easy it becomes to match `if-else` pairs if the code is correctly indented (with or without using braces).

| Correct code indentation | Correct code indentation (with braces) |
|---|---|
| ```
if (score > 200)
    if (score < 400)
        if (score > 300)
            System.out println(1);
        else
            System.out println(2);
    else
        System.out println(3);
``` | ```
if (score > 200) {
    if (score < 400) {
        if (score > 300) {
            System.out println(1);
        } else {
            System.out println(2);
        }
    } else {
        System.out println(3);
    }
}
``` |

**Figure 5.5   Correct code indentation (with or without braces) makes the code more readable.**

 **NOTE**   As a good programming practice, indent all your code properly. Also use braces to improve readability.

You can also use the ternary construct to evaluate an expression and assign a value to a variable, depending on the result of a `boolean` expression, covered in the next section.

### 5.1.6   *Ternary construct*

You can use a ternary operator, `?:`, to define a ternary construct. A ternary construct can be compared to a compact `if-else` construct, used to assign a value to a variable depending on a `boolean` expression.

**CORRECT USAGE**

In the following example, the variable `discount` is assigned the value 15 if the expression (`bill > 2000`) evaluates to `true` but 10 otherwise:

```
int bill = 2000;
int discount = (bill > 2000)? 15 : 10;        ① Uses ternary
System.out.println(discount);                    operator
                                               Outputs 10
```

Figure 5.6 compares a ternary construct ① used in the preceding example with an `if-else` construct.

| Ternary construct | if-else construct |
|---|---|
| `int bill = 2000;`<br>`int discount = (bill > 2000)? 15 : 10;` | `int bill = 2000;`<br>`int discount`<br>`if (bill > 2000)`<br>`        discount = 15;`<br>`else`<br>`        discount = 10;` |

**Figure 5.6   Comparing a ternary construct with an `if-else` construct**

The parentheses enclosing a `boolean` expression are optional and are used for better readability. The code will work without them:

```
int bill = 2000;
int discount = bill > 2000? 15 : 10;        OK; boolean expression
                                            not enclosed within ()
```

The variable `discount` might or might not be declared in the same statement that includes the ternary operator:

```
int bill = 2000;
int discount;                               OK; variable discount isn't
discount = (bill > 2000)? 15 : 10;          declared in this statement
```

You can also assign an expression to the variable `discount` using a ternary operator. Here's the modified code:

```
int bill = 2000;
int discount = (bill > 2000)? bill-150 : bill - 100;   Assign expression to
System.out.println(discount);                          variable discount
                                                       Outputs 1900
```

A method that returns a value can also be used to initialize a variable in a ternary construct:

```
class Ter{
    public void ternaryConstruct() {
        int bill = 2000;
        int discount = (bill > 2000)? getSpecDisc(): getRegDisc();      ◄─┐
        System.out.println(discount);                                      │
    }                                                            Return value
    int getRegDisc() {                                           using a method│
        return 11;
    }
    int getSpecDisc() {
        return 15;
    }
}
```

### INCORRECT USAGE

If the expression used to evaluate a ternary operator doesn't return a `boolean` or a `Boolean` value, the code won't compile:

```
int bill = 2000;
int qty = 10;                                      Won't compile; ++qty
int discount = ++qty ? 10: 20;         ◄─┘          isn't a boolean type
```

All three parts of a ternary operator are mandatory:

- The `boolean` expression
- The value returned if the `boolean` expression evaluates to `true`
- The value returned if the `boolean` expression evaluates to `false`

Unlike an `if` construct, a ternary can't drop its `else` part. The following code won't compile:

```
int discount = (bill > 2000)? 15;        ◄──── Won't compile
```

In chapter 3, you created methods that return values. It's not mandatory to assign values returned from these methods, but the same doesn't apply to ternary constructs. The value returned by a ternary operator must be assigned to a variable or the code won't compile:

```
(5000 > 2000)? 15 : 10;          ◄──── Won't compile; not a statement
```

Because a ternary operator must return values, which are assigned to a variable, it can't include code blocks. The following code won't compile:

```
int bill = 2000;
int discount = (bill > 2000)? {bill-150} : {bill - 100};      ◄──── Won't compile
```

A method that doesn't return a value can't be used to initialize variables in a ternary construct:

```
class TernaryConst{
    public void invalidTernaryConstruct() {
        int bill = 2000;
        int discount = (bill > 2000)? 10 : getRegularDiscount();        ⟵┐
        System.out.println(discount);
    }                                                        Won't compile; getRegDisc
    void getRegularDiscount() {}                                doesn't return a value
}
```

### INCORRECT ASSIGNMENTS

In the exam, watch out for compatibility of the value that's returned by a ternary operator and the variable to which it's assigned. The following code won't compile because it's trying to assign a long value to an int variable:

```
long bill = 2000;                                     │ Won't compile;
int discount = (bill > 2000)? bill-100 : bill - 50;   ⟵┘ bill-100 is of type long
```

Also, look out for conversions between primitive and wrapper classes. The following code won't compile because Integer can't be assigned to Long and vice versa:

```
                                                                       │ Won't
Long discount = (5000 > 2000)? new Integer(10) : new Integer(15);  ⟵┤ compile
```

### NESTED TERNARY CONSTRUCTS

In the following example, the *if* part of the ternary operator includes another ternary operator. Watch out for nested ternary constructs on the exam:

```
int bill = 2000;
int qty = 10;
int discount = (bill > 1000)? (qty > 11)? 10 : 9 : 5;   ⟵┘ Outputs 9
System.out.println(discount);
```

Here's a simple but effective method to split and indent a ternary construct into its components to determine which value belongs to which operator. Let's first indent a simple ternary construct in which its boolean expression, if and else values, are placed on separate lines:

```
int discount = (bill > 1000)?
                    10
                    :9;
```

Now let's apply this indentation technique to the example used in the beginning of this section:

```
int bill = 2000;
int qty = 10;
```

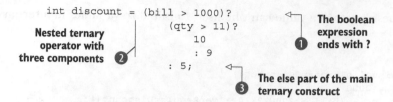

```
int discount = (bill > 1000)?
                    (qty > 11)?
                         10
                           : 9
               : 5;
```

**Nested ternary operator with three components** **②**

**The boolean expression ends with ?** **①**

**The else part of the main ternary construct** **③**

In the preceding code, **①** ends with ?, that is, the `boolean` expression. The code at **②** includes all three components of the nested ternary operator. The code at **②** will execute if the `boolean` expression at **①** returns `true`. The code at **③** starts with : and includes the *else* part of the ternary operator at **①**.

Let's apply the preceding indentation technique to another example. Here's the code before the indentation:

```
int bill = 2000;
int qty = 10;
int days = 10;
int discount = (bill > 1000)? (qty > 11)? 10 : days > 9? 20 : 30 : 5;
System.out.println(discount);
```

Here's the same code with the indentation:

```
int bill = 2000;
int qty = 10;
int days = 10;
int discount = (bill > 1000)?
                    (qty > 11)?
                         10
                           : days > 9 ? 20 : 30
                    : 5;
System.out.println(discount);                    ⤶ Outputs 20
```

You can also use the `switch` statement to execute code conditionally. Even though both `if-else` constructs and `switch` statements are used to execute statements selectively, they differ in their usage, which you'll notice as you work with the `switch` statement in the next section.

## 5.2   *The switch statement*

 [3.4]   Use a switch statement

In this section, you'll learn how to use the `switch` statement and see how it compares to nested `if-else` constructs. You'll learn the right ingredients for defining values that are passed to the `switch` labels and the correct use of the `break` statement in these labels.

### 5.2.1 Create and use a switch statement

You can use a switch statement to compare the value of a variable with multiple values. For each of these values, you can define a set of statements to execute.

The following example uses a switch statement to compare the value of the variable marks with the literal values 10, 20, and 30, defined using the case keyword:

```java
int marks = 20;
switch (marks) {
    case 10: System.out.println(10);
        break;
    case 20: System.out.println(20);
        break;
    case 30: System.out.println(30);
        break;
    default: System.out.println("default");
        break;
}
```

Compare value of marks

Values that are compared to variable marks

Marks the end of a case label

Default case to execute if no matching cases found

A switch statement can define multiple case labels within its switch block but only a single default label. The default label executes when no matching value is found in the case labels. A break statement is used to exit a switch statement, after the code completes its execution for a matching case.

### 5.2.2 Comparing a switch statement with multiple if-else constructs

A switch statement can improve the readability of your code by replacing a set of (rather complicated-looking) related if-else-if-else statements with a switch and multiple case statements.

Examine the following code, which uses if-else-if-else statements to check the value of a String variable day and display an appropriate message:

```java
String day = "SUN";
if (day.equals("MON") || day.equals("TUE") ||
    day.equals("WED") || day.equals("THU"))
    System.out.println("Time to work");
else if (day.equals("FRI"))
    System.out.println("Nearing weekend");
else if (day.equals("SAT") || day.equals("SUN"))
    System.out.println("Weekend!");
else
    System.out.println("Invalid day?");
```

Multiple comparisons

Now examine this implementation of the preceding code using the switch statement:

```java
String day = "SUN";
switch (day) {
    case "MON":
    case "TUE":
```

```
        case "WED":
        case "THU": System.out.println("Time to work");
                    break;
        case "FRI": System.out.println("Nearing weekend");
                    break;
        case "SAT":
        case "SUN": System.out.println("Weekend!");
                    break;
        default: System.out.println("Invalid day?");
}
```

The two preceding snippets of code perform the same function of comparing the value of the variable day and printing an appropriate value. But the latter code, which uses the switch statement, is simpler and easier to read and follow.

Note that the preceding switch statement doesn't define code for all the case values. What happens if the value of the variable day matches TUE? When control of the code enters the label matching TUE in the switch construct, it'll execute all the code until it encounters a break statement or it reaches the end of the switch statement.

Figure 5.7 depicts the execution of the multiple if-else-if-else statements used in the example code in this section. You can compare it to a series of questions and answers that continue until a match is found or all the conditions are evaluated.

**Figure 5.7  The if-else-if-else construct is like a series of questions and answers.**

As opposed to an if-else-if-else construct, you can compare a switch statement to asking a single question and evaluating its answer to determine which code to execute. Figure 5.8 illustrates the switch statement and its case labels.

  **EXAM TIP**  The if-else-if-else construct evaluates all the conditions until it finds a match. A switch construct compares the argument passed to it with its labels.

See if you can find the twist in the next exercise. Hint: It defines code to compare String values (answer can be found in the appendix).

Figure 5.8 A `switch` statement is like asking a question and acting on the answer.

---

**Twist in the Tale 5.2**

Modify the code used in the previous example as follows. What's the output of this code?

```
String day = new String("SUN");
switch (day) {
    case "MON":
    case "TUE":
    case "WED":
    case "THU": System.out.println("Time to work");
                break;
    case "FRI": System.out.println("Nearing weekend");
                break;
    case "SAT":
    case "SUN": System.out.println("Weekend!");
                break;
    default: System.out.println("Invalid day?");
}
```

a  Time to work
b  Nearing weekend
c  Weekend!
d  Invalid day?

---

### 5.2.3  Arguments passed to a switch statement

You can't use the `switch` statement to compare all types of values, such as all types of objects and primitives. There are limitations on the types of arguments that a `switch` statement can accept.

Figure 5.9 shows the types of arguments that can be passed to a switch statement and to an if construct.

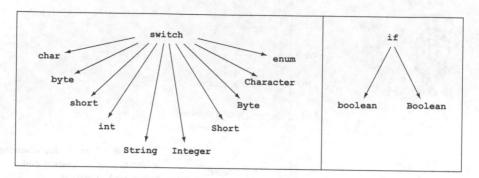

**Figure 5.9   Types of arguments that can be passed to a switch statement and an if construct**

A switch statement accepts arguments of types char, byte, short, int, and String (starting in Java version 7). It also accepts arguments and expressions of types enum, Character, Byte, Integer, and Short. Because enums aren't on the OCA Java SE 8 Programmer I exam objectives, I won't discuss them any further. The switch statement doesn't accept arguments of type long, float, or double, or any object besides String.

Apart from passing a variable to a switch statement, you can also pass an expression to the switch statement as long as it returns one of the allowed types. The following code is valid:

```
int score =10, num = 20;
switch (score+num) {
    // ..code
}
```
◁─┤ **Type of score+num is int and can thus be passed as an argument to the switch statement**

The following code won't compile because the type of history is double, which is a type that isn't accepted by the switch statement:

```
double history = 20;
switch (history) {
    // ..code
}
```
◁─┐ **double variable can't be passed as an argument to a switch statement**

 **EXAM TIP**   Watch out for questions in the exam that try to pass a primitive decimal type such as float or double to a switch statement. Code that tries to do so will not compile.

For nonprimitive types, that is, `String` and wrapper types, the `switch` argument must not be `null`, which would cause a `NullPointerException` to be thrown:

```
Integer value = null;
switch (value) {
    default: System.out.println("value is not 10");
            break;
    case 10: System.out.println("value is 10");
            break;
}
```

**Throws NullPointerException because value is null**

In the preceding code, if the variable `value` is assigned the value 10, the code will output value is 10.

**EXAM TIP**   For nonprimitive types, that is, `String` and wrapper types, the `switch` argument must not be `null`, which would cause a `NullPointer-Exception` to be thrown.

### 5.2.4   *Values passed to the label case of a switch statement*

You're constrained in a couple of ways when it comes to the value that can be passed to the `case` label in a `switch` statement, as the following subsections explain.

#### CASE VALUES SHOULD BE COMPILE-TIME CONSTANTS

The value of a `case` label must be a compile-time constant value; that is, the value should be known at the time of code compilation:

```
int a=10, b=20, c=30;
switch (a) {
    case b+c: System.out.println(b+c); break;
    case 10*7: System.out.println(10*7512+10); break;
}
```

**❶ Not allowed**

**❷ Allowed**

Note that b+c in the preceding code defined at ❶ can't be determined at the time of compilation and isn't allowed. But `10*7` defined at ❷ is a valid `case` label value.

You can use variables in an expression if they're marked `final` because the value of `final` variables can't change once they're initialized:

```
final int a = 10;
final int b = 20;
final int c = 30;
switch (a) {
    case b+c: System.out.println(b+c); break;
}
```

**❶ Expression b+c is compile-time constant**

Because the variables b and c are `final` variables here, at ❶ the value of b+c can be known at compile time. This makes it a compile-time constant value, which can be used in a `case` label.

You may be surprised to learn that if you don't assign a value to a final variable with its declaration, it isn't considered a compile-time constant:

```
final int a = 10;
final int b = 20;             ❶  final variable c is defined
final int c;                      but not initialized           ❸  Code doesn't compile; b+c
c = 30;                                                             isn't considered a constant
switch (a) {                  ◄—❷  c is initialized                expression because the
                                                                   variable c wasn't initialized
    case b+c: System.out.println(b+c); break;                      with its declaration.
}
```

This code defines a final variable c at line ❶ but doesn't initialize it. The final variable c is initialized at line ❷. Because the final variable c isn't initialized with its declaration, at ❸ the expression b+c isn't considered a compile-time constant, so it can't be used as a case label.

**CASE VALUES SHOULD BE ASSIGNABLE TO THE ARGUMENT PASSED TO THE SWITCH STATEMENT**
Examine the following code, in which the type of argument passed to the switch statement is byte and the case label value is of the type float. Such code won't compile:

```
byte myByte = 10;
switch (myByte) {                                       Floating-point number can't
    case 1.2: System.out.println(1); break;             be assigned to byte variable
}
```

**NULL ISN'T ALLOWED AS A CASE LABEL**
Code that tries to compare the variable passed to the switch statement with null won't compile, as demonstrated in the following code:

```
String name = "Paul";
switch (name) {
    case "Paul": System.out.println(1);
            break;                                       null isn't allowed
    case null: System.out.println("null");              as a case label.
}
```

**ONE CODE BLOCK CAN BE DEFINED FOR MULTIPLE CASES**
It's acceptable to define a single code block for multiple case labels in a switch statement, as shown by the following code:

```
int score =10;
switch (score) {
    case 100:
    case 50 :                                           You can define
    case 10 : System.out.println("Average score");      multiple cases, which
          break;                                        should execute the
                                                        same code block.
```

```
    case 200: System.out.println("Good score");
}
```

This example code will output Average score if the value of the variable score matches any of the values 100, 50, and 10.

### 5.2.5 Use of break statements within a switch statement

In the previous examples, note the use of break to exit the switch construct once a matching case is found. In the absence of the break statement, control will *fall through* the remaining code and execute the code corresponding to all the *remaining* cases that *follow* that matching case.

Consider the examples shown in figure 5.10—one with a break statement and the other without a break statement. Examine the flow of code (depicted using arrows) in this figure when the value of the variable score is equal to 50.

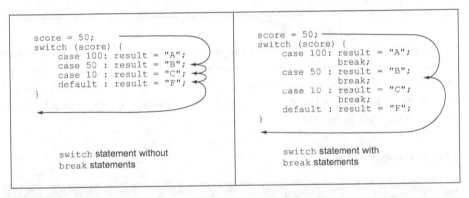

**Figure 5.10** Differences in code flow for a switch statement with and without break statements

Our (hypothetical) enthusiastic programmers, Harry and Selvan, who are also preparing for this exam, sent in some of their code. Can you choose the correct code for them in the following Twist in the Tale exercise? (The answer is in the appendix.)

---

**Twist in the Tale 5.3**

---

Which of the following code submissions by our two hypothetical programmers, Harry and Selvan, examines the value of the long variable dayCount and prints out the name of any one month that matches the day count?

**a** Submission by Harry:

```
long dayCount = 31;
if (dayCount == 28 || dayCount == 29)
    System.out.println("Feb");
else if (dayCount == 30)
    System.out.println("Apr");
else if (dayCount == 31)
    System.out.println("Jan");
```

**b** Submission by Selvan:

```
long dayCount = 31;
switch (dayCount) {
    case 28:
    case 29: System.out.println("Feb"); break;
    case 30: System.out.println("Apr"); break;
    case 31: System.out.println("Jan"); break;
}
```

---

In the next section, I'll cover the iteration statements known as loop statements. Just as you'd like to repeat the action of "eating an ice cream" every day, loops are used to execute the same lines of code multiple times. You can use a for loop, an enhanced for (for-each) loop, or the do-while and while loops to repeat a block of code. Let's start with the for loop.

## 5.3 *The for loop*

[5.2]   Create and use for loops including the enhanced for loop

In this section, I'll cover the regular or traditional for loop. The enhanced for loop is covered in the next section.

A for loop is *usually* used to execute a set of statements a fixed number of times. It takes the following form:

```
for (initialization; condition; update) {
    statements;
}
```

Here's a simple example:

```
int tableOf = 25;
for (int ctr = 1; ctr <= 5; ctr++) {
    System.out.println(tableOf * ctr);
}
```

 **Executes
multiple times**

The output of the preceding code is as follows:

```
25
50
75
100
125
```

In the preceding example, the code at ❶ will execute five times. It'll start with an initial value of 1 for the variable ctr and execute while the value of the variable ctr is less than or equal to 5. The value of variable ctr will increment by 1 (ctr++) after the execution of the code at ❶.

The code at ❶ executes for ctr values 1, 2, 3, 4, and 5. Because 6 <= 5 evaluates to false, the for loop completes its execution without executing the code at ❶ any further.

In the preceding example, notice that the for loop defines three types of statements separated with semicolons (;), as follows:

- Initialization statements
- Termination condition
- Update clause (executable statement)

This loop is depicted as a flowchart in figure 5.11. The statements defined within the loop body execute until the termination condition is false.

One important point to note with respect to the for loop is that the update clause executes after all the statements defined within the for loop body. In other words, you can consider the update clause to be a last statement in the for loop. The initialization section, which executes only once, may define multiple initialization statements. Similarly, the update clause may define multiple statements. But there can be only one termination condition for a for loop.

In figure 5.12, I've provided a code snippet and a flowchart that depicts the corresponding flow of execution of statements to explain the previous concept.

Let's explore the initialization block, termination condition, and update clause of a for loop in detail.

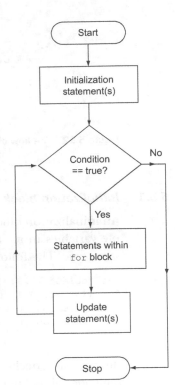

**Figure 5.11  The flow of control in a for loop**

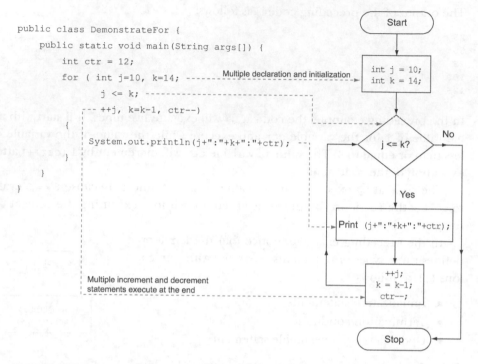

**Figure 5.12   The flow of control in a `for` loop using a code example**

### 5.3.1   *Initialization block*

An initialization block executes only once. A `for` loop can declare and initialize multiple variables in its initialization block, but the variables it declares should be of the same type. The following code is valid:

```
int tableOf = 25;
for (int ctr = 1, num = 100000; ctr <= 5; ++ctr) {      Define and assign
    System.out.println(tableOf * ctr);                   multiple variables
    System.out.println(num * ctr);
}
```

But you can't declare variables of different types in an initialization block. The following code will fail to compile:

```
for (int j=10, long longVar = 10; j <= 1; ++j) { }      Can't define variables of different
                                                         types in an initialization block
```

It's a common programming mistake to try to use the variables defined in a `for`'s initialization block outside the `for` block. Please note that the scope of the variables declared in the initialization block is limited to the `for` block. An example follows:

```
int tableOf = 25;
for (int ctr = 1; ctr <= 5; ++ctr) {         Variable ctr is accessible
    System.out.println(tableOf * ctr);       only within for loop body
}
ctr = 20;                      Variable ctr isn't accessible
                               outside for loop
```

### 5.3.2  Termination condition

The termination condition is evaluated once for each iteration before executing the statements defined within the body of the loop. The `for` loop terminates when the termination condition evaluates to `false`:

```
for (int ctr = 1; ctr <= 5; ++ctr) {      1  for loop body
    System.out.println(ctr);
}                                          2  Code following
...                                           the for loop
```

The termination condition—`ctr <= 5` in this example—is checked before ❶ executes. If the condition evaluates to `false`, control is transferred to ❷. A `for` loop can define exactly one termination condition—no more, no less.

### 5.3.3  The update clause

Usually, you'd use this block to manipulate the value of the variable that you used to specify the termination condition. In the previous example, I defined the following code:

```
++ctr;
```

Code defined in this block executes *after* all the code defined in the body of the `for` loop. The previous code increments the value of the variable `ctr` by 1 after the following code executes:

```
System.out.println(ctr);
```

The termination condition is evaluated next. This execution continues until the termination condition evaluates to `false`.

You can define multiple statements in the update clause, including calls to other methods. The only limit is that these statements will execute in the order in which they appear, at the end of all the statements defined in the `for` block. Examine the following code, which calls a method in the update block:

```
public class ForIncrementStatements {
    public static void main(String args[]) {           The increment
        String line = "ab";                            block can also
        for (int i=0; i < line.length(); ++i, printMethod())    call methods.
            System.out.println(line.charAt(i));
    }
```

```
    private static void printMethod() {
        System.out.println("Happy");
    }
}
```

> **printMethod is called by the for loop's increment block.**

The output of this code is as follows:

```
a
Happy
b
Happy
```

### 5.3.4  *Optional parts of a for statement*

All three parts of a for statement—that is, initialization block, termination condition, and update clause—are optional. But you must specify that you aren't including a section by just including a semicolon. In the following example, the initialization block doesn't include any code:

```
int a = 10;
for(; a < 5; ++a) {
    System.out.println(a);
}
```

> **Valid for loop without any code in the initialization block**

Removing the semicolon that marks the end of the initialization block prevents the code from compiling:

```
int a = 10;
for(a < 5; ++a) {
    System.out.println(a);
}
```

> **Won't compile**

In the following example, the termination condition is missing, resulting in a *potentially* infinite loop (*potentially* because it can be stopped with a break statement or an exception):

```
for(int a = 10; ; ++a) {
    System.out.println(a);
}
```

> **Missing termination condition implies infinite loop**

Again, if you remove the semicolon that marks the end of the termination condition, the code won't compile:

```
for(int a = 10; ++a) {
    System.out.println(a);
}
```

> **Won't compile**

The following code doesn't include code in its update clause but compiles successfully:

```
for(int a = 10; a > 5; ) {
    System.out.println(a);
}
```

> **Missing update clause**

But removing the semicolon that marks the start of the update clause prevents the code from compiling:

```
for(int a = 10; a > 5) {            Won't
    System.out.println(a);         compile
}
```

It's interesting to note that the following code is valid:

```
for(;;)
    System.out.println(1);
```

**EXAM TIP**   All three parts of a `for` statement—initialization block, termination condition, and update clause—are optional. A missing termination condition implies an infinite loop.

### 5.3.5   Nested for loop

If a loop encloses another loop, they are called *nested loops*. The loop that encloses another loop is called the *outer loop*, and the enclosed loop is called the *inner loop*. Theoretically, there are no limits on the levels of nesting `for` loops.

Let's get started with a single-level nested loop. For an example, you can compare the hour hand of a clock to an outer loop and its minute hand to an inner loop. Each hour can be compared with an iteration of the outer loop, and each minute can be compared with an iteration of the inner loop. Because an hour has 60 minutes, the inner loop should iterate 60 times *for each iteration* of the outer loop. This comparison between a clock and a nested loop is shown in figure 5.13.

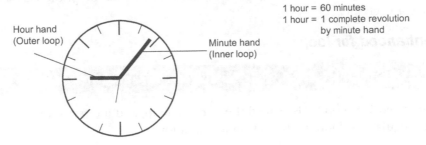

**Figure 5.13   Comparison of the hands of a clock to a nested loop**

You can use the following nested `for` loops to print out each minute (1 to 60) for hours from 1 to 6:

```
for (int hrs = 1; hrs <= 6; hrs++) {           Outer loop iterates for
    for (int min = 1; min <= 60; min++) {      values 1 through 6
        System.out.println(hrs + ":" + min);   Inner loop iterates for
    }                                          values 1 through 60
}                                              Executes 6 × 60 times (total outer loop
                                               iterations × total inner loop iterations)
```

Nested loops are often used to initialize or iterate multidimensional arrays. The following code initializes a multidimensional array using nested for loops:

```
int multiArr[][];                                    Array declaration
multiArr = new int[2][3];                            Array allocation
for (int i = 0; i < multiArr.length; i++) {
    for (int j = 0; j < multiArr[i].length; j++) {    Outer for loop
        multiArr[i][j] = i + j;                       Inner for loop
    }
}                              Inner for loop ends
                   Outer for loop ends
```

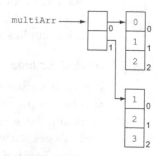

Figure 5.14  **The array multiArr after its initialization**

❶ defines a two-dimensional array multiArr. ❷ allocates this array, creating two rows and three columns, and assigns all array members the default int value of 0. Figure 5.14 illustrates the array multiArr after it's initialized using the preceding code.

❸ defines an outer for loop. Because the value of multi-Arr.length is 2 (the value of the first subscript at ❷), the outer for loop executes twice, with the variable i having the values 0 and 1. The inner for loop is defined at ❹. Because the length of each of the rows of the multiArr array is 3 (the value of the second subscript at ❷), the inner loop executes three times for each iteration of the outer for loop, with the variable j having the values 0, 1, and 2.

In the next section, I'll discuss another flavor of the for loop: the *enhanced* for loop or for-each loop.

## 5.4   *The enhanced for loop*

[5.2]   Create and use for loops including the enhanced for loop

The enhanced for loop is also called the *for-each* loop, and it offers some advantages over the regular for loop. It also has some limitations.

### 5.4.1   *Iteration with enhanced for loop*

To start with, the regular for loop is cumbersome to use when it comes to iterating through a collection or an array. You need to create a looping variable and specify the start and end positions of the collection or the array, even if you want to iterate through the complete collection or list. The enhanced for loop makes the previously mentioned routine task quite a breeze, as the following example demonstrates for the ArrayList myList:

```
ArrayList<String> myList= new ArrayList<String>();
myList.add("Java");
myList.add("Loop");
```

The following code uses the regular `for` loop to iterate through this list:

```
for(Iterator<String> i = myList.iterator(); i.hasNext();)
    System.out.println(i.next());
```

This code uses the enhanced `for` loop to iterate through the list `myList`:

```
for (String val : myList)
    System.out.println(val);
```

You can read the colon (`:`) in a for-each loop as "in."

The for-each loop is a breeze to implement: there's no code clutter, and the code is easy to write and comprehend. In the preceding example, the for-each loop is read as "for each element `val` in collection `myList`, print the value of `val`."

You can also easily iterate through *nested collections* using the enhanced `for` loop. In this example, assume that an `ArrayList` of exams, levels, and grades is defined as follows:

```
ArrayList<String> exams= new ArrayList<String>();
exams.add("Java");
exams.add("Oracle");
ArrayList<String> levels= new ArrayList<String>();
levels.add("Basic");
levels.add("Advanced");
ArrayList<String> grades= new ArrayList<String>();
grades.add("Pass");
grades.add("Fail");
```

The following code creates a nested `ArrayList`, `nestedArrayList`, every element of which is itself an `ArrayList` of `String` objects:

```
ArrayList<ArrayList<String>> nestedArrayList =
                    new ArrayList< ArrayList<String>>();

nestedArrayList.add(exams);
nestedArrayList.add(levels);
nestedArrayList.add(grades);
```

**ArrayList of ArrayList**

**Add object of ArrayList to nestedArrayList**

The `nestedArrayList` can be compared to a multidimensional array, as shown in figure 5.15.

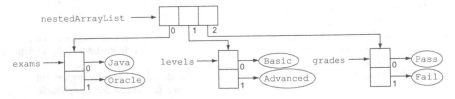

**Figure 5.15  Pictorial representation of `nestedArrayList`**

A nested enhanced `for` loop can be used to iterate through the nested `ArrayList` nestedArrayList. Here's the relevant code:

```
for (ArrayList<String> nestedListElement : nestedArrayList)
    for (String element : nestedListElement)
        System.out.println(element);
```

The output of this code is as follows:

```
Java
Oracle
Basic
Advanced
Pass
Fail
```

The enhanced `for` loop is again a breeze to use to iterate through *nested* or *non-nested* arrays. For example, you can use the following code to iterate through an array of elements and calculate its total:

```
int total = 0;
int primeNums[] = {2, 3, 7, 11};
for (int num : primeNums)
    total += num;
```

What happens when you try to modify the value of the loop variable in an enhanced `for` loop? The result depends on whether you're iterating through a collection of primitive values or objects. If you're iterating through an array of primitive values, manipulation of the loop variable will never change the value of the array being iterated because the primitive values are passed by value to the loop variable in an enhanced `for` loop.

When you iterate through a collection of objects, the value of the collection is passed by reference to the loop variable. Therefore, if the value of the loop variable is manipulated by executing methods on it, the modified value will be reflected in the collection of objects being iterated:

```
StringBuilder myArr[] = {
                new StringBuilder("Java"),
                new StringBuilder("Loop")
              };
for (StringBuilder val : myArr)                    Iterates through array myArr
    System.out.println(val);                       and prints Java and Loop

for (StringBuilder val : myArr)                    Appends Oracle to value
    val.append("Oracle");                          referenced by loop variable val

for (StringBuilder val : myArr)                    Iterates through array myArr and
    System.out.println(val);                       prints JavaOracle and LoopOracle
```

The output of the preceding code is

```
Java
Loop
JavaOracle
LoopOracle
```

Let's modify the preceding code. Instead of calling the method append on the loop variable val, let's assign to it another StringBuilder object. In this case, the original elements of the array being iterated won't be affected and will remain the same:

```
StringBuilder myArr[] = {
                new StringBuilder("Java"),
                new StringBuilder("Loop")
                };
or (StringBuilder val : myArr)          Iterates through array myArr
    System.out.println (val);           and prints Java and Loop
for (StringBuilder val : myArr)
    val = new StringBuilder("Oracle");  Assigns new StringBuilder object to
                                        reference variable val with value Oracle
for (StringBuilder val : myArr)
    System.out.println (val);           Iterates through array myArray
                                        and still prints Java and Loop
```

The output of the preceding code is

```
Java
Loop
Java
Loop
```

**EXAM TIP** Watch out for code that uses an enhanced for loop and its loop variable to change the values of elements in the collection that it iterates. This behavior often serves as food for thought for the exam authors.

### 5.4.2 Limitations of the enhanced for loop

Although a for-each loop is a good choice for iterating through collections and arrays, it can't be used in some places.

#### CAN'T BE USED TO INITIALIZE AN ARRAY AND MODIFY ITS ELEMENTS

Can you use an enhanced for loop in place of the regular for loop in the following code?

```
int[] myArray = new int[5];              Declare      count=length
for (int i=0; i<myArray.length; ++i) {   array        of the array
    myArray[i] = i;
    if ((myArray[i]%2)==0)                Initialize array
        myArray[i] = 20;                  elements
}                                Modify array
                                 elements
```

The simple answer is no. Although you can define a counter outside the enhanced for loop and use it to initialize and modify the array elements, this approach defeats the purpose of the for-each loop. The traditional for loop is easier to use in this case.

#### CAN'T BE USED TO DELETE OR REMOVE THE ELEMENTS OF A COLLECTION

Because the for loop hides the *iterator* used to iterate through the elements of a collection, you can't use it to remove or delete the existing collection values because you can't call the remove method.

If you assign a null value to the loop variable, it won't remove the element from a collection:

```
ArrayList<StringBuilder> myList= new ArrayList<>();
myList.add(new StringBuilder("One"));
myList.add(new StringBuilder("Two"));
for (StringBuilder val : myList)
    System.out.println (val);                          Doesn't remove an object
for (StringBuilder val : myList)                        from list; sets value of
    val = null;                                ⟵⎦      loop variable to null
for (StringBuilder val : myList)
    System.out.println(val);
```

The output of the preceding code is

```
One
Two
One
Two
```

#### CAN'T BE USED TO ITERATE OVER MULTIPLE COLLECTIONS OR ARRAYS IN THE SAME LOOP

Although it's perfectly fine for you to iterate through nested collections or arrays using a for loop, you can't iterate over multiple collections or arrays in the same for-each loop because the for-each loop allows for the creation of only one looping variable. Unlike the regular for loop, you can't define multiple looping variables in a for-each loop.

> **EXAM TIP**  Use the for-each loop to iterate over arrays and collections. Don't use it to initialize, modify, or filter them.

### 5.4.3   *Nested enhanced for loop*

First of all, working with a nested collection is not the same as working with a nested loop. A nested loop can also work with unrelated collections.

As discussed in section 5.3.4, loops defined within another loop are called *nested loops*. The loop that defines another loop within itself is called the *outer loop*, and the loop that's defined within another loop is called the *inner loop*. Theoretically, the level of nesting for any of the loops has no limits, including the enhanced for loop.

In this section, we'll work with three nested, enhanced for loops. You can compare a three-level nested loop with a clock that has hour, minute, and second hands. The second hand of the clock completes a full circle each minute. Similarly, the minute hand completes a full circle each hour. This comparison is shown in figure 5.16.

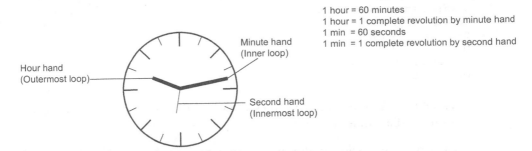

**Figure 5.16  Comparison between a clock with three hands and the levels of a nested `for` loop**

The following is a coding example of the nested, enhanced `for` loop, which I discussed in a previous section:

```
ArrayList<String> exams= new ArrayList<String>();        ◁─┐  First ArrayList
exams.add("Java"); exams.add("Oracle");
ArrayList<String> levels= new ArrayList<String>();       ◁───  Second ArrayList
levels.add("Basic"); levels.add("Advanced");
ArrayList<String> grades= new ArrayList<String>();       ❶  Outermost
grades.add("Pass"); grades.add("Fail");                     loop
for (String exam : exams)                                ◁─┘        ❷  Inner
    for (String level : levels)                          ◁─┘           nested
        for (String grade : grades)                      ◁─┐           loop
            System.out.println(exam+":"+level+":"+grade);   │
                                                          ❸  Innermost
                                                             nested loop
```

*Third Array-List* ↳

An inner loop in a nested loop executes for each iteration of its outer loop. The preceding example defines three enhanced `for` loops: the outermost loop at ❶, the inner nested loop at ❷, and the innermost loop at ❸. The complete innermost loop at ❸ executes for each iteration of its immediate outer loop defined at ❷. Similarly, the complete inner loop defined at ❷ executes for each iteration of its immediate outer loop defined at ❶. Figure 5.17 shows the loop values for which all of these loops iterate.

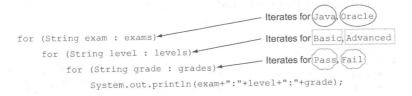

**Figure 5.17  Nested `for` loop with the loop values for which each of these nested loops iterates**

The output of the preceding code is as follows:

```
Java:Basic:Pass
Java:Basic:Fail
Java:Advanced:Pass
Java:Advanced:Fail
Oracle:Basic:Pass
Oracle:Basic:Fail
Oracle:Advanced:Pass
Oracle:Advanced:Fail
```

 **EXAM TIP**   A nested loop executes all its iterations for each single iteration of its immediate outer loop.

Apart from the for loops, the other looping statements on the exam are while and do-while, which are discussed in the next section.

## 5.5    *The while and do-while loops*

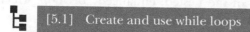 [5.1]    Create and use while loops

[5.3]    Create and use do-while loops

You'll learn about while and do-while loops in this section. Both of these loops execute a set of statements as long as their condition evaluates to true. Both of these loops work in the same manner except for one difference: the while loops checks its condition before evaluating its loop body, and the do-while loop checks its condition after executing the statements defined in its loop body.

Does this difference in behavior make a difference in their execution? Yes, it does, and in this section, you'll see how.

### 5.5.1    *The while loop*

A while loop is used to repeatedly execute a set of statements as long as its condition evaluates to true. This loop checks the condition *before* it starts the execution of the statement.

For example, at the famous fast-food chain Superfast Burgers, an employee may be instructed to prepare burgers as long as buns are available. In this example, the availability of buns is the while condition and the preparation of burgers is the while's loop body. You can represent this in code as follows:

```
boolean bunsAvailable = true;
while (bunsAvailable) {
    /* ... prepare burger ...*/
    if (noMoreBuns)
        bunsAvailable = false;
}
```

The preceding example is for demonstration purposes only, because the loop body isn't completely defined. The condition used in the `while` loop to check whether or not to execute the loop body again should evaluate to `false` at some point; otherwise, the loop will execute indefinitely. The value of this loop variable may be changed by the `while` loop or by another method if it's an instance or a `static` variable.

The `while` loop accepts arguments of type `boolean` or `Boolean`. In the preceding code, the loop body checks whether more buns are available. If none are available, it sets the value of the variable `bunsAvailable` to `false`. The loop body doesn't execute for the next iteration because `bunsAvailable` evaluates to `false`.

The execution of the preceding `while` loop is shown in figure 5.18 as a simple flowchart to help you understand the concept better.

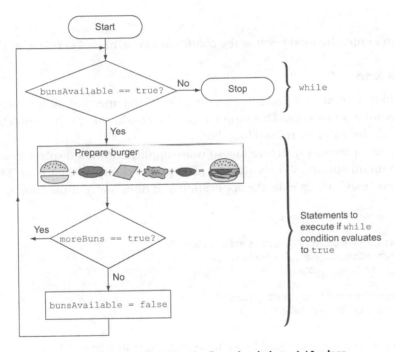

**Figure 5.18   A flowchart depicting the flow of code in a `while` loop**

Now, let's examine another simple example that uses the `while` loop:

```
int num = 9;
boolean divisibleBy7 = false;
while (!divisibleBy7) {
    System.out.println(num);
    if (num % 7 == 0) divisibleBy7 = true;
    --num;
}
```

The output of this code is as follows:

```
9
8
7
```

What happens if you change the code as follows (changes in bold)?

```
int num = 9;
boolean divisibleBy7 = true;
while (divisibleBy7 == false) {
    System.out.println(num);
    if (num % 7 == 0) divisibleBy7 = true;
    --num;
}
```

The code won't enter the loop because the condition `divisibleBy7==false` isn't true.

### 5.5.2　*The do-while loop*

A `do-while` loop is used to repeatedly execute a set of statements until the condition that it uses evaluates to `false`. This loop checks the condition *after* it completes the execution of all the statements in its loop body.

You could compare this structure to a software application that displays a menu at startup. Each menu option will execute a set of steps and redisplay the menu. The last menu option is "exit," which exits the application and does not redisplay the menu:

```
boolean exitSelected = false;
do {
    String selectedOption = displayMenuToUser();
    if (selectedOption.equals("exit"))
        exitSelected = true;
    else
        executeCommand(selectedOption);
} while (exitSelected == false);
```

The preceding code is represented by a simple flowchart in figure 5.19 that will help you to better understand the code.

The preceding example is for demonstration purposes only because the methods used in the `do-while` loop aren't defined. As discussed in the previous section on `while` loops, the condition that's used in the `do-while` loop to check whether or not to execute the loop body again should evaluate to `false` at some point, or the loop will execute indefinitely. The value of this loop variable may be changed by the `while` loop or by another method, if it's an instance or `static` variable.

 **NOTE**　Don't forget to use a semicolon (`;`) to end the `do-while` loop after specifying its condition. Even some experienced programmers overlook this step!

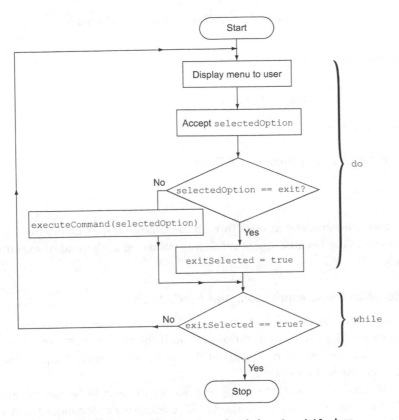

**Figure 5.19 Flowchart showing the flow of code in a do-while loop**

The do-while loop accepts arguments of type boolean or Boolean.

Let's modify the example used in section 5.5.1 to use the do-while loop instead of a while loop, as follows:

```
int num = 9;
boolean divisibleBy7 = false;
do {
    System.out.println(num);
    if (num % 7 == 0) divisibleBy7 = true;
    num--;
} while (divisibleBy7 == false);
```

The output of this code is as follows:

```
9
8
7
```

What happens if you change the code as follows (changes in bold)?

```
int num = 9;
boolean divisibleBy7 = true;
do {
    System.out.println(num);
    if (num % 7 == 0) divisibleBy7 = true;
    num--;
} while (divisibleBy7 == false);
```

The output of the preceding code is as follows:

```
9
```

The do-while loop executes once, even though the condition specified in the do-while loop evaluates to false because the condition is evaluated at the end of execution of the loop body.

### 5.5.3   *while and do-while block, expression, and nesting rules*

You can use the curly braces {} with while and do-while loops to define multiple lines of code to execute for every iteration. Without the use of curly braces, only the first line of code will be considered a part of the while or do-while loop, as specified in the if-else construct in section 5.1.3.

Similarly, the rules that define an appropriate expression to be passed to while and do-while loops are the same as for the if-else construct in section 5.1.4. Also, the rules for defining nested while and do-while loops are the same as for the if-else construct in section 5.1.5.

## 5.6   *Comparing loop constructs*

 [5.4]   Compare loop constructs

In this section, I'll discuss the differences and similarities between the following looping constructs: do-while, while, for, and enhanced for.

### 5.6.1   *Comparing do-while and while loops*

Both do-while and while loops execute a set of statements until their termination condition evaluates to false. The only difference between these two statements is that the do-while loop executes the code at least once, even if the condition evaluates to false. The do-while loop evaluates the termination condition *after* executing the statements, whereas the while loop evaluates the termination condition *before* executing its statements.

The forms taken by these statements are depicted in figure 5.20.

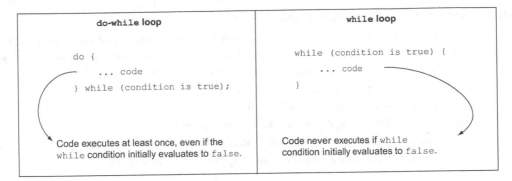

**Figure 5.20** Comparing do-while and while loops

What do you think the output of the following code is?

```
int num=10;
do {
    num++;
} while (++num > 20);
System.out.println (num);
```

**Value of num incremented to 11 is incremented by 1**

**Evaluate condition ++num > 20**

The output of the preceding code is as follows:

```
12
```

What do you think the output of the following code is?

```
int num=10;
while (++num > 20) {
    num++;
}
System.out.println(num);
```

**Because 11 isn't > 20, num++ doesn't execute.**

The output of the preceding code is as follows:

```
11
```

### 5.6.2 *Comparing for and enhanced for loops*

The regular for loop, although cumbersome to use, is much more powerful than the enhanced for loop (as mentioned in section 5.4.1):

- The enhanced for loop can't be used to initialize an array and modify its elements.
- The enhanced for loop can't be used to delete the elements of a collection.
- The enhanced for loop can't be used to iterate over multiple collections or arrays in the same loop.

### 5.6.3 *Comparing for and while loops*

You should *try* to use a for loop when you know the number of iterations—for example, when you're iterating through a collection or an array or when you're executing a loop for a fixed number of times, say, to ping a server five times.

You should *try* to use a do-while or a while loop when you don't know the number of iterations beforehand and when the number of iterations depends on a condition being true—for example, when accepting passport renewal applications from applicants until there are no more applicants. In this case, you'd be unaware of the number of applicants who have submitted their applications on a given day.

## 5.7    *Loop statements: break and continue*

 [5.5]   Use break and continue

Imagine that you've defined a loop to iterate through a list of managers, and you're looking for at least one manager whose name starts with the letter *D*. You'd like to exit the loop after you find the first match, but how? You can do this by using the break statement in your loop.

Now imagine that you want to iterate through all the folders on your laptop and scan any files larger than 10 MB for viruses. If all those files are found to be OK, you want to upload them to a server. But what if you'd like to skip the steps of *virus checking* and *file uploading* for file sizes less than 10 MB yet still proceed with the remaining files on your laptop? You can! You'd use the continue statement in your loop.

In this section, I'll discuss the break and continue statements, which you can use to exit a loop completely or to skip the remaining statements in a loop iteration. At the end of this section, I'll discuss labeled statements.

### 5.7.1 *The break statement*

The break statement is used to *exit*—or *break out of*—the for, for-each, do, and do-while loops, as well as switch constructs. Alternatively, the continue statement can be used to skip the remaining steps in the current iteration and start with the next loop iteration.

The difference between these statements can be best demonstrated with an example. You could use the following code to browse and print all the values of a String array:

```
String[] programmers = {"Paul", "Shreya", "Selvan", "Harry"};
for (String name : programmers) {
    System.out.println(name);
}
```

The output of the preceding code is as follows:

```
Paul
Shreya
Selvan
Harry
```

Let's modify the preceding code to exit the loop when the array value is equal to Shreya. Here's the required code:

```
String[] programmers = {"Paul", "Shreya", "Selvan", "Harry"};
for (String name : programmers) {
    if (name.equals("Shreya"))
        break;                          ⟵  Break out
    System.out.println(name);               of the loop
}
```

The output of the preceding code is as follows:

```
Paul
```

As soon as a loop encounters a break, it exits the loop. Hence, only the first value of this array—that is, Paul—is printed. As mentioned in the section on the switch construct, the break statement can be defined after every case in order for the control to exit the switch construct once it finds a matching case.

    The preceding code snippets are depicted in figure 5.21, which shows the transfer of control upon execution of the break statement.

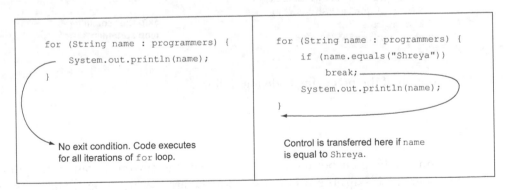

**Figure 5.21**    **The flow of control when the break statement executes within a loop**

When you use the break statement with nested loops, it exits the inner loop. The next Twist in the Tale exercise looks at a small code snippet to see how the control transfers when you use a break statement in nested for loops (answer in the appendix).

---

**Twist in the Tale 5.4**

Modify the code used in the previous example as follows. What is the output of this code?

```
String[] programmers = {"Outer", "Inner"};
for (String outer : programmers) {
    for (String inner : programmers) {
        if (inner.equals("Inner"))
            break;
        System.out.print(inner + ":");
    }
}
```

a  Outer:Outer:

b  Outer:Inner:Outer:Inner:

c  Outer:

d  Outer:Inner:

e  Inner:Inner:

---

## 5.7.2   *The continue statement*

The continue statement is used to skip the remaining steps in the current iteration and start with the next loop iteration. Let's replace the break statement in the previous example with continue and examine its output:

```
String[] programmers = {"Paul", "Shreya", "Selvan", "Harry"};
for (String name : programmers) {
    if (name.equals("Shreya"))
        continue;                        ⊲──┤  Skip the remaining
    System.out.println(name);               │  loop statements
}
```

The output of the preceding code is as follows:

```
Paul
Selvan
Harry
```

As soon as a loop encounters continue, it exits the current iteration of the loop. In this example, it skips the printing step for the array value Shreya. Unlike the break statement, continue doesn't exit the loop—it restarts with the next loop iteration, printing the remaining array values (that is, Selvan and Harry).

When you use the continue statement with nested loops, it exits the current iteration of the inner loop.

Figure 5.22 compares how the control transfers out of the loop and to the next iteration when break and continue statements are used.

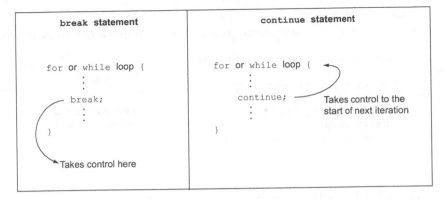

**Figure 5.22  Comparing the flow of control when using `break` and `continue` statements in a loop**

### 5.7.3  *Labeled statements*

In Java, you can add labels to the following types of statements:

- A code block defined using {}
- All looping statements (`for`, enhanced `for`, `while`, `do-while`)
- Conditional constructs (`if` and `switch` statements)
- Expressions
- Assignments
- `return` statements
- `try` blocks
- `throws` statements

An example of a labeled loop is given here:

```
String[] programmers = {"Outer", "Inner"};
outer:
for (int i = 0; i < programmers.length; i++) {
}
```

You can't add labels to declarations. The following labeled declaration won't compile:

```
outer :
    int[] myArray = {1,2,3};
```
**Variable declaration that fails compilation**

It's interesting to note that the preceding declaration can be defined within a block statement, as follows:

**Start definition of block**
```
outer : {
    int[] myArray = {1,2,3};
}
```
**Variable declaration, compiles**

**End block**

### LABELED BREAK STATEMENTS

You can use a labeled break statement to exit an outer loop. Here's an example:

```
String[] programmers = {"Outer", "Inner"};
outer:
for (String outer : programmers) {
    for (String inner : programmers) {
        if (inner.equals("Inner"))
            break outer;                            Exits the outer loop,
        System.out.print(inner + ":");              marked with label outer
    }
}
```

The output of the preceding code is

```
Outer:
```

When this code executes break outer;, control transfers to the line of text that marks the end of this block. It doesn't transfer control to the label outer.

### LABELED CONTINUE STATEMENTS

You can use a labeled continue statement to skip an iteration of the outer loop. Here's an example:

```
String[] programmers = {"Paul", "Shreya", "Selvan", "Harry"};
outer:
for (String name1 : programmers) {
    for (String name : programmers) {               Skips remaining code for current
        if (name.equals("Shreya"))                  iteration of outer loop and starts
            continue outer;                          with its next iteration
        System.out.println(name);
    }
}
```

The output of the preceding code is

```
Paul
Paul
Paul
Paul
```

 **NOTE**    Please use labels sparingly and only if they *really* seem to increase the readability of your code.

## 5.8   Summary

We started this chapter with the selection statements if and switch and ternary constructs. We covered the different flavors of the if construct. Then we looked at the switch construct, which accepts a limited set of argument types including byte, char, short, int, and String. The humble if-else construct can define virtually any set of simple or complicated conditions.

You also saw how you can execute your code using all types of loops: for, for-each, do, and do-while. The for, do, and do-while loops have been around since the Java language was first introduced, whereas the enhanced for loop (the for-each loop) was added to the language as of Java version 5.0. I recommend that you use the for-each loop to iterate through arrays and collections.

At the end of this chapter, we looked at the break and continue statements. You use the break statement to *exit*—or *break out of*—a for, for-each, do, do-while, or switch construct. You use the continue statement to skip the remaining steps in the current iteration and start with the next loop iteration.

## 5.9 Review notes

if and if-else constructs:

- The if statement enables you to execute a set of statements in your code based on the result of a condition, which should evaluate to a boolean or a Boolean value.
- The multiple flavors of an if statement are if, if-else, and if-else-if-else.
- The if construct doesn't use the keyword *then* to define code to execute when an if condition evaluates to true. The *then* part of the if construct follows the if condition.
- An if construct may or may not define its else part.
- The else part of an if construct can't exist without the definition of its *then* part.
- It's easy to get confused with the common *if-else* syntax used in other programming languages. The if-elsif and if-elseif statements aren't used in Java to define if-else-if-else constructs. The correct keywords are if and else.
- You can execute a single statement or a block of statements for corresponding true and false conditions. A pair of braces marks a block of statements: {}.
- If an if construct doesn't use {} to define a block of code to execute for its *then* or else part, only the first line of code is part of the if construct.
- An assignment of a boolean variable can also be passed as an argument to the if construct. It's valid because the resultant value is boolean, which is accepted by if constructs.
- Theoretically, nested if and if-else constructs have no limits on their levels. When using nested if-else constructs, be careful about matching the else part with the right if part.

Ternary constructs:

- You can use a ternary operator, ?:, to define a compact if-else construct to assign value to a variable depending on a boolean expression.
- The parentheses enclosing a boolean expression are optional for better readability. The code will work without them.
- You can assign a literal value or an expression to a variable using a ternary operator.
- A method that returns a value can be used to initialize a variable in a ternary construct.

- If the expression used to evaluate a ternary operator doesn't return a `boolean` or `Boolean` value, the code won't compile.
- All three parts of a ternary operator are mandatory.
- The value returned by a ternary operator must be assigned to a variable, or the code won't compile.
- Because a ternary operator must return values, which are assigned to a variable, it can't include code blocks.
- A method that doesn't return a value can't be used to initialize variables in a ternary construct.
- The value returned by a ternary construct must be compatible with the variable type to which the value is being assigned.
- Ternary operators can be nested to any level.

`switch` statements:

- A `switch` statement is used to compare the value of a variable with multiple predefined values.
- A `switch` statement accepts arguments of type `char`, `byte`, `short`, `int`, and `String`. It also accepts arguments of wrapper classes: `Character`, `Byte`, `Short`, `Integer`, and `Enum`.
- A `switch` statement can be compared with multiple related `if-else-if-else` constructs.
- You can pass an expression as an argument to a `switch` statement, as long as the type of the expression is one of the acceptable data types.
- The case value should be a compile-time constant, assignable to the argument passed to the `switch` statement.
- The case value can't be the literal value `null`.
- The case value can define expressions that use literal values; that is, they can be evaluated at compile time, as in 7+2.
- One code block can be defined to execute for multiple `case` values in a `switch` statement.
- A `break` statement is used to exit a `switch` construct once a matching case is found and the required code statements have executed.
- In the absence of the `break` statement, control will *fall through* all the remaining case values in a `switch` statement until the first `break` statement is found, evaluating the code for the `case` statements in order.

`for` loops:

- A traditional `for` loop is usually used to execute a set of statements a fixed number of times.
- A `for` loop defines three types of statements separated by semicolons (`;`): initialization statements, termination condition, and update clause.

- The definition of any of the three `for` statements—initialization statements, termination condition, and update clause—is optional. For example, `for (;;);` and `for (;;){}` are valid code for defining a `for` loop. Also, defining any one of these statements is also valid code.
- An initialization block executes only once. A `for` loop can declare and initialize multiple variables in its initialization block, but the variables that it declares should be of the same type.
- The termination condition is evaluated once, for each iteration, before the statements defined within the body of the loop are executed.
- The `for` loop terminates when the termination condition evaluates to `false`.
- The update block is usually used to increment or decrement the value of the variables that are defined in the initialization block. It can also execute multiple other statements, including method calls.
- Nested `for` loops have no limits on levels.
- Nested `for` loops are frequently used to work with multidimensional arrays.

Enhanced `for` loops:

- The enhanced `for` loop is also called the `for`-each loop.
- The enhanced `for` loop offers some benefits over the regular `for` loop, but it's not as flexible as the regular `for` loop.
- The enhanced `for` loop offers simple syntax to iterate through a collection of values—an array, `ArrayList`, or other classes from Java's Collection framework that store a collection of values.
- The enhanced `for` loop can't be used to initialize an array and modify its elements.
- The enhanced `for` loop can't be used to delete the elements of a collection.
- The enhanced `for` loop can't be used to iterate over multiple collections or arrays in the same loop.
- Nested enhanced `for` loops have no limits on levels.

`while` and `do-while` loops:

- A `while` loop is used to keep executing a set of statements until the condition that it uses evaluates to `false`. This loop checks the condition *before* it starts the execution of the statement.
- A `do-while` loop is used to keep executing a set of statements until the condition that it uses evaluates to `false`. This loop checks the condition *after* it completes the execution of all the statements in its loop body.
- The levels of nested `do-while` or `while` loops have no limitations.
- Both `do-while` and `while` loops can define either a single line of code or a code block to execute. The latter is defined by using curly braces {}.

Comparing loop constructs:

- Both the `do-while` and `while` loops execute a set of statements until the termination condition evaluates to `false`. The only difference between these two statements is that the do-while loop executes the code at least once, even if the condition evaluates to false.

- The regular for loop, though cumbersome to use, is much more powerful than the enhanced for loop.
- The enhanced for loop can't be used to initialize an array and modify its elements. The enhanced for loop can't be used to delete or remove the elements of a collection.
- The enhanced for loop can't be used to iterate over multiple collections or arrays in the same loop.
- You should try to use a for loop when you know the number of iterations—for example, iterating through a collection or an array, or executing a loop for a fixed number of times, say, to ping a server five times.
- You should try to use a do-while or a while loop when you don't know the number of iterations beforehand and the number of iterations depends on a condition being true—for example, accepting passport renewal applications until all applicants have been attended to.

Loop statements (break and continue):

- The break statement is used to *exit*—or *break out of*—the for, for-each, do, and do-while loops and the switch construct.
- The continue statement is used to skip the remaining steps in the current iteration and start with the next loop iteration. The continue statement works with the for, for-each, do, and do-while loops and the switch construct.
- When you use the break statement with nested loops, it exits the corresponding loop.
- When you use the continue statement with nested loops, it exits the current iteration of the corresponding loop.

Labeled statements:

- You can add labels to a code block defined using braces, {}, all looping statements (for, enhanced for, while, do-while), conditional constructs (if and switch statements), expressions and assignments, return statements, try blocks, and throws statements.
- You can't add labels to declarations of variables.
- You can use a labeled break statement to exit an outer loop.
- You can use a labeled continue statement to skip the iteration of the outer loop.

## 5.10  *Sample exam questions*

**Q5-1.** What's the output of the following code?

```
class Loop2 {
    public static void main(String[] args) {
        int i = 10;
```

```
        do
            while (i < 15)
                i = i + 20;
        while (i < 2);
        System.out.println(i);
    }
}
```

a  10

b  30

c  31

d  32

**Q5-2.** What's the output of the following code?

```
class Loop2 {
    public static void main(String[] args) {
        int i = 10;
        do
            while (i++ < 15)
                i = i + 20;
        while (i < 2);
        System.out.println(i);
    }
}
```

a  10

b  30

c  31

d  32

**Q5-3.** Which of the following statements is true?

a  The enhanced for loop can't be used within a regular for loop.

b  The enhanced for loop can't be used within a while loop.

c  The enhanced for loop can be used within a do-while loop.

d  The enhanced for loop can't be used within a switch construct.

e  All of the above statements are false.

**Q5-4.** What's the output of the following code?

```
int a =  10;
if (a++ > 10) {
    System.out.println("true");
}
{
    System.out.println("false");
}
System.out.println("ABC");
```

a   true
    false
    ABC

b   false
    ABC

c   true
    ABC

d   Compilation error

**Q5-5.** Given the following code, which of the optional lines of code can individually replace the //INSERT CODE HERE line so that the code compiles successfully?

```
class EJavaGuru {
    public static void main(String args[]) {
        int num = 10;
        final int num2 = 20;
        switch (num) {
            // INSERT CODE HERE
            break;
            default: System.out.println("default");
        }
    }
}
```

a   case 10*3: System.out.println(2);
b   case num: System.out.println(3);
c   case 10/3: System.out.println(4);
d   case num2: System.out.println(5);

**Q5-6.** What's the output of the following code?

```
class EJavaGuru {
    public static void main(String args[]) {
        int num = 20;
        final int num2;
        num2 = 20;
        switch (num) {
            default: System.out.println("default");
            case num2: System.out.println(4);
            break;
        }
    }
}
```

a   default
b   default
    4

c   4

d   Compilation error

**Q5-7.** What's the output of the following code?

```
class EJavaGuru {
    public static void main(String args[]) {
        int num = 120;
        switch (num) {
            default: System.out.println("default");
            case 0: System.out.println("case1");
            case 10*2-20: System.out.println("case2");
            break;
        }
    }
}
```

  **a**  default
      case1
      case2

  **b**  case1
      case2

  **c**  case2

  **d**  Compilation error

  **e**  Runtime exception

**Q5-8.** What's the output of the following code?

```
class EJavaGuru3 {
    public static void main(String args[]) {
        byte foo = 120;
        switch (foo) {
            default: System.out.println("ejavaguru"); break;
            case 2: System.out.println("e"); break;
            case 120: System.out.println("ejava");
            case 121: System.out.println("enum");
            case 127: System.out.println("guru"); break;
        }
    }
}
```

  **a**  ejava
      enum
      guru

  **b**  ejava

  **c**  ejavaguru
      e

  **d**  ejava
      enum
      guru
      ejavaguru

**Q5-9.** What's the output of the following code?

```
class EJavaGuru4 {
    public static void main(String args[]) {
        boolean myVal = false;
        if (myVal=true)
        for (int i = 0; i < 2; i++) System.out.println(i);
        else System.out.println("else");
    }
}
```

   a  else

   b  0
      1
      2

   c  0
      1

   d  Compilation error

**Q5-10.** What's the output of the following code?

```
class EJavaGuru5 {
    public static void main(String args[]) {
        int i = 0;
        for (; i < 2; i=i+5) {
            if (i < 5) continue;
            System.out.println(i);
        }
        System.out.println(i);
    }
}
```

   a  Compilation error

   b  0
      5

   c  0
      5
      10

   d  10

   e  0
      1
      5

   f  5

## 5.11  *Answers to sample exam questions*

**Q5-1.** What's the output of the following code?

```
class Loop2 {
    public static void main(String[] args) {
        int i = 10;
        do
            while (i < 15)
                i = i + 20;
        while (i < 2);
        System.out.println(i);
    }
}
```

  a  10
  b  **30**
  c  31
  d  32

Answer: b

Explanation: The condition specified in the do-while loop evaluates to false (because 10<2 evaluates to false). But the control enters the do-while loop because the do-while loop executes at least once—its condition is checked at the end of the loop. The while loop evaluates to true for the first iteration and adds 20 to i, making it 30. The while loop doesn't execute for the second time. Hence, the value of the variable i at the end of the execution of the previous code is 30.

**Q5-2.** What's the output of the following code?

```
class Loop2 {
    public static void main(String[] args) {
        int i = 10;
        do
            while (i++ < 15)
                i = i + 20;
        while (i < 2);
        System.out.println(i);
    }
}
```

  a  10
  b  30
  c  31
  d  **32**

Answer: d

Explanation: If you attempted to answer question 5-1, it's likely that you would select the same answer for this question. I deliberately used the same question text and variable names (with a small difference) because you may encounter a similar pattern in the OCA Java SE 8 Programmer I exam. This question includes one difference: unlike question 5-1, it uses a postfix unary operator in the while condition.

The condition specified in the do-while loop evaluates to false (because 10<2 evaluates to false). But the control enters the do-while loop because the do-while loop executes at least once—its condition is checked at the end of the loop. This question prints out 32, not 30, because the condition specified in the while loop (which has an increment operator) executes twice.

In this question, the while loop condition executes twice. For the first evaluation, i++ < 15 (that is, 10<15) returns true and increments the value of variable i by 1 (due to the postfix increment operator). The loop body modifies the value of i to 31. The second condition evaluates i++<15 (that is, 31<15) to false. But because of the postfix increment operator value of i, the value increments to 32. The final value is printed as 32.

**Q5-3.** Which of the following statements is true?

a  The enhanced for loop can't be used within a regular for loop.
b  The enhanced for loop can't be used within a while loop.
c  **The enhanced for loop can be used within a do-while loop.**
d  The enhanced for loop can't be used within a switch construct.
e  All of the above statements are false.

Answer: c

Explanation: The enhanced for loop can be used within all types of looping and conditional constructs. Notice the use of "can" and "can't" in the answer options. It's important to take note of these subtle differences.

**Q5-4.** What's the output of the following code?

```
int a =  10;
if (a++ > 10) {
    System.out.println("true");
}
{
    System.out.println("false");
}
System.out.println("ABC");
```

a  true
   false
   ABC

b  **false**
   **ABC**

   **c**  true
       ABC

   **d**  Compilation error

Answer: b

Explanation: First of all, the code has no compilation errors. This question has a trick—the following code snippet isn't part of the if construct:

```
{
    System.out.println("false");
}
```

Hence, the value false will print no matter what, regardless of whether the condition in the if construct evaluates to true or false.

    Because the opening and closing braces for this code snippet are placed right after the if construct, it leads you to believe that this code snippet is the else part of the if construct. Also, note that an if construct uses the keyword else to define the else part. This keyword is missing in this question.

    The if condition (that is, a++ > 10) evaluates to false because the postfix increment operator (a++) increments the value of the variable a immediately after its earlier value is used. 10 isn't greater than 10, so this condition evaluates to false.

**Q5-5.** Given the following code, which of the optional lines of code can individually replace the //INSERT CODE HERE line so that the code compiles successfully?

```
class EJavaGuru {
    public static void main(String args[]) {
        int num = 10;
        final int num2 = 20;
        switch (num) {
            // INSERT CODE HERE
            break;
            default: System.out.println("default");
        }
    }
}
```

   **a**  `case 10*3: System.out.println(2);`

   **b**  `case num: System.out.println(3);`

   **c**  `case 10/3: System.out.println(4);`

   **d**  `case num2: System.out.println(5);`

Answer: a, c, d

Explanation: Option (a) is correct. Compile-time constants, including expressions, are permissible in the case labels.

Option (b) is incorrect. The case labels should be compile-time constants. A non-final variable isn't a compile-time constant because it can be reassigned a value during the course of a class's execution. Although the previous class doesn't assign a value to it, the compiler still treats it as a changeable variable.

Option (c) is correct. The value specified in the case labels should be assignable to the variable used in the switch construct. You may think that 10/3 will return a decimal number, which can't be assigned to the variable num, but this operation discards the decimal part and compares 3 with the variable num.

Option (d) is correct. The variable num2 is defined as a final variable and assigned a value on the same line of code, with its declaration. Hence, it's considered to be a compile-time constant.

**Q5-6.** What's the output of the following code?

```
class EJavaGuru {
    public static void main(String args[]) {
        int num = 20;
        final int num2;
        num2 = 20;
        switch (num) {
            default: System.out.println("default");
            case num2: System.out.println(4);
            break;
        }
    }
}
```

  a  default

  b  default
     4

  c  4

  d  **Compilation error**

Answer: d

Explanation: The code will fail to compile. The case labels require compile-time constant values, and the variable num2 doesn't qualify as such. Although the variable num2 is defined as a final variable, it isn't assigned a value with its declaration. The code assigns a literal value 20 to this variable after its declaration, but it isn't considered to be a compile-time constant by the Java compiler.

**Q5-7.** What's the output of the following code?

```
class EJavaGuru {
    public static void main(String args[]) {
        int num = 120;
        switch (num) {
            default: System.out.println("default");
            case 0: System.out.println("case1");
```

```
                    case 10*2-20: System.out.println("case2");
                    break;
            }
        }
    }
```

**a** `default`
   `case1`
   `case2`

**b** `case1`
   `case2`

**c** `case2`

**d** **Compilation error**

**e** Runtime exception

Answer: d

Explanation: The expressions used for both case labels—0 and `10*2-20`—evaluate to the constant value 0. Because you can't define duplicate case labels for the `switch` statement, the code will fail to compile with an error message that states that the code defines a duplicate case label.

**Q5-8.** What's the output of the following code?

```
class EJavaGuru3 {
    public static void main(String args[]) {
        byte foo = 120;
        switch (foo) {
            default: System.out.println("ejavaguru"); break;
            case 2: System.out.println("e"); break;
            case 120: System.out.println("ejava");
            case 121: System.out.println("enum");
            case 127: System.out.println("guru"); break;
        }
    }
}
```

**a** **ejava**
   **enum**
   **guru**

**b** `ejava`

**c** `ejavaguru`
   `e`

**d** `ejava`
   `enum`
   `guru`
   `ejavaguru`

Answer: a

Explanation: For a switch case construct, control enters the case labels when a matching case is found. The control then falls through the remaining case labels until it's terminated by a break statement. The control exits the switch construct when it encounters a break statement or it reaches the end of the switch construct.

In this example, a matching label is found for case label 120. The control executes the statement for this case label and prints ejava to the console. Because a break statement doesn't terminate the case label, the control falls through to case label 121. The control executes the statement for this case label and prints enum to the console. Because a break statement doesn't terminate this case label also, the control falls through to case label 127. The control executes the statement for this case label and prints guru to the console. This case label is terminated by a break statement, so the control exits the switch construct.

**Q5-9.** What's the output of the following code?

```
class EJavaGuru4 {
    public static void main(String args[]) {
        boolean myVal = false;
        if (myVal=true)
        for (int i = 0; i < 2; i++) System.out.println(i);
        else System.out.println("else");
    }
}
```

   **a**  else

   **b**  0
      1
      2

   **c**  0
      1

   **d**  Compilation error

Answer: c

Explanation: First of all, the expression used in the if construct isn't comparing the value of the variable myVal with the literal value true—it's assigning the literal value true to it. The assignment operator (=) assigns the literal value. The comparison operator (==) is used to compare values. Because the resulting value is a boolean value, the compiler doesn't complain about the assignment in the if construct.

The code is deliberately poorly indented because you may encounter similarly poor indentation in the OCA Java SE 8 Programmer I exam. The for loop is part of the if construct, which prints 0 and 1. The else part doesn't execute because the if condition evaluates to true. The code has no compilation errors.

**Q5-10.** What's the output of the following code?

```
class EJavaGuru5 {
    public static void main(String args[]) {
        int i = 0;
        for (; i < 2; i=i+5) {
            if (i < 5) continue;
            System.out.println(i);
        }
        System.out.println(i);
    }
}
```

    a  Compilation error

    b  0
        5

    c  0
        5
        10

    d  10

    e  0
        1
        5

    f  **5**

Answer: f

Explanation: First, the following line of code has no compilation errors:

```
for (; i < 2; i=i+5) {
```

Using the initialization block is optional in a for loop. In this case, using a semicolon (;) terminates it.

For the first for iteration, the variable i has a value of 0. Because this value is less than 2, the following if construct evaluates to true and the continue statement executes:

```
if (i < 5) continue;
```

Because the continue statement ignores all the remaining statements in a for loop iteration, the control doesn't print the value of the variable i, which leads the control to move on to the next for iteration. In the next for iteration, the value of the variable i is 5. The for loop condition evaluates to false and the control moves out of the for loop. After the for loop, the code prints out the value of the variable i, which increments once using the code i=i+5.

# Working with inheritance

6

| Exam objectives covered in this chapter | What you need to know |
|---|---|
| [7.1] Describe inheritance and its benefits. | The need for inheriting classes.<br>How to implement inheritance using classes. |
| [7.2] Develop code that demonstrates the use of polymorphism; including overriding and object type versus reference type. | How to implement polymorphism with classes and interfaces.<br>How to define polymorphic or overridden methods.<br>How to determine the valid types of the variables that can be used to refer to an object.<br>How to determine the differences in the members of an object, which ones are accessible, and when an object is referred to using a variable of an inherited base class or an implemented interface. |
| [7.3] Determine when casting is necessary. | The need for casting.<br>How to cast an object to another class or an interface. |
| [7.4] Use super and this to access objects and constructors. | How to access variables, methods, and constructors using super and this.<br>What happens if a derived class tries to access variables of a base class when the variables aren't accessible to the derived class. |
| [7.5] Use abstract classes and interfaces. | The role of abstract classes and interfaces in implementing polymorphism. |
| [9.5] Write a simple Lambda expression that consumes a Lambda Predicate expression | Syntax and usage of lambda expressions. Usage of Predicate class. |

All living beings inherit the characteristics and behaviors of their parents. The off-spring of a fly looks and behaves like a fly, and that of a lion looks and behaves like a lion. But despite being similar to their parents, all offspring are also different and unique in their own ways. In addition, a single action may have different meanings for different beings. For example, the action "eat" has different meanings for a fly than a lion. A fly eats nectar, whereas a lion eats an antelope.

Something similar happens in Java. The concept of inheriting characteristics and behaviors from parents can be compared to classes inheriting variables and methods from a parent class. Being different and unique in one's own way is similar to how a class can both inherit from a parent and define additional variables and methods. Single actions having different meanings can be compared to polymorphism in Java.

In the OCA Java SE 8 Programmer I exam, you'll be asked questions on how to implement inheritance and polymorphism and how to use classes and interfaces. Hence, this chapter covers the following:

- Understanding and implementing inheritance
- Developing code that demonstrates the use of polymorphism
- Differentiating between the type of a reference and an object
- Determining when casting is required
- Using super and this to access objects and constructors
- Using abstract classes and interfaces

## 6.1 Inheritance with classes

> [7.1] Describe inheritance and its benefits

> [7.5] Use abstract classes and interfaces

When we discuss inheritance in the context of an object-oriented programming language such as Java, we talk about how a class can inherit the properties and behavior of another class. The class that inherits from another class can also define additional properties and behaviors. The exam will ask you explicit questions about the need to inherit classes and how to implement inheritance using classes.

Let's get started with the need to inherit classes.

### 6.1.1 The need to inherit classes

Imagine the positions *Programmer* and *Manager* within an organization. Both of these positions have a common set of properties, including name, address, and phone number. These positions also have different properties. A *Programmer* may be concerned with a project's programming languages, whereas a *Manager* may be concerned with project status reports.

Let's assume you're supposed to store details of all Programmers and Managers in your office. Figure 6.1 shows the properties and behavior that you may have identified for a Programmer and a Manager, together with their representations as classes.

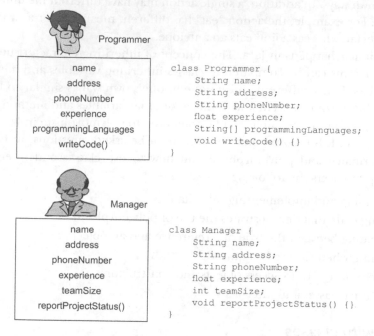

```
class Programmer {
    String name;
    String address;
    String phoneNumber;
    float experience;
    String[] programmingLanguages;
    void writeCode() {}
}
```

```
class Manager {
    String name;
    String address;
    String phoneNumber;
    float experience;
    int teamSize;
    void reportProjectStatus() {}
}
```

**Figure 6.1   Properties and behavior of a Programmer and a Manager, together with their representations as classes**

Did you notice that the classes `Programmer` and `Manager` have common properties, namely, `name`, `address`, `phoneNumber`, and `experience`? The next step is to pull out these common properties into a new position and name it something like *Employee*. This step is shown in figure 6.2.

This new position, Employee, can be defined as a new class, `Employee`, which is inherited by the classes `Programmer` and `Manager`. A class uses the keyword `extends` to *inherit* a class, as shown in figure 6.3.

Inheriting a class is also referred to as *subclassing*. In figure 6.3, the inherited class `Employee` is also referred to as the *superclass, base class*, or *parent class*. The classes `Programmer` and `Manager` that inherit the class `Employee` are called *subclasses, derived classes, extended classes*, or *child classes*.

Why do you think you need to pull out the common properties and behaviors into a separate class `Employee` and make the `Programmer` and `Manager` classes inherit it? The next section covers the benefits of inheriting classes.

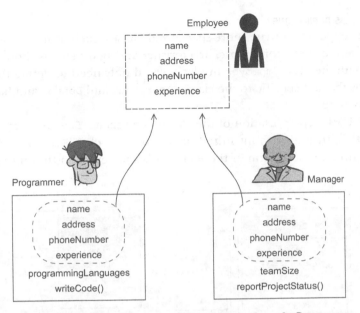

**Figure 6.2    Identify common properties and behaviors of a Programmer and a Manager, pull them out into a new position, and name it Employee.**

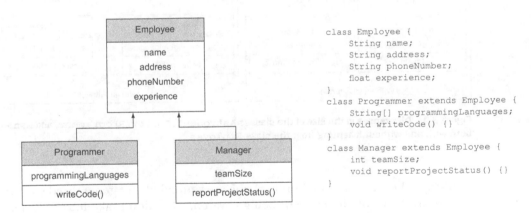

**Figure 6.3    The classes `Programmer` and `Manager` extend the class `Employee`.**

## 6.1.2    Benefits

Do you know that all classes in Java inherit class `java.lang.Object`, either implicitly or explicitly? Extending a class offers multiple benefits. Let's revisit the examples used in the previous section to highlight the benefits of inheriting classes.

### SMALLER DERIVED CLASS DEFINITIONS

What if you were supposed to write more-specialized classes, such as `Astronaut` and `Doctor`, which have the same common characteristics and behaviors as those of the class `Employee`? With the class `Employee` in place, you'd only need to define the variables and methods that are specific to the classes `Astronaut` and `Doctor` and have the classes inherit `Employee`.

Figure 6.4 is a UML representation of the classes `Astronaut`, `Doctor`, `Programmer`, and `Manager`, both with and without inheritance from the class `Employee`. As you can see in this figure, the definition of these classes is smaller when they inherit the class `Employee`.

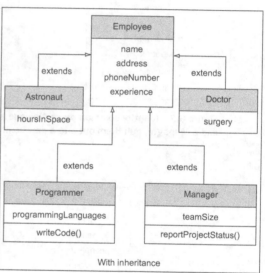

**Figure 6.4   Differences in the size of the classes** `Astronaut`, `Doctor`, `Programmer`, **and** `Manager`, **both with and without inheriting from the class** `Employee`

   **NOTE**   The examples used in this book are simplified and generalized so that you can focus on the concept being covered. They don't take into consideration all real-world scenarios. For example, on a particular project, an astronaut or a doctor might not be an employee of some organization.

### EASE OF MODIFICATION TO COMMON PROPERTIES AND BEHAVIOR

What happens if your boss steps in and tells you that all of these specialized classes—`Astronaut`, `Doctor`, `Programmer`, and `Manager`—should now have a property `facebookId`? Figure 6.5 shows that with the base class `Employee` in place, you just need to add this variable to that base class. If you haven't inherited from the class `Employee`, you'll need to add the variable `facebookId` to *each* of these four classes.

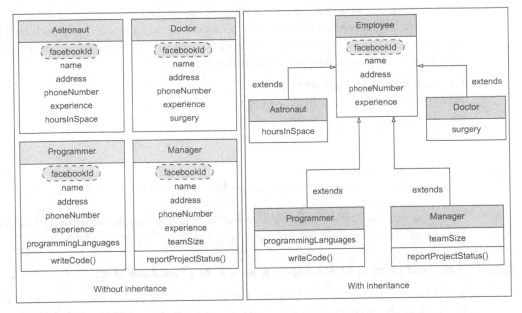

**Figure 6.5** **Adding a new property, `facebookId`, to all classes, with and without the base class `Employee`**

Note that common code can be modified and deleted from the base class `Employee` fairly easily.

### EXTENSIBILITY

Code that works with the base class in a hierarchy tree can work with all classes that are added using inheritance later.

Assume that an organization needs to send out invitations to all its employees and that it uses the following method to do so:

```
class HR {
    void sendInvitation(Employee emp) {
        System.out.println("Send invitation to" +
                            emp.name + " at " + emp.address);
    }
}
```

Because the method `sendInvitation` accepts an argument of type `Employee`, you can also pass to it a subclass of `Employee`. Essentially, this design means that you can use the previous method with a class defined later that has `Employee` as its base class. Inheritance makes code extensible.

### USE TRIED-AND-TESTED CODE FROM A BASE CLASS

You don't need to reinvent the wheel. With inheritance in place, subclasses can use tried-and-tested code from a base class.

### CONCENTRATE ON THE SPECIALIZED BEHAVIOR OF YOUR CLASSES

Inheriting a class enables you to concentrate on the variables and methods that define the special behavior of your class. Inheritance lets you make use of existing code from a base class without having to define it yourself.

### LOGICAL STRUCTURES AND GROUPING

When multiple classes inherit a base class, this creates a logical group. For an example, see figure 6.5. The classes Astronaut, Doctor, Programmer, and Manager are all grouped as types of the class Employee.

> **EXAM TIP**   Inheritance enables you to reuse code that has already been defined by a class. Inheritance can be implemented by extending a class.

The next section solves the mystery of how you can access the inherited members of a base class directly in a derived class.

## 6.1.3   *A derived class contains within it an object of its base class*

The classes Programmer and Manager inherit the nonprivate variables and methods defined in the class Employee and use them directly, as if they were defined in their own classes. Examine the following code:

```
class Employee {
    protected String name;
    protected String address;
    protected String phoneNumber;
    protected float experience;
}
class Manager extends Employee {
    protected int teamSize;
    public void reportProjectStatus() {}
}
class Programmer extends Employee {
    private String[] programmingLanguages;
    public void writeCode() {}
    public void accessBaseClassMembers() {
        name = "Programmer";
    }
}
```

Derived class Programmer can directly access members of its superclass

How can the class Programmer assign a value to a variable that's defined in the class Employee? You can think of this arrangement as follows: When a class inherits another class, it encloses within it an object of the inherited class. Hence, all the nonprivate members (variables and methods) of the inherited class are available to the class, as shown in figure 6.6.

But a derived class can't inherit all the members of its base class. The next two sections discuss which base class members are and aren't inherited by a derived class.

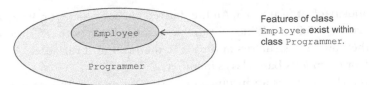

**Figure 6.6** An object of a derived class can access features of its base class object.

### 6.1.4 Which base class members are inherited by a derived class?

The access modifiers play an important role in determining the inheritance of base class members in derived classes. A derived class can inherit only what it can see. A derived class inherits all the nonprivate members of its base class. A derived class inherits base class members with the following accessibility levels:

- *Default*—Members with default access can be accessed in a derived class only if the base and derived classes reside in the same package.
- `protected`—Members with `protected` access are accessible to all the derived classes, regardless of the packages in which the base and derived classes are defined.
- `public`—Members with `public` access are visible to all other classes.

**EXAM TIP** A derived class can inherit only what it can see.

### 6.1.5 Which base class members aren't inherited by a derived class?

A derived class doesn't inherit the following members:

- `private` members of the base class.
- Base class members with default access, if the base class and derived classes exist in separate packages.
- Constructors of the base class. A derived class can call a base class's constructors, but it doesn't inherit them (section 6.5 discusses how a derived class can call a base class's constructors using the implicit reference `super`).

Apart from inheriting the properties and behavior of its base class, a derived class can also define additional properties and behaviors, as discussed in the next section.

### 6.1.6 Derived classes can define additional properties and behaviors

Although derived classes are similar to their base classes, they generally also have differences. Derived classes can define additional properties and behaviors. You may see explicit questions on the exam about how a derived class can differ from its base class.

Take a quick look back at figure 6.5. All the derived classes—Manager, Programmer, Doctor, and Astronaut—define additional variables, methods, or both. Derived classes can also define their own constructors and static methods and variables. A derived class can also *hide* or *override* its base class's members.

When a derived class defines an instance or class variable with the same name as one defined from its base class, only these new variables and methods are visible to code using the derived class. When a derived class defines different code for a method inherited from a base class by defining the method again, this method is treated as a special method—an *overridden* method.

You can implement inheritance by using either a concrete class or an abstract class as a base class, but there are some important differences that you should be aware of. These are discussed in the next section.

### 6.1.7  *Abstract base class versus concrete base class*

Figures 6.2 and 6.3 showed how you can pull out the common properties and behavior of a Programmer and Manager and represent these as a new class, Employee. You can define the class Employee as an abstract class, if you think that it's only a categorization and no real Employee exists in real life—that is, if all Employees are really either *Programmers* or *Managers*. That's the essence of an abstract class: it groups the common properties and behavior of its derived classes, but it prevents itself from being instantiated. Also, an abstract class can *force* all its derived classes to define their own implementations for a behavior by defining it as an abstract method (a method without a body).

**NOTE**  Section 6.6.1 includes an example of usage of abstract classes: how it forces its derived classes to implement the abstract methods.

It isn't mandatory for an abstract class to define an abstract method. But if an abstract base class defines one or more abstract methods, the class must be marked as abstract and the abstract methods must be implemented in all its concrete derived classes. If a derived class doesn't implement all the abstract methods defined by its base class, then it also needs to be an abstract class.

For the exam, you need to remember the following important points about implementing inheritance using an abstract base class:

- You can never create objects of an abstract class.
- A base class can be defined as an abstract class, even if it doesn't define any abstract methods.
- A derived class should implement all the abstract methods of its base class. If it doesn't, it must be defined as an abstract derived class.
- You can use variables of an abstract base class to refer to objects of its derived class (discussed in detail in section 6.3).

The first Twist in the Tale exercise for this chapter queries you on the relationship between base and derived classes (answer in the appendix).

**Twist in the Tale 6.1**

Modify the code used in the previous example as follows. Which of the options is correct for this modified code?

```
class Employee {
    private String name;
    String address;
    protected String phoneNumber;
    public float experience;
}
class Programmer extends Employee {
    Programmer (String val) {
        name = val;
    }
    String getName() {
        return name;
    }
}
class Office {
    public static void main(String args[]) {
        new Programmer ("Harry").getName();
    }
}
```

a   The class `Office` prints `Harry`.

b   The derived class `Programmer` can't define a getter method for a variable defined in its base class `Employee`.

c   The derived class `Programmer` can't access variables of its base class in its constructors.

d   `new Programmer ("Harry").getName();` isn't the right way to create an object of class `Programmer`.

e   Compilation error.

---

**TERMS AND DEFINITIONS TO REMEMBER**

Following is a list of terms and their corresponding definitions that you should remember; they're used throughout the chapter, and you'll come across them while answering questions on inheritance in the OCA Java SE 8 Programmer I exam.

- *Base class*—A class inherited by another class. The class `Employee` is a *base class* for the classes `Programmer` and `Manager` in the previous examples.
  - *Superclass*—A base class is also known as a *superclass*.
  - *Parent class*—A base class is also known as a *parent class*.

- *Derived class*—A class that inherits from another class. The classes `Programmer` and `Manager` are *derived classes* in the previous examples.
  - *Subclass*—A derived class is also known as a *subclass*.
  - *Extended class*—A derived class is also known as an *extended class*.
  - *Child class*—A derived class is also known as a *child class*.
- *IS-A relationship*—A relationship shared by base and derived classes. In the previous examples, a `Programmer` IS-A `Employee`. A `Manager` IS-A `Employee`. Because a derived class represents a specialized type of a base class, a derived class *IS-A* kind of base class.
- `extends`—The keyword used by a class to inherit another class and by an interface to inherit another interface.
- `implements`—The keyword used by a class to implement an interface (interfaces are covered in the next section).

> **NOTE**   The terms *base class*, *superclass*, and *parent class* are used interchangeably. Similarly, the terms *derived class* and *subclass* are also used interchangeably.

In this section, you learned that an `abstract` class may define `abstract` methods. Let's take it a step further to interfaces. In the next section, we'll discuss why you need interfaces and how to use them.

## 6.2   Use interfaces

[7.1]   Describe inheritance and its benefits

[7.5]   Use abstract classes and interfaces

We all use interfaces quite often in our lives. For example, when you refer to someone as a *runner*, do you care whether that person is also an orator, a parent, or an entrepreneur? You care only that the person is able to *run*. The term *runner* enables you to refer to unrelated individuals, by opening a small window to each person and accessing behavior that's applicable to *only* that person's capacity as a runner. Someone can be referred to as a runner only if that person supports characteristics relevant to running, though the specific behavior can depend on the person.

In the preceding example, you can compare the term *runner* to a Java interface, which defines the required behavior *run*. An interface can define a set of behaviors (methods) and constants. Usually it delegates the implementation of the behavior to the classes that implement it. Interfaces are used to refer to multiple related or unrelated objects that share the same set of behaviors. Figure 6.7 compares the interface *runner* with a small *window* to an object, which is concerned only about the running capabilities of that object.

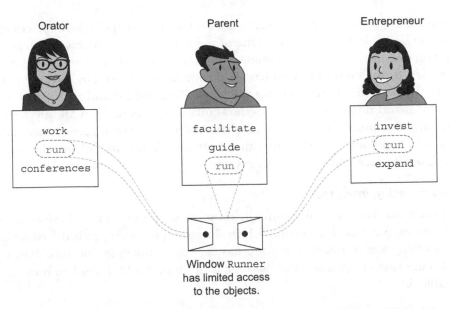

**Figure 6.7   You can compare an interface with a window that can connect multiple objects but has limited access to them.**

Similarly, when you design your application by using interfaces, you can use similar windows (also referred to as *specifications* or *contracts*) to specify the behavior that you need from an object, without caring about the specific types of objects.

> **NOTE**   You can compare a *contract* with a set of rules or deliverables that are mutually accepted by persons. A contract might include a set of rules to abide by or deliverables to be made accessible by a certain date. A contract usually doesn't include *how* the rules stated would be abided by or *how* the deliverables would be made accessible. It states *what* and not *how*. Similarly, an interface defines *what* behavior would be supported by the classes that implement it.

Separating the required behavior from its implementation has many benefits. As an application designer, you can use interfaces to *establish* the behavior that's required from objects, promoting flexibility in the design (new classes that implement an interface can be created and used later). Interfaces make an application manageable, extensible, and less prone to propagation of errors due to changes to existing types.

Now imagine you created an interface in an application some time ago. The application needs to be upgraded, which requires additional behavior to be added to some of its interfaces. This wouldn't have been possible with Java 7 or its earlier versions. But with Java 8, you can add methods to an interface without breaking the existing implementations. Prior to Java 8, an interface could only define abstract methods. With Java 8, an interface can define the default implementation for its methods (so it doesn't stop the existing classes that implement it from compiling). Interfaces in Java 8 can also define `static` methods. One of the main reasons for this language change (adding default and `static` methods to interfaces) was to improve the aging Collections API, especially with Stream-based functionalities (covered by the OCP exam).

In this section, you'll come to understand the need for and importance of using interfaces and different types of methods that can be defined in an interface. You'll work with the implicit and explicit properties of interface members—its constants and methods. You'll also see why inheriting multiples classes isn't allowed but inheriting multiple interfaces is allowed. Let's get started with the need for interfaces.

### 6.2.1   *Need for using interfaces*

You need interfaces to enable multiple classes to support a set of behaviors. Let's work with the example used in section 6.1. In this example, `Employee` is the base class and classes `Programmer` and `Manager` subclass `Employee`. Imagine that your boss steps in and states that `Programmer` and `Manager` *must* support additional behaviors, as listed in table 6.1.

**Table 6.1   Additional behaviors that need to be supported by the classes `Programmer` and `Manager`**

| Entity | New expected behavior |
|--------|----------------------|
| Programmer | Attend training |
| Manager | Attend training, conduct interviews |

How will you accomplish this task? One approach you can take is to define all the relevant methods in the class `Employee`. Because both `Programmer` and `Manager` extend the class `Employee`, they'd be able to access these methods. But wait: `Programmer` doesn't need the behavior of the conducting interview task; only `Manager` should support the functionality of conducting interviews.

Another obvious approach would be to define the relevant methods in the desired classes. You could define methods to conduct interviews in `Manager` and methods to attend training in both `Programmer` and `Manager`. Again, this isn't an ideal solution. What will happen if your boss later informs you that all the `Employees` who attend training should accept a *training schedule*; that is, there's a change in the signature of the method that defines the behavior "attend training"? Can you define separate classes for this behavior and make the classes `Programmer` and `Manager` implement them? No, you can't. Java doesn't allow a class to inherit multiple classes (covered in a later section in this chapter).

Let's try interfaces. Create two interfaces to define the specified behavior:

```
interface Trainable {
    public void attendTraining();
}
```

```
interface Interviewer {
    public void conductInterview();
}
```

Although Java doesn't allow a class to inherit from more than one class, it allows a class to implement multiple interfaces. A class uses the keyword `implements` to implement an interface. In the following code, the classes `Programmer` and `Manager` implement the relevant interfaces (the modified code is in bold):

```
class Employee {
    String name;
    String address;
    String phoneNumber;
    float experience;
}
class Manager extends Employee implements Interviewer, Trainable {
    int teamSize;
    void reportProjectStatus() {}
    public void conductInterview() {
        System.out.println("Mgr - conductInterview");
    }
    public void attendTraining() {
        System.out.println("Mgr - attendTraining");
    }
}
class Programmer extends Employee implements Trainable{
    String[] programmingLanguages;
    void writeCode() {}
    public void attendTraining() {
        System.out.println("Prog - attendTraining");
    }
}
```

**Manager implements Interviewer and Trainable**

**Programmer implements only Trainable**

Figure 6.8 displays the relationships between these classes in a UML diagram.

 **NOTE** An interface can be represented in UML diagrams using either a rectangle with the text <<interface>> or simply a circle. Both notations are popular; you may see them in various websites or books.

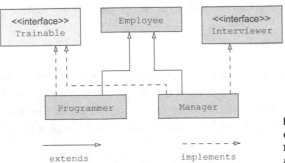

**Figure 6.8  Relationships among the classes** `Employee`, `Programmer`, **and** `Manager` **and the interfaces** `Trainable` **and** `Interviewer`

The preceding relationships can also be represented as depicted in figure 6.9, where the interfaces are defined as circles.

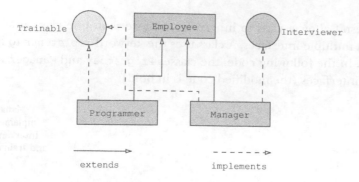

**Figure 6.9   Relationships among the classes** `Employee`, `Programmer`, **and** `Manager` **and the interfaces** `Trainable` **and** `Interviewer`, **with interfaces represented by circles**

## 6.2.2   *Defining interfaces*

You can define methods and constants in an interface. Declaring an interface is simple, but don't let this simplicity take you for a ride. For the exam, it's important to understand the implicit modifiers that are added to the members of an interface. All methods of an interface are implicitly `public`. The interface variables are implicitly `public`, `static`, and `final`. Let's define an interface `Runner` that defines an abstract method speed and a variable `distance`. Figure 6.10 shows how implicit modifiers are added to the members of interface `Runner` during the compilation process.

```
interface Runner{
    int speed();
    double distance = 70;
}
```
Becomes
```
interface Runner{
    (public)(abstract) int speed();
    (public)(static)(final) double distance = 70;
}
```

**Figure 6.10   All the methods of an interface are implicitly public. Its variables are implicitly public, static, and final.**

Why do you think these implicit modifiers are added to the interface members? Because an interface is used to define a contract, it doesn't make sense to limit access to its members—and so they are implicitly public. An interface can't be instantiated, and so the value of its variables should be defined and accessible in a static context, which makes them implicitly static.

The exam will also test you on the various components of an interface declaration, including access and nonaccess modifiers. Here's the complete list of the components of an interface declaration:

- Access modifiers
- Nonaccess modifiers
- Interface name
- All extended interfaces, if the interface is extending any interfaces
- Interface body (variables and methods), included within a pair of curly braces { }

To include all the possible components, let's modify the declaration of the interface `Runner`:

```
public strictfp interface Runner extends Athlete, Walker {}
```

The components of the interface `Runner` are shown in figure 6.11. To declare any interface, you *must* include the keyword `interface`, the name of interface, and its body, marked by { }.

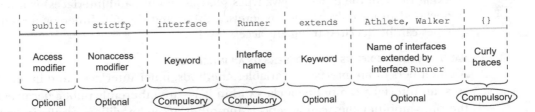

**Figure 6.11   Components of an interface declaration**

The optional and compulsory components of an interface can be summarized as listed in table 6.2.

**Table 6.2   Optional and compulsory components of an interface declaration**

| Compulsory | Optional |
|---|---|
| Keyword `interface` | Access modifier |
| Name of the interface | Nonaccess modifier |
| Interface body, marked by the opening and closing curly braces { } | Keyword `extends`, together with the name of the base interface(s) (Unlike a class, an interface can extend multiple interfaces.) |

 **EXAM TIP**   The declaration of an interface can't include a class name. An interface can never extend any class.

Can you define a top-level, *protected* interface? No, you can't. For the exam, you must know the answer to questions about the correct values for each component that can be used with an interface declaration. Let's dive into these nuances.

### VALID ACCESS MODIFIERS FOR AN INTERFACE

You can declare a *top-level interface* (the one that isn't declared within any other class or interface), with only the following access levels:

- public
- No modifier (default access)

If you try to declare your top-level interfaces by using the other access modifiers (protected or private), your interface will fail to compile. The following definitions of the interface MyInterface won't compile:

```
private interface MyInterface{}
```
← **Top-level interface can't be defined as private**

```
protected interface MyInterface {}
```
← **Top-level interface can't be defined as protected**

 **EXAM TIP**   All the top-level Java types (classes, enums, and interfaces) can be declared using only two access levels: public and default. Inner or nested types can be declared using any access level.

### VALID ACCESS MODIFIERS FOR MEMBERS OF AN INTERFACE

All members of an interface—variables, methods, inner interfaces, and inner classes (yes, an interface can define a class within it!)—are inherently public because that's the only modifier they can accept. Using other access modifiers results in compilation errors:

```
interface MyInterface {
    private int number = 10;
    protected void aMethod();
    interface interface2{}
    public interface interface4{}
}
```
❶ **Won't compile**

← **Won't compile**

**interface2 is implicitly prefixed with public**

**Interface member can be prefixed with public**

The code at ❶ fails compilation with the following error message:

```
illegal combination of modifiers: public and private
    private int number = 10;
```

### VALID NONACCESS MODIFIERS FOR AN INTERFACE

You can declare a top-level interface with only the following nonaccess modifiers:

- abstract
- strictfp

**NOTE** The `strictfp` keyword guarantees that results of all floating-point calculations are identical on all platforms.

If you try to declare your top-level interfaces by using the other nonaccess modifiers (`final`, `static`, `transient`, `synchronized`, or `volatile`), the interface will fail to compile. All the following interface declarations fail to compile because they use invalid nonaccess modifiers:

```
final interface MyInterface {}
static interface MyInterface {}
transient interface MyInterface {}
synchronized interface MyInterface {}
volatile interface MyInterface {}
```
Won't compile; invalid nonaccess modifiers used with interface declaration

### 6.2.3 Types of methods in an interface

Oracle has made fundamental changes to interfaces in Java 8. Apart from `abstract` methods, an interface can define methods with default implementations. It can also define `static` methods. Here's a quick list of the types of methods that can be defined in an interface (in Java 8):

- `abstract` methods
- Default methods (new in Java 8)
- `static` methods (new in Java 8)

Let's examine each of these in detail.

**NOTE** The default methods are also referred to as *defender* or *virtual extension methods*. But the most popular term to refer them is *default methods* because the `default` keyword is used to identify them.

**ABSTRACT METHODS**

Most jobs require a candidate to be interviewed, and the interviewer can be a CEO, a technical leader, or a programmer. Although each of these categories supports the behavior of an *interviewer*, it will `conductInterview` in its own specific manner.

An abstract method is used to *specify* a behavior (set of methods), which must be defined by the class that implements it. It's another way of stating "a class *supports* a behavior, but in its own manner" in the way it likes. In the following example, the interface `Interviewer` defines an `abstract` method `conductInterview`.

An abstract method is defined without a method body:

```
interface Interviewer {
    void conductInterview();
}
```
Doesn't include the keyword abstract

You might include the keyword `abstract` to define an `abstract` method in an interface. The following definition of the method `conductInterview` is the same as its definition in the preceding code:

```
interface Interviewer {
    abstract void conductInterview();          ⟵  Includes keyword
}                                                   abstract
```

**EXAM TIP** Interface methods are implicitly `abstract`. To define *default* or *static* methods, you must explicitly use the keyword `default` or `static` with the method declaration in an interface. Default and `static` methods include their implementation in an interface.

When a class implements an interface with `abstract` methods, the class must implement all the methods, or else the class won't compile. A developer can't add `abstract` methods to an interface without breaking existing implementations. It can only be done with default methods.

### DEFAULT METHODS

Imagine you need to add a behavior—*submit interview status*—to the interface `Interviewer`, *after* its publication. This wouldn't have been possible with Java 7 and its earlier versions without implying the need to provide an implementation for each existing concrete class (either directly or through a superclass). *Default methods* can rescue you here. Starting with Java 8, interfaces can be augmented by adding methods with default implementation. Implementing classes might choose to override these methods to define their own specific behavior. If they don't choose to override them, the default implementation from the interface is used. The definition of a default method *must* include the keyword `default`:

```
interface Interviewer {
    abstract void conductInterview();
    default void submitInterviewStatus() {        ⟵  Inclusion of
        System.out.println("Accept");                  keyword default
    }
}
```

I deliberately oversimplified `submitInterviewStatus()` in the preceding code so that the code focuses on the definition of default methods and not on its implementation details.

**NEW IN JAVA 8** Interface methods can define an implementation by using *default* methods.

Because the return type of the preceding method, `submitInterviewStatus`, is void, the following definition of method `submitInterviewStatus` is valid:

```
interface Interviewer {
    default void submitInterviewStatus() {}       ⟵  Empty method body
}                                                      != abstract method
```

Even though the method in the preceding example doesn't define any code in its body, it isn't equivalent to an abstract method. Declaration of a default method must be followed by the method body marked using { }. The following code won't compile:

```
interface Interviewer {
    default void submitInterviewStatus();          ⟵  Won't compile;
}                                                       missing {}
```

Just like regular methods, the return type of a default method must match the type of the value that it returns. The following won't compile:

```
interface Interviewer {
    default void submitInterviewStatus() {
        return 0;                                   ⟵  Won't compile; can't return
    }                                                   0 for return type void
}
```

## STATIC METHODS

Revisit the interface Interviewer used in the preceding section. Imagine that you need a utility (static) method that can be used to book a conference hall for an interview on a particular date and time. With Java 8, you can add static methods to an interface. Prior to Java 8, interfaces weren't allowed to define static methods. In such a case, you'd need to define the required static method in a separate class. This is one of the main reasons why static methods have been allowed in the interfaces—to improve the aging Collections API, which includes a few classes just to define static methods (like Collections and Paths).

> **NOTE** static interface methods enable you to define utility methods in the interfaces that they belong to.

Let's add a static method bookConferenceRoom to the interface Interviewer (in bold):

```
interface Interviewer {
    abstract void conductInterview();
    default void submitInterviewStatus() {
        System.out.println("Accept");
    }
    static void bookConferenceRoom(LocalDateTime dateTime, int duration) {
        System.out.println("Interview scheduled on:" + dateTime);
        System.out.println("Book conference room for: "+duration + " hrs");
    }
}
```

The method bookConferenceRoom() must be called by prefixing its call with the interface name. You can't call it using a reference variable of the type Interviewer or of the class that implements this interface. Let's define the class Manager that implements `Interviewer` and the class `Project` that tries to call the method `book-ConferenceRoom`:

```
class Manager implements Interviewer {}

class Project {
    public static void main(String[] args) {
        Interviewer inv = new Manager();
        inv.bookConferenceRoom(LocalDateTime.now(), 2);

        Manager mgr = new Manager();
        mgr.bookConferenceRoom(LocalDateTime.now(), 2);

        Interviewer.bookConferenceRoom(LocalDateTime.now(), 2);
    }
}
```

Won't
compile

Compiles
successfully

It's interesting to note that for `mgr.bookConferenceRoom()`, the compiler states that the method `bookConferenceRoom` is not defined for the type `Manager`.

 **EXAM TIP**   A `static` method in an interface can't be called using a reference variable. It *must* be called using the interface name.

In contrast to the preceding code, you can call a `static` method defined in a class either by using reference variables or by the name of the class:

```
class Employee {
    static void defaultPlan() {
        System.out.println("Basic");
    }
}
class Programmer extends Employee {}

class Project {
    public static void main(String[] args) {
        Employee emp = new Programmer();
        emp.defaultPlan();

        Programmer pgr = new Programmer();
        pgr.defaultPlan();

        Employee.defaultPlan();
        Programmer.defaultPlan();
    }
}
```

Static method in
class Employee

Programmer
subclasses Employee

Compiles; static method
accessed using variable emp

Compiles; static method
accessed using variable pgr

Compiles; static method accessed
using Employee and Programmer

In the preceding example, the `static` method `defaultPlan` is defined in the class `Employee`, which is subclassed by the class `Programmer`. The class `Project` defines reference variables of the type `Employee` and `Programmer` and initializes them using `Programmer` instances. To execute `defaultPlan()`, you can use the reference variables `emp` and `pgr` of types `Employee` and `Programmer`, respectively. You can also call `default-Plan()` by using the class name: `Employee` or `Programmer`.

```
class Manager implements Interviewer {
    static String bookConferenceRoom(LocalDateTime dateTime, int dur) {
        System.out.println("Manager-bookConferenceRoom");
        return null;
    }
}
```

**Compiles
successfully**

**EXAM TIP** static methods in a class and the interface that it implements are not related to each other. A static method in a class doesn't hide or override the static method in the interface that it implements.

Why do you think Java doesn't allow a class to inherit multiple classes but allows a class to implement multiple interfaces? I'll cover that in detail in the next sections.

## 6.2.5 *A class can't extend multiple classes*

In Java, a class can't extend multiple classes. Let's examine the reason using an example, in which the class Programmer *is* allowed to inherit two classes: Employee and Philanthropist. Figure 6.12 shows the relationship between these classes and the corresponding code.

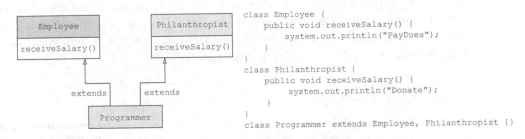

**Figure 6.12 What happens if a class is allowed to extend multiple classes?**

If the class Programmer inherited the method receiveSalary, defined in both Employee and Philanthropist, what do you think a Programmer would do with their salary: pay dues (like an Employee) or donate it (like a Philanthropist)? What do you think would be the output of the following code?

```
class Test {
    public static void main(String args[]) {
        Programmer p = new Programmer();
        p.receiveSalary();
    }
}
```

**Would this print
"PayDues" or "Donate"?**

In this case, the class Programmer can access two receiveSalary methods with identical method signatures but different implementations, so it's impossible to resolve this method call. This is why classes aren't allowed to inherit multiple classes in Java.

**EXAM TIP**   Because a derived class may inherit different implementations for the same method signature from multiple base *classes*, multiple inheritance isn't allowed in Java.

### 6.2.6   *A class can implement multiple interfaces*

In the preceding section, we discussed that a class can't inherit multiple classes. But a class can implement multiple interfaces. Why is this allowed, when Java doesn't allow a class to extend multiple classes? Prior to Java 8, an interface could define only `abstract` methods. So even if a class inherited methods with the same name from different interfaces, it came without an implementation.

But with Java 8, an interface can also define default methods—methods that include an implementation. So when a class implements multiple interfaces, it must adhere to a set of rules.

**EXAM TIP**   A class can extend multiple interfaces only if a set of rules is adhered to.

#### IMPLEMENTING MULTIPLE INTERFACES WITH THE SAME CONSTANT NAMES

A class can implement multiple interfaces with the same constant name, as long as a call to these interfaces isn't ambiguous. In the following example, the class `Animal` compiles successfully. It doesn't use the constant `MIN_DISTANCE` defined in the interfaces `Moveable` and `Jumpable` that it implements:

```
interface Jumpable {
    int MIN_DISTANCE = 10;
}
interface Moveable {
    String MIN_DISTANCE = "SMALL";
}
class Animal implements Jumpable, Moveable {}
```
Compiles successfully; no ambiguous implicit reference to **MIN_DISTANCE**

If you modify the implementation details of the class `Animal` so that it refers to the variable `MIN_DISTANCE` without prefixing it with the interface name, then it won't compile:

```
interface Jumpable {
    int MIN_DISTANCE = 10;
}
interface Moveable {
    String MIN_DISTANCE = "SMALL";
}
class Animal implements Jumpable, Moveable {
    Animal() {
        System.out.println(MIN_DISTANCE);
    }
}
```
Won't compile; implicit reference to **MIN_DISTANCE** is ambiguous

When prefixed with the interface name, the reference to MIN_DISTANCE is no longer ambiguous:

```
interface Jumpable {
    int MIN_DISTANCE = 10;
}
interface Moveable {
    String MIN_DISTANCE = "SMALL";
}
class Animal implements Jumpable, Moveable {
    Animal() {
        System.out.println(Jumpable.MIN_DISTANCE);
    }
}
```

← **Compiles successfully; the reference to MIN_DISTANCE is not ambiguous**

If an implicit reference to a constant defined in an interface(s) isn't ambiguous, the class that implements the interface can refer to it without prefixing it with the interface name:

```
interface Jumpable {
    int MIN_DISTANCE = 10;
}
interface Moveable {
    String MAX_DISTANCE = "SMALL";
}
class Animal implements Jumpable, Moveable {
    Animal() {
        System.out.println(MIN_DISTANCE);
    }
}
```

← **Compiles successfully; implicit reference to MIN_DISTANCE is not ambiguous**

**EXAM TIP**  A class can implement multiple interfaces with the same constant names, *only if* a reference to the constants isn't ambiguous.

### IMPLEMENTING MULTIPLE INTERFACES WITH THE SAME ABSTRACT METHOD NAMES

An abstract method doesn't define a body. It's acceptable for a class to extend multiple interfaces that define abstract methods with the same signature because when a class implements the abstract method, it seems to implement the abstract method from all the interfaces:

```
interface Jumpable {
    abstract String currentPosition();
}
interface Moveable {
    abstract String currentPosition();
}
class Animal implements Jumpable, Moveable {
    public String currentPosition() {
        return "Home";
    }
}
```

But you can't make a class extend multiple interfaces that define methods with the same name that don't seem to be a correct combination of overloaded methods. If you change the return type of the method currentPosition() from String to void in the interface Moveable, the class Animal won't compile. It would need to implement methods currentPosition, which differ only in their return type, which isn't acceptable:

```
interface Jumpable {
    abstract String currentPosition();
}
interface Moveable {
    abstract void currentPosition();
}
class Animal implements Jumpable, Moveable {          ⬅──┤ Won't
    public String currentPosition() {                        compile
        return "Home";
    }
}
```

 **EXAM TIP**   A class can implement multiple interfaces with the same abstract method names if they have the same signature or form an overloaded set of methods.

### IMPLEMENTING MULTIPLE INTERFACES WITH THE SAME DEFAULT METHOD NAMES

Imagine a class, Animal, that extends multiple interfaces, Moveable and Jumpable, which define default methods with the same name, relax(). If the class Animal doesn't override the default implementation of relax(), it won't compile:

```
interface Jumpable {
    default void relax() {
        System.out.println("No jumping");
    }
}
interface Moveable {
    default void relax() {
        System.out.println("No moving");          Won't compile; inherits
    }                                              unrelated defaults for
}                                                  relax() from Jumpable
class Animal implements Jumpable, Moveable { }  ⬅──┘ and Moveable
```

Let's modify the preceding code, so that the class Animal overrides the default implementation of relax(). In this case, it will compile successfully:

```
interface Jumpable {
    default void relax() {
        System.out.println("No jumping");
    }
}
interface Moveable {
    default void relax() {
        System.out.println("No moving");
    }
}
```

```
class Animal implements Jumpable, Moveable {
    public void relax() {                              ←┐  Compiles
        System.out.println("Watch movie");              │  successfully
    }
}
```

The default methods that a class inherits from the interfaces that it implements must
form a correct set of overloaded methods, or else the class won't compile:

```
interface Jumpable {
    default void relax() {
        System.out.println("No jumping");
    }
}
interface Moveable {
    default String relax() {
        System.out.println("No moving");         Won't compile;
        return null;                              relax in Jumpable
    }                                             and Moveable have
}                                                 unrelated return types
class Animal implements Jumpable, Moveable { }  ←┘
```

 **EXAM TIP** A class can implement multiple interfaces with the same default
method name and signature, if it overrides its default implementation.

**IMPLEMENTING MULTIPLE INTERFACES WITH THE SAME STATIC METHOD NAMES**
A class can implement multiple interfaces that define static methods with the same
name, even if they don't qualify as correctly overloaded or overridden methods. This
is because they're not inherited by the class that implements the interfaces:

```
interface Jumpable {
    static int maxDistance() {
        return 100;
    }
}
interface Moveable {
    static String maxDistance() {
        return "forest";
    }                                              Compiles
}                                                  successfully
class Animal implements Jumpable, Moveable { }  ←┘
```

 **EXAM TIP** A class can implement multiple interfaces with the same static
method names, irrelevant of their return types or signature.

### 6.2.7 *Extending interfaces*

An interface can extend multiple interfaces. When an interface extends another
interface, it must follow a set of rules.

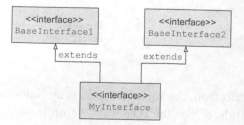

**Figure 6.13**   The interface `MyInterface` extends the interfaces `BaseInterface1` and `BaseInterface2`.

### EXTENDING MULTIPLE INTERFACES WITH THE SAME ABSTRACT METHOD NAMES

An `abstract` method doesn't define a body. Consider the following code, whose UML representation is shown in figure 6.13. Which of the `getName` methods will be inherited by the interface `MyInterface`? Will `MyInterface` inherit the `getName` method defined in `BaseInterface1` or the one defined in `BaseInterface2`?

```
interface BaseInterface1 {
    String getName();
}
interface BaseInterface2 {
    String getName();
}
interface MyInterface extends BaseInterface1, BaseInterface2 {}
```

Because neither of the `getName` methods defined in `BaseInterface1` and `BaseInterface2` define a method body (as shown in figure 6.14), the question of which of the methods `MyInterface` inherits is irrelevant. The interface `MyInterface` has access to a single `getName` method, which must be implemented by all the concrete classes that implement `MyInterface`.

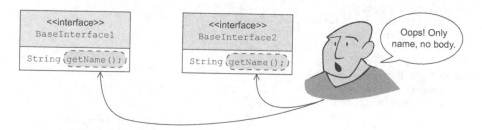

**Figure 6.14**   Methods defined in an interface don't have a method body.

Let's make the `Employee` class implement the interface `MyInterface`, as follows:

```
class Employee implements MyInterface {
    String name;
    public String getName() {          Employee defines a body for
        return name;                   the method getName, inherited
    }                                  from the interface MyInterface
}
```

## EXTENDING MULTIPLE INTERFACES WITH THE SAME NAME DEFAULT METHOD NAMES

When an interface extends multiple interfaces, Java ensures that it shouldn't inherit multiple method implementations for the same method. In the following example, interface `MyInterface` won't compile because it inherits unrelated defaults for `get-Name()` from types `BaseInterface1` and `BaseInterface2`:

```
interface BaseInterface1 {
    default void getName() {
        System.out.println("Base 1");
    }
}
interface BaseInterface2 {
    default void getName() {
        System.out.println("Base 2");
    }
}
interface MyInterface extends BaseInterface1, BaseInterface2 {}
```

← Won't compile

If you override the default implementation of the method `getName()` in `MyInterface`, it will compile successfully:

```
interface BaseInterface1 {
    default void getName() { System.out.println("Base 1"); }
}
interface BaseInterface2 {
    default void getName() { System.out.println("Base 2"); }
}
interface MyInterface extends BaseInterface1, BaseInterface2 {
    default void getName() { System.out.println("Just me"); }
}
```

← Compiles successfully

In the preceding code, the `getName` method in `MyInterface` can refer to a superinterface method by using the `super` keyword:

- `BaseInterface1.super.getName();`
- `BaseInterface2.super.getName();` (This would work as well if `MyInterface` were a class implementing both interfaces.) Other methods too can invoke a superinterface method this way.

Here are three resolution rules in case of multiple inheritance:

- Classes always win: a method implemented in a class always has priority over an interface default method.
- Otherwise, subinterfaces always win: a method implemented in a more specific interface has precedence over one defined in a more general interface (for example, a superinterface).
- Otherwise, if there's an ambiguity that can't be resolved by the previous rules, then you get to the case presented earlier: the targeted superinterface must be specified, using the `super` keyword.

**EXAM TIP**   When an interface extends multiple interfaces, Java ensures that it shouldn't inherit multiple method implementations for the same method.

**EXTENDING MULTIPLE INTERFACES WITH THE SAME STATIC METHOD NAMES**
An interface can extend multiple interfaces with the same static method name:

```
interface BaseInterface1 {
    static void status() { System.out.println("Base 1"); }
}
interface BaseInterface2 {
    static void status() { System.out.println("Base 2"); }
}
interface MyInterface extends BaseInterface1, BaseInterface2 {}      ◁───  Compiles
                                                                           successfully
```

The following code also compiles successfully, even though the return types of the methods status() in BaseInterface1 and BaseInterface2 are unrelated:

```
interface BaseInterface1 {
    static void status() {
        System.out.println("Base 1");
    }
}
interface BaseInterface2 {
    static String status() {
        System.out.println("Base 2");
        return null;
    }
}
interface MyInterface extends BaseInterface1, BaseInterface2 {      ◁───  Compiles
}                                                                         successfully
```

**EXAM TIP**   An interface can extend multiple interfaces, which define static methods with the same name; the signatures of these methods don't matter. This is because static methods are never inherited, so no conflicts can occur.

### 6.2.8   *Modifying existing methods of an interface*

What happens if you modify the declaration of the methods in an interface? Because you can define multiple types of methods in an interface—abstract, default, and static—these modifications would have different implications.

The modifications to existing methods of an interface can break the code of the classes that implement it or the interfaces that extend it. The modifications must follow the rules of implementing or extending interfaces, as covered in detail in the previous sections.

In this section, you'll see what happens when you modify an interface by changing the type of its method (abstract, default, or static). This change can affect the classes that implement the interface or the code that calls the modified methods.

### CHANGING STATIC METHOD TO DEFAULT OR ABSTRACT

In an interface, if you change a static method to a default method, the implementing class will continue to compile, but the code that calls the method won't compile. It you change a static method to an abstract method, the implementing class might not compile. The code, changes, and results are shown in figure 6.15.

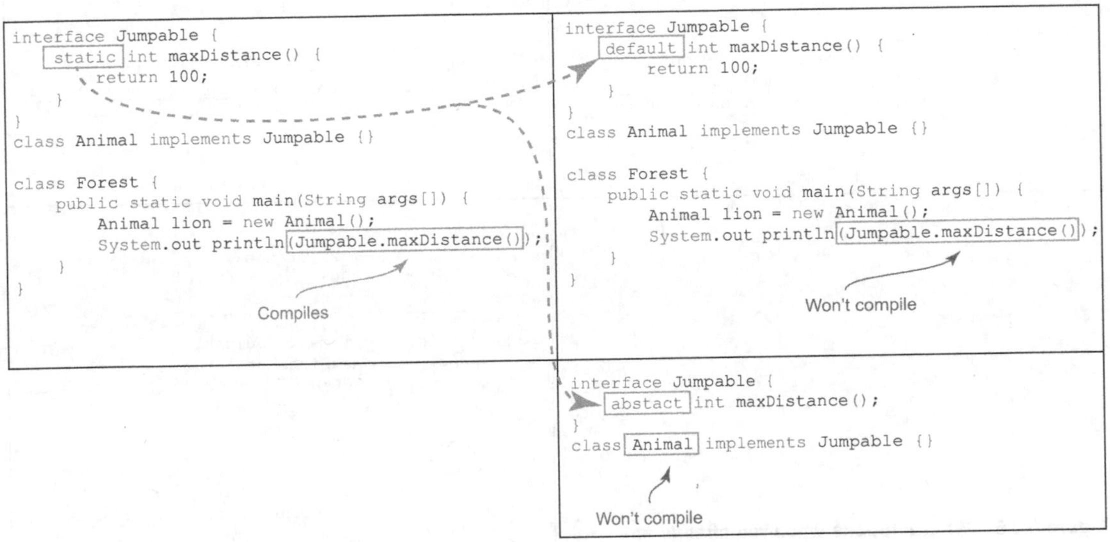

**Figure 6.15**   **What happens when you change a static method in an interface to a default or abstract method**

### CHANGING AN ABSTRACT METHOD TO DEFAULT OR STATIC

If you modify an interface by changing its abstract method to a default method, the code that calls the method will continue to compile. But if you change an abstract method into a static method, the code that calls the method won't compile. This is because static methods of an interface are called by prefixing the method name with the interface name. The code, modifications, and its results are shown in figure 6.16.

### CHANGING A DEFAULT METHOD TO ABSTRACT OR STATIC

If you modify an interface and change its default method to an abstract method, a class that implements it *might* fail to compile. The implementing class will fail to compile, if it doesn't override the default method of the interface. If you modify the default method to a static method in an interface, the code that calls the method won't compile. The code, changes, and results are shown in figure 6.17.

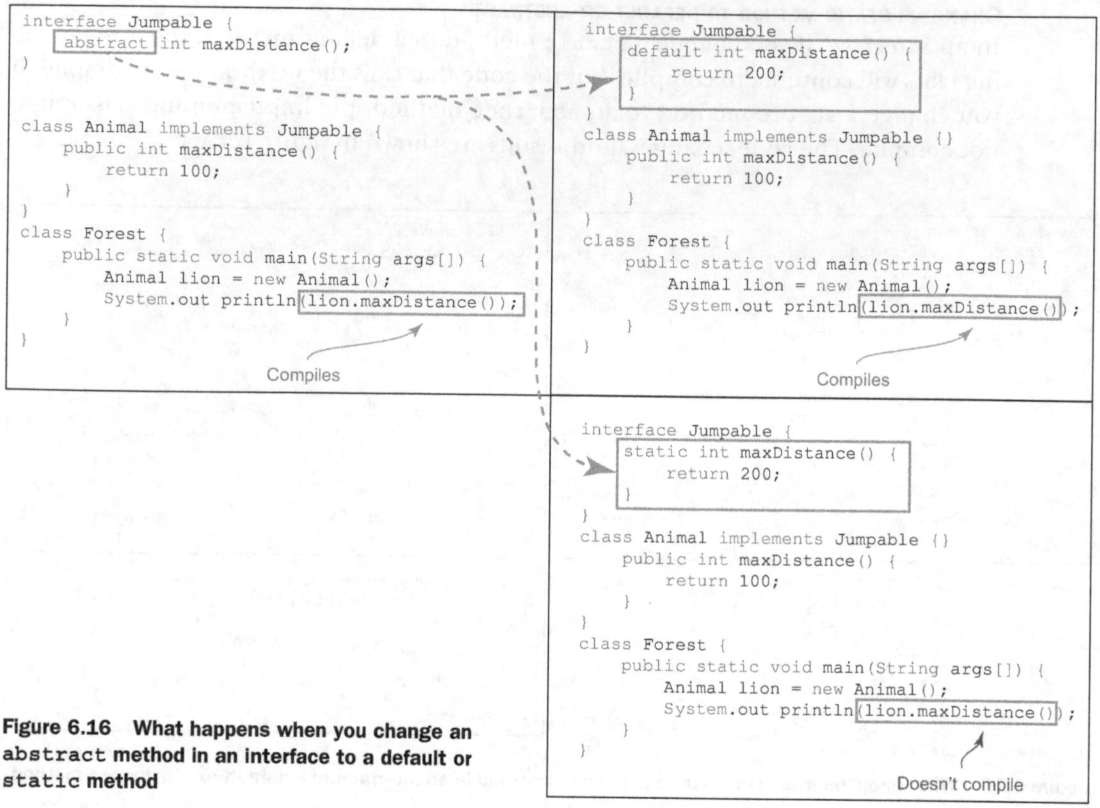

Figure 6.16  **What happens when you change an abstract method in an interface to a default or static method**

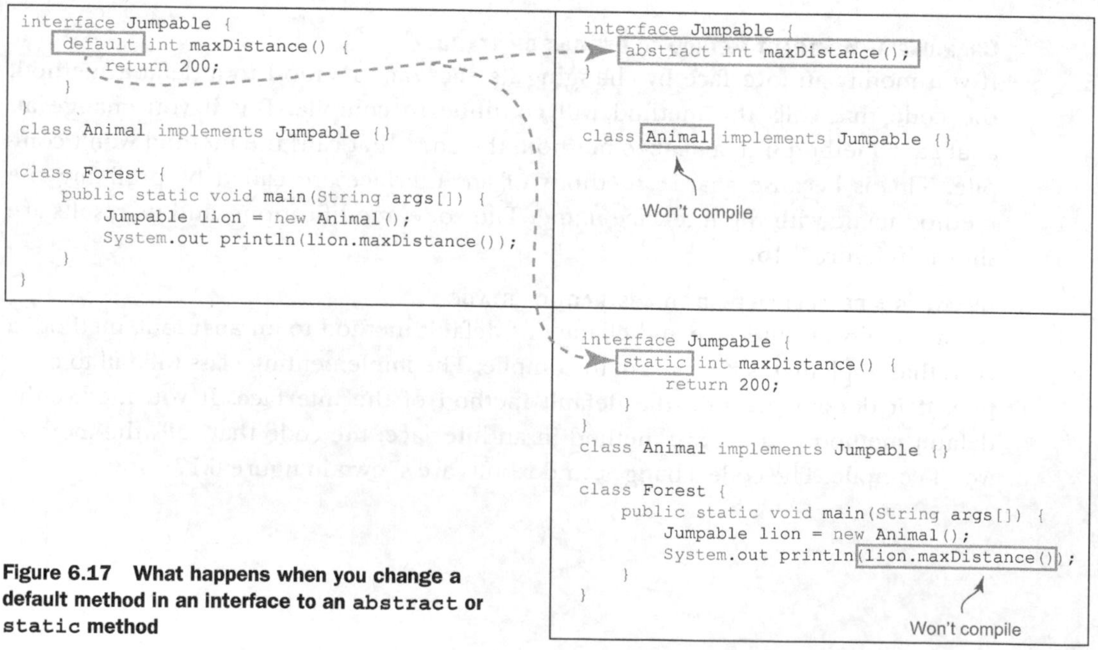

Figure 6.17  **What happens when you change a default method in an interface to an abstract or static method**

### 6.2.9 *Properties of members of an interface*

An interface can define constants and methods, which are implicitly assigned a set of properties.

**INTERFACE CONSTANTS**

As you've already seen, the variables of an interface are implicitly `public`, `final`, and `static`. So the following definition of the interface `MyInterface`

```
interface MyInterface {
    int age = 10;
}
```

is equivalent to the following definition:

```
interface MyInterface {
    public static final int AGE = 10;      ◁──  public, static, and final
}                                                modifiers are implicitly
                                                 added to variables
                                                 defined in an interface
```

You must initialize all variables in an interface, or your code won't compile:

```
interface MyInterface {
    int AGE;                      ◁──  Won't compile; should assign
}                                      a value to a final variable
```

**INTERFACE METHODS**

The methods of an interface are implicitly `public`. When you implement an interface, you must implement all its methods by using the access modifier `public`. A class that implements an interface can't make the interface's methods more restrictive. Although the following class and interface definitions look acceptable, they're not:

```
interface Relocatable {
    void move();                  ◁───  Implicitly public
}
class CEO implements Relocatable {      Won't compile; can't assign weaker
    void move() {}                ◁──  access (default access) to public
}                                       method move in class CEO
```

The following code is correct and compiles happily:

```
interface Relocatable {
    void move();                  ◁───  Implicitly public
}
class CEO implements Relocatable {
    public void move() {}         ◁───  Will compile
}
```

### INTERFACE CONSTRUCTORS

Unlike a class, an interface can't define constructors.

You can use a reference variable of a base class to refer to an object of its derived class. Similarly, you can use a reference variable of an interface to refer to an object of a class that implements it. It's interesting to note that these variables can't access all the variables and methods defined in the derived class or the class that implements the interface.

Let's dig into some more details about this in the next section.

## 6.3   *Reference variable and object types*

> [7.2]   Develop code that demonstrates the use of polymorphism; including overriding and object type versus reference type

For this exam objective, you need to understand that when you refer to an object, the type of the *object reference variable* and the type of the *object* being referred to may be different. But there are rules on *how different* these can be. This concept may take a while to sink in, so don't worry if you don't get it on your first attempt.

In the same way in which you can refer to a person using their first name, last name, or both names, objects of derived classes can be referred to using a reference variable of any of the following types:

- *Its own type*—An object of a class HRExecutive can be referred to using an object reference variable of type HRExecutive.
- *Its superclass*—If the class HRExecutive inherits the class Employee, an object of the class HRExecutive can be referred to using a variable of type Employee. If the class Employee inherits the class Person, an object of the class HRExecutive can also be referred to using a variable of type Person.
- *Implemented interfaces*—If the class HRExecutive implements the interface Interviewer, an object of the class HRExecutive can be referred to using a variable of type Interviewer.

There are differences, however, when you try to access an object using a reference variable of its own type, its base class, or an implemented interface. Let's start with accessing an object with a variable of its own type.

### 6.3.1   *Using a variable of the derived class to access its own object*

Let's start with the code of the class HRExecutive, which inherits the class Employee and implements the interface Interviewer, as follows:

```
class Employee {
    String name;
    String address;
    String phoneNumber;
    float experience;
}
```

```
interface Interviewer {
    public void conductInterview();
}
class HRExecutive extends Employee implements Interviewer {
    String[] specialization;
    public void conductInterview() {
        System.out.println("HRExecutive - conducting interview");
    }
}
```

**Class HRExecutive inherits class Employee and implements interface Interview**

Here's some code that demonstrates that an object of the class HRExecutive can be referred to using a variable of type HRExecutive:

```
class Office {
    public static void main(String args[]) {
        HRExecutive hr = new HRExecutive();
    }
}
```

**A variable of type HRExecutive can be used to refer to its object**

You can access fields and methods defined in the class Employee, the class HRExecutive, and the interface Interviewer using the variable hr (with the type HRExecutive), as follows:

```
class Office {
    public static void main(String args[]) {
        HRExecutive hr = new HRExecutive();
        hr.specialization = new String[] {"Staffing"};
        System.out.println(hr.specialization[0]);
        hr.name = "Pavni Gupta";
        System.out.println(hr.name);
        hr.conductInterview();
    }
}
```

**Access variable defined in class HRExecutive**

**Access variable defined in class Employee**

**Access method defined in interface Interviewer**

When you access an object of the class HRExecutive using its own type, you can access all the variables and methods that are defined in its base class and interface—the class Employee and the interface Interviewer. Can you do the same if the type of the reference variable is changed to the class Employee, as defined in the next section?

### 6.3.2 *Using a variable of a superclass to access an object of a derived class*

Let's access an object of type HRExecutive using a reference variable of type Employee, as follows:

```
class Office {
    public static void main(String args[]) {
        Employee emp = new HRExecutive();
    }
}
```

**Variable of type Employee can also be used to refer to an object of class HRExecutive because class HRExecutive extends Employee**

Now let's see whether changing the type of the reference variable makes any difference when accessing the members of the class `Employee`, the class `HRExecutive`, or the interface `Interviewer`. Will the following code compile successfully?

**Type of variable emp is Employee**

**❶ Variable emp can't access member specialization defined in class HRExecutive**

```
class Office {
    public static void main(String args[]) {
        Employee emp = new HRExecutive();
        emp.specialization = new String[] {"Staffing"};
        System.out.println(emp.specialization[0]);
        emp.name = "Pavni Gupta";
        System.out.println(emp.name);
        emp.conductInterview();
    }
}
```

**Variable emp can access member name defined in class Employee**

**Variable emp can't access method conductInterview defined in interface Interviewer**

The code at ❶ fails to compile because the type of the variable `emp` is defined as `Employee`. Picture it like this: the variable `emp` can see only the `Employee` object. Hence, it can access only the variables and methods defined in the class `Employee`, as illustrated in figure 6.18.

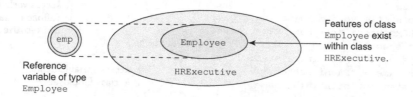

**Reference variable of type Employee**

**Features of class Employee exist within class HRExecutive.**

**Figure 6.18**  A variable of type `Employee` can see only the members defined in the class `Employee`.

### 6.3.3  *Using a variable of an implemented interface to access a derived class object*

Here's another interesting equation: what happens when you change the type of the reference variable to the interface `Interviewer`? A variable of type `Interviewer` can also be used to refer to an object of the class `HRExecutive` because the class `HRExecutive` implements `Interviewer`. See the following code:

```
class Office {
    public static void main(String args[]) {
        Interviewer interviewer = new HRExecutive();
    }
}
```

Now try to access the same set of variables and methods using the variable inter-viewer, which refers to an object of the class HRExecutive:

**Variable interviewer can't access members of class Employee or HRExecutive** ❶

```
class Office {
    public static void main(String args[]) {
        Interviewer interviewer = new HRExecutive();
        interviewer.specialization = new String[] {"Staffing"};
        System.out.println(interviewer.specialization[0]);
        interviewer.name = "Pavni Gupta";
        System.out.println(interviewer.name);
        interviewer.conductInterview();
    }
}
```

**Type of variable interviewer is Interviewer**

**Variable interviewer can access method conductInterview defined in interface Interviewer**

The code at ❶ doesn't compile because the type of the variable interviewer is defined as Interviewer. Picture it like this: the variable interviewer can only *access* the methods defined in the interface Interviewer, as illustrated in figure 6.19.

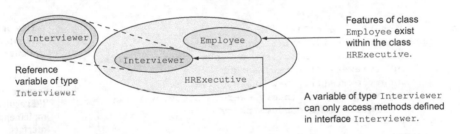

Reference variable of type Interviewer

Features of class Employee exist within the class HRExecutive.

A variable of type Interviewer can only access methods defined in interface Interviewer.

**Figure 6.19** A variable of type Interviewer can see only the members defined in the interface Interviewer.

### 6.3.4 *The need for accessing an object using the variables of its base class or implemented interfaces*

You may be wondering why you need a reference variable of a base class or an implemented interface to access an object of a derived class if a variable can't access all the members that are available to an object of a derived class. The simple answer is that you might not be interested in *all* the members of a derived class.

Confused? Compare it with the following situation. When you enroll in flying classes, do you care whether the instructor can cook Italian cuisine or knows how to swim? No! You don't care about characteristics and behavior that are unrelated to flying. Here's another example. At an office party, all the Employees are welcome, whether they are Programmers, HRExecutives, or Managers, as shown in figure 6.20.

The same logic applies when you access an object of the class HRExecutive using a reference variable of type Interviewer. When you do so, you're only concerned about the behavior of HRExecutive that relates to its capability as an Interviewer.

— Employees

**Figure 6.20   All types of Employees can attend an office party.**

This arrangement also makes it possible to create an array (or a list) of the objects that refers to different types of objects grouped by a common base class or an interface. The following code segment defines an array of type Interviewer and stores in it objects of the classes HRExecutive and Manager:

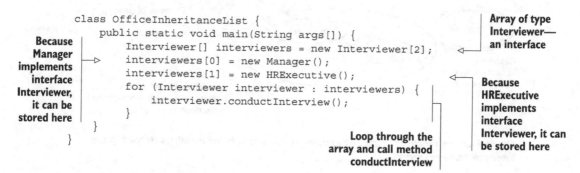

```
class OfficeInheritanceList {
    public static void main(String args[]) {
        Interviewer[] interviewers = new Interviewer[2];
        interviewers[0] = new Manager();
        interviewers[1] = new HRExecutive();
        for (Interviewer interviewer : interviewers) {
            interviewer.conductInterview();
        }
    }
}
```

**Array of type Interviewer— an interface**

**Because Manager implements interface Interviewer, it can be stored here**

**Because HRExecutive implements interface Interviewer, it can be stored here**

**Loop through the array and call method conductInterview**

The class HRExecutive extends the class Employee and implements the interface Interviewer. Hence, you can assign an object of HRExecutive to any of the following types of variables:

- HRExecutive
- Employee
- Interviewer
- Object

Please note that the reverse of these assignments will fail compilation. To start with, you can't refer to an object of a base class by using a reference variable of its derived class. Because *all* members of a derived class can't be accessed using an object of the base class, it isn't allowed. The following statement won't compile:

```
HRExecutive hr = new Employee();
```

**Not allowed— won't compile**

Because you can't create an object of an interface, the following line of code will also fail to compile:

```
HRExecutive hr = new Interviewer();
```
◁─┤ **Not allowed—won't compile**

It's now time for you to try to add objects of the previously defined related classes—Employee, Manager, and HRExecutive—to an array in your next Twist in the Tale exercise (answers in the appendix).

**Twist in the Tale 6.2**

Given the following definition of the classes Employee, Manager, and HRExecutive and the interface Interviewer, select the correct options for the class TwistInTale2:

```
class Employee {}
interface Interviewer {}
class Manager extends Employee implements Interviewer {}
class HRExecutive extends Employee implements Interviewer {}

class TwistInTale2 {
    public static void main (String args[]) {
        Interviewer[] interviewer = new Interviewer[] {
                new Manager(),          // Line 1
                new Employee(),         // Line 2
                new HRExecutive(),      // Line 3
                new Interviewer()       // Line 4
            };
    }
}
```

a An object of the class Manager can be added to an array of the interface Interviewer. Code on line 1 will compile successfully.

b An object of the class Employee can be added to an array of the interface Interviewer. Code on line 2 will compile successfully.

c An object of the class HRExecutive can be added to an array of the interface Interviewer. Code on line 3 will compile successfully.

d An object of the interface Interviewer can be added to an array of the interface Interviewer. Code on line 4 will compile successfully.

 **EXAM TIP** You may see multiple questions in the exam that try to assign an object of a base class to a reference variable of a derived class. Note that a derived class can be referred to using a reference variable of a superclass. The reverse is not allowed and won't compile.

In this section, you learned that the variables of a base class or interface are unable to access all the members of the object to which they refer. Don't worry; this can be resolved by *casting* a reference variable of a base class or an interface to the exact type of the object they refer to, as discussed in the next section.

## 6.4   *Casting*

[7.3]   Determine when casting is necessary

*Casting* is the process of forcefully making a variable behave as a variable of another type. If a class shares an IS-A or inheritance relationship with another class or interface, their variables can be cast to each other's type.

In section 6.3, you learned that you can't access all the members of the class HRExecutive (derived class) if you refer to it via a variable of type Interviewer (implemented interface) or Employee (base class). In this section, you'll learn how to cast a variable of type Interviewer to access variables defined in the class HRExecutive and why you'd want to.

### 6.4.1   *How to cast a variable to another type*

We'll start with the definitions of the interface Interviewer and the classes HRExecutive and Manager:

```
class Employee {}
interface Interviewer {
    public void conductInterview();
}
class HRExecutive extends Employee implements Interviewer {
    String[] specialization;
    public void conductInterview() {
        System.out.println("HRExecutive - conducting interview");
    }
}
class Manager implements Interviewer{
    int teamSize;
    public void conductInterview() {
        System.out.println("Manager - conducting interview");
    }
}
```

Create a variable of type Interviewer and assign to it an object of type HRExecutive (as depicted in figure 6.21):

```
Interviewer interviewer = new HRExecutive();
```

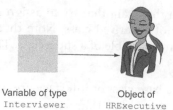

Variable of type
Interviewer

Object of
HRExecutive

**Figure 6.21   A reference variable of the interface Interviewer referring to an object of the class HRExecutive**

Try to access the variable `specialization` defined in the class `HRExecutive` using the previous variable:

```
interviewer.specialization = new String[] {"Staffing"};          ◄──── Won't compile
```

The previous line of code won't compile. The compiler knows that the type of the variable `interviewer` is `Interviewer` and that the interface `Interviewer` doesn't define any variable with the name `specialization` (as shown in figure 6.22).

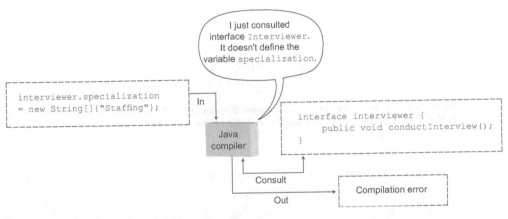

**Figure 6.22  The Java compiler doesn't compile code if you try to access the variable `specialization`, defined in the class `HRExecutive`, by using a variable of the interface `Interviewer`.**

On the other hand, the JRE knows that the object referred to by the variable `interviewer` is of type `HRExecutive`, so you can use casting to get past the Java compiler and access the members of the object being referred to, as follows (see also figure 6.23):

```
((HRExecutive)interviewer).specialization = new String[] {"Staffing"};
```

In the previous example code, `(HRExecutive)` is placed just before the name of the variable, `interviewer`, to cast it to `HRExecutive`. A pair of parentheses surrounds `HRExecutive`, which lets Java know you're sure that the object being referred to is an object of the class `HRExecutive`. Casting is another method of telling Java, "Look, I know that the actual object being referred to is `HRExecutive`, even though I'm using a reference variable of type `Interviewer`."

The parentheses that surround the whole `(HRExecutive)interviewer` token are required to bypass the Java operator precedence rules, according to which the casting

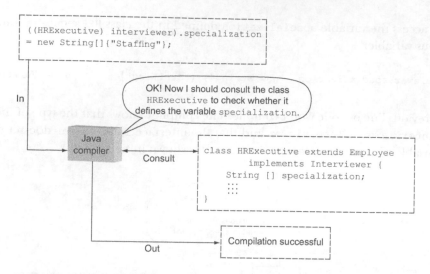

**Figure 6.23   Casting can be used to access the variable** `specialization`**, defined in the class** `HRExecutive`**, by using a variable of the interface** `Interviewer`**.**

"operator" (the parentheses) has lower priority than the dot "operator" (used to access an object field or invoke a method).

### 6.4.2   *Need for casting*

In section 6.3.4, I discussed the need to use a reference variable of an inherited class or an implemented interface to refer to an object of a derived class. I also used an example of enrolling in flying classes, where you don't care about whether the instructor can cook Italian cuisine or knows how to swim. You don't care about characteristics and behavior that are unrelated to flying.

But think about a situation in which you do care about the swimming skills of your instructor. Imagine that when you're attending flying classes, your friend inquires about whether your flying instructor also conducts swimming classes, and if so, whether your friend could enroll. In this case, a *need* arises to inquire about the swimming skills of your flying instructor.

Let's apply this situation to Java. You can't access all the members of an object if you access it using a reference variable of any of its implemented interfaces or of a base class. But when a need arises (as mentioned in the preceding paragraph), you *might* choose to access some of the members of a derived class, which aren't explicitly available, by using the reference variable of the base type or the implemented interface. This is where casting comes in!

It's time to see this in code. Here's an example that exhibits the need for casting. An application maintains a list of interviewers, and depending on the type of interviewer (`HRExecutive` or `Manager`), it performs a different set of actions. If the interviewer is a

Manager, the code calls conductInterview only if the value for the Manager's teamSize is greater than 10. Here's the code that implements this logic:

Store object of
HRExecutive at
array position 1

If object referred to
by interviewer is of
class Manager, use
casting to retrieve
value for its teamSize

If interviewer's
teamSize > 10, call
conductInterview

```
class OfficeWhyCasting {
    public static void main(String args[]) {
        Interviewer[] interviewers = new Interviewer[2];
        interviewers[0] = new Manager();
        interviewers[1] = new HRExecutive();
        for (Interviewer interviewer : interviewers) {
            if (interviewer instanceof Manager) {
                int teamSize =((Manager)interviewer).teamSize;
                if (teamSize > 10) {
                    interviewer.conductInterview();
                } else {
                    System.out.println("Mgr can't " +
                        "interview with team size less than 10");
                }
            } else if (interviewer instanceof HRExecutive) {
                interviewer.conductInterview();
            }
        }
    }
}
```

Array to store objects of
classes that implement
interface Interviewer

Store object of Manager
at array position 0

Loop through
values of array
interviewers

If interviewer's
teamSize <= 10,
print message

Otherwise, if object stored is of class
HRExecutive, call conductInterview
method on object; no casting is
required in this case

The preceding code shows a best practice when it comes to casting a variable, that is, interviewer instanceof Manager. If you omit this test, you run the risk of code throwing a ClassCastException (covered in section 7.5.2 in detail).

## 6.5    *Use this and super to access objects and constructors*

[7.4]   Use super and this to access objects and constructors

In this section, you'll use the this and super keywords to access objects and constructors. this and super are *implicit* object references. These variables are defined and initialized by the JVM for every object in its memory.

Let's examine the capabilities and use of each of these reference variables.

### 6.5.1    *Object reference: this*

The this reference always points to an object's *own instance*. Any object can use the this reference to refer to its own instance. Think of the words *me, myself,* and *I:* anyone using those words is always referring to oneself, as shown in figure 6.24.

> this = I, me, myself

**Figure 6.24   The keyword `this` can be compared to the words *me*, *myself*, and *I*.**

### USING THIS TO ACCESS VARIABLES AND METHODS

You can use the keyword `this` to refer to all methods and variables that are accessible to a class. For example, here's a modified definition of the class `Employee`:

```
class Employee {
    String name;
}
```

The variable `name` can be accessed in the class `Programmer` (which extends the class `Employee`) as follows:

```
class Programmer extends Employee {
    void accessEmployeeVariables() {
        name = "Programmer";
    }
}
```

Because there exist members of the class `Employee` within the class `Programmer`, the variable `name` is accessible to an object of `Programmer`. The variable `name` can also be accessed in the class `Programmer` as follows:

```
class Programmer extends Employee {
    void accessEmployeeVariables() {
        this.name = "Programmer";
    }
}
```

The `this` reference is required only when code executing within a method block needs to differentiate between an instance variable and its local variable or method parameters. But some developers use the keyword `this` all over their code, even when it's not required. Some use `this` as a means to differentiate instance variables from local variables or method parameters.

Figure 6.25 shows the constructor of the class `Employee`, which uses the reference variable `this` to differentiate between the local and instance variables `name`, which are declared with the same name.

In the previous example, the class `Employee` defines an instance variable `name`. The `Employee` class constructor also defines a method parameter `name`, which is effectively a local variable defined within the scope of the method block. Hence, within the scope of the previously defined `Employee` constructor, there's a clash of names, and

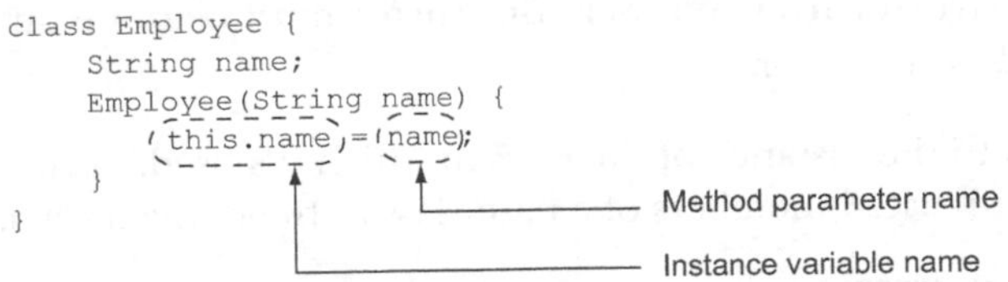

```
class Employee {
    String name;
    Employee(String name) {
        this.name = name;
    }
}
```

Method parameter name

Instance variable name

**Figure 6.25  Using the keyword this to differentiate between the method parameter and the instance variable**

the local variable will take precedence (covered in section 3.1). Using name within the scope of the Employee class constructor block will implicitly refer to that method's parameter, not the instance variable. In order to refer to the instance variable name from within the scope of the Employee class constructor, you are obliged to use a this reference.

#### USING THIS TO ACCESS CONSTRUCTORS

You can also reference one constructor from another by using the keyword this. Here's an example in which the class Employee defines two constructors, with the second constructor calling the first one:

```
class Employee {
    String name;
    String address;
    Employee(String name) {
        this.name = name;
    }
    Employee(String name, String address) {
        this(name);
        this.address = address;
    }
}
```

Constructor that accepts name and address

Instance variables are name and address

Constructor that accepts only name

Calls constructor that accepts only name

Assigns value of method parameter address to instance variable

To call the default constructor (one that doesn't accept any method parameters), call this(). Here's an example:

```
class Employee {
    String name;
    String address;
    Employee() {
        name = "NoName";
        address = "NoAddress";
    }
    Employee(String name, String address) {
        this();
        if (name != null) this.name = name;
        if (address != null) this.address = address;
    }
}
```

Calls constructor that doesn't accept any arguments. Must be the first statement in this method.

Instance variables are name and address

Constructor that doesn't accept any arguments

Constructor that accepts name and address

Assigns value of not-null method parameters

If present, a call to a constructor from another constructor must be done on the first line of code of the calling constructor.

> **EXAM TIP**    this refers to the instance of the class in which it's used. this can be used to access the inherited members of a base class in the derived class.

### USING THE KEYWORD THIS IN AN INTERFACE

With Java 8, you can use the keyword this in an interface's default method to access its constants and other default and abstract methods. In the following example, the interface Interviewer defines a default method submitInterviewStatus. This method uses this to access itself and its constants or methods:

```java
interface Interviewer {
    int MIN_SAL = 9999;
    default void submitInterviewStatus() {
        System.out.println(this);
        System.out.println(this.MIN_SAL);
        System.out.println(this.print());
    }
    String print();
}
class Manager implements Interviewer {
    public String print() {
        return("I am " + this);
    }
}
class Foo {
    public static void main(String rags[]) {
        Interviewer m = new Manager();
        m.submitInterviewStatus();
    }
}
```

You might see a similar output for the preceding code:

```
Manager@19e0bfd
9999
I am Manager@19e0bfd
```

> **EXAM TIP**    With Java 8, you can use the keyword this in a default method to access the methods of an interface and its constants.

You can't use the this keyword to access static methods of an interface.

### 6.5.2    *Object reference: super*

In the previous section, I discussed how this refers to the object instance itself. Similarly, super is also an object reference, but super refers to the direct parent or base class of a class. Think of the words *my parent, my base*: anyone using those terms is always referring to their direct parent or the base class, as shown in figure 6.26.

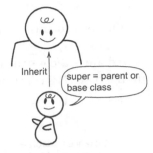

**Figure 6.26** When a class mentions super, it refers to its direct parent or the base class.

## USING SUPER TO ACCESS VARIABLES AND METHODS OF THE BASE CLASS

The variable reference super can be used to access a variable or method from the base class if there's a clash between these names. This situation normally occurs when a derived class defines variables and methods with the same name as the base class.

Here's an example:

```
class Employee {
    String name;                              ← Instance variable—
}                                               name, in Employee
class Programmer extends Employee {
    String name;                              ← Instance variable—
    void setNames() {                           name, in Programmer
        this.name = "Programmer";             ← Assign value to instance variable—
        super.name = "Employee";                name, defined in Employee
    }
    void printNames() {
        System.out.println(super.name);       ← Print value of instance variable—
        System.out.println(this.name);          name, defined in Employee
    }                                         ← Print value of instance
}                                               variable—name, defined
class UsingThisAndSuper {                        in Programmer
    public static void main(String[] args) {
        Programmer programmer = new Programmer();  ← Create an object of
        programmer.setNames();                        class Programmer
        programmer.printNames();
    }
}
```

Left margin annotation: **Assign value to instance variable— name, defined in Programmer**

The output of the preceding code is as follows:

```
Employee
Programmer
```

Similarly, you can use the reference variable super to access a method defined with the same name in the base or the parent class.

**USING SUPER TO ACCESS CONSTRUCTORS OF BASE CLASS**

The reference variable super can also be used to refer to the constructors of the base class in a derived class.

Here's an example in which the base class, Employee, defines a constructor that assigns default values to its variables. Its derived class calls the base class constructor in its own constructor.

```
class Employee {
    String name;
    String address;
    Employee(String name, String address) {
        this.name = name;
        this.address = address;
    }
}
class Programmer extends Employee {
    String progLanguage;
    Programmer(String name, String address, String progLang) {
        super(name, address);
        this.progLanguage = progLang;
    }
}
```

*Instance variables—name and address*

*Constructor that accepts name and address*

*Instance variable—progLanguage*

*Constructor that accepts values for superclass variables also*

**❶** *Calls Employee constructor*

The code at ❶ calls the superclass constructor by passing it the reference variables, name and address, which it accepts itself.

**EXAM TIP**   If present, a call to a superclass's constructor must be the first statement in a derived class's constructor. Otherwise, a call to super(); (the no-argument constructor) is inserted automatically by the compiler.

**USING SUPER AND THIS IN STATIC METHODS**

The keywords super and this are implicit object references. Because static methods belong to a class, not to objects of a class, you can't use this and super in static methods. Code that tries to do so won't compile:

```
class Employee {
    String name;
}
class Programmer extends Employee {
    String name;
    static void setNames() {
        this.name = "Programmer";
        super.name = "Employee";
    }
}
```

*Instance variable—name, in Employee*

*Instance variable—name, in Programmer*

*Won't compile—can't use super in static method*

*Won't compile—can't use this in static method*

It's time to attempt the next Twist in the Tale exercise, using the this and super keywords (answer in the appendix).

**Twist in the Tale 6.3**

Let's modify the definition of the Employee and Programmer classes as follows. What is the output of the class TwistInTale3?

```java
class Employee {
    String name = "Emp";
    String address = "EmpAddress";
}
class Programmer extends Employee{
    String name = "Prog";
    void printValues() {
        System.out.print(this.name + ":");
        System.out.print(this.address + ":");
        System.out.print(super.name + ":");
        System.out.print(super.address);
    }
}
class TwistInTale3 {
    public static void main(String args[]) {
        new Programmer().printValues();
    }
}
```

    **a**  Prog:null:Emp:EmpAddress

    **b**  Prog:EmpAddress:Emp:EmpAddress

    **c**  Prog::Emp:EmpAddress

    **d**  Compilation error

---

Similarly, you can't use the keyword this in a static method, defined in an interface:

```java
interface Interviewer {
    int MIN_SAL = 9999;
    static int getMinSalary() {          ◁─| Won't compile; can't use
        return this.MIN_SAL;               | keyword this in a static method
    }
}
```

Now let's move to one of the very important programming concepts: polymorphism. In the next section, you'll use abstract classes and interfaces to implement it.

## 6.6    *Polymorphism*

> [7.5]   Use abstract classes and interfaces

> [7.2]   Develop code that demonstrates the use of polymorphism; including overriding and object type versus reference type

The literal meaning of the word *polymorphism* is "many forms." At the beginning of this chapter, I used a practical example to explain the meaning of polymorphism; the same action may have different meanings for different living beings. The action *eat* has a different meaning for a *fly* and a *lion*. A *fly* may eat *nectar,* whereas a *lion* may eat an antelope. Reacting to the same action in one's own unique manner in living beings can be compared to polymorphism in Java.

For the exam, you need to know what polymorphism in Java is, why you need it, and how to implement it in code.

### 6.6.1    *Polymorphism with classes*

Polymorphism with classes comes into the picture when a class inherits another class and both the base and the derived classes define methods with the same method signature (the same method name and method parameters). As discussed in the previous section, an object can also be referred to using a reference variable of its base class. In this case, depending on the type of the object used to execute a method, the Java runtime executes the method defined in the base or derived class.

Let's consider polymorphism using the classes `Employee`, `Programmer`, and `Manager`, where the classes `Programmer` and `Manager` inherit the class `Employee`. Figure 6.27 shows a UML diagram depicting the relationships among these classes.

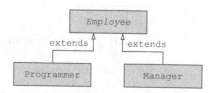

We'll start with the `Employee` class, which is not quite sure about what must be done to start work on a project (execute method `startProjectWork`). Hence, the method `startProjectWork` is defined as an abstract method, and the class `Employee` is defined as an abstract class, as follows:

**Figure 6.27   Relationships among the classes `Employee`, `Programmer`, and `Manager`**

```
abstract class Employee {
    public void reachOffice() {
        System.out.println("reached office - Gurgaon, India");
    }
    public abstract void startProjectWork();          ⊲—|  Doesn't know how to
}                                                        |  work on a project
```

The class `Programmer` extends the class `Employee`, which essentially means that it has access to the method `reachOffice` defined in `Employee`. `Programmer` must also implement the abstract method startProjectWork, inherited from Employee. How do you think a Programmer will typically start work on a programming project? Most probably, the Programmer will define classes and unit test them. This behavior is contained in the definition of the class Programmer, which implements the method start-ProjectWork, as follows:

```java
class Programmer extends Employee {
    public void startProjectWork() {
        defineClasses();
        unitTestCode();
    }
    private void defineClasses() { System.out.println("define classes"); }
    private void unitTestCode() { System.out.println("unit test code"); }
}
```

We're fortunate to have another special type of Employee, a Manager, who knows how to start work on a project. How do you think a Manager will typically start work on a programming project? Most probably, the Manager will meet with the customers, define a project schedule, and assign work to the team members. Here's the definition of the class Manager that extends the class Employee and implements the method startProjectWork:

```java
class Manager extends Employee {
    public void startProjectWork() {
        meetingWithCustomer();
        defineProjectSchedule();
        assignRespToTeam();
    }
    private void meetingWithCustomer() {
        System.out.println("meet Customer");
    }
    private void defineProjectSchedule() {
        System.out.println("Project Schedule");
    }
    private void assignRespToTeam() {
        System.out.println("team work starts");
    }
}
```

Let's see how this method behaves with different types of Employees. Here's the relevant code:

```java
class PolymorphismWithClasses {
    public static void main(String[] args)  {
        Employee emp1 = new Programmer();
        Employee emp2 = new Manager();
        emp1.reachOffice();
        emp2.reachOffice();
        emp1.startProjectWork();
        emp2.startProjectWork();
    }
}
```

**①** emp1 refers to Programmer

**②** emp2 refers to Manager

**③** No confusion here because reachOffice is defined only in class Employee

**④** Method from Programmer

**⑤** Method from Manager

Here's the output of the code (blank lines added for clarity):

```
reached office - Gurgaon, India
reached office - Gurgaon, India

define classes
unit test code

meet Customer
Project Schedule
team work starts
```

The code at ❶ creates an object of the class `Programmer` and assigns it to a variable of type `Employee`. ❷ creates an object of the class `Manager` and assigns it to a variable of type `Employee`. So far, so good!

Now comes the complicated part. ❸ executes the method `reachOffice`. Because this method is defined only in the class `Employee`, there isn't any confusion and the same method executes, printing the following:

```
reached office - Gurgaon, India
reached office - Gurgaon, India
```

The code at ❹ executes the code `emp1.startProjectWork()` and calls the method `startProjectWork` defined in the class `Programmer`, because `emp1` refers to an object of the class `Programmer`. Here's the output of this method call:

```
define classes
unit test code
```

The code at ❺ executes `emp2.startProjectWork()` and calls the method `start-ProjectWork` defined in the class `Manager`, because `emp2` refers to an object of the class `Manager`. Here's the output of this method call:

```
meet Customer
Project Schedule
team work starts
```

Figure 6.28 illustrates this code.

As discussed in the beginning of this section, the usefulness of polymorphism lies in the ability of an object to behave in its own specific manner when the same action is passed to it. In the previous example, reference variables (`emp1` and `emp2`) of type `Employee` are used to store objects of the classes `Programmer` and `Manager`. When the same action—that is, the method call `startProjectWork`—is invoked on these reference variables (`emp1` and `emp2`), each method call results in the method defined in the respective classes being executed.

**Figure 6.28** The objects are aware of their own type and execute the overridden method defined in their own class, even if a base class variable is used to refer to them.

## POLYMORPHIC METHODS ARE ALSO CALLED OVERRIDDEN METHODS

Take a quick look at the method startProjectWork, as defined in the following classes Employee, Programmer, and Manager (only the relevant code is shown):

```
abstract class Employee {
    public abstract void startProjectWork();        Method
}                                                    startProjectWork in
class Programmer extends Employee {                  class Employee
    public void startProjectWork() {
                                                     Method
        ...                                          startProjectWork in
    }                                                class Programmer
}
class Manager extends Employee {
    public void startProjectWork() {                Method
                                                     startProjectWork
        ...                                          in class Manager
    }
}
```

Note that the name of the method startProjectWork is same in all these classes. Also, it accepts the same number of method arguments and defines the same return type in all three classes: Employee, Programmer, and Manager. This is a contract specified to define overridden methods. Failing to use the same method name, same argument list, or same return type won't mark a method as an overridden method.

### RULES TO REMEMBER TO OVERRIDE METHODS

Here's the set of rules to note to define overriding methods:

- Overridden methods are defined by classes and interfaces that share inheritance relationships.
- The name of the overridden method in the base class and the overriding method in the subclass must be the same.
- The argument list passed to the overridden method in the base class must be the same as the argument list passed to the overriding method in the subclass.
- The return type of an overriding method in the subclass can be the same as or a subclass of the return type of the overridden method in the base class. When the overriding method returns a subclass of the return type of the overridden method, it's known as a *covariant return type*.
- An overridden method defined in the base class can be an `abstract` method or a non-`abstract` method.
- A derived class can override only non-`final` methods.
- Access modifiers for an overriding method can be the same as or less restrictive than the method being overridden, but they can't be more restrictive.

### DO POLYMORPHIC METHODS ALWAYS HAVE TO BE ABSTRACT?

No, polymorphic methods don't always have to be `abstract`. You can define the class `Employee` as a concrete class and the method `startProjectWork` as a non-abstract method and still get the same results (changes in bold):

```
class Employee {
    public void reachOffice() {
        System.out.println("reached office - Gurgaon, India");
    }
    public void startProjectWork() {
        System.out.println("procure hardware");
        System.out.println("install software");
    }
}
```

Because there's no change in the definition of the rest of the classes—`Programmer`, `Manager`, and `PolymorphismWithClasses`—I haven't listed them here. If you create an object of the class `Employee` (not of any of its derived classes), you can execute the method `startProjectWork` as follows:

```
Employee emp = new Employee();       ◄─┐  Object of class Employee,
emp.startProjectWork();                 │  not its derived classes
                                     ◄─┐  Call method startProjectWork,
                                        │  defined in Employee
```

**EXAM TIP**   To implement polymorphism with classes, you can define `abstract` or non-abstract methods in the base class and override them in the derived classes.

### CAN POLYMORPHISM WORK WITH OVERLOADED METHODS?

No, polymorphism works only with overridden methods. Overridden methods have the same number and type of method arguments, whereas overloaded methods define a method argument list with either a different number or type of method parameters.

Overloaded methods share only the same name; the JRE treats them like different methods. In the case of overridden methods, the JRE decides at runtime which method should be called based on the exact type of the object on which it's called.

It's time for the next Twist in the Tale exercise. As usual, you can find the answers in the appendix.

---

**Twist in the Tale 6.4**

Given the following definition of classes `Employee` and `Programmer`, which of the options when inserted at `//INSERT CODE HERE//` will define the method `run` as a polymorphic method?

```
class Employee {
    //INSERT CODE HERE// {
        System.out.println("Emp-run");
        return null;
    }
}
class Programmer extends Employee{
    String run() {
        System.out.println("Programmer-run");
        return null;
    }
}
class TwistInTale4 {
    public static void main(String args[]) {
        new Programmer().run();
    }
}
```

   a  `String run()`

   b  `void run(int meters)`

   c  `void run()`

   d  `int run(String race)`

---

### 6.6.2 *Binding of variables and methods at compile time and runtime*

You can use reference variables of a base class to refer to an object of a derived class. But there's a major difference in how Java accesses the variables and methods for these objects. With inheritance, the instance variables bind at compile time and the methods bind at runtime.

**NOTE**    *Binding* refers to resolving of variables or methods that would be called for a reference variable.

Examine the following code:

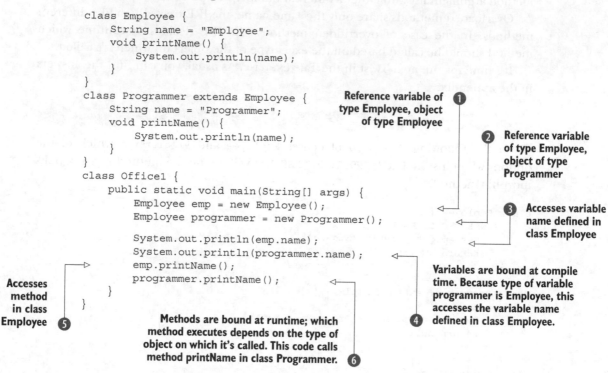

```
class Employee {
    String name = "Employee";
    void printName() {
        System.out.println(name);
    }
}
class Programmer extends Employee {
    String name = "Programmer";
    void printName() {
        System.out.println(name);
    }
}
class Office1 {
    public static void main(String[] args) {
        Employee emp = new Employee();
        Employee programmer = new Programmer();

        System.out.println(emp.name);
        System.out.println(programmer.name);
        emp.printName();
        programmer.printName();
    }
}
```

Callout ❶ **Reference variable of type Employee, object of type Employee**

Callout ❷ **Reference variable of type Employee, object of type Programmer**

Callout ❸ **Accesses variable name defined in class Employee**

Callout ❹ **Variables are bound at compile time. Because type of variable programmer is Employee, this accesses the variable name defined in class Employee.**

Callout ❺ **Accesses method in class Employee**

Callout ❻ **Methods are bound at runtime; which method executes depends on the type of object on which it's called. This code calls method printName in class Programmer.**

The output of the preceding code is as follows:

```
Employee
Employee
Employee
Programmer
```

Let's see what's happening in the code, step by step:

- ❶ creates an object of the class Employee, referenced by a variable of its own type—Employee.
- ❷ creates an object of the class Programmer, referenced by a variable of its base type—Employee.
- ❸ accesses the variable name defined in the class Employee and prints Employee.
- ❹ also prints Employee. The type of the variable programmer is Employee. Because the variables are bound at compile time, the type of the object that's referenced by the variable emp doesn't make a difference. programmer.name will access the variable name defined in the class Employee.

- ⑤ prints `Employee`. Because the type of the reference variable `emp` and the type of object referenced by it are the same (`Employee`), there's no confusion with the method call.
- ⑥ prints `Programmer`. Even though the method `printName` is called using a reference of type `Employee`, the JRE is aware that the method is invoked on a `Programmer` object and hence executes the overridden `printName` method in the class `Programmer`.

**EXAM TIP**    Watch out for code in the exam that uses variables of the base class to refer to objects of the derived class and then accesses variables and methods of the referenced object. Remember that variables bind at compile time, whereas methods bind at runtime.

### 6.6.3 *Polymorphism with interfaces*

Polymorphism can also be implemented using interfaces. Whereas polymorphism with classes has a class as the base class, polymorphism with interfaces requires a class to implement an interface. Polymorphism with interfaces involves `abstract` or default methods from the implemented interface. An interface can also define static methods, but static methods never participate in polymorphism.

#### POLYMORPHISM WITH ABSTRACT METHODS

Let's start with an example. Here's an interface, `MobileAppExpert`, that defines an abstract method, `deliverMobileApp`:

```
interface MobileAppExpert {
    void deliverMobileApp();
}
```

Here's a simplified version of the classes `Programmer` and `Manager` that implement this interface and the method `deliverMobileApp`:

```
class Employee {}
class Programmer extends Employee implements MobileAppExpert {
    public void deliverMobileApp() {
        System.out.println("testing complete on real device");
    }
}
class Manager extends Employee implements MobileAppExpert {
    public void deliverMobileApp() {
        System.out.println("QA complete");
        System.out.println("code delivered with release notes");
    }
}
```

The relationships among the two classes and the interface are shown in figure 6.29.

In the real world, the delivery of a mobile application would have different meanings for a programmer and a manager. For a *programmer*, the delivery of a mobile

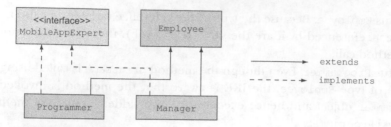

**Figure 6.29   Relationships among classes** `Employee`, `Programmer`, **and** `Manager` **and the interface** `MobileAppExpert`

application may require the completion of testing on the real mobile device. But for a *manager*, the delivery of a mobile application may mean completing the QA process and handing over code to the client along with any release notes. The bottom line is that the same message, `deliverMobileApp`, results in the execution of different sets of steps for a programmer and a manager.

Here's a class, `PolymorphismWithInterfaces`, that creates objects of the classes `Programmer` and `Manager` and calls the method `deliverMobileApp`:

```
class PolymorphismWithInterfaces {
    public static void main(String[] args)  {
        MobileAppExpert expert1 = new Programmer();
        MobileAppExpert expert2 = new Manager();
        expert1.deliverMobileApp();
        expert2.deliverMobileApp();
    }
}
```

❶ **Reference type of variables expert1 and expert2 is MobileAppExpert**

The output of the preceding code is as follows:

```
testing complete on real device
QA complete
code delivered with release notes
```

At ❶, the type of the variable is `MobileAppExpert`. Because the classes `Manager` and `Programmer` implement the interface `MobileAppExpert`, a reference variable of type `MobileAppExpert` can also be used to store objects of the classes `Programmer` and `Manager`.

Because both these classes also extend the class `Employee`, you can use a variable of type `Employee` to store objects of the classes `Programmer` and `Manager`. But in this case you won't be able to call the method `deliverMobileApp` because it isn't visible to the class `Employee`. Examine the following code:

```
class PolymorphismWithInterfaces {
    public static void main(String[] args)  {
        Employee expert1 = new Programmer();
```

**Employee can't see deliverMobileApp**

```
        Employee expert2 = new Manager();
        expert1.deliverMobileApp();
        expert2.deliverMobileApp();
    }
}
```
**Won't compile**

Let's see what happens if you modify the class `Employee` to implement the interface `MobileAppExpert`, as follows:

```
class Employee implements MobileAppExpert {
    // code
}
interface MobileAppExpert {
    // code
}
```

Now the classes `Programmer` and `Manager` can just extend the class `Employee`. They no longer need to implement the interface `MobileAppExpert` because their base class, `Employee`, implements it:

```
class Programmer extends Employee {
    // code
}
class Manager extends Employee {
    // code
}
```

With the modified code, the new relationships among the classes `Employee`, `Manager`, and `Programmer` and the interface `MobileAppExpert` are shown in figure 6.30.

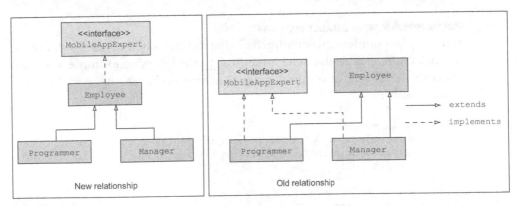

**Figure 6.30  Modified relationships among the classes `Employee`, `Manager`, and `Programmer`, and the interface `MobileAppExpert`**

Let's try to access the method `deliverMobileApp` using a reference variable of type Employee class, as follows:

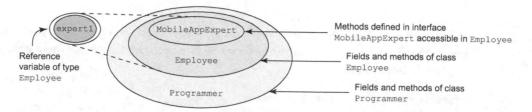

```
class PolymorphismWithInterfaces {
    public static void main(String[] args)  {
        Employee expert1 = new Programmer();
        Employee expert2 = new Manager();
        expert1.deliverMobileApp();
        expert2.deliverMobileApp();
    }
}
```

**Employee can see deliverMobileApp**

**Will work!**

Figure 6.31 shows what's accessible to the variable `expert1`.

Figure 6.31 shows what's accessible to the variable expert1 diagram:

expert1

MobileAppExpert

Employee

Programmer

Reference variable of type Employee

Methods defined in interface `MobileAppExpert` accessible in Employee

Fields and methods of class Employee

Fields and methods of class Programmer

**Figure 6.31   What's accessible to the variable `expert1`**

**EXAM TIP**   Watch out for overloaded methods that seem to participate in polymorphism—overloaded methods don't participate in polymorphism. Only overridden methods—methods with the same method signatures—participate in polymorphism.

### POLYMORPHISM WITH DEFAULT METHODS

When a class implements an interface that defines a default method, the class might or might not override the default method. In the following example, the class `Manager` overrides the default method `submitInterviewStatus`, defined in the interface `Interviewer`:

```
interface Interviewer {
    default Object submitInterviewStatus() {
        System.out.println("Interviewer:Accept");
        return null;
    }
}
class Manager implements Interviewer {
    public String submitInterviewStatus() {
        System.out.println("Manager:Accept");
        return null;
    }
}
```

```
class Project {
    public static void main(String args[]) {
        Interviewer interviewer = new Manager();
        interviewer.submitInterviewStatus();

        Manager mgr = new Manager();
        mgr.submitInterviewStatus();
    }
}
```

Here's the output of the preceding code:

```
Manager:Accept
Manager:Accept
```

In the preceding code, even though the class Project uses a reference variable of the interface Interviewer and the class Manager to refer to a Manager instance, the call to submitInterviewStatus() is delegated to the overriding method defined in the class Manager.

Here's an interesting situation. Imagine that two interfaces, BaseInterface1 and BaseInterface2, define default methods with the same name, getName(). These interfaces are extended by another interface, MyInterface, which overrides the method getName. Now, imagine that a class, MyClass, implements all three interfaces. What is the output when you call getName() on the MyClass instance? Will it compile?

```
interface BaseInterface1 {
    default void getName() { System.out.println("Base 1"); }
}
interface BaseInterface2 {
    default void getName() { System.out.println("Base 2"); }
}
interface MyInterface extends BaseInterface1, BaseInterface2 {
    default void getName() { System.out.println("Just me"); }
}
class MyClass implements BaseInterface1, BaseInterface2, MyInterface {
    public static void main(String ar[]) {
        new MyClass().getName();
    }
}
```

The preceding code compiles successfully and outputs Just me. Using the interface names BaseInterface1, BaseInterface2 in the declaration of class MyClass is redundant (duplicate) because MyInterface already extends BaseInterface1 and BaseInterface2. So MyClass doesn't inherit three implementations of the default method getName. It inherits just one of them, getName(), which is defined in the interface MyInterface.

## 6.7    *Simple lambda expressions*

> [9.5]   Write a simple Lambda expression that consumes a Lambda
>         Predicate expression

This exam includes working with simple lambda expressions to enable you to get started with *functional-style programming* in Java. Functional programming enables you to write declarative code. It lets you define *what* to do, rather than focusing on *how* to do it. With functional programming, you can pass code to your methods as arguments. Let's get the hang of it by comparing passing of variable or literal values to methods with passing code to them.

### 6.7.1   *Comparing passing values with passing code to methods*

Imagine that you need to write methods to print values of a range of numbers, like 1 to 10, 10 to 20, and so on, *without* passing parameters to methods. Here's how you might write your code:

```
class NoMethodParameters{
    void print1To10() {
        for (int i = 1; i <= 10; i++)
            System.out.println(i);
    }
    void print10To20() {
        for (int i = 10; i <= 20; i++)
            System.out.println(i);
    }
    void print1To99() {
        for (int i = 1; i <= 99; i++)
            System.out.println(i);
    }
}
```

Because you know how to define method parameters for a method, you're sure to think it's insane to define the methods as shown in the preceding code. So here's a method that accepts method arguments:

```
class WithMethodParameters {
    void printNumbers(int start, int end) {
        for (int i = start; i <= end; i++)
            System.out.println(i);
    }
}
```

Here's how you would call the methods to print integers, defined in the preceding code:

```
NoMethodParameters noParameters = new NoMethodParameters();
noParameters.print10To20();
noParameters.print1To99();

WithMethodParameters withParameters = new WithMethodParameters();
withParameters.printNumbers(10, 20);
```

```
withParameters.printNumbers(1, 99);
withParameters.printNumbers(100, 200);
withParameters.printNumbers(500, 1000);
```

Note how you can define just *one* method, `printNumbers`, and call it with multiple values. Let's apply the same logic to defining just one method, passing it code so that we don't need its multiple implementations.

Before using lambdas, let's work with an example that doesn't use them, to highlight their benefits. The following example defines the class `Emp` (with a few instance variables). It also defines an interface, `Validate`, which defines just one `abstract` method, `check`. It's meant to check the state of an `Emp` instance and return a `boolean` value:

```
interface Validate {
    boolean check(Emp emp);
}
class Emp {
    String name;
    int performanceRating;
    double salary;
    Emp(String nm, int rating, double sal) {
        name = nm;
        performanceRating = rating;
        salary = sal;
    }
    public String getName() { return name; }
    public int getPerformanceRating() { return performanceRating; }
    public double getSalary() { return salary; }
    public String toString() {
        return name + ":" + performanceRating + ":" + salary;
    }
}
```

To use the interface `Validate` (without using lambdas), you can either define a class that implements it or define anonymous classes. Because anonymous classes aren't on this exam, I'll define a class that implements the interface `Validate`. In the following code, the class `ValidatePerformanceRating` checks an `Emp` instance, returning `true` if the `performanceRating` of an `Emp` instance is greater than or equal to 5:

```
class ValidatePerformanceRating implements Validate{
    public boolean check(Emp emp) {
        return (emp.getPerformanceRating() >= 5);
    }
}
```

What happens if you want to check another attribute of an `Emp` instance, say, name? You'll need another class:

```
class ValidateName implements Validate{
    public boolean check(Emp emp) {
        return (emp.getName.startsWith("P"));
    }
}
```

Compare the preceding classes—ValidateName and ValidatePerformanceRating—with multiple print*XXX* methods in the class NoMethodParameters. Note how just the boolean condition is changing in the check methods in the classes ValidateName and ValidatePerformanceRating. Here's how you would use instances of ValidateName or ValidatePerformanceRating in a method, say, filter:

```
class Test {
    public static void main(String args[]) {
        Emp e1 = new Emp("Shreya", 5, 9999.00);
        Emp e2 = new Emp("Paul", 4, 1234.00);
        Emp e3 = new Emp("Harry", 5, 8769.00);
        Emp e4 = new Emp("Selvan", 1, 2769.00);

        ArrayList<Emp> empArrList = new ArrayList<>();
        empArrList.add(e1);
        empArrList.add(e2);
        empArrList.add(e3);
        empArrList.add(e4);

        filter(empArrList, new ValidatePerformanceRating());
    }
    static void filter(ArrayList<Emp> list, Validate rule) {
        for (Emp e : list) {
            if (rule.check(e)) {
                System.out.println(e);
            }
        }
    }
}
```

In the preceding code, the filter method accepts an ArrayList of Emp and outputs the ones that return true when an Emp instance is checked with the method check of the interface Validate.

As mentioned previously, you'll need to create multiple classes (that implement the interface Validate) to use different validity rules. Apart from being mostly repetitive, it's verbose too. Lambdas to the rescue! Let's remove the definition of the classes ValidateName and ValidatePerformanceRating. To define the validation condition, we'll use lambdas (the modified code is in bold):

```
class Test {
    public static void main(String args[]) {
        Emp e1 = new Emp("Shreya", 5, 9999.00);
        Emp e2 = new Emp("Paul", 4, 1234.00);
        Emp e3 = new Emp("Harry", 5, 8769.00);
        Emp e4 = new Emp("Selvan", 1, 2769.00);

        ArrayList<Emp> empArrList = new ArrayList<>();
        empArrList.add(e1);
        empArrList.add(e2);
        empArrList.add(e3);
        empArrList.add(e4);
```

```
        Validate validatePerfor = e -> e.getPerformanceRating() >= 5;
        filter(empArrList, validatePerfor);
    }
    static void filter(ArrayList<Emp> list, Validate rule) {
        for (Emp e : list) {
            if (rule.check(e)) {
                System.out.println(e);
            }
        }
    }
}
```

**Use lambda expressions**

In the preceding code, there isn't any change to the method `filter` that accepts a method parameter of type `Validate` (an interface). The code at ❶ defines a lambda expression. It defines code to be passed to the method `filter`. Map the lambda expression to the method signature of `check` in `Validate`. The method `check` accepts only one method parameter and so does the lambda expression, that is, `(e)`. The method `check` returns a `boolean` value and so does the expression `e.getPerformanceRating() >= 5` in the lambda expression.

 **NOTE** Lambdas work only with *functional interfaces*—interfaces that define exactly one `abstract` method.

Let's dive into the details of lambda expressions in the next section.

### 6.7.2 *Syntax of lambda expressions*

Let's revisit the lambda expression used in the previous expression:

```
Validate validatePerfor = e -> e.getPerformanceRating() >= 5;
```

The preceding code includes only the mandatory sections of a lambda, as shown in figure 6.32.

```
(e) -> e.getPerformanceRating() >= 5;
```

Parameter name    Arrow    Lambda body

**Figure 6.32  A Lambda expression and its mandatory sections**

Each lambda expression has multiple optional and mandatory sections:

- Parameter type (optional)
- Parameter name (mandatory)
- Arrow (mandatory)
- Curly braces (optional)
- Keyword `return` (optional)
- Lambda body (mandatory)

The following are valid variations of the preceding lambda expression (modifications in bold):

```
Validate validate = (e) -> e.getPerformanceRating() >= 5;
Validate validate = (Emp e) -> e.getPerformanceRating() >= 5;
Validate validate = (e) -> { return (e.getPerformanceRating() >= 5); };
```

On the exam, you'll need to identify invalid lambda expressions. The return value of the lambda expression must match or must be compatible with the return value of the only abstract method in the interface. The method check in the interface Validate declares its return type as boolean. So the following would be invalid:

```
Validate validatePerformance = (Emp e) -> 5;        ⟵──  Doesn't compile;
                                                         invalid return type
```

If you try to pass an incorrect count of method parameters to the lambda expression, the code won't compile:

```
Validate validatePerformance = (e, f) -> { return true; };    ⟵──  Doesn't compile;
                                                                   mismatch in
                                                                   parameter count
```

Java 8 has added multiple functional interfaces for your convenience. This exam covers just one of these—interface Predicate—discussed in the next section.

### 6.7.3    *Interface Predicate*

Predicate is a functional interface. Here's the partial definition of this interface:

```
public interface Predicate<T> {
    /**
     * Evaluates this predicate on the given argument.
     *
     * @param t the input argument
     * @return {@code true} if the input argument matches the predicate,
     * otherwise {@code false}
     */
    boolean test(T t);
    // rest of the code
}
```

In the preceding code, the class declaration includes <T>, which declares that Predicate is a generic interface, which isn't limited to a particular type. It can be used with multiple types. Generics are covered in detail in the OCP Java SE 8 Programmer II exam.

To use Predicate in your code, your method must accept a parameter of type Predicate and you must use its public method test to evaluate an argument. Let's modify the example used in section 6.7.1 to use `Predicate` instead of `Validate` (changes in bold):

```
class Test {
    public static void main(String args[]) {
        Emp e1 = new Emp("Shreya", 5, 9999.00);
        Emp e2 = new Emp("Paul", 4, 1234.00);
        Emp e3 = new Emp("Harry", 5, 8769.00);
        Emp e4 = new Emp("Selvan", 1, 2769.00);

        ArrayList<Emp> empArrList = new ArrayList<>();
        empArrList.add(e1);
        empArrList.add(e2);
        empArrList.add(e3);
        empArrList.add(e4);

        Predicate<Emp> predicate = e -> e.getPerformanceRating() >= 5;
        filter(empArrList, predicate);
    }
    static void filter(ArrayList<Emp> list, Predicate<Emp> rule) {
        for (Emp e : list) {
            if (rule.test(e)) {
                System.out.println(e);
            }
        }
    }
}
```

Java 8 has also modified many of its existing API methods, which work with functional interfaces like `Predicate`. For example, the class `ArrayList` defines the method `removeIf`, which accepts a method parameter of type `Predicate`. The following example shows the use of `removeIf`:

```
Emp e1 = new Emp("Shreya", 5, 9999.00);
Emp e2 = new Emp("Paul", 4, 1234.00);
Emp e3 = new Emp("Harry", 5, 8769.00);
Emp e4 = new Emp("Selvan", 1, 2769.00);

ArrayList<Emp> empArrList = new ArrayList<>();
empArrList.add(e1);
empArrList.add(e2);
empArrList.add(e3);
empArrList.add(e4);

for (Emp e : empArrList)
    System.out.println(e);

System.out.println("After deletion..");

empArrList.removeIf(e -> e.getName().startsWith("S"));

for (Emp e : empArrList)
    System.out.println(e);
```

Here's the output of the preceding code:

```
Shreya:5:9999.0
Paul:4:1234.0
Harry:5:8769.0
Selvan:1:2769.0
After deletion..
Paul:4:1234.0
Harry:5:8769.0
```

As you can see, the use of `Predicate` and lambda expressions in the preceding code enabled you to write code declaratively.

## 6.8   Summary

We started the chapter with a discussion of inheritance and polymorphism, using an example from everyday life: all creatures inherit the properties and behavior of their parents, and the same action (such as *reproduce*) may have different meanings for different species. Inheritance enables the reuse of existing code, and it can be implemented using classes and interfaces. A class can't extend more than one class, but it can implement more than one interface. Inheriting a class is also called *subclassing*, and the inherited class is referred to as the *base* or *parent class*. A class that inherits another class or implements an interface is called a *derived class* or *subclass*.

Just as it's common to address someone using a last name or family name, an object of a derived class can be referred to with a variable of a base class or an interface that it implements. But when you refer to an object using a variable of the base class, the variable can access only the members defined in the base class. Similarly, a variable of type interface can access only the members defined in that interface. Even with this limitation, you may wish to refer to objects using variables of their base class to work with multiple objects that have common base classes.

Objects of related classes—the ones that share an inheritance relationship—can be cast to another object. You may wish to cast an object when you wish to access its members that aren't available by default using the variable that's used to refer to the object.

The keywords `this` and `super` are object references and are used to access an object and its base class, respectively. You can use the keyword `this` to access a class's variables, methods, and constructors. Similarly, the keyword `super` is used to access a base class's variables, methods, and constructors.

Polymorphism is the ability of objects to execute methods defined in a superclass or base class, depending on their type. Classes that share an inheritance relationship exhibit polymorphism. The polymorphic method should be defined in both the base class and the inherited class.

You can implement polymorphism by using either classes or interfaces. In the case of polymorphism with classes, the base class can be either an abstract class or a concrete class. The method in question here also need not be an `abstract` method. When you implement polymorphism using interfaces, you must use an `abstract` method from the interface.

Java 8 enables you to write code declaratively. We covered lambda expressions, their syntax, and the interface `Predicate`.

## 6.9 Review notes

Inheritance with classes:

- A class can inherit the properties and behavior of another class.
- A class can implement multiple interfaces.
- An interface can inherit zero or more interfaces. An interface can't inherit a class.
- Inheritance enables you to use existing code.
- Inheriting a class is also known as subclassing.
- A class that inherits another class is called a derived class or subclass.
- A class that's inherited is called a parent or base class or superclass.
- Private members of a base class can't be inherited in the derived class.
- A derived class can only inherit members with the default access modifier if both the base class and the derived class are in the same package.
- A class uses the keyword `extends` to inherit a class.
- A class uses the keyword `implements` to implement an interface.
- A class can implement multiple interfaces but can inherit only one class.
- An `abstract` class can inherit a concrete class, and a concrete class can inherit an `abstract` class.

Use interfaces:

- An interface uses the keyword `extends` to inherit another interface.
- An interface can extend multiple interfaces.
- Although interfaces can define a default implementation for their methods in Java 8, it's not compulsory for them to do so. Interfaces can also define `abstract` methods.
- The declaration of an interface can't include a class name. An interface can never extend any class.
- All the top-level Java types (classes, enums, and interfaces) can be declared using only two access levels: public and default. Inner or nested types can be declared using any access level.
- The `strictfp` keyword guarantees that results of all floating-point calculations are identical on all platforms.
- Interface methods are implicitly abstract. To define default or `static` methods, you must use the keyword `default` or `static`.
- Interface methods can define an implementation by using default methods.

- A static method in an interface can't be called using a reference variable. It must be called using the interface name.
- Unlike an interface, if you define a static method in a base class, it can be accessed using either a reference variable or the class name.
- You must implement an abstract method of an interface using the explicit access modifier public.
- While overriding a default method, you must not use the keyword default. The rules for overriding default and regular methods are same.
- static methods in a class and the interface that it implements are not related to each other. A static method in a class doesn't hide or override the static method in the interface that it implements.
- Because a derived class may inherit different implementations for the same method signature from multiple base classes, multiple inheritance is not allowed in Java.
- A class can extend multiple interfaces, only if a set of rules is adhered to:
  - A class can implement multiple interfaces with the same constant names only if the reference to the constants is not ambiguous.
  - A class can implement multiple interfaces with the same abstract method names if they have the same signature or form an overloaded set of methods.
  - A class can implement multiple interfaces with the same default method name if it overrides its default implementation.
  - A class can implement multiple interfaces with the same static method name regardless of their return types or signature.
- When an interface extends multiple interfaces, Java ensures that it doesn't inherit multiple method implementations for the same method.
- An interface can extend multiple interfaces that define static methods with the same name; the signatures of these methods don't matter.
- The variables of an interface are implicitly public, final, and static.
- The methods of an interface are implicitly public.
- An interface can't define any constructors.

Reference variable and object types:

- With inheritance, you can also refer to an object of a derived class using a variable of a base class or interface.
- An object of a base class can't be referred to using a reference variable of its derived class.
- When an object is referred to by a reference variable of a base class, the reference variable can access only the variables and members that are defined in the base class.
- When an object is referred to by a reference variable of an interface implemented by a class, the reference variable can access only the variables and methods defined in the interface.

- You may need to access an object of a derived class using a reference variable of the base class to group and use all the classes with common parent classes or interfaces.

The need for casting:

- Casting is the process of forcefully making a variable behave as a variable of another type.
- If the class Manager extends the class Employee, and a reference variable emp of type Employee is used to refer to an object of the class Manager, ((Manager)emp) will cast the variable emp to Manager.

Using super and this to access objects and constructors:

- The keywords super and this are object references. These variables are defined and initialized by the JVM for every object in its memory.
- The this reference always points to an object's *own instance.*
- You can use the keyword this to refer to all methods and variables that are accessible to a class.
- If a method defines a local variable or method parameter with the same name as an instance variable, the keyword this must be used to access the instance variable in the method.
- You can call one constructor from another constructor by using the keyword this.
- With Java 8, you can use the keyword this in a default method to access the methods of an interface and its constants.
- The static methods of an interface can't be accessed using the keyword this.
- super, an object reference, refers to the parent class or the base class of a class.
- The reference variable super can be used to access a variable or method from the base class if there's a clash between these names. This situation normally occurs when a derived class defines variables and methods with the same names as in the base class.
- The reference variable super can also be used to refer to the constructors of the direct parent class in a derived class.

Polymorphism with classes:

- The literal meaning of the word *polymorphism* is "many forms."
- In Java, polymorphism comes into the picture when there's an inheritance relationship between classes, and both the base and derived classes define methods with the same name.
- The polymorphic methods are also called overridden methods.
- Overridden methods should define methods with the same name, same argument list, and same list of method parameters. The return type of the overriding method can be the same, or it can be a subclass of the return type of the

overridden method in the base class, which is also known as the covariant return type.

- Access modifiers for an overriding method can be equally or less restrictive but can't be more restrictive than the method being overridden.

- A derived class is said to override a method in the base class if it defines a method with the same name, same parameter list, and same return type as in the derived class.

- If a method defined in a base class is overloaded in the derived classes, then these two methods (in the base class and the derived class) are not called polymorphic methods.

- When implementing polymorphism with classes, a method defined in the base class may or may not be abstract.

- When implementing polymorphism with interfaces, a method defined in the base interface could be an abstract method or a non-abstract method with a default implementation.

- Static methods in interfaces don't participate in polymorphism.

Simple lambda expressions:

- Lambdas work only with functional interfaces—interfaces that define exactly one abstract method.

- Each lambda expression has multiple optional and mandatory sections:
  - Parameter type (optional)
  - Parameter name (mandatory)
  - Arrow (mandatory)
  - Curly braces (optional)
  - Keyword return (optional)
  - Lambda body (mandatory)

## 6.10  *Sample exam questions*

**Q6-1.** What is the output of the following code?

```
class Animal {
    void jump() { System.out.println("Animal"); }
}
class Cat extends Animal {
    void jump(int a) { System.out.println("Cat"); }
}
class Rabbit extends Animal {
    void jump() { System.out.println("Rabbit"); }
}
class Circus {
    public static void main(String args[]) {
        Animal cat = new Cat();
        Rabbit rabbit = new Rabbit();
        cat.jump();
```

```
        rabbit.jump();
    }
}
```

   **a**  Animal
      Rabbit

   **b**  Cat
      Rabbit

   **c**  Animal
      Animal

   **d**  None of the above

**Q6-2.** Given the following code, select the correct statements:

```
class Flower {
    public void fragrance() {System.out.println("Flower"); }
}
class Rose {
    public void fragrance() {System.out.println("Rose"); }
}
class Lily {
    public void fragrance() {System.out.println("Lily"); }
}
class Bouquet {
    public void arrangeFlowers() {
        Flower f1 = new Rose();
        Flower f2 = new Lily();
        f1.fragrance();
    }
}
```

   **a**  The output of the code is

      `Flower`

   **b**  The output of the code is

      `Rose`

   **c**  The output of the code is

      `Lily`

   **d**  The code fails to compile.

**Q6-3.** Examine the following code and select the correct method declaration to be inserted at //INSERT CODE HERE:

```
interface Movable {
    void move();
}
```

```
class Person implements Movable {
    public void move() { System.out.println("Person move"); }
}
class Vehicle implements Movable {
    public void move() { System.out.println("Vehicle move"); }
}
class Test {
    // INSERT CODE HERE
        movable.move();
    }
}
```

    **a**  `void walk(Movable movable) {`

    **b**  `void walk(Person movable) {`

    **c**  `void walk(Vehicle movable) {`

    **d**  `void walk() {`

**Q6-4.** Select the correct statements:

    **a**  Only an abstract class can be used as a base class to implement polymorphism with classes.

    **b**  Polymorphic methods are also called overridden methods.

    **c**  In polymorphism, depending on the exact type of object, the JVM executes the appropriate method at compile time.

    **d**  None of the above.

**Q6-5.** Given the following code, select the correct statements:

```
class Person {}
class Employee extends Person {}
class Doctor extends Person {}
```

    **a**  The code exhibits polymorphism with classes.

    **b**  The code exhibits polymorphism with interfaces.

    **c**  The code exhibits polymorphism with classes and interfaces.

    **d**  None of the above.

**Q6-6.** Which of the following statements are true?

    **a**  Inheritance enables you to reuse existing code.

    **b**  Inheritance saves you from having to modify common code in multiple classes.

    **c**  Polymorphism passes special instructions to the compiler so that the code can run on multiple platforms.

    **d**  Polymorphic methods can't throw exceptions.

**Q6-7.** Given the following code, which of the options are true?

```
class Satellite {
    void orbit() {}
}
class Moon extends Satellite {
    void orbit() {}
}
class ArtificialSatellite extends Satellite {
    void orbit() {}
}
```

a  The method orbit defined in the classes Satellite, Moon, and Artificial-Satellite is polymorphic.

b  Only the method orbit defined in the classes Satellite and Artificial-Satellite is polymorphic.

c  Only the method orbit defined in the class ArtificialSatellite is polymorphic.

d  None of the above.

**Q6-8.** Examine the following code:

```
class Programmer {
    void print() {
        System.out.println("Programmer - Mala Gupta");
    }
}
class Author extends Programmer {
    void print() {
        System.out.println("Author - Mala Gupta");
    }
}
class TestEJava {
    public static void main(String[] args) {
        Programmer a = new Programmer();
        // INSERT CODE HERE
        a.print();
        b.print();
    }
}
```

Which of the following lines of code can be individually inserted at //INSERT CODE HERE so that the output of the code is as follows?

```
Programmer - Mala Gupta
Author - Mala Gupta
```

a  Programmer b = new Programmer();

b  Programmer b = new Author();

c  Author b = new Author();

d  Author b = new Programmer();

```
e   Programmer b = ((Author)new Programmer());
f   Author b = ((Author)new Programmer());
```

**Q6-9.** Given the following code, which of the options, when applied individually, will make it compile successfully?

```
Line1>    interface Employee {}
Line2>    interface Printable extends Employee {
Line3>        String print();
Line4>    }
Line5>    class Programmer {
Line6>        String print() { return("Programmer - Mala Gupta"); }
Line7>    }
Line8>    class Author extends Programmer implements Printable, Employee {
Line9>        String print() { return("Author - Mala Gupta"); }
Line10>   }
```

  a  Modify the code on line 2 to interface Printable{
  b  Modify the code on line 3 to publicStringprint();
  c  Define the accessibility of the print methods to public on lines 6 and 9.
  d  Modify the code on line 8 so that it implements only the interface Printable.

**Q6-10.** What is the output of the following code?

```
class Base {
    String var = "EJava";
    void printVar() {
        System.out.println(var);
    }
}
class Derived extends Base {
    String var = "Guru";
    void printVar() {
        System.out.println(var);
    }
}
class QReference {
    public static void main(String[] args) {
        Base base = new Base();
        Base derived = new Derived();
        System.out.println(base.var);
        System.out.println(derived.var);
        base.printVar();
        derived.printVar();
    }
}
```

  a  EJava
     EJava
     EJava
     Guru

  b  EJava
     Guru
     EJava
     Guru

  c  EJava
     EJava
     EJava
     EJava

  d  EJava
     Guru
     Guru
     Guru

## 6.11 *Answers to sample exam questions*

**Q6-1.** What is the output of the following code?

```
class Animal {
    void jump() { System.out.println("Animal"); }
}
class Cat extends Animal {
    void jump(int a) { System.out.println("Cat"); }
}
class Rabbit extends Animal {
    void jump() { System.out.println("Rabbit"); }
}
class Circus {
    public static void main(String args[]) {
        Animal cat = new Cat();
        Rabbit rabbit = new Rabbit();
        cat.jump();
        rabbit.jump();
    }
}
```

  a  **Animal**
     **Rabbit**

  b  Cat
     Rabbit

  c  Animal
     Animal

  d  None of the above

Answer: a

Explanation: Although the classes Cat and Rabbit seem to override the method jump, the class Cat doesn't override the method jump() defined in the class Animal. The class Cat defines a method parameter with the method jump, which makes it an overloaded method, not an overridden method. Because the class Cat extends the class Animal, it has access to the following two overloaded jump methods:

```
void jump() { System.out.println("Animal"); }
void jump(int a) { System.out.println("Cat"); }
```

The following lines of code create an object of class Cat and assign it to a variable of type Animal:

```
Animal cat = new Cat();
```

When you call the method jump on the previous object, it executes the method jump, which doesn't accept any method parameters, printing the following value:

```
Animal
```

The following code will also print Animal and not Cat:

```
Cat cat = new Cat();
cat.jump();
```

**Q6-2.** Given the following code, select the correct statements:

```
class Flower {
    public void fragrance() {System.out.println("Flower"); }
}
class Rose {
    public void fragrance() {System.out.println("Rose"); }
}
class Lily {
    public void fragrance() {System.out.println("Lily"); }
}
class Bouquet {
    public void arrangeFlowers() {
        Flower f1 = new Rose();
        Flower f2 = new Lily();
        f1.fragrance();
    }
}
```

a  The output of the code is

```
Flower
```

b  The output of the code is

```
Rose
```

c  The output of the code is

```
Lily
```

d  **The code fails to compile.**

Answer: d

Explanation: Although the code seems to implement polymorphism using classes, note that neither of the classes Rose or Lily *extends* the class Flower. Hence, a variable of type Flower can't be used to store objects of the classes Rose or Lily. The following lines of code will fail to compile:

```
Flower f1 = new Rose();
Flower f2 = new Lily();
```

**Q6-3.** Examine the following code and select the correct method declaration to be inserted at //INSERT CODE HERE:

```
interface Movable {
    void move();
}
class Person implements Movable {
    public void move() { System.out.println("Person move"); }
}
class Vehicle implements Movable {
    public void move() { System.out.println("Vehicle move"); }
}
class Test {
    // INSERT CODE HERE
        movable.move();
    }
}
```

    **a**  **void walk(Movable movable) {**

    **b**  **void walk(Person movable) {**

    **c**  **void walk(Vehicle movable) {**

    **d**  void walk() {

Answer: a, b, c

Explanation: You need to insert code in the class Test that makes the following line of code work:

```
movable.move();
```

Hence, option (d) is incorrect. Because class Test doesn't define any instance methods, the only way that the question's line of code can execute is when a method parameter movable is passed to the method walk.

    Option (a) is correct. Because the interface Movable defines the method move, you can pass a variable of its type to the method move.

    Option (b) is correct. Because the class Person implements the interface Movable and defines the method move, you can pass a variable of its type to the method walk. With this version of the method walk, you can pass it an object of the class Person or any of its subclasses.

Option (c) is correct. Because the class `Vehicle` implements the interface `Movable` and defines the method `move`, you can pass a variable of its type to the method `walk`. With this version of method `walk`, you can pass it an object of the class `Vehicle` or any of its subclasses.

**Q6-4.** Select the correct statements:

a  Only an `abstract` class can be used as a base class to implement polymorphism with classes.

b  **Polymorphic methods are also called overridden methods.**

c  In polymorphism, depending on the exact type of object, the JVM executes the appropriate method at compile time.

d  None of the above.

Answer: b

Option (a) is incorrect. To implement polymorphism with classes, either an `abstract` class or a concrete class can be used as a base class.

Option (c) is incorrect. First of all, no code execution takes place at compile time. Code can only execute at runtime. In polymorphism, the determination of the exact method to execute is deferred until runtime and is determined by the exact type of the object on which a method needs to be called.

**Q6-5.** Given the following code, select the correct statements:

```
class Person {}
class Employee extends Person {}
class Doctor extends Person {}
```

a  The code exhibits polymorphism with classes.

b  The code exhibits polymorphism with interfaces.

c  The code exhibits polymorphism with classes and interfaces.

d  **None of the above.**

Answer: d

Explanation: The given code doesn't define any method in the class `Person` that is redefined or implemented in the classes `Employee` and `Doctor`. Although the classes `Employee` and `Doctor` extend the class `Person`, all three polymorphism concepts or design principles are based on a method, which is missing in these classes.

**Q6-6.** Which of the following statements are true?

a  **Inheritance enables you to reuse existing code.**

b  **Inheritance saves you from having to modify common code in multiple classes.**

    **c** Polymorphism passes special instructions to the compiler so that the code can run on multiple platforms.

    **d** Polymorphic methods can't throw exceptions.

Answer: a, b

Explanation: Option (a) is correct. Inheritance can allow you to reuse existing code by extending a class. In this way, the functionality that's already defined in the base class need not be defined in the derived class. The functionality offered by the base class can be accessed in the derived class as if it were defined in the derived class.

    Option (b) is correct. Common code can be placed in the base class, which can be extended by all the derived classes. If any changes need to be made to this common code, it can be modified in the base class. The modified code will be accessible to all the derived classes.

    Option (c) is incorrect. Polymorphism doesn't pass any special instructions to the compiler to make the Java code execute on multiple platforms. Java code can execute on multiple platforms because the Java compiler compiles to virtual machine code, which is platform neutral. Different platforms implement this virtual machine.

    Option (d) is incorrect. Polymorphic methods can throw exceptions.

**Q6-7.** Given the following code, which of the options are true?

```
class Satellite {
    void orbit() {}
}
class Moon extends Satellite {
    void orbit() {}
}
class ArtificialSatellite extends Satellite {
    void orbit() {}
}
```

    **a** **The method orbit defined in the classes Satellite, Moon, and Artificial-Satellite is polymorphic.**

    **b** Only the method orbit defined in the classes Satellite and Artificial-Satellite is polymorphic.

    **c** Only the method orbit defined in the class ArtificialSatellite is polymorphic.

    **d** None of the above.

Answer: a

Explanation: All these options define classes. When methods with the same method signature are defined in classes that share an inheritance relationship, the methods are considered polymorphic.

**Q6-8.** Examine the following code:

```java
class Programmer {
    void print() {
        System.out.println("Programmer - Mala Gupta");
    }
}
class Author extends Programmer {
    void print() {
        System.out.println("Author - Mala Gupta");
    }
}
class TestEJava {
    public static void main(String[] args) {
        Programmer a = new Programmer();
        // INSERT CODE HERE
        a.print();
        b.print();
    }
}
```

Which of the following lines of code can be individually inserted at //INSERT CODE HERE so that the output of the code is as follows?

```
Programmer - Mala Gupta
Author - Mala Gupta
```

   **a**  Programmer b = new Programmer();

   **b**  **Programmer b = new Author();**

   **c**  **Author b = new Author();**

   **d**  Author b = new Programmer();

   **e**  Programmer b = ((Author)new Programmer());

   **f**  Author b = ((Author)new Programmer());

Answer: b, c

Explanation: Option (a) is incorrect. This code will compile, but because both the reference variable and object are of type Programmer, calling print on this object will print Programmer - Mala Gupta, not Author - Mala Gupta.

Option (d) is incorrect. This code will not compile. You can't assign an object of a base class to a reference variable of a derived class.

Option (e) is incorrect. This line of code will compile successfully, but it will fail at runtime with a ClassCastException. An object of a base class can't be cast to an object of its derived class.

Option (f) is incorrect. The expression ((Author)new Programmer()) is evaluated before it can be assigned to a reference variable of type Author. This line of code also tries to cast an object of the base class, Programmer, to an object of its derived class, Author. This code will also compile successfully but will fail at runtime with a ClassCastException. Using a reference variable of type Author won't make a difference here. What matters here is the type that follows the new operator.

**Q6-9.** Given the following code, which of the options, when applied individually, will make it compile successfully?

```
Line1>     interface Employee {}
Line2>     interface Printable extends Employee {
Line3>         String print();
Line4>     }
Line5>     class Programmer {
Line6>         String print() { return("Programmer - Mala Gupta"); }
Line7>     }
Line8>      class Author extends Programmer implements Printable, Employee {
Line9>         String print() { return("Author - Mala Gupta"); }
Line10>    }
```

   **a**  Modify the code on line 2 to interface Printable {

   **b**  Modify the code on line 3 to public String print();

   **c**  **Define the accessibility of the print methods to public on lines 6 and 9.**

   **d**  Modify the code on line 8 so that it implements only the interface Printable.

Answer: c

Explanation: The methods in an interface are implicitly public. A non-abstract class that implements an interface must implement all the methods defined in the interface. While overriding or implementing the methods, the accessibility of the implemented method must be public. An overriding method can't be assigned a weaker access privilege than public.

Option (a) is incorrect. There are no issues with the interface Printable extending the interface Employee and the class Author implementing both of these interfaces.

Option (b) is incorrect. Adding the access modifier to the method print on line 3 won't make any difference to the existing code. The methods defined in an interface are implicitly public.

Option (d) is incorrect. There are no issues with a class implementing two interfaces when one of the interfaces extends the other interface.

**Q6-10.** What is the output of the following code?

```
class Base {
    String var = "EJava";
    void printVar() {
        System.out.println(var);
    }
}
class Derived extends Base {
    String var = "Guru";
    void printVar() {
        System.out.println(var);
    }
}
class QReference {
    public static void main(String[] args) {
```

```
        Base base = new Base();
        Base derived = new Derived();
        System.out.println(base.var);
        System.out.println(derived.var);
        base.printVar();
        derived.printVar();
    }
}
```

a  **EJava**
   **EJava**
   **EJava**
   **Guru**

b  EJava
   Guru
   EJava
   Guru

c  EJava
   EJava
   EJava
   EJava

d  EJava
   Guru
   Guru
   Guru

Answer: a

Explanation: With inheritance, the instance variables bind at compile time and the methods bind at runtime. The following line of code refers to an object of the class Base, using a reference variable of type Base. Hence, both of the following lines of code print EJava:

```
System.out.println(base.var);
base.printVar();
```

But the following line of code refers to an object of the class Derived using a reference variable of type Base:

```
Base derived = new Derived();
```

Because the instance variables bind at compile time, the following line of code accesses and prints the value of the instance variable defined in the class Base:

```
System.out.println(derived.var);     // prints EJava
```

In derived.printVar(), even though the method printVar is called using a reference of type Base, the JVM is aware that the method is invoked on a Derived object and so executes the overridden printVar method in the class Derived.

# Exception handling

7

| Exam objectives covered in this chapter | What you need to know |
|---|---|
| **[8.3]** Describe the advantages of Exception handling. | The need for and advantages of exception handlers. |
| **[8.1]** Differentiate among checked exceptions, unchecked exceptions, and `Errors`. | Differences and similarities between checked exceptions, `RuntimeExceptions`, and `Errors`. Differences and similarities in the way these exceptions and errors are handled in code. |
| **[8.2]** Create a `try-catch` block and determine how exceptions alter normal program flow. | How to create a `try-catch-finally` block. Understand the flow of code when the enclosed code throws an exception or error. How to create nested `try-catch-finally` blocks. |
| **[8.4]** Create and invoke a method that throws an exception. | How to create methods that throw exceptions. Rules that cover when overriding or overridden methods throw or don't throw exceptions. How to determine the flow of control when an invoked method throws an exception. How to apply this to cases when one is thrown without a `try` block and from a `try` block (with appropriate and insufficient exception handlers). The difference in calling methods that throw or don't throw exceptions. |
| **[8.5]** Recognize common exception classes (such as NullPointerException, Arithmetic-Exception, ArrayIndexOutOfBounds-Exception, ClassCastException) | How to recognize the code that can throw these exceptions and handle them appropriately. |

Imagine you're about to board an airplane to Geneva to attend an important conference. At the last minute, you learn that the flight has been cancelled because the pilot isn't feeling well. Fortunately, the airline quickly arranges for an alternative pilot, allowing the flight to take off at its originally scheduled time. What a relief!

This example illustrates how exceptional conditions can modify the initial flow of an action and demonstrates the need to handle those conditions appropriately. In Java, an exceptional condition (like the illness of a pilot) can affect the normal code flow (airline flight operation). In this context, the arrangement for an alternative pilot can be compared to an exception handler.

Depending on the nature of the exceptional condition, you may or may not be able to recover completely. For example, would airline management have been able to get your flight off the ground if, instead, an earthquake had damaged much of the airport?

In the exam, you'll be asked similar questions with respect to Java code and exceptions. With that in mind, this chapter covers the following:

- Understanding and identifying exceptions arising in code
- Determining how exceptions alter the normal program flow
- Understanding the need to handle exceptions separately in your code
- Using try-catch-finally blocks to handle exceptions
- Differentiating between checked exceptions, unchecked exceptions, and errors
- Invoking methods that may throw exceptions
- Recognizing common exception categories and classes

You might feel like we're covering a lot in this chapter, but remember that we aren't going to delve into too much background information because I assume you already know the definitions and uses of classes and methods, class inheritance, arrays, and ArrayLists. Our focus in this chapter is on the exam objectives and what you need to know about exceptions.

In this chapter, I won't discuss a try statement with multiple catch clauses, automatic closing of resources with a try-with-resources statement, or the creation of custom exceptions. These topics are covered in the next level of Java certification (in the OCP Java SE 8 Programmer II exam).

## 7.1    Exceptions in Java

 [8.3]   Describe the advantages of Exception handling

In this section, you'll learn what exceptions are in Java, why you need to handle exceptions separately from the main code, and all about their advantages and disadvantages.

### 7.1.1    A taste of exceptions

In figure 7.1, do you think the code in bold in the classes ArrayAccess, OpenFile, and MethodAccess has anything in common?

```
public class ArrayAccess      {
    public static void main(String args[]) {
        String[] students = {"Shreya", "Joseph", null};
        System.out.println(students[5].length());
    }
}
```

```
public class OpenFile {
    public static void main(String args[]) {
        FileInputStream fis = new FileInputStream("file.txt");
    }
}
```

Examine these lines of code.

```
public class MethodAccess {
    public static void main(String  args[]) {
        myMethod();
    }
    public static void myMethod() {
        System.out.println("myMethod");
        myMethod();
    }
}
```

**Figure 7.1   Getting a taste of exceptions in Java**

I'm sure, given this chapter's title, that this question was easy to answer. Each of these three statements is associated with throwing an exception or an error. Let's look at them individually:

- *Class* ArrayAccess—Because the length of the array students is 3, trying to access the element at array position 5 is an exceptional condition, as shown in figure 7.2.

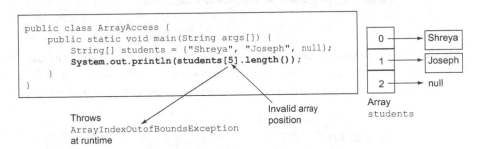

Throws
ArrayIndexOutofBoundsException
at runtime

Invalid array position

Array students

**Figure 7.2   An example of ArrayIndexOutOfBoundsException**

- *Class* OpenFile—The constructor of the class FileInputStream throws a checked exception, FileNotFoundException (as shown in figure 7.3). If you try to compile this code without enclosing it within a try block and catching it, or marking it to be thrown by the method `main` (by using the `throws` statement), or catching this exception, your code will fail to compile. (I'll discuss checked exceptions in detail in section 7.2.3.)

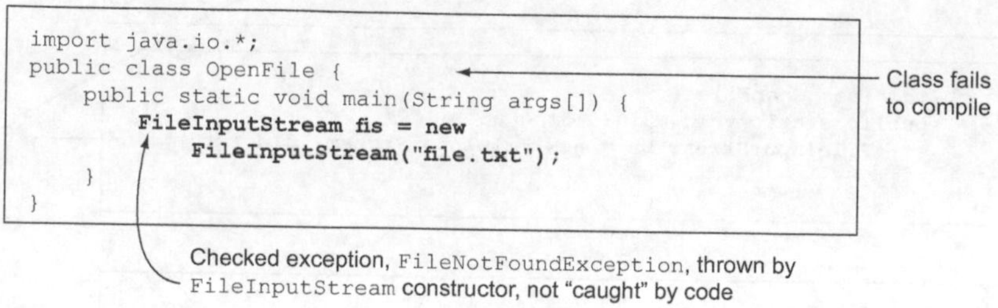

```
import java.io.*;
public class OpenFile {                          ←———————— Class fails
    public static void main(String args[]) {                to compile
        FileInputStream fis = new
            FileInputStream("file.txt");
    }
}
```

Checked exception, `FileNotFoundException`, thrown by `FileInputStream` constructor, not "caught" by code

**Figure 7.3** An example of `FileNotFoundException`

- *Class* `MethodAccess`—As you can see in figure 7.4, the method `myMethod` calls itself recursively, without specifying an exit condition. These recursive calls result in a `StackOverflowError` at runtime.

```
public class MethodAccess {
    public static void main(String args[]) {        Throws
        myMethod();  ————————————————————————→      StackOverflowError at
    }                                                runtime
    public static void myMethod() {
        System.out.println("myMethod");            Calls itself recursively
        myMethod();  ←————————————————————          without an exit condition
    }
}
```

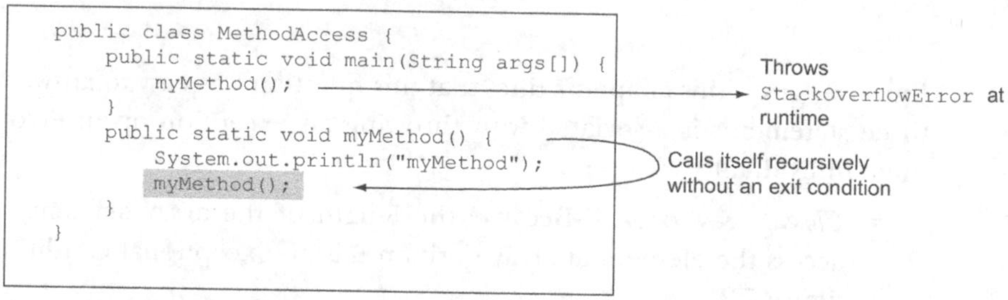

**Figure 7.4** An example of `StackOverflowError`

These examples of exceptions are typical of what you'll find on the OCA Java SE 8 Programmer I exam. Let's move on and explore exceptions and their handling in Java so that you can spot code that throws exceptions and handle them accordingly.

---

### File I/O in Java

File I/O isn't covered on this exam, but you may notice it mentioned in questions related to exception handling. I'll cover it quickly here just to the extent required for this exam.

File I/O involves multiple classes that enable you to read data from and write it to a source. This data source can be persistent storage, memory, or even network connections. Data can be read and written as streams of binary or character data. Some file I/O classes only read data from a source, some write data to a source, and some do both.

In this chapter, you'll work with three classes from the file I/O API: `java.io.File`, `java.io.FileInputStream`, and `java.io.FileOutputStream`. `File` is an abstract representation of file and directory pathnames. You can *open* a `File` and then read from and write to it. A `FileInputStream` obtains input bytes using an object of the class `File`. It defines the methods `read` to read bytes and `close` to close this stream. A `FileOutputStream` is an output stream for writing data to a `File`. It defines the methods `write` to write bytes and `close` to close this stream.

Creating an object of the class `FileInputStream` or `FileOutputStream` can throw the checked exception `java.io.FileNotFoundException`. The methods `read`, `write`, and `close` defined in classes `FileInputStream` and `FileOutputStream` can throw the checked exception `java.io.IOException`. Note that `FileNotFound-Exception` subclasses `IOException`.

## 7.1.2 *Why handle exceptions separately?*

Imagine you want to post some comments on a blogging website. To make a comment, you must complete the following steps:

1. Access the blogging website.
2. Log into your account.
3. Select the blog you want to comment on.
4. Post your comments.

The preceding list might seem like an ideal set of steps. In actual conditions, you may have to verify whether you've completed a previous step before you can progress with the next step. Figure 7.5 modifies the previous steps.

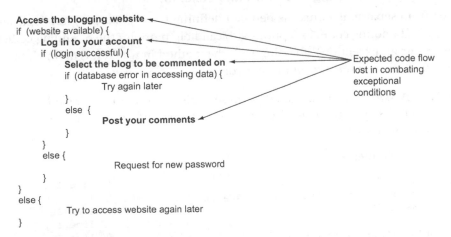

**Figure 7.5  Expected code flow lost in combating exception conditions, without separate exception handlers**

The modified logic (figure 7.5) requires the code to check conditions before a user can continue with the next step. This checking of conditions at multiple places introduces new steps for users and also new paths of execution of the original steps. The difficult part of these modified paths is that they may leave users confused about the steps involved in the tasks they're trying to accomplish. Figure 7.6 shows how exception handling can help.

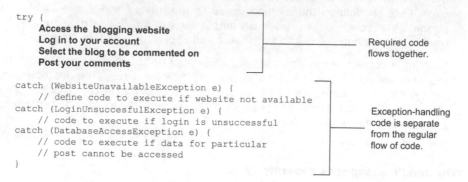

**Figure 7.6   Defining exception-handling code separate from the main code logic**

The code in figure 7.6 defines the original steps required to post comments to a blog, along with some exception-handling code. Because the exception handlers are defined separately, any confusion with what steps you need to accomplish to post comments on the website has been clarified. In addition, this code doesn't compromise on checking the completion of a step before moving on to the next step, courtesy of appropriate exception handlers.

### 7.1.3   *Does exception handling offer any other benefits?*

Apart from separating concerns between defining the regular program logic and the exception-handling code, exceptions also can help pinpoint the offending code (code that throws an exception), together with the method in which it is defined, by providing a stack trace of the exception or error.

   **NOTE**   A *stack* trace is so called because it gives you a way to trace back the stack—the sequence of method calls that generated the error (covered in detail in section 7.2).

Here's an example:

```
public class Trace {                              // line 1
    public static void main(String args[]) {      // line 2
        method1();                                 // line 3
    }                                              // line 4
    public static void method1() {                 // line 5
        method2();                                 // line 6
    }                                              // line 7
```

```
public static void method2() {                    // line 8
    String[] students = {"Shreya", "Joseph"};      // line 9
    System.out.println(students[5]);               // line 10
}                                                  // line 11
}                                                  // line 12
```

method2() tries to access the array element of students at index 5, which is an invalid index for the array students, so the code throws the exception ArrayIndexOutOf-BoundsException at runtime. Figure 7.7 shows the stack trace when this exception is thrown. It includes the runtime exception message and the list of methods that were involved in calling the code that threw the exception, starting from the entry point of this application, the main method. You can match the line numbers specified in the stack trace in figure 7.7 to the line numbers in the code.

```
Exception in thread "main"
java.lang.ArrayIndexOutOfBoundsException: 5        Offending code in method2 (line 10)
    at Trace.method2(Trace.java:10)  ◄──────────
    at Trace.method1(Trace.java:6)   ◄─────────── method2 called by method1 (line 6)
    at Trace.main(Trace.java:3)      ◄──────────┐
                                                 method1 called by main (line 3)
```

**Figure 7.7   Tracing the line of code that threw an exception at runtime**

**NOTE**   The stack trace gives you a trace of the methods that were called when the JVM encountered an unhandled exception. Stack traces are read from the bottom up. In figure 7.7, the trace starts with the main method (the last line of the stack trace) and continues up to the method containing the code that threw the exception. Depending on the complexity of your code, a stack trace can range from a few lines to hundreds of lines of code. A stack trace works with handled and unhandled exceptions.

Let's move on and look at more details of exception propagation and at the creation of try-catch-finally blocks to take care of exceptions in code.

Before diving into the details of exception handling, let's look at the multiple flavors of exceptions.

## 7.2   *Categories of exceptions*

> [8.1]   Differentiate among checked exceptions, unchecked exceptions, and Errors

The Java compiler and its runtime treat the exception categories in a different manner. This implies that separate rules exist to define methods that throw exceptions and code that handles them.

In this section, you'll learn about the categories of exceptions in Java: checked exceptions, runtime exceptions, and errors.

### 7.2.1   *Identifying exception categories*

As depicted in figure 7.8, exceptions can be divided into three main categories:

- Checked exceptions
- Runtime exceptions
- Errors

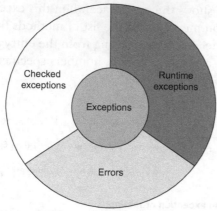

Unchecked exceptions = Runtime exception + Errors

**Figure 7.8   Categories of exceptions: checked exceptions, runtime exceptions, and errors**

 **NOTE**   Runtime exceptions and errors are collectively referred to as unchecked exceptions.

Of these three types, checked exceptions require most of your attention when it comes to coding and using methods. Runtime exceptions represent programming errors. Checks should be inserted to prevent runtime exceptions from being thrown. There are few options you can use for the errors, because they're thrown by the JVM.

For the OCA Java SE 8 Programmer I exam, it's important to have a crystal-clear understanding of these three categories of exceptions, including their similarities and differences.

### 7.2.2   *Class hierarchy of exception classes*

Exception categories are related to each other; all extend the class java.lang.Throwable (as shown in the class hierarchy in figure 7.9).

Here's the categorization of exceptions based on their class hierarchy:

- *Checked exceptions*—java.lang.Exception and its subclasses (excluding java.lang.RuntimeException and its subclasses)
- *Runtime exceptions*—java.lang.RuntimeException and its subclasses
- *Errors*—java.lang.Error and its subclasses

Let's examine each of these categories in detail.

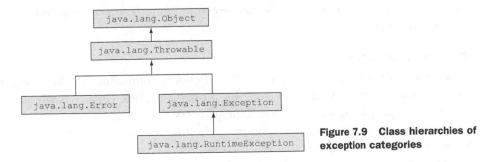

**Figure 7.9  Class hierarchies of exception categories**

### 7.2.3  Checked exceptions

When we talk about handling exceptions, *checked* exceptions take up most of our attention.

What is a checked exception?

- A checked exception is an unacceptable condition *foreseen* by the author of a method but outside their immediate control. For an example, FileNotFound-Exception is a checked exception. This exception is thrown if the file that the code is trying to access can't be found. A method, say, readFile(), can declare it to be thrown when it's unable to access the target file.
- Checked exceptions are so named because they're checked during compilation. If a method call throws a checked exception, the compiler checks and ensures that the calling method is either handling the exception or declaring it to be rethrown.
- A checked exception is a subclass of the class java.lang.Exception, but it's not a subclass of java.lang.RuntimeException. It's interesting to note, however, that the class java.lang.RuntimeException itself is a subclass of the class java.lang.Exception.

**EXAM TIP**  In this exam, you may have to select which type of reference variable to use to store the object of the thrown checked exception in a handler. To answer such questions correctly, remember that a checked exception subclasses java.lang.Exception but not java.lang.RuntimeException.

A checked exception is part of the API and is well documented. For a quick example, here's the declaration of the constructor of the class java.io.FileInputStream in the Java API:

```
public FileInputStream(File file)
            throws FileNotFoundException
```

Checked exceptions are unacceptable conditions that a programmer *foresees* at the time of writing a method. By declaring these exceptions as checked exceptions, the author of the method makes its users aware of the exceptional conditions that can arise from its use. The user of a method with a checked exception must handle the exceptional condition accordingly.

### 7.2.4   Runtime exceptions

Although you'll spend most of your time and energy combating checked exceptions, the runtime exceptions will give you the most headaches. This is particularly true when you're preparing to work on real-life projects. Some examples of runtime exceptions are `NullPointerException` (the most common one), `ArrayIndexOutOfBounds-Exception`, and `ClassCastException`.

What is a runtime exception?

- A runtime exception is a representation of a programming error. These occur from inappropriate use of a piece of code. For example, `NullPointerException` is a runtime exception that occurs when a piece of code tries to execute some code on a variable that hasn't been assigned an object and points to `null`. Another example is `ArrayIndexOutOfBoundsException`, which is thrown when a piece of code tries to access an array element at a nonexistent position.
- A runtime exception is named so because it isn't feasible to determine whether a method call will throw a runtime exception until it executes.
- A runtime exception is a subclass of `java.lang.RuntimeException`.
- It's optional to declare a runtime exception in the signature of a method. It's up to the person who writes the code to decide whether to declare it explicitly or not.

 **EXAM TIP**   Together, runtime exceptions and errors are referred to as unchecked exceptions.

### 7.2.5   Errors

Whether you're preparing for this exam or your real-life projects, you need to know when the JVM throws errors. These errors are considered to be *serious* exceptional conditions and they can't be directly controlled by your code.

What is an error?

- An error is a serious exception thrown by the JVM as a result of an error in the environment state that processes your code. For example, `NoClassDefFound-Error` is an error thrown by the JVM when it's unable to locate the .class file that it's supposed to run. `StackOverflowError` is another error thrown by the JVM when the size of the memory required by the stack of a Java program is greater than what the JRE has offered for the Java application. This error might also occur as a result of infinite or highly nested loops.
- An error is a subclass of class `java.lang.Error`.
- An error need not be a part of a method signature.
- An error can be caught by an exception handler, but it shouldn't be.

Let's move on to creating methods that throw exceptions.

## 7.3   Creating a method that throws an exception

[8.4]   Create and invoke a method that throws an exception

In this section, you'll explore the need to create methods that throw exceptions. You'll also work with the `throw` and `throws` keywords to define methods that throw exceptions.

Why do you need methods that throw exceptions? Imagine that you're assigned the task of finding a specific book and then reading and explaining its contents to a class of students. The required sequence looks like the following:

1   Get the specified book.
2   Read aloud its contents.
3   Explain the contents to a class of students.

But what happens if you can't find the specified book? You can't proceed with the rest of the actions without it, so you need to report back to the person who assigned the task to you. This unexpected event (the missing book) prevents you from completing your task. By reporting it, you want the *originator* of this request to take corrective or alternate steps.

Let's code the preceding task as the `teachClass` method, as shown in figure 7.10, which uses the `throw` statement and `throws` clause. This example code is for demonstration purposes only, because it uses the `BookNotFoundException` exception and the `locateBook()`, `readBook()`, and `explainContents()` methods, which aren't defined.

The code in figure 7.10 is simple to follow. On execution of the code `throw new BookNotFoundException()`, the execution of `teachClass()` halts. The JVM creates an instance of `BookNotFoundException` and sends it off to the caller of `teachClass()` so alternate arrangements can be made.

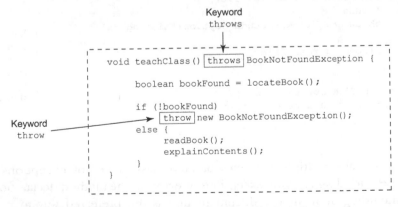

**Figure 7.10   Using *throw* and *throws* to create methods that can throw exceptions**

The throw statement is used to *throw* an instance of BookNotFoundException. The throws statement is used in the declaration of the teachClass() method to signal that it can throw BookNotFoundException.

Why does a method choose to throw an exception as opposed to handling it itself? It's a contract between the *calling* method and the *called* method. Referring to the teachClass() method shown in figure 7.9, the *caller* of teachClass would like to be informed if teachClass() is unable to find the specified book. The teachClass() method doesn't handle BookNotFoundException because its responsibilities don't include working around a missing book.

The preceding example helps identify a situation when you'd *want* a method to throw an exception, rather than handling it itself. It shows you how to use and compare the statements throw and throws—to *throw* exceptions and to signal that a method *might* throw an exception. The example also shows that a calling method can define alternate code, when the called method doesn't complete successfully and throws an exception. Apart from testing this logic, the exam will test you on how to create and use methods that throw checked or unchecked exceptions and errors, along with several other rules.

### 7.3.1 *Create a method that throws a checked exception*

Let's create a simple method that doesn't handle the checked exception thrown by it, by using the statements throw and throws. The class DemoThrowsException defines the readFile() method, which includes a throws clause in its method declaration. The actual throwing of an exception is accomplished by the throw statement:

> **The throws statement indicates the method can throw FileNotFoundException or one of its subclasses**

```
import java.io.FileNotFoundException;
class DemoThrowsException {
    public void readFile(String file) throws FileNotFoundException {
        boolean found = findFile(file);
        if (!found)
            throw new FileNotFoundException("Missing file");
        else {
            //code to read file
        }
    }
    boolean findFile(String file) {
        //code to return true if file can be located
    }
}
```

> **If file can't be found, code creates and throws instance of FileNotFoundException by using the throw statement**

A method can have multiple comma-separated class names of exceptions in its throws clause. Including runtime exceptions or errors in the method declaration isn't required. Including them in the documentation is the preferred way to mention them. A method can still throw runtime exceptions or errors, without including them in its throws clause.

**EXAM TIP**  Syntactically, you don't always need a combination of `throw` and `throws` statements to create a method that throws an exception (checked or unchecked). You can replace the `throw` statement with a method that throws an exception.

### 7.3.2  Handle-or-declare rule

To use a method that throws a *checked exception*, you must do one of the following:

- *Handle the exception*—Enclose the code within a try block and *catch* the thrown exception.
- *Declare it to be thrown*—Declare the exception to be thrown by using the `throws` clause.
- *Handle and declare*—Implement both of the preceding options together.

**EXAM TIP**  The rule of either handling or declaring an exception is also referred to as the *handle-or-declare rule*. To use a method that throws a checked exception, you must either handle the exception or declare it to be thrown. But this rule applies only to checked exceptions and not to unchecked exceptions.

### 7.3.3  Creating a method that throws runtime exceptions or errors

When creating a method that throws a runtime exception or error, including the exception or error name in the `throws` clause isn't required. A method that throws a runtime exception or error isn't subject to the handle-or-declare rule.

Let's see this concept in action by modifying the preceding example so the `read-File()` method throws `NullPointerException` (a runtime exception) when a `null` value is passed to it (code changes are shown in bold in this example and throughout the rest of the chapter):

```
                                            The throws clause indicates that this
                                            method can throw FileNotFoundException

import java.io.FileNotFoundException;
class DemoThrowsException {
    public void readFile(String file) throws FileNotFoundException {
        if (file == null)
            throw new NullPointerException();          Code throws
        boolean found = findFile(file);                NullPointerException,
        if (!found)                                    but it's not included
            throw new FileNotFoundException("Missing file");   in the throws clause
        else {
            //code to read file
        }
    }
    boolean findFile(String file) {
        //code to return true if file can be located
    }
}
```

The exam might trick you by including the names of runtime exceptions and errors in one method's declaration and leaving them out in another. (You *can* include the name of unchecked exceptions in the `throws` clause, but you don't have to.) Assuming that the rest of the code remains the same, the following method declaration is correct:

```
public void readFile(String file)
                throws NullPointerException, FileNotFoundException {
    //rest of the code remains same
}
```

Though not required, including runtime exceptions in the throws clause is valid.

> **EXAM TIP**  Adding runtime exceptions or errors to a method's declaration isn't required. A method can throw a runtime exception or error irrespective of whether its name is included in its `throws` clause.

### 7.3.4   *A method can declare to throw all types of exceptions, even if it doesn't*

In the following example, the class `ThrowExceptions` defines multiple methods, which declare to throw different exception types. The class `ThrowExceptions` compiles successfully, even though its methods don't include the code that might throw these exceptions:

```
class ThrowExceptions {
    void method1() throws Error {}
    void method2() throws Exception {}
    void method3() throws Throwable {}
    void method4() throws RuntimeException {}
    void method5() throws FileNotFoundException {}
}
```

Although a `try` block can define a handler for unchecked exceptions not thrown by it, it can't do so for checked exceptions (other than `Exception`):

```
class HandleExceptions {
    void method6() {
        try {}
        catch (Error e) {}
    }
    void method7() {
        try {}
        catch (Exception e) {}
    }
    void method8() {
        try {}
        catch (Throwable e) {}
    }
    void method9() {
        try {}
        catch (RuntimeException e) {}
    }
```

```
    void method10() {
        try {}                                          Won't
        catch (FileNotFoundException e) {}      ←┘      compile
    }
}
```

In the preceding code, `method6()`, `method7()`, `method8()`, and `method9()` compile even though their `try` block doesn't define code to throw the exception being handled by its `catch` block. But `method10()` won't compile.

**EXAM TIP** A method can declare to throw any type of exception, checked or unchecked, even if it doesn't do so. But a `try` block can't define a `catch` block for a checked exception (other than `Exception`) if the `try` block doesn't throw that checked exception or use a method that declares to throw that checked exception.

In the next section, we'll detail what happens when an exception is thrown and how to handle that.

## 7.4 *What happens when an exception is thrown?*

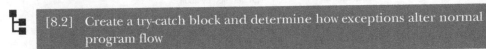

[8.2]  Create a try-catch block and determine how exceptions alter normal program flow

[8.4]  Create and invoke a method that throws an exception

In this section, we'll uncover what happens when an exception is thrown in Java. We'll work through several examples to understand how the normal flow of code is disrupted when an exception is thrown. We'll also define an alternative program flow for code that may throw exceptions using `try-catch-finally` blocks.

As with all other Java objects, an exception is an object. All types of exceptions subclass `java.lang.Throwable`. When a piece of code hits an obstacle in the form of an exceptional condition, it creates an object of the class `java.lang.Throwable` (at runtime, an object of the most appropriate subtype is created), initializes it with the necessary information (such as its type, an optional textual description, and the offending program's state), and hands it over to the JVM. The JVM blows a siren in the form of this exception and looks for an appropriate code block that can "handle" this exception. The JVM keeps account of all the methods that were called when it hit the offending code, so to find an appropriate exception handler it looks through all the tracked method calls.

Reexamine the class `Trace` and the `ArrayIndexOutOfBoundsException` thrown by it, as mentioned in section 7.1.3. Figure 7.11 illustrates the propagation of the exception `ArrayIndexOutOfBoundsException` thrown by `method2` through all the methods.

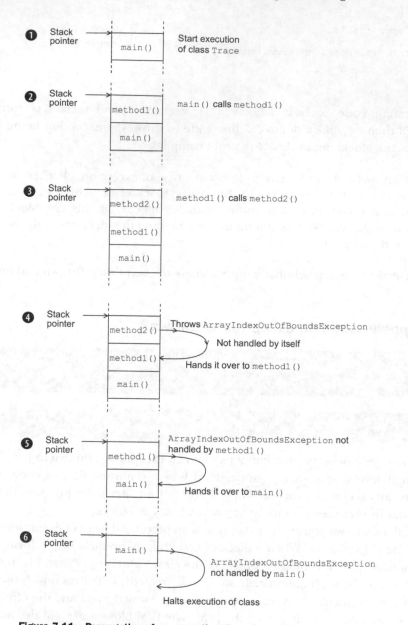

**Figure 7.11    Propagation of an exception through multiple method calls**

To understand how an exception propagates through method calls, it's important to understand how method calls work. An application starts its execution with the method main, and main may call other methods. When main calls another method, the called method should complete its execution before main can complete its own execution.

An operating system (OS) keeps track of the code that it needs to execute using a *stack*. A stack is a type of list in which the items that are added last to it are the first ones to be taken off it—last in, first out. This stack uses a *stack pointer* to point to the instructions that the OS should execute.

Now that you have this basic information under your belt, here's a step-by-step discussion of exception propagation, as shown in figure 7.11:

1 When the method `main` starts its execution, its instructions are pushed onto the stack.

2 The method `main` calls the method `method1`, and instructions for `method1` are pushed onto the stack.

3 `method1` calls `method2`; instructions for `method2` are pushed onto the stack.

4 `method2` throws an exception: `ArrayIndexOutOfBoundsException`. Because `method2` doesn't handle this exception itself, it's passed to the method that called it—`method1`.

5 `method1` doesn't define any exception handler for `ArrayIndexOutOfBounds-Exception`, so it hands this exception over to its calling method—`main`.

6 There are no exception handlers for `ArrayIndexOutOfBoundsException` in `main`. Because there are no further methods that handle `ArrayIndexOutOfBounds-Exception`, execution of the class `Trace` stops.

You can use `try-catch-finally` blocks to define code to execute when an exception is thrown, as discussed in the next section.

### 7.4.1 Creating try-catch-finally blocks

When you work with exception handlers, you often hear the terms `try`, `catch`, and `finally`. Before you start to work with these concepts, I'll answer three simple questions:

- *Try what?*
  First, you *try* to execute your code. If it doesn't execute as planned, you handle the exceptional conditions using a `catch` block.

- *Catch what?*
  You *catch* the exceptional event arising from the code enclosed within the `try` block and handle the event by defining appropriate exception handlers.

- *What does finally do?*
  Finally, you execute a set of code, in all conditions, regardless of whether the code in the `try` block throws any exceptions.

Let's compare a `try-catch-finally` block with a real-life example. Imagine you're going river rafting on your vacation. Your instructor informs you that while rafting, you *might* fall off the raft into the river while crossing the rapids. In such a condition, you should try to use your oar or the rope thrown toward you to get back into the raft. You *might* also drop your oar into the river while rowing your raft. In such a condition, you should not panic and should stay seated. Whatever happens, you're paying for this adventure sport.

Compare this to Java code:

- You can compare river rafting to a class whose methods *might* throw exceptions.
- Crossing the rapids and rowing a raft are methods that *might* throw exceptions.
- Falling off the raft and dropping your oar are the exceptions.
- The steps for getting back into the raft and not panicking are the exception handlers—code that executes when an exception arises.
- The fact that you pay for the sport, whether you stay in the boat or not, can be compared to the finally block.

Let's implement the previous real-life examples by defining appropriate classes and methods. To start with, here are two barebones exception classes—FallInRiver-Exception and DropOarException—that can be thrown by methods in the class RiverRafting:

```
class FallInRiverException extends Exception {}
class DropOarException extends Exception {}
```

**NOTE**  You can create an exception of your own—a custom exception—by extending the class Exception (or any of its subclasses). Although the creation of custom classes is not on this exam, you may see questions in the exam that create and use custom exceptions. Perhaps these are included because hardly any checked exceptions from the Java API are on this exam. Coding questions on the exam may create and use custom exceptions.

Following is a definition of class RiverRafting. Its methods crossRapid and rowRaft may throw exceptions of type FallInRiverException and DropOarException:

```
class RiverRafting {
    void crossRapid(int degree) throws FallInRiverException {      ◄
        System.out.println("Cross Rapid");
        if (degree > 10) throw new FallInRiverException();
    }
    void rowRaft(String state) throws DropOarException {           ◄
        System.out.println("Row Raft");
        if (state.equals("nervous")) throw new DropOarException();
    }
}
```

**Method crossRapid may throw FallInRiverException** ❶

**Method rowRaft may throw DropOar-Exception** ❷

The method crossRapid at ❶ throws the exception FallInRiverException. When you call this method, you should define an exception handler for this exception. Similarly, the method rowRaft at ❷ throws the exception DropOarException. When you call this method, you should define an exception handler for this exception.

When you execute methods that may throw *checked exceptions* (exceptions that don't extend the class RuntimeException), enclose the code within a try block. catch blocks that follow a try block should handle all the checked exceptions thrown by the code enclosed in the try block (checked exceptions are covered in detail in section 7.2.3).

The code shown in figure 7.12 uses the class `RiverRafting` as defined previously and depicts the flow of control when the code on line 3 (`riverRafting.cross-Rapid(11);`) throws an exception of type `FallInRiverException`.

```
1> RiverRafting riverRafting = new RiverRafting();
2> try {
3>     riverRafting.crossRapid(11);
4>     riverRafting.rowRaft("happy");
5>     System.out.println("Enjoy River Rafting");
6> }
7> catch (FallingRiverException e1) {
8>     System.out.println("Get back in the raft");
9> }
10> catch (DropOarException e2) {
11>     System.out.println("Do not panic");
12> }
13> finally {
14>     System.out.println("Pay for the sport");
15> }
16> System.out.println("After the try block");
```

1. Execute code on line 3.

Code on lines 4 and 5 won't execute if line 3 throws an exception.

2. Combat exception thrown by code on line 3. Execute exception handler for `FallInRiverException`.

3. `finally` block always executes, whether line 3 throws any exception or not.

4. Control transfers to the statement following the `try-catch-finally` block.

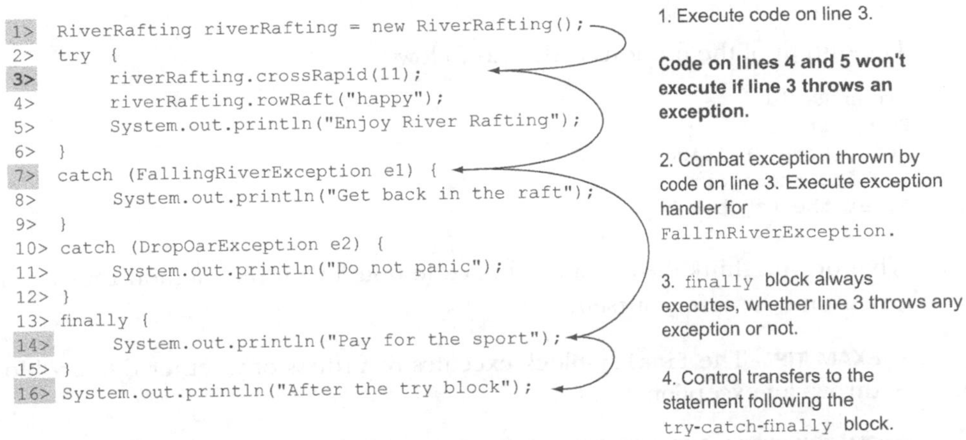

**Figure 7.12  Modified flow of control when an exception is thrown**

The example in figure 7.12 shows how exceptions alter the normal program flow. If the code on line 3 throws an exception (`FallInRiverException`), the code on lines 4 and 5 won't execute. In this case, control is transferred to the code block that handles `FallInRiverException`. Then control is transferred to the `finally` block. After the execution of the `finally` block, the code that follows the `try-catch-finally` block is executed. The output of the previous code is as follows:

```
Cross Rapid
Get back in the raft
Pay for the sport
After the try block
```

If you modify the previous example code as follows, no exceptions are thrown by the code on line 3 (modifications in bold):

```
class TestRiverRafting {
    public static void main(String args[]) {
        RiverRafting riverRafting = new RiverRafting();
        try {
            riverRafting.crossRapid(7);
            riverRafting.rowRaft("happy");
            System.out.println("Enjoy River Rafting");
        } catch (FallInRiverException e1) {
            System.out.println("Get back in the raft");
        } catch (DropOarException e2) {
            System.out.println("Do not panic");
        } finally {
```

No exceptions thrown by this line of code

```
            System.out.println("Pay for the sport");
        }
        System.out.println("After the try block");
    }
}
```

The output of the previous code is as follows:

```
Cross Rapid
Row Raft
Enjoy River Rafting
Pay for the sport
After the try block
```

What do you think the output of the code would be if the method rowRaft threw an exception? Try it for yourself!

**EXAM TIP**    The finally block executes regardless of whether the try block throws an exception.

### SINGLE TRY BLOCK, MULTIPLE CATCH BLOCKS, AND A FINALLY BLOCK

For a try block, you can define multiple catch blocks but only a single finally block. Multiple catch blocks are used to handle different types of exceptions. A finally block is used to define *cleanup* code—code that closes and releases resources, such as file handlers and database or network connections.

When it comes to code, it makes sense to verify a concept by watching it in action. Let's work through a simple example so that you can better understand how to use the try-catch-finally block.

In the following listing, the constructor of the class FileInputStream may throw a FileNotFoundException, and calling the method read on an object of FileInput-Stream, such as fis, may throw an IOException.

**Listing 7.1   Code flow with multiple catch statements and a finally block**

```
import java.io.*;
public class MultipleExceptions {
    public static void main(String args[]) {
        FileInputStream fis = null;
        try {
            fis = new FileInputStream("file.txt");       ⟵  May throw
            System.out.println("File Opened");              FileNotFoundException
            fis.read();                                  ⟵  May throw
            System.out.println("Read File ");               IOException
        } catch (FileNotFoundException fnfe) {
            System.out.println("File not found");
        } catch (IOException ioe) {
            System.out.println("I/O Exception");            Positioning of
        } finally {                                         catch and
            System.out.println("finally");                  finally blocks
            //code to close fis                             can't be
        }                                                   interchanged
```

```
            System.out.println("Next task..");
        }
    }
}
```

Table 7.1 compares the code output that occurs depending on whether the system is able or unable to open (and read) file.txt.

**Table 7.1** Output of code in listing 7.1 when the system is unable to open file.txt and when the system is able to open file.txt but unable to read it

| Output if the system is unable to open file.txt | Output if the system is able to open file.txt but unable to read it |
|---|---|
| `File not found`<br>`finally`<br>`Next task..` | `File Opened`<br>`File Closing Exception`<br>`finally`<br>`Next task..` |

In either of the cases described in table 7.1, the `finally` block executes, and after its execution, control is transferred to the statement following the `try-catch` block. Here's the output of the class `MultipleExceptions` if none of its code throws an exception:

```
File Opened
Read File
finally
Next task..
```

It's time now to attempt this chapter's first Twist in the Tale exercise. When you execute the code in this exercise, you'll understand what happens when you change the placement of the exception handlers (answers are in the appendix).

**Twist in the Tale 7.1**

Let's modify the placement of the `finally` block in listing 7.1 and see what happens.

Given that file.txt doesn't exist on your system, what is the output of the following code?

```
import java.io.*;
public class MultipleExceptions {
    public static void main(String args[]) {
        FileInputStream fis = null;
        try {
            fis = new FileInputStream("file.txt");
            System.out.println("File Opened");
            fis.read();
            System.out.println("Read File");
        } finally {
            System.out.println("finally");
```

```
        } catch (FileNotFoundException fnfe) {
            System.out.println("File not found");
        } catch (IOException ioe) {
            System.out.println("File Closing Exception");
        }
        System.out.println("Next task..");
    }
}
```

**a**  The code prints

```
File not found
finally
Next task..
```

**b**  The code prints

```
File Opened
File Closing Exception
finally
Next task..
```

**c**  The code prints File not found.
**d**  The code fails to compile.

---

### 7.4.2   *Using a method that throws a checked exception*

To use a method that throws a *checked exception,* you must follow the handle-or-declare rule (section 7.3.2). In the following code, the method main in the class TestRiver-Rafting won't compile because it doesn't handle or declare the checked exception FallInRiverException declared to be thrown by the method crossRapid:

```
class FallInRiverException extends Exception {}          ◄──┤  FallInRiverException is
                                                             a checked exception
class RiverRafting {
    void crossRapid(int degree) throws FallInRiverException {   ◄──
        System.out.println("Cross Rapid");                         crossRapid
        if (degree > 10) throw new FallInRiverException();         declares
    }                                                              to throw
}                                                                  FallInRiver-
                                                                   Exception
class TestRiverRafting {
    public static void main(String args[]) {
        RiverRafting riverRafting = new RiverRafting();
        riverRafting.crossRapid(9);          ◄─────
    }                                          Won't compile; main neither handles
}                                              nor declares FallInRiverException
```

The `main` method in the classes `Handle`, `Declare`, and `HandleAndDeclare` compiles successfully because they follow the handle-or-declare rule:

```java
class Handle {
    public static void main(String args[]) {
        RiverRafting riverRafting = new RiverRafting();
        try {
            riverRafting.crossRapid(9);
        } catch (FallInRiverException e) {
            System.out.println("Exception : " + e);
        }
    }
}
class Declare {
    public static void main(String args[]) throws FallInRiverException {
        RiverRafting riverRafting = new RiverRafting();
        riverRafting.crossRapid(9);
    }
}
class HandleAndDeclare {
    public static void main(String args[]) throws FallInRiverException {
        RiverRafting riverRafting = new RiverRafting();
        try {
            riverRafting.crossRapid(9);
        } catch (FallInRiverException e) {
            System.out.println("Exception : " + e);
        }
    }
}
```

 **EXAM TIP**   To use a method that throws a *checked exception*, you must follow the handle-or-declare rule.

### 7.4.3   *Using a method that throws a runtime exception*

If a method throws a runtime exception, the exception name isn't required to be included in the method's declaration (though it is allowed). To use a method that throws a runtime exception, you don't need to follow the declare-or-handle rule. Here's an example:

```java
class FeelingHungryException extends RuntimeException {}   ◄──

class Trip {
    void goTrekking(LocalTime startTime) {   ◄─┐
        // compare time now and start time
        // throw FeelingHungryException if difference is > 2 hrs
        int hrs = LocalTime.now().getHour() - startTime.getHour();
        if (hrs >= 2) throw new FeelingHungryException();
    }
}
class TestTrip {
    public static void main(String args[]) {
        Trip trip = new Trip();
```

FeelingHungry-Exception is a runtime exception

goTrekking throws FeelingHungry-Exception (without including it in the method signature)

```
        trip.goTrekking(LocalTime.of(11,24));
    }
}
```

> ← **Compiles successfully even though main neither handles nor declares FeelingHungryException**

Here's another example. Examine the following code, which throws a runtime exception (ArrayIndexOutOfBoundsException):

```
public class InvalidArrayAccess {
    public static void main(String args[]) {
        String[] students = {"Shreya", "Joseph"};
        System.out.println(students[5]);
        System.out.println("All seems to be well");
    }
}
```

> ← **students[5] tries to access nonexistent array position; exception thrown: ArrayIndexOutOfBoundsException**

The preceding code doesn't print output from System.out.println("All seems to be well"). The code execution halts with the exception thrown by the code that tries to output the value of students[5].

It's possible to create an exception handler for the exception ArrayIndexOutOfBoundsException thrown by the previous example code, as follows:

```
public class InvalidArrayAccess {
    public static void main(String args[]) {
        String[] students = {"Shreya", "Joseph"};
        try {
            System.out.println(students[5]);
        } catch (ArrayIndexOutOfBoundsException e){
            System.out.println("Exception");
        }
        System.out.println("All seems to be well");
    }
}
```

The output of the previous code is as follows:

```
Exception
All seems to be well
```

In the same way you can *catch* a checked exception, you can also catch a RuntimeException. On real projects, the preferred approach is to avoid runtime exceptions by including appropriate checks. For example, in the previous code, you can prevent ArrayIndexOutOfBoundsException from being thrown by using appropriate checks:

```
public class InvalidArrayAccess {
    public static void main(String args[]) {
        String[] students = {"Shreya", "Joseph"};
        int pos = 10;
        if (pos > 0 && pos < students.length)
            System.out.println(students[pos]);
    }
}
```

> ← **This line won't execute because pos is greater than length of array students**

### 7.4.4 Using a method that throws an error

Errors are serious exceptions thrown by the JVM, such as when it runs out of stack memory or can't find the definition of a class. You shouldn't define code to handle errors. You should instead let the JVM handle the errors.

In the remainder of this section, we'll look at some frequently asked questions on try-catch-finally blocks that often overwhelm certification aspirants.

### 7.4.5 Will a finally block execute even if the catch block defines a return statement?

Imagine the following scenario: a guy promises to buy diamonds for his girlfriend and treat her to coffee. The girl inquires about what will happen if he meets with an exceptional condition during the diamond purchase, such as inadequate funds. To the girl's disappointment, the boy replies that he'll still treat her to coffee.

You can compare the try block to the purchase of diamonds and the finally block to the coffee treat. The girl gets the coffee treat regardless of whether the boy successfully purchases the diamonds. Figure 7.13 shows this conversation.

**Figure 7.13   A little humor to help you remember that a finally block executes regardless of whether an exception is thrown**

It's interesting to note that a finally block will execute even if the code in the try block or any of the catch blocks defines a return statement. Examine the code in figure 7.14 and its output, and note when the class ReturnFromCatchBlock is unable to open file.txt.

As you can see from figure 7.14's code output, the flow of control doesn't return to the method main when the return statement executes in the catch handler of File-NotFoundException. It continues with the execution of the finally block before control is transferred back to the main method. Note that control isn't transferred to the println statement "Next task.. " that follows the try block because the return statement is encountered in the catch block, as mentioned previously.

```java
import java.io.*;
public class ReturnFromCatchBlock {
    public static void main(String args[]) {
        openFile();
    }
    private static void openFile() {
        FileInputStream fis = null;
        try {
            fis = new FileInputStream("file.txt");
        }
        catch (FileNotFoundException fnfe) {
            System.out.println("file not found");
            return;
        }
        finally {
            System.out.println("finally");
        }
        System.out.println("Next task..");
    }
}
```

The `return` statement does not return the control to the `main` method before execution of the `finally` block completes.

**Code output:**
file not found
finally

**Figure 7.14 The `finally` block executes even if an exception handler defines a `return` statement.**

Going back to the example of the guy and his girlfriend, a few tragic conditions, such as an earthquake or tornado, can cancel the coffee treat. Similarly, there are a few scenarios in Java in which a `finally` block does not execute:

- *Application termination*—The `try` or the `catch` block executes `System.exit`, which immediately terminates the application.
- *Fatal errors*—A crash of the JVM or the OS occurs.

In the exam, you may be questioned on the correct order of two or more exception handlers. Does order matter? See for yourself in section 7.4.9.

### 7.4.6 What happens if both a catch and a finally block define return statements?

In the previous section, you saw that the `finally` block executes even if a `catch` block defines a `return` statement. For a method that defines a `try-catch-finally` block, what is returned to the calling method if both `catch` and `finally` return a value?

Here's an example:

```java
class MultipleReturn {
    int getInt() {
        try {
            String[] students = {"Harry", "Paul"};
            System.out.println(students[5]);
        } catch (Exception e) {
            return 10;
        } finally {
            return 20;
        }
    }
```

- `System.out.println(students[5]);` — Throws ArrayIndexOutOfBoundsException
- `return 10;` — Returns value 10 from catch block
- `return 20;` — Returns value 20 from finally block

```
    public static void main(String args[]) {
        MultipleReturn var = new MultipleReturn();
        System.out.println(var.getInt());
    }
}
```

The output of the preceding code is

```
20
```

If both the catch and finally blocks define return statements, the calling method will receive a value from the finally block.

### 7.4.7 *What happens if a finally block modifies the value returned from a catch block?*

If a catch block returns a primitive data type, the finally block can't modify the value being returned by it. Here's an example:

```
class MultipleReturn {
    int getInt() {
        int returnVal = 10;
        try {
            String[] students = {"Harry", "Paul"};        ←  Throws
            System.out.println(students[5]);                  ArrayIndexOutOfBoundsException
        } catch (Exception e) {
            System.out.println("About to return :" + returnVal);  ←  Returns value 10
            return returnVal;                                         from catch block
        } finally {
            returnVal += 10;                                          ←
            System.out.println("Return value is now :" + returnVal);
        }
        return returnVal;                                      Modifies value
    }                                                          of variable to
    public static void main(String args[]) {                   be returned in
        MultipleReturn var = new MultipleReturn();             finally block
        System.out.println("In Main:" + var.getInt());
    }
}
```

The output of the preceding code is as follows:

```
About to return :10
Return value is now :20
In Main:10
```

Even though the finally block adds 10 to the variable returnVal, this modified value is not returned to the method main. Control in the catch block *copies* the value of returnVal to be returned before it executes the finally block, so the returned value is not modified when finally executes.

Will the preceding code behave in a similar manner if the method returns an object? See for yourself:

```
class MultipleReturn {
    StringBuilder getStringBuilder() {
        StringBuilder returnVal = new StringBuilder("10");
        try {
            String[] students = {"Harry", "Paul"};
            System.out.println(students[5]);
        } catch (Exception e) {
            System.out.println("About to return :" + returnVal);
            return returnVal;
        } finally {
            returnVal.append("10");
            System.out.println("Return value is now :" + returnVal);
        }
        return returnVal;
    }
    public static void main(String args[]) {
        MultipleReturn var = new MultipleReturn();
        System.out.println("In Main:" + var.getStringBuilder());
    }
}
```

**Returns StringBuilder object value from catch block**

**Throws ArrayIndexOutOfBoundsException**

**Modifies value of variable to be returned in finally block**

This is the output of the preceding code:

```
About to return :10
Return value is now :1010
In Main:1010
```

In this case, the catch block returns an object of the class StringBuilder. When the finally block executes, it can access the value of the object referred to by the variable returnVal and can modify it. The modified value is returned to the method main. Remember that primitives are passed by value and objects are passed by reference.

**EXAM TIP**   Watch out for code that returns a value from the catch block and modifies it in the finally block. If a catch block returns a primitive data type, the finally block can't modify the value being returned by it. If a catch block returns an object, the finally block can modify the state of the object being returned by it.

### 7.4.8   Can a try block be followed only by a finally block?

Syntactically, you can define a try block that might only be followed by a finally block:

```
class NoCatchOnlyFinally {
    public static void main(String args[]) {
        String name = null;
        try {
            System.out.println("Try block : open resource 1");
            System.out.println("Try block : open resource 2");
```

```
        System.out.println("in try : " + name.length());
        System.out.println("Try block : close resources");
    } finally {
        System.out.println("finally : close resources");
    }
}
}
```

Here's the output of the preceding code:

```
Try block : open resource 1
Try block : open resource 2
finally : close resources
Exception in thread "main" java.lang.NullPointerException
    at NoCatchOnlyFinally.main(NoCatchOnlyFinally.java:7)
```

Because `main()` in the preceding code throws an unchecked exception, `NullPointer-Exception`, it compiles successfully. But if the code enclosed within a `try` block declares to throw a checked exception, either it must be followed by a `catch` block, or the method in which it is defined must declare to throw it.

### 7.4.9 Does the order of the exceptions caught in the catch blocks matter?

Order doesn't matter for unrelated classes. But it does matter for related classes sharing an IS-A relationship because `catch` blocks are checked from the top down to find a suitable one to handle a given exception.

In the latter case, if you try to catch an exception of the base class before an exception of the derived class, your code will fail to compile. This behavior may seem bizarre, but there's a valid reason for it. As you know, an object of a derived class can be assigned to a variable of a base class. Similarly, if you try to catch an exception of a base class before its derived class, the exception handler for the derived class can never be reached, so the code will fail to compile.

Examine the code in figure 7.15, which has been modified by defining the `catch` block for `IOException` before the `catch` block for `FileNotFoundException`.

Figure 7.16 depicts an interesting way to remember that order matters. As you know, a thrown exception looks for an appropriate exception handler, starting with the first handler and working toward the last. Let's compare a thrown exception to a tiger and the exception handlers to doors that allow certain types of creatures to enter. Like a thrown exception, the tiger should start with the first door and move on to the rest of the doors until a match is found.

The tiger starts with the first door, which allows all animals to enter. Voilà! The tiger enters the first door and never reaches the second door, which is meant specifically for tigers. In Java, when such a condition arises, the Java compiler refuses to compile the code because the later exception handler code will never execute. Java doesn't compile code if it contains unreachable statements.

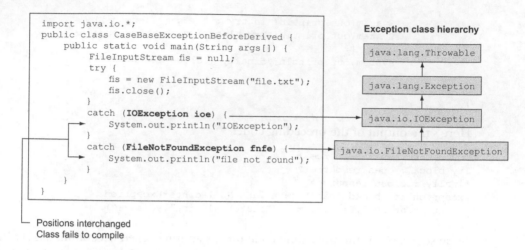

```
import java.io.*;
public class CaseBaseExceptionBeforeDerived {
    public static void main(String args[]) {
        FileInputStream fis = null;
        try {
            fis = new FileInputStream("file.txt");
            fis.close();
        }
        catch (IOException ioe) {
            System.out.println("IOException");
        }
        catch (FileNotFoundException fnfe) {
            System.out.println("file not found");
        }
    }
}
```

**Exception class hierarchy**

java.lang.Throwable

java.lang.Exception

java.io.IOException

java.io.FileNotFoundException

Positions interchanged
Class fails to compile

**Figure 7.15   The order of placement of exception handlers is important.**

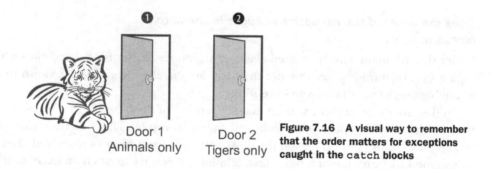

**❶**  Door 1
Animals only

**❷**  Door 2
Tigers only

**Figure 7.16   A visual way to remember that the order matters for exceptions caught in the `catch` blocks**

### RULES TO REMEMBER

Here are a few more rules you'll need to answer the questions in the OCA Java SE 8 Programmer I exam:

- A try block may be followed by multiple catch blocks, and the catch blocks may be followed by a single finally block.
- A try block may be followed by either a catch or a finally block or both. But a finally block alone won't suffice if code in the try block throws a checked exception. In this case, you need to catch the checked exception or declare it to be thrown by your method. Otherwise, your code won't compile.
- The try, catch, and finally blocks can't exist independently.
- The finally block can't appear before a catch block.
- A finally block always executes, regardless of whether the code throws an exception.

### 7.4.10　*Can I rethrow an exception or the error I catch?*

You can do whatever you want with an exception. Rethrow it, pass it on to a method, assign it to another variable, upload it to a server, send it in an SMS, and so on. Examine the following code:

```
import java.io.*;
public class ReThrowException {
    FileInputStream soccer;
    public void myMethod() {
        try {
            soccer = new FileInputStream("soccer.txt");
        } catch (FileNotFoundException fnfe) {
            throw fnfe;                              ◁─┐  Use throw keyword to
        }                                              │  throw exception caught
    }                                                  │  in exception handler
}
```

Oops! The previous code fails to compile, and you get the following compilation error message:

```
ReThrowException.java:9: unreported exception java.io.FileNotFoundException;
    must be caught or declared to be thrown
            throw fnfe;
            ^
```

When you rethrow a checked exception, it's treated like a regular thrown checked exception, meaning that all the rules of handling a checked exception apply to it. In the previous example, the code neither caught the rethrown `FileNotFoundException` exception nor declared that the method `myMethod` would throw it using the throw clause. Hence, the code failed to compile.

The following (modified) code declares that the method `myMethod` throws a File-NotFoundException, and it compiles successfully:

```
import java.io.*;                                      Throws
public class ReThrowException {            FileNotFoundException
    FileInputStream soccer;
    public void myMethod() throws FileNotFoundException {   ◁─
        try {
            soccer = new FileInputStream("soccer.txt");
        } catch (FileNotFoundException fnfe) {
            throw fnfe;                              ◁─┐  Exception
        }                                              │  rethrown
    }
}
```

Another interesting point to note is that the previous code doesn't apply to a `Runtime-Exception`. You can rethrow a runtime exception, but you're not required to catch it, nor must you modify your method signature to include the `throws` clause. The simple reason for this rule is that `RuntimeExceptions` aren't checked exceptions, and they may not be caught or declared to be thrown by your code (exception categories are discussed in detail in section 7.2).

### 7.4.11 Can I declare my methods to throw a checked exception instead of handling it?

If a method doesn't wish to handle the checked exceptions thrown by a method it calls, it can declare to *throw* these exceptions using the throws clause in its own method declaration. Examine the following example, in which the method myMethod doesn't include an exception handler; instead, it rethrows the IOException thrown by a constructor of the class FileInputStream using the throws clause in its declaration:

```
import java.io.*;
public class ReThrowException2 {
    public void myMethod() throws IOException {        ← myMethod throws
        FileInputStream soccer = new FileInputStream("soccer.txt");   checked exception
        soccer.close();
    }
}
```

Any method that calls myMethod must now either catch the exception IOException or declare that it will be rethrown in its method signature.

### 7.4.12 I can create nested loops, so can I create nested try-catch blocks too?

The simple answer is yes, you can define a try-catch-finally block within another try-catch-finally block. Theoretically, the levels of nesting for the try-catch-finally blocks have no limits.

In the following example, another set of try-catch blocks is defined in the try and finally blocks of the outer try block:

```
import java.io.*;
public class NestedTryCatch {
    FileInputStream players, coach;
    public void myMethod() {
        try {                                                    Outer try
            players = new FileInputStream("players.txt");        block
            try {                                                Inner try
                coach = new FileInputStream("coach.txt");        block
                //.. rest of the code
            } catch (FileNotFoundException e) {
                System.out.println("coach.txt not found");
            }
            //.. rest of the code
        }                                                        Outer
        catch (FileNotFoundException fnfe) {                     catch
            System.out.println("players.txt not found");         block
        }                                                        Outer finally
        finally {                                                block
```

```
        try {                          ←——  Another Inner
            players.close();                 try block
            coach.close();
        } catch (IOException ioe) {
            System.out.println(ioe);
        }
    }
  }
}
```

Now comes another Twist in the Tale exercise that'll test your understanding of the exceptions thrown and caught by nested try-catch blocks. In this one, an inner try block defines code that throws a NullPointerException. But the inner try block doesn't define an exception handler for this exception. Will the outer try block catch this exception? See for yourself (answer in the appendix).

**Twist in the Tale 7.2**

Given that players.txt exists on your system and that the assignment of players, shown in bold, doesn't throw any exceptions, what's the output of the following code?

```
import java.io.*;
public class TwistInTaleNestedTryCatch {
    static FileInputStream players, coach;
    public static void main(String args[]) {
        try {
            players = new FileInputStream("players.txt");
            System.out.println("players.txt found");
            try {
                coach.close();
            } catch (IOException e) {
                System.out.println("coach.txt not found");
            }
        } catch (FileNotFoundException fnfe) {
            System.out.println("players.txt not found");
        } catch (NullPointerException ne) {
            System.out.println("NullPointerException");
        }
    }
}
```

a  The code prints

```
players.txt found
NullPointerException
```

b  The code prints

```
players.txt found
coach.txt not found
```

c  The code throws a runtime exception.

d  The code fails to compile.

### 7.4.13  *Should I handle errors?*

Although you can define code to handle errors, you shouldn't. You should instead let the JVM handle the errors. The following example shows how it's possible to catch an error:

```java
public class CatchError {
    public static void main(String args[]) {
        try {
            myMethod();
        } catch (StackOverflowError s) {
            System.out.println(s);
        }
    }
    public static void myMethod() {
        System.out.println("myMethod");
        myMethod();
    }
}
```

> A class can catch and handle an error, but it shouldn't.

Though you shouldn't handle errors in your code, what happens if you do? Will the exception handler that handles the code execute? See for yourself by answering the question in the following Twist in the Tale exercise (answer in the appendix).

**Twist in the Tale 7.3**

Will the code in the error-handling block execute? What do you think is the output of the following code?

```java
public class TwistInTaleCatchError {
    public static void main(String args[]) {
        try {
            myMethod();
        } catch (StackOverflowError s) {
            for (int i=0; i<2; ++i)
                System.out.println(i);
        }
    }
    public static void myMethod() {
        myMethod();
    }
}
```

a   0

b   java.lang.StackOverFlowError

c   0
    1

d   0
    1
    2
    java.lang.StackOverFlowError

In the next section, you'll work with specific exception classes and errors that are on the exam.

## 7.5 *Common exception classes and categories*

[8.5] "Recognize common exception classes (such as NullPointerException, ArithmeticException, ArrayIndexOutOfBoundsException, ClassCastException)"

In this section, we'll take a look at common exception classes and categories of exceptions. You'll also learn about the scenarios in which these exceptions are thrown and how to handle them.

For this exam, you should be familiar with the scenarios that lead to these commonly thrown exception classes and categories and how to handle them. Table 7.2 lists common errors and exceptions. Although the exam specifically lists four runtime exceptions, you might see the other common exception and error classes on the exam.

**Table 7.2  Common errors and exceptions**

| Runtime exceptions | Errors |
|---|---|
| ArrayIndexOutOfBoundsException | ExceptionInInitializerError |
| IndexOutOfBoundsException | StackOverflowError |
| ClassCastException | NoClassDefFoundError |
| IllegalArgumentException | OutOfMemoryError |
| ArithmeticException | |
| NullPointerException | |
| NumberFormatException | |

The OCA Java SE 8 Programmer I exam objectives require that you understand which of the previously mentioned errors and exceptions are thrown by the JVM and which should be thrown programmatically. From the discussion of errors earlier in this chapter, you know that errors represent issues associated with the JRE, such as OutOfMemoryError. As a programmer, you *shouldn't* throw or catch these errors—leave them for the JVM. The definition of runtime exceptions notes that these are the kinds of exceptions that are thrown by the JVM, which shouldn't be thrown by you programmatically.

Let's review each of these in detail.

### 7.5.1   *ArrayIndexOutOfBoundsException and IndexOutOfBoundsException*

As shown in figure 7.17, `ArrayIndexOutOfBoundsException` and `IndexOutOfBounds-Exception` are runtime exceptions, which share an IS-A relationship. `IndexOutOfBoundsException` is subclassed by `ArrayIndexOutOfBoundsException`.

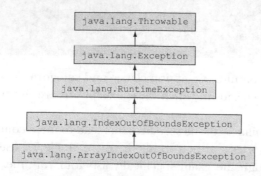

**Figure 7.17   Class hierarchy of `ArrayIndexOutOfBoundsException`**

An `ArrayIndexOutOfBoundsException` is thrown when a piece of code tries to access an array out of its bounds (either an array is accessed at a position less than 0 or at a position greater than or equal to its length). An `IndexOutOfBoundsException` is thrown when a piece of code tries to access a list, like an `ArrayList`, using an illegal index.

Assume that an array and list have been defined as follows:

```
String[] season = {"Spring", "Summer"};
ArrayList<String> exams = new ArrayList<>();
exams.add("SCJP");
exams.add("SCWCD");
```

The following lines of code will throw an `ArrayIndexOutOfBoundsException`:

```
System.out.println(season[5]);      ←——  Can't access position
                                          >= array length
System.out.println(season[-9]);     ←——  Can't access array at
                                          negative position
```

The following lines of code will throw an `IndexOutOfBoundsException`:

```
System.out.println(exams.get(-1));  ←——  Can't access list at
                                          negative position
System.out.println(exams.get(4));   ←——  Can't access list at
                                          position >= its size
```

Why do you think the JVM has taken the responsibility on itself to throw this exception? One of the main reasons is that this exception isn't known until runtime and depends on the array or list position that's being accessed by a piece of code. Most often, a variable is used to specify this array or list position, and its value may not be known until runtime.

> **NOTE** When you try to access an invalid array position, `ArrayIndexOutOf-BoundsException` is thrown. When you try to access an invalid `ArrayList` position, `IndexOutOfBoundsException` is thrown.

You can avoid these exceptions from being thrown if you check whether the index position you're trying to access is greater than or equal to 0 and less than the size of your array or `ArrayList`.

### 7.5.2 *ClassCastException*

Before I start discussing the example I'll use for this exception, take a quick look at figure 7.18 to review the class hierarchy of this exception.

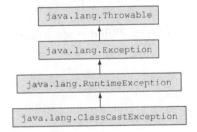

**Figure 7.18 Class hierarchy of** `ClassCastException`

Examine the code in the next listing, where the line of code that throws the `Class-CastException` is shown in bold.

**Listing 7.2 An example of code that throws `ClassCastException`**

```
import java.util.ArrayList;
public class ListAccess {
    public static void main(String args[]) {
        ArrayList<Ink> inks = new ArrayList<Ink>();
        inks.add(new ColorInk());
        inks.add(new BlackInk());
        Ink ink = (BlackInk)inks.get(0);           ⟵——— Throws
    }                                                      ClassCastException
}
class Ink{}
class ColorInk extends Ink{}
class BlackInk extends Ink{}
```

A `ClassCastException` is thrown when an object fails an IS-A test with the class type to which it's being cast. In the preceding example, class `Ink` is the base class for classes

ColorInk and BlackInk. The JVM throws a ClassCastException in the previous case because the code in bold tries to explicitly cast an object of ColorInk to BlackInk.

Note that this line of code avoided the compilation error because the variable inks defines an ArrayList of type Ink, which can store objects of type Ink and all its subclasses. The code then correctly adds the permitted objects: one each of BlackInk and ColorInk. If the code had defined an ArrayList of type BlackInk or ColorInk, the code would have failed the compilation, as follows:

```java
import java.util.ArrayList;
public class Invalid {
    public static void main(String args[]) {
        ArrayList<ColorInk> inks = new ArrayList<ColorInk>();
        inks.add(new ColorInk());
        Ink ink = (BlackInk)inks.get(0);        ⟵⎯┐ Compilation
    }                                                 │ issues
}
class Ink{}
class ColorInk extends Ink{}
class BlackInk extends Ink{}
```

Here's the compilation error thrown by the previously modified piece of code:

```
Invalid.java:6: inconvertible types
found   : ColorInk
required: BlackInk
        Ink ink = (BlackInk)inks.get(0);
                  ^
```

You can use the instanceof operator to verify whether an object can be cast to another class before casting it. Assuming that the definition of classes Ink, ColorInk, and BlackInk are the same as defined in the previous example, the following lines of code will avoid the ClassCastException:

```java
import java.util.ArrayList;
public class AvoidClassCastException {
    public static void main(String args[]) {
        ArrayList<Ink> inks = new ArrayList<Ink>();
        inks.add(new ColorInk());
        inks.add(new BlackInk());
        if (inks.get(0) instanceof BlackInk) {             No
            BlackInk ink = (BlackInk)inks.get(0);    ⟵⎯┐ ClassCastException
        }
    }
}
```

In the previous example, the condition (inks.get(0) instanceof BlackInk) evaluates to false, so the then part of the if statement doesn't execute.

In the following Twist in the Tale exercise, I'll introduce an interface used in the casting example in listing 7.2 (answer in the appendix).

**Twist in the Tale 7.4**

Let's introduce an interface used in listing 7.2 and see how it behaves. Following is the modified code. Examine the code and select the correct options:

```
class Ink{}
interface Printable {}
class ColorInk extends Ink implements Printable {}
class BlackInk extends Ink{}

class TwistInTaleCasting {
    public static void main(String args[]) {
        Printable printable = null;
        BlackInk blackInk = new BlackInk();
        printable = (Printable)blackInk;
    }
}
```

**a** `printable = (Printable)blackInk` will throw compilation error

**b** `printable = (Printable)blackInk` will throw runtime exception

**c** `printable = (Printable)blackInk` will throw checked exception

**d** The following line of code will fail to compile:

```
printable = blackInk;
```

### 7.5.3 *IllegalArgumentException*

As the name of this exception suggests, Illegal-ArgumentException is thrown to specify that a method has passed illegal or inappropriate arguments. Its class hierarchy is shown in figure 7.19.

Even though it's a runtime exception, programmers usually use this exception to validate the arguments that are passed to a method. The exception constructor is passed a descriptive message, specifying the exception details. Examine the following code:

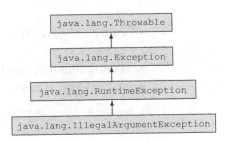

**Figure 7.19  Class hierarchy of IllegalArgumentException**

```
public void login(String username, String pwd, int maxLoginAttempt) {
    if (username == null || username.length() < 6)
        throw new IllegalArgumentException
                    ("Login:username can't be shorter than 6 chars");
    if (pwd == null || pwd.length() < 8)
        throw new IllegalArgumentException
                    ("Login: pwd cannot be shorter than 8 chars");
    if (maxLoginAttempt < 0)
        throw new IllegalArgumentException
                    ("Login: Invalid loginattempt val");
```

```
    //.. rest of the method code
}
```

The previous method validates the various method parameters passed to it and throws an appropriate IllegalArgumentException if they don't meet the requirements of the method. Each object of the IllegalArgumentException is passed a different String message that briefly describes it.

### 7.5.4   *NullPointerException*

The NullPointerException, shown in figure 7.20, is the quintessential exception.

I imagine that almost all Java programmers have had a taste of this exception, but let's look at an explanation for it.

This exception is thrown by the JVM if you try to access a non-static method or a variable through a null value. The exam can have interesting code combinations to test you on whether a particular piece of code will throw a NullPointerException. The key is to ensure that the reference variable has been assigned a non-null value. In particular, I'll address the following cases:

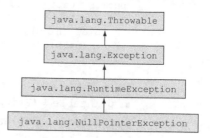

**Figure 7.20   Class hierarchy of NullPointerException**

- Accessing members of a reference variable that is explicitly assigned a null value
- Using an uninitialized local variable, which may *seem* to throw a NullPointer-Exception
- Attempting to access nonexistent array positions
- Using members of an array element that are assigned a null value

Let's get started with the first case, in which a variable is explicitly assigned a null value:

```
import java.util.ArrayList;
class ThrowNullPointerException {                          list is null
    static ArrayList<String> list = null;
    public static void main(String[] args) {
        list.add("1");                            Attempt to call method
    }                                             add on list throws
}                                                 NullPointerException
```

The preceding code tries to access the method add on the variable list, which has been assigned a null value. It throws an exception, as follows:

```
Exception in thread "main" java.lang.NullPointerException
    at ThrowNullPointerException.main(ThrowNullPointerException.java:5)
```

By default, the static and instance variables of a class are assigned a null value. In the previous example, the static variable list is assigned an explicit null value. To help you clarify the code and avoid any possible doubt, list is assigned an explicit null value. When the method main tries to execute the method add on the variable list, it calls a method on a null value. This call causes the JVM to throw a NullPointerException (which is a RuntimeException). If you define the variable list as an instance variable and don't assign an explicit value to it, you'll get the same result (NullPointerException being thrown at runtime). Because the static method main can't access the instance variable list, you'll need to create an object of the class ThrowNullPointerException to access it:

```
import java.util.ArrayList;
class ThrowNullPointerException {                          list is implicitly
    ArrayList<String> list;                                assigned a null value
    public static void main(String[] args) {
        ThrowNullPointerException obj = new ThrowNullPointerException();
        obj.list.add("1");                    Attempt to call method
    }                                         add on list throws
}                                             NullPointerException
```

You can prevent a NullPointerException from being thrown by checking whether an object is null before trying to access its member:

```
import java.util.ArrayList;
class ThrowNullPointerException {
    static ArrayList<String> list;
    public static void main(String[] args) {
        if (list!=null)                       Ascertain that
            list.add("1");                    list is not null
    }
}
```

What happens if you modify the previous code as follows? Will it still throw a NullPointerException?

```
import java.util.ArrayList;
class ThrowNullPointerException {
    public static void main(String[] args) {
        ArrayList<String> list;
        if (list!=null)
            list.add("1");          Fails to
    }                               compile
}
```

Interestingly, the previous code fails to compile. list is defined as a local variable inside the method main, and by default local variables aren't assigned a value—not even a null value. If you attempt to use an uninitialized local variable, your code will fail to compile. Watch out for similar questions in the exam.

Another set of conditions when code may throw the `NullPointerException` involves the use of arrays:

```
class ThrowAnotherNullPointerException {
    static String[] oldLaptops;
    public static void main(String[] args) {
        System.out.println(oldLaptops[1]);                    Throws
    }                                                         NullPointerException
}
```

In the preceding code, the static variable `oldLaptops` is assigned a `null` value by default. Its array elements are neither initialized nor assigned a value. The code that tries to access the array's second element throws a `NullPointerException`.

In the following code, two array elements of the variable `newLaptops` are initialized and assigned a default value of `null`. If you call the method `toString` on the second element of the variable `newLaptops`, it results in a `NullPointerException` being thrown:

```
class ThrowNullPointerException {
    public static void main(String[] args) {
        String[] newLaptops = new String[2];
        System.out.println(newLaptops[1].toString());    ①   Throws
    }                                                         NullPointerException
}
```

If you modify the code at ❶ as follows, it won't throw an exception—it'll print the value `null`. This is because the object-based `System.out.println()` overload calls the object-based `String.valueOf()` overload, which itself checks whether the object to "print" is `null`, in which case it will output `null` without calling any `toString()` method:

```
System.out.println(newLaptops[1]);        ◄————   No RuntimeException; prints "null"
```

**EXAM TIP**   In the exam, watch out for code that tries to use an uninitialized local variable. Because such variables aren't initialized with even a `null` value, you can't print their value using the `System.out.println` method. Such code *won't* compile.

Let's modify the previous code that uses the variable `oldLaptops` and check your understanding of `NullPointerExceptions`. Here's another Twist in the Tale hands-on exercise for you (answers in the appendix).

### Twist in the Tale 7.5

Let's check your understanding of the `NullPointerException`. Here's a code snippet. Examine the code and select the correct answers.

```
class TwistInTaleNullPointerException {
    public static void main(String[] args) {
        String[][] oldLaptops =
```

```
                { {"Dell", "Toshiba", "Vaio"}, null,
{"IBM"}, new String[10] };
        System.out.println(oldLaptops[0][0]);        // line 1
        System.out.println(oldLaptops[1]);           // line 2
        System.out.println(oldLaptops[3][6]);        // line 3
        System.out.println(oldLaptops[3][0].length()); // line 4
        System.out.println(oldLaptops);              // line 5
    }
}
```

**a**  Code on line 1 will throw `NullPointerException`

**b**  Code on lines 1 and 3 will throw `NullPointerException`

**c**  Only code on line 4 will throw `NullPointerException`

**d**  Code on lines 3 and 5 will throw `NullPointerException`

### 7.5.5  *ArithmeticException*

When the JVM encounters an exceptional mathematical condition, like dividing an integer by zero, it throws `ArithmeticException` (the class hierarchy shown in figure 7.21). Note that division by 0 is not the same as division by 0.0. In this section, we'll cover the results of division of integers and decimals by 0 and 0.0.

The following summarizes the cause of an `ArithmeticException`:

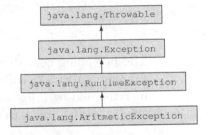

**Figure 7.21  Class hierarchy of `ArithmeticException`**

- A division will be performed as an integer division as long as only integers are involved.
  As soon as there's a floating-point number, then everything is computed in floating-point arithmetic (true for all arithmetic operations, by the way).
- An integer division by zero throws an `ArithmeticException`.
- A floating-point division by zero won't throw any exception but rather will return ±`Infinity` or `NaN`, depending on the first operand.

**DIVISION OF AN INTEGER VALUE BY 0**

Although it might seem simple to spot an occurrence of this exception, assumptions can be wrong. Let's start with a simple and explicit example (which is easy to spot):

```
class ThrowArithmeticEx {
    public static void main(String args[]) {
        System.out.println(77/0);         ← ⌐ Division
    }                                         by 0
}
```

On execution, the previous code will throw an `ArithmeticException` with a similar message:

```
Exception in thread "main" java.lang.ArithmeticException: / by zero
    at ThrowArithmeticEx.main(ThrowArithmeticEx.java:3)
```

Here's an example of comparatively complex code that you might see on the exam. Do you think it will throw an `ArithmeticException`? Also, do you think that the answer seems obvious like in the preceding code?

```java
class ThrowArithmeticEx {
    public static void main(String args[]) {
        int a = 10;
        int y = a++;
        int z = y--;

        int x1 = a - 2*y - z;
        int x2 = a - 11;
        int x = x1/ x2;

        System.out.println(x);
    }
}
```

The preceding code throws `ArithmeticException` for the operation x1/x2 because the value of x2 is 0. With the initialization of the variable y, the value of variable a is incremented by 1, from 10 to 11 (due to the post-fix increment operator). The variable x2 is initialized with a value that's equal to 11 and less than a, which is 0.

**EXAM TIP**   In the exam, watch out for division with integers. If the divisor is 0, the integer value that's being divided doesn't matter. Such an operation will throw an `ArithmeticException`.

What do you think would be the answer if you divide 0 by 0? What do you think is the output of the following code: 1, 0, or `ArithmeticException`?

```java
class ThrowArithmeticEx {
    public static void main(String args[]) {
        int x = (int)(7.3/10.6);
        int y = (int)(100.76/123.87);

        int z = x/y;

        System.out.println(x);
    }
}
```

Division of an integer number by 0 will result in an `ArithmeticException`. So the preceding code will also throw an `ArithmeticException`.

**EXAM TIP**   Division of a negative or positive integer value by 0 will result in an `ArithmeticException`.

Here's an explicit example of dividing 0 by 0:

```
System.out.println(0/0);                  ⟵———— Throws ArithmeticException
```

> **EXAM TIP**   Division of 0 by 0 results in an `ArithmeticException`.

#### DIVISION OF A DECIMAL VALUE BY 0

If you divide a positive decimal number by 0, the answer is `Infinity`:

```
class DivideDecimalNumberByZero {
    public static void main(String args[]) {
        System.out.println(77.0/0);            ⟵——⌐ Outputs
    }                                                │ Infinity
}
```

If you divide a negative decimal number by 0, the answer is `-Infinity`:

```
class DivideNegativeDecimalNumberByZero {
    public static void main(String args[]) {
        System.out.println(-77.0/0);           ⟵——⌐ Outputs
    }                                                │ -Infinity
}
```

> **EXAM TIP**   If you divide a positive decimal value by 0, the result is `Infinity`. If you divide a negative decimal value by 0, the result is `-Infinity`.

Here's an interesting question: what do you think is the result of division of 0.0 by 0? Here's a quick code snippet:

```
System.out.println(0.0/0);                ⟵———— Outputs NaN
```

> **EXAM TIP**   Division of 0.0 by 0 results in `NaN` (Not a Number).

Any mathematical operation with a `NaN` results in `NaN`.

#### DIVISION OF INTEGERS OR DECIMALS BY 0.0

Dividing by 0 and dividing by 0.0 don't give you the same results. Let's revisit the previous examples, starting with the modified version of the first example in this section:

```
class DivideIntegerByZeroPointZero {
    public static void main(String args[]) {
        System.out.println(77/0.0);            │ Outputs
        System.out.println(77.0/0.0);          │ Infinity
    }
}
```

The preceding code doesn't throw an `ArithmeticException`. It outputs `Infinity`.

> **EXAM TIP**   When a positive integer or decimal value is divided by 0.0, the result is `Infinity`.

Here's another modified example:

```
class DivideByZeroPointZero {
    public static void main(String args[]) {
        int a = 10;
        int y = a++;
        int z = y--;

        int x1 = a - 2*y - z;
        int x2 = a - 11;
        double x3 = x2;

        double x = x1/ x3;

        System.out.println(x);
        System.out.println(x1);
        System.out.println(x3);
    }
}
```

Here's the output of the preceding code:

```
-Infinity
-17
0.0
```

The preceding code doesn't throw an `ArithmeticException`. The variable x1 is assigned a negative integer value, that is, `-17`. The variable x2 is assigned the value `0`. When the variable x3 of type `double` is initialized with the value of x2, it's promoted to a `double` value, assigning `0.0` to x3. When a negative integer value is divided by 0.0, the result is `-Infinity`.

**EXAM TIP** When a negative integer or decimal value is divided by 0.0, the result is `-Infinity`.

### 7.5.6 *NumberFormatException*

What happens if you try to convert "87" and "9m#" to numeric values? The former value is OK, but you can't convert the latter value to a numeric value unless it's an encoded value, straight from a James Bond movie, that can be converted to anything.

As shown in figure 7.22, `NumberFormat-Exception` is a runtime exception. It's thrown to indicate that the application tried to convert a string (with an inappropriate format) to one of the numeric types.

Multiple classes in the Java API define parsing methods. One of the most frequently used

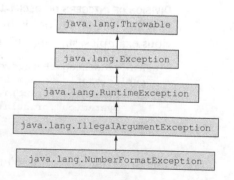

**Figure 7.22 Class hierarchy of `NumberFormatException`**

methods is parseInt from the class Integer. It's used to parse a String argument as a signed (negative or positive) decimal integer. Here are some examples:

Valid String values that can be converted to numeric values

```
System.out.println(Integer.parseInt("-123"));
System.out.println(Integer.parseInt("123"));
System.out.println(Integer.parseInt("+123"));
System.out.println(Integer.parseInt("123_45"));
System.out.println(Integer.parseInt("12ABCD"));
```

**Will throw NumberFormatException. Use of underscores in string values isn't allowed.**

**Will throw NumberFormatException. Characters ABCD can't be converted to integers in base 10.**

Starting in Java 7, you can use underscores (_) in numeric literal values. But you can't use them in String values passed to the method parseInt. The letters ABCD aren't used in the decimal number system, but they can be used in the hexadecimal number system, so you can convert the hexadecimal literal value "12ABCD" to the decimal number system by specifying the base of the number system as 16:

```
System.out.println(Integer.parseInt("123ABCD", 16));     ◄────── Prints 19114957
```

Note that the argument 16 is passed to the method parseInt, not to the method println. The following will not compile:

```
System.out.println(Integer.parseInt("123ABCD"), 16);     ◄────── Won't compile
```

You may throw NumberFormatException from your own method to indicate that there's an issue with the conversion of a String value to a specified numeric format (decimal, octal, hexadecimal, binary), and you can add a customized exception message. One of the most common candidates for this exception is methods that are used to convert a command-line argument (accepted as a String value) to a numeric value. Please note that all command-line arguments are accepted in a String array as String values.

The following is an example of code that throws a NumberFormatException programmatically:

```
public class ThrowNumberFormatException {
    public static int convertToNum(String val) {
        int num = 0;
        try {
            num = Integer.parseInt(val, 16);
        } catch (NumberFormatException e) {
            throw new NumberFormatException(val+
                " cannot be converted to hexadecimal number");
        }
        return num;
    }
```

**In the exception handler, creates and throws new NumberFormatException with a custom message**

```
public static void main(String args[]) {
    System.out.println(convertToNum("16b"));
    System.out.println(convertToNum("65v"));
}
}
```

The conversion of the hexadecimal literal 16b to the decimal number system is successful. But the conversion of the hexadecimal literal 65v to the decimal number system fails, and the previous code will give the following output:

```
363
Exception in thread "main" java.lang.NumberFormatException: 65v cannot be
    converted to hexadecimal number
    at
    ThrowNumberFormatException.convertToNum(ThrowNumberFormatException.java:8)
    at ThrowNumberFormatException.main(ThrowNumberFormatException.java:14)
```

Now let's take a look at some of the common errors that are covered on this exam.

### 7.5.7  *ExceptionInInitializerError*

The `ExceptionInInitializerError` error is typically thrown by the JVM when a static initializer in your code throws any type of `RuntimeException`. Figure 7.23 shows the class hierarchy of `ExceptionInInitializer-Error`.

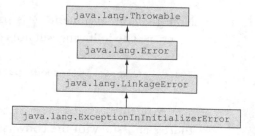

**Figure 7.23  Class hierarchy of ExceptionInInitializerError**

A static initializer block is defined using the keyword `static`, followed by curly braces, in a class. This block is defined within a class but not within a method. It's usually used to execute code when a class loads for the first time. Runtime exceptions arising from any of the following will throw this error:

- Execution of an anonymous `static` block
- Initialization of a `static` variable
- Execution of a `static` method (called from either of the previous two items)

The static initializer block of the class defined in the following example will throw a `NumberFormatException`, and when the JVM tries to load this class, it'll throw an `ExceptionInInitializerError`:

```
public class DemoExceptionInInitializerError {
    static {
        int num = Integer.parseInt("sd", 16);
    }
}
```

Following is the error message when the JVM tries to load the class DemoExceptionIn-InitializerError:

```
java.lang.ExceptionInInitializerError
Caused by: java.lang.NumberFormatException: For input string: "sd"
    at
    java.lang.NumberFormatException.forInputString(NumberFormatException.jav
    a:48)
    at java.lang.Integer.parseInt(Integer.java:447)
    at
    DemoExceptionInInitializerError.<clinit>(DemoExceptionInInitializerError
    .java:3)
```

 **EXAM TIP** Beware of code that seems to be simple in the OCA Java SE 8 Programmer I exam. The class DemoExceptionInInitializerError (mentioned previously) seems deceptively simple, but it's a good candidate for an exam question. As you know, this class throws the error ExceptionInInitializerError when the JVM tries to load it.

In the following example, initialization of a static variable results in a NullPointerException being thrown. When this class is loaded by the JVM, it throws an ExceptionInInitializerError:

```
public class DemoExceptionInInitializerError1 {
    static String name = null;
    static int nameLength = name.length();
}
```

The error message when the JVM tries to load the DemoExceptionInInitializerError1 class is as follows:

```
java.lang.ExceptionInInitializerError
Caused by: java.lang.NullPointerException
    at
    DemoExceptionInInitializerError1.<clinit>(DemoExceptionInInitializerErro
    r1.java:3)
Exception in thread "main"
```

Now let's move on to the exception thrown by a static method, which may be called by the static initializer block or to initialize a static variable. Examine the following code, in which MyException is a user-defined RuntimeException:

```
public class DemoExceptionInInitializerError2 {
    static String name = getName();
    static String getName() {
        throw new MyException();          ◄——  MyException is a
    }                                           runtime exception.
}
class MyException extends RuntimeException{}
```

This is the error thrown by the class `DemoExceptionInInitializerError2`:

```
java.lang.ExceptionInInitializerError
Caused by: MyException
    at
    DemoExceptionInInitializerError2.getName(DemoExceptionInInitializerError
    2.java:4)
    at
    DemoExceptionInInitializerError2.<clinit>(DemoExceptionInInitializerErro
    r2.java:2)
```

Did you notice that the error `ExceptionInInitializerError` can be caused only by a runtime exception? This happens for valid reasons, of course.

If a static initializer block throws an error, it doesn't recover from it to come back to the code to throw an `ExceptionInInitializerError`. This error can't be thrown if a static initializer block throws an object of a checked exception because the Java compiler is intelligent enough to determine this condition and doesn't allow you to throw an unhandled checked exception from a static initialization block.

**EXAM TIP** `ExceptionInInitializerError` can be caused by an object of `RuntimeException` only. It can't occur as the result of an error or checked exception thrown by the static initialization block.

### 7.5.8   *StackOverflowError*

The `StackOverflowError` error extends `Virtual-MachineError` (as shown in figure 7.24). As its name suggests, you should leave it to be managed by the JVM.

This error is thrown by the JVM when a Java program calls itself so many times that the memory stack allocated to execute the Java program "overflows" (*overflows* means that the stack exceeds a certain size). Examine the following code, in which a method calls itself recursively without an exit condition:

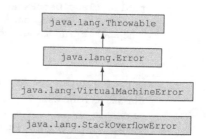

**Figure 7.24   Class hierarchy of `StackOverflowError`**

```
public class DemoStackOverflowError{
    static void recursion() {
        recursion();
    }
    public static void main(String args[]) {
        recursion();
    }
}
```

**Calls itself recursively, without exit condition**

The following error is thrown by the previous code:

```
Exception in thread "main" java.lang.StackOverflowError
    at DemoStackOverflowError.recursion(DemoStackOverflowError.java:3)
```

### 7.5.9    *NoClassDefFoundError*

What would happen if you failed to set your class-path and, as a result, the JVM was unable to load the class that you wanted to access or execute? Or what would happen if you tried to run your application before compiling it (and so no .class file would be found for the class you were trying to use)? In both these conditions, the JVM would throw a `NoClassDefFoundError` (the class hierarchy shown in figure 7.25).

This is what the Java API documentation says about this error:

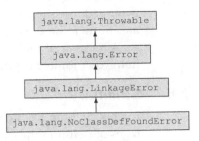

**Figure 7.25    Class hierarchy of `NoClassDefFoundError`**

> *Thrown if the Java Virtual Machine or a* `ClassLoader` *instance tries to load in the definition of a class (as part of a normal method call or as part of creating a new instance using the* new *expression) and no definition of the class could be found.*[1]

Because this particular error isn't a coding issue, I don't have a coding example for you. As you can see from the error hierarchy diagram in figure 7.25, this is a linkage error arising from a missing class file definition at runtime. Like every system error, this error shouldn't be handled by the code and should be left to be handled exclusively by the JVM.

> **NOTE**    Don't confuse the exception thrown by `Class.forName()`, used to load the class, and `NoClassDefFoundError`, thrown by the JVM. `Class.for-Name()` throws `ClassNotFoundException`.

### 7.5.10    *OutOfMemoryError*

What happens if you create and use a *lot* of objects in your application—for example, if you load a large chunk of persistent data to be processed by your application? In such a case, the JVM may run out of memory *on the heap*, and the garbage collector may not be able to free more memory for the JVM. In this case, the JVM is unable to create any more objects on the heap. An `OutOfMemoryError` will be thrown (the class hierarchy shown in figure 7.26).

You'll always work with a finite heap size, no matter what platform you work on, so you can't create

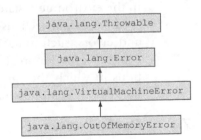

**Figure 7.26    Class hierarchy of `OutOfMemoryError`**

---

[1]  The `NoClassDefFoundError` documentation can be found in the Javadoc: http://docs.oracle.com/javase/8/docs/api/java/lang/NoClassDefFoundError.html.

and use an unlimited number of objects in your application. To get around this error, you need to either limit the number of resources or objects that your application creates or increase the heap size on the platform you're working with.

A number of tools are available (which are beyond the scope of this book) that can help you monitor the number of objects created in your application.

## 7.6    Summary

In this chapter, we discussed the need for exception handling, as well as the advantages of defining the exception-handling code separately from the program logic. You saw how this approach helps separate concerns about defining the regular program logic and exception-handling code. We also looked at the code syntax, specifically try-catch-finally blocks, for implementing exception-handling code. Code that throws an exception should be enclosed within a try block that's immediately followed by a catch and/or a finally block. A try block can be followed by multiple catch blocks but only a single finally block. A finally block can't be placed before a try block. A try block must be followed by at least one catch or finally block. The try, catch, and finally blocks can't exist independently.

Next, we delved into the different categories of exceptions: checked exceptions, runtime or unchecked exceptions, and errors. Checked exceptions are subclasses of the class java.lang.Exception. Unchecked exceptions are subclasses of the class java.lang.RuntimeException, which itself is a subclass of the class java.lang.Exception. Errors are subclasses of java.lang.Error. All of these exceptions are subclasses of java.lang.Throwable.

A checked exception is an unacceptable condition foreseen by the author of a method but outside the immediate control of the code. A runtime exception represents a programming error—these occur because of inappropriate use of another piece of code. Errors are serious exceptions, thrown by the JVM, as a result of an error in the environment state that processes your code.

In the final sections of this chapter, we covered commonly occurring exceptions and errors, such as NullPointerException, IllegalArgumentException, StackOverflowError, and more. For each of these errors and exceptions, I explained the conditions in which they may be thrown in code and whether they should be explicitly handled in exception handlers.

## 7.7    Review notes

This section lists the main points of all the sections covered in this chapter.

Why handle exceptions separately:

- Handling exceptions separately enables you to define the main logic of your code together.
- Without the use of separate exception handlers, the main logic of your code would be lost in combating the exceptional conditions. (See figure 7.5 for an example.)

- Exception handlers separate the concerns of defining regular program logic from exception-handling code.
- Exceptions help pinpoint the offending code, together with the method in which it's defined, by providing a stack trace of the exception or error.
- The JVM may send the stack trace of an unhandled exception to the Java console.

Categories of exceptions:

- Exceptions are divided into three categories: checked exceptions, runtime (or unchecked exceptions), and errors. These three categories share IS-A relationships (inheritance).
- Subclasses of the class java.lang.RuntimeException are categorized as runtime exceptions.
- Subclasses of the class java.lang.Error are categorized as errors.
- Subclasses of the class java.lang.Exception are categorized as checked exceptions if they're not subclasses of the class java.lang.RuntimeException.
- The class java.lang.RuntimeException is a subclass of the class java.lang.Exception.
- The class java.lang.Exception is a subclass of the class java.lang.Throwable.
- The class java.lang.Error is also a subclass of the class java.lang.Throwable.
- The class java.lang.Throwable inherits the class java.lang.Object.

Checked exceptions:

- A checked exception is an unacceptable condition foreseen by the author of a method but outside the immediate control of the code.
- A checked exception is a subclass of the java.lang.Exception class but not a subclass of java.lang.RuntimeException. It's interesting to note, however, that the class java.lang.RuntimeException itself is a subclass of the class java.lang.Exception.
- If a method calls another method that may throw a checked exception, either it must be enclosed within a try-catch block, or the method should declare this exception to be thrown in its method signature.

Runtime exceptions:

- Runtime exceptions represent programming errors. These occur from inappropriate use of another piece of code. For example, NullPointerException is a runtime exception that occurs when a piece of code tries to execute some code on a variable that hasn't been assigned an object and points to null. Another example is ArrayIndexOutOfBoundsException, which is thrown when a piece of code tries to access an array of list elements at a nonexistent position.
- A runtime exception is a subclass of java.lang.RuntimeException.

- A runtime exception might not be a part of the method signature, even if a method may throw it.
- A runtime exception may not necessarily be caught by a try-catch block.

Errors:

- An error is a serious exception, thrown by the JVM as a result of an error in the environment state, which processes your code. For example, NoClassDefFound-Error is an error thrown by the JVM when it's unable to locate the .class file it's supposed to run.
- StackOverflowError is another error, thrown by the JVM when the size of the memory required by the stack of the Java program is greater than what the JRE has offered for the Java application. This error usually occurs as a result of infinite or highly nested loops.
- An error is a subclass of the class java.lang.Error.
- An error need not be a part of a method signature.
- Although you can handle errors syntactically, there's little that you can do when these errors occur. Usually, ordinary programs aren't expected to recover from errors.

Creating a method that throws an exception:

- A method uses a throw statement to throw an exception or error.
- A method uses a throws clause in its signature to declare that it might throw an exception.
- A method can have multiple comma-separated class names of exceptions in its throws clause. Including runtime exceptions or errors in the method declaration isn't required.
- Syntactically, you don't always need a combination of throw and throws statements to create a method that throws an exception (checked or unchecked). You can replace the throw statement with a method that throws an exception.
- To use a method that throws a checked exception, you must do one of the following:
  - *Handle the exception*—Enclose the code within a try block and catch the thrown exception.
  - *Declare it to be thrown*—Declare the exception to be thrown by using the throws clause.
  - *Handle and declare*—Implement both of the preceding options together.
- While creating a method that throws a runtime exception or error, including the exception or error name in the throws clause isn't required.
- A method that throws a runtime exception or error isn't subject to the handle-or-declare rule.

- A method can declare to throw all types of exceptions, even if it doesn't. But a `try` block can't define a `catch` block for a checked exception (other than `Exception`) if the `try` block doesn't throw that checked exception or use a method that declares to throw that checked exception.

What happens when an exception is thrown:

- An exception is an object of the class `java.lang.Throwable`.
- When a piece of code hits an obstacle in the form of an exceptional condition, it creates an object of subclass `java.lang.Throwable`, initializes it with the necessary information (such as its type and optionally a textual description and the offending program's state), and hands it over to the JVM.
- Enclose the code that may throw an exception within a `try` block.
- Define `catch` blocks to include alternative code to execute when an exceptional condition arises.
- A `try` block can be followed by one or more `catch` blocks.
- The `catch` blocks must be followed by zero or one `finally` block.
- The `finally` block executes regardless of whether the code in the `try` block throws an exception.
- The order in which the `catch` blocks are placed matters. If the caught exceptions have an inheritance relationship, the base class exceptions can't be caught before the derived class exceptions. An attempt to do this will result in compilation failure.
- A `finally` block will execute even if a `try` or `catch` block defines a `return` statement.
- If both `catch` and `finally` blocks define `return` statements, the calling method will receive the value from the `finally` block.
- If a `catch` block returns a primitive data type, a `finally` block can't modify the value being returned by it.
- If a `catch` block returns an object, a `finally` block can modify the value being returned by it.
- A `finally` block alone won't suffice with a `try` block if code in the `try` block throws a checked exception. In this case, you'll need to catch the checked exception or define in the method signature that the exception is thrown, or your code won't compile.
- None of the `try`, `catch`, and `finally` blocks can exist independently.
- The `finally` block can't appear before a `catch` block.
- You can rethrow an error that you *catch* in an exception handler.
- You can either handle an exception or declare it to be thrown by your method. In the latter case, you need not handle the exception in your code. This applies to checked exceptions.
- You can create nested exception handlers.

- A try, catch, or finally block can define another try-catch-finally block. Theoretically, there's no limit on the allowed level of nesting of try-catch-finally blocks.

Commonly occurring exceptions, categories, and classes:

- In typical programming conditions, the ArrayIndexOutOfBoundsException shouldn't be thrown programmatically.

- One of the main reasons for the JVM taking the responsibility on itself for throwing this exception is that this exception isn't known until runtime and depends on the array or list position that's being accessed by a piece of code. Most often, a variable is used to specify this array or list position, and its value may not be known until runtime.

- ClassCastException is a runtime exception. java.lang.ClassCastException extends java.lang.RuntimeException.

- ClassCastException is thrown when an object fails an IS-A test with the class type it is being cast to.

- You can use the operator instanceof to verify whether an object can be cast to another class before casting it.

- IllegalArgumentException is a runtime exception. java.lang.Illegal-ArgumentException extends java.lang.RuntimeException.

- An IllegalArgumentException is thrown to specify that a method has been passed illegal or inappropriate arguments.

- Even though IllegalArgumentException is a runtime exception, programmers usually use this exception to validate the arguments that are passed to a method, and the exception constructor is passed a descriptive message specifying the exception details.

- As a programmer, you can throw an IllegalStateException to signal to the calling method that the method that's being requested for execution isn't ready to start its execution or is in a state in which it can't execute.

- NullPointerException is a runtime exception. The class java.lang.Null-PointerException extends java.lang.RuntimeException.

- A NullPointerException is thrown by the JVM if you try to access a method or variable of an uninitialized reference variable.

- When the JVM encounters an exceptional mathematical condition, like dividing a number by zero, it throws an ArithmeticException.

- In division with integers, if the divisor is 0, the integer value that's being divided doesn't matter. Such an operation will throw an ArithmeticException.

- Division of a negative or positive integer value by 0 will result in an Arithmetic-Exception.

- Division of 0 by 0 results in an ArithmeticException.

- If you divide a positive decimal value by 0, the result is Infinity. If you divide a negative decimal value by 0, the result is -Infinity.

- Division of 0.0 by 0 results in `NaN` (Not a Number).
- When a positive integer or decimal value is divided by 0.0, the result is `Infinity`.
- When a negative integer or decimal value is divided by 0.0, the result is `-Infinity`.
- `NumberFormatException` is a runtime exception. `java.lang.NumberFormat-Exception` extends `java.lang.IllegalArgumentException`. `java.lang.Illegal-ArgumentException` extends `java.lang.RuntimeException`.
- You can throw a `NumberFormatException` from your own method to indicate that there's an issue with the conversion of a `String` value to a specified numeric format (decimal, octal, hexadecimal, or binary).
- Runtime exceptions arising from any of the following may throw an `Exception-InInitializerError`:
  - Execution of an anonymous `static` block
  - Initialization of a `static` variable
  - Execution of a `static` method (called from either of the previous two items)
- The error `ExceptionInInitializerError` can be thrown only by an object of a runtime exception.
- `ExceptionInInitializerError` can't be thrown if a `static` initializer block throws an object of a checked exception, because the Java compiler is intelligent enough to determine this condition, and it doesn't allow you to throw an unhandled checked exception from a `static` initialization block.
- `StackOverflowError` is an error. `java.lang.StackOverflowError` extends `java.lang.VirtualMachineError`.
- Because `StackOverflowError` extends `VirtualMachineError`, it should be left to be managed by the JVM.
- The `StackOverflowError` error is thrown by the JVM when a Java program calls itself so many times that the memory stack allocated to execute the Java program "overflows."
- `NoClassDefFoundError` is an `Error`. `java.lang.NoClassDefFoundError` extends `java.lang.LinkageError`. `java.lang.LinkageError` extends `java.lang.Error`.
- A `NoClassDefFoundError` is thrown by the JVM or a `ClassLoader` when it's unable to load the definition of a class required to create an object of the class.
- Don't confuse the exception thrown by `Class.forName()`, used to load the class, and `NoClassDefFoundError`, thrown by the JVM. `Class.forName()` throws a `ClassNotFoundException`.
- An `OutOfMemoryError` is thrown by the JVM when it's unable to create objects on the heap and the garbage collector may not be able to free more memory for the JVM.

## 7.8    Sample exam questions

**Q7-1.** What is the output of the following code:

```
class Course {
    String courseName;
    Course() {
        Course c = new Course();
        c.courseName = "Oracle";
    }
}
class EJavaGuruPrivate {
    public static void main(String args[]) {
        Course c = new Course();
        c.courseName = "Java";
        System.out.println(c.courseName);
    }
}
```

   **a**  The code will print `Java`.

   **b**  The code will print `Oracle`.

   **c**  The code will not compile.

   **d**  The code will throw an exception or an error at runtime.

**Q7-2.** Select the correct option(s):

   **a**  You cannot handle runtime exceptions.

   **b**  You should not handle errors.

   **c**  If a method throws a checked exception, it must be either handled by the method or specified in its `throws` clause.

   **d**  If a method throws a runtime exception, it may include the exception in its `throws` clause.

   **e**  Runtime exceptions are checked exceptions.

**Q7-3.** Examine the following code and select the correct option(s):

```
class EJavaGuruExcep {
    public static void main(String args[]) {
        EJavaGuruExcep var = new EJavaGuruExcep();
        var.printArrValues(args);
    }
    void printArrValues(String[] arr) {
        try {
            System.out.println(arr[0] + ":" + arr[1]);
        } catch (NullPointerException e) {
            System.out.println("NullPointerException");
        } catch (IndexOutOfBoundsException e) {
            System.out.println("IndexOutOfBoundsException");
        } catch (ArrayIndexOutOfBoundsException e) {
            System.out.println("ArrayIndexOutOfBoundsException");
```

```
        }
      }
  }
```

**a** If the class EJavaGuruExcep is executed using the following command, it prints NullPointerException:

```
java EJavaGuruExcep
```

**b** If the class EJavaGuruExcep is executed using the following command, it prints IndexOutOfBoundsException:

```
java EJavaGuruExcep
```

**c** If the class EJavaGuruExcep is executed using the following command, it prints ArrayIndexOutOfBoundsException:

```
java EJavaGuruExcep one
```

**d** The code will fail to compile.

**Q7-4.** What is the output of the following code?

```
class EJava {
    void method() {
        try {
            guru();
            return;
        } finally {
            System.out.println("finally 1");
        }
    }
    void guru() {
        System.out.println("guru");
        throw new StackOverflowError();
    }
    public static void main(String args[]) {
        EJava var = new EJava();
        var.method();
    }
}
```

**a** guru
finally 1

**b** guru
finally 1
Exception in thread "main" java.lang.StackOverflowError

**c** guru
Exception in thread "main" java.lang.StackOverflowError

**d** guru

**e** The code fails to compile.

**Q 7-5.** What is the output of the following code?

```
class Quest5 {
    public static void main(String args[]) {
        int arr[] = new int[5];
        arr = new int[]{1,2,3,4};

        int x = arr[1]-- + arr[0]-- /arr[0] * arr[4];
        System.out.println(x);
    }
}
```

   **a**  The code outputs a value.

   **b**  The code outputs a value followed by an exception.

   **c**  `ArithmeticException`

   **d**  `NullPointerException`

   **e**  `IndexOutOfBoundsException`

   **f**  `ArrayIndexOutOfBoundsException`

   **g**  Compilation error

   **h**  None of the above

**Q7-6.** Which of the following methods will not compile?

   **a**
```
private void method1(String name) {
    if (name.equals("star"))
        throw new IllegalArgumentException(name);
}
```

   **b**
```
private void method2(int age) {
    if (age > 30)
        throw Exception();
}
```

   **c**
```
public Object method3(boolean accept) {
    if (accept)
        throw new StackOverflowError();
    else
        return new StackOverflowError();
}
```

   **d**
```
protected double method4() throws Exception {
    throw new Throwable();
}
```

   **e**
```
public double method5() throws Exception {
    return 0.7;
}
```

**Q7-7.** What is the output of the following code?

```
class TryFinally {
    int tryAgain() {
        int a = 10;
        try {
            ++a;
```

```
        } finally {
            a++;
        }
        return a;
    }
    public static void main(String args[]) {
        System.out.println(new TryFinally().tryAgain());
    }
}
```

a 10

b 11

c 12

d Compilation error

e Runtime exception

**Q7-8.** What is the output of the following code?

```
class EJavaBase {
    void myMethod() throws ExceptionInInitializerError {
        System.out.println("Base");
    }
}
class EJavaDerived extends EJavaBase {
    void myMethod() throws RuntimeException {
        System.out.println("Derived");
    }
}
class EJava3 {
    public static void main(String args[]) {
        EJavaBase obj = new EJavaDerived();
        obj.myMethod();
    }
}
```

a Base

b Derived

c Derived
Base

d Base
Derived

e Compilation error

**Q7-9.** Which of the following statements are true?

a A user-defined class may not throw an `IllegalStateException`. It must be thrown only by Java API classes.

b `System.out.println` will throw a `NullPointerException` if an uninitialized instance variable of type `String` is passed to it to print its value.

  c   NumberFormatException is thrown by multiple methods from the Java API when invalid numbers are passed on as Strings to be converted to the specified number format.

  d   ExceptionInInitializerError may be thrown by the JVM when a static initializer in your code throws a NullPointerException.

**Q7-10.** What is the output of the following code?

```java
class EJava {
    void foo() {
        try {
            String s = null;
            System.out.println("1");
            try {
                System.out.println(s.length());
            } catch (NullPointerException e) {
                System.out.println("inner");
            }
            System.out.println("2");
        } catch (NullPointerException e) {
            System.out.println("outer");
        }
    }
    public static void main(String args[]) {
        EJava obj = new EJava();
        obj.foo();
    }
}
```

  a   1
       inner
       2
       outer

  b   1
       outer

  c   1
       inner

  d   1
       inner
       2

## 7.9    *Answers to sample exam questions*

**Q7-1.** What is the output of the following code:

```java
class Course {
    String courseName;
    Course() {
        Course c = new Course();
        c.courseName = "Oracle";
    }
}
```

```
class EJavaGuruPrivate {
    public static void main(String args[]) {
        Course c = new Course();
        c.courseName = "Java";
        System.out.println(c.courseName);
    }
}
```

  a  The code will print `Java`.

  b  The code will print `Oracle`.

  c  The code will not compile.

  d  **The code will throw an exception or an error at runtime.**

Answer: d

Explanation: This class will throw a `StackOverflowError` at runtime. The easiest way to look for a `StackOverflowError` is to locate recursive method calls. In the question's code, the constructor of the class `Course` creates an object of the class `Course`, which will call the constructor again. Hence, this becomes a recursive call and ends up throwing a `StackOverflowError` at runtime. (As you know, an exception or an error can be thrown only at runtime, not compile time.)

**Q7-2.** Select the correct option(s):

  a  You cannot handle runtime exceptions.

  b  **You should not handle errors.**

  c  **If a method throws a checked exception, it must be either handled by the method or specified in its `throws` clause.**

  d  **If a method throws a runtime exception, it may include the exception in its `throws` clause.**

  e  Runtime exceptions are checked exceptions.

Answer: b, c, d

Explanation: Option (a) is incorrect. You can handle runtime exceptions the way you can handle a checked exception in your code: using a `try-catch` block.

    Option (b) is correct. You shouldn't try to handle errors in your code. Or, to put it another way, you can't do much when an error is thrown by your code. Instead of trying to handle errors in your code, you should resolve the code that results in these errors. For example, `StackOverflowError` is an error that will be thrown by your code if your code executes a method recursively without any exit condition. This repetition will consume all the space on the stack and result in a `StackOverflowError`.

    Option (c) is correct. If you fail to implement either of these options, your code won't compile.

    Option (d) is correct. It isn't mandatory for runtime exceptions to be included in a method's `throws` clause. Usually this inclusion is unnecessary, but if you do include it, your code will execute without any issues.

Option (e) is incorrect. A runtime exception and all its subclasses are *not* checked exceptions.

**Q7-3.** Examine the following code and select the correct option(s):

```
class EJavaGuruExcep {
    public static void main(String args[]) {
        EJavaGuruExcep var = new EJavaGuruExcep();
        var.printArrValues(args);
    }
    void printArrValues(String[] arr) {
        try {
            System.out.println(arr[0] + ":" + arr[1]);
        } catch (NullPointerException e) {
            System.out.println("NullPointerException");
        } catch (IndexOutOfBoundsException e) {
            System.out.println("IndexOutOfBoundsException");
        } catch (ArrayIndexOutOfBoundsException e) {
            System.out.println("ArrayIndexOutOfBoundsException");
        }
    }
}
```

a  If the class EJavaGuruExcep is executed using the following command, it prints NullPointerException:

   `java EJavaGuruExcep`

b  If the class EJavaGuruExcep is executed using the following command, it prints IndexOutOfBoundsException:

   `java EJavaGuruExcep`

c  If the class EJavaGuruExcep is executed using the following command, it prints ArrayIndexOutOfBoundsException:

   `java EJavaGuruExcep one`

d  **The code will fail to compile.**

Answer: d

Explanation: The key to answering this question is to be aware of the following two facts:

- Exceptions are classes. If an exception's base class is used in a catch block, it can catch all the exceptions of its derived class. If you try to catch an exception from its derived class afterward, the code won't compile.
- ArrayIndexOutOfBoundsException is a derived class of IndexOutOfBounds-Exception.

The rest of the points try to trick you into believing that the question is based on the arguments passed to a main method.

**Q7-4.** What is the output of the following code?

```
class EJava {
    void method() {
        try {
            guru();
            return;
        } finally {
            System.out.println("finally 1");
        }
    }
    void guru() {
        System.out.println("guru");
        throw new StackOverflowError();
    }
    public static void main(String args[]) {
        EJava var = new EJava();
        var.method();
    }
}
```

a guru
  finally 1

b **guru**
  **finally 1**
  **Exception in thread "main" java.lang.StackOverflowError**

c guru
  Exception in thread "main" java.lang.StackOverflowError

d guru

e The code fails to compile.

Answer: b

Explanation: No compilation errors exist with the code.

The method guru throws StackOverflowError, which is not a checked exception. Even though your code shouldn't throw an error, it is possible syntactically. Your code will compile successfully.

The call to the method guru is immediately followed by the keyword return, which is supposed to end the execution of the method method. But the call to guru is placed within a try-catch block, with a finally block. Because guru doesn't handle the error StackOverflowError itself, the control looks for the exception handler in the method method. This calling method doesn't handle this error but defines a finally block. The control then executes the finally block. Because the code can't find an appropriate handler to handle this error, it propagates to the JVM, which abruptly halts the code.

**Q 7-5.** What is the output of the following code?

```
class Quest5 {
    public static void main(String args[]) {
        int arr[] = new int[5];
        arr = new int[]{1,2,3,4};
```

```
    int x = arr[1]-- + arr[0]-- /arr[0] * arr[4];
    System.out.println(x);
  }
}
```

a   The code outputs a value.

b   The code outputs a value followed by an exception.

c   **ArithmeticException**

d   NullPointerException

e   IndexOutOfBoundsException

f   ArrayIndexOutOfBoundsException

g   Compilation error

h   None of the above

Answer: c

Explanation: Apart from testing your exception-handling skills, this question also tests you in operator precedence. The code throws an ArithmeticException in an attempt to evaluate the following expression:

```
int x = arr[1]-- + arr[0]-- /arr[0] * arr[4];
```

Before execution of the preceding line of code, arr[1] stores value 2, arr[0] stores value 1, and arr[4] isn't initialized. So an attempt to access arr[4] would result in an ArrayIndexOutOfBoundsException.

In an arithmetic operation, post- and pre-increment operators have the highest precedence. So the first pass reduces this equation to

```
int x = 2 + 1 /0 * undefined;
```

Both * and / have equal precedence level here. What matters beyond operator precedence is reading the same-level operations from left to right. This is why / is computed before * in the present expression. So an attempt to execute 1/0 throws an ArithmeticException.

**Q7-6.** Which of the following methods will not compile?

a
```
private void method1(String name) {
    if (name.equals("star"))
        throw new IllegalArgumentException(name);
}
```

b
```
private void method2(int age) {
    if (age > 30)
        throw Exception();
}
```

```
c  public Object method3(boolean accept) {
       if (accept)
           throw new StackOverflowError();
       else
           return new StackOverflowError();
   }
d  protected double method4() throws Exception {
       throw new Throwable();
   }
e  public double method5() throws Exception {
       return 0.7;
   }
```

Answer: b, d

Explanation: Methods that compile successfully might not be implemented correctly. This question only asks about the methods that will follow the syntax rules so that they compile successfully.

Option (a) code compiles successfully. Because `IllegalArgumentException` is a runtime exception, `method1()` can throw it without declaring it to be thrown in its `throws` statement.

Option (b) code won't compile. `method2()` throws a checked exception, that is, `Exception`, without declaring it to be thrown in its `throws` statement.

Although the code in option (c) makes little sense, it will compile successfully. A method can throw a `StackOverflowError` (an unchecked exception) without including it in the `throws` clause of its method declaration.

Option (d) code won't compile. If a method declares to throw a checked exception, its body can't throw a more general exception in its body. `method4()` declares to throw `Exception` but throws `Throwable`, which is not allowed (`Exception` subclasses `Throwable`).

Option (e) code will compile successfully. If a method declares to throw `Exception`, it might not actually throw it. This only applies to `Exception` (because `Runtime-Exception` subclasses it), runtime exceptions, and errors.

**Q7-7.** What is the output of the following code?

```
class TryFinally {
    int tryAgain() {
        int a = 10;
        try {
            ++a;
        } finally {
            a++;
        }
        return a;
    }
```

```
    public static void main(String args[]) {
        System.out.println(new TryFinally().tryAgain());
    }
}
```

    a   10

    b   11

    c   **12**

    d   Compilation error

    e   Runtime exception

Answer: c

Explanation: The `try` block executes, incrementing the value of variable a to 11. This step is followed by execution of the `finally` block, which also increments the value of variable a by 1, to 12. The method `tryAgain` returns the value 12, which is printed by the method `main`.

There are no compilation issues with the code. A `try` block can be followed by a `finally` block without any `catch` blocks. Even though the `try` block doesn't throw any exceptions, it compiles successfully. The following is an example of a `try-catch` block that won't compile because it tries to *catch* a checked exception that's never thrown by the `try` block:

```
try {
    ++a;
} catch (java.io.FileNotFoundException e) {
}
```

**Q7-8.** What is the output of the following code?

```
class EJavaBase {
    void myMethod() throws ExceptionInInitializerError {
        System.out.println("Base");
    }
}
class EJavaDerived extends EJavaBase {
    void myMethod() throws RuntimeException {
        System.out.println("Derived");
    }
}
class EJava3 {
    public static void main(String args[]) {
        EJavaBase obj = new EJavaDerived();
        obj.myMethod();
    }
}
```

    a   `Base`

    b   `Derived`

   c  `Derived`
      `Base`

   d  `Base`
      `Derived`

   e  Compilation error

Answer: b

Explanation: The rule that if a base class method doesn't throw an exception, an over-riding method in the derived class can't throw an exception applies only to checked exceptions. It doesn't apply to runtime (unchecked) exceptions or errors. A base or overridden method is free to throw any error or runtime exception.

**Q7-9.** Which of the following statements are true?

   a  A user-defined class may not throw an `IllegalStateException`. It must be thrown only by Java API classes.

   b  `System.out.println` will throw a `NullPointerException` if an uninitialized instance variable of type `String` is passed to it to print its value.

   c  **`NumberFormatException` is thrown by multiple methods from the Java API when invalid numbers are passed on as `Strings` to be converted to the specified number format.**

   d  **`ExceptionInInitializerError` may be thrown by the JVM when a `static` initializer in your code throws a `NullPointerException`.**

Answer: c, d

Option (a) is incorrect. A user-defined class can throw any exception from the Java API.

    Option (b) is incorrect. An uninitialized instance variable of type `String` will be assigned a default value of `null`. When you pass this variable to `System.out.println` to print it, it will print `null`. If you try to access any non-static member (variable or method) of this `null` object, then a `NullPointerException` will be thrown.

**Q7-10.** What is the output of the following code?

```
class EJava {
    void foo() {
        try {
            String s = null;
            System.out.println("1");
            try {
                System.out.println(s.length());
            } catch (NullPointerException e) {
                System.out.println("inner");
            }
            System.out.println("2");
```

```
        } catch (NullPointerException e) {
            System.out.println("outer");
        }
    }
    public static void main(String args[]) {
        EJava obj = new EJava();
        obj.foo();
    }
}
```

a  1
   inner
   2
   outer

b  1
   outer

c  1
   inner

d  1
   **inner**
   2

Answer: d

Explanation: First of all, nested try-catch statements don't throw compilation errors.

Because the variable s hasn't been initialized, an attempt to access its method length() will throw a NullPointerException. The inner try-catch block handles this exception and prints inner. The control then moves on to complete the remaining code in the outer try-catch block, printing 2. Because the NullPointerException was already handled in the inner try-catch block, it's not handled in the outer try-catch block.

# Full mock exam 8

**This chapter covers**

- Complete mock exam with 77 questions
- Answers to all mock exam questions with extensive explanations and the subobjective on which each exam question is based

On the real exam, each question displays the count of correct options that you should select. The exam engine won't allow you to select more answer options than are specified by this number. If you try to do so, a warning will be displayed. The questions in this mock exam also specify the correct number of answer options to align it more closely with the real exam.

## 8.1 Mock exam

**ME-Q1)** Given the following definition of the classes Animal, Lion, and Jumpable, select the correct combinations of assignments of a variable that don't result in compilation errors or runtime exceptions (select 2 options).

```
interface Jumpable {}
class Animal {}
class Lion extends Animal implements Jumpable {}
```

```
☐ a  Jumpable var1 = new Jumpable();
☐ b  Animal var2 = new Animal();
☐ c  Lion var3 = new Animal();
☐ d  Jumpable var4 = new Animal();
☐ e  Jumpable var5 = new Lion();
☐ f  Jumpable var6 = (Jumpable)(new Animal());
```

**ME-Q2)** Given the following code, which option, if used to replace /* INSERT CODE HERE */, will make the code print 1? (Select 1 option.)

```
try {
    String[][] names = {{"Andre", "Mike"}, null, {"Pedro"}};
    System.out.println (names[2][1].substring(0, 2));
} catch (/*INSERT CODE HERE*/) {
    System.out.println(1);
}
```

- ○ a  IndexPositionException e
- ○ b  NullPointerException e
- ○ c  ArrayIndexOutOfBoundsException e
- ○ d  ArrayOutOfBoundsException e

**ME-Q3)** What is the output of the following code? (Select 1 option.)

```
public static void main(String[] args) {
    int a = 10; String name = null;
    try {
        a = name.length();                  //line1
        a++;                                //line2
    } catch (NullPointerException e){
        ++a;
        return;
    } catch (RuntimeException e){
        a--;
        return;
    } finally {
        System.out.println(a);
    }
}
```

- ○ a  5
- ○ b  6
- ○ c  10
- ○ d  11
- ○ e  12
- ○ f  Compilation error
- ○ g  No output
- ○ h  Runtime exception

**ME-Q4)** Given the following class definition,

```
class Student { int marks = 10; }
```

what is the output of the following code? (Select 1 option.)

```
class Result {
    public static void main(String... args) {
        Student s = new Student();
        switch (s.marks) {
            default: System.out.println("100");
            case 10: System.out.println("10");
            case 98: System.out.println("98");
        }
    }
}
```

&#9673; **a** 100
    10
    98

&#9673; **b** 10
    98

&#9673; **c** 100

&#9673; **d** 10

**ME-Q5)** Given the following code, which code can be used to create and initialize an object of the class `ColorPencil`? (Select 2 options.)

```
class Pencil {}
class ColorPencil extends Pencil {
    String color;
    ColorPencil(String color) {this.color = color;}
}
```

&#9744; **a** `ColorPencil var1 = new ColorPencil();`
&#9744; **b** `ColorPencil var2 = new ColorPencil(RED);`
&#9744; **c** `ColorPencil var3 = new ColorPencil("RED");`
&#9744; **d** `Pencil var4 = new ColorPencil("BLUE");`

**ME-Q6)** What is the output of the following code? (Select 1 option.)

```
class Doctor {
    protected int age;
    protected void setAge(int val) { age = val; }
    protected int getAge() { return age; }
}
class Surgeon extends Doctor {
    Surgeon(String val) {
        specialization = val;
    }
```

```
        String specialization;
        String getSpecialization() { return specialization; }
}
class Hospital {
    public static void main(String args[]) {
        Surgeon s1 = new Surgeon("Liver");
        Surgeon s2 = new Surgeon("Heart");
        s1.age = 45;
        System.out.println(s1.age + s2.getSpecialization());
        System.out.println(s2.age + s1.getSpecialization());
    }
}
```

    a   45Heart
        0Liver

    b   45Liver
        0Heart

    c   45Liver
        45Heart

    d   45Heart
        45Heart

    e   Class fails to compile.


**ME-Q7)** What is the output of the following code? (Select 1 option.)

```
class RocketScience {
    public static void main(String args[]) {
        int a = 0;
        while (a == a++) {
            a++;
            System.out.println(a);
        }
    }
}
```

    a   The while loop won't execute; nothing will be printed.

    b   The while loop will execute indefinitely, printing all numbers, starting from 1.

    c   The while loop will execute indefinitely, printing all even numbers, starting from 0.

    d   The while loop will execute indefinitely, printing all even numbers, starting from 2.

    e   The while loop will execute indefinitely, printing all odd numbers, starting from 1.

    f   The while loop will execute indefinitely, printing all odd numbers, starting from 3.

**ME-Q8)** Given the following statements,

- com.ejava is a package
- class Person is defined in package com.ejava
- class Course is defined in package com.ejava

which of the following options correctly import the classes Person and Course in the class MyEJava? (Select 3 options.)

☐ **a** 
```
import com.ejava.*;
class MyEJava {}
```

☐ **b** 
```
import com.ejava;
class MyEJava {}
```

☐ **c** 
```
import com.ejava.Person;
import com.ejava.Course;
class MyEJava {}
```

☐ **d** 
```
import com.ejava.Person;
import com.ejava.*;
class MyEJava {}
```

**ME-Q9)** Given that the following classes Animal and Forest are defined in the same package, examine the code and select the correct statements (select 2 options).

```
line1>    class Animal {
line2>        public void printKing() {
line3>            System.out.println("Lion");
line4>        }
line5>    }

line6>    class Forest {
line7>        public static void main(String... args) {
line8>            Animal anAnimal = new Animal();
line9>            anAnimal.printKing();
line10>        }
line11>    }
```

☐ **a** The class Forest prints Lion.

☐ **b** If the code on line 2 is changed as follows, the class Forest will print Lion:

```
private void printKing() {
```

☐ **c** If the code on line 2 is changed as follows, the class Forest will print Lion:

```
void printKing() {
```

☐ **d** If the code on line 2 is changed as follows, the class Forest will print Lion:

```
default void printKing() {
```

**ME-Q10)** Given the following code,

```
class MainMethod {
    public static void main(String... args) {
        System.out.println(args[0]+":"+ args[2]);
    }
}
```

what is its output if it's executed using the following command? (Select 1 option.)

```
java MainMethod 1+2 2*3 4-3 5+1
```

- a  java:1+2
- b  java:3
- c  MainMethod:2*3
- d  MainMethod:6
- e  1+2:2*3
- f  3:3
- g  6
- h  1+2:4-3
- i  31
- j  4

**ME-Q11)** What is the output of the following code? (Select 1 option.)

```
interface Moveable {
    int move(int distance);
}
class Person {
    static int MIN_DISTANCE = 5;
    int age;
    float height;
    boolean result;
    String name;
}
public class EJava {
    public static void main(String arguments[]) {
        Person person = new Person();
        Moveable moveable = (x) -> Person.MIN_DISTANCE + x;
        System.out.println(person.name + person.height + person.result
                                        + person.age + moveable.move(20));
    }
}
```

- a  null0.0false025
- b  null0false025
- c  null0.0ffalse025
- d  0.0false025

○ e 0false025

○ f 0.0ffalse025

○ g null0.0true025

○ h 0true025

○ i 0.0ftrue025

○ j Compilation error

○ k Runtime exception

**ME-Q12)** Given the following code, which option, if used to replace /* INSERT CODE HERE */, will make the code print the value of the variable pagesPerMin? (Select 1 option.)

```
class Printer {
    int inkLevel;
}
class LaserPrinter extends Printer {
    int pagesPerMin;
    public static void main(String args[]) {
        Printer myPrinter = new LaserPrinter();
        System.out.println(/* INSERT CODE HERE */);
    }
}
```

○ a (LaserPrinter)myPrinter.pagesPerMin

○ b myPrinter.pagesPerMin

○ c LaserPrinter.myPrinter.pagesPerMin

○ d ((LaserPrinter)myPrinter).pagesPerMin

**ME-Q13)** What is the output of the following code? (Select 1 option.)

```
interface Keys {
    String keypad(String region, int keys);
}
public class Handset {
    public static void main(String... args) {
        double price;
        String model;
        Keys varKeys = (region, keys) ->
                    {if (keys >= 32)
                        return region; else return "default";};
        System.out.println(model + price + varKeys.keypad("AB", 32));
    }
}
```

○ a null0AB

○ b null0.0AB

○ c null0default

○ d null0.0default

○ **e** 0

○ **f** 0.0

○ **g** Compilation error

**ME-Q14)** What is the output of the following code? (Select 1 option.)

```
public class Sales {
    public static void main(String args[]) {
        int salesPhone = 1;
        System.out.println(salesPhone++ + ++salesPhone +
                                            ++salesPhone);
    }
}
```

○ **a** 5

○ **b** 6

○ **c** 8

○ **d** 9

**ME-Q15)** Which of the following options defines the correct structure of a Java class that compiles successfully? (Select 1 option.)

○ **a** 
```
package com.ejava.guru;
package com.ejava.oracle;
class MyClass {
    int age = /* 25 */ 74;
}
```

○ **b** 
```
import com.ejava.guru.*;
import com.ejava.oracle.*;
package com.ejava;
class MyClass {
    String name = "e" + "Ja /*va*/ v";
}
```

○ **c** 
```
class MyClass {
    import com.ejava.guru.*;
}
```

○ **d** 
```
class MyClass {
    int abc;
    String course = //this is a comment
                "eJava";
}
```

○ **e** None of the above

**ME-Q16)** What is the output of the following code? (Select 1 option.)

```
class OpPre {
    public static void main(String... args) {
        int x = 10;
        int y = 20;
```

```
        int z = 30;
        if (x+y%z > (x+(-y)*(-z))) {
            System.out.println(x + y + z);
        }
    }
}
```

- ◉ **a** 60
- ◉ **b** 59
- ◉ **c** 61
- ◉ **d** No output.
- ◉ **e** The code fails to compile.

**ME-Q17)** Select the most appropriate definition of the variable name and the line number on which it should be declared so that the following code compiles successfully (choose 1 option).

```
class EJava {
    // LINE 1
    public EJava() {
        System.out.println(name);
    }
    void calc() {
        // LINE 2
        if (8 > 2) {
            System.out.println(name);
        }
    }
    public static void main(String... args) {
        // LINE 3
        System.out.println(name);
    }
}
```

- ◉ **a** Define static String name; on line 1.
- ◉ **b** Define String name; on line 1.
- ◉ **c** Define String name; on line 2.
- ◉ **d** Define String name; on line 3.

**ME-Q18)** Examine the following code and select the correct statement (choose 1 option).

```
line1>    class Emp {
line2>        Emp mgr = new Emp();
line3>    }
line4>    class Office {
line5>        public static void main(String args[]) {
line6>            Emp e = null;
line7>            e = new Emp();
line8>            e = null;
line9>        }
line10>    }
```

⊙ **a** The object referred to by object e is eligible for garbage collection on line 8.

⊙ **b** The object referred to by object e is eligible for garbage collection on line 9.

⊙ **c** The object referred to by object e isn't eligible for garbage collection because its member variable mgr isn't set to null.

⊙ **d** The code throws a runtime exception and the code execution never reaches line 8 or line 9.

**ME-Q19)** Given the following,

```
long result;
```

which options are correct declarations of methods that accept two String arguments and an int argument and whose return value can be assigned to the variable result? (Select 3 options.)

☐ **a** `Short myMethod1(String str1, int str2, String str3)`

☐ **b** `Int myMethod2(String val1, int val2, String val3)`

☐ **c** `Byte myMethod3(String str1, str2, int a)`

☐ **d** `Float myMethod4(String val1, val2, int val3)`

☐ **e** `Long myMethod5(int str2, String str3, String str1)`

☐ **f** `Long myMethod6(String... val1, int val2)`

☐ **g** `Short myMethod7(int val1, String... val2)`

**ME-Q20)** Which of the following will compile successfully? (Select 3 options.)

☐ **a** `int eArr1[] = {10, 23, 10, 2};`

☐ **b** `int[] eArr2 = new int[10];`

☐ **c** `int[] eArr3 = new int[] {};`

☐ **d** `int[] eArr4 = new int[10] {};`

☐ **e** `int eArr5[] = new int[2] {10, 20};`

**ME-Q21)** Assume that Oracle has asked you to create a method that returns the concatenated value of two String objects. Which of the following methods can accomplish this job? (Select 2 options.)

☐ **a**
```
public String add(String 1, String 2) {
    return str1 + str2;
}
```

☐ **b**
```
private String add(String s1, String s2) {
    return s1.concat(s2);
}
```

☐ **c**
```
protected String add(String value1, String value2) {
    return value2.append(value2);
}
```

```
    d String subtract(String first, String second) {
            return first.concat(second.substring(0));
    }
```

**ME-Q22)** Given the following,

```
int ctr = 10;
char[] arrC1 = new char[]{'P','a','u','l'};
char[] arrC2 = {'H','a','r','r','y'};
//INSERT CODE HERE
System.out.println(ctr);
```

which options, when inserted at //INSERT CODE HERE, will output 14? (Choose 2 options.)

```
    a for (char c1 : arrC1) {
            for (char c2 : arrC2) {
                if (c2 == 'a') break;
                ++ctr;
            }
    }
    b for (char c1 : arrC1)
            for (char c2 : arrC2) {
                if (c2 == 'a') break;
                ++ctr;
            }
    c for (char c1 : arrC1)
            for (char c2 : arrC2)
                if (c2 == 'a') break;
                ++ctr;
    d for (char c1 : arrC1) {
            for (char c2 : arrC2) {
                if (c2 == 'a') continue;
                ++ctr;
            }
    }
```

**ME-Q23)** Given the following definitions of the class ChemistryBook, select the statements that are correct individually (choose 2 options).

```
import java.util.ArrayList;
class ChemistryBook {
    public void read() {}                       //METHOD1
    public String read() { return null; }       //METHOD2
    ArrayList read(int a) { return null; }       //METHOD3
}
```

    a Methods marked with //METHOD1 and //METHOD2 are correctly overloaded methods.

    b Methods marked with //METHOD2 and //METHOD3 are correctly overloaded methods.

☐ c Methods marked with //METHOD1 and //METHOD3 are correctly overloaded methods.

☐ d All the methods—methods marked with //METHOD1, //METHOD2, and //METHOD3—are correctly overloaded methods.

**ME-Q24)** Given the following,

```
final class Home {
    String name;
    int rooms;
    //INSERT CONSTRUCTOR HERE
}
```

which options, when inserted at //INSERT CONSTRUCTOR HERE, will define valid overloaded constructors for the class Home? (Choose 3 options.)

☐ a `Home() {}`

☐ b `Float Home() {}`

☐ c `protected Home(int rooms) {}`

☐ d `final Home() {}`

☐ e `private Home(long name) {}`

☐ f `float Home(int rooms, String name) {}`

☐ g `static Home() {}`

**ME-Q25)** Given the following code, which option, if used to replace // INSERT CODE HERE, will make the code print numbers that are completely divisible by 14? (Select 1 option.)

```
for (int ctr = 2; ctr <= 30; ++ctr) {
    if (ctr % 7 != 0)
        //INSERT CODE HERE
    if (ctr % 14 == 0)
        System.out.println(ctr);
}
```

○ a `continue;`

○ b `exit;`

○ c `break;`

○ d `end;`

**ME-Q26)** What is the output of the following code? (Select 1 option.)

```
import java.util.function.Predicate;
public class MyCalendar {
    public static void main(String arguments[]) {
        Season season1 = new Season();
        season1.name = "Spring";
```

```
        Season season2 = new Season();
        season2.name = "Autumn";

        Predicate<String> aSeason = (s) -> s == "Summer" ?
                                  season1.name : season2.name;

        season1 = season2;
        System.out.println(season1.name);
        System.out.println(season2.name);
        System.out.println(aSeason.test(new String("Summer")));
    }
}
class Season {
    String name;
}
```

- a String
  Autumn
  false

- b Spring
  String
  false

- c Autumn
  Autumn
  false

- d Autumn
  String
  true

- e Compilation error

- f Runtime exception

**ME-Q27)** What is true about the following code? (Select 1 option.)

```
class Shoe {}
class Boot extends Shoe {}
class ShoeFactory {
    ShoeFactory(Boot val) {
        System.out.println("boot");
    }
    ShoeFactory(Shoe val) {
        System.out.println("shoe");
    }
}
```

- a The class ShoeFactory has a total of two overloaded constructors.

- b The class ShoeFactory has three overloaded constructors, two user-defined constructors, and one default constructor.

- c The class ShoeFactory will fail to compile.

- d The addition of the following constructor will increment the number of constructors of the class ShoeFactory to 3:

  ```
  private ShoeFactory (Shoe arg) {}
  ```

**ME-Q28)** Given the following definitions of the classes ColorPencil and TestColor, which option, if used to replace //INSERT CODE HERE, will initialize the instance variable color of the reference variable myPencil with the String literal value "RED"? (Select 1 option.)

```java
class ColorPencil {
    String color;
    ColorPencil(String color) {
        //INSERT CODE HERE
    }
}
class TestColor {
    ColorPencil myPencil = new ColorPencil("RED");
}
```

    ◎ **a** `this.color = color;`

    ◎ **b** `color = color;`

    ◎ **c** `color = RED;`

    ◎ **d** `this.color = RED;`

**ME-Q29)** What is the output of the following code? (Select 1 option.)

```java
class EJavaCourse {
    String courseName = "Java";
}
class University {
    public static void main(String args[]) {
        EJavaCourse courses[] = { new EJavaCourse(), new EJavaCourse() };
        courses[0].courseName = "OCA";
        for (EJavaCourse c : courses) c = new EJavaCourse();
        for (EJavaCourse c : courses) System.out.println(c.courseName);
    }
}
```

    ◎ **a** Java
        Java

    ◎ **b** OCA
        Java

    ◎ **c** OCA
        OCA

    ◎ **d** None of the above

**ME-Q30)** What is the output of the following code? (Select 1 option.)

```java
class Phone {
    static void call() {
        System.out.println("Call-Phone");
    }
}
```

```
class SmartPhone extends Phone{
    static void call() {
        System.out.println("Call-SmartPhone");
    }
}
class TestPhones {
    public static void main(String... args) {
        Phone phone = new Phone();
        Phone smartPhone = new SmartPhone();
        phone.call();
        smartPhone.call();
    }
}
```

- a  Call-Phone
      Call-Phone

- b  Call-Phone
      Call-SmartPhone

- c  Call-Phone
      null

- d  null
      Call-SmartPhone

**ME-Q31)** Given the following code, which of the following statements are true? (Select 3 options.)

```
class MyExam {
    void question() {
        try {
            question();
        } catch (StackOverflowError e) {
            System.out.println("caught");
        }
    }
    public static void main(String args[]) {
        new MyExam().question();
    }
}
```

- a  The code will print caught.
- b  The code won't print caught.
- c  The code would print caught if StackOverflowError were a runtime exception.
- d  The code would print caught if StackOverflowError were a checked exception.
- e  The code would print caught if question() throws the exception NullPointer-Exception.

**ME-Q32)** A class Student is defined as follows:

```
public class Student {
    private String fName;
    private String lName;
```

```
    public Student(String first, String last) {
        fName = first; lName = last;
    }
    public String getName() { return fName + lName; }
}
```

The creator of the class later changes the method getName as follows:

```
    public String getName() {
        return fName + " " + lName;
    }
```

What are the implications of this change? (Select 2 options.)

- [ ] a The classes that were using the class Student will fail to compile.
- [ ] b The classes that were using the class Student will work without any compilation issues.
- [ ] c The class Student is an example of a well-encapsulated class.
- [ ] d The class Student exposes its instance variable outside the class.

**ME-Q33)** What is the output of the following code? (Select 1 option.)

```
class ColorPack {
    int shadeCount = 12;
    static int getShadeCount() {
        return shadeCount;
    }
}
class Artist {
    public static void main(String args[]) {
        ColorPack pack1 = new ColorPack();
        System.out.println(pack1.getShadeCount());
    }
}
```

- a 10
- b 12
- c No output
- d Compilation error

**ME-Q34)** Paul defined his Laptop and Workshop classes to upgrade his laptop's memory. Do you think he succeeded? What is the output of this code? (Select 1 option.)

```
class Laptop {
    String memory = "1 GB";
}
class Workshop {
    public static void main(String args[]) {
        Laptop life = new Laptop();
        repair(life);
```

```
        System.out.println(life.memory);
    }
    public static void repair(Laptop laptop) {
        laptop.memory = "2 GB";
    }
}
```

- ⊙ **a** 1 GB
- ⊙ **b** 2 GB
- ⊙ **c** Compilation error
- ⊙ **d** Runtime exception

**ME-Q35)** What is the output of the following code? (Select 1 option.)

```
public class Application {
    public static void main(String... args) {
        double price = 10;
        String model;
        if (price > 10)
            model = "Smartphone";
        else if (price <= 10)
            model = "landline";
        System.out.println(model);
    }
}
```

- ⊙ **a** landline
- ⊙ **b** Smartphone
- ⊙ **c** No output
- ⊙ **d** Compilation error

**ME-Q36)** What is the output of the following code? (Select 1 option.)

```
class EString {
    public static void main(String args[]) {
        String eVal = "123456789";
        System.out.println(eVal.substring(eVal.indexOf("2"),
    ➥ eVal.indexOf("0")).concat("0"));
    }
}
```

- ⊙ **a** 234567890
- ⊙ **b** 34567890
- ⊙ **c** 234456789
- ⊙ **d** 3456789
- ⊙ **e** Compilation error
- ⊙ **f** Runtime exception

**ME-Q37)** Examine the following code and select the correct statements (choose 2 options).

```
class Artist {
    Artist assistant;
}
class Studio {
    public static void main(String... args) {
        Artist a1 = new Artist();
        Artist a2 = new Artist();
        a2.assistant = a1;
        a2 = null;          // Line 1
    }
      // Line 2
}
```

    **a** At least two objects are garbage collected on line 1.

    **b** At least one object is garbage collected on line 1.

    **c** No objects are garbage collected on line 1.

    **d** The number of objects that are garbage collected on line 1 is unknown.

    **e** At least two objects are eligible for garbage collection on line 2.

**ME-Q38)** What is the output of the following code? (Select 1 option.)

```
class Book {
    String ISBN;
    Book(String val) {
        ISBN = val;
    }
}
class TestEquals {
    public static void main(String... args) {
        Book b1 = new Book("1234-4657");
        Book b2 = new Book("1234-4657");
        System.out.print(b1.equals(b2) +":");
        System.out.print(b1 == b2);
    }
}
```

    **a** true:false

    **b** true:true

    **c** false:true

    **d** false:false

    **e** Compilation error—there is no equals method in the class Book.

    **f** Runtime exception.

**ME-Q39)** Which of the following statements are correct? (Select 2 options.)

☐ **a** `StringBuilder sb1 = new StringBuilder()` will create a `StringBuilder` object with no characters but with an initial capacity to store 16 characters.

☐ **b** `StringBuilder sb1 = new StringBuilder(5*10)` will create a `StringBuilder` object with a value of 50.

☐ **c** Unlike the class `String`, the `concat` method in `StringBuilder` modifies the value of a `StringBuilder` object.

☐ **d** The `insert` method can be used to insert a character, number, or `String` at the start or end or a specified position of a `StringBuilder`.

**ME-Q40)** Given the following definition of the class `Animal` and the interface `Jump`, select the correct array declarations and initialization (choose 3 options).

```
interface Jump {}
class Animal implements Jump {}
```

☐ **a** `Jump eJump1[] = {null, new Animal()};`

☐ **b** `Jump[] eJump2 = new Animal()[22];`

☐ **c** `Jump[] eJump3 = new Jump[10];`

☐ **d** `Jump[] eJump4 = new Animal[87];`

☐ **e** `Jump[] eJump5 = new Jump()[12];`

**ME-Q41)** What is the output of the following code? (Select 1 option.)

```
import java.util.*;
class EJGArrayL {
    public static void main(String args[]) {
        ArrayList<String> seasons = new ArrayList<>();
        seasons.add(1, "Spring"); seasons.add(2, "Summer");
        seasons.add(3, "Autumn"); seasons.add(4, "Winter");
        seasons.remove(2);

        for (String s : seasons)
            System.out.print(s + ", ");
    }
}
```

○ **a** `Spring, Summer, Winter,`

○ **b** `Spring, Autumn, Winter,`

○ **c** `Autumn, Winter,`

○ **d** Compilation error

○ **e** Runtime exception

**ME-Q42)** What is the output of the following code? (Select 1 option.)

```
class EIf {
    public static void main(String args[]) {
        bool boolean = false;
        do {
            if (boolean = true)
                System.out.println("true");
            else
                System.out.println("false");
        }
        while(3.3 + 4.7 > 8);    }
}
```

- ⊙ a  The class will print true.
- ⊙ b  The class will print false.
- ⊙ c  The class will print true if the if condition is changed to boolean == true.
- ⊙ d  The class will print false if the if condition is changed to boolean != true.
- ⊙ e  The class won't compile.
- ⊙ f  Runtime exception.

**ME-Q43)** How many Fish did the Whale (defined as follows) manage to eat? Examine the following code and select the correct statements (choose 2 options).

```
class Whale {
    public static void main(String args[]) {
        boolean hungry = false;
        while (hungry=true) {
            ++Fish.count;
        }
        System.out.println(Fish.count);
    }
}
class Fish {
    static byte count;
}
```

- ☐ a  The code doesn't compile.
- ☐ b  The code doesn't print a value.
- ☐ c  The code prints 0.
- ☐ d  Changing ++Fish.count to Fish.count++ will give the same results.

**ME-Q44)** Given the following code, which option, if used to replace /* REPLACE CODE HERE */, will make the code print the name of the phone with the position at which it's stored in the array phones? (Select 1 option.)

```
class Phones {
    public static void main(String args[]) {
        String phones[]= {"BlackBerry", "Android", "iPhone"};
```

```
        for (String phone : phones)
            /* REPLACE CODE HERE */
    }
}
```

- **a** `System.out.println(phones.count + ":" + phone);`
- **b** `System.out.println(phones.counter + ":" + phone);`
- **c** `System.out.println(phones.getPosition() + ":" + phone);`
- **d** `System.out.println(phones.getCtr() + ":" + phone);`
- **e** `System.out.println(phones.getCount() + ":" + phone);`
- **f** `System.out.println(phones.pos + ":" + phone);`
- **g** None of the above

**ME-Q45)** Given the following code,

```
Byte b1 = (byte)100;                    // 1
Integer i1 = (int)200;                  // 2
Long l1 = (long)300;                    // 3
Float f1 = (float)b1 + (
     0int)l1;              // 4
String s1 = 300;                        // 5
if (s1 == (b1 + i1))                    // 6
    s1 = (String)500;                   // 7
else                                    // 8
    f1 = (int)100;                      // 9
System.out.println(s1 + ":" + f1);      // 10
```

what is the output? Select 1 option.

- **a** Code fails compilation at line numbers 1, 3, 4, 7.
- **b** Code fails compilation at line numbers 6, 7.
- **c** Code fails compilation at line numbers 7, 9.
- **d** Code fails compilation at line numbers 4, 5, 6, 7, 9.
- **e** No compilation error—outputs 500:300.
- **f** No compilation error—outputs 300:100.
- **g** Runtime exception.

**ME-Q46)** What is the output of the following code? (Select 1 option.)

```
class Book {
    String ISBN;
    Book(String val) {
        ISBN = val;
    }
    public boolean equals(Object b) {
        if (b instanceof Book) {
            return ((Book)b).ISBN.equals(ISBN);
        }
```

```
        else
            return false;
    }
}

class TestEquals {
    public static void main(String args[]) {
        Book b1 = new Book("1234-4657");
        Book b2 = new Book("1234-4657");
        LocalDate release = null;
        release = b1.equals(b2) ? b1 == b2? LocalDate.of(2050,12,12):
        LocalDate.parse("2072-02-01"):LocalDate.parse("9999-09-09");
        System.out.print(release);
    }
}
```

- ⊙ **a** 2050-12-12
- ⊙ **b** 2072-02-01
- ⊙ **c** 9999-09-09
- ⊙ **d** Compilation error
- ⊙ **e** Runtime exception

**ME-Q47)** What is the output of the following code? (Select 1 option.)

```
int a = 10;
for (; a <= 20; ++a) {
    if (a%3 == 0) a++; else if (a%2 == 0) a=a*2;
    System.out.println(a);
}
```

- ⊙ **a** 11
     13
     15
     17
     19

- ⊙ **b** 20
- ⊙ **c** 11
     14
     17
     20

- ⊙ **d** 40
- ⊙ **e** Compilation error

**ME-Q48)** Given the following code, which option, if used to replace // INSERT CODE HERE, will define an overloaded rideWave method? (Select 1 option.)

```
class Raft {
    public String rideWave() { return null; }
    //INSERT CODE HERE
}
```

- **a** `public String[] rideWave() { return null; }`
- **b** `protected void riceWave(int a) {}`
- **c** `private void rideWave(int value, String value2) {}`
- **d** `default StringBuilder rideWave (StringBuffer a) { return null; }`

**ME-Q49)** Given the following code, which option, if used to replace // INSERT CODE HERE, will correctly calculate the sum of all the even numbers in the array num and store it in the variable sum? (Select 1 option.)

```
int num[] = {10, 15, 2, 17};
int sum = 0;
for (int number : num) {
    //INSERT CODE HERE
    sum += number;
}
```

- **a** `if (number % 2 == 0)`
       `continue;`
- **b** `if (number % 2 == 0)`
       `break;`
- **c** `if (number % 2 != 0)`
       `continue;`
- **d** `if (number % 2 != 0)`
       `break;`

**ME-Q50)** What is the output of the following code? (Select 1 option.)

```
class Op {
    public static void main(String... args) {
        int a = 0;
        int b = 100;
        Predicate<Integer> compare = (var) -> var++ == 10;
        if (!b++ > 100 && compare.test(a)) {
            System.out.println(a+b);
        }
    }
}
```

- **a** 100
- **b** 101
- **c** 102
- **d** Code fails to compile.
- **e** No output is produced.

**ME-Q51)** Choose the option that meets the following specification: Create a well-encapsulated class Pencil with one instance variable model. The value of model should be accessible and modifiable outside Pencil. (Select 1 option.)

a class Pencil {
```
        public String model;
    }
```

b class Pencil {
```
        public String model;
        public String getModel() { return model; }
        public void setModel(String val) { model = val; }
    }
```

c class Pencil {
```
        private String model;
        public String getModel() { return model; }
        public void setModel(String val) { model = val; }
    }
```

d class Pencil {
```
        public String model;
        private String getModel() { return model; }
        private void setModel(String val) { model = val; }
    }
```

**ME-Q52)** What is the output of the following code? (Select 1 option.)

```
class Phone {
    void call() {
        System.out.println("Call-Phone");
    }
}
class SmartPhone extends Phone{
    void call() {
        System.out.println("Call-SmartPhone");
    }
}
class TestPhones {
    public static void main(String[] args) {
        Phone phone = new Phone();
        Phone smartPhone = new SmartPhone();
        phone.call();
        smartPhone.call();
    }
}
```

a Call-Phone
Call-Phone

b Call-Phone
Call-SmartPhone

c Call-Phone
null

d null
Call-SmartPhone

**ME-Q53)** What is the output of the following code? (Select 1 option.)

```
class Phone {
    String keyboard = "in-built";
}
class Tablet extends Phone {
    boolean playMovie = false;
}
class College2 {
    public static void main(String args[]) {
        Phone phone = new Tablet();
        System.out.println(phone.keyboard + ":" + phone.playMovie);
    }
}
```

- **a** in-built:false
- **b** in-built:true
- **c** null:false
- **d** null:true
- **e** Compilation error

**ME-Q54)** What is the output of the following code? (Select 1 option.)

```
public class Wall {
    public static void main(String args[]) {
        double area = 10.98;
        String color;
        if (area < 5)
            color = "red";
        else
            color = "blue";
        System.out.println(color);
    }
}
```

- **a** red
- **b** blue
- **c** No output
- **d** Compilation error

**ME-Q55)** What is the output of the following code? (Select 1 option.)

```
class Diary {
    int pageCount = 100;
    int getPageCount() {
        return pageCount;
    }
    void setPageCount(int val) {
        pageCount = val;
    }
}
```

```
class ClassRoom {
    public static void main(String args[]) {
        System.out.println(new Diary().getPageCount());
        new Diary().setPageCount(200);
        System.out.println(new Diary().getPageCount());
    }
}
```

      a   100
          200

      b   100
          100

      c   200
          200

      d   Code fails to compile.

**ME-Q56)** How many times do you think you can shop with the following code (that is, what's the output of the following code)? (Select 1 option.)

```
class Shopping {
    public static void main(String args[]) {
        boolean bankrupt = true;
        do System.out.println("enjoying shopping"); bankrupt = false;
        while (!bankrupt);
    }
}
```

      a   The code prints enjoying shopping once.
      b   The code prints enjoying shopping twice.
      c   The code prints enjoying shopping in an infinite loop.
      d   The code fails to compile.

**ME-Q57)** Which of the following options are valid for defining multidimensional arrays? (Choose 4 options.)

      a   `String ejg1[][] = new String[1][2];`
      b   `String ejg2[][] = new String[][] { {}, {} };`
      c   `String ejg3[][] = new String[2][2];`
      d   `String ejg4[][] = new String[][]{{null},new String[]{"a","b","c"},`
          `{new String()}};`
      e   `String ejg5[][] = new String[][2];`
      f   `String ejg6[][] = new String[][]{"A", "B"};`
      g   `String ejg7[][] = new String[]{{"A"}, {"B"}};`

**ME-Q58)** What is the output of the following code? (Select 1 option.)

```
class Laptop {
    String memory = "1GB";
}
class Workshop {
    public static void main(String args[]) {
        Laptop life = new Laptop();
        repair(life);
        System.out.println(life.memory);
    }
    public static void repair(Laptop laptop) {
        laptop = new Laptop();
        laptop.memory = "2GB";
    }
}
```

- ⊙ **a** 1 GB
- ⊙ **b** 2 GB
- ⊙ **c** Compilation error
- ⊙ **d** Runtime exception

**ME-Q59)** Given the following code, which option, if used to replace //INSERT CODE HERE, will enable a reference variable of type Roamable to refer to an object of the Phone class? (Select 1 option.)

```
interface Roamable{}
class Phone {}
class Tablet extends Phone implements Roamable {
    //INSERT CODE HERE
}
```

- ⊙ **a** Roamable var = new Phone();
- ⊙ **b** Roamable var = (Roamable)Phone();
- ⊙ **c** Roamable var = (Roamable)new Phone();
- ⊙ **d** Because the interface Roamable and the class Phone are unrelated, a reference variable of type Roamable can't refer to an object of the class Phone.

**ME-Q60)** What is the output of the following code? (Select 1 option.)

```
class Paper {
    Paper() {
        this(10);
        System.out.println("Paper:0");
    }
    Paper(int a) { System.out.println("Paper:1"); }
}
class PostIt extends Paper {}
```

```
class TestPostIt {
    public static void main(String[] args) {
        Paper paper = new PostIt();
    }
}
```

- **a** Paper:1

- **b** Paper:0

- **c** Paper:0
  Paper:1

- **d** Paper:1
  Paper:0

**ME-Q61)** Examine the following code and select the correct statement (choose 1 option).

```
line1> class StringBuilders {
line2>     public static void main(String... args) {
line3>         StringBuilder sb1 = new StringBuilder("eLion");
line4>         String ejg = null;
line5>         ejg = sb1.append("X").substring(sb1.indexOf("L"),
    sb1.indexOf("X"));
line6>         System.out.println(ejg);
line7>     }
line8> }
```

- **a** The code will print LionX.

- **b** The code will print Lion.

- **c** The code will print Lion if line 5 is changed to the following:

  ```
  ejg = sb1.append("X").substring(sb1.indexOf('L'), sb1.indexOf('X'));
  ```

- **d** The code will compile only when line 4 is changed to the following:

  ```
  StringBuilder ejg = null;
  ```

**ME-Q62)** Given the following code,

```
interface Jumpable {
    int height = 1;
    default void worldRecord() {
        System.out.print(height);
    }
}
interface Moveable {
    int height = 2;
    static void worldRecord() {
        System.out.print(height);
    }
}
```

```
class Chair implements Jumpable, Moveable {
    int height = 3;
    Chair() {
        worldRecord();
    }
    public static void main(String args[]) {
        Jumpable j = new Chair();
        Moveable m = new Chair();
        Chair c = new Chair();
    }
}
```

what is the output? Select 1 option.

- a 111
- b 123
- c 333
- d 222
- e Compilation error
- f Runtime exception

**ME-Q63)** Given the following code, which option, if used to replace /* INSERT CODE HERE */, will enable the class Jungle to determine whether the reference variable animal refers to an object of the class Lion and print 1? (Select 1 option.)

```
class Animal{ float age; }
class Lion extends Animal { int claws;}
class Jungle {
    public static void main(String args[]) {
        Animal animal = new Lion();
        /* INSERT CODE HERE */
            System.out.println(1);
    }
}
```

- a if (animal instanceof Lion)
- b if (animal instanceOf Lion)
- c if (animal == Lion)
- d if (animal = Lion)

**ME-Q64)** Given that the file Test.java, which defines the following code, fails to compile, select the reasons for the compilation failure (choose 2 options).

```
class Person {
    Person(String value) {}
}
class Employee extends Person {}
```

```
class Test {
    public static void main(String args[]) {
        Employee e = new Employee();
    }
}
```

- ☐ a The class Person fails to compile.
- ☐ b The class Employee fails to compile.
- ☐ c The default constructor can call only a no-argument constructor of a base class.
- ☐ d The code that creates the object of the class Employee in the class Test did not pass a String value to the constructor of the class Employee.

**ME-Q65)** Examine the following code and select the correct statements (choose 2 options).

```
class Bottle {
    void Bottle() {}
    void Bottle(WaterBottle w) {}
}
class WaterBottle extends Bottle {}
```

- ☐ a A base class can't pass reference variables of its defined class as method parameters in constructors.
- ☐ b The class compiles successfully—a base class can use reference variables of its derived class as method parameters.
- ☐ c The class Bottle defines two overloaded constructors.
- ☐ d The class Bottle can access only one constructor.

**ME-Q66)** Given the following code, which option, if used to replace /* INSERT CODE HERE */, will cause the code to print 110? (Select 1 option.)

```
class Book {
    private int pages = 100;
}
class Magazine extends Book {
    private int interviews = 2;
    private int totalPages() { /* INSERT CODE HERE */ }

    public static void main(String[] args) {
        System.out.println(new Magazine().totalPages());
    }
}
```

- ○ a return super.pages + this.interviews*5;
- ○ b return this.pages + this.interviews*5;
- ○ c return super.pages + interviews*5;

    **d** `return pages + this.interviews*5;`

    **e** None of the above

**ME-Q67)** Given the following code,

```
class NoInkException extends Exception {}
class Pen{
    void write(String val) throws NoInkException {
        int c = (10 - 7)/ (8 - 2 - 6);
    }
    void article() {
        //INSERT CODE HERE
    }
}
```

which of the options, when inserted at `//INSERT CODE HERE`, will define a valid use of the method `write` in the method `article`? (Select 2 options.)

    **a**
```
try {
        new Pen().write("story");
    } catch (NoInkException e) {}
```

    **b**
```
try {
        new Pen().write("story");
    } finally {}
```

    **c**
```
try {
        write("story");
    } catch (Exception e) {}
```

    **d**
```
try {
        new Pen().write("story");
    } catch (RuntimeException e) {}
```

**ME-Q68)** What is the output of the following code? (Select 1 option.)

```
class EMyMethods {
    static String name = "m1";
    void riverRafting() {
        String name = "m2";
        if (8 > 2) {
            String name = "m3";
            System.out.println(name);
        }
    }
    public static void main(String[] args) {
        EMyMethods m1 = new EMyMethods();
        m1.riverRafting();
    }
}
```

    **a** m1

    **b** m2

    **c** m3

    **d** The code fails to compile.

**ME-Q69)** What is the output of the following code? (Select 1 option.)

```java
class EBowl {
    public static void main(String args[]) {
        String eFood = "Corn";
        System.out.println(eFood);
        mix(eFood);
        System.out.println(eFood);
    }
    static void mix(String foodIn) {
        foodIn.concat("A");
        foodIn.replace('C', 'B');
    }
}
```

- a  Corn
  BornA

- b  Corn
  CornA

- c  Corn
  Born

- d  Corn
  Corn

**ME-Q70)** Which statement is true for the following code? (Select 1 option.)

```java
class SwJava {
    public static void main(String args[]) {
        String[] shapes = {"Circle", "Square", "Triangle"};
        switch (shapes) {
            case "Square": System.out.println("Circle"); break;
            case "Triangle": System.out.println("Square"); break;
            case "Circle": System.out.println("Triangle"); break;
        }
    }
}
```

- a  The code prints `Circle`.
- b  The code prints `Square`.
- c  The code prints `Triangle`.
- d  The code prints

  ```
  Circle
  Square
  Triangle
  ```

- e  The code prints

  ```
  Triangle
  Circle
  Square
  ```

- f  The code fails to compile.

**ME-Q71)** Given the following definition of the classes Person, Father, and Home, which option, if used to replace //INSERT CODE HERE, will cause the code to compile successfully? (Select 3 options.)

```
class Person {}
class Father extends Person {
    public void dance() throws ClassCastException {}
}
class Home {
    public static void main(String args[]) {
        Person p = new Person();
        try {
            ((Father)p).dance();
        }
        //INSERT CODE HERE
    }
}
```

- **a** `catch (NullPointerException e) {}`
  `catch (ClassCastException e) {}`
  `catch (Exception e) {}`
  `catch (Throwable t) {}`

- **b** `catch (ClassCastException e) {}`
  `catch (NullPointerException e) {}`
  `catch (Exception e) {}`
  `catch (Throwable t) {}`

- **c** `catch (ClassCastException e) {}`
  `catch (Exception e) {}`
  `catch (NullPointerException e) {}`
  `catch (Throwable t) {}`

- **d** `catch (Throwable t) {}`
  `catch (Exception e) {}`
  `catch (ClassCastException e) {}`
  `catch (NullPointerException e) {}`

- **e** `finally {}`

**ME-Q72)** What is the output of the following code? (Select 1 option.)

```
import java.time.*;
class Camera {
    public static void main(String args[]) {
        int hours;
        LocalDateTime now = LocalDateTime.of(2020, 10, 01, 0 , 0);
        LocalDate before = now.toLocalDate().minusDays(1);
        LocalTime after = now.toLocalTime().plusHours(1);

        while (before.isBefore(after) && hours < 4) {
            ++hours;
        }
        System.out.println("Hours:" + hours);
    }
}
```

    ○ **a** The code prints `Camera:null`.

    ○ **b** The code prints `Camera:Adjust settings manually`.

    ○ **c** The code prints `Camera:`.

    ○ **d** The code will fail to compile.

**ME-Q73)** The output of the class `TestEJavaCourse`, defined as follows, is `300`:

```
class Course {
    int enrollments;
}
class TestEJavaCourse {
    public static void main(String args[]) {
        Course c1 = new Course();
        Course c2 = new Course();
        c1.enrollments = 100;
        c2.enrollments = 200;
        System.out.println(c1.enrollments + c2.enrollments);
    }
}
```

What will happen if the variable `enrollments` is defined as a `static` variable? (Select 1 option.)

    ○ **a** No change in output. `TestEJavaCourse` prints `300`.

    ○ **b** Change in output. `TestEJavaCourse` prints `200`.

    ○ **c** Change in output. `TestEJavaCourse` prints `400`.

    ○ **d** The class `TestEJavaCourse` fails to compile.

**ME-Q74)** What is the output of the following code? (Select 1 option.)

```
String ejgStr[] = new String[][]{{null},new String[]{"a","b","c"},{new
    String()}}[0] ;
String ejgStr1[] = null;
String ejgStr2[] = {null};

System.out.println(ejgStr[0]);
System.out.println(ejgStr2[0]);
System.out.println(ejgStr1[0]);
```

    ○ **a** `null`
       `NullPointerException`

    ○ **b** `null`
       `null`
       `NullPointerException`

    ○ **c** `NullPointerException`

    ○ **d** `null`
       `null`
       `null`

**ME-Q75)** Examine the following code and select the correct statement (choose 1 option).

```java
import java.util.*;
class Person {}
class Emp extends Person {}

class TestArrayList {
    public static void main(String[] args) {
        ArrayList<Object> list = new ArrayList<>();
        list.add(new String("1234"));                //LINE1
        list.add(new Person());                       //LINE2
        list.add(new Emp());                          //LINE3
        list.add(new String[]{"abcd", "xyz"});        //LINE4
        list.add(LocalDate.now().plus(1));            //LINE5
    }
}
```

    **a** The code on line 1 won't compile.

    **b** The code on line 2 won't compile.

    **c** The code on line 3 won't compile.

    **d** The code on line 4 won't compile.

    **e** The code on line 5 won't compile.

    **f** None of the above.

    **g** All the options from (a) through (e).

**ME-Q76)** What is the output of the following code? (Select 1 option.)

```java
public class If2 {
    public static void main(String args[]) {
        int a = 10; int b = 20; boolean c = false;
        if (b > a) if (++a == 10) if (c!=true) System.out.println(1);
        else System.out.println(2); else System.out.println(3);
    }
}
```

    **a** 1

    **b** 2

    **c** 3

    **d** No output

**ME-Q77)** Given the following code,

```java
interface Movable {
    default int distance() {
        return 10;
    }
}
interface Jumpable {
    default int distance() {
```

```
            return 10;
        }
    }
```

which options correctly define the class `Person` that implements interfaces `Movable` and `Jumpable`? (Select 1 option.)

- **a** `class Person implements Movable, Jumpable {}`

- **b**
  ```
  class Person implements Movable, Jumpable {
      default int distance() {
          return 10;
      }
  }
  ```

- **c**
  ```
  class Person implements Movable, Jumpable {
      public int distance() {
          return 10;
      }
  }
  ```

- **d**
  ```
  class Person implements Movable, Jumpable {
      public long distance() {
          return 10;
      }
  }
  ```

- **e**
  ```
  class Person implements Movable, Jumpable {
      int distance() {
          return 10;
      }
  }
  ```

## 8.2 Answers to mock exam questions

This section contains answers to all the mock exam questions in section 8.1. Also, each question is preceded by the exam objectives that the question is based on.

> [7.2]　Develop code that demonstrates the use of polymorphism; including overriding and object type versus reference type

> [7.3]　Determine when casting is necessary

> [8.5]　"Recognize common exception classes (such as NullPointerException, ArithmeticException, ArrayIndexOutOfBoundsException, ClassCastException)"

**ME-Q1)** Given the following definition of the classes `Animal`, `Lion`, and `Jumpable`, select the correct combinations of assignments of a variable that don't result in compilation errors or runtime exceptions (select 2 options).

```
interface Jumpable {}
class Animal {}
class Lion extends Animal implements Jumpable {}
```

☐ **a** `Jumpable var1 = new Jumpable();`

☑ **b** `Animal var2 = new Animal();`

☐ **c** `Lion var3 = new Animal();`

☐ **d** `Jumpable var4 = new Animal();`

☑ **e** `Jumpable var5 = new Lion();`

☐ **f** `Jumpable var6 = (Jumpable)(new Animal());`

Answer: b, e

Explanation: Option (a) is incorrect. An `interface` can't be instantiated.

Option (c) is incorrect. A reference variable of a derived class can't be used to refer to an object of its base class.

Option (d) is incorrect. A reference variable of type `Jumpable` can't be used to refer to an object of the class `Animal` because `Animal` doesn't implement the interface `Jumpable`.

Option (f) is incorrect. Although this line of code will compile successfully, it will throw a `ClassCastException` at runtime. You can explicitly cast *any* object to an interface, even if it doesn't implement it to make the code compile. But if the object's class doesn't implement the interface, the code will throw a `ClassCastException` at runtime.

> **[8.2]** Create a try-catch block and determine how exceptions alter normal program flow

**ME-Q2)** Given the following code, which option, if used to replace `/*INSERT CODE HERE*/`, will make the code print 1? (Select 1 option.)

```
try {
    String[][] names = {{"Andre", "Mike"}, null, {"Pedro"}};
    System.out.println (names[2][1].substring(0, 2));
} catch (/*INSERT CODE HERE*/) {
    System.out.println(1);
}
```

○ **a** `IndexPositionException e`

○ **b** `NullPointerException e`

◉ **c** `ArrayIndexOutOfBoundsException e`

○ **d** `ArrayOutOfBoundsException e`

Answer: c

Explanation: Options (a) and (d) are incorrect because the Java API doesn't define any exception classes with these names.

Here's a list of the array values that are initialized by the code in this question:

```
names[0][0] = "Andre"
names[0][1] = "Mike"
names[1] = null
names[2][0] = "Pedro"
```

Because the array position [2][1] isn't defined, any attempt to access it will throw an ArrayIndexOutOfBoundsException.

An attempt to access any position of the second array—that is, names[1][0]—will throw a NullPointerException because names[1] is set to null.

 **[8.2]   Create a try-catch block and determine how exceptions alter normal program flow**

**ME-Q3)** What is the output of the following code? (Select 1 option.)

```java
public static void main(String[] args) {
    int a = 10; String name = null;
    try {
        a = name.length();                    //line1
        a++;                                  //line2
    } catch (NullPointerException e){
        ++a;
        return;
    } catch (RuntimeException e){
        a--;
        return;
    } finally {
        System.out.println(a);
    }
}
```

- ○ **a** 5
- ○ **b** 6
- ○ **c** 10
- ◉ **d** 11
- ○ **e** 12
- ○ **f** Compilation error
- ○ **g** No output
- ○ **h** Runtime exception

Answer: d

Explanation: Because the variable name isn't assigned a value, you can't call an instance method (length()) using it. The following line of code will throw a Null-PointerException:

```
name.length();
```

When an exception is thrown, the control is transferred to the exception handler, skipping the execution of the remaining lines of code in the try block. So the code (a++) doesn't execute at the comment marked with line2.

The code defines an exception handler for both NullPointerException and RuntimeException. When an exception is thrown, more than one exception handler won't execute. In this case, the exception handler for NullPointerException will execute because it's more specific and it's defined earlier than RuntimeException. The exception handler for NullPointerException includes the following code:

```
++a;
return;
```

The preceding code increments the value of the variable a by 1; and before it exits the method main, due to the call to the statement return, it executes the finally block, outputting the value 11. A finally block executes even if the catch block includes a return statement.

## [3.4]   Use a switch statement

**ME-Q4)** Given the following class definition,

```
class Student { int marks = 10; }
```

what is the output of the following code? (Select 1 option.)

```
class Result {
    public static void main(String... args) {
        Student s = new Student();
        switch (s.marks) {
            default: System.out.println("100");
            case 10: System.out.println("10");
            case 98: System.out.println("98");
        }
    }
}
```

- ○ **a** 100
      10
      98

- ◉ **b** 10
      98

- ○ **c** 100

- ○ **d** 10

Answer: b

Explanation: The default case executes only if no matching values are found. In this case, a matching value of 10 is found and the case label prints 10. Because a break statement doesn't terminate this case label, the code execution continues and executes the remaining statements within the `switch` block, until a `break` statement terminates it or it ends.

**[7.4]**    Use super and this to access objects and constructors

**ME-Q5)** Given the following code, which code can be used to create and initialize an object of the class `ColorPencil`? (Select 2 options.)

```
class Pencil {}
class ColorPencil extends Pencil {
    String color;
    ColorPencil(String color) {this.color = color;}
}
```

☐ **a**  `ColorPencil var1 = new ColorPencil();`

☐ **b**  `ColorPencil var2 = new ColorPencil(RED);`

☑ **c**  `ColorPencil var3 = new ColorPencil("RED");`

☑ **d**  `Pencil var4 = new ColorPencil("BLUE");`

Answer: c, d

Explanation: Option (a) is incorrect because `new ColorPencil()` tries to invoke the no-argument constructor of the class `ColorPencil`, which isn't defined in the class `ColorPencil`.

Option (b) is incorrect because `new ColorPencil(RED)` tries to pass a variable `RED`, which isn't defined in the code.

**[2.3]**    Know how to read or write to object fields

**ME-Q6)** What is the output of the following code? (Select 1 option.)

```
class Doctor {
    protected int age;
    protected void setAge(int val) { age = val; }
    protected int getAge() { return age; }
}
class Surgeon extends Doctor {
    Surgeon(String val) {
        specialization = val;
    }
    String specialization;
    String getSpecialization() { return specialization; }
}
class Hospital {
    public static void main(String args[]) {
        Surgeon s1 = new Surgeon("Liver");
```

```
        Surgeon s2 = new Surgeon("Heart");
        s1.age = 45;
        System.out.println(s1.age + s2.getSpecialization());
        System.out.println(s2.age + s1.getSpecialization());
    }
}
```

⦿ **a** **45Heart**
　　 **0Liver**

◍ **b** 45Liver
　　 0Heart

◍ **c** 45Liver
　　 45Heart

◍ **d** 45Heart
　　 45Heart

◍ **e** Class fails to compile.

Answer: a

Explanation: The constructor of the class Surgeon assigns the values "Liver" and "Heart" to the variable specialization of objects s1 and s2. The variable age is protected in the class Doctor. Also, the class Surgeon extends the class Doctor. Hence, the variable age is accessible to reference variables s1 and s2. The code assigns a value of 45 to the member variable age of reference variable s1. The variable age of reference variable s2 is initialized to the default value of an int, which is 0. Hence, the code prints the values mentioned in option (a).

 [3.1]　Use Java operators; including parentheses to override operator precedence

**ME-Q7)** What is the output of the following code? (Select 1 option.)

```
class RocketScience {
    public static void main(String args[]) {
        int a = 0;
        while (a == a++) {
            a++;
            System.out.println(a);
        }
    }
}
```

◍ **a** The while loop won't execute; nothing will be printed.
◍ **b** The while loop will execute indefinitely, printing all numbers, starting from 1.
◍ **c** The while loop will execute indefinitely, printing all even numbers, starting from 0.

○ d **The while loop will execute indefinitely, printing all even numbers, starting from 2.**

○ e The while loop will execute indefinitely, printing all odd numbers, starting from 1.

○ f The while loop will execute indefinitely, printing all odd numbers, starting from 3.

Answer: d

Explanation: The while loop will execute indefinitely because the condition a == a++ will always evaluate to true. The postfix unary operator will increment the value of the variable a after it's used in the comparison expression. a++ within the loop body will increment the value of a by 1. Hence, the value of a increments by 2 in a single loop.

**[1.4]    Import other Java packages to make them accessible in your code**

**ME-Q8)** Given the following statements,

- com.ejava is a package
- class Person is defined in package com.ejava
- class Course is defined in package com.ejava

which of the following options correctly import the classes Person and Course in the class MyEJava? (Select 3 options.)

☑ a `import com.ejava.*;`
  `class MyEJava {}`

☐ b `import com.ejava;`
  `class MyEJava {}`

☑ c `import com.ejava.Person;`
  `import com.ejava.Course;`
  `class MyEJava {}`

☑ d `import com.ejava.Person;`
  `import com.ejava.*;`
  `class MyEJava {}`

Answer: a, c, d

Explanation: Option (a) is correct. The statement `import com.ejava.*;` imports all the public members of the package com.ejava in the class MyEJava.

Option (b) is incorrect. Because com.ejava is a package, to import all the classes defined in this package, the package name should be followed by .*:

```
import com.ejava.*;
```

Option (c) is correct. It uses two separate import statements to import each of the classes Person and Course individually, which is correct.

Option (d) is also correct. The first import statement imports only the class Person in MyClass. But the second import statement imports both the Person and Course classes from the package com.ejava. You can import the same class more than once in a Java class with no issues. This code is correct.

In Java, the import statement makes the imported class *visible* to the Java compiler, allowing it to be referred to by the class that's importing it. In Java, the import statement doesn't embed the imported class in the target class.

## [6.4] Apply access modifiers

**ME-Q9)** Given that the following classes Animal and Forest are defined in the same package, examine the code and select the correct statements (select 2 options).

```
line1>    class Animal {
line2>        public void printKing() {
line3>            System.out.println("Lion");
line4>        }
line5>    }

line6>    class Forest {
line7>        public static void main(String... args) {
line8>            Animal anAnimal = new Animal();
line9>            anAnimal.printKing();
line10>       }
line11>   }
```

☑ **a The class Forest prints Lion.**

☐ b If the code on line 2 is changed as follows, the class Forest will print Lion:

```
private void printKing() {
```

☑ **c If the code on line 2 is changed as follows, the class Forest will print Lion:**

```
void printKing() {
```

☐ d If the code on line 2 is changed as follows, the class Forest will print Lion:

```
default void printKing() {
```

Answer: a, c

Explanation: Option (a) is correct. The code will compile successfully and print Lion.

Option (b) is incorrect. The code won't compile if the access modifier of the method printKing is changed to private. private members of a class can't be accessed outside the class.

Option (c) is correct. The classes Animal and Forest are defined in the same package, so changing the access modifier of the method printKing to default access will still make it accessible in the class Forest. The class will compile successfully and print Lion.

Option (d) is incorrect. "default" isn't a valid access modifier or keyword in Java. In Java, the default accessibility is marked by the absence of any explicit access modifier. This code will fail to compile.

 [1.3]   Create executable Java applications with a main method; run a Java program from the command line; including console output.

**ME-Q10)** Given the following code,

```java
class MainMethod {
    public static void main(String... args) {
        System.out.println(args[0]+":"+ args[2]);
    }
}
```

what's its output if it's executed using the following command? (Select 1 option.)

```
java MainMethod 1+2 2*3 4-3 5+1
```

- a  java:1+2
- b  java:3
- c  MainMethod:2*3
- d  MainMethod:6
- e  1+2:2*3
- f  3:3
- g  6
- h  1+2:4-3
- i  31
- j  4

Answer: h

Explanation: This question tests you on multiple points.

1  *The arguments that are passed on to the main method*—The keyword java and the name of the class (MainMethod) aren't passed as arguments to the main method. The arguments following the class name are passed to the main method. In this case, four method arguments are passed to the main method, as follows:

```
args[0]: 1+2
args[1]: 2*3
args[2]: 4-3
args[3]: 5+1
```

2 *The type of the arguments that are passed to the main method*—The main method accepts arguments of type `String`. All the numeric expressions—1+2, 2*3, 5+1, and 4-3—are passed as literal `String` values. These won't be evaluated when you try to print their values. Hence, `args[0]` won't be printed as 3. It will be printed as 1+2.

3 *+ operations with `String` array elements*—Because the array passed to the `main` method contains all the `String` values, using the + operand with its individual values will concatenate its values. It won't add the values, if they are numeric expressions. Hence, `"1+2"+"4-3"` won't evaluate to 31 or 4.

[2.2]   Differentiate between object reference variables and primitive variables

[9.5]   Write a simple Lambda expression that consumes a Lambda Predicate expression

**ME-Q11)** What is the output of the following code? (Select 1 option.)

```java
interface Moveable {
    int move(int distance);
}
class Person {
    static int MIN_DISTANCE = 5;
    int age;
    float height;
    boolean result;
    String name;
}
public class EJava {
    public static void main(String arguments[]) {
        Person person = new Person();
        Moveable moveable = (x) -> Person.MIN_DISTANCE + x;
        System.out.println(person.name + person.height + person.result
                                    + person.age + moveable.move(20));

    }
}
```

- ◉ **a** `null0.0false025`
- ○ **b** `null0false025`
- ○ **c** `null0.0ffalse025`
- ○ **d** `0.0false025`
- ○ **e** `0false025`
- ○ **f** `0.0ffalse025`
- ○ **g** `null0.0true025`
- ○ **h** `0true025`

- l   0.0ftrue025
- j   Compilation error
- k   Runtime exception

Answer: a

Explanation: The instance variables of a class are all assigned default values if no explicit value is assigned to them. Here are the default values of the primitive data types and the objects:

- char -> \u0000
- byte, short, int -> 0
- long -> 0L
- float-> 0.0f
- double -> 0.0d
- boolean -> false
- objects -> null

Moveable is a functional interface. The example code defines the code to execute for its functional method move by using the Lambda expression (x) -> Person.MIN _DISTANCE + x.

Calling moveable.move(20) passes 20 as an argument to the method move. It returns 25 (the sum of Person.MIN_DISTANCE, which is 5, and the method argument 20).

## [7.3]   Determine when casting is necessary

**ME-Q12)** Given the following code, which option, if used to replace /* INSERT CODE HERE */, will make the code print the value of the variable pagesPerMin? (Select 1 option.)

```
class Printer {
    int inkLevel;
}
class LaserPrinter extends Printer {
    int pagesPerMin;
    public static void main(String args[]) {
        Printer myPrinter = new LaserPrinter();
        System.out.println(/* INSERT CODE HERE */);
    }
}
```

- a  (LaserPrinter)myPrinter.pagesPerMin
- b  myPrinter.pagesPerMin
- c  LaserPrinter.myPrinter.pagesPerMin
- **d  ((LaserPrinter)myPrinter).pagesPerMin**

Answer: d

Explanation: Option (a) is incorrect because (LaserPrinter) tries to cast myPrinter .pagesPerMin (variable of primitive type int) to LaserPrinter, which is incorrect. This code won't compile.

Option (b) is incorrect. The type of reference variable myPrinter is Printer. myPrinter refers to an object of the class LaserPrinter, which extends the class Printer. A reference variable of the base class can't access the variables and methods defined in its subclass without an explicit cast.

Option (c) is incorrect. LaserPrinter.myPrinter treats LaserPrinter as a variable, although no variable with this name exists in the question's code. This code fails to compile.

 [2.1]  Declare and initialize variables (including casting of primitive data types)

 [9.5]  Write a simple Lambda expression that consumes a Lambda Predicate expression

**ME-Q13)** What is the output of the following code? (Select 1 option.)

```
interface Keys {
    String keypad(String region, int keys);
}
public class Handset {
    public static void main(String... args) {
        double price;
        String model;
        Keys varKeys = (region, keys) ->
                        {if (keys >= 32)
                            return region; else return "default";};
        System.out.println(model + price + varKeys.keypad("AB", 32));
    }
}
```

- ⊙ **a** null0AB
- ⊙ **b** null0.0AB
- ⊙ **c** null0default
- ⊙ **d** null0.0default
- ⊙ **e** 0
- ⊙ **f** 0.0
- ⦿ **g** **Compilation error**

Answer: g

Explanation: The local variables (variables that are declared within a method) aren't initialized with their default values. If you try to print the value of a local variable before initializing it, the code won't compile.

The Lambda expression used in the code is correct.

 **[3.1]** Use Java operators; including parentheses to override operator precedence

**ME-Q14)** What is the output of the following code? (Select 1 option.)

```
public class Sales {
    public static void main(String args[]) {
        int salesPhone = 1;
        System.out.println(salesPhone++ + ++salesPhone +
                                        ++salesPhone);
    }
}
```

- a  5
- b  6
- c  8
- d  9

Answer: c

Explanation: Understanding the following rules will enable you to answer this question correctly:

- An arithmetic expression is evaluated from left to right.
- When an expression uses the unary increment operator (++) in postfix notation, its value increments just *after* its original value is used in an expression.
- When an expression uses the unary increment operator (++) in prefix notation, its value increments just *before* its value is used in an expression.

The initial value of the variable salesPhone is 1. Let's evaluate the result of the arithmetic expression salesPhone++ + ++salesPhone + ++salesPhone step by step:

1  The first occurrence of salesPhone uses ++ in postfix notation, so its value is used in the expression *before* it's incremented by 1. This means that the expression evaluates to

    1 + ++salesPhone + ++salesPhone

2  Note that the previous usage of ++ in postfix increments has already incremented the value of salesPhone to 2. The second occurrence of salesPhone

uses ++ in prefix notation, so its value is used in the expression *after* it's incremented by 1, to 3. This means that the expression evaluates to

```
1 + 3 + ++salesPhone
```

3 The third occurrence of salesPhone again uses ++ in prefix notation, so its value is used in the expression *after* it's incremented by 1, to 4. This means that the expression evaluates to

```
1 + 3 + 4
```

The preceding expression evaluates to 8.

**[1.2]** Define the structure of a Java class

**[1.4]** Import other Java packages to make them accessible in your code

**ME-Q15)** Which of the following options defines the correct structure of a Java class that compiles successfully? (Select 1 option.)

```
a  package com.ejava.guru;
   package com.ejava.oracle;
   class MyClass {
       int age = /* 25 */ 74;
   }
b  import com.ejava.guru.*;
   import com.ejava.oracle.*;
   package com.ejava;
   class MyClass {
       String name = "e" + "Ja /*va*/ v";
   }
c  class MyClass {
       import com.ejava.guru.*;
   }
d  class MyClass {
       int abc;
       String course = //this is a comment
                   "eJava";
   }
e  None of the above
```

Answer: d

Explanation: This question requires you to know

- Correct syntax and usage of comments
- Usage of import and package statements

None of the code fails to compile due to the end-of-line or multiline comments. All the following lines of code are valid:

```
int age = /* 25 */ 74;
String name = "e" + "Ja /*va*/ v";
String course = //this is a comment
                "eJava";
```

In the preceding code, the variable age is assigned an integer value 74, the variable name is assigned a string value "eJa /*va*/ v", and course is assigned a string value "eJava". A multiline comment delimiter is ignored if put inside a string definition. Let's see how all the options perform on the usage of package and import statements:

Option (a) is incorrect. A class can't define more than one package statement.

Option (b) is incorrect. Although a class can import multiple packages in a class, the package statement must be placed before the import statement.

Option (c) is incorrect. A class can't define an import statement within its class body. The import statement appears before the class body.

Option (d) is correct. In the absence of any package information, this class becomes part of the default package.

 **[3.1]** Use Java operators; including parentheses to override operator precedence

**ME-Q16)** What is the output of the following code? (Select 1 option.)

```
class OpPre {
    public static void main(String... args) {
        int x = 10;
        int y = 20;
        int z = 30;
        if (x+y%z > (x+(-y)*(-z))) {
            System.out.println(x + y + z);
        }
    }
}
```

  a  60
  b  59
  c  61
● d  **No output.**
  e  The code fails to compile.

Answer: d

Explanation: x+y%z evaluates to 30; (x+(y%z)) and (x+(-y)*(-z)) evaluate to 610. The if condition returns false and the line of code that prints the sum of x, y, and z doesn't execute. Hence, the code doesn't provide any output.

[1.1]   Define the scope of variables

 [6.2]   Apply the static keyword to methods and fields

**ME-Q17)** Select the most appropriate definition of the variable name and the line number on which it should be declared so that the following code compiles successfully (choose 1 option).

```
class EJava {
    // LINE 1
    public EJava() {
        System.out.println(name);
    }
    void calc() {
        // LINE 2
        if (8 > 2) {
            System.out.println(name);
        }
    }
    public static void main(String... args) {
        // LINE 3
        System.out.println(name);
    }
}
```

- a **Define static String name; on line 1.**
- b Define String name; on line 1.
- c Define String name; on line 2.
- d Define String name; on line 3.

Answer: a

Explanation: The variable name must be accessible in the instance method calc, the class constructor, and the static method main. A non-static variable can't be accessed by a static method. Hence, the only appropriate option is to define a static variable name that can be accessed by all: the constructor of the class EJava and the methods calc and main.

 [2.4]   Explain an Object's Lifecycle (creation, "dereference by reassignment" and garbage collection)

**ME-Q18)** Examine the following code and select the correct statement (choose 1 option).

```
line1>    class Emp {
line2>        Emp mgr = new Emp();
line3>    }
```

```
line4>     class Office {
line5>         public static void main(String args[]) {
line6>             Emp e = null;
line7>             e = new Emp();
line8>             e = null;
line9>         }
line10>    }
```

- a The object referred to by object e is eligible for garbage collection on line 8.
- b The object referred to by object e is eligible for garbage collection on line 9.
- c The object referred to by object e isn't eligible for garbage collection because its member variable mgr isn't set to null.
- **d The code throws a runtime exception and the code execution never reaches line 8 or line 9.**

Answer: d

Explanation: The code throws `java.lang.StackOverflowError` at runtime. Line 7 creates an instance of class `Emp`. Creation of an object of the class `Emp` requires the creation of an instance variable `mgr` and its initialization with an object of the same class. As you can see, the `Emp` object creation calls itself recursively (without an exit condition), resulting in a `java.lang.StackOverflowError`.

 [2.5]   Develop code that uses wrapper classes such as Boolean, Double, and Integer.

 [6.1]   Create methods with arguments and return values; including overloaded methods

**ME-Q19)** Given the following,

```
long result;
```

which options are correct declarations of methods that accept two `String` arguments and an `int` argument and whose return value can be assigned to the variable `result`? (Select 3 options.)

- ☑ a `Short myMethod1(String str1, int str2, String str3)`
- ☐ b `Int myMethod2(String val1, int val2, String val3)`
- ☐ c `Byte myMethod3(String str1, str2, int a)`
- ☐ d `Float myMethod4(String val1, val2, int val3)`
- ☑ e `Long myMethod5(int str2, String str3, String str1)`
- ☐ f `Long myMethod6(String... val1, int val2)`
- ☑ g `Short myMethod7(int val1, String... val2)`

Answer: a, e, g

Explanation: The placement of the type of method parameters and the name of the method parameters doesn't matter. You can accept two String variables and then an int variable or a String variable followed by int and again a String. The name of an int variable can be str2. As long as the names are valid identifiers, any name is acceptable. The return type of the method must be assignable to a variable of type long.

Option (a) is correct. The value of a Short instance can be assigned to a variable of the primitive type long.

Option (b) is incorrect. It won't compile because Int is not defined in the Java API. The correct wrapper class name for the int data type is Integer.

Options (c) and (d) are incorrect. Unlike the declaration of multiple variables, which can be preceded by a single occurrence of their data type, each and every method argument *must* be preceded by its type. The declaration of the following variables is valid:

```
int aa, bb;
```

But the declaration of the method parameters in the following declaration isn't:

```
Byte myMethod3(String str1, str2, int a) { /*code*/ }
```

Option (e) is correct. The value of a Long instance can be assigned to a variable of primitive type long.

Option (f) won't compile. If varargs is used to define method parameters, it must be the last one.

Option (g) is correct. The method parameter val2, a variable argument, can accept two String arguments. Also, the return value of method7(), a Short, can be assigned to a variable of type long.

[4.1]   Declare, instantiate, initialize, and use a one-dimensional array

**ME-Q20)** Which of the following will compile successfully? (Select 3 options.)

☑ a `int eArr1[] = {10, 23, 10, 2};`
☑ b `int[] eArr2 = new int[10];`
☑ c `int[] eArr3 = new int[] {};`
☐ d `int[] eArr4 = new int[10] {};`
☐ e `int eArr5[] = new int[2] {10, 20};`

Answer: a, b, c

Explanation: Option (d) is incorrect because it defines the size of the array while using { }, which isn't allowed. Both of the following lines of code are correct:

```
int[] eArr4 = new int[10];
int[] eArr4 = new int[]{};
```

Option (e) is incorrect because it's invalid to specify the size of the array within the square brackets when you're declaring, instantiating, and initializing an array in a single line of code.

> **[6.1]**    Create methods with arguments and return values; including overloaded methods

> **[9.2]**    Create and manipulate strings

**ME-Q21)** Assume that Oracle has asked you to create a method that returns the concatenated value of two `String` objects. Which of the following methods can accomplish this job? (Select 2 options.)

  ☐ **a** `public String add(String 1, String 2) {`
       `return str1 + str2;`
    `}`

  ☑ **b** `private String add(String s1, String s2) {`
       `return s1.concat(s2);`
    `}`

  ☐ **c** `protected String add(String value1, String value2) {`
       `return value2.append(value2);`
    `}`

  ☑ **d** `String subtract(String first, String second) {`
       `return first.concat(second.substring(0));`
    `}`

Answer: b, d

Explanation: Option (a) is incorrect. This method defines method parameters with invalid identifier names. Identifiers can't start with a digit.

    Option (b) is correct. The method requirements don't talk about the access modifier of the required method. It can have any accessibility.

    Option (c) is incorrect because the class `String` doesn't define any `append` method.

    Option (d) is correct. Even though the name of the method—`subtract`—isn't an appropriate name for a method that tries to concatenate two values, it does accomplish the required job.

**[3.3]** Create if and if/else and ternary constructs

**[5.2]** Create and use for loops including the enhanced for loop

**[5.5]** Use break and continue

**ME-Q22)** Given the following,

```
int ctr = 10;
char[] arrC1 = new char[]{'P','a','u','l'};
char[] arrC2 = {'H','a','r','r','y'};
//INSERT CODE HERE
System.out.println(ctr);
```

which options, when inserted at //INSERT CODE HERE, will output 14? (Choose 2 options.)

☑ **a** 
```
for (char c1 : arrC1) {
    for (char c2 : arrC2) {
        if (c2 == 'a') break;
        ++ctr;
    }
}
```

☑ **b** 
```
for (char c1 : arrC1)
    for (char c2 : arrC2) {
        if (c2 == 'a') break;
        ++ctr;
    }
```

☐ **c** 
```
for (char c1 : arrC1)
    for (char c2 : arrC2)
        if (c2 == 'a') break;
        ++ctr;
```

☐ **d** 
```
for (char c1 : arrC1) {
    for (char c2 : arrC2) {
        if (c2 == 'a') continue;
        ++ctr;
    }
}
```

Answer: a, b

Explanation: Options (a) and (b) differ only in the usage of {} for the outer for construct. You can use {} to group the statements to execute for iteration constructs like do, do-while, and for. {} are also used with conditional constructs like switch and if-else.

The initial value of the variable ctr is 10. The size of array arrC1 is 4 and the size of array arrC2 is 5 with 'a' at the second position. The outer loop executes four times.

Because the second character referred to by arrC2 is `'a'`, the inner loop will increment the value of variable ctr for its first element. The inner loop won't execute `++ctr` for its second element because `c2=='a'` returns true and the break statement, and exits the inner loop. The inner loop increments the value ctr four times, incrementing its value to 14.

Option (c) is incorrect. Because the inner for loop doesn't use {} to group the lines of code that must execute for it, the code `++ctr` isn't a part of the inner for loop.

Option (d) is incorrect. The code `++ctr` just executes once, after the completion of the outer and inner for loops, because it isn't a part of the looping constructs.

---

**[6.1]**    Create methods with arguments and return values; including overloaded methods

---

**ME-Q23)** Given the following definitions of the class ChemistryBook, select the statements that are correct individually (choose 2 options):

```
import java.util.ArrayList;
class ChemistryBook {
    public void read() {}                   //METHOD1
    public String read() { return null; }     //METHOD2
    ArrayList read(int a) { return null; }    //METHOD3
}
```

- ☐ **a** Methods marked with //METHOD1 and //METHOD2 are correctly overloaded methods.
- ☑ **b** **Methods marked with //METHOD2 and //METHOD3 are correctly overloaded methods.**
- ☑ **c** **Methods marked with //METHOD1 and //METHOD3 are correctly overloaded methods.**
- ☐ **d** All the methods—methods marked with //METHOD1, //METHOD2, and //METHOD3— are correctly overloaded methods.

Answer: b, c

Explanation: Options (a) and (d) are incorrect because the methods read marked with //METHOD1 and //METHOD2 differ only in their return types, void and String. Overloaded methods can't be defined with only a change in their return types; hence, these methods don't qualify as correctly overloaded methods.

Note that the presence of methods marked with //METHOD1 and //METHOD2 together will cause a compilation error.

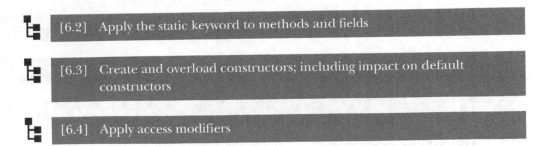

**ME-Q24)** Given the following,

```
final class Home {
    String name;
    int rooms;
    //INSERT CONSTRUCTOR HERE
}
```

which options, when inserted at `//INSERT CONSTRUCTOR HERE`, will define valid over-loaded constructors for the class `Home`? (Choose 3 options.)

☑ **a** `Home() {}`

☐ **b** `Float Home() {}`

☑ **c** `protected Home(int rooms) {}`

☐ **d** `final Home() {}`

☑ **e** `private Home(long name) {}`

☐ **f** `float Home(int rooms, String name) {}`

☐ **g** `static Home() {}`

Answer: a, c, e

Explanation: A constructor must not define an explicit return type. It you use it to do so, it's no longer a constructor. A constructor can be defined using any access level—private, default, protected, and public—irrespective of the access level that's used to declare the class.

Options (b) and (f) are incorrect because they define explicit return types: `Float` or `float`. The code in these options defines a method with the name `Home`, not constructors.

Options (d) and (g) are incorrect. The code won't compile because a constructor can't be defined using non-access modifiers `static`, `abstract`, or `final`.

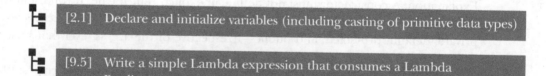

**[3.3]** Create if and if/else and ternary constructs

**[5.2]** Create and use for loops including the enhanced for loop

**[5.5]** Use break and continue

**ME-Q25)** Given the following code, which option, if used to replace //INSERT CODE HERE, will make the code print numbers that are completely divisible by 14? (Select 1 option.)

```
for (int ctr = 2; ctr <= 30; ++ctr) {
    if (ctr % 7 != 0)
        //INSERT CODE HERE
    if (ctr % 14 == 0)
        System.out.println(ctr);
}
```

- ● **a** `continue;`
- ○ **b** `exit;`
- ○ **c** `break;`
- ○ **d** `end;`

Answer: a

Explanation: Options (b) and (d) are incorrect because `exit` and `end` aren't valid statements in Java.

Option (c) is incorrect. Using `break` will terminate the `for` loop for the first iteration of the `for` loop so that no output is printed.

**[2.1]** Declare and initialize variables (including casting of primitive data types)

**[9.5]** Write a simple Lambda expression that consumes a Lambda Predicate expression

**ME-Q26)** What is the output of the following code? (Select 1 option.)

```
import java.util.function.Predicate;
public class MyCalendar {
    public static void main(String arguments[]) {
        Season season1 = new Season();
        season1.name = "Spring";

        Season season2 = new Season();
        season2.name = "Autumn";
```

```
        Predicate<String> aSeason = (s) -> s == "Summer" ?
                            season1.name : season2.name;

        season1 = season2;
        System.out.println(season1.name);
        System.out.println(season2.name);
        System.out.println(aSeason.test(new String("Summer")));
    }
}
class Season {
    String name;
}
```

- **a** `String`
  `Autumn`
  `false`

- **b** `Spring`
  `String`
  `false`

- **c** `Autumn`
  `Autumn`
  `false`

- **d** `Autumn`
  `String`
  `true`

- **e** **Compilation error**
- **f** Runtime exception

Answer: e

Explanation: The return type of the functional method `test` in the functional inter-face `Predicate` is `boolean`. The following Lambda expression is trying to return a `String` value and so the code fails compilation:

```
Predicate<String> aSeason = (s) -> s == "Summer" ?
                        season1.name : season2.name;
```

This question also covers another important topic: multiple variable references can refer to the same instances. Let's assume that you modify the preceding Lambda expression as follows:

```
Predicate<String> aSeason = (s) -> s == "Summer";
```

In this case, the code will output the following:

```
Autumn
Autumn
false
```

This is because multiple variable references can point to the same object. The following lines of code define a reference variable season1, which refers to an object that has the value of its instance variable (name) set to Spring:

```
Season season1 = new Season();
season1.name = "Spring";
```

The following lines of code define a reference variable season2, which refers to an object that has the value of its instance variable (name) set to Autumn:

```
Season season2 = new Season();
season2.name = "Autumn";
```

The following line of code reinitializes the reference variable season1 and assigns it to the object referred to by the variable season2:

```
season1 = season2;
```

Now the variable season1 refers to the object that's also referred to by the variable season2. Both of these variables refer to the same object—the one that has the value of the instance variable set to Autumn. Hence, the output of the modified code is as follows:

```
Autumn
Autumn
false
```

A quick reminder for the reason for the preceding output: a String object with the value "Summer", created with the new operator, is never pooled by the JVM. Here, such an instance is compared to the pooled "Summer" instance through the == operator.

[6.3]   Create and overload constructors; including impact on default
        constructors

**ME-Q27)** What is true about the following code? (Select 1 option.)

```
class Shoe {}
class Boot extends Shoe {}
class ShoeFactory {
    ShoeFactory(Boot val) {
        System.out.println("boot");
    }
    ShoeFactory(Shoe val) {
        System.out.println("shoe");
    }
}
```

  **a** **The class `ShoeFactory` has a total of two overloaded constructors.**

  **b** The class `ShoeFactory` has three overloaded constructors, two user-defined constructors, and one default constructor.

  **c** The class `ShoeFactory` will fail to compile.

  **d** The addition of the following constructor will increment the number of constructors of the class `ShoeFactory` to 3:

```
private ShoeFactory (Shoe arg) {}
```

Answer: a

Explanation: Java accepts changes in the objects of base-derived classes as a sole criterion to define overloaded constructors and methods.

Option (b) is incorrect because Java doesn't generate a default constructor for a class that has already defined a constructor.

Option (c) is incorrect. All classes defined for this example compile successfully.

Option (d) is incorrect. The class `ShoeFactory` already defines a constructor that accepts a method argument of type `Shoe`. You can't overload a constructor with a mere change in its access modifier.

### [7.4]   Use super and this to access objects and constructors

**ME-Q28)** Given the following definitions of the classes `ColorPencil` and `TestColor`, which option, if used to replace `//INSERT CODE HERE`, will initialize the instance variable `color` of the reference variable `myPencil` with the `String` literal value `"RED"`? (Select 1 option.)

```
class ColorPencil {
    String color;
    ColorPencil(String color) {
        //INSERT CODE HERE
    }
}
class TestColor {
    ColorPencil myPencil = new ColorPencil("RED");
}
```

  **a** **`this.color = color;`**

  **b** `color = color;`

  **c** `color = RED;`

  **d** `this.color = RED;`

Answer: a

Explanation: Option (b) is incorrect. This line of code will assign the value of the method parameter to itself. The constructor of the class `ColorPencil` defines a method parameter with the same name as its instance variable, color. To access an instance variable in the constructor, it must be prefixed with the keyword this, or it will refer to the method parameter color.

Options (c) and (d) are incorrect. They try to access the value of the variable RED, which isn't defined in the code.

## [2.3]   Know how to read or write to object fields

**ME-Q29)** What is the output of the following code? (Select 1 option.)

```
class EJavaCourse {
    String courseName = "Java";
}
class University {
    public static void main(String args[]) {
        EJavaCourse courses[] = { new EJavaCourse(), new EJavaCourse() };
        courses[0].courseName = "OCA";
        for (EJavaCourse c : courses) c = new EJavaCourse();
        for (EJavaCourse c : courses) System.out.println(c.courseName);
    }
}
```

    a  Java
      Java

    b  **OCA**
      **Java**

    c  OCA
      OCA

    d  None of the above

Answer: b

Explanation: This question tests you on multiple concepts: how to read from and write to object fields, how to use arrays, the enhanced for loop, and assigning a value to a loop variable.

The code defines an array of the class EJavaCourse with two elements. The default value of the variable courseName—Java—is assigned to each of these two elements. courses[0].courseName = "OCA" changes the value courseName for the object stored at array position 0. c = new EJavaCourse() assigns a new object to the loop variable c. This assignment doesn't reassign new objects to the array reference variables. System.out.println(c.courseName) prints the name of the courseName of the objects initially stored by the array, using the loop variable c.

The loop variable in the enhanced for loop refers to a copy of the array or list element. If you modify the state of the loop variable, the modified object state will be reflected in the array. But if you assign a new object to the loop variable, it won't be reflected in the list or the array that's being iterated. You can compare this behavior of the enhanced `for` loop variable with the behavior of object references passed as arguments to a method.

 [6.2] Apply the static keyword to methods and fields

 [7.2] Develop code that demonstrates the use of polymorphism; including overriding and object type versus reference type

**ME-Q30)** What is the output of the following code? (Select 1 option.)

```java
class Phone {
    static void call() {
        System.out.println("Call-Phone");
    }
}
class SmartPhone extends Phone{
    static void call() {
        System.out.println("Call-SmartPhone");
    }
}
class TestPhones {
    public static void main(String... args) {
        Phone phone = new Phone();
        Phone smartPhone = new SmartPhone();
        phone.call();
        smartPhone.call();
    }
}
```

- ⦿ **a** `Call-Phone`
     `Call-Phone`

- ◌ **b** `Call-Phone`
     `Call-SmartPhone`

- ◌ **c** `Call-Phone`
     `null`

- ◌ **d** `null`
     `Call-SmartPhone`

Answer: a

Explanation: Invocation of a `static` method is tied to the type of the reference variable and doesn't depend on the type of the object that's assigned to the reference variable. The `static` method belongs to a class, not to its objects. Reexamine the following code:

```java
Phone smartPhone = new SmartPhone();
smartPhone.call();
```

In the preceding code, the type of the reference variable `smartPhone` is `Phone`. Because `call` is a `static` method, `smartPhone.call()` calls the method `call` defined in the class `Phone`.

**[8.1]**　Differentiate among checked exceptions, unchecked exceptions, and Errors

**ME-Q31)** Given the following code, which of the following statements are true? (Select 3 options.)

```
class MyExam {
    void question() {
        try {
            question();
        } catch (StackOverflowError e) {
            System.out.println("caught");
        }
    }
    public static void main(String args[]) {
        new MyExam().question();
    }
}
```

- ☑ **a** **The code will print `caught`.**
- ☐ **b** The code won't print `caught`.
- ☑ **c** **The code would print `caught` if `StackOverflowError` were a runtime exception.**
- ☑ **d** **The code would print `caught` if `StackOverflowError` were a checked exception.**
- ☐ **e** The code would print `caught` if `question()` throws the exception `NullPointer-Exception`.

Answer: a, c, d

Explanation: Option (a) is correct. The control will be transferred to the exception handler for `StackOverflowError` when it's encountered. Hence it will print `caught`.

Options (c) and (d) are correct. Exception handlers execute when the corresponding checked or runtime exceptions are thrown.

Option (e) is incorrect. An exception handler for the class `StackOverflow` can't handle exceptions of the class `NullPointerException` because `NullPointerException` is not a superclass of `StackOverflowError`.

**[6.5]**　Apply encapsulation principles to a class

**ME-Q32)** A class `Student` is defined as follows:

```
public class Student {
    private String fName;
    private String lName;
```

```
    public Student(String first, String last) {
        fName = first; lName = last;
    }
    public String getName() { return fName + lName; }
}
```

The creator of the class later changes the method getName as follows:

```
public String getName() {
    return fName + " " + lName;
}
```

What are the implications of this change? (Select 2 options.)

☐ **a** The classes that were using the class Student will fail to compile.

☑ **b** **The classes that were using the class Student will work without any compilation issues.**

☑ **c** **The class Student is an example of a well-encapsulated class.**

☐ **d** The class Student exposes its instance variable outside the class.

Answer: b, c

Explanation: This is an example of a well-encapsulated class. There's no change in the signature of the method getName after it's modified. Hence, none of the code that uses this class and method will face any compilation issues. Its instance variables (fName and lName) aren't exposed outside the class. They're available only via a public method: getName.

## [6.2]  Apply the static keyword to methods and fields

**ME-Q33)** What is the output of the following code? (Select 1 option.)

```
class ColorPack {
    int shadeCount = 12;
    static int getShadeCount() {
        return shadeCount;
    }
}
class Artist {
    public static void main(String args[]) {
        ColorPack pack1 = new ColorPack();
        System.out.println(pack1.getShadeCount());
    }
}
```

○ **a** 10

○ **b** 12

○ **c** No output

◉ **d** **Compilation error**

Answer: d

Explanation: A static method can't access non-static instance variables of a class. Hence, the class ColorPack fails to compile.

> **[6.6]**   Determine the effect upon object references and primitive values when they are passed into methods that change the values

**ME-Q34)** Paul defined his Laptop and Workshop classes to upgrade his laptop's memory. Do you think he succeeded? What is the output of this code? (Select 1 option.)

```
class Laptop {
    String memory = "1 GB";
}
class Workshop {
    public static void main(String args[]) {
        Laptop life = new Laptop();
        repair(life);
        System.out.println(life.memory);
    }
    public static void repair(Laptop laptop) {
        laptop.memory = "2 GB";
    }
}
```

- ○ **a** 1 GB
- ◉ **b** 2 GB
- ○ **c** Compilation error
- ○ **d** Runtime exception

Answer: b

Explanation: The method repair defined in this example modifies the state of the method parameter laptop that's passed to it. It does so by modifying the value of the instance variable memory.

When a method modifies the state of an object reference variable that's passed to it, the changes made are visible in the calling method. The method repair makes changes to the state of the method parameter laptop; these changes are visible in the method main. Hence, the method main prints the value of life.memory as 2 GB.

> **[2.1]**   Declare and initialize variables (including casting of primitive data types)

**ME-Q35)** What is the output of the following code? (Select 1 option.)

```
public class Application {
    public static void main(String... args) {
        double price = 10;
```

```
        String model;
        if (price > 10)
            model = "Smartphone";
        else if (price <= 10)
            model = "landline";
        System.out.println(model);
    }
}
```

    ◯ **a** `landline`
    ◯ **b** `Smartphone`
    ◯ **c** No output
    ◉ **d** **Compilation error**

Answer: d

Explanation: The local variables aren't initialized with default values. Code that tries to print the value of an uninitialized local variable fails to compile.

    In this code, the local variable `model` is only declared, not initialized. The initialization of the variable `model` is placed within the `if` and `else-if` constructs. If you initialize a variable within an `if` or `else-if` construct, the compiler can't be sure whether these conditions will evaluate to `true`, resulting in no initialization of the local variable. Because there's no `else` at the bottom and the compiler can't tell whether the `if` and `else-if` are mutually exclusive, the code won't compile.

    If you remove the condition `if (price <= 10)` from the previous code, the code will compile successfully:

```
public class Application {
    public static void main(String... args) {
        double price = 10;
        String model;
        if (price > 10)
            model = "Smartphone";
        else
            model = "landline";
        System.out.println(model);
    }
}
```

In this code, the compiler can be sure about the initialization of the local variable `model`.

## [9.2] Create and manipulate strings

**ME-Q36)** What is the output of the following code? (Select 1 option.)

```
class EString {
    public static void main(String args[]) {
        String eVal = "123456789";
```

```
        System.out.println(eVal.substring(eVal.indexOf("2"),
            eVal.indexOf("0")).concat("0"));
    }
}
```

⊙ a  234567890

⊙ b  34567890

⊙ c  234456789

⊙ d  3456789

⊙ e  Compilation error

⊙ f  **Runtime exception**

Answer: f

Explanation: When multiple methods are chained on a single code statement, the methods execute from left to right, not from right to left. `eVal.indexOf("0")` returns a negative value because, as you can see, the `String eVal` doesn't contain the digit `0`. Hence, `eVal.substring` is passed a negative `end` value, which results in a runtime exception.

[2.4]   Explain an Object's Lifecycle (creation, "dereference by reassignment" and garbage collection)

**ME-Q37)** Examine the following code and select the correct statements (choose 2 options).

```
class Artist {
    Artist assistant;
}
class Studio {
    public static void main(String... args) {
        Artist a1 = new Artist();
        Artist a2 = new Artist();
        a2.assistant = a1;
        a2 = null;          // Line 1
    }
    // Line 2
}
```

☐ a  At least two objects are garbage collected on line 1.

☐ b  At least one object is garbage collected on line 1.

☐ c  No objects are garbage collected on line 1

☑ d  **The number of objects that are garbage collected on line 1 is unknown.**

☑ e  **At least two objects are eligible for garbage collection on line 2.**

Answer: d, e

Explanation: Options (a), (b), and (c) are incorrect.

When an object reference is marked as null, the object is marked for garbage collection. But you can't be sure exactly when a garbage collector will kick in to garbage collect the objects. A garbage collector is a low-priority thread, and its exact execution time will depend on the OS. The OS will start this thread if it needs to claim unused space. You can be sure only about the number of objects that are eligible for garbage collection. You can never be sure about which objects have been garbage collected, so any statement that asserts that a particular number of objects *have* been garbage collected is incorrect.

Option (d) is correct. As mentioned previously, the exact number of objects garbage collected at any point in time can't be determined.

Option (e) is correct. If you marked this option incorrect, think again. The question wants you to select the correct statements, and this is a correct statement. You may argue that at least two objects were already made eligible for garbage collection at line 1, and you're correct. But because nothing changes on line 2, at least two objects are still eligible for garbage collection.

**[3.2]  Test equality between Strings and other objects using == and equals()**

**ME-Q38)** What is the output of the following code? (Select 1 option.)

```
class Book {
    String ISBN;
    Book(String val) {
        ISBN = val;
    }
}
class TestEquals {
    public static void main(String... args) {
        Book b1 = new Book("1234-4657");
        Book b2 = new Book("1234-4657");
        System.out.print(b1.equals(b2) +":");
        System.out.print(b1 == b2);
    }
}
```

- a true:false
- b true:true
- c false:true
- **d false:false**
- e Compilation error—there is no equals method in the class Book.
- f Runtime exception

Answer: d

Explanation: The comparison operator determines whether the reference variables refer to the same object. Because the reference variables `b1` and `b2` refer to different objects, `b1==b2` prints `false`.

The method `equals` is a `public` method defined in the class `java.lang.Object`. Because the class `Object` is the superclass for all the classes in Java, the method `equals` is inherited by all classes. Hence, the code compiles successfully. The default implementation of the method `equals` in the base class compares the object references and returns `true` if both reference variables refer to the same object, and `false` otherwise.

Because the class `Book` doesn't override this method, the method `equals` in the base class `Object` is called for `b1.equals(b2)`, which returns `false`. Hence, the code prints

```
false:false
```

### [9.1]   Manipulate data using the StringBuilder class and its methods

**ME-Q39)** Which of the following statements are correct? (Select 2 options.)

&#9745; a `StringBuilder sb1 = new StringBuilder()` **will create a** `StringBuilder` **object with no characters but with an initial capacity to store 16 characters.**

&#9744; b `StringBuilder sb1 = new StringBuilder(5*10)` will create a `StringBuilder` object with a value of 50.

&#9744; c Unlike the class `String`, the `concat` method in `StringBuilder` modifies the value of a `StringBuilder` object.

&#9745; d **The** `insert` **method can be used to insert a character, number, or** `String` **at the start or end or a specified position of a** `StringBuilder`**.**

Answer: a, d

Explanation: There is no `concat` method in the `StringBuilder` class. It defines a whole army of `append` methods (overloaded methods) to add data at the end of a `StringBuilder` object.

`new StringBuilder(50)` creates a `StringBuilder` object with no characters but with an initial capacity to store 50 characters.

### [4.1]   Declare, instantiate, initialize, and use a one-dimensional array

**ME-Q40)** Given the following definition of the class `Animal` and the interface `Jump`, select the correct array declarations and initialization (choose 3 options).

```
interface Jump {}
class Animal implements Jump {}
```

&#9745; a `Jump eJump1[] = {null, new Animal()};`

&#9744; b `Jump[] eJump2 = new Animal()[22];`

☑ c `Jump[] eJump3 = new Jump[10];`

☑ d `Jump[] eJump4 = new Animal[87];`

☐ e `Jump[] eJump5 = new Jump()[12];`

Answer: a, c, d

Explanation: Option (b) is incorrect because the right side of the expression is trying to create a single object of the class `Animal` by using parentheses `()`. At the same time, it's also using the square brackets `[]` to define an array. This combination is invalid.

Option (e) is incorrect. Apart from using an invalid syntax to initialize an array (as mentioned previously), it also tries to create objects of the interface `Jump`. Objects of interfaces can't be created.

 [9.4]   Declare and use an ArrayList of a given type

 [8.5]   "Recognize common exception classes (such as NullPointerException, ArithmeticException, ArrayIndexOutOfBoundsException, ClassCastException)"

**ME-Q41)** What is the output of the following code? (Select 1 option.)

```java
import java.util.*;
class EJGArrayL {
    public static void main(String args[]) {
        ArrayList<String> seasons = new ArrayList<>();
        seasons.add(1, "Spring"); seasons.add(2, "Summer");
        seasons.add(3, "Autumn"); seasons.add(4, "Winter");
        seasons.remove(2);

        for (String s : seasons)
            System.out.print(s + ", ");
    }
}
```

⊙ a `Spring, Summer, Winter,`

⊙ b `Spring, Autumn, Winter,`

⊙ c `Autumn, Winter,`

⊙ d Compilation error

⦿ e **Runtime exception**

Answer: e

Explanation: The code throws a runtime exception, `IndexOutOfBoundsException`, because the `ArrayList` is trying to insert its first element at position 0. Before the first call to the method `add`, the size of the `ArrayList` seasons is 0. Because season's first element is stored at position 0, a call to store its first element at position 1 will throw a

RuntimeException. The elements of an ArrayList can't be added to a higher position if lower positions are available.

 **[2.1]**    Declare and initialize variables (including casting of primitive data types)

 **[3.3]**    Create if and if/else and ternary constructs

 **[5.3]**    Create and use do-while loops

**ME-Q42)** What is the output of the following code? (Select 1 option.)

```
class EIf {
    public static void main(String args[]) {
        bool boolean = false;
        do {
            if (boolean = true)
                System.out.println("true");
            else
                System.out.println("false");
        }
        while(3.3 + 4.7 > 8);      }
}
```

   ◉ **a** The class will print true.
   ◉ **b** The class will print false.
   ◉ **c** The class will print true if the if condition is changed to boolean == true.
   ◉ **d** The class will print false if the if condition is changed to boolean != true.
   ◉ **e** **The class won't compile.**
   ◉ **f** Runtime exception

Answer: e

Explanation: This question tries to trick you on two points. First, there's no data type bool in Java. Second, the name of an identifier can't be the same as a reserved word. The code tries to define an identifier of type bool with the name boolean.

 **[5.1]**    Create and use while loops

**ME-Q43)** How many Fish did the Whale (defined as follows) manage to eat? Examine the following code and select the correct statements (choose 2 options).

```
class Whale {
    public static void main(String args[]) {
        boolean hungry = false;
```

```
        while (hungry=true) {
            ++Fish.count;
        }
        System.out.println(Fish.count);
    }
}
class Fish {
    static byte count;
}
```

   ☐ **a** The code doesn't compile.

   ☑ **b** **The code doesn't print a value.**

   ☐ **c** The code prints 0.

   ☑ **d** **Changing ++Fish.count to Fish.count++ will give the same results.**

Answer: b, d

Explanation: Option (a) is incorrect because the code compiles successfully.

Option (c) is incorrect. This question tries to trick you by comparing a boolean value when it's assigning a boolean value in the while construct. Because the while loop assigns the value true to the variable hungry, it will always return true, incrementing the value of the variable count and thus getting stuck in an infinite loop.

Option (d) is correct because when the unary increment operator (++) is not part of an expression, postfix and prefix notation behave in exactly the same manner.

**[5.2]** Create and use for loops including the enhanced for loop

**ME-Q44)** Given the following code, which option, if used to replace /* REPLACE CODE HERE */, will make the code print the name of the phone with the position at which it's stored in the array phones? (Select 1 option.)

```
class Phones {
    public static void main(String args[]) {
        String phones[]= {"BlackBerry", "Android", "iPhone"};
        for (String phone : phones)
            /* REPLACE CODE HERE */
    }
}
```

   ◉ **a** System.out.println(phones.count + ":" + phone);

   ◉ **b** System.out.println(phones.counter + ":" + phone);

   ◉ **c** System.out.println(phones.getPosition() + ":" + phone);

   ◉ **d** System.out.println(phones.getCtr() + ":" + phone);

   ◉ **e** System.out.println(phones.getCount() + ":" + phone);

   ◉ **f** System.out.println(phones.pos + ":" + phone);

   ◉ **g** **None of the above**

Answer: g

Explanation: The enhanced for loop doesn't provide you with a variable to access the position of the array that it's being used to iterate over. This facility comes with the regular for loop.

**[2.5]** Develop code that uses wrapper classes such as Boolean, Double, and Integer.

**[3.2]** Test equality between Strings and other objects using == and equals()

**[7.3]** Determine when casting is necessary

**[9.2]** Create and manipulate strings

**ME-Q45)** Given the following code,

```
Byte b1 = (byte)100;                        // 1
Integer i1 = (int)200;                      // 2
Long l1 = (long)300;                        // 3
Float f1 = (float)b1 + (int)l1;             // 4
String s1 = 300;                            // 5
if (s1 == (b1 + i1))                        // 6
    s1 = (String)500;                       // 7
else                                        // 8
    f1 = (int)100;                          // 9
System.out.println(s1 + ":" + f1);          // 10
```

what is the output? Select 1 option.

- a Code fails compilation at line numbers 1, 3, 4, 7.
- b Code fails compilation at line numbers 6, 7.
- c Code fails compilation at line numbers 7, 9.
- **d Code fails compilation at line numbers 4, 5, 6, 7, 9.**
- e No compilation error—outputs 500:300.
- f No compilation error—outputs 300:100.
- g Runtime exception

Answer: d

Explanation: This question tests you on multiple concepts:

- Autoboxing and unboxing wrapper classes
- The difference between casting primitive values and wrapper classes, for example, from long to int and casting Long to int

- Implicit and explicit casting of primitives and objects
- Exception thrown due to invalid explicit casting (implicit casting doesn't throw any exception)

The code on lines 1, 2, and 3 doesn't throw a compilation error or runtime exceptions. You can explicitly cast all numeric primitive data types to one another. For example, a `double` primitive value can be implicitly cast to a `byte`. A `char` primitive can be explicitly cast to any other numeric data type:

```
char c = 100;
Float f = (float)c;
```

The code at line 4 will throw a compilation error. The code `(int)l1` isn't casting primitive `long` to `int`. It's trying to cast `Long` to primitive `int`. You can explicitly cast a wrapper object to only the type that it wraps.

The code at line 5 doesn't compile because you can't assign `int` values to `String` reference variables by using the assignment operator. You can use the `String` method `valueOf()`, passing it a numeric value (integer or decimal) to return a `String` instance.

The code at line 6 doesn't compile because you can't compare `String` instances with instances of wrapper classes.

The code at line 7 doesn't compile. You can't explicitly cast a numeric literal value to convert it to a `String` value.

The code at line 9 doesn't compile because `int` can't be converted to `Float`.

[3.2]  Test equality between Strings and other objects using == and equals()

[3.3]  Create if and if/else and ternary constructs

[9.3]  Create and manipulate calendar data using classes from java.time.LocalDateTime, java.time.LocalDate, java.time.LocalTime, java.time.format.DateTimeFormatter, java.time.Period

**ME-Q46)** What is the output of the following code? (Select 1 option.)

```
class Book {
    String ISBN;
    Book(String val) {
        ISBN = val;
    }
    public boolean equals(Object b) {
        if (b instanceof Book) {
            return ((Book)b).ISBN.equals(ISBN);
        }
```

```
        else
            return false;
    }
}

class TestEquals {
    public static void main(String args[]) {
        Book b1 = new Book("1234-4657");
        Book b2 = new Book("1234-4657");
        LocalDate release = null;
        release = b1.equals(b2) ? b1 == b2? LocalDate.of(2050,12,12):
        LocalDate.parse("2072-02-01"):LocalDate.parse("9999-09-09");
        System.out.print(release);
    }
}
```

   a   2050-12-12

   **b   2072-02-01**

   c   9999-09-09

   d   Compilation error

   e   Runtime exception

Answer: b

Explanation: This question tests you on multiple concepts:

- Usage of equals() and the comparison operator == to determine object equality
- Usage of the ternary operator
- Correct method and syntax to instantiate LocalDate

The comparison operator determines whether the reference variables refer to the same object. Because the reference variables b1 and b2 refer to different objects, b1==b2 will return false.

The method equals is a public method defined in the class java.lang.Object. Because the class Object is the superclass for all the classes in Java, equals is inherited by all classes. The default implementation of equals in the base class compares the object references and returns true if both reference variables refer to the same object and false otherwise. If a class has overridden this method, it returns a boolean value depending on the logic defined in this class. The class Book overrides the equals method and returns true if the Book object defines the same ISBN value as the Book object being compared to. Because the ISBN object value of both variables b1 and b2 is the same, b1.equals(b2) returns true.

Here's the syntax of the ternary operator:

```
variable = booleanValue? returnValueIfTrue : returnValueIfFalse;
```

All the components of a ternary operator are compulsory. Unlike an if construct, you can't leave out the else part in a ternary operator. The code in this question uses a nested ternary operator. Let's indent the code, which will make it easy to evaluate the expression:

```
release = b1.equals(b2) ?
            b1 == b2?
                LocalDate.of(2050,12,12):
                LocalDate.parse("2072-02-01"):
            LocalDate.parse("9999-09-09");
```

Because `b1.equals(b2)` returns `true`, the control evaluates the nested ternary operator. Because `b1 == b2` returns `false`, the code returns the `LocalDate` instance created in the `else` part of the ternary operator, `2072-02-01`.

[5.2]   Create and use for loops including the enhanced for loop

**ME-Q47)** What is the output of the following code? (Select 1 option.)

```
int a = 10;
for (; a <= 20; ++a) {
    if (a%3 == 0) a++; else if (a%2 == 0) a=a*2;
    System.out.println(a);
}
```

- a  11
    13
    15
    17
    19

- ● **b  20**

- c  11
    14
    17
    20

- d  40

- e  Compilation error

Answer: b

Explanation: This question requires multiple skills: understanding the declaration of a `for` loop, the use of operators, and the use of the `if-else` construct.

The `for` loop is correctly defined in the code. The `for` loop in this code doesn't use its variable initialization block; it starts with `;` to mark the absence of its variable initialization block. The code for the `if` construct is deliberately incorrect, because you may encounter similar code in the exam.

For the first iteration of the `for` loop, the value of the variable a is 10. Because a <= 20 evaluates to `true`, control moves on to the execution of the `if` construct. This `if` construct can be indented properly as follows:

```
if (a%3 == 0)
    a++;
else if (a%2 == 0)
    a=a*2;
```

(a%3 == 0) evaluates to `false` and (a%2 == 0) evaluates to `true`, so a value of 20 (a*2) is assigned to a. The subsequent line prints the value of a as 20.

The increment part of the loop statement, (++a), increments the value of variable a to 21. For the next loop iteration, its condition evaluates to `false` (a <= 20), and the loop terminates.

[6.1]   Create methods with arguments and return values; including overloaded methods

**ME-Q48)** Given the following code, which option, if used to replace //INSERT CODE HERE, will define an overloaded `rideWave` method? (Select 1 option.)

```
class Raft {
    public String rideWave() { return null; }
    //INSERT CODE HERE
}
```

    ◉ **a** `public String[] rideWave() { return null; }`
    ◉ **b** `protected void riceWave(int a) {}`
    ◉ **c** `private void rideWave(int value, String value2) {}`
    ◉ **d** `default StringBuilder rideWave (StringBuffer a) { return null; }`

Answer: c

Explanation: Option (a) is incorrect. Making a change only in the return value of a method doesn't define a valid overloaded method.

Option (b) is incorrect. The name of the method in this option is `riceWave` and not `rideWave`. Overloaded methods should have the same method name.

Option (d) is incorrect. `default` isn't a valid access modifier. The default modifier is marked by the absence of an access modifier.

[5.2]   Create and use for loops including the enhanced for loop

[5.5]   Use break and continue

**ME-Q49)** Given the following code, which option, if used to replace //INSERT CODE HERE, will correctly calculate the sum of all the even numbers in the array num and store it in the variable sum? (Select 1 option.)

```
int num[] = {10, 15, 2, 17};
int sum = 0;
for (int number : num) {
    //INSERT CODE HERE
    sum += number;
}
```

○  **a** if (number % 2 == 0)
          continue;

○  **b** if (number % 2 == 0)
          break;

◉  **c** if (number % 2 != 0)
          continue;

○  **d** if (number % 2 != 0)
          break;

Answer: c

Explanation: To find the sum of the even numbers, you first need to determine whether a number is an even number. Then you need to add the even numbers to the variable sum.

Option (c) determines whether the array element is completely divisible by 2. If it isn't, it skips the remaining statements in the for loop by using the continue statement, which starts execution of the for loop with the next array element. If the array element is completely divisible by 2, continue doesn't execute, and the array number is added to the variable sum.

[3.1]   Use Java operators; including parentheses to override operator precedence

[9.5]   Write a simple Lambda expression that consumes a Lambda Predicate expression

**ME-Q50)** What is the output of the following code? (Select 1 option.)

```
import java.util.function.Predicate;
class Op {
    public static void main(String... args) {
```

```
        int a = 0;
        int b = 100;
        Predicate<Integer> compare = (var) -> var++ == 10;
        if (!b++ > 100 && compare.test(a)) {
            System.out.println(a+b);
        }
    }
}
```

- ○ **a** 100
- ○ **b** 101
- ○ **c** 102
- ◉ **d** **Code fails to compile.**
- ○ **e** No output is produced.

Answer: d

Explanation: The code defines the Lambda expression correctly.

Although it may seem that the unary negation operator ! is being applied to the expression b++ > 100, it's actually being applied to the variable b of type int. Because a unary negation operator ! can't be applied to a variable of type int, the code fails to compile. The correct if condition would be as follows:

```
if (!(b++ > 100) && compare.test(a)) {
```

**[6.5]   Apply encapsulation principles to a class**

**ME-Q51)** Choose the options that meets the following specification: Create a well-encapsulated class Pencil with one instance variable model. The value of model should be accessible and modifiable outside Pencil. (Select 1 option.)

- ○ **a**
  ```
  class Pencil {
      public String model;
  }
  ```
- ○ **b**
  ```
  class Pencil {
      public String model;
      public String getModel() { return model; }
      public void setModel(String val) { model = val; }
  }
  ```
- ◉ **c**
  ```
  class Pencil {
      private String model;
      public String getModel() { return model; }
      public void setModel(String val) { model = val; }
  }
  ```
- ○ **d**
  ```
  class Pencil {
      public String model;
      private String getModel() { return model; }
      private void setModel(String val) { model = val; }
  }
  ```

Answer: c

Explanation: A well-encapsulated class's instance variables shouldn't be directly accessible outside the class. They should be accessible via non-private getter and setter methods.

 **[7.2]**   Develop code that demonstrates the use of polymorphism; including overriding and object type versus reference type

**ME-Q52)** What is the output of the following code? (Select 1 option.)

```
class Phone {
    void call() {
        System.out.println("Call-Phone");
    }
}
class SmartPhone extends Phone{
    void call() {
        System.out.println("Call-SmartPhone");
    }
}
class TestPhones {
    public static void main(String[] args) {
        Phone phone = new Phone();
        Phone smartPhone = new SmartPhone();
        phone.call();
        smartPhone.call();
    }
}
```

    **a** `Call-Phone`
        `Call-Phone`

    **b** **`Call-Phone`**
        **`Call-SmartPhone`**

    **c** `Call-Phone`
        `null`

    **d** `null`
        `Call-SmartPhone`

Answer: b

Explanation: The method `call` is defined in the base class `Phone`. This method `call` is inherited and overridden by the derived class `SmartPhone`. The type of both reference variables, phone and smartphone, is `Phone`. But the reference variable phone refers to an object of the class `Phone`, and the variable `smartPhone` refers to an object of the class `SmartPhone`. When the method `call` is called on the reference variable `smartPhone`, it calls the method `call` defined in the class `SmartPhone`, because a call to an overridden method is resolved at runtime and is based on the type of the object on which a method is called.

**[7.2]**   Develop code that demonstrates the use of polymorphism; including overriding and object type versus reference type

**ME-Q53)** What is the output of the following code? (Select 1 option.)

```
class Phone {
    String keyboard = "in-built";
}
class Tablet extends Phone {
    boolean playMovie = false;
}
class College2 {
    public static void main(String args[]) {
        Phone phone = new Tablet();
        System.out.println(phone.keyboard + ":" + phone.playMovie);
    }
}
```

- ⦿ **a** `in-built:false`
- ⦿ **b** `in-built:true`
- ⦿ **c** `null:false`
- ⦿ **d** `null:true`
- ⦿ **e** **Compilation error**

Answer: e

Explanation: This code won't compile. The object reference variable `phone`, of type `Phone`, can be used to refer to an object of its derived type, `Tablet`. But variables of a base class can't access variables and methods of its derived classes without an explicit cast to the object of the derived class. So `phone` can access `keyboard` but not `playMovie`.

**[2.1]**   Declare and initialize variables (including casting of primitive data types)

**ME-Q54)** What is the output of the following code? (Select 1 option.)

```
public class Wall {
    public static void main(String args[]) {
        double area = 10.98;
        String color;
        if (area < 5)
            color = "red";
        else
            color = "blue";
        System.out.println(color);
    }
}
```

⊙ **a** red
◉ **b** **blue**
⊙ **c** No output
⊙ **d** Compilation error

Answer: b

Explanation: When you answer a question that includes accessing the value of a local variable, check whether it has been initialized or not. Code that tries to access an uninitialized local variable won't compile.

In this question, the local variable color is initialized using an if-else construct. The variable color will be initialized as the value "red" if the value of another local variable (area) is less than 5 but will be initialized as "blue" otherwise. So, irrespective of the value of area, color will be initialized for sure. In an if-else construct, at least one of the two blocks of code, corresponding to if and else, is sure to execute. The code will execute successfully, printing blue.

Watch out for code that initializes a local variable using a conditional statement. If the compiler can't seem to guarantee initialization of a local variable, *code that tries to access it* won't compile. Here's a modified version of the code (modifications in bold) included in this question, which doesn't compile:

```java
public class Wall {
    public static void main(String args[]) {
        double area = 10.98;
        String color;
        if (area < 5)
            color = "red";
        if (area >= 5)
            color = "blue";
        System.out.println(color);
    }
}
```

**[2.3]   Know how to read or write to object fields**

**ME-Q55)** What is the output of the following code? (Select 1 option.)

```java
class Diary {
    int pageCount = 100;
    int getPageCount() {
        return pageCount;
    }
    void setPageCount(int val) {
        pageCount = val;
    }
}
```

```
class ClassRoom {
    public static void main(String args[]) {
        System.out.println(new Diary().getPageCount());
        new Diary().setPageCount(200);
        System.out.println(new Diary().getPageCount());
    }
}
```

    a  100
       200

    **b  100**
       **100**

    c  200
       200

    d  The code fails to compile.

Answer: b

Explanation: The constructor of a class creates and returns an object of the class in which it's defined. This returned object can be assigned to a reference variable. In case the returned object isn't assigned to any reference variable, none of the variables or methods of this object can be accessed again. This is what happens in the class ClassRoom. All calls to the methods getPageCount and setPageCount in the example operate on unrelated objects.

## [5.3]   Create and use do-while loops

**ME-Q56)** How many times do you think you can shop with the following code (that is, what's the output of the following code)? (Select 1 option.)

```
class Shopping {
    public static void main(String args[]) {
        boolean bankrupt = true;
        do System.out.println("enjoying shopping"); bankrupt = false;
        while (!bankrupt);
    }
}
```

    a  The code prints enjoying shopping once.

    b  The code prints enjoying shopping twice.

    c  The code prints enjoying shopping in an infinite loop.

    **d  The code fails to compile.**

Answer: d

Explanation: The code fails to compile because it's trying to stuff two lines of code between the do and while statements without using curly braces.

[4.2]  Declare, instantiate, initialize, and use a multidimensional array

**ME-Q57)** Which of the following options are valid for defining multidimensional arrays? (Choose 4 options.)

☑ **a** `String ejg1[][] = new String[1][2];`

☑ **b** `String ejg2[][] = new String[][] { {}, {} };`

☑ **c** `String ejg3[][] = new String[2][2];`

☑ **d** `String ejg4[][] = new String[][]{{null},new String[]{"a","b","c"},`
    `{new String()}};`

☐ **e** `String ejg5[][] = new String[][2];`

☐ **f** `String ejg6[][] = new String[][]{"A", "B"};`

☐ **g** `String ejg7[][] = new String[]{{"A"}, {"B"}};`

Answer: a, b, c, d

Explanation: Options (a), (b), (c), and (d) define a multidimensional array correctly.

Option (e) is incorrect because the size in the first square bracket is missing.

Option (f) is incorrect. The correct code must use an additional pair of {} on the right-hand side, as follows:

```
String ejg6[][] = new String[][]{{"A"}, {"B"}};
```

Option (g) is incorrect. The correct code must use an additional [] on the right-hand side as follows:

```
String ejg7[][] = new String[][]{{"A"}, {"B"}};
```

[6.6]  Determine the effect upon object references and primitive values when they are passed into methods that change the values

**ME-Q58)** What is the output of the following code? (Select 1 option.)

```
class Laptop {
    String memory = "1GB";
}
class Workshop {
    public static void main(String args[]) {
        Laptop life = new Laptop();
        repair(life);
        System.out.println(life.memory);
    }
    public static void repair(Laptop laptop) {
        laptop = new Laptop();
        laptop.memory = "2GB";
    }
}
```

- ⦿ **a** 1 GB
- ○ **b** 2 GB
- ○ **c** Compilation error
- ○ **d** Runtime exception

Answer: a

Explanation: The method `repair` defined in this example assigns a new object to the method parameter `laptop` that's passed to it. Then it modifies the state of this new assigned object by assigning 1 GB to its instance variable, `memory`.

When a method reassigns an object reference variable that's passed to it, the changes made to its state aren't visible in the calling method. This is because the changes are made to a new object and not to the one that was initially passed to this method. The method `repair` assigns a new object to the reference variable `laptop` that's passed to it and then modifies its state. Hence, the changes made to the state of the method parameter `laptop` aren't visible in method `main`, and it prints the value of `life.memory` as 1 GB.

---

### [7.3]  Determine when casting is necessary

**ME-Q59)** Given the following code, which option, if used to replace `//INSERT CODE HERE`, will enable a reference variable of type `Roamable` to refer to an object of the Phone class? (Select 1 option.)

```
interface Roamable{}
class Phone {}
class Tablet extends Phone implements Roamable {
    //INSERT CODE HERE
}
```

- ○ **a** `Roamable var = new Phone();`
- ○ **b** `Roamable var = (Roamable)Phone();`
- ⦿ **c** `Roamable var = (Roamable)new Phone();`
- ○ **d** Because the interface `Roamable` and the class `Phone` are unrelated, a reference variable of the type `Roamable` can't refer to an object of the class `Phone`.

Answer: c

Explanation: Option (a) is incorrect. Without explicit casting, a reference variable of type `Roamable` can't refer to an object of the class `Phone`.

Option (b) is incorrect because this is an invalid line of code that will fail to compile.

Option (d) is incorrect because a reference variable of the type `Roamable` can refer to an object of the class `Phone` with an explicit cast.

Note that although option (c) will compile, it will throw a `ClassCastException` if it's executed.

**[7.4]** Use super and this to access objects and constructors

**ME-Q60)** What is the output of the following code? (Select 1 option.)

```
class Paper {
    Paper() {
        this(10);
        System.out.println("Paper:0");
    }
    Paper(int a) { System.out.println("Paper:1"); }
}
class PostIt extends Paper {}
class TestPostIt {
    public static void main(String[] args) {
        Paper paper = new PostIt();
    }
}
```

◯ **a** Paper:1

◯ **b** Paper:0

◯ **c** Paper:0
    Paper:1

◉ **d Paper:1**
    **Paper:0**

Answer: d

Explanation: new PostIt() creates an object of the class PostIt by calling its com-
piler-provided no-argument constructor. The no-argument constructor of the class
PostIt calls its base class no-argument constructor, which calls the other constructor
that accepts one int method argument. The constructor that accepts an int argument prints Paper:1 and then returns control to the no-argument constructor. The
no-argument constructor then prints Paper:0.

**[9.1]** Manipulate data using the StringBuilder class and its methods

**ME-Q61)** Examine the following code and select the correct statement (choose 1 option).

```
line1> class StringBuilders {
line2>     public static void main(String... args) {
line3>         StringBuilder sb1 = new StringBuilder("eLion");
line4>         String ejg = null;
line5>         ejg = sb1.append("X").substring(sb1.indexOf("L"),
    sb1.indexOf("X"));
line6>         System.out.println(ejg);
line7>     }
line8> }
```

   a  The code will print LionX.

   **b  The code will print Lion.**

   c  The code will print Lion if line 5 is changed to the following:

```
ejg = sb1.append("X").substring(sb1.indexOf('L'), sb1.indexOf('X'));
```

   d  The code will compile only when line 4 is changed to the following:

```
StringBuilder ejg = null;
```

Answer: b

Explanation: Option (a) is incorrect and option (b) is correct. The substring method doesn't include the character at the end position in the result that it returns. Hence, the code prints Lion.

Option (c) is incorrect. If line 5 is changed as suggested in this option, the code won't compile. You can't pass a char to StringBuilder's method indexOf; it accepts String.

Option (d) is incorrect because there are no compilation issues with the code.

## [7.5]    Use abstract classes and interfaces

**ME-Q62)** Given the following code,

```
interface Jumpable {
    int height = 1;
    default void worldRecord() {
        System.out.print(height);
    }
}
interface Moveable {
    int height = 2;
    static void worldRecord() {
        System.out.print(height);
    }
}
class Chair implements Jumpable, Moveable {
    int height = 3;
    Chair() {
        worldRecord();
    }
    public static void main(String args[]) {
        Jumpable j = new Chair();
        Moveable m = new Chair();
        Chair c = new Chair();
    }
}
```

what is the output? Select 1 option.

◉ **a** 111
◎ **b** 123
◎ **c** 333
◎ **d** 222
◎ **e** Compilation error
◎ **f** Runtime exception

Answer: a

Explanation: The constructor of the class Chair invokes the default non-static method defined in the interface Jumpable. Moreover, if only the static world-Record() method in the interface Moveable were defined, its invocation would have to be qualified (that is, Moveable.worldRecord();) for the class Chair to compile.

**[7.3]    Determine when casting is necessary**

**ME-Q63)** Given the following code, which option, if used to replace /* INSERT CODE HERE */, will enable the class Jungle to determine whether the reference variable animal refers to an object of the class Lion and print 1? (Select 1 option.)

```
class Animal{ float age; }
class Lion extends Animal { int claws;}
class Jungle {
    public static void main(String args[]) {
        Animal animal = new Lion();
        /* INSERT CODE HERE */
            System.out.println(1);
    }
}
```

◉ **a** `if (animal instanceof Lion)`
◎ **b** `if (animal instanceOf Lion)`
◎ **c** `if (animal == Lion)`
◎ **d** `if (animal = Lion)`

Answer: a

Explanation: Option (b) is incorrect because the correct operator name is instanceof and not instanceOf (note the capitalized O).

Options (c) and (d) are incorrect. Neither of these lines of code will compile because they are trying to compare and assign a class name to a variable, which isn't allowed.

[6.3]   Create and overload constructors; including impact on default
                constructors

**ME-Q64)** Given that the file Test.java, which defines the following code, fails to compile, select the reasons for the compilation failure (choose 2 options).

```
class Person {
    Person(String value) {}
}
class Employee extends Person {}
class Test {
    public static void main(String args[]) {
        Employee e = new Employee();
    }
}
```

- ☐ **a** The class Person fails to compile.
- ☑ **b** **The class Employee fails to compile.**
- ☑ **c** **The default constructor can call only a no-argument constructor of a base class.**
- ☐ **d** The code that creates an object of the class Employee in the class Test did not pass a String value to the constructor of the class Employee.

Answer: b, c

Explanation: The class Employee doesn't compile, so the class Test can't use a variable of type Employee, and it fails to compile.

While trying to compile the class Employee, the Java compiler generates a default constructor for it, which looks like the following:

```
Employee() {
    super();
}
```

Note that a derived class constructor must always call a base class constructor. When Java generates the previous default constructor for the class Employee, it fails to compile because the base class doesn't have a no-argument constructor. The default constructor that's generated by Java can only define a call to a no-argument constructor in the base class. It can't call any other base class constructor.

**[6.3]** Create and overload constructors; including impact on default constructors

**ME-Q65)** Examine the following code and select the correct statements (choose 2 options).

```
class Bottle {
    void Bottle() {}
    void Bottle(WaterBottle w) {}
}
class WaterBottle extends Bottle {}
```

- ☐ **a** A base class can't pass reference variables of its defined class as method parameters in constructors.
- ☑ **b** **The class compiles successfully—a base class can use reference variables of its derived class as method parameters.**
- ☐ **c** The class `Bottle` defines two overloaded constructors.
- ☑ **d** **The class `Bottle` can access only one constructor.**

Answer: b, d

Explanation: A base class can use reference variables and objects of its derived classes. Note that the methods defined in the class `Bottle` aren't constructors but regular methods with the name `Bottle`. The return type of a constructor isn't void.

**[7.4]** Use super and this to access objects and constructors

**ME-Q66)** Given the following code, which option, if used to replace /* INSERT CODE HERE */, will cause the code to print 110? (Select 1 option.)

```
class Book {
    private int pages = 100;
}
class Magazine extends Book {
    private int interviews = 2;
    private int totalPages() { /* INSERT CODE HERE */ }

    public static void main(String[] args) {
        System.out.println(new Magazine().totalPages());
    }

}
```

- ◉ **a** `return super.pages + this.interviews*5;`
- ◉ **b** `return this.pages + this.interviews*5;`
- ◉ **c** `return super.pages + interviews*5;`

○ **d** `return pages + this.interviews*5;`

◉ **e** **None of the above**

Answer: e

Explanation: The variable `pages` has `private` access in the class `Book`, and it can't be accessed from outside this class.

**[8.4]** Create and invoke a method that throws an exception

**[8.5]** "Recognize common exception classes (such as NullPointerException, ArithmeticException, ArrayIndexOutOfBoundsException, ClassCastException)"

**ME-Q67)** Given the following code,

```
class NoInkException extends Exception {}
class Pen{
    void write(String val) throws NoInkException {
        int c = (10 - 7)/ (8 - 2 - 6);
    }
    void article() {
        //INSERT CODE HERE
    }
}
```

which of the options, when inserted at `//INSERT CODE HERE`, will define a valid use of the method `write` in the method `article`? (Select 2 options.)

☑ **a** 
```
try {
    new Pen().write("story");
} catch (NoInkException e) {}
```

☐ **b** 
```
try {
    new Pen().write("story");
} finally {}
```

☑ **c** 
```
try {
    write("story");
} catch (Exception e) {}
```

☐ **d** 
```
try {
    new Pen().write("story");
} catch (RuntimeException e) {}
```

Answer: a, c

Explanation: On execution, the method `write` will always throw an `Arithmetic-Exception` (a `RuntimeException`) due to division by 0. But this method declares to throw a `NoInkException`, which is a checked exception.

Because `NoInkException` extends the class `Exception` and not `RuntimeException`, `NoInkException` is a checked exception. When you call a method that throws a checked exception, you can either handle it using a `try-catch` block or declare it to be thrown in your method signature.

Option (a) is correct because a call to the method `write` is enclosed within a `try` block. The `try` block is followed by a `catch` block, which defines a handler for the exception `NoInkException`.

Option (b) is incorrect. The call to the method `write` is enclosed within a `try` block, followed by a `finally` block. The `finally` block isn't used to handle an exception.

Option (c) is correct. Because `NoInkException` is a subclass of `Exception`, an exception handler for the class `Exception` can handle the exception `NoInkException` as well.

Option (d) is incorrect. This option defines an exception handler for the class `RuntimeException`. Because `NoInkException` is not a subclass of `RuntimeException`, this code won't handle `NoInkException`.

## [1.1]   Define the scope of variables

**ME-Q68)** What is the output of the following code? (Select 1 option.)

```
class EMyMethods {
    static String name = "m1";
    void riverRafting() {
        String name = "m2";
        if (8 > 2) {
            String name = "m3";
            System.out.println(name);
        }
    }
    public static void main(String[] args) {
        EMyMethods m1 = new EMyMethods();
        m1.riverRafting();
    }
}
```

- a  m1
- b  m2
- c  m3
- **d  The code fails to compile.**

Answer: d

Explanation: The class `EMyMethods` defines three variables with the name `name`:

- The `static` variable name with the value `"m1"`
- The local variable name in the method `riverRafting` with the value `"m2"`
- The variable name, local to the `if` block in the method `riverRafting`, with the value `"m3"`

The code fails to compile due to the definition of two local variables with the same name (name) in the method riverRafting. If this code were allowed to compile, the scope of these local variables would overlap—the variable name defined outside the if block would be accessible to the complete method riverRafting. The scope of the local variable name, defined within the if block, would be limited to the if block.

Within the if block, how do you think the code would differentiate between these local variables? Because there's no way to do so, the code fails to compile.

 **[9.2]   Create and manipulate strings**

**ME-Q69)** What is the output of the following code? (Select 1 option.)

```
class EBowl {
    public static void main(String args[]) {
        String eFood = "Corn";
        System.out.println(eFood);
        mix(eFood);
        System.out.println(eFood);
    }
    static void mix(String foodIn) {
        foodIn.concat("A");
        foodIn.replace('C', 'B');
    }
}
```

- a  Corn
   BornA
- b  Corn
   CornA
- c  Corn
   Born
- ● **d  Corn**
   **Corn**

Answer: d

Explanation: String objects are immutable. This implies that using any method can't change the value of a String variable. In this case, the String object is passed to a method, which seems to, but doesn't, change the contents of String.

**[3.4]   Use a switch statement**

**ME-Q70)** Which statement is true for the following code? (Select 1 option.)

```
class SwJava {
    public static void main(String args[]) {
        String[] shapes = {"Circle", "Square", "Triangle"};
```

```
        switch (shapes) {
            case "Square": System.out.println("Circle"); break;
            case "Triangle": System.out.println("Square"); break;
            case "Circle": System.out.println("Triangle"); break;
        }
    }
}
```

- a The code prints `Circle`.
- b The code prints `Square`.
- c The code prints `Triangle`.
- d The code prints

    ```
    Circle
    Square
    Triangle
    ```

- e The code prints

    ```
    Triangle
    Circle
    Square
    ```

- **f The code fails to compile.**

Answer: f

Explanation: The question tries to trick you; it passes a `String[]` value to a `switch` construct by passing it an array of `String` objects. The code fails to compile because an array isn't a valid argument to a `switch` construct. The code would have compiled if it passed an element from the array shapes (`shapes[0]`, `shapes[1]`, or `shapes[2]`).

---

**[8.4]** Create and invoke a method that throws an exception

**ME-Q71)** Given the following definition of the classes `Person`, `Father`, and `Home`, which options, if used to replace `//INSERT CODE HERE`, will cause the code to compile successfully? (Select 3 options.)

```
class Person {}
class Father extends Person {
    public void dance() throws ClassCastException {}
}
class Home {
    public static void main(String args[]) {
        Person p = new Person();
        try {
            ((Father)p).dance();
        }
        //INSERT CODE HERE
    }
}
```

☑ **a** `catch (NullPointerException e) {}`
   `catch (ClassCastException e) {}`
   `catch (Exception e) {}`
   `catch (Throwable t) {}`

☑ **b** `catch (ClassCastException e) {}`
   `catch (NullPointerException e) {}`
   `catch (Exception e) {}`
   `catch (Throwable t) {}`

☐ **c** `catch (ClassCastException e) {}`
   `catch (Exception e) {}`
   `catch (NullPointerException e) {}`
   `catch (Throwable t) {}`

☐ **d** `catch (Throwable t) {}`
   `catch (Exception e) {}`
   `catch (ClassCastException e) {}`
   `catch (NullPointerException e) {}`

☑ **e** `finally {}`

Answer: a, b, e

Explanation: Because `NullPointerException` and `ClassCastException` don't share a base class–derived class relationship, these can be placed before or after each other.

The class `Throwable` is the base class of `Exception`. Hence, the exception handler for the class `Throwable` can't be placed before the exception handler of the class `Exception`. Similarly, `Exception` is a base class for `NullPointerException` and `ClassCastException`. Hence, the exception handler for the class `Exception` can't be placed before the exception handlers of the class `ClassCastException` or `NullPointerException`.

Option (e) is OK because no checked exceptions are defined to be thrown.

[2.1]   Declare and initialize variables (including casting of primitive data types)

[5.1]   Create and use while loops

[9.3]   Create and manipulate calendar data using classes from java.time.LocalDateTime, java.time.LocalDate, java.time.LocalTime, java.time.format.DateTimeFormatter, java.time.Period

**ME-Q72)** What is the output of the following code? (Select 1 option.)

```java
import java.time.*;
class Camera {
    public static void main(String args[]) {
        int hours;
        LocalDateTime now = LocalDateTime.of(2020, 10, 01, 0 , 0);
```

```
        LocalDate before = now.toLocalDate().minusDays(1);
        LocalTime after = now.toLocalTime().plusHours(1);

        while (before.isBefore(after) && hours < 4) {
            ++hours;
        }
        System.out.println("Hours:" + hours);
    }
}
```

- ○ **a** The code prints `Camera:null`.
- ○ **b** The code prints `Camera:Adjust settings manually`.
- ○ **c** The code prints `Camera:`.
- ◉ **d** **The code fails to compile.**

Answer: d

Explanation: Note the type of the variables now, before, and after—they aren't the same. The code fails compilation because the code `before.isBefore(after)` calls the `isBefore` method on an instance of `LocalDate`, passing it a `LocalTime` instance, which isn't allowed.

The local variable `hours` isn't initialized prior to being referred to in the while condition (`hours < 4`), which is another reason why the class doesn't compile.

---

**[6.2]** Apply the static keyword to methods and fields

**ME-Q73)** The output of the class `TestEJavaCourse`, defined as follows, is `300`:

```
class Course {
    int enrollments;
}
class TestEJavaCourse {
    public static void main(String args[]) {
        Course c1 = new Course();
        Course c2 = new Course();
        c1.enrollments = 100;
        c2.enrollments = 200;
        System.out.println(c1.enrollments + c2.enrollments);
    }
}
```

What will happen if the variable `enrollments` is defined as a `static` variable? (Select 1 option.)

- ○ **a** No change in output. `TestEJavaCourse` prints `300`.
- ○ **b** Change in output. `TestEJavaCourse` prints `200`.
- ◉ **c** **Change in output. `TestEJavaCourse` prints 400.**
- ○ **d** The class `TestEJavaCourse` fails to compile.

Answer: c

Explanation: The code doesn't fail compilation after the definition of the variable enrollments is changed to a static variable. A static variable can be accessed using a variable reference of the class in which it's defined. All the objects of a class share the same copy of the static variable. When the variable enrollments is modified using the reference variable c2, c1.enrollments is also equal to 200. Hence, the code prints the result of 200 + 200, that is, 400.

 [4.2]   Declare, instantiate, initialize, and use a multidimensional array

**ME-Q74)** What is the output of the following code? (Select 1 option.)

```
String ejgStr[] = new String[][]{{null},new String[]{"a","b","c"},{new
    String()}}[0] ;
String ejgStr1[] = null;
String ejgStr2[] = {null};

System.out.println(ejgStr[0]);
System.out.println(ejgStr2[0]);
System.out.println(ejgStr1[0]);
```

    ○ **a** `null`
        `NullPointerException`

    ◉ **b** **null**
        **null**
        **NullPointerException**

    ○ **c** `NullPointerException`

    ○ **d** `null`
        `null`
        `null`

Answer: b

Explanation: The trickiest assignment in this code is the assignment of the variable ejgStr. The following line of code may *seem* to (but doesn't) assign a two-dimensional String array to the variable ejgStr:

```
String ejgStr[] = new String[][]{{null},new String[]{"a","b","c"},{new
    String()}}[0] ;
```

The preceding code assigns the first element of a two-dimensional String array to the variable ejgStr. The following indented code will make the previous statement easier to understand:

```
String ejgStr[] = new String[][]{
                     {null},
                     new String[]{"a","b","c"},
                     {new String()}
```

**First element of two-dimensional array—an array of length 1**

**Second element of two-dimensional array—an array of length 3**

**Third element of two-dimensional array—an array of length 1**

So let's look at the simplified assignment:

```
String ejgStr[] = {null};
String ejgStr1[] = null;
String ejgStr2[] = {null};
```

Revisit the code that prints the array elements:

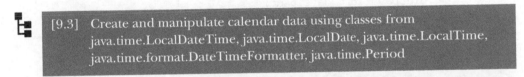

```
System.out.println(ejgStr[0]);
System.out.println(ejgStr2[0]);
System.out.println(ejgStr1[0]);
```

Because `ejgStr` refers to an array of length 1 (`{null}`), `ejgStr[0]` prints `null`. `ejgStr2` also refers to an array of length 1 (`{null}`), so `ejgStr2[0]` also prints `null`. `ejgStr1` refers to `null`, not to an array. An attempt to access the first element of `ejgStr1` throws a `NullPointerException`.

[9.3] Create and manipulate calendar data using classes from java.time.LocalDateTime, java.time.LocalDate, java.time.LocalTime, java.time.format.DateTimeFormatter, java.time.Period

[9.4] Declare and use an ArrayList of a given type

**ME-Q75)** Examine the following code and select the correct statement (choose 1 option).

```
import java.util.*;
class Person {}
class Emp extends Person {}

class TestArrayList {
    public static void main(String[] args) {
        ArrayList<Object> list = new ArrayList<>();        //LINE1
        list.add(new String("1234"));                      //LINE2
        list.add(new Person());                            //LINE3
        list.add(new Emp());                               //LINE4
        list.add(new String[]{"abcd", "xyz"});             //LINE5
        list.add(LocalDate.now().plus(1));
    }
}
```

- a  The code on line 1 won't compile.
- b  The code on line 2 won't compile.
- c  The code on line 3 won't compile.
- d  The code on line 4 won't compile.
- **e  The code on line 5 won't compile.**
- f  None of the above.
- g  All the options from (a) to (e).

Answer: e

Explanation: The type of an `ArrayList` determines the type of the objects that can be added to it. An `ArrayList` can add to it all the objects of its derived class. Options (a) to (d) will compile because the class `Object` is the superclass of all Java classes; the `ArrayList` list as defined in this question will accept all types of objects, including arrays, because they are also objects.

Although a `LocalDate` instance can be added to an `ArrayList`, the code in option (e) won't compile. `LocalDate.now()` returns a `LocalDate` instance. But the class `LocalDate` doesn't define a `plus()` method, which accepts an integer value to be added to it—there's actually one plus method that accepts a `TemporalAmount` instance. You can use any of the following methods to add days, months, weeks, or years to `Local-Date`, passing it `long` values:

- `plusDays(long daysToAdd)`
- `plusMonths(long monthsToAdd)`
- `plusWeeks(long weeksToAdd)`
- `plusYears(long yearsToAdd)`

You can also use the following method to add a duration of days to `LocalDate`, passing it an instance of `Period` (`Period` implements `TemporalAmount`):

```
plus(TemporalAmount amountToAdd)
```

 **[3.3]   Create if and if/else and ternary constructs**

**ME-Q76)** What is the output of the following code? (Select 1 option.)

```
public class If2 {
    public static void main(String args[]) {
        int a = 10; int b = 20; boolean c = false;
        if (b > a) if (++a == 10) if (c!=true) System.out.println(1);
        else System.out.println(2); else System.out.println(3);
    }
}
```

- a  1
- b  2

&#9673; **c** 3

&#9673; **d** No output

Answer: c

Explanation: The key to answering questions about unindented code is to indent it. Here's how:

```
if (b > a)
    if (++a == 10)
        if (c!=true)
            System.out.println(1);
        else
            System.out.println(2);
    else System.out.println(3);
```

Now the code becomes much simpler to look at and understand. Remember that the last else statement belongs to the inner if (++a == 10). As you can see, if (++a == 10) evaluates to false, the code will print 3.

---

**[7.5]   Use abstract classes and interfaces**

**ME-Q77)** Given the following code,

```
interface Movable {
    default int distance() {
        return 10;
    }
}
interface Jumpable {
    default int distance() {
        return 10;
    }
}
```

which options correctly define the class Person that implements interfaces Movable and Jumpable? (Select 1 option.)

&#9673; **a** class Person implements Movable, Jumpable {}

&#9673; **b** class Person implements Movable, Jumpable {
            default int distance() {
                return 10;
            }
        }

&#9673; **c** class Person implements Movable, Jumpable {
            public int distance() {
                return 10;
            }
        }

```
   d class Person implements Movable, Jumpable {
         public long distance() {
             return 10;
         }
     }

   e class Person implements Movable, Jumpable {
         int distance() {
             return 10;
         }
     }
```

Answer: c

Explanation: Option (a) is incorrect because the class Person can't implement both interfaces, Jumpable and Movable, which define the method distance with the same signatures and a default implementation. The class Person must override the default implementation of distance() to implement both these interfaces.

Option (b) is incorrect. When a class overrides the default implementation of a method that it inherits from an interface, it can't use the keyword default. Such code won't compile.

Option (d) is incorrect. The method distance() with the return type long can't override distance() with the return type int.

Option (e) is incorrect and this code won't compile. The class Person is trying to decrease the accessibility of distance(), from public to the *default* access level.

# *appendix*
# *Answers to Twist*
# *in the Tale exercises*

Chapters 1 through 7 include multiple Twist in the Tale exercises. The answers to these exercises, along with comprehensive explanations, are given in this appendix. The answers to each exercise include the following elements:

- *Purpose*—The aim of the exercise (the *twist* to which each exercise is trying to draw your attention)
- *Answer*—The correct answer
- *Explanation*—A comprehensive explanation of the answer

Let's get started with the first chapter.

## A.1 Chapter 1: Java basics

Chapter 1 includes four Twist in the Tale exercises.

### A.1.1 Twist in the Tale 1.1

Purpose: This exercise encourages you to practice code with a combination of the correct contents (classes and interfaces) of a Java source code file.

Answer: c, d

Explanation: Options (a) and (b) are incorrect.

Option (c) is correct because a Java source code file can define multiple interfaces and classes.

Option (d) is correct because a `public` interface or class can be defined in a Java source code file with a matching name. The `public` interface `Printable` can't be defined in the Java source code file, Multiple.java. It must be defined in Printable.java.

## A.1.2   *Twist in the Tale 1.2*

Purpose: Though similar to Twist in the Tale 1.1, this question is different in terms of its wording and intent. It asks you to select the options that are correct *individually*. Selecting an option that's correct individually means that an option should be correct on its own and not in combination with any other option. You may get to answer similar questions in the real exam.

Answer: a, c, d

Explanation: Option (a) is correct and (b) is incorrect because Multiple2.java won't compile. Multiple2.java can't define a `public` class `Car`.

Option (c) is correct because removal of the definition of the `public` class `Car` from Multiple2.java will leave only one `public` interface in Multiple2.java—`Multiple2`. Because the names of the `public` interface `Multiple2` and the source code file match, Multiple2.java will compile successfully.

Option (d) is correct. Changing the `public` class `Car` to a non-public class will leave only one `public` interface in Multiple2.java—`Multiple2`. Because the names of the public interface `Multiple2` and source code file match, Multiple2.java will compile successfully.

Option (e) is incorrect. If you change the access modifier of the `public` interface `Multiple2` to non-public, Multiple2.java will contain a definition of a `public` class `Car`, which isn't allowed.

## A.1.3   *Twist in the Tale 1.3*

Purpose: This exercise encourages you to execute the code in the options to understand the correct method signature of the method `main` together with the method parameters that are passed to it.

Answer: a, b

Explanation: All the options in this question are supposed to execute using the command `javaEJava java one one`. The purpose of each of these terms is as follows:

- Term 1, `java`—Used to execute a Java class
- Term 2, `EJava`—Name of class to execute
- Term 3, `java`—Passed as the first argument to the method `main`
- Term 4, `one`—Passed as the second argument to `main`
- Term 5, `one`—Passed as the third argument to `main`

To output `java one`, the `main` method should output the first and either the second or third method parameters passed to it.

Options (a) and (b) are correct because they use the correct method signature of the method `main`. The name of the method parameter need not be `args`. It can be any other valid identifier. Option (a) outputs the values of the first and third terms passed to it. Option (b) outputs the values of the first and second terms passed to it.

Option (c) is incorrect because this `main` method accepts a two-dimensional array. Hence, it won't be treated as *the* `main` method.

Option (d) is incorrect because this code won't compile. The access modifier of a method (`public`) should be placed before its return type (`void`); otherwise, the code won't compile.

### A.1.4   Twist in the Tale 1.4

Purpose: Apart from determining the right access modifier that can limit the visibility of a class within a package, this exercise wants you to try out different access modifiers that can be used to declare a class.

Answer: The code submitted by Harry.

Explanation: The code submitted by Paul is incorrect because when the class `Curtain` is defined with the `public` access modifier, it will be accessible outside the package `building`.

The code submitted by Shreya and Selvan is incorrect because the class `Curtain` is a top-level class (it's not defined within another class), so it can't be defined using the access modifiers `protected` and `private`.

## A.2   Chapter 2: Working with Java data types

Chapter 2 includes four Twist in the Tale exercises. Twist in the Tale 2.1 has two parts.

### A.2.1   Twist in the Tale 2.1 (part 1)

Purpose: By default, `System.out.println()` will print out a number in its decimal base. It does so regardless of the base number system that you use to initialize a number.

Answer: The code prints the following output:

```
534
534
```

Explanation: Often programmers are tricked by similar questions. If a variable is assigned a value using `0b100001011` (a number in the binary number system), a programmer might believe that `System.out.println()` will print out numbers in the binary number system, which is incorrect. By default, `System.out.println()` will print out a number in its decimal base. All four variables `baseDecimal`, `octVal`, `hexVal`, and `binVal` represent the decimal value `267` in the decimal, octal, hexadecimal, and binary number systems. The addition operation adds these values and prints `534` twice.

You can use a method from the class `Integer` to print out a value in the binary number system as follows:

```
System.out.println(Integer.toBinaryString(0b100001011));
```

Note that the class `Integer` isn't on this exam and you won't be asked any questions on it. This class is mentioned only for your reference.

### A.2.2    *Twist in the Tale 2.1 (part 2)*

Purpose: A new Java 7 language feature is the use of the underscore in literal number values. This exercise's purpose is to help you get familiar with this feature if you haven't worked with underscores in literal number values before.

Answer: Only `var1`, `var6`, and `var7` correctly define a literal integer value.

Explanation: The literal value `0_x_4_13` defined by `var2` is incorrect because it uses underscores after the starting 0 and after the letter x, neither of which is allowed. The correct value is `0x4_13`.

The literal value `0b_x10_BA_75` defined by `var3` is incorrect. You can't place an underscore right after the prefixes `0b` and `0B` that are used to define binary literal values. Also, a binary value can contain only the digits 1 and 0.

The literal value `0b_10000_10_11` defined by value `var4` is incorrect. You can't place an underscore right after the prefixes `0b` and `0B` used to define binary literal values. The correct value is `0b10000_10_11`.

The literal value `0xa10_AG_75` defined by `var5` is incorrect because it uses the letter G, which isn't allowed in a hexadecimal number system. A correct value is `0xa10_A_75`.

The literal integer defined by `var1` is valid. But 0 (for octal literals) is an exception to the rule stating that a radix prefix can't be isolated by an underscore (for example, `0x_100_267_760` and `0b_100_110` are invalid expressions).

### A.2.3    *Twist in the Tale 2.2*

Purpose: To reinforce the following concepts:

- Multiple variables of the *same type* can be defined on the same line of code.
- Variable assignment rule: if multiple variables of *similar types* are assigned values on the same line, assignment starts from right to left. Also, unlike other programming languages such as C, the literal value 0 can't be assigned to a variable of type `boolean`.
- Questions that ask you to select incorrect answers or code can be confusing. It's common to start by determining the incorrect options and then selecting the correct options. Make note of such questions.

Answer: a, b, c, e

Explanation: Options (a) and (b) are incorrect statements. You can define multiple variables of the same type on the same line. Also, you can assign values to variables of compatible types on the same line of code. Assignment starts from right to left. For proof, the following lines of code will compile:

```
int int1;
long long2;
long2 = int1 = 10;
```

But the following lines of code won't compile:

```
int i1;
long 12;
int1 = long2 = 10;
```

In the final line of the preceding code, a literal value 10 is assigned to the variable long2 of type long, which is acceptable. An attempt to assign the value of the variable long2 to int1 fails because it would need an explicit cast.

Option (c) is an incorrect statement because a literal value 0 can't be assigned to a variable of type boolean.

Option (d) is a correct statement.

Option (e) is an incorrect statement. The code doesn't define a variable with the name yes and thus seems to treat it like a literal value. Java doesn't define a literal value yes, so the code doesn't compile.

## A.2.4 *Twist in the Tale 2.3*

Purpose: The exercise encourages you to

- Try code with increment and decrement postfix and prefix unary operators
- Get the hang of how variables are evaluated in an expression that has multiple occurrences of unary operators in postfix and prefix notation

Answer: 32

Explanation: The actual task is to evaluate the following expression:

```
int a = 10;
a = ++a + a + --a - --a + a++;
System.out.println(a);
```

This is the actual task because the question asks you to replace all occurrences of ++a with a++, --a with a--, and vice versa. This expression is depicted in figure A.1:

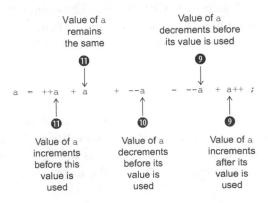

**Figure A.1 Evaluation of an expression that has multiple unary operators in postfix and prefix notation**

## A.2.5    *Twist in the Tale 2.4*

Purpose: To determine whether the operands of an expression that uses the short-circuit operators && and || will evaluate.

Answer: The operands that will execute are circled and the ones that won't are enclosed in rectangles in figure A.2.

```
class TwistInTaleLogicalOperators {
    public static void main(String args[]){
        int a=10;
        int b=20;
        int c=40;

        System.out.println(a++>10 || ++b<30);                //line1
        System.out.println(a>90 && ++b<30);
        System.out.println(!(c>20) && a==10);
        System.out.println(a>=99 || a<=33 && b==10);
        System.out.println(a>=99 && a<=33 || b==10);
    }
}
```

**Figure A.2    In an expression that uses the short-circuit operators && and ||, the operands that are evaluated are circled and the ones that aren't evaluated are enclosed in rectangles.**

Explanation: Both of the short-circuit operators, && and ||, will evaluate their first operand. For the short-circuit operator &&, if the first operand evaluates to false, it won't evaluate the second operator. For the short-circuit operator ||, if the first operand evaluates to true, it won't evaluate the second operator.

For the expression (a++ > 10 || ++b < 30), because a++ > 10 evaluates to false, both operands will evaluate.

For the expression (a > 90 && ++b < 30), because a > 90 evaluates to false, the second operand won't execute.

For expression (!(c > 20) && a == 10), because !(c > 20) evaluates to false, the second operand won't execute.

The expression (a >= 99 || a <= 33 && b == 10) has three operands together with the OR (||) and AND (&&) short-circuit operators. Because the short-circuit operator AND has higher operator precedence than the short-circuit operator OR, the expression is evaluated as follows:

```
(a >= 99 || (a <= 33 && b == 10))
```

Evaluation of the preceding expression starts with the evaluation of (a <= 33 && b == 10). Because a <= 33 evaluates to true, the operator && evaluates the second operand (b == 10) to determine whether (a <= 33 && b == 10) will return true or false. a <= 33 returns true and b == 10 returns false, so the expression (a <= 33 && b == 10) returns false.

The original expression—(a >= 99 || (a <= 33 && b == 10))—is now reduced to the following expression:

```
(a >= 99 || false)
```

The short-circuit operator OR (||) executes its first operand (even if the value of the second operand is known), evaluating a >= 99. So for this expression, all three operands are evaluated.

The expression (a >= 99 && a <= 33 || b == 10) also has three operands, together with OR and AND short-circuit operators. Because the short-circuit operator AND has a higher operator precedence than the short-circuit operator OR, this expression is evaluated as follows:

```
((a >= 99 && a <= 33) || b == 10 )
```

a >= 99 evaluates to false, so the next operand (a <= 33) isn't evaluated. Because the first operand to operator ||, a >= 99 && a <= 33), evaluates to false, b == 10 is evaluated.

## A.3 Chapter 3: Methods and encapsulation

Chapter 3 includes three Twist in the Tale exercises.

### A.3.1 Twist in the Tale 3.1

Purpose: In the same way that the class TestPhone in this exercise defines a local variable with the same name as its instance variable, I strongly recommend that you try out different combinations of defining variables with the same name in a class, but with different scope.

Answer: a

Explanation: The class Phone defines an instance variable with the name phoneNumber. The method setNumber also defines a local variable phoneNumber and assigns a value to its local variable. A local variable takes precedence over an instance variable defined in the class with the same names. Because there is no change in the value of the instance variable phoneNumber, 123456789 is printed to the console from the method main, defined in the class TestPhone.

### A.3.2 Twist in the Tale 3.2

Purpose: To learn that *recursive* or *circular* calls to constructors aren't allowed.

Answer: The code fails to compile, with the following compilation error message:

```
Employee.java:4: error: recursive constructor invocation
    Employee() {
    ^
1 error
```

Explanation: A method calling itself is called *recursion*. Two or more methods calling each other, in a circular manner, is called *circular method calling*.

Starting in Java version 1.4.1, the Java compiler won't compile code with *recursive* or *circular* constructors. A constructor is used to initialize an object, so it doesn't make sense to allow recursive calls to a constructor. You can initialize an object once and then modify it. You can't initialize an object multiple times.

In case you're wondering whether you can call a constructor conditionally from another constructor, you can't. A call to a constructor must be the first statement:

```
class Employee {
    String name;
    int age;
    Employee() {
        if (7<2)
            this();
    }
    Employee(String newName, int newAge) {
        name = newName;
        age = newAge;
    }
}
```

> Won't compile—conditional execution of constructors isn't allowed. The call to this must be the first statement in the constructor.

Also, circular constructor calls aren't allowed:

```
class Employee {
    String name;
    int age;
    Employee() {
        this(null, 0);
    }
    Employee(String newName, int newAge) {
        this();
        name = newName;
        age = newAge;
    }
}
```

> Won't compile. This constructor calls back the no-argument constructor, resulting in a circular constructor call.

The previous example doesn't compile, with the following compilation error message:

```
Employee.java:8: error: recursive constructor invocation
    Employee(String newName, int newAge) {
    ^
1 error
```

Note that similar recursive or circular calls defined in methods don't result in compilation errors.

### A.3.3   *Twist in the Tale 3.3*

Purpose: A class with `public` instance variable(s) can never be designated as a well-encapsulated class.

Answer: e

Explanation: This question tries to trick you by defining options that play with multiple access modifiers for methods `getWeight` and `setWeight`. Because the instance variable `model` of the class `Phone` is defined using the `public` access modifier (and no proposed options address this issue), it's accessible outside this class. So `Phone` isn't a well-encapsulated class.

## A.4 Chapter 4: Selected classes from the Java API and arrays

Chapter 4 includes four Twist in the Tale exercises.

### A.4.1 Twist in the Tale 4.1

Purpose: To remind you to be careful with the overloaded methods of the class `String` that accept either `char` or `String` or both, the code in this exercise passes an invalid method argument—a `char`—to method `startsWith`.

Answer: e

Explanation: When it comes to the `String` class, it's easy to confuse the methods that accept `char` or `String` values as method arguments. For example, the overloaded method `indexOf` can accept both `String` and `char` values to search for a target value in a `String`. The methods `startsWith` and `endsWith` accept only arguments of type `String`. The method `charAt` accepts only method arguments of type `int`. Hence, this method can be passed `char` values, which are stored as unsigned integer values.

### A.4.2 Twist in the Tale 4.2

Purpose: This exercise has multiple purposes:

- To confuse you with the use of method names, which are used in the Java API by other classes to create their objects.
- To encourage you to refer to the Java API documentation when you work with classes from the Java API. The Java API documentation is an extensive source of information and facts that are often not included in most books (because it's practically impossible to do so).

Answer: d

Explanation: The correct way to create an object of class `StringBuilder` with a default capacity of 16 characters is to call `StringBuilder`'s no-argument constructor, as follows:

```
StringBuilder name = StringBuilder();
```

### A.4.3    *Twist in the Tale 4.3*

Purpose: Identify the difference between an array element that isn't initialized and an array element that doesn't exist. A pictorial representation of a multidimensional array is quick to draw, and you can easily refer to its nonexistent or null array elements. This concept is shown in figure A.3.

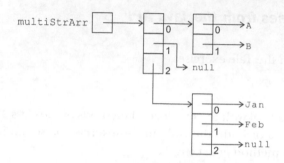

**Figure A.3    Array** `multiStrArr` **and its elements**

Answer: b, d

Explanation: Option (a) is incorrect. Initializing a row of array `multiStrArr` with `{"Jan","Feb",null}` and `{"Jan","Feb",null,null}` isn't the same. The former option defines *three* array elements with the last array element assigned to `null`. The latter option defines *four* array elements with the last two array elements assigned to `null`.

   Option (b) is correct. The array element at the position exists but isn't assigned any value. It's assigned to `null`.

   Option (c) is incorrect. Because `multiStrArr[1]` refers to `null`, `multiStrArr[1][1]` doesn't exist.

   Option (d) is correct. As shown in figure A.3, the array `multiStrArr` doesn't define an equal number of elements in each row, so it's asymmetric.

### A.4.4    *Twist in the Tale 4.4*

Purpose: This exercise tries to trick you by using multiple objects of `ArrayList`, assigning the object reference of one `ArrayList` to another, and modifying the value of the `ArrayList` objects. `String` objects are immutable—you can't change their values.

Answer: a

Explanation: Option (a) is correct, and options (b), (c), and (d) are incorrect. The `ArrayLists` `myArrList` and `yourArrList` contain `String` objects. The value of `String` objects can't be modified once created.

## A.5 Chapter 5: Flow control

Chapter 5 includes four Twist in the Tale exercises.

### A.5.1 Twist in the Tale 5.1

Purpose: To emphasize multiple points:

- A variable of any type can be (re)assigned a value in an expression used in an `if` condition.
- `if-else-if` statements execute each `if` condition as control is passed to them, changing the value of any variable that's manipulated in the evaluation of the expression.
- An expression used in an `if` condition should evaluate to a `boolean` value.

Answer: f

Explanation: The flow of execution of code statements in this exercise is shown in figure A.4.

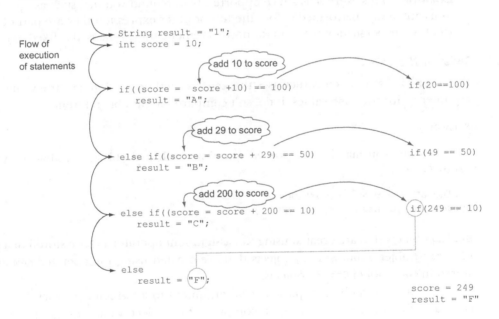

**Figure A.4  Flow of execution of code in Twist in the Tale 5.1**

The arrows on the left in figure A.4 show the flow of execution of statements for this code snippet. The `if` conditions on the right show the actual values that are compared after the expression used in the `if` statements is evaluated. Following is a detailed description:

- The initial value of variable `score` is 10. The first condition (`(score = score + 10) == 100`) reassigns the value of variable `score` to 20 and then compares it to the literal integer value 100. The expression 20 == 100 returns a boolean value false. The control doesn't evaluate the *then* part of the if construct and moves on to the evaluation of the second if condition defined in the else part.

- The second condition ((score = score + 29) == 50) adds 29 to the existing value 20 of variable score and then compares the new value 49 with 50. The expression 49 == 50 returns false again. The control doesn't evaluate the *then* part of the if construct and moves on to evaluation of the second if condition defined in the else part.

- The third condition ((score = score + 200) == 10) adds a value of 200 to the existing value 49 of variable score, making it 249, and compares that with the integer literal value 10. Because 249 == 10 evaluates to false, control moves to the else part. The else part assigns a literal value F to the variable result. At the end of execution of the if-else-if statement, the variable score is assigned a value of 249 and result is assigned a value of F. The code outputs F:249.

**EXAM TIP**   This exercise is a nice opportunity to remind you that such assignations are always performed before the test or other expression they are part of (that is, preassignments) except for post-incrementations (that is, postfixed ++).

## A.5.2    *Twist in the Tale 5.2*

Purpose: The switch construct uses the equals method to compare the value of its argument with the case values. It doesn't compare the variable references.

Answer: c

Explanation: You may have answered questions with code like the following, which prints false:

```
String aDay = new String("SUN");
System.out.println(aDay == "SUN");
```

String objects that are created using the assignment operator (=) are stored in a pool of String objects, but String objects that are created using the operator new aren't stored in the pool of String objects.

When a String object is passed as an argument to a switch construct, it doesn't compare the object references; it compares the object values using the equals method. In the code snippet shown in the question, a match is found for the String literal value SUN, so the code prints Weekend!, executes the break statement, and exits the block.

## A.5.3    *Twist in the Tale 5.3*

Purpose: Note the type of the variable that's passed as an argument to the switch construct. Among the primitive data types, you can pass on variables of types byte, short, char, and int to a switch construct. Other data types that you can pass to a switch construct are Byte, Short, Integer, Character, enum, and String.

This question tries to take your attention off this simple basic requirement and to move your focus to the logic of the question.

Answer: The submission by Harry.

Explanation: Paul's submission doesn't compile because a `switch` construct doesn't accept an argument of the `long` primitive data type.

### A.5.4    Twist in the Tale 5.4

Purpose: When an unlabeled `break` statement is used within nested loops (for any combinations of `for`, `do-while`, or `while` loops), a `break` statement will end the execution of the *inner loop*, not all the nested loops. The *outer loop* will continue to execute, starting with its *next* iteration value.

Answer: a

Explanation: Let's start with the *outer loop*'s first iteration. In the first iteration, the value of the variable `outer` is `Outer`.

For the outer loop's first iteration, the inner loop should execute for the values `Outer` and `Inner` for the variable `inner`. For the first iteration of the inner loop, the value of the variable `inner` is `Outer`, so the condition `inner.equals("Inner")` evaluates to `false` and the break statement doesn't execute. The code prints the value of the variable `inner`, which is `Outer:`, and starts with the next iteration of the inner loop. In the second iteration of the inner loop, the value of the variable `inner` is `Inner`, so the condition `inner.equals("Inner")` evaluates to `true` and the `break` statement executes, ending the execution of the inner loop and skipping the code that prints out the value of the variable `inner`.

The outer loop starts its execution with the second iteration. In this iteration, the value of the variable `outer` is `Outer`. For the outer loop's iteration, the inner loop executes twice in the same manner as mentioned in the previous paragraph. This iteration of the outer loop again prints the value of the variable `inner` when it's equal to `Outer`.

The nested loops included in the question print out the value `Outer:` twice:

```
Outer:Outer:
```

## A.6    Chapter 6: Working with inheritance

Chapter 6 includes four Twist in the Tale exercises.

### A.6.1    Twist in the Tale 6.1

Purpose: This question is an example of a simple concept (`private` members are not accessible to a derived class) that is made to look complex by including code and options that try to divert your attention. Expect similar questions on the exam.

Answer: e

Explanation: The code fails to compile because the `private` members of a class can't be accessed outside a class—not even by its derived class. The compiler can detect such attempts; this code won't compile.

### A.6.2  Twist in the Tale 6.2

Purpose: To help you to work with a combination of

- Arrays
- Assigning an object of a derived class to a reference variable of the base class
- Assigning an object of a class that implements an interface to a reference variable of the interface

Answer: a, c

Explanation: The rules you need to follow to assign a value to an array element are the same rules you follow when you assign an object to a reference variable. Because the type of array `interviewer` is `Interviewer`, you can assign objects of classes that implement this interface. The inheritance of classes `Employee`, `Manager`, and `HRExecutive` and the interface `Interviewer` are shown in figure A.5.

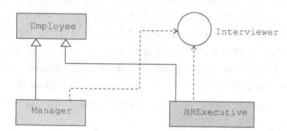

**Figure A.5  UML notation of inheritance hierarchy of the classes `Employee`, `Manager`, and `HRExecutive` and the interface `Interviewer`**

As you can see in figure A.5, the classes `Manager` and `HRExecutive` implement the interface `Interviewer`. The class `Employee` doesn't implement the interface `Interviewer`; hence, an object of the class `Employee` can't be added to an array of type `Interviewer`.

From this explanation, it's apparent that options (a) and (c) are correct and option (b) is incorrect.

Option (d) is incorrect because you can't create objects of an interface. Option (d) tries to create an object of the interface `Interviewer`. Code that tries to create an instance of an interface won't compile.

### A.6.3  Twist in the Tale 6.3

Purpose: If there is no collision with the name of a variable defined in the base class or derived class, the variable can be accessed using both `super` and `this` references from a derived class. If there is a collision, the base class variable can be accessed using the `super` reference.

Answer: b

Explanation: In a derived class, you'd normally use the implicit reference super to refer to a method or variable of a base class. Similarly, you'd normally use the implicit reference this to refer to a method or variable defined in the same class. A derived class contains within it an object of its base class and can access non-private members of its base class. A derived class can *also* refer to the members of its base class as its own members using the reference this. This approach is acceptable only if the same member isn't defined in the derived class, that is, if there are no name collisions.

The base class Employee defines two non-private variables, name and address, which are accessible in Employee's derived class Programmer. The class Programmer also defines an instance variable name, so the variable name should be prefixed with the explicit references super and this to refer to the variable name defined in the classes Employee and Programmer. The variable address can be referred to using both super and this in the derived class Programmer.

Option (a) is incorrect. The derived class Programmer can refer to the variable address defined in the base class using this.address. This value won't print null.

Option (c) is incorrect. this.address won't print blank when accessed from the derived class Programmer.

Option (d) is incorrect. The code has no compilation issues.

## A.6.4 *Twist in the Tale 6.4*

Purpose: Polymorphic methods should define a method's overriding rules.

Answer: a

Explanation: Polymorphic methods exist when classes or interfaces share an inheritance relationship. A polymorphic method can be defined by a derived class if

- The derived class implements an abstract method defined in a base class or interface
- The derived class overrides a non-abstract method defined in a base class

Options (b) and (d) are incorrect. A method can't be overridden if it defines a different parameter list.

Option (c) is incorrect. The return type of the overridden method must be the same in the base class and the derived class.

## A.7 *Chapter 7: Exception handling*

Chapter 7 includes five Twist in the Tale exercises.

## A.7.1 *Twist in the Tale 7.1*

Purpose: A finally block can't be placed before the catch blocks. A number of programmers have compared this question with placing the label default before the label `case` in a `switch` construct. Though the latter approach works, the `finally` and `catch` blocks aren't so flexible.

Answer: d

Explanation: Options (a), (b), and (c) are incorrect because code that defines a `finally` block before `catch` blocks won't compile.

### A.7.2    *Twist in the Tale 7.2*

Purpose: Unhandled exceptions thrown by an inner exception handler are passed on to the outer `try-catch` block to handle.

Answer: a

Explanation: Options (b), (c), and (d) are incorrect. The question assumes that a text file players.txt exists on your system so that the following code won't throw a `FileNot-FoundException` exception:

```
players = new FileInputStream("players.txt");
```

The code defined for this question doesn't initialize the `static` variable `coach` before executing the following code, which is bound to throw a `NullPointerException`:

```
coach.close();
```

The previous line of code is defined in the inner `try` block, which doesn't define an exception handler for the exception `NullPointerException`. This exception is propagated to the outer exception-handler block. The outer exception handler *catches* the `NullPointerException` thrown by the inner `try` block and executes the appropriate exception handler. Hence, the code prints the following:

```
players.txt found
NullPointerException
```

### A.7.3    *Twist in the Tale 7.3*

Purpose: To determine whether exception-handling code for errors will execute.

Answer: b

Explanation: We know that typically errors shouldn't be handled programmatically and that they should be left for the JVM to take care of. Also, you can't be sure that error-handling code for all the errors will execute. For example, error-handling code for `StackOverFlowError` may execute but (as the name suggests) may not execute for `VirtualMachineError`.

### A.7.4   *Twist in the Tale 7.4*

Purpose: `ClassCastException` is a runtime exception. As you know, a runtime exception can be thrown only by the JVM.

Answer: b, d

Explanation: Options (a) and (c) are incorrect because the code throws `ClassCast-Exception`, which is a runtime exception, for the following code:

```
printable = (Printable)blackInk;
```

Option (d) is correct because neither the class `BlackInk` nor any of its base classes implement the interface `Printable`. Thus, the code that assigns `blackInk` to `printable` without an explicit cast will fail to compile.

### A.7.5   *Twist in the Tale 7.5*

Purpose: Trying to access a nonexistent position of an array throws an `ArrayIndex-OutOfBoundsException`. Calling a member on a `null` value stored in an array throws a `NullPointerException`.

Answer: c

Explanation: Let's indent the assignment of the two-dimensional array `oldLaptops` so that it's easier to understand the values that are assigned to it:

```
String[][] oldLaptops = {
                          {"Dell", "Toshiba", "Vaio"},
                          null,
                          {"IBM"},
                          new String[10]
                        };
```

The preceding code results in the following assignments:

```
oldLaptops[0] = {"Dell", "Toshiba", "Vaio"};
oldLaptops[1] = null;
oldLaptops[2] = {"IBM"};
oldLaptops[3] = new String[10];
```

A pictorial representation of the two-dimensional `String` array `oldLaptops` is shown in figure A.6.

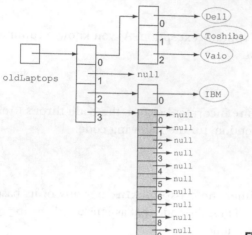

**Figure A.6   The array oldLaptops**

As you can see, oldLaptops[3] is an array of 10 uninitialized String objects. All the members (from index position 0 to 9) of the array oldLaptops[3] are assigned a null value. The code on line 4 tries to call the method length on the first element of array oldLaptops[0], which is null, throwing a NullPointerException.

# index